Ian Sinclair, born 1932 in Tayport, Fife, was educated at Madras College, St Andrews, and the University of St Andrews, where he read chemistry, mainly because there were no courses in electronic engineering available at the time. He joined the Research Department of the English Electric Valve Co. in 1956, working on electron optics and photoelectric devices and contributing articles to technical magazines. In 1966 he became a lecturer, first at Havering Technical College and subsequently at Braintree College of Further Education, teaching physics and electronics and writing books on these topics. The interest in computing, first aroused by a course in FORTRAN programming in 1964, surfaced again in San Francisco in 1977 when microcomputers became available, and he wrote for several US magazines until microcomputers became available in the UK. He has to date written about 200 books on electronics and computing topics and has been a full-time writer since 1982.

Collins · DICTIONARY

Electronics

DEFINITIONS FOR THE DIGITAL AGE

Collins · DICTIONARY

Electronics

DEFINITIONS FOR THE DIGITAL AGE

HarperCollins*Publishers*
Westerhill Road, Glasgow G64 2QT

The Collins website is www.collins.co.uk

First published 1988
Second edition published 2004

© Ian Sinclair 1998, 2004

Reprint 10 9 8 7 6 5 4 3 2 1 0

ISBN 0-00-717801-8

A catalogue record for this book is available from the British Library

Typeset by Davidson Pre-Press Graphics Ltd, Glasgow

Printed and bound in Great Britain by Clays Ltd, St Ives plc.

CONTENTS

PREFACE TO THE SECOND EDITION

The first edition of this dictionary was published in 1988, and the vast changes in Electronics since then are reflected by the larger size of this volume and the number of new terms and illustrations that have been added. In addition, I have taken the opportunity to recast the book in accordance with what I believe to be its main objectives.

A dictionary, above all, should provide an easy and rapid explanation of an unfamiliar term. A dictionary is not a textbook, so that an academic explanation is totally inappropriate, and for some abbreviations all that is needed is an explanation of the term, some of which need no elaboration (like POTS, meaning plain old telephone service). Above all, the dictionary entry should point out the general application of an unfamiliar term and its relationship to other parts of Electronics knowledge. I hope that I have achieved a good balance between the brief but inadequate and the verbose but incomprehensible. Some unavoidably academic topics are dealt with by referring the reader to a suitable textbook.

Although the foundations of electronics were laid in the late nineteenth century, the technology that we know as electronics is very much a product of the twentieth century, and the most rapid development of electronics has occurred in the years following the 1950s. Prior to that time, the word *electronics* had not been coined and the topics that we now consider as being part of electronics were then classed as part of radio engineering. Electronics has changed from being a development of radio engineering into an all-pervading subject in its own right, spawning various subdivisions and tangential topics as its growth exceeded that of any other engineering science. The rapid rise in the use of electronic devices has been brought about by the ubiquitous silicon crystal and the integrated circuit, products of the years since the Second World War. The integrated circuit itself was a by-product of the space race, one whose effect has been much further-reaching than the landing of a man on the moon.

As happens with any science that has been the subject of a rapid expansion, explanations and definitions have lagged behind the development of the technology. Each new development has brought with it a huge quantity of new terms, some of them slang words which have vanished almost as soon as they appeared, others of lasting value, and a few that, like *feedback*, have been assimilated into everyday English, though usually in an incorrect sense. Although the rate of growth of electronics has not really abated, the flow of new terms has been reduced to a level at which it becomes easier to take stock and select which terms are of lasting use and which were transient. There are still dictionaries which present slang words of the Second World War period as if they were a part of modern-day electronics; in contrast, the present volume is an attempt to define and explain the terms which I believe to be relevant to modern electronics. This now includes much (such as telephony) that once was regarded as separate from electronics, and new domestic devices such as the DVD recorder that were only being dreamt of at the time when the first edition was being prepared.

The book is intended to cater for anyone who needs to know the definitions of electronics terms. This of course includes the student, whether at school or in the early years of a university, polytechnic, or technical college course, but it is important to remember the needs of the non-specialist. To an ever-increasing extent, electronic devices and methods are impinging on studies that at one time would have appeared to be unlikely users of such devices. From archaeology to music, from medicine to navigation, electronic measurements and methods now need to be understood by students and practitioners of subjects that appear to have very little in common. The need for, and use of, electronics now transcends all the artificial divisions of subject matter, and makes a dictionary of electronics that is expressed in plain language a necessity rather than a luxury. Even the student of Electronics will have need to look up terms that are unfamiliar because the breadth of the subject makes it impossible to be aware of all its ramifications.

This book has therefore been designed with more than the needs of the traditional electronics student in mind. Each explanation is couched in accessible terms, avoiding the use of mathematics except where a note on the mathematical aspect of a topic is necessary as a reminder to the prospective designer as distinct from the user of electronics. The form of the dictionary has been set out so as to make it easier to find an explanation of a device or principle under one heading rather than requiring the user to flit from one heading to another, picking up pollen-fragments of learning from each. Additionally, cross references (indicated by SMALL CAPITAL LETTERS) guide the user to related entries. I am most grateful to Edwin Moore, of HarperCollins Publishers, for his unstinting efforts in working this book into its final form from the material on CD-R disc, for it is his efforts that have made this a readable and usable dictionary.

Ian Sinclair 2004

A

AA see AUTOANSWER.

AAC see ADVANCED AUDIO CODING.

AAUI Apple attachment unit interface: a port and connector unit for Apple computers.

a-b box or **ab switch** a switch that allows a PERIPHERAL such as a printer to be shared by two computers, or to allow a computer the use of two printers.

abbreviated dialling or **speed dialling** a telephone dialling system in which the full number is held in memory and the user dials only a shorter access number such as #2.

aberration any distortion of an image by a lens system. In electronics the term denotes distortions in the electron lenses of TV CAMERA TUBES, CATHODE-RAY TUBES, ELECTRON MICROSCOPES, etc. See also BARREL DISTORTION; ELECTROMAGNETIC LENS; ELECTROSTATIC LENS; PINCUSHION DISTORTION.

abnormally quiet days (AQD) days when solar activity that affects radio communications is greatly reduced.

abrupt junction a JUNCTION (sense 2) in which there is a sudden change of MAJORITY CARRIER, in which one material is lightly doped (either as DONOR or ACCEPTOR) with the other material heavily doped in the opposite polarity.

abscissa another name for the X-COORDINATE of a graph.

absolute maximum ratings the ratings of maximum voltage, current and POWER DISSIPATION for a device that must not be exceeded, even momentarily.

absolute scale or **Kelvin scale** the scale of temperature that uses ABSOLUTE ZERO as its zero point.

absolute tab a tabulation point, the position of which is measured from the left-hand edge of the paper or screen rather than from the margin line.

absolute temperature a temperature measured in the ABSOLUTE SCALE, with

ABSOLUTE ZERO at around –273°C. All fundamental equations in electronics that make use of temperature will require the units of temperature to be in the absolute scale.

absolute value the value of a number, ignoring any sign. For example, the absolute value of –6.7 is 6.7.

absolute value circuit a circuit that provides a positive output equal to the magnitude of the input signal. See also BRIDGE RECTIFIER.

absolute zero the zero of the ABSOLUTE SCALE. The temperature is calculated theoretically from the behaviour of gases and is the point at which THERMAL NOISE ceases. In practice, the value is confirmed from the fact that the absolute zero temperature can never be exactly attained, though it is possible to achieve temperatures within a fraction of a degree of absolute zero.

absorption the extraction of ENERGY, usually from a WAVE. A radio CARRIER (sense 1) is absorbed by many materials, resulting in the conversion of the absorbed energy into heat or some other form of energy. The alternatives to absorption are TRANSMISSION, REFLECTION and REFRACTION.

absorption loss a measure of the amount of power loss caused by ABSORPTION. The absorption loss is usually quoted in DECIBELS, and is equal to 20 log (power lost/power input).

absorption, dielectric see SOAKAGE.

ab switch see A-B BOX.

a/b switching a method of comparing systems that have the same input by switching between them and observing any change in output. For example, two LOUDSPEAKERS fed from the same amplifier can be a/b switched to hear differences in rendering of the same music.

AC see ALTERNATING CURRENT.

AC bias an ANALOGUE audio tape recording system used in the RECORDING OF SOUND. A graph of the retained magnetism (REMANENCE) of a magnetic material plotted against the AMPERE-TURNS of the magnetizing coils is never a straight line. When a high-frequency sine wave AC signal is applied to the recording head, the lower frequency signal that is to be recorded can be mixed with this signal. The result is that the signal to be recorded causes values of remanent magnetism to be generated which lie on a comparatively straight part of the graph. On playback, the high-frequency signals can be filtered out. The use of digital recording methods is a better solution, but has been rendered obsolescent by the use of recordable CD and DVD discs.

ACC see AUTOMATIC COLOUR CONTROL.

accelerated graphics port (AGP) a type of hardware BUS that allows the use of a fast GRAPHICS adapter on a PERSONAL COMPUTER, replacing the PCI bus connection formerly used, and using a slightly longer EXPANSION SLOT. The use of an AGP connection is essential if THREE-DIMENSIONAL GRAPHICS with rapid movement are required.

accelerated life test a LIFE TEST that is conducted under unusually harsh conditions. This normally implies the use of a supply voltage higher than normal, or greater than normal dissipation. The aim is to check that samples have consistent lifetimes, rather than to predict actual life under normal conditions. If sufficient statistical evidence is available, however, it may be possible to correlate expected life with the results of accelerated life tests.

accelerating anode or **first anode** a metal cylinder that is maintained at a positive voltage relative to the CATHODE (sense 1) of a CATHODE-RAY TUBE. The resulting electric field accelerates the electrons to high speeds, but because of the shape of this anode, few electrons strike it. The current that flows to the electrode is therefore negligible compared to the current to the FINAL

ANODE, which is normally the aluminized screen surface.

acceleration factor a number calculated from temperature and other data that can predict the relationship between working life of a device in normal use and the life found in an ACCELERATED LIFE TEST.

acceleration of gravity the value, in metres per second^2, of gravitational acceleration, particularly applicable in the relationship between mass and weight. The standard value at the Earth's surface is taken as 9.81 ms^{-2}.

acceleration sensing detection of acceleration using a TRANSDUCER such as a PIEZOELECTRIC CRYSTAL accelerometer.

acceleration time or **latency** the time required for a magnetic or optical DISK to reach its normal rotating speed when it has been called into action. This particularly affects FLOPPY DISKS and CD-ROM, since a HARD DRIVE is normally rotating for as long as a computer is switched on, though energy-saving systems usually provide for a hard drive to be at rest when not in use. See also LATENCY.

acceleration voltage or **accelerating voltage** the steady voltage, measured with respect to the CATHODE (sense 1) voltage, that is applied to the accelerating ANODE of an electron beam device such as a CATHODE-RAY TUBE or X-RAY TUBE.

accelerator card a PRINTED CIRCUIT BOARD, now obsolete, that contains a MICROPROCESSOR and associated chips. When plugged into an EXPANSION SLOT or replacing the existing microprocessor of the computer, the accelerator board provides faster operation without the need to upgrade to a different computer. Accelerator cards have in the past also been used to provide faster GRAPHICS and FLOATING POINT arithmetic actions.

accelerator, thermostat a resistor placed inside a bimetallic thermostat casing and wired so that current flows while the thermostat contacts are closed. This increases the rate of heating and thus reduces HYSTERESIS effects that cause an unaccelerated thermostat to overshoot its set temperature.

accelerometer　a device that senses or measures the ACCELERATION applied to it, usually with an electrical output.

acceptable quality level (AQL)　a figure derived from a graph of probability of batch acceptance plotted against actual percentage defects in a batch. This allows a producer to calculate the risk that a batch will be rejected; the risk fraction (usually expressed as a percentage) is 1/AQL.

acceptance angle　the maximum angle, measured relative to the optical axis of a PHOTOCELL, at which light can strike the cell and still cause a useful output.

acceptance testing　a scheme for checking that an electronics system will perform as intended. A large and elaborate system, whose cost may amount to many millions of pounds, cannot simply be put in place and switched on. It is extensively tested with the type of inputs that will eventually be used with it. During the time of this testing, the operators of the system will also undergo training in its use.

acceptor　a P-TYPE material for DOPING a pure semiconductor that accepts electrons into its structure, thus releasing positive charges (HOLES) in the semiconductor. Contrast DONOR.

acceptor atoms　atoms that possess three electrons in their outer shell, and can accept another electron, creating a HOLE. Chemically, acceptor atoms are of TRIVALENT ELEMENTS.

access control　(in a security system) the method of ensuring that only authorized personnel can have access to a building, but providing easy exit in case of emergency.

access delay　for a PACKET SWITCHED NETWORK, this is the time for which a DATA PACKET may be delayed before a suitable time gap appears.

access protocols　for a satellite data system, the factors of acceptable transmission delay, data rate, acceptable message failure rate and message format.

access time　**1.** see MEMORY ACCESS TIME.
2. for a computer HARD DRIVE, the time

required to start reading from or writing to a selected TRACK on a PLATTER.

AC circuit analysis　a description of a circuit in terms of impedance and frequency for a continuous wave input.

AC coupling　any method of transferring a signal between stages that blocks DC, such as a capacitor or a transformer.

accumulator　**1.** the main REGISTER of a microprocessor. Each of the operations of addition, subtraction, AND, OR and XOR will affect a byte in the accumulator and a byte taken from memory. The result of the action is then stored back in the accumulator. **2.** see LEAD-ACID CELL.

accuracy, meter　the percentage figure of error for a METER on a given range.

AC/DC　(of electric motors and electronic equipment) being able to operate on either ALTERNATING CURRENT or DIRECT CURRENT supply. The term originally denoted radios and TV receivers that could be connected direct to the supply mains and which used no transformers. Nowadays the term usually denotes equipment that can be operated either from mains AC, using a transformer, or from low-voltage DC, such as a car battery.

ACE head　the audio and control signal head of a VIDEO CASSETTE RECORDER. During fast search actions, the tape is lifted away from the rotating head into a loop that makes contact with the ACE head so that signals such as those indicating the start of a recording can be found.

AC erase　the use of a high-frequency sine wave signal to supply the erase head of a tape recorder in order to demagnetize the tape.

acetone　a volatile liquid used for cleaning or as a solvent. Acetone is a fire and toxicity hazard.

AC feedback　connection of an output terminal to an input terminal through a path that blocks DC. Either POSITIVE FEEDBACK or NEGATIVE FEEDBACK may be used.

AC generator　any device or circuit that generates ALTERNATING CURRENT. The term usually denotes a rotating machine, such as an ALTERNATOR. A purely electronic circuit that generates AC is more commonly described as a waveform or SIGNAL GENERATOR.

achromatic lens a lens suitable for colour imaging that has the same focal point for all colours, made by cementing together two lenses using different types of glass.

ACIA see ASYNCHRONOUS COMMUNICATIONS INTERFACE ADAPTER.

ACK/NACK protocol a communications method for ensuring accuracy of transmission. When a DATA PACKET is decoded and has no errors, the ACK signal is sent; when errors are present the NACK signal is sent and the same packet is re-transmitted.

AC load line a graph line that shows the possible values of input and output signals obtainable from an amplifying stage using a particular LOAD.

AC mains the power supply for mains-operated electronic equipment. In the UK this is nominally 240V 50Hz; in the USA it is 115V 60Hz.

AC motor any form of motor that requires an AC supply, i.e. all types of INDUCTION, SYNCHRONOUS and SHADED-POLE motors. Motors that use wound rotors and COMMUTATORS are generally described as AC/DC or universal motors.

acoustically transparent (of a material) allowing sound to pass freely.

acoustic construction, microphone the physical arrangement of the TRANSDUCER in a MICROPHONE that will determine the type of response. Typically, if a sound wave can strike only one surface of the transducer the microphone will be omnidirectional (see PRESSURE OPERATED MICROPHONE), but if both surfaces are affected the microphone will be unidirectional (see VELOCITY OPERATED MICROPHONE).

acoustic coupler an obsolete method of transmitting BINARY data over telephone lines or radio links. To transmit computer data over narrow-band telephone lines, the data must be converted into electrical audio tone signals, and sent at a comparatively low rate. If direct connection of electrical equipment to the telephone system is prohibited, an acoustic coupler converts the electrical signals into musical notes that are sent and received by the normal telephone microphone and earpiece. This is done by placing the hand-piece of the telephone over a pair of rubber cups, one that contains a loudspeaker, the other containing a microphone. Problems of this arrangement include slow speed, interference from other sounds, and inefficient coupling that lead to data errors. Acoustic couplers are used only where a direct connection to the telephone system is impossible, such as in some hotel rooms or in telephone boxes. A direct electrical connection to the telephone system is greatly preferable. See also MODEM.

acoustic delay line a method of delaying electrical signals by converting them into ULTRASONIC signals. A TRANSDUCER converts the electrical signals into acoustic (vibration) signals. These travel along a material at the speed of sound, which is much slower than the speed of electromagnetic waves, and are reconverted into electrical signals by another transducer. The original acoustic delay lines used mercury as the wave medium, and were known as *mumble-tubs*. At one time, acoustic delay lines were manufactured from glass for use in COLOUR TELEVISION receivers to equalize the time taken by colour signals which have different bandwidths. Acoustic waves are also used in wave FILTERS. See DELAY LINE; SURFACE ACOUSTIC WAVE.

acoustic feedback the unwanted feedback of sound waves. The most common form is the squealing (or *howl-around*) which is caused when a PUBLIC ADDRESS system is used with a loudspeaker placed too close to a microphone. This is a form of POSITIVE FEEDBACK in which the sound wave from the loudspeaker reaches the microphone to be amplified over again, resulting in oscillation. The cure is to use very strongly directional microphones, or circuits which ensure that the PHASE of acoustically fed back signals is always incorrect for oscillation. Acoustic feedback can also affect ANALOGUE gramophone PICKUPS that are placed too close to loudspeakers.

acoustic wave any wave of alternate compression and rarefaction in a material in the form of a sound wave, whether the result can be detected by ear or not.

acoustic wave device any electronic device that makes use of ACOUSTIC WAVES. See also ACOUSTIC DELAY LINE; SURFACE ACOUSTIC WAVE.

ACPI see ADVANCED CONFIGURATION AND POWER INTERFACE.

AC power analyzer a measuring instrument that detects and records deviations from the normal constant-amplitude SINE WAVE mains supply.

AC power supply or **power supply unit** or **PSU** a circuit that rectifies an AC input and smoothes the resulting output to DC for use with electronic equipment.

acquisition time the time required for a device to respond to an input, particularly a set of data signals on a BUS.

AC regulator a circuit that use devices such as SATURABLE REACTORS and/or TRIACS to maintain a constant output of AC voltage for a varying input.

AC resistance a quantity obtained by dividing AC voltage by AC current value. In a circuit that contains only resistive components, this value will be equal to DC resistance, but the value will be very different if the circuit contains REACTIVE CURRENT components because of the PHASE DIFFERENCE between voltage and current. See IMPEDANCE; REACTANCE.

ACSSB see AMPLITUDE COMPANDED SINGLE SIDE BAND.

AC3 or **Dolby Digital** a five-channel SURROUND SOUND digital sound reproducing system that is often used as part of a home cinema installation.

activated cathode a hot CATHODE (sense 1) of the oxide-coated type in a THERMIONIC VALVE. See THERMIONIC CATHODE.

active making use of active components that require a power supply to function. Compare PASSIVE.

active aerial (or **antenna)** a TRANSMITTING AERIAL that is supplied with radio frequency power. See also AERIAL; DIRECTOR; PASSIVE AERIAL; REFLECTOR.

active area the area within a rectifier JUNCTION (sense 2) that actually passes current.

active circuit any circuit that uses one or more ACTIVE COMPONENTS requiring a power supply. Contrast PASSIVE CIRCUIT.

active component or **active device** a circuit component that is capable of increasing the power of a signal. An active component requires a power supply in order to operate, and can have a measurable POWER GAIN, as distinct from voltage gain or current gain. Contrast PASSIVE COMPONENT.

active crossover a signal FILTER using ACTIVE components to separate drive currents to TWEETER and WOOFER loudspeakers.

active current see IN-PHASE COMPONENT (sense 1).

active device see ACTIVE COMPONENT.

active filter a form of FILTER that uses ACTIVE COMPONENTS, usually OPERATIONAL AMPLIFIERS. The PASSIVE COMPONENTS that decide the filter performance are part of a FEEDBACK CONTROL LOOP round the active device. See Fig. 1.

active infra-red detector a security device in which breaking a beam of infra-red light aimed at a detector will activate an alarm. Compare PASSIVE INFRA-RED (PIR) devices.

active load an ACTIVE COMPONENT used as a power-dissipating load. Since a TRANSISTOR, bipolar or FET, is a form of variable resistor, it can be used as a load whose resistance value is variable.

active loudspeaker a loudspeaker (usually one of a pair) that contains its own power supply and audio amplifier, so that the input signals, from a computer or a miniature cassette or CD player, can be of small amplitude and low power.

active low (of an electronic signal) having a valid effect when its voltage level is low. The opposite is *active high*.

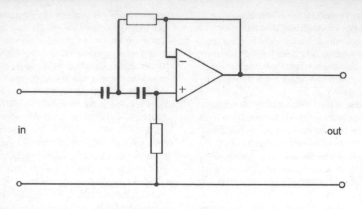

Fig. I. **active filter**

active-low line a connector, part of a BUS, that provides an input to an IC when its voltage value becomes low (logic 0).

active matrix screen see ACTIVE-MATRIX LCD.

active matrix display a form of LCD screen in which each unit is controlled by a separate TRANSISTOR or set of (usually thin-film) transistors. An active matrix display is more difficult to construct than the older type, but the display is much more controllable, allowing better resolution and contrast, and making colour display possible. See also TFT.

active matrix LCD an LCD display in which each cell unit is controlled by a separate IC or TFT unit.

active network a set of components that includes an ACTIVE COMPONENT. The term usually denotes any FILTER network that includes a transistor, operational amplifier, or other device with power gain.

active picture technology see TOUCH SCREEN.

active region for a semiconductor amplifying device, the region between CUTOFF and SATURATION CURRENT value that can be used for amplification.

active sideband optimization or **ASO** a technique, due to Nokia, applied to the playback CARRIER (sense 1) in a video cassette recorder which speeds up the transitions between levels, giving better-defined pictures.

active smoothing a form of SERIES REGULATION circuit used in a POWER SUPPLY unit (PSU) to improve smoothing.

active speaker a loudspeaker, usually one of a stereo pair, that contains a power supply and AMPLIFIER so that the speakers can be operated with a low-level input, such as from a miniature cassette or disc player or from the sound output of a computer sound card.

active tone control a form of TONE CONTROL that makes use of active components, such as the BAXANDALL TONE CONTROL.

active transducer a form of transducer with power gain. Most transducers are PASSIVE COMPONENTS, but a transducer that is based on a transistor (such as a PHOTOTRANSISTOR) can supply power gain in addition to energy conversion.

active voltage see IN-PHASE COMPONENT (sense 1).

activity a measure of the efficiency of a QUARTZ CRYSTAL. A crystal oscillator provides a driving voltage which sets the crystal into natural oscillation or resonance. The PEAK signal voltage across the crystal is many times greater than the driving voltage, and the ratio of peak crystal voltage to peak driving voltage is the activity figure of the crystal under these conditions. Activity figures of tens of thousands are common.

activity factor   the fraction of an hour for which a message handling system will be occupied.

activity light   an indicator light that is lit to indicate an action, typically the use of a HARD DRIVE or a CD-ROM DRIVE in a computer.

actuator   any electrically operated device that performs a mechanical action. The term is extensively used in control systems and ROBOTICS. An actuator can be a simple solenoid, or a very elaborate system of motors.

adapter, IC   a clip fitted with contacts and a cable connection that can be placed over the top of an IC, making contact to the pins so that voltage and waveform measurements can be made. This avoids having to make connections to the PRINTED CIRCUIT BOARD.

adaption header   part of an MPEG DATA PACKET for digital television that contains synchronizing and timing data.

adaptive and real time channel evaluation   a system for optimizing radio communications by using several frequencies and constantly switching to a frequency that offers best characteristics.

adaptive channel allocation or **adaptive routing**   a system of communications in which communications links are allocated according to demand rather than being fixed.

adaptive delta modulation (ADM)   a modification (by Dolby laboratories) of the DELTA MODULATION system that allows BIT RATE REDUCTION and higher SAMPLING frequencies.

adaptive differential pulse code modulation or **adaptive digital pulse code modulation (ADPCM)**   a method of COMPRESSING and digitizing (see DIGITIZE) AUDIO data that operates by RECORDING the difference between samples. Overloading is avoided by limiting the number of steps of amplitude sampling and sending a code for step size along with the signal.

adaptive equalizer   a circuit that can automatically correct data transmission problems caused by NON-LINEAR amplitude, phase and frequency response of a transmission path.

adaptive filter   a FILTER, used for noise reduction in an ANALOGUE audio circuit, that will alter its FREQUENCY RESPONSE according to the signal amplitude, mimicking the response of the ear.

adaptive pulse code modulation (APCM)   a system of digitizing (see DIGITIZE) an ANALOGUE waveform by SAMPLING and RECORDING the difference between samples.

adaptive quantization   a method of reducing the amount of data in a digitized (see DIGITIZE) TV signal.

adaptive RADAR   a RADAR system in which characteristics such as pulse rate, pulse width and pulse spectrum can be varied so as to obtain optimum results.

adaptive routing   1. or **dynamic routing** a method of switching signals in a NETWORK (sense 2) so that the quickest route is always used. 2. see ADAPTIVE CHANNEL ALLOCATION.

adaptive slicer   a control circuit for a SAMPLING stage that picks the optimum point for taking each sample.

adaptive threshold, hearing   an important factor for compressing digital audio signals. The threshold of hearing is the level of amplitude at which a sound can just be heard, and this amplitude is not fixed; it depends on the amount of other sound levels and on the frequency of the signals. By removing all sound data that would be below the threshold for any given part of a sound track, a considerable reduction in the number of bits needed per sample can be achieved.

adaptive transform acoustic coding (ATRAC)   a method for digitizing (see DIGITIZE) AUDIO signals that achieves DIGITAL COMPRESSION by ignoring low-amplitude signals that are present at the same time as high-amplitude signals.

ADC   see ANALOGUE TO DIGITAL CONVERTER.

ADCCP   see ADVANCED DATA. COMMUNICATIONS CONTROL PROTOCOL.

A/D converter   see ANALOGUE TO DIGITAL CONVERTER.

added noise signal   see DITHER.

adder a LOGIC CIRCUIT that provides the binary adding action that is summarized by the table of Fig. 2. An adder circuit that provides for a carry bit *into* the addition is called a FULL ADDER, and if this carry-in is not provided for, the device is called a HALF-ADDER.

add direct memory access co-processor (ADMA) a chip that can be used for direct access (see DMA) to memory, particularly intended for older computers that are IBM COMPATIBLE. See also UDMA.

addition, binary see BINARY ADDITION.

additive light mixing, colour the process of adding three primary light colours to obtain any desired colour, used in colour TV displays. Contrast SUBTRACTIVE LIGHT MIXING.

address a number that is used to activate a MEMORY LOCATION or a PORT (sense 1) connected to a MICROPROCESSOR. The microprocessor controls other parts of the system by using a set of connections called the ADDRESS BUS. Each line in an address bus links the microprocessor to each of the memory and port units in a system. When a set of binary signals is placed on the address bus by the

microprocessor, this is used to locate one unique port or part of memory. Each address number therefore corresponds to one memory unit or one port. When a device is addressed by putting its address number on the bus, it can then be read from (data copied from the device to the microprocessor) or written to (data copied from the microprocessor to the device).

addressability the degree to which the PIXELS on a graphics SCREEN can be individually controlled. Older graphics systems appeared to control small single pixels, but in fact dealt with pixels in groups. High addressability, as used on modern VGA systems, requires a very large amount of memory dedicated to graphics use; see VIDEO MEMORY.

address bus the set of connectors that carries binary ADDRESS numbers to all parts of a MICROPROCESSOR system.

address decoder a chip on the MOTHERBOARD of a computer that allocates an address number to the correct chip(s) (such as RAM, ROM, ports) and ensures that signals are read from or written to the correct chips.

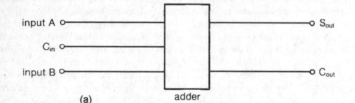

(a)   adder

A	B	C_{in}	S	C_{out}
0	0	0	0	0
0	0	1	1	0
0	1	0	1	0
0	1	1	0	1
1	0	0	1	0
1	0	1	0	1
1	1	0	0	1
1	1	1	1	1

(b)

Fig. 2. **adder**

address selected system (ADSEL)
a form of RADAR system in which the
ground station can send interrogating
codes to an aircraft which will then reply
with coded data for altitude, course, fuel
supply, and speed.

addressable chip   an IC device that can
be activated by sending an ADDRESS code
over BUS lines or by a SERIAL TRANSFER link.

addressable memory   memory to which
access can be obtained when a binary
number is placed in bit form on the lines
of an ADDRESS BUS. Typically an IC will use
a set of address pins and a set of data
pins, and various portions of the memory
can be read or written when both buses
contain valid binary numbers.

**Addressing Communications and
Reporting System (ACARS)** or
**Aeronautical Public Correspondence
(APC)** or **IMMERSAT aeronautical
mobile system**   a digital communications
system for aircraft use operating in the
bands 1545 to 1555 MHz and 1646.5 to
1656.5 MHz, using a satellite relay.

adjacent channel interference
interference to a transmitted signal caused
by frequency beating with the CARRIER
(sense 1) or SIDEBANDS of a signal in an
adjacent channel. See also CO-CHANNEL
INTERFERENCE.

adjustable voltage regulator   a form of
VOLTAGE REGULATOR, usually an IC, whose
output can be adjusted within limits by
a POTENTIOMETER (sense 1) connected to
the circuit.

adjustment, offset   see OFFSET.

ADM   see ADAPTIVE DELTA MODULATION.

admittance   the reciprocal of IMPEDANCE,
symbol Y, unit SIEMENS (formerly mho).
For circuits in which it is more convenient
to work with currents than with voltages,
the equation $Y = G + jB$ is used rather
than the more familiar $Z = R + jX$.
The symbol G is used for conductance
(1/resistance), and B for susceptance
(1/reactance). See also COMPLEX NUMBER.

admittance gap   the hole in a WAVEGUIDE
or CAVITY RESONATOR at which an electron
beam and a resonant microwave signal
can interact.

ADPCM   see ADAPTIVE DIFFERENTIAL PULSE
CODE MODULATION.

ADR   see ASTRA DIGITAL RADIO.

ADSEL   see ADDRESS SELECTED SYSTEM.

ADSL   see ASYMMETRIC DIGITAL SUBSCRIBER
LINE.

ADTRAC   see ADAPTIVE TRANSFORM
ACOUSTIC CODING.

advanced audio coding (AAC)   a system
of COMPRESSING audio signals that allows
lower bit rates (see BIT RATE) to be used
and with more consistent quality as
compared to MP3.

**advanced configuration and power
interface (ACPI)**   a standard method
for power management for a PERSONAL
COMPUTER. Typically this implements
systems for shutting down the MONITOR
and HARD DRIVE when not required, and
for other power-saving actions.

advanced intelligent tape (AIT)   a form
of computer-controlled tape drive or
STREAMER for storing very large amounts
of data, with fast data transfer rates.

advanced power management (AMP)
a software program that, given suitable
hardware, can reduce the use of power
on PORTABLE and other battery-operated
computers or other electronic equipment.
This software shuts down (hibernates)
parts of the system that are not currently
in use, as for example, a HARD DRIVE motor
when disk access is not required. See also
ADVANCED CONFIGURATION AND POWER
INTERFACE, a more wide-ranging system.

**advanced research project agency
network (ARPANET)**   one of the earliest
LONG-HAUL NETWORK applications of the
MESH type used in research and defence
studies in the USA. This was the model
for the development of the INTERNET.

advanced RISC machine (ARM)
a MICROPROCESSOR using RISC techniques
developed initially by ACORN computing.

advanced run-length limiting (ARLL)
a way of coding information into
magnetic signals on a HARD DRIVE that
achieves tighter packing of data and faster
operation. See also RLL.

**advanced SCSI peripheral interface
(ASPI)**   a set of software routines that

provides an interface between MICROSOFT WINDOWS and SCSI devices.

advanced technology attachment (ATA) a drive interface system for the PC that was based on the 16-bit bus used on the IBM PC-AT machine. This was used on many PC machines as a low-cost alternative to SCSI for interfacing hard drives (see IDE) and other devices. The later versions are comparable in performance with SCSI but do not allow for as many devices to be connected.

advanced technology attachment interface with extensions (ATA-2) a development of the ATA standard that allows faster data transfer, 32-bit working, and the use of DMA. See also EIDE.

advection an atmospheric condition of temperature inversion causing VHF/UHF signals to be carried well beyond their normal range so that interference can occur between signals that do not usually have enough range to interfere.

aerial or **antenna** a transmitting or receiving device for radiated waves. The aerial acts as a form of MATCHING TRANSFORMER for waves along a line and waves in space so that the maximum transfer of ENERGY can be achieved. Achieving high efficiency in an aerial system is of great importance both for transmitting and for receiving. Because of the very great differences in the wavelengths of radio waves at the extremes of the spectrum, aerials can take a great variety of shapes and sizes. For low radio frequencies, aerials require long wires, well clear of the ground. For the VHF and UHF range, rod aerials, cut to tuned lengths, are used, and these may be of the YAGI type in order to be directional. At microwave frequencies, aerials consist of sections of launching waveguide with horn ends and parabolic reflectors. See also DIPOLE AERIAL; DIRECTIVITY; MARCONI AERIAL; RADIATION PATTERN.

aerial (or antenna) array a set of aerials arranged to transmit or receive in one particular direction. This is done by using the correct spacing between aerials, and the correct phasing of signals, so that the waves from each separate aerial will reinforce each other in the chosen direction. A BROADSIDE ARRAY concentrates its energy in a direction that is at right angles to the line of aerials. An ENDFIRE ARRAY concentrates radiated ENERGY in the direction of the aerial line. An array can be said to have a figure of gain as compared to a single element, and this figure is a good measure of both efficiency and directional qualities. See also DIRECTIVITY; MAJOR LOBE; RADIATION PATTERN; YAGI.

aerial (or antenna) element any of a set of rods or wires constituting an aerial, such as a REFLECTOR or DIRECTOR. See also YAGI.

aerial (or antenna) current the radio-frequency current in an aerial. This is measured as the ROOT MEAN SQUARE (sense 2) value of the CARRIER (sense 1) frequency at some point in the AERIAL FEEDER. For an UNTUNED AERIAL, the current is usually measured at the feeder connection, otherwise the current is measured at the voltage standing wave NODE (sense 2), which is the maximum-current position.

aerial (or antenna) efficiency the percentage power-radiation efficiency of an aerial. This is measured at the CARRIER (sense 1) frequency of radiation, and is the percentage of power radiated as compared to power supplied to the aerial. A low aerial efficiency implies a poor STANDING WAVE RATIO.

aerial (or antenna) feeder the TRANSMISSION LINE that connects an aerial to a transmitter or to a receiver.

aerial (or antenna) gain a measure of the efficiency of an aerial in comparison to a standard reference aerial. The efficiency is measured in terms of the power radiated or received as compared to the standard under the same conditions. For VHF and UHF aerials, the standard is a simple DIPOLE AERIAL. For lower frequencies, a notional 'infinite wire' standard is sometimes used, whose radiated energy figures are theoretically calculated.

aerial (or antenna) group a classification of UHF TV aerials using letter and colour codes to indicate the range of channels. See Table 1.

Group	A	B	C/D	E	K	W
Channels	21–37	35–53	48–68	53–68	21–48	21–68
Colour	Red	Yellow	Green	Brown	Grey	Black

Table 1. **UHF TV aerial groups**

aerial (or **antenna**) **impedance** a COMPLEX NUMBER relating signal voltage to signal current at a point on the aerial. The aerial impedance will not be a constant, particularly for a TUNED AERIAL. The figure for impedance is therefore usually measured at the aerial FEED POINT, and is often referred to as *feed-point impedance*.

aerial (or **antenna**) **polar diagram** see POLAR DIAGRAM PLOT.

aerial (or **antenna**) **resistance** a quantity obtained by dividing aerial power by the square of current. If the power figure is of radiated power, the resulting figure is of *aerial radiation resistance*. If the power figure that is used is of supplied power, then the resistance figure is of *aerial resistance*.

aerial, ferrite rod see FERRITE ROD.

aerial, radio see AERIAL.

aerial, telescopic see TELESCOPIC AERIAL.

aeronautical mobile system a satellite service that links aircraft with ground stations.

AES/EBU interface a standardized form of connection for digital signals, often using an isolating transformer.

AF see AUDIO FREQUENCY.

AF amplifier an AMPLIFIER whose intended signal FREQUENCY BAND is the AUDIO RANGE.

AFC see AUTOMATIC FREQUENCY CONTROL.

affine transform a MATRIX operation that is used for compressing and encoding digital images into very small files, but at a slow rate.

AF IC a semiconductor IC whose intended signal FREQUENCY BAND is the AUDIO RANGE.

AFM or **audio fm** a method of RECORDING the sound part of a TV signal in a VIDEO CASSETTE RECORDER in a way that ensures higher quality. Typically, this involves frequency modulating the sound and recording at high amplitude before the conventional audio track is recorded.

This FM track is not completely obliterated by the ordinary audio track and can be demodulated (see DEMODULATION).

AFSK AUDIO FREQUENCY SHIFT KEYING.

afterglow the light pattern that can be seen from the PHOSPHOR of a CATHODE-RAY TUBE screen after the electron beam has been cut off. For radar use, a long afterglow (of several seconds) is useful in allowing the tracks of moving objects to show up as a trail. For TV use, the afterglow must be short enough to avoid any appearance of trail. At the same time, some afterglow is desirable to avoid excessive FLICKER. Other forms of display screens for digital pictures need not possess afterglow because the picture elements are continually energized.

AF transformer a TRANSFORMER intended for use with signals in the AUDIO RANGE.

AGC see AUTOMATIC GAIN CONTROL.

ageing or **burn-in** the operating of a component until its characteristics become stable. The term is usually applied to transmitting THERMIONIC VALVES and other vacuum devices using a hot CATHODE (sense 1), in which small changes occur in the characteristics during the first few hundred hours of life. This process can sometimes be speeded up by using more stringent conditions, such as raised voltage supply, higher input power, higher operating temperature, etc. A few types of PASSIVE COMPONENTS can also benefit from ageing.

AGP see ACCELERATED GRAPHICS PORT.

AGP slot the slot connector in a PC machine that can be used for a GRAPHICS card of the ACCELERATED GRAPHICS PORT type.

air-break switch a switch whose contacts separate in air, as distinct from vacuum or oil.

air capacitor a capacitor that uses air as its only DIELECTRIC. The device is used for some variable capacitors and for some high-voltage transmitter capacitors. See also VACUUM CAPACITOR.

air-compression sensor a sensor that uses the pressure exerted on a DIAPHRAGM to operate an electronic TRANSDUCER so as to sense air pressure.

air core a core for an INDUCTOR or TRANSFORMER that is hollow, with no high-permeability material enclosed.

air discharge a flow of current through air that has been ionized (see IONIZATION).

airflow the path and speed of cooling air over electronic devices.

air gap any air-filled discontinuity in a material, particularly in a MAGNETIC CORE (sense 1).

airport surveillance RADAR (ASR) a ground radar system that provides distance and bearing information for air traffic control by scanning the air space around it.

air purity sensor a TRANSDUCER using a SEMICONDUCTOR surface whose electrical characteristics are altered by changes in air quality.

air time the time for which a communications service needs to use a radio link.

AIT see ADVANCED INTELLIGENT TAPE.

alarm loop a form of security system wiring in which alarm detectors are connected into a loop, ensuring that any activated device will operate the alarm.

alarm verification a SOFTWARE method of remotely checking an alarm system to ensure that it has been correctly set.

A-law see POTENTIOMETER LAW.

ALC see AUTOMATIC LEVEL CONTROL.

Alcomax™ a magnetic material consisting of an alloy of iron, nickel, aluminium, cobalt and copper that has exceptionally high coercive force (see MAGNETIC HYSTERESIS). It is used mainly in making permanent magnets for loudspeakers and for MAGNETRONS.

algorithm a formulaic method of solving a problem.

algorithmic converter a fast method of A TO D conversion using current operated

stages in a SUCCESSIVE APPROXIMATION CONVERSION system. This provides high conversion speed and is easily implemented in ICs.

aliasing a problem encountered in ANALOGUE TO DIGITAL CONVERTER use denoting the transmission of an analogue signal at too high a frequency compared to the sampling rate. The digital signal then corresponds to an 'alias' of the true signal, and this alias is usually a subharmonic of the true signal. See also SHANNON'S SAMPLING THEOREM.

aliasing noise noise due to some frequencies in a digitized (see DIGITIZE) signal being higher than half of the digitizing frequency, creating ALIASING effects.

alignment the action of aligning mechanisms or electronic circuits. A set of RESONANT CIRCUITS are said to be aligned if they are all tuned to the same FREQUENCY or frequency band.

alignment, aerial adjustment of the direction of an aerial to produce the optimum signals strength from the local transmitter.

alignment tape a test tape recorded by a VIDEO CASSETTE RECORDER manufacturer and used to ensure that a recorder has its heads and guides perfectly aligned for optimum signal pickup.

alkaline cell a cell such as the manganese alkaline type, that uses an alkaline ELECTROLYTE.

alligator clip a spring clip with distinctive jaw shape used to make a temporary connection such as to a meter or oscilloscope.

alloy a mixture of two or more metals, such as SOLDER, or COMPOUND SEMICONDUCTOR material.

alloyed junction a JUNCTION (sense 2) produced by depositing metal on a SEMICONDUCTOR material that is then heated to form an alloy. The method was once used to produce germanium transistors that had better high-frequency characteristics than the earlier diffused junction type.

all-pass filter (APF) a circuit that passes signals of all frequencies equally.

Contrast a normal FILTER, that has PASS BANDS and STOP-BANDS.

all-points addressable display (APA) a SCREEN display in which each PIXEL on the screen can have its colour and brightness controlled by reference to an ADDRESS number.

almanac data transmitted by a satellite containing information on present and predicted orbits.

Alnico™ a magnetic material, an alloy of aluminium, nickel and iron (with copper and cobalt) that is used for permanent magnets.

alpha (α) for a BIPOLAR JUNCTION TRANSISTOR, the ratio of COLLECTOR current to EMITTER (sense 1) current at constant collector voltage.

alpha cut-off the conventional limit of operating frequency for a transistor. COMMON BASE connection of a transistor allowing operation up to the highest possible frequency that the construction of the transistor allows. The alpha cut-off frequency is the frequency at which the voltage gain of the transistor in a common-base circuit has fallen to 0.707 of the voltage gain at lower frequencies.

alphanumeric (of a character set, code, or file of data) consisting of alphabetical and numerical symbols.

alpha particle the ionized (see IONIZATION) helium nucleus which has a very short range, but is strongly ionizing. Detection requires a device such as a GEIGER-MÜLLER TUBE with a very thin entry window.

alternate mark inversion a form of three-level digital code in which 0 is represented by no voltage transition, and 1 by alternate positive and negative transitions.

alternating current (AC) a current that flows in each of two opposite directions alternately. The term usually implies that the time between current reversals is constant, so that the FREQUENCY of the current reversal is constant. The WAVEFORM of current plotted against time is also assumed to be symmetrical around zero. The term is normally reserved to denote the *mains power supply*. See also MARK-SPACE RATIO; PULSE.

alternating voltage a voltage that is alternately higher than or lower than its median level. If the median level is zero, meaning that there is no DC component, the voltage swings are alternately positive and negative. See also FREQUENCY; MARK-SPACE RATIO; PULSE; WAVEFORM.

alternator a mechanical generator of ALTERNATING CURRENT. The principle of the alternator is of a coil of wire rotating in a magnetic field. If the connections to the ends of the coil are made through sliprings to ensure continuous contact, the waveform that is generated will be alternating current whose voltage at time t is given by the expression $V = -\omega BaCos(\omega t)$ where a is the side length of a square coil rotating with angular velocity ω.

altimeter, radar a device for measuring height above the Earth's surface using radio beam reflection.

alu see ARITHMETIC AND LOGIC UNIT.

aluminium electrolytic the common type of ELECTROLYTIC CAPACITOR which uses aluminium, usually in corrugated and/or etched form, as one plate and an aluminium can as the other plate. See also TANTALUM ELECTROLYTIC (tantalytic).

aluminium film, CRT see ALUMINIZED SCREEN.

aluminium solder a specialized form of SOLDER with a high lead content and about 2% of silver, melting at 270°C; or an alloy using 10% silver with a melting point of 370°C. Either of these alloys can be used to solder aluminium but they require a soldering iron that runs at a higher temperature than normal, or the use of a small gas torch.

aluminized screen a CATHODE-RAY TUBE screen whose brightness is increased by coating the PHOSPHOR with a thin film of aluminium, slightly spaced from the phosphor. Light from an excited part of the phosphor that would normally shine back inside the tube is thus reflected forward, increasing the total light output from the screen. The aluminium film must be thick enough to reflect efficiently, but not so thick as to absorb too great a proportion of the electrons that strike it.

AM see AMPLITUDE MODULATION.

AM alignment adjustment of the tuning of circuits in an AMPLITUDE MODULATION receiver so that they respond to the correct frequency, particularly the IF circuits.

amateur bands the SHORTWAVE bands in the radio spectrum that are reserved for use of licensed amateur operators. At one time, the short-wave bands were regarded as useless, and it was only the experiments of amateur enthusiasts that demonstrated that these bands were, in fact, the most efficient method of long-distance transmission available before the use of satellites. Governments then took possession of the shortwave bands, but selected parts were made available to amateurs in recognition of their achievements. Licensed amateurs continue to make many significant discoveries in radio communication.

ambient noise the level of noise, electrical or acoustic, that is due to the surroundings in which the signal is received.

ambient temperature the temperature of the air surrounding a device or unit.

AM/CW RADAR a radar system using CONTINUOUS WAVES at two frequencies. By detecting the PHASE SHIFT between the two returned frequencies, the range can be calculated with no ambiguities.

AM demodulation see DEMODULATION.

AM detector see DEMODULATION.

American National Standards Institute or **ANSI** a standardizing body that has defined electronic symbols and character sets for computer use.

American Standard Code for Information Interchange (ASCII) the code system using seven binary bits for the alphabetical, numerical and other symbols for computer use. An extended form using 8 bits is now more common, allowing for other alphabet sets and characters to be added.

americium-241 a radioactive source of ALPHA PARTICLES, used in the IONIZATION type of smoke detector.

AM/FM IF amplifier an IF AMPLIFIER whose stages are connected by a network

tuned to both the AM IF of 470 kHz and the FM IF of 10.7 MHz.

AM/FM radio a radio that can receive both AMPLITUDE MODULATION and FREQUENCY MODULATION signals.

ammeter *abbrev. for* ampere-meter, a meter used for current measurements. At one time, most ammeters used MOVING-COIL METER movements, shunted (see SHUNT, sense 1) to the appropriate range. AC ammeters generally made use of RECTIFIERS along with moving coil movements. These types have now been replaced by digital instruments. THERMOAMMETERS (hot-wire ammeters) are used for some radio-frequency current measurements, such as AERIAL current measurements.

ammonium perborate a slightly acidic salt used in jelly form as the ELECTROLYTE in an ELECTROLYTIC CAPACITOR.

amp see AMPERE.

AM/PM-VSB a FACSIMILE (fax) communications system, now obsolete, that uses a combination of amplitude and phase modulation with vestigial sideband transmission.

amorphous (of a material) having no crystal structure.

ampere or **amp** the unit of electric current, defined in terms of force between a pair of parallel wires. Symbol: A. The definition imagines two infinitely long straight parallel wires of negligible diameter, suspended in a vacuum, and with an identical current flowing in each wire. When the force between the wires is 2×10^{-7} newtons per metre length of wire, then the current flowing in the wires is one ampere. This definition is another way of stating that the BIOT-SAVART LAW is held to be the defining equation for magnetic FLUX DENSITY. The unit is named after André Marie Ampère (1775–1836), the French physicist and mathematician who made major discoveries in the fields of magnetism and electricity.

amperage amount of current in AMPERE units.

ampere hour the unit of battery capacity, the product of the steady discharge current in units of amperes multiplied by the time in hours for which the current can be maintained.

ampere per metre the unit of MAGNETIC FIELD strength, symbol **H**.

Ampere's law see BIOT-SAVART LAW.

ampere-turn the unit of MAGNETOMOTIVE FORCE (mmf) for a coil. The mmf of a coil is found by multiplying the number of turns by the current flowing. The size of magnetomotive force can then be related to the flux density by using the equation: mmf = reluctance × flux.

amplification see GAIN.

amplification factor the absolute value of small signal GAIN. Symbol: μ (Greek mu). The amplification factor for a transistor or other amplifying device is defined as change of output voltage divided by change of input voltage, disregarding sign.

amplified Zener a simple form of VOLTAGE REGULATOR circuit. The circuit uses a Zener diode with a power transistor connected to carry the main regulated current. See Fig. 3.

amplifier a circuit that provides power GAIN. Amplifiers can be classed as voltage amplifiers, current amplifiers, TRANSCONDUCTANCE AMPLIFIERS or TRANSRESISTANCE AMPLIFIERS according to their design and use. A voltage amplifier provides voltage gain at constant current, a current amplifier provides current gain at constant voltage. A transconductance amplifier has an output current proportional to its input voltage and a transresistance amplifier has an output voltage proportional to its input current.

amplifier, angle of flow see ANGLE OF FLOW.

amplifier, audio see AUDIO AMPLIFIER.

amplifier, bridge see BRIDGE AMPLIFIER.

amplifier, cascode see CASCODE.

amplifier class a system of nomenclature for amplifiers, based on the degree of linearity (see LINEAR AMPLIFIER), so that a Class A amplifier is, in theory, perfectly linear, but a Class C amplifier is cut off for a large part of the cycle of a wave. Class-B and Class-C operation relies on using another device to complete the wave output; a second amplifying device for Class-B or a tuned circuit for Class-C.

amplifier, common base see COMMON BASE CONNECTION.

amplifier, commutating auto-zero (CAZ) see CHOPPER STABILIZED AMPLIFIER.

amplifier crossover distortion see CROSSOVER DISTORTION.

amplifier, Darlington see DARLINGTON PAIR.

amplifier frequency response see FREQUENCY RESPONSE.

amplifier, long-tailed pair see DIFFERENTIAL AMPLIFIER.

amplifier, non-inverting see NON-INVERTING AMPLIFIER.

amplifier protection a circuit designed to cut off a POWER AMPLIFIER (sense 3) in the event of overload.

amplifier stage a single section of an amplifier that consists of several sections.

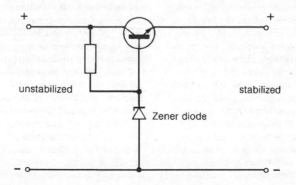

Fig. 3. **amplified Zener**

amplifier, transconductance see TRANSCONDUCTANCE AMPLIFIER.

amplifier, transresistance see TRANSRESISTANCE AMPLIFIER.

amplifier, tuned see TUNED AMPLIFIER.

amplify to increase the AMPLITUDE of a signal. In fact, the action is one of making a copy of the input signal at a greater value of amplitude.

amplifying connections the connections of COMMON-EMITTER, COMMON-BASE and common-collector (see EMITTER FOLLOWER) and the corresponding MOSFET connections that can be used in different configurations of a BIPOLAR JUNCTION TRANSISTOR or MOS device.

amplitude the size of a WAVE at a given time. For a VOLTAGE wave, this will mean the voltage, positive or negative, of the wave at an instant. The PEAK AMPLITUDE is the amplitude measured from zero to one peak of the wave. The PEAK-TO-PEAK AMPLITUDE (as measured by an oscilloscope) is the amplitude measured between the positive peak and the negative peak of the wave. For a sine wave, the amplitude A_t at time t is given by $A_t = A_0 \mathrm{Sin}(\omega t + \phi)$ where A_0 = peak amplitude, ω = ANGULAR FREQUENCY and ϕ = PHASE ANGLE.

amplitude companded single side band (ACSSB) a transmission system used for speech transmission over portable satellite links.

amplitude compensation the alteration of relative amplitudes of an AUDIO signal for VINYL DISC recording. The lowest frequencies must be attenuated to avoid excessive groove width, and the amplitudes of the highest frequencies must be boosted so that they are well above the INTRINSIC (sense 1) noise level of the disc surface. See also RIAA CURVE.

amplitude modulation (AM) a form of encoding that provides one method of carrying information by a radio wave. The AMPLITUDE of a high frequency (radio) wave (see CARRIER, sense 1) is increased or decreased by the amount of the amplitude of a low-frequency wave (audio or video). This results in the outline, or ENVELOPE, of

the high-frequency wave taking the shape of the low-frequency wave. See also FREQUENCY MODULATION; SINGLE SIDEBAND; VESTIGIAL SIDEBAND.

amplitude network analyzer or **scalar network analyzer** a form of SPECTRUM ANALYZER consisting of a CATHODE-RAY OSCILLOSCOPE and printer controlled by a MICROPROCESSOR system, providing digital processing and paper printouts.

amplitude response the graph of wave AMPLITUDE plotted against FREQUENCY for a circuit, particularly a FILTER.

amplitude shift keying (ASK) or **on-off keying (OOK)** a method of modulating a CARRIER (sense 1) with a DIGITAL signal in which two or more values of carrier amplitude are used to represent the digital values. The most common version is OOK, in which zero carrier amplitude represents 0 and any other amplitude represents 1. See also PHASE SHIFT KEYING.

amplitude-stabilizing circuit a circuit used in a low-frequency OSCILLATOR to limit the amplitude of oscillation, preventing the sine wave from degenerating into a square wave. Amplitude stabilization for a high-frequency oscillator is provided by the action of the LC TANK CIRCUIT, but LC methods cannot be used for low frequencies due to the size of the components required.

AM radio a radio system that makes use of AMPLITUDE MODULATION, such as broadcasts on the MEDIUM WAVE band.

AM rejection ratio the ratio of FM signal to AM signal existing after DEMODULATION of an FM signal, usually 1000:1 (60 dB) for a good receiver design.

amyl acetate a solvent and cleaning agent which is volatile and flammable, with toxic fumes.

analogue (of a signal or device) using continuous waveforms whose AMPLITUDE, PHASE and FREQUENCY can be continually varying, and in which one or more of these factors is used to convey data. Contrast DIGITAL.

analogue camcorder a CAMCORDER that uses the same methods as an analogue VIDEO CASSETTE RECORDER for storing the signals from the video pickup unit (of the CHARGE COUPLED DEVICE type). Contrast DIGITAL CAMCORDER.

analogue card a PRINTED CIRCUIT BOARD, particularly for a computer, that contains ANALOGUE TO DIGITAL CONVERTER circuits for converting varying analogue signals into digital form.

analogue circuit a circuit whose output signal voltage is proportional to its input signal voltage, i.e. any circuit that, supplied with a varying input of suitable frequency, will produce an output whose voltage at any time bears a fixed relationship to the voltage at the input.

analogue computer a form of computer in which waveforms are used to represent quantities, and mathematical operations and active circuits such as amplifiers are used to represent mathematical operations. The analogue computer uses the AMPLITUDE of a wave to represent the size of a quantity, making linearity of amplification extremely important (see LINEAR AMPLIFIER). Mathematical actions, such as integration and differentiation, are represented by the correspondingly named electrical operations on a waveform. The basic circuit of the analogue computer is the OPERATIONAL AMPLIFIER, a very high-gain linear amplifier whose characteristics can be modified by using NEGATIVE FEEDBACK. Contrast DIGITAL COMPUTER.

analogue demodulation the recovery of an ANALOGUE signal from a modulated (see MODULATION) RF transmission, usually AM or FM.

analogue device a device whose input and output signals are continuously variable rather than varying in steps. See also ANALOGUE; DIGITAL.

analogue filter a filter intended to separate continuous wave signals of differing frequencies. See also ALL-PASS FILTER; BAND-PASS FILTER; DIGITAL FILTER; HIGH-PASS FILTER; LOW-PASS FILTER.

analogue ground or **analogue earth** a separate common earthing point for all analogue portions of a circuit that also includes a digital section. By using a single analogue earth and a single digital

earth, connecting these two points will avoid malfunction that can arise because of EARTH LOOPS.

analogue high definition television (HDTV) any of a number of systems proposed for higher definition analogue TV broadcasting; now overtaken by the rapid spread of digital television.

analogue meter a meter that uses electro-mechanical methods, such as a moving-coil movement, to measure electrical quantities and indicate the size using a pointer over a scale.

analogue mixing the addition of ANALOGUE signals to produce a composite that should contain no frequencies other than those that have been mixed.

analogue modulation the modification of a high frequency CARRIER (sense 1) wave by a low frequency (signal) wave so that the signal information can be transmitted over long distances.

analogue monitor a TV type of display whose inputs are ANALOGUE colour signals, usually red, green and blue. This is the type of monitor used along with modern computers, often indicated by VGA or SVGA.

analogue multimeter an ANALOGUE METER that provides a switch-selected set of different measuring ranges of voltage, current and resistance.

analogue oscilloscope the conventional form of CATHODE-RAY OSCILLOSCOPE that uses analogue amplifiers and displays an input signal waveform. Contrast DIGITAL STORAGE OSCILLOSCOPE.

analogue real time (ART) the conventional CATHODE-RAY TUBE form of oscilloscope design, in which a TRANSIENT signal can be examined only if a suitable camera is used to photograph the trace.

analogue sat-box the SET-TOP BOX for reception of analogue satellite signals, decoding these signals for use by the circuits of a TV receiver.

analogue signal any signal for which the AMPLITUDE and PHASE of waves carries information.

analogue switch a switch circuit, typically implemented using CMOS devices, that will switch an analogue input on or off at its output with minimum distortion of the signal by the switching pulses.

analogue to digital converter or **AD** or **A/D** or **ADC**   a circuit that converts the ANALOGUE signals of any waveform into DIGITAL (usually binary) signals. The digital signal gives the amplitude of the analogue signal at each instant. The conversion is achieved by sampling the analogue wave at many intervals during the course of a wave, and converting each of the measurements into binary code. The sampling rate must be considerably greater than the frequency of the wave that is being sampled. See also ALIASING; COUNTING A/D CONVERTER; DELTA MODULATION; DUAL SLOPE ADC; DUAL-CONVERTER; FLASH CONVERTER; FLOATING POINT CONVERTER; INTEGRATOR A-D CONVERTER; QUANTIZATION; SINGLE SLOPE A/D; SUCCESSIVE APPROXIMATION CONVERTER; VOLTAGE ADDING CONVERTER.

analogue video   the signals, either as analogue RGB or analogue COMPOSITE SIGNAL form, used to send a picture to an analogue monitor or TV receiver.

analysis, gate circuit   any process that will predict the action of a gate circuit, usually in the form of a TRUTH TABLE or a BOOLEAN expression.

analyzer, logic   see LOGIC ANALYZER.

analyzing gate circuit   see ANALYSIS, GATE CIRCUIT.

anastigmatic lens   a lens that is manufactured in a way that makes it free from ASTIGMATISM.

anchor frame   see I-FRAME.

AND   a logical operation in which a TRUE (1) output is obtained only if all the inputs are at the TRUE (1) level. See also BOOLEAN ALGEBRA; OR; NOT.

and function or **logical product**   the AND logical operation as represented in a BOOLEAN EXPRESSION by the use of the × sign. See also OR FUNCTION.

AND gate   an electronic circuit whose action carries out AND logic. The output of the AND gate is at logic level 1 only when each input is simultaneously at logic level 1. See Fig. 4.

anemometer   a wind-strength gauge. Electronic anemometers have largely replaced the older types for navigational purposes. The simplest system uses a TACHO-GENERATOR driven by a propeller to measure wind speed, and a wind vane mounted on a POTENTIOMETER (sense 1) or SELSYN to transmit directional signals to the receiver. The advantage of electronic methods is that the distance between transmitter and receiver is unimportant.

angle   the difference in direction between two lines, expressed in degrees or radians.

angle modulation   a form of modulation in which the PHASE ANGLE of the CARRIER (SENSE 1) is affected by the amplitude of

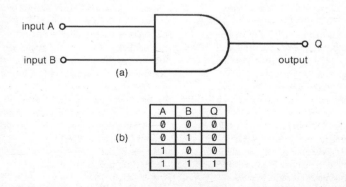

Fig. 4. **AND gate**

the modulating signal. Angle modulation is often used as a means of achieving FREQUENCY MODULATION, and an angle-modulated signal can usually be demodulated by an FM radio receiver.

angle of flow the fraction of a radio-frequency CYCLE for that current flows in an amplifying device. The term is used mainly of CLASS C transmitting stages. Conduction at all parts of the cycle corresponds to an angle of flow of 360°, conduction for half of a cycle to an angle of flow of 180° and so on. Class C amplifiers normally have angles of conduction of considerably less than 180°.

angle of incidence 1. The angle at which a wave is launched into space, measured from the vertical (which is angle 0°). 2. The angle at which a light beam or an electron beam hits a surface, measured from the normal (a line perpendicular to the surface).

angle of radiation the angle between a signal path from a transmitter and the Earth's surface.

angle of view for a lens, the range of angle of approaching light that will form a focused image of the correct size, expressed as the angle subtended at the centre of the lens by the extreme diagonals of the image.

angström unit a unit of length, symbol Å equal to 10^{-10} metres, seldom used now because it has not been standardized as an SI unit. See NANOMETRE.

angular frequency a wave frequency expressed in radians per second. The cycle of a wave is considered as a revolution of a circle, with one revolution tracing out the angle 2π. The angular frequency is therefore the frequency in hertz multiplied by 2π.

anion a negatively charged ION. The term is so called because such an ion will move, if free to do so, to a positively charged electrode or ANODE. Contrast CATION.

anisochronous signal a form of DIGITAL signal in which BITS are not clocked, so that the time between bits is variable.

anisochronous transmission see ASYNCHRONOUS TRANSMISSION.

anisotropic (of a material) having characteristics that depend on direction. A simple example is wood, in that the strength depends on grain direction. In electronics, the word is applied to crystals and to magnetic materials whose magnetic or electrical properties are different along different axes.

annunciator any form of sound or visual warning or reminder used to alert a user to the need for action.

anode 1. or **plate** (US) a conductor that is held at a positive potential. The term is used in electronics to mean an electron-collector in a vacuum device, such as a THERMIONIC VALVE or CATHODE-RAY TUBE. 2. the positive electrode of a diode or thyristor. 3. the cell ELECTRODE that loses electrons to the electrolyte and is therefore positive. Compare CATHODE (sense 3).

anode, crt see ELECTRON GUN.

anode current the amount of electron current flowing from the electron source to the ANODE. Since the conventional direction of current is positive to negative, this is described as a current flowing from anode to cathode.

anode slope resistance (R_a) for a THERMIONIC VALVE, the slope of the value of ANODE current plotted against anode voltage for a constant GRID voltage.

anodizing the protecting of aluminium with a skin of oxide. This also serves as an electrical insulator, but is not a good heat insulator. Anodized aluminium surfaces can therefore be used as HEAT SINKS that also provide electrical insulation.

Ansaphone™ see TELEPHONE ANSWERING MACHINE.

ANSI see AMERICAN NATIONAL STANDARDS INSTITUTE.

antenna see AERIAL.

anti-aliasing filter a steep-cut FILTER intended to remove harmonics from an analogue signal prior to SAMPLING, to avoid ALIASING effects from harmonics that are at frequencies higher than the sampling frequency.

anti-bounce circuit a circuit, often a form of R-S FLIP-FLOP, that can be used to eliminate the problem of pulses generated by switch contacts that bounce when closing. The output from the flip-flop is a single change of voltage even if the input from the switch changes several times.

anticathode see TARGET.

anticoincidence circuit a form of XOR gate (see EXCLUSIVE OR) that has an output when there is a pulse at one input only, but no output when there are pulses at both inputs. The circuit, used in particle counters, can usually be adjusted to reject input pulses at the two inputs that are within a specified time apart.

anti fuse a form of connector use in the manufacture of PROGRAMMABLE LOGIC DEVICES (PLD). An anti-fuse link is initially non-conductive, but can be made conductive by applying a voltage that will break the insulation and join tracks.

anti-hunting circuit a part of the circuitry of a SERVO control system designed to damp out this oscillation around a set level. See DAMPED; HUNTING.

anti-interference aerial a RECEIVING AERIAL that is connected to the receiver by balanced TWIN CABLE or by COAXIAL CABLE. The aerial is placed well clear of man-made interference, and the link between the aerial and the receiver is designed so that it does not pick up any signals.

antijamming any form of measure to reduce deliberate interference with electronic signals. This can include rapid changes of frequency, the use of DIGITAL coding or of very DIRECTIONAL AERIALS, or the use of satellite repeaters. See also SPREAD SPECTRUM.

antilog the inverse of a LOGARITHM. The antilog of 2.4, for example, is (approx.) 251.88, because the logarithm (base 10) of 251.88 is (approx.) 2.4.

antilog law a POTENTIOMETER LAW or taper that produces a graph of resistance plotted against shaft rotation that follows the shape of an antilog curve.

antinode a point in a STANDING WAVE pattern that has maximum voltage amplitude. On a TRANSMISSION LINE or AERIAL FEEDER, this is the point of minimum current and maximum resistance.

antinoise the use of a noise signal in ANTIPHASE as a way of counteracting noise when all other methods have failed. Modern antinoise methods for reducing acoustic noise pick up a sample of noise from a microphone, invert the phase and rebroadcast the signal from loudspeakers to create a zone that is virtually noise-free. See also HUMBUCKER COIL.

antiphase in PHASE opposition (180°) to an existing WAVE. The term is sometimes loosely used to mean *inverse*, but the two are identical only for sine waves. See Fig. 5.

anti-reversal circuit a circuit used to block current and prevent damage to equipment if a battery or other DC power source is connected the wrong way round.

anti-shake system see ELECTRONIC IMAGE STABILIZER.

anti-skating force or **bias compensation** a force applied, often through a weight, thread and set of pulleys, to a TONE ARM so as to counteract the force exerted by the side of the VINYL DISC groove on the STYLUS.

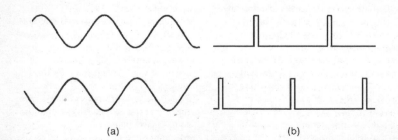

(a)   (b)

Fig. 5. **antiphase**

antistatic   (of a material) having sufficient conductivity so that it will not accumulate a static charge when rubbed.

antistatic mat   a mat of material that is an electrical conductor, used to rest CHIPs (sense 1) or circuit cards that are susceptible to ELECTROSTATIC damage.

antitamper loop or **tamper loop**   a method of wiring security devices so that any attempt to interfere with wiring (by cutting a wire or shorting connections) will activate the alarm.

anti-tinkle suppression   circuitry used in a MODEM that prevents telephones on the same line from ringing briefly when the modem is used for dialling out.

antitracking   a silicone resin solution with good insulating properties. This material is used to paint onto surfaces around a high-voltage connector to avoid leakage current, or TRACKING (sense 5).

anti-transmit/receive switch (ATR) a device used in a radar system that will short-circuit the receiver input during transmission and open-circuit the transmitter during reception, so as to avoid destroying the receiver circuits with the power of the transmitter.

APC   automatic picture control: see AUTOMATIC GAIN CONTROL.

APCM   see ADAPTIVE PULSE CODE MODULATION.

aperiodic circuit or **nonresonant circuit** an untuned circuit, i.e. any circuit that responds to a wide range of frequencies without a noticeable resonance.

aperiodic coupling   any method of passing signals from one STAGE to another without emphasizing any one frequency, so that no resonant circuit is involved. See also R-C coupling.

aperiodic oscillator   any oscillating circuit that has no resonant (see RESONANT CIRCUIT) components, so that its output is not a sine wave. See also ASTABLE; MULTIVIBRATOR.

aperture or **lens aperture**   the effective diameter of the opening of a lens (often measured as a fraction of the focal length) that determines how much light will enter the lens.

aperture correction   a circuit for adding OVERSHOOT and UNDERSHOOT pulses before and after a signal level transition, so partially correcting for the loss of detail due to APERTURE DISTORTION.

aperture delay   for a SAMPLING circuit, the time between holding a signal and acquiring the signal value.

aperture distortion   the blurring of a scanned TV picture due to the finite spot diameter of a scanning beam or PIXELs in the CCD device. This makes a sharp transition from dark to light or light to dark in a TELEVISION CAMERA impossible to achieve.

aperture effect   the distortion of a DIGITAL signal caused by the finite width of the SAMPLING pulse.

aperture efficiency   a figure for the reception efficiency of an aerial in terms of the effective area of the aerial divided by the actual physical area of aerial, usually between 50% and 75% for parabolic aerials. See also RADIATION EFFICIENCY for a TRANSMITTING AERIAL.

aperture grille   a metal mask in a TV colour PICTURE TUBE that is etched with a pattern of narrow slits. The electron beams from the three guns of the colour tube cross over at a slit, and so strike the correct PHOSPHORs to achieve coloured light outputs. See also COLOUR CRT. See Fig. 6.

APM   see ADVANCED POWER MANAGEMENT.

apogee   the highest point above the Earth's surface that a satellite reaches in its elliptical orbit. Contrast PERIGEE.

apparent power   the figure of power that is obtained from multiplying voltage by current. For an alternating signal, this will be equal to true power only if the phase angle is zero. *True power* in an AC circuit is obtained when apparent power is multiplied by the cosine of the phase angle.

Appleton layer   see F LAYER.

application specific integrated circuit or **ASIC**   a form of IC that is manufactured for one particular set of actions as distinct from the use of general-purpose ICs, often designed for use by one manufacturer of equipment.

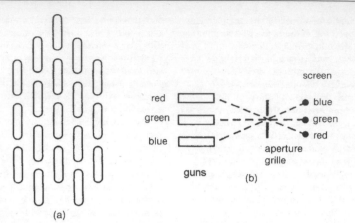

red green blue
guns

screen
blue
green
red
aperture grille

(a)   (b)

Fig. 6. aperture grille

approved case   a computer case whose layout, POWER SUPPLY unit and cooling arrangement have been approved by a manufacturer of CPUs for use with fast processors.

arc   a conducting path in air or other gas. This requires the air or other gas to be ionized (see IONIZATION), and is more likely to occur with DC than with low-frequency AC because at the zero-voltage portion of an AC wave, there will be no arc current, and the air can de-ionize in this time. An arc causes severe radio frequency interference, and also evaporation of metal from the conductors between which the arc takes place.

architecture   the way in which HARDWARE or SOFTWARE is designed and constructed, either on the overall scale (architecture of a computer system) or in detail (architecture of a microprocessor).

arcing   see ARCOVER.

arcover or **arcing**   the appearance of an ARC between two terminals with a large potential difference. Arcover is common in all high-voltage devices, such as high-voltage switches, X-RAY TUBES, CATHODE-RAY TUBES, transmitting valves etc. Arcover is treated by using insulation around high-voltage connectors, painting surfaces with ANTITRACKING material, and the removal of dust and moisture.

arc suppression   any system for reducing ARCING. Switch contacts in DC circuits are arc-suppressed by using resistor-capacitor networks. For large switches, an airblast when the contacts open can be used to blow out the arc, or the contacts can be completely immersed in oil (*oil-quenched contacts*).

Argand diagram   a two-dimensional graph plot that represents a COMPLEX NUMBER ($a+jb$) by plotting real values (a) on the x-axis and imaginary values (b) on the y-axis.

arithmetic and logic unit (ALU)   the portion of a MICROPROCESSOR that deals with arithmetic (such as addition and subtraction) and logic (such as AND, OR) actions carried out on two BINARY NUMBERS.

ARLL   see ADVANCED RUN-LENGTH LIMITING.

ARM   see ADVANCED RISC MACHINE.

armature   any moving piece of SOFT MAGNETIC MATERIAL such as the rotating part of an AC or DC generator or the moving part of a RELAY.

Armstrong, Edwin   (1890–1954) the inventor in 1918 of the SUPERHETERODYNE principle and in 1934 of FM broadcasting. Unable to interest commercial broadcasting stations, he personally financed a transmitter near New York in 1939 to prove the benefits of the system. By 1940,

150 applications for FM broadcast stations had been submitted in the USA and in 1954 the BBC launched its wideband FM service, now challenged by DIGITAL AUDIO BROADCASTING. Armstrong profited very little from his remarkable achievements, and died by his own hand.

Armstrong method the first method, devised by Edwin Armstrong, used to create a purely frequency-modulated signal. A CARRIER (sense 1) and the modulating signal are mixed to produce a double-sideband suppressed carrier signal. Adding the original carrier, phase shifted by 90°, to the sidebands and then limiting produces a pure FM signal with no trace of AM.

Armstrong oscillator An oscillator that uses a transformer to couple output to input in phase.

ARPANET see ADVANCED RESEARCH PROJECT AGENCY NETWORK.

ARQ see AUTOMATIC REQUEST FOR REPEAT.

array 1. a set of related values that can be treated in the same way. 2. see AERIAL ARRAY.

array factor the ratio of radiated FIELD STRENGTH for an aerial ARRAY (sense 2) to that of a simple dipole for the same total RF power supplied.

array processor a type of computer circuit that uses a large number of linked processors. This allows ARRAY (sense 1) data to be manipulated very rapidly, with one processor handling each part of the array.

Arrhenius model see ACCELERATION FACTOR.

arrow the symbol used to indicate flow direction, such as current flow in a DIODE or transistor or signal flow in a BLOCK DIAGRAM.

ART see ANALOGUE REAL TIME.

artifact a defect in an ANALOGUE or DIGITAL TELEVISION picture, such as flickering, patterning or colour bands.

artificial aerial or **dummy antenna** a network of PASSIVE COMPONENTS that acts as a load for a transmitter. The component values are chosen so that the network simulates the action of an aerial at the frequency of transmission, but with no

radiation. The transmitter power is dissipated as heat, and the resistors in the artificial aerial must be capable of dissipating this power. The use of an artificial aerial allows final adjustments and measurements to be made to a transmitter before connecting to its real aerial.

artificial line or **artificial delay line** a network of PASSIVE COMPONENTS that has the same characteristics as a TRANSMISSION LINE. See also LUMPED PARAMETER.

artificial noise radiated man-made noise due mainly to electric motors, switches, and other unsuppressed sparking devices.

artwork the drawings that will be used to form the etch patterns for PRINTED CIRCUITS or INTEGRATED CIRCUITS. These will be reproduced photographically, with any reduction of scale that is needed.

ASCII see AMERICAN STANDARD CODE FOR INFORMATION INTERCHANGE.

ASIC see APPLICATION SPECIFIC INTEGRATED CIRCUIT.

ASK see AMPLITUDE SHIFT KEYING.

ASK demodulation recovery of DIGITAL DATA from an ASK signal, usually by a simple diode and filter, or using a SQUARE-LAW DETECTOR and LOW-PASS FILTER.

ASO see ACTIVE SIDEBAND OPTIMIZATION.

aspect ratio the ratio of width to height for a TV or computer monitor picture or any other image. A value of 4:3 was once universal, but 16:9 has been standardized for DIGITAL TELEVISION, though not for computer monitors.

aspheric lens a form of lens that eliminates SPHERICAL ABERRATION so as to produce very sharp images even at large aperture (see LENS APERTURE) settings.

ASPI see ADVANCED SCSI PERIPHERAL INTERFACE.

ASR see AIRPORT SURVEILLANCE RADAR.

assemble editing the editing of analogue VIDEO CASSETTE RECORDER tape by connecting one recorder to play and another connected machine to record, and editing by using the RECORD and PAUSE keys, or by implementing these actions electrically from an editing controller. See also LINEAR EDITING.

assembler a computer program that can translate commands into machine code for systems software. The commands must be written in assembly language, that uses simple mnemonic abbreviations (*mnemonics*) for machine code instructions.

assembly a set of components, usually on a single PRINTED CIRCUIT BOARD, that performs a distinct circuit action. The alternative to using assemblies is to have single-board construction.

assembly language a programming language that uses word abbreviations for actions that the microprocessor can carry out. A program written in assembly language can be converted by another program (an *assembler*) into number codes that the microprocessor will obey.

associative law the algebraic law summarized as (A+B)+C = A+(B+C); true for BOOLEAN ALGEBRA as well as for everyday arithmetic.

astable (of an oscillator) oscillating continually for as long as power is supplied because it has no stable state. See also BISTABLE; MONOSTABLE; MULTIVIBRATOR.

astigmatic lens a lens that has a focus point in one plane that is not identical to the focus point for a plane at right angles, so that either vertical or horizontal lines will be slightly out of focus.

astigmatism a defect in an optical or ELECTRON-OPTICS system in which the image of a circular spot is elliptical rather than circular. Astigmatism in a CATHODE-RAY OSCILLOSCOPE tube causes the effect that vertical lines appear thicker than horizontal lines, or vice versa. Astigmatism in a TV CAMERA TUBE or receiver tube makes pictures appear to be out of focus in one direction.

ASTM American Society for Testing Materials.

Astra the group name for a set of satellites used for entertainment signals.

Astra digital radio (ADR) the early format of digital radio broadcasting, superseded by DAB.

astronomical time the time scale developed from long-term observation

of the Earth's orbit around the sun in approximately 365.25 days.

asymmetric digital subscriber line (ADSL) a digital connection that allocates more BANDWIDTH for communication in one direction than in another. This is ideal for the common situation where data is sent from a keyboard in one direction and from a server computer in the other direction.

asymmetrical modulation (of a communications system) allocating more of the available BANDWIDTH to the MODEM that is transmitting the larger amount of information.

asymmetrical waveform a waveform that has no axis of symmetry, or that has a DC component so that its axis of symmetry is a steady voltage.

asymmetric network a network whose input and outputs cannot be reversed because their characteristics are not identical.

asynchronous (of a signal) being unsynchronized to any other signal in a circuit. Contrast SYNCHRONOUS; see also UNCLOCKED.

asynchronous character a set of BITS of equal time duration that are transmitted using start and stop characters so that there can be unequal times between characters.

asynchronous communications interface adapter (ACIA) a circuit, usually in a single chip, that provides a PORT (sense 1) that can be used for serial communications to and from a computer without the need for a continuous stream of synchronizing signals.

asynchronous connection a data connection that is not synchronized to a CLOCK, typically the system used by a MODEM.

asynchronous counter or **serial counter** a counter in which the input pulses are applied only to the first stage of the counter, and the output of each stage is used as the input for the following stage. If such a counter is incremented from, for example, 0111 to 1000 in binary the stages will not change simultaneously. See also SYNCHRONOUS COUNTER.

asynchronous decade counter   a form of ASYNCHRONOUS COUNTER in which the count, normally to 16, is gated so as to end at 9, making the overall action that of a DECADE COUNTER.

asynchronous demodulation or **non-coherent demodulation**   any method of demodulating a DIGITAL signal that does not depend on the use of a synchronizing clock signal.

asynchronous logic   a form of LOGIC CIRCUIT design in which no CLOCK pulse is used, so that data is output from the stage as soon as it is available.

asynchronous serial interface (ASI) a standardized method of connecting serial (see SERIAL TRANSFER) MPEG digital TV signals as 10-bit words transmitted over copper cables or FIBRE OPTICS cables.

asynchronous transfer mode (ATM) a communications system that uses a DATA PACKET of fixed size and allocates BANDWIDTH dynamically.

asynchronous transmission or **anisochronous transmission**   any DIGITAL transmission in which the time between BITS is not fixed, so that start and stop bits are required for each character.

AT   advanced technology; the initials applied by IBM in 1982 to the ARCHITECTURE of their PC-AT, successor to the original PC-XT machines. The AT architecture later became the basis of industry standard architecture (ISA).

ATA   see ADVANCED TECHNOLOGY ATTACHMENT.

ATA-2   see ADVANCED TECHNOLOGY ATTACHMENT INTERFACE WITH EXTENSIONS.

AT bus   the standard set of signal lines used originally in the IBM PC-AT computer and now widely used by many other COMPATIBLE and CLONE computers. This form of circuit was used on machines with the Intel 80286, 80386, 80486, Pentium™ and later MICROPROCESSOR chips and is now known as ISA (industry standard architecture). See also EISA (sense 2); MCA; PERIPHERAL COMPONENTS INTERCONNECT BUS; VLB.

at casing   the older form of casing for the PC type of computer, now obsolete. See ATX CASING.

AT cut crystal   the form of cutting a QUARTZ CRYSTAL that results in the lowest (often zero) TEMPERATURE COEFFICIENT of frequency change.

ATE   see AUTOMATIC TEST EQUIPMENT.

ATF   see AUTOMATIC TRACK FINDING.

Athlon™   the tradename for fast processors manufactured by Advanced Micro Devices Inc. (AMD).

ATM   **1.** see ASYNCHRONOUS TRANSFER MODE. **2.** acronym for *automated teller machine*, the familiar cash dispensing machine ('hole-in-the-wall') often found on an outer wall of a bank.

atmosphere   the space, subdivided into TROPOSPHERE and STRATOSPHERE, extending to about 40 km above the Earth's surface, in which both temperature and pressure fall almost linearly with increasing height. See also IONOSPHERE.

atmospheric noise   radio NOISE due mainly to the presence of water vapour and oxygen molecules in the ATMOSPHERE.

A to D   see ANALOGUE TO DIGITAL CONVERTER.

atom   the smallest possible particle of an element, consisting of a positively charged core of PROTONS and NEUTRONS with outer layers (shells) of ELECTRONS.

atomic clock   a signal generator whose standard of frequency is derived from the stable natural oscillations within an atom. The stable frequency can be counted down to give a very precise time indication.

atomic number   for an atom, the number of positive charges (protons) in the nucleus that gives the atom its distinctive chemical nature.

ATRAC   see ADAPTIVE TRANSFORM ACOUSTIC CODING.

attached processor   an auxiliary MICROPROCESSOR in a computer. The attached processor is a separate processor under the control of the main processor, and is used for auxiliary actions so as to allow the main processor to operate faster.

attack   the first part of the waveform for a musical note in which the amplitude rises steeply from zero. See also DECAY; RELEASE; SUSTAIN.

attack, AGC   the time needed for an AUTOMATIC GAIN CONTROL to take effect, a balance between a slow change which might not follow rapid FADING, and fast change which will attenuate bass notes.

attenuate to reduce the amplitude of a signal. See also AMPLIFY.

attenuation a reduction of signal power, the opposite of gain. Attenuation, like gain, is measured in decibels (dB). Attenuation of signals in circuits is caused by RESISTORS and other energy-dissipating components.

attenuation band the range of frequencies over which a FILTER attenuates signals.

attenuation characteristic the graph of ATTENUATION (in dB) and GROUP DELAY for a TRANSMISSION LINE plotted against frequency.

attenuation constant the real part of the PROPAGATION CONSTANT for a transmission line. If the propagation constant is expressed as the COMPLEX NUMBER $\alpha + j\beta$, then α is the attenuation constant in units of NEPERS per unit length.

attenuation, slope see SLOPE OF ATTENUATION.

attenuator a circuit that attenuates a signal by a known amount. A switched attenuator uses a resistive LADDER network, and will be calibrated in decibels (dB). POTENTIOMETERS (sense 1) can be used as attenuators, but calibration is less easy. See Fig. 7.

attenuator, cro probe a COMPENSATED ATTENUATOR using resistors and capacitors that is attached to the input of a CRO to form a low-loss input that can be applied to points on a PRINTED CIRCUIT BOARD.

atto prefix meaning 10^{-18}.

attosecond a time unit of 10^{-18} seconds.

A20 line the ADDRESS BUS line in a 16-bit IBM-AT or CLONE PC that controls the high memory area.

ATX casing a modern case design for PC computers in which ventilation and layout are improved compared to the older AT design, and the power supply unit has more voltage supplies.

ATX motherboard the modern type of PC MOTHERBOARD, designed for better cooling and access to components as compared to the obsolete AT type.

AT/XT bus or **PC bus** the BUS link design used in PC machines. The original XT bus was 8 bits wide with a transfer rate of 800 KB/s; the later AT bus is 16 bits wide and operates at 1.6 MB/s. Faster bus rates are used in more modern machines, along with specialized buses such as AGP.

audible effect see LOUDNESS.

audio (of any system) making use of frequencies that can be heard by the human ear. This range is taken as approximately 16 Hz. to 20 kHz.

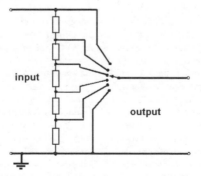

Fig. 7. **attenuator**

audio amplifier   an AMPLIFIER designed to work with the AUDIO FREQUENCY range.

audio board, sound board or **audio card** a PRINTED CIRCUIT BOARD added to a computer by way of an EXPANSION SLOT so as to add sound capabilities to the computer. This includes the ability to convert incoming analogue signals into digital sound signals. Many computers have this facility built into the MOTHERBOARD and require no added sound board unless high-power audio outputs are required.

audio cassette   a tape cassette that is primarily intended for recording sound, and not suitable for data recordings.

audio connector   any connector designed for use with AUDIO signals, usually RCA or DIN connectors for consumer use or the XLR type for professional use.

audio coupling   the method used to pass an AUDIO signal from one STAGE of an amplifier to the next; usually by way of a capacitor.

audio distortion   changes in the WAVEFORM shape of an AUDIO signal, or restriction of its BANDWIDTH, caused by an amplifier.

audio dropout   a problem affecting both Nicam stereo TV and DIGITAL TELEVISION transmissions in which sound is intermittent, though vision may not be noticeably affected. The dropout is often due to momentary loss of signal.

audio file format   any system for storing digitized (see DIGITIZE) audio data as computer files. These are known by their file extension names such as WAV, AU, AIFF, MPEG, and VOC.

audio frequency or **AF**   the range of frequencies between about 15Hz and 20kHz. This corresponds to the range of sound wave frequencies that can be heard by a 'perfect' human ear.

audio frequency shift keying   see FREQUENCY SHIFT KEYING.

audio interface, PC   see AUDIO BOARD.

audiometer   an instrument used to measure acuity of human hearing. The older type used signals into earphones and required a response from the person being tested. This is not suitable for very young children, and later models have

operated on a system that uses a pulsed note to set the eardrum into resonance. The sound radiated by the resonating eardrum can then be picked up, recorded, and analyzed to give much more information about the ear than could be obtained by the earlier type of instrument.

audio mixer   a device that will accept input signals from a variety of audio sources, such as CD, tape, vinyl disc etc., and allow the VOLUME (sense 2) of each to be controlled. The mixed output is then available for amplification. An audio mixer is normally implemented in hardware for analogue sound signals, but software control is used for digitally coded sound.

audion   the first TRIODE THERMIONIC VALVE, invented by Lee de Forest.

audio output stage or **audio power amplifier**   the final POWER OUTPUT STAGE of an audio amplifier, driven by an audio input signal and connected to loudspeakers.

audio range   the range of sound frequencies that the (perfect) human ear can detect, often taken as 15 Hz to 20 kHz.

audio signal generator   an OSCILLATOR that operates in the AUDIO RANGE, delivering an output of variable and precise amplitude and frequency for testing audio equipment.

audio signals   electronic signals in the AUDIO RANGE.

audio tracks   separate tracks on a magnetic tape used to record the sound portion of a TV signal.

audio video interleave (AVI)   a MICROSOFT WINDOWS standard for MULTIMEDIA video computer files that consist of alternate DIGITAL VIDEO and sound samples.

auditory masking   the principle that loud sounds can conceal softer sounds even if the loud sound occurs just ahead of the softer sound. This allows AUDIO data in digital form to be compressed (see BIT REDUCTION) by omitting the data for the softer sounds that are masked.

aurora or **northern lights**   a visible light in the IONOSPHERE due to intense IONIZATION, visible usually near the poles.

auroral oval region   the shape and size of the AURORA over the North pole.

authorization code   a digital code contained in SMART CARD for satellite video receivers that ensures that only 32-byte instructions from the authorized user will be obeyed. This defeats attempts to copy the card.

authorization key   a code encryption process that allows access to scrambled (see SCRAMBLER) satellite broadcasts.

auto answer (AA)   a feature of a FACSIMILE (fax) machine or computer-controlled messaging service that will answer an incoming call without the need for human intervention.

autobaud   see AUTOMATIC BAUD RATE DETECTION.

autochanger   a unit, formerly used for VINYL DISC recordings that can hold a stack of discs and will play each in turn. Latterly autochangers for CDs have been used, particularly in car audio systems, but these are likely to become obsolete when car CD players can use MP-3 coded discs.

auto correlation function   an algebraic expression that describes the similarity between an original signal and its appearance after a delay.

auto detect   a system, usually part of a computer, that will detect when a CD has been loaded and will play the CD.

auto-diagnosis   a system built into some TV receivers that allows the use of a 'service' mode that will check for faults.

auto dial   a MODEM facility that will dial telephone numbers from the computer.

autodialer or **autoredialer**   a feature of a MODEM that allows a telephone number to be re-dialled at intervals until an answer is obtained.

autodyne   see DIRECT CONVERSION RECEIVER.

auto-editor   a video editing system in which the editing actions are controlled by an edit decision list prepared by the operator.

auto grey scale   a circuit for controlling the BLACK LEVEL for each gun in a colour CATHODE-RAY TUBE, making it possible to allow for the changes due to tube ageing.

auto idle   a CLOCK rate management system for a MICROPROCESSOR that reduces the clock rate at times when the processor is waiting for data.

auto-install or **auto set-up** or **auto-tuning**   a tuning system for a TV RECEIVER or SET-TOP BOX in which entering a search mode will automatically tune in the strongest available signals and allocate them to channel numbers.

auto-loopback connection   a form of connection for a SERIAL TRANSMISSION cable that dispenses with HANDSHAKING signals and can be used for testing purposes.

automated bias setting   a system used in some audio tape or cassette recorders, using the first 11 seconds of tape run to check and set optimum settings for BIAS and then resetting and starting a RECORDING.

automated teller machine   see ATM (sense 2).

automated test equipment   see AUTOMATIC TEST EQUIPMENT.

automatic baud rate detection (ABRD) or **autobaud**   a feature of a MODEM that can determine the speed and other features of an incoming message and adjust itself for the PROTOCOL that is in use.

automatic call distribution (ACD)   a queue management system for communications that experience a large number of incoming calls.

automatic colour control (ACC)   the use of a BIAS signal derived from the COLOUR BURST to control the gain of the CHROMINANCE AMPLIFIER stages in a colour TV receiver.

automatic control   any control system that uses electrical input signals to control devices without human intervention. The electrical signals into the controller will arise from TRANSDUCERS such as photocells, strain gauges, limit switches, level switches and so on. The output will usually consist of high-power supplies for electric motors, heaters and similar devices. Most control systems depend on the application of overall NEGATIVE FEEDBACK.

automatic debit   a system used for road-toll charging by detecting the identity of a road user and billing the owner of the vehicle.

automatic frequency control (AFC)
a system of LOCAL OSCILLATOR control in a SUPERHETERODYNE receiver for FREQUENCY MODULATED signals. The local oscillator is made voltage dependent, usually by making a VARACTOR diode part of the tuned circuit. At the demodulator, a DISCRIMINATOR (sense 1) circuit gives a DC voltage that varies according to the frequency of the IF signal. This DC voltage is connected (sometimes with a stage of amplification) to the varactor diode. If the receiver is perfectly tuned, this DC voltage should be zero. If not, then the voltage applied to the varactor diode will adjust the oscillator frequency until the receiver is in tune.

automatic gain control (AGC), automatic volume control (AVC), automatic picture control (APC)   a system for counteracting input signal amplitude fluctuations in a radio-frequency signal. The scheme applies mainly to AM signals, and makes use of the DC level at the demodulator. This DC level is proportional to the amplitude of the CARRIER (sense 1) wave, and will vary as the carrier amplitude varies. By using this voltage to control the gain of several stages (usually RF and IF stages), the amount of IF signal at the detector can be made almost constant despite large variations in carrier amplitude.

automatic level control (ALC)   1. the system used to maintain the constancy of the amplitude level of signal from a microphone (or other varying source), to avoid excessive or inadequate amplitude levels. 2. a form of automatic gain control for TV signals, in which the BLACK LEVEL of the picture is held at a constant level.

automatic noise level sensing   a system used in PUBLIC ADDRESS equipment that senses the level of AMBIENT NOISE and adjusts the amplitude and treble boost of speech signals to make announcements intelligible.

automatic noise limiter   a circuit that clips IMPULSE (sense 1) noise peaks from any signal. The circuit makes use of the

principle of charging a capacitor to the PEAK signal voltage, and using this voltage to operate a CLIPPER. Any pulse of more than the PEAK AMPLITUDE is clipped.

automatic noise reduction, FM
a system, used particularly on in-car FM radios, that blends STEREO and MONOPHONIC signals so that as the SIGNAL TO NOISE RATIO becomes lower, the mono signal (which uses a lower BANDWIDTH, so is less noisy) predominates.

automatic power control (APC)   a circuit used in a CD player to maintain constant output power from the LASER, usually in the region of 120 microwatts.

automatic request for repeat (ARQ)
a code generated by an error detection system in a digital transmission which requires the sender to repeat a section of code.

automatic test equipment (ATE)
computer monitoring system for monitoring and logging test data for production equipment or communications links.

automatic track finding (ATF)   a method of maintaining head ALIGNMENT for a video cassette recorder that uses guidance signals recorded in the video tracks, first used in the (now obsolete) Philips/Grundig V2000 recorder format, subsequently used in the Video-8 format.

automatic tracking   a form of automatic control for a RADAR aerial. This keeps the transmitted beam on the target while the range is computed. This is nowadays achieved electronically (by altering the phasing of signals to different parts of the aerial) rather than entirely by mechanical control of aerial movement.

automatic tuning or **search tuning**
a method of tuning a receiver to a set of input signals so that station selection by pushbutton or remote control can be easily implemented. The digitally controlled tuner sweeps over the range of frequencies (radio, or TV) and stores the data for the strongest signals which are then allocated to pushbuttons or to numbers on a remote control. These

settings can be changed manually to allow a favourite channel to be allocated to a particular button or number.

automatic voice recognition (AVR) or **speech recognition** a system that uses a microphone to pick up the sound of speech, and a set of circuits and software to convert this speech into text. This works well with languages like Japanese, in which the sounds of speech are standardized, but less well with flexible languages like English, though its use is now well established. Each user of a speech recognition system needs to log on to the system, and a new user must go through an initial period of repeating words that are shown on the screen so that differences in accents and intonation can be accommodated.

automatic white balance (AWB) a CAMCORDER circuit that samples the white content of the light of a scene and adjusts the colour amplifiers accordingly to compensate for different illumination.

automation the replacement of human labour with machines, now generally computer-controlled. The positive aspects of automation include elimination of drudgery, raising of standards of workmanship (machineship?), and increased productivity, that should lead to higher living standards. Its undesirable aspects include unemployment, particularly for the lower-skilled, and the feeling that you are 'tied to a machine' if you work in an extensively automated environment.

automaton see ROBOT.

auto ranging, meter a feature of a DIGITAL MULTIMETER design that allows the instrument to be connected to any voltage or current within its range without the need to alter range switches.

autoredialer see AUTODIALER.

auto-reset module part of a security system that will automatically reset alarms following an alarm that has proved false.

auto-reverse cassette player an AUDIO CASSETTE player, usually for in-car use, that will automatically reverse the tape

direction at the end of one side and switch the HEAD connections so that the other set of STEREO tracks of the tape can be played.

auto-rewind a VIDEO CASSETTE RECORDER action which rewinds the tape automatically when a RECORDING has reached the end of the tape.

autorun a software system that will play a CD automatically once it has been placed in a drive.

auto scan a MODEM feature that will detect the speed of incoming signals and adjust the modem to read at that speed.

autospec the ten-bit coding system used with the five-bit BAUDOT CODE for ERROR CORRECTION, using five PARITY bits.

autostop see CASSETTE END DETECTION.

auto tracking see AUTOMATIC TRACK FINDING.

autotransformer a transformer with a single winding that can be tapped at any point. At mains frequency the device is used mainly for testing equipment that must operate with a range of supply voltages. Autotransformers are also found in RF amplifiers functioning as tuned transformers.

auto-tuning see AUTO-INSTALL.

auto widescreen switching the action of switching a TV display between widescreen (16:9) and conventional (4:3) according to the ASPECT RATIO of the input signal.

auxiliary battery a battery used as backup when mains power is interrupted (see also UPS) or as a means of retaining essential data in a computer memory when the main battery is exhausted.

auxiliary unit any unit that will provide power to electronics equipment in the event of failure of the mains supply. Battery-powered units are usually referred to as UPS (UNINTERRUPTIBLE POWER SUPPLY) and the name *auxiliary unit* should be reserved for a generator operated by a petrol, diesel or gas-powered engine.

A/V or **AV** audio-visual: a set of signals containing both sound and picture information.

availability a measure of RELIABILITY equal to MTTF/(MTTF + MTTR). Unavailability is defined as (1 – availability).

avalanche the uncontrollable BREAKDOWN of insulation, particularly of a gas or a SEMICONDUCTOR. An avalanche occurs in a gas when IONS are formed in a gas in which there is a strong electric field. The acceleration of the ions by the electric field can cause them to reach such speeds that collisions with gas molecules will generate more ions, that in turn are accelerated. This leads to total IONIZATION of the gas in a very short time. The initial ionization can be triggered by a charged particle from a radioactive material, as in a Geiger-Müller tube, or by light or other radiation.

avalanche breakdown a form of AVALANCHE effect in a semiconductor JUNCTION (sense 2). Avalanche breakdown occurs in a reverse biased junction at a very sharply defined voltage level. The effect is used in the manufacture of voltage reference diodes. These diodes are usually named ZENER DIODES, but ZENER BREAKDOWN is not identical to avalanche breakdown, being more gradual.

avalanche injection programming a method of user-programming a MOS logic device in which a charge can be injected beneath selected GATE (sense 1) electrodes. The charge can be neutralized to reuse the device.

avalanche photodiode (APD) a form of PHOTODIODE that uses the AVALANCHE effect to obtain high current gains of the order of 1000 times that of a simple photodiode.

AVC see AUTOMATIC GAIN CONTROL.

AV cable a cable set with connectors used for carrying audio and video signals, such as the commonly used (and hated!) SCART system, and the serial IEE1394 (*Firewire*) system that will probably replace SCART for digital signals.

AV connector the connector, such as the Peritel (SCART) type, used at each end of an AV cable.

average access time an ACCESS TIME (sense 2) figure for a computer HARD DRIVE equal to half of the worst-case access time.

average detector a demodulator whose output responds to slow changes in carrier level as distinct from (more rapid) modulation. Typically, this can be achieved by following a peak detector with a low-pass filter, as is used to obtain an AGC signal. See also PEAK DETECTOR.

average failure rate for a quality control test, the ratio of the number of devices failing per device hour to the total number of devices.

average information or **source entropy** a figure for the amount of information carried by a set of transmitted symbols related to the certainty of information. See INFORMATION THEORY.

averaging see ENSEMBLE AVERAGING.

average noise factor for a transmission, the NOISE FACTOR for the bandwidth used.

average seek time the time required to find a TRACK on a COMPACT DISC.

average traffic a measure of TRAFFIC flow in a communications system, measured in units called ERLANG, where the Erlang is defined as a permanently engaged line.

AVI file see AUDIO VIDEO INTERLEAVE.

avionics the application of electronics to aviation. This covers all aspects of airborne radar, communications, control systems and on-board computers.

AWB see AUTOMATIC WHITE BALANCE.

AWG American Wire Gauge: a system that uses a single number to indicate the diameter of wire (in inch units). The UK equivalent is SWG (Standard Wire Gauge), but modern usage specifies the diameter of the wire directly in millimetre units.

axes of graph see X-AXIS; Y-AXIS; Z-AXIS.

axis a line defining direction on a graph, see X-AXIS; Y-AXIS; Z-AXIS.

azimuth angle 1. the angle of tilt of a tape recording or replay HEAD. The head is at azimuth zero when the line of the magnetic gap is at 90° to the line of motion of the tape. A tape recorded by a head with an azimuth angle error will replay poorly on a machine with a correctly aligned head. This is particularly important if the tape is used for digital signals. See Fig. 8.

2. the angle in the horizontal plane between a direction and the direction of North or South pole.

azimuth error the result of an incorrect tape head AZIMUTH ANGLE (sense 1) that causes faint recording or replay.

azimuth recording a technique developed for DIGITAL AUDIO TAPE that allows TRACKS to be much closer spaced. The two HEADS on the revolving DRUM (sense 1) are at different AZIMUTH ANGLES (sense 1), so that if a head is not perfectly on a track it will pick up very little from the next track that was recorded by the other head.

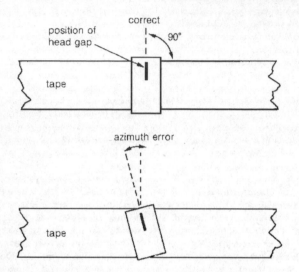

Fig. 8. **azimuth angle**

B

Babbage, Charles (1792–1871) the English engineer who conceived of the general stored program computer, which he called a *difference engine*. His designs were entirely mechanical and the technology of the time was not sufficiently advanced for physical realization of the machine, though a working model has now been constructed and used. Babbage is credited with being the father of modern computing, though in fact his designs were lost and were rediscovered only in the late 1930s, and a model of his computer is now in the Science Museum. See also COLOSSUS.

babble or **crosstalk** interference between two CHANNELS (sense 1) that are transmitting data

baby AT board a smaller version of the format of MOTHERBOARD used on the original IBM PC-AT computer of 1983. The baby AT format was widely used until superseded by the modern ATX type.

baby AT case a casing designed to be used along with the BABY AT BOARD, now obsolete.

back EMF a voltage that is set up in opposition to a supplied voltage, for example the reverse ELECTROMOTIVE FORCE generated in an INDUCTOR when current changes, and the EMF developed in the ARMATURE coils of a DC motor when the armature revolves.

backbone the common top level circuits of a hierarchical NETWORK (sense 2) to which all other data-carrying circuits are connected.

back end processor or **back-end processor** a processor used in a MULTIPROCESSOR SYSTEM to handle the bulk of repetitive processing as distinct from input and output.

background count the count of ionizing (see IONIZATION) particles per minute in the absence of known radiating material. The background count is the natural count due to the Earth's own radioactivity, and also to the bombardment of particles from outer space. This background is irregular, varies considerably from one place to another, and very careful measurements are needed to distinguish it from any additional radiation from a weak radioactive source. See also IONIZATION.

background memory system a large DYNAMIC RAM memory used in a TELETEXT receiver to store data and so reduce the time needed to gain access.

background noise the NOISE signal, due to natural or manmade sources, that is always present in any transmission.

back heating an effect used in a MAGNETRON to continue electron emission. Electron emission is started by heating the cathode of a magnetron. When the magnetron is running, however, the path of many electrons causes them to return to the cathode. The bombardment of the cathode by returning (*back*) electrons causes heating, so that the auxiliary heating can be reduced or switched off.

backing store a store for data that is not a working part of the memory of a computer. Typical examples are a HARD DRIVE or a CD-ROM. A backing store can be used to hold programs and data that can be read and used by the computer during the course of a main program.

backlight a light placed behind an LCD display so that the display can be seen in dim surroundings. Without a backlight, the display may be visible only in a well-lit room.

back-lighting a diffuse light source placed behind an LCD display to make the display visible under poor lighting conditions, particularly for computer monitor screens.

backlit display a form of LIQUID CRYSTAL DISPLAY that can be lit from behind so as to make it visible in poor lighting conditions.

back lobe the pattern of strong radiation from a DIRECTIONAL AERIAL that is in the reverse direction to the intended direction. See LOBE; RADIATION PATTERN.

back-off period the time delay after a DATA COLLISION on a NETWORK (sense 2), during which both data transmitters halt. After the backup period, normal network use can restart.

backplane see MOTHERBOARD.

back plate the signal electrode of a TV CAMERA TUBE. The term was applied originally to tubes in which this electrode was at the rear of the tube. For the more modern types of camera pickup tube, such as the VIDICON, the back plate is a conducting layer at the front of the tube.

back porch the portion of the SYNCHRONIZING PULSE for a TV signal waveform that immediately follows the line sync pulse. On a monochrome signal, the back porch consists of 2.25 microseconds of BLACK LEVEL. On a colour signal, the COLOUR BURST of 10 cycles of subcarrier takes place in this time. This portion of subcarrier signal is used to synchronize the colour subcarrier oscillator in the receiver.

back projection a system of projecting images on to the rear of a translucent screen that is viewed from the front, used in large-screen TV displays.

back scatter the reflection of radar waves from a target to the TRANSMITTING AERIAL. Compare FORWARD SCATTER.

backside cache a form of SECONDARY CACHE that can be read directly by the MICROPROCESSOR of the computer system.

backswing see UNDERSHOOT.

back-tension the tensioning force applied to tape in the cassette of a VIDEO CASSETTE RECORDER at a point before the tape is wrapped around the DRUM (sense 1).

backup a copy of important data retained safely in case of problems with a HARD DRIVE.

backup battery a battery, usually a lithium-ion (see LITHIUM-ION CELL) or nickel-cadmium type, built into equipment in order to maintain a supply to low-consumption parts (such as memory) in the event of mains power failure, or to maintain the memory storage of some data in a computer while the machine is switched off.

backup capacitor a high-capacity CAPACITOR, usually of low working voltage, used to supply power for a limited period to a memory circuit in the event of failure of the mains supply.

backup switching a circuit in a POWER SUPPLY unit that will automatically connect to battery supply when the mains fails or when mains voltage drops to an unacceptable level.

backward diode a diode in which both regions are heavily doped (see DOPING). This has the effect of allowing the diode to conduct better in the reverse direction than in the forward direction, and with very small voltage drop. There is virtually no CARRIER STORAGE, so response speeds are very high. The backward diode is used for DEMODULATION, particularly of low-level microwave signals. See also TUNNEL DIODE.

backward echo a transmission that has travelled around the world arriving at a receiver some time after the DIRECT WAVE and from the opposite direction.

backward-wave oscillator see CARCINOTRON.

backward-wave tube a form of TRAVELLING-WAVE TUBE oscillator in which the electromagnetic wave travels in the opposite direction from the electron beam. See also CARCINOTRON.

Bailey clamp a form of protection for transistors in a POWER OUTPUT STAGE designed by A. R. Bailey in which a clamp transistor monitors the voltage across output transistors and also the output current. If the combination of the two is enough to turn on the clamp transistor it will shunt the input signal and avoid output transistor damage.

Baird, John Logie (1888–1946) Scots engineer who was the first to construct a form of mechanical television system following the principles suggested by Nipkov and Rosing at St. Petersburg.

balance the symmetry or equality of signals. STEREO audio signals are said to be balanced in a stereo amplifier if they produce a sound that appears centrally between the loudspeakers when both channels are fed with the same signals. A WAVEFORM is said to be balanced about earth if the shape of the wave form is symmetrical with the zero voltage line as the axis of symmetry.

balance condition, bridge the condition in which the voltages across a BRIDGE, which can be regarded as a pair of VOLTAGE DIVIDERS, are equal, so that no current will flow through a sensitive detector. (See also Fig. 14.)

balance control a ganged POTENTIOMETER (sense 1) set, often now omitted, used in a stereo amplifier to alter the allocation of signal power between the main channels.

balanced about earth the condition of a circuit using inputs and outputs that are in ANTIPHASE, so that the sum of voltages on a pair will at any time be zero. See also PARAPHASE AMPLIFIER.

balanced amplifier an amplifier whose two inputs are a signal and its inverse balanced about earth. There is no output if the signals at both inputs are identical. The advantage is a very great immunity to interference from supply-line noise or radiated noise. See also PARAPHASE AMPLIFIER.

balanced bridge see BALANCE CONDITION, BRIDGE.

balanced connections the use of two signal-carrying wires with balanced signals, usually with an earth screen.

balanced feeder an aerial transmission line that uses a BALANCED LINES pair rather than a coaxial cable.

balanced lines transmission lines using two identical lines at a constant spacing fed from a centre-tapped transformer with the centre tap earthed so that the line signals are balanced about earth.

balanced mixer a MIXER circuit that uses two semiconductors in a BRIDGE form of circuit so that the local oscillator signal is balanced out of the output.

balanced power supply a power supply whose output is DC of equal and opposite polarity voltage, such as +15V and −15V, used for OPERATIONAL AMPLIFIER circuits.

ball grid array (BGA) a form of mounting for soldering a SURFACE MOUNTED DEVICE (SMD), usually with several hundred ball-shaped connectors on the PCB to which the SMD is soldered.

ballast a resistor that was used in early radio and electronic circuits to absorb supply SURGES. A ballast resistor was wired in series with a DC supply. Because the resistor ran hot, and had a large positive TEMPERATURE COEFFICIENT of resistance, any increase in current through the resistor caused an increase in its resistance value. This stabilized the value of current through the ballast. Tungsten-filament lamps were often used as ballast resistors.

ballistic characteristics the rate of response of a RECORDING LEVEL INDICATOR to fast TRANSIENT signal level changes.

ballooning a TV picture fault, caused by poor EHT REGULATION, in which the picture size changes as the overall brightness changes.

balun *acronym for* balanced-unbalanced transformer: a transformer designed to match an unbalanced line to a balanced line with minimum power loss. Its main use is to connect a (balanced) DIPOLE AERIAL to an (unbalanced) COAXIAL feeder.

banana plug an obsolete form of plug, once used for low-voltage connections. The banana plug has now been superseded by the 4mm plug and socket that is universally used for educational apparatus in the UK.

band 1. a range of frequencies. 2. in SEMICONDUCTOR theory, a range of permitted energy levels, see ENERGY BANDS.

band, energy see ENERGY BAND.

band, frequency see FREQUENCY BAND.

bandgap (of a semiconductor) having a difference in energy between the conduction band and the next lower energy bands. Typically, this is about 1.2 electron-volts for silicon at room temperature.

bandgap diode a form of low-voltage REFERENCE DIODE that uses the forward voltage across a JUNCTION (sense 2), typically 1.2V. This voltage is very stable and precise.

band-limited noise WHITE NOISE that has been passed through a FILTER to restrict its range of frequencies. See also GAUSSIAN NOISE; PINK NOISE; RAYLEIGH DISTRIBUTED NOISE; RED NOISE.

band-pass coupled circuits COUPLED TUNED CIRCUITS that have a flat response over a range of frequencies rather than a PEAK response at a single frequency.

band-pass filter a filter designed to pass a range of frequencies, excluding the lower and the higher values.

band switch a manual switch for changing the tuning of a receiver or transmitter from one frequency range to another. This is usually done by changing the connections to inductors.

band-stop filter (BSF) a filter that stops a range of frequencies but allows signals of below or above this range to pass.

bandwidth the range of frequencies in a BAND (sense 1). For radio frequencies this is usually quoted in terms of the difference between the highest and the lowest frequencies in the band.

bandwidth, aerial the range of radio frequencies over which an aerial has sufficient gain to be useful. See also AERIAL GROUP.

bandwidth, cro the range of signal frequencies that can be displayed and measured on a CATHODE-RAY OSCILLOSCOPE.

bandwidth, extending the bandwidth of a TUNED AMPLIFIER can be extended by adding DAMPING RESISTORS or by STAGGER-TUNING. For an untuned amplifier, bandwidth is extended by using low-resistance loads and by adding inductors to resonate (see RESONANT CIRCUIT) with stray capacitance.

bandwidth-length product the product of signal BANDWIDTH and cable length for a FIBRE OPTIC CABLE; a measure of data carrying capacity.

bandwidth, resonant circuit the range of frequencies for which a circuit is resonant, defined as the range of frequencies between the 3dB points on the response curve. See Fig. 9.

bang-bang control a form of control, such as a simple BIMETAL THERMOSTAT, that uses on-off switching as distinct from LINEAR CONTROL.

bank a set of controls arranged together. The controls (switches, potentiometers, variable capacitors) may be ganged (see GANGED CIRCUITS) by electrical or mechanical connection so that all of them are altered by one single control.

bank-switching the switching of RAM memory, usually in 64 megabyte 'banks' so that different portions of RAM can be allocated to the same ADDRESS range.

bar code an information storage system using a set of printed black and white bars of varying width, used in particular for product identification.

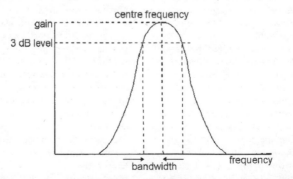

Fig. 9. **bandwidth, resonant circuit**

bar-code reader   a device for automatically reading BAR CODES in DIGITAL form. The reader generally uses a LASER beam that is scanned to and fro over the bar code with a PHOTOCELL detecting the bars. The software will usually provide for accepting the value that is most frequently found on a number of scans, to avoid the possibility of error on a single scan.

bare bones   (of a computer) supplied without monitor, printer, keyboard, mouse or other attachments, intended to allow the user to upgrade only the main computing components.

bare metal   totally new and un-programmed computer HARDWARE, such as a newly designed computer with no PROM or BIOS chips so that it cannot be used until these items are designed, created and added.

bargraph display   a form of measuring display, often used for volume control indications, that uses the length of a bar to indicate the amplitude of a signal or other quantity.

BARITT (barrier injection transit time) diode   a form of diode formed with a Schottky PNP structure, used for generating microwave energy. See also IMPATT DIODE.

barium titanate   a PIEZOELECTRIC CRYSTAL material, used in acceleration and acoustic TRANSDUCERS.

Barlow-Wadley loop or **drift-cancelling oscillator**   a form of DOUBLE SUPERHET receiver that uses both a VARIABLE FREQUENCY OSCILLATOR and a CRYSTAL OSCILLATOR with their outputs connected to two MIXERS, so cancelling the effects of DRIFT (sense 2) in the variable frequency oscillator.

barrage reception   see DIVERSITY RECEPTION.

barrel   the outer cover of a JACK PLUG.

barrel distortion   the distortion of a TV picture in which the normally rectangular shape is distorted to one in which the sides are bowed outwards. Contrast PINCUSHION DISTORTION.

barrel shifter   a REGISTER circuit using a set of parallel shift registers permitting shifts either within a register or from one register to another, used to apply scaling factors to digital numbers.

barrier potential   the voltage across a forward-biased PN JUNCTION (sense 2). This represents a barrier to a CARRIER (sense 2) moving in the reverse direction.

barrier region   see DEPLETION REGION.

Bartlett window   see WINDOW FUNCTION.

base   one electrode of a BIPOLAR JUNCTION TRANSISTOR (BJT). For maximum voltage gain, the signal input will be to the BASE, and the output from the COLLECTOR. In some applications, the base is held at AC zero potential, and the signal input is to the EMITTER (sense 1).

baseband   (of a DIGITAL signal) that has not been modulated (see MODULATION) and is transmitted in its original form, as in a local area network.

baseband distribution   distribution of video and audio signals among a NETWORK (sense 2) of receivers, providing better quality than RF DISTRIBUTION.

baseband signal   the ANALOGUE signal that is sampled to provide a DIGITAL output.

base current   the current flowing between the BASE and EMITTER (sense 1) terminals of a BIPOLAR JUNCTION TRANSISTOR (BJT).

base-emitter Zener effect   the ZENER limiting of voltage between BASE and EMITTER (sense 1) of a silicon BIPOLAR JUNCTION TRANSISTOR (BJT) when reverse-biased. This can cause CLIPPING of an applied signal that overdrives the transistor, typically in a MULTIVIBRATOR circuit, so that frequency becomes affected by the collector-emitter voltage. The remedy is to use a high-reverse voltage diode in series with the base.

base level   the voltage level from which a PULSE starts and to which it returns. In most pulse-generating circuits the base level will either be EARTH or supply voltage level.

baseline, wave   the line around which a WAVEFORM is symmetrical, the zero voltage line for a signal waveform with no DC COMPONENT.

base standards   the internationally agreed standards for telecommunications systems and equipment.

base station   a fixed transmitter/receiver and aerial unit used to connect CELLULAR PHONES to fixed lines or other radio networks.

base stopper   a resistor of low value that is wired in series with the base of a TRANSISTOR in order to damp PARASITIC OSCILLATIONS. The base stopper is generally wired as close to the base terminal as is physically possible.

base unit   a unit, usually mains powered, connected to a fixed telephone line to act as a transmitter, receiver and charger for cordless phone units.

basic frequency   see FUNDAMENTAL FREQUENCY.

basic rate access (BRA)   the most common class of ISDN service, allowing two 64 Kbit/s voice and data channels and a 16 Kbit/s digital signalling channel.

bass   the lowest pitched AUDIO frequency notes in the region 15Hz to 200Hz (approximately). These frequencies are attenuated by the normal capacitor coupling in amplifier circuits, and the lower bass frequencies are not well reproduced by loudspeakers, particularly by small loudspeakers.

bass boost   a selective gain increase for the BASS frequencies. Bass boost is often used to compensate for the ATTENUATION of bass frequencies in the amplifier coupling capacitors and in the loudspeakers.

bass response   the relative gain of a device for the BASS frequencies, usually quoted in decibels relative to the response for a 1kHz signal.

batch counter   a mechanism for counting items, usually passing on an assembly line.

bath tub diagram or **bathtub curve**   the shape of the graph of observed failure rate plotted against time for a manufactured device follows a bathtub shape, with a high incidence of early failures and also a higher rate in later life, but a low incidence between these limits. See Fig. 10.

battery   a group of identical devices. The term usually denotes a group of voltaic CELLS connected so as to provide either higher voltage or (unusually) higher current than a single cell. Series connection provides voltage levels that are equal to the cell voltage multiplied by the number of series cells. Parallel connection allows higher currents to be delivered, because the total internal resistance is equal to the internal resistance of a cell divided by the number of cells. Parallel connection, however, can be troublesome unless the cells are truly identical, and a faulty cell can cause a rapid discharge of the other cells as they pass current into the faulty cell.

battery backup   see BACK-UP BATTERY.

battery charging   applying a voltage to a battery of SECONDARY CELLS to cause reversal of the chemical actions that take place during discharge of a battery, so that the battery is capable of further use.

battery memory or **voltage depression**   the loss of capacity of a RECHARGEABLE CELL, particularly the older nickel-cadmium type, if it is often recharged after being only partially discharged.

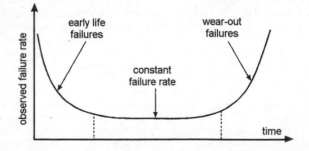

Fig. 10. **bath tub diagram**

baud   the unit of rate of transmission of signals along telegraph lines. One baud means one signal cycle per second. The unit is named after the pioneer telegraph engineer, Jean Baudot (d. 1903).

Baudot code   a five-bit digital code that represents 64 characters, used for TELEPRINTERS.

Baud rate   the rate of carrying of signal, equal to the CARRIER (sense 1) frequency. The SYMBOL RATE can be higher and is expressed in BITS PER SECOND. For example, if the carrier phase can be modulated (see MODULATION) using four values of phase, then the symbol rate will be four times the Baud rate. See also QAM.

Baxandall tone control   a form of TREBLE and BASS adjustment circuit using NEGATIVE FEEDBACK methods, devised by Peter Baxandall and used extensively.

bay   a slot in the (usually) front part of a computer casing, intended for drives such as hard drives, FLOPPY DRIVE, CD-ROM drive, DVD drive etc. An external bay has its front open so that the front panel of the drive is accessible; an internal bay, used for a hard drive, has no external accessibility.

Bayes theorem   an equation that can be used to calculate the uncertainty of transmission of a SYMBOL along a data link in the presence of noise.

bayonet fitting   any form of locking connector that is attached by a plug-in and twist action.

BCD   see BINARY CODED DECIMAL.

BCD counter   an electronic counter whose output is in four-bit BINARY CODED DECIMAL, ideally suited to interfacing with electronic displays.

BCD decoder   a decoder circuit whose input is a four-bit BCD code and whose output is suitable for direct application to display devices.

B-channel or **bearer channel**   the data or voice channel for an ISDN transmission.

BCH code   see BOSE-CHAUDHURI-HOCQUENGHEM CODE.

B-Crypt   an ALGORITHM for a scrambled (see SCRAMBLER) video system for TELECONFERENCING use, devised by GPT Video Systems Ltd.

beacon or **radio beacon**   the radio-wave equivalent of a lighthouse. Signals sent out from a beacon transmitter are used for identification of the transmitter (*code beacon*), for location and guidance (*homing beacon*), and for more specialized purposes such as aircraft blind landing.

bead thermistor   a form of THERMISTOR in the shape of a small sphere with two leads.

beam   a confined path through space for radio waves or electrons. The term beam implies that the shape of the path is almost parallel-sided and straight.

beam angle   the angle of divergence of ELECTRONS emerging from the GUN of a CATHODE-RAY TUBE.

beam bending   a form of distortion in TV CAMERA TUBES. The electron beam scans over areas that are electrostatically charged by the action of light. The discharge current provided by the beam then constitutes the output video signal. The differences in charge, however, can cause the low-velocity beam to be deflected in the direction of more positive charge. The effect on the signal of this beam bending is to exaggerate the size of bright areas in the picture.

beam current limiting   restriction of electron beam current in a colour CATHODE-RAY TUBE to avoid distortion and overheating of the SHADOWMASK or APERTURE GRILLE.

beamer   any type of video projector connected to a computer as if it were a monitor, but producing a large image on a screen.

beam intensity   the electron beam current in a CATHODE-RAY TUBE, controlled by varying the grid-cathode voltage.

beam lead   a connection on a transistor or IC that is resistant to vibration. This is achieved by supporting the connection at the centre so that it is balanced.

beam switching   a method of obtaining more than one TRACE from a single electron gun of a CATHODE-RAY TUBE. This is done by very rapid alternation of the vertical position of the trace so that to the eye it appears to be more than one trace.

The signals to the DEFLECTION PLATES are also switched at the same rate, making it appear that completely independent traces are being used.

beam tetrode or **beam power valve** a form of transmitting THERMIONIC VALVE in which the electron flow from CATHODE (sense 1) to ANODE is formed into a beam by beam-forming plates. This results in lower losses than the use of an additional GRID.

beamwidth for an AERIAL, the angle between the directions at which the BEAM power is 3dB below its beam-centre power.

beat see BEAT FREQUENCY.

beat frequency or **beat note** a signal that is produced as a result of mixing two other signals. When two signals, frequencies f_1 and f_2 are mixed in a NONLINEAR device, the output contains these frequencies along with the sum frequency (f_1+f_2) and the difference frequency $(f_1-f_2$ or f_2-f_1, whichever is positive). These sum and difference frequencies are both beat frequencies, but the difference frequency is the one that is normally used and referred to as a beat frequency or beat note.

beat-frequency oscillator (BFO) a part of a receiver for CW (continuous wave, meaning Morse code) signals that operates at a frequency slightly above or below the INTERMEDIATE FREQUENCY. The difference in frequencies is usually about 400Hz to 1kHz, so the beat frequency is an audio note. The BFO output is applied to the demodulator, so that Morse signals sound as audio notes in the AF sections of the receiver. The term can also denote an audio SIGNAL GENERATOR that makes use of two radio frequency oscillators mixed so as to produce a wide range of beat signals.

beating the production of signals from the mixing of higher frequencies.

beat note see BEAT FREQUENCY.

BEDO dram or **burst EDO dram** a variety of PC memory, now obsolete.

bed of nails a connector used along with AUTOMATIC TEST EQUIPMENT (ATE) to make contact with a large number of points on a circuit.

bel a unit for comparing two power levels, equal to the logarithm (base 10) of the ratio of the power levels. See DECIBEL.

bell curve the shape of the NORMAL DISTRIBUTION curve of a set of statistics.

bell, self-activating (SAB) see SELF-ACTIVATING BELL.

bell timer an electronic timing circuit that ensures that an alarm bell will not ring for more than the permitted 20 minute interval.

belt slipping a problem encountered in tape mechanisms, usually due to jamming or stiffness of rotating parts.

bend losses the loss of power in a FIBRE OPTIC CABLE due to excessive curvature of the line.

benzene a volatile, toxic and flammable solvent used for degreasing.

BER see BIT ERROR RATE.

BERT BIT ERROR RATE test.

beryllium oxide a solid electrical insulator used in power semiconductors because of its heat conductivity. Beryllium oxide is highly toxic, and a power transistor or power IC should never be opened.

Bessel approximation a form of filter response that is most closely described by a Bessel function. See also BUTTERWORTH RESPONSE; TCHEBYSHEV RESPONSE.

beta or h_{fe} the ratio of collector current to base current for a BIPOLAR JUNCTION TRANSISTOR (BJT).

beta gain an old term for the COMMON EMITTER current gain of a BIPOLAR JUNCTION TRANSISTOR.

Betamax™ or **Beta recorder** the Sony version of video cassette recording system, eclipsed by VHS in the UK but more successful elsewhere, and employed for professional camcorders until recently.

beta particle an old name for an ELECTRON.

beta ray see ELECTRON BEAM.

Beverage aerial or **antenna** a long-wire vertical aerial (at least one wavelength long), used for reception of LONG WAVE signals.

bezel the front cover surround of any instrument, often engraved with names for controls or other text.

BFO   see BEAT FREQUENCY OSCILLATOR.

B frame or **B-frame** or **bi-directional predicted frame**   a form of difference frame in an MPEG-2 set, accounting for eight of the frames in a set of twelve. The information in a B-frame is interpolated from the nearest adjacent I-FRAME and P-FRAME so that its data content is usually small. See also DIFFERENCE FRAME; GROUP OF PICTURES.

BGA   see BALL GRID ARRAY.

B-H curve   a graph of flyback converter FLUX DENSITY (B) plotted against MAGNETIC FIELD STRENGTH (H). Such a graph for a FERROMAGNETIC material will show MAGNETIC HYSTERESIS.

bi-amping   the use of separate POWER AMPLIFIERS (sense 3) for loudspeakers, usually so that one amplifier is used for bass and another for higher frequencies.

bias   a DC voltage applied to a device in order to control its linearity (see LINEAR). The output-input characteristic of most ACTIVE COMPONENTs is seldom linear, and bias is used to select a position in the characteristic curve that will give reasonably linear results. Bias can also be used to provide deliberate NONLINEARITY, so that only the tip of a pulse, for example, will operate a circuit (see CLIPPER).

bias circuit   a circuit, usually a resistive potential divider, used to apply BIAS to a semiconductor.

bias compensation   see ANTI-SKATING FORCE.

biased switch   a form of toggle switch that is held by a spring in one position, returning to that position after being operated manually.

biasing   see BIAS.

bias, magnetic   see BIAS, TAPE.

bias noise or **noise behind signal** or **modulation noise**   NOISE caused because of the random magnetic nature of the coating of a MAGNETIC TAPE. This causes the amplitude of the noise to be modulated by the signal so that when the signal disappears the added noise also stops.

bias oscillator   a circuit used to generate a pure high-frequency SINE WAVE as a bias (see BIAS, TAPE) signal for a TAPE RECORDER.

bias, tape   a high-frequency AC signal applied to the RECORDING HEAD of a TAPE RECORDER in order to make the RECORDING action more linear.

BiCMOS   a SEMICONDUCTOR manufacturing process that uses a mixture of techniques to provide low power consumption along with high output current.

bi-directional   (of a conducting path) able to be used for signals in either direction.

bi-directional cable   a cable, particularly intended for connecting a computer to a printer, that allows signals to be passed in either direction. This enables, for example, the printer to signal that the ink level is low.

bi-directional counter   a digital COUNTER that can count up or down depending on the setting of a control line.

bi-directional frame   see B-FRAME.

bi-directional microphone   a microphone whose response curve resembles a figure of 8 with two strong LOBEs in opposite directions.

bi-directional port   a computer PORT (sense 1) that allows signals to pass in either direction.

bi-directional transistor   a transistor in which the COLLECTOR and EMITTER (sense 1) regions have identical doping levels and geometry, so that the collector and emitter leads can be interchanged. Many small-signal transistors are reasonably bi-directional.

bifilar winding   a method of coil winding that reduces stray INDUCTANCE losses. The usual scheme is to wind both the primary and the secondary wires together round the core.

big iron   see SUPERCOMPUTER.

bilateral triode switch   see TRIAC™.

bilinear compander   a Dolby design of COMPRESSOR and EXPANDER for NOISE REDUCTION CIRCUITRY that uses the same differential circuit in both compressor and expander portions.

bilinear transform   a mathematical approximation for determining the design of a DIGITAL FILTER in order to provide the action of an analogue filter.

bimetallic disc   a temperature sensing device formed by welding two discs of different metals. A change of temperature will cause the compound disc to buckle, and this change of shape can be used to operate a switch.

bimetallic strip a metal strip that will bend when its temperature changes. The strip is a composite of two metals with different expansivity values. The bending of the strip is normally used as a method of switching for thermostats, temperature limit switches, etc.

bimetallic switch a switch, used in thermostats and thermal cutouts, that has a BIMETALLIC STRIP or BIMETALLIC DISC as one contact arm.

bimorph a sandwich of oppositely polarized PIEZOELECTRIC CRYSTAL slabs joined into a single unit and used as the sensor for a MICROPHONE.

binary **1.** of or relating to any code or counting system consisting of only two components. In computing, the term always refers to the number system which uses digits 0 and 1. See BIT. **2.** another name for FLIP-FLOP.

binary addition the addition of digital bits, following the rules: 0+0=0; 0+1=1; 1+1=0 (carry 1).

binary code or **binary** any system of representing numbers with only the digits 0 and 1. The term denotes codes such as Gray code and Excess-three code, but is normally used to denote 8-4-2-1 binary code in which the position of a digit in a number indicates its power-of-2 significance.

binary coded decimal (BCD) a method of expressing a DENARY number by using the binary equivalent of each digit individually, rather than converting the whole number to binary. For example, denary 512 in BCD is 010100010010, the separate codes for 5, 1 and 2, whereas in pure binary it is 1000000000. Arithmetic using BCD is difficult, but it is well suited to driving denary number displays.

binary counter a counting circuit whose input is a series of pulses and whose outputs are BINARY DIGITS on a set of lines, so that the digits at the output represent the pulse count.

binary data a set of number codes in the range 0 to 255, used for program or image information as opposed to text characters that correspond to ASCII code.

binary digit or **bit** a signal representing the number 0 or 1 in a digital device.

binary fraction a fractional number expressed as digits following the (binary) point and consisting of units of $1/2$, $1/4$, $1/8$, $1/16$ and so on.

binary number a number expressed in BINARY CODE.

binary number stream a set of BINARY DIGITS on a single line, one following another in SERIAL form.

binary numeration see BINARY WEIGHTING.

binary phase shift keying (BPSK) see PHASE SHIFT KEYING (PSK).

binary point the binary equivalent of a decimal point, marking the change between power of 2 and powers of $1/2$.

binary scale the counting scale that uses the digits 0 and 1 only, so that DENARY 2 is expressed as 10, denary 4 as 100 and so on.

binary subtraction the action of subtracting one BINARY NUMBER from another, using the same basic principles of subtract and borrow as DENARY subtraction.

binary to denary conversion the conversion of a BINARY NUMBER into its scale of ten (DENARY) equivalent, either manually or electronically.

binary-to-denary converter an electronic circuit which for a set of BINARY (sense 1) inputs will provide outputs (typically BCD) that can be used in a scale-of-ten display.

binary weighted resistor network a set of resistors in an ATTENUATOR with values arranged in a 1, 2, 4, 8, 16, 32…series. This can be used for DIGITAL TO ANALOGUE CONVERTER, but has the disadvantage that the resistor values need to be impossibly large and precise for 16-bit operation.

binary weighting or **binary numeration** the weighting of value of digits according to their position in a BINARY NUMBER. See also LEAST SIGNIFICANT BIT; MOST SIGNIFICANT BIT.

binding post a form of connection, often used for loudspeaker cable, in which the cable is threaded through a hole in a metal rod and clamped by a spring-loaded collar.

binit   see BIT.

BIOS   basic input output system part of the operating system of a computer, stored in ROM on the main motherboard and used to control the input and output of data to and from PERIPHERALS such as disk drives, keyboard, monitor.

biosensor   a SEMICONDUCTOR device, used mainly for detecting vapours, that has a thin film of an organic chemical deposited on the surface and capable of altering the conductivity of the SUBSTRATE when affected by other chemicals.

Biot-Savart law   the relationship between the amount of current flowing between two points and the MAGNETIC FLUX DENSITY that it creates; formerly called Ampere's Law in the UK. The law is stated in a form that is physically impossible to achieve, and only formulae deduced from the law can be tested. See a textbook of electromagnetism for full details. See Fig. 11.

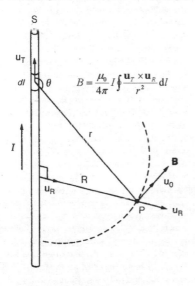

$$B = \frac{\mu_0}{4\pi} I \oint \frac{\mathbf{u}_T \times \mathbf{u}_R}{r^2} \, \mathrm{d}l$$

Fig. 11. **Biot-Savart law**

biphase code   general classification for BINARY CODES of the MANCHESTER CODE type using two code bits for each single bit of the original signal.

bi-phase half-wave   the type of RECTIFIER circuit that requires a centre-tapped TRANSFORMER feeding two DIODEs. The circuit is seldom used now that BRIDGE PACKAGES are readily available at low cost.

bipolar   (of a semiconductor) using both P-type and N-type material.

bipolar CMOS (BiCMOS)   an IC that is formed from both bipolar (see BIPOLAR TRANSISTOR) and CMOS transistors, combining the speed of bipolar devices with the low power consumption of CMOS.

bipolar code   any code system for DIGITAL DATA that can lead to long sequences of a single digit which affect the synchronization of the receiver CLOCK. See BNZS code.

bipolar device   any SEMICONDUCTOR device that uses both ELECTRON and HOLE carriers.

bipolar IC   a form of IC in which the transistors are bipolar (see BIPOLAR JUNCTION TRANSISTOR) rather than field-effect types.

bipolar junction transistor (bjt) or **bipolar transistor**   a form of TRANSISTOR that makes use of two close-spaced junctions (sense 2) in a single CRYSTAL to form a P-N-P or N-P-N sandwich of layers. The central section is called the BASE and the outer regions are the EMITTER (sense 1) and the COLLECTOR. In general the collector is of larger area than the emitter, otherwise the transistor construction is symmetrical.

With a steady voltage applied between the collector and the emitter, no current can flow unless a current is also flowing between the base and emitter. The connector-emitter current is very much greater than the base-emitter current, but is proportional to the base-emitter current over a very large current range. For a P-N-P transistor, the controlled current consists of holes, and the collector and base voltages are negative with respect to the emitter. The N-P-N transistor uses electrons as carriers, and operates with collector and base voltage levels that are positive with respect to the emitter. Compare FIELD EFFECT TRANSISTOR.

BIPS   billions of instructions per second: a measure of computing speed.

B-ISDN   *abbrev. for* BROADBAND ISDN.

BIST (built in self-test) a feature of some MICROPROCESSOR chips that allows testing to be carried out for consistency of values whenever power is applied to the chip.

bistable (of a circuit) possessing two stable states. The term denotes the FLIP-FLOP type of circuit that can be switched from one stable state to the other by a TRIGGER pulse. Contrast STABLE STATE. See also MULTIVIBRATOR; STEERING DIODE.

bistable multivibrator see BISTABLE.

bistatic RADAR a RADAR system in which a low-power transmitter and a sensitive receiver are located in different places, making the combination difficult to detect and attack.

bisynchronous transmission use of two defined digital characters for synchronizing a data stream.

bit *abbrev. for* binary digit, i.e. one of the two possible digits, 0 or 1, in a BINARY NUMBER. Also (in information theory) called *binit* or *Shannon*.

bit bus a form of low-speed master-slave BUS system that can be used for long-length buses.

bit cell the time interval allocated for transmitting or recording a single BIT of data. In a recording, the voltage change representing the bit may occur (have a transition) at the start, end, or centre of the cell time.

bit error an error in a single bit of data so that a 1 becomes a 0 and a 0 becomes a 1.

bit error rate (BER) or **error rate** for a digital transmission, the ratio of number of error bits to total transmitted bits in one second.

bitmap a representation of an image in which one or more BITS will be used to represent the brightness and colour of each PICTURE ELEMENT (pixel) of the image.

bit mapping a system of reducing the bit content of a DIGITAL AUDIO signal, typically from 20-bit to 16-bit, by using a LOOK-UP TABLE for translation. See also BIT RATE REDUCTION.

bit oriented any CODING (sense 1) system that can be coded in bit-sized units, typically using one bit for each item.

bit position the position or significance of a bit in a byte or word. See also LEAST SIGNIFICANT BIT; MOST SIGNIFICANT BIT.

bit rate the speed of transmission of data, expressed as the number of BITS PER SECOND. See also BAUD RATE, SYMBOL RATE.

bit rate reduction (BRR) a form of LOSSY COMPRESSION in which bits that do not contribute significantly to the data are omitted, so reducing the total number of bits required for storage and transmission. See also AUDITORY MASKING.

bit reduction or **compression** or **compaction** the reduction in the number of bits required to describe an analogue signal, particularly an image. Image information in particular contains a large amount of redundancy that can be considerably reduced, see JPEG; MPEG. Compare BIT RATE REDUCTION.

bit robbing see BIT STEALING.

bit slice a method of constructing a MICROPROCESSOR from 4-bit ICs that can be connected in parallel to make use of a WORD of any size.

bit, soldering see SOLDERING IRON.

bits per inch (BPI) the measurement of RECORDING DENSITY on a medium such as tape or disk.

bits per number the number of bits used in an ANALOGUE/DIGITAL CONVERTER to represent each analogue number.

bits per second (BPS) the measurement of rate of data transmission, usually preceded by a multiplier such as k (kilo) or M (mega).

bit stealing the use of a bit within a PULSE CODE MODULATION time slot for other than its intended purpose, usually for control signals.

bitstream a serial stream of digital bits forming a message. Also applied to a fast stream of bits generated by OVERSAMPLING.

bitstream method a system used for a DIGITAL TO ANALOGUE CONVERTER by changing the digital representation to a SERIAL stream of bits, so that the ratio of 1s to 0s in the stream represents the size of analogue signal.

bit stuffing or **digital filling** or **justification** or **rate adaptation** the addition of meaningless BITS to a signal to adjust the data rate.

Bitter pattern　a method of investigating the magnetism of a material. A liquid that contains fine magnetic particles is applied to the surface of a magnetic material. The particles then form into a pattern that reveals how the material is magnetized.

bi-wiring　the practice of feeding the TWEETER portion of a loudspeaker set using a separate cable, on the (dubious) assumption that this will avoid INTERMODULATION from the lower frequency signals.

BJT　see BIPOLAR JUNCTION TRANSISTOR.

black body　a theoretical ideal radiating material to which any other heat radiator can be compared.

black box　a method of treating the behaviour of a circuit or other device in which the internal construction is ignored, and only the inputs and outputs are considered. By treating a device as a 'black box', its effect in the circuit can be studied rather than its internal action. Components such as INTEGRATED CIRCUITS generally have to be treated as black boxes, because their internal construction is known only to their manufacturers. Contrast WHITE BOX.

black box testing or **closed box testing** or **functional testing**　testing of a system using random data or observing inputs and output, with no knowledge of the working of the system. Contrast WHITE BOX TESTING.

black death　a failure mechanism of early ICs in which migration of gold into an aluminium region formed a black high-resistance region.

black level　a voltage level in a TV VIDEO SIGNAL that results in the electron beam being just cut off. Signals below this level cannot produce any effect on the screen of the CATHODE-RAY TUBE.

black level clamp　a circuit used to ensure that the BLACK LEVEL in a TV picture signal is maintained at a steady level that determines the overall brightness of the picture.

blackout　1. a sudden loss of circuit gain. This is normally the result of nonlinear

action that charges capacitors to CUT-OFF bias levels. The cause of the nonlinear action is usually an excessive pulse input. **2.** loss of data or services due to power line fluctuations or total loss of power.

blanking　the suppression of an electron beam. This is normally done to prevent an unwanted display as, for example, when the FLYBACK part of a TIMEBASE is being traced.

blanking level　the voltage level in a VIDEO signal that corresponds to electron beam cut-off. See also BLACK LEVEL.

blasting　a severe distortion of an audio output caused by excessive input signal.

Blattnerphone　the original (1930) form of TAPE RECORDER, using huge lengths of steel tape, typically several miles for a short recording.

B-law　a form of non-linear POTENTIOMETER LAW or taper.

bleeder current　a steady current drawn from a supply, usually for bias purposes.

Bletchley Park　the site of the decoding centre in World War II, now a suburb of Milton Keynes, where the first working electronic computer (see COLOSSUS) was designed and constructed by Tommy Flowers (1905–1999) in 1943.

block　1. a unit in a BLOCK DIAGRAM. **2.** a set of bits transmitted as a unit set in a digital circuit.

block address　the ADDRESS number used to locate a BLOCK (sense 2) of data on a HARD DRIVE so that data can be assembled from blocks that are in totally different positions.

block code　the complete set of binary numbers for a code. For a code using k bits, the size of the block code is 2^k.

block diagram　an overall diagram for a system. A block diagram shows no circuit details. Each part of the circuit is shown as a BLOCK (sense 1), with drawings of the waveforms in and out to illustrate the actions. In this way, the overall action is easier to understand, and a fault can often be isolated to one particular block. See also BLACK BOX; CIRCUIT DIAGRAM.

blocked impedance　a form of impedance found in an electromechanical TRANSDUCER.

When a signal is applied to a loudspeaker or other electro-mechanical device, the measured impedance is greater than the electrical resistance of the coil windings. This is because of the power conversion to mechanical power. If the motion is prevented, the impedance changes to the lower value that is called the blocked impedance. See also MOTIONAL IMPEDANCE.

blocking reduction of the SENSITIVITY of a radio receiver due to a very strong signal that is off-channel.

blocking capacitor a CAPACITOR whose main action is to pass signal frequencies between parts of a circuit that are at different DC levels without passing DC current.

blocking losses or **masking losses** or **shadow losses** or **shadowing losses** the shadowing of signal to or from a PARABOLIC DISH, caused by the support structure for the FEED UNIT.

blocking oscillator a form of oscillator that is used for pulse generation. A blocking oscillator makes use of a capacitor in the BIAS circuit. After one cycle of high-frequency oscillation, the capacitor has charged so as to bias off the oscillator completely, so that no further oscillation can occur until the charge has leaked away. The leakage is slow in comparison to the time of oscillation, so the circuit generates pulses with a low DUTY FACTOR. See also SQUEGGING. See Fig. 12.

blocking ratio 1. the level of signal 20 kHz distant in frequency from a received channel that causes a 3dB reduction in the wanted signal due to BLOCKING.

2. see CALL CONGESTION RATIO.

block matching an image processing action in which sets (blocks) of PIXELs, typically 8×8 or 16×16 are compared.

block symbols symbols, mostly rectangular, used in a BLOCK DIAGRAM for stages in a circuit or to show signal ranges.

block systematic code a variant of BLOCK CODE in which original data bits are used unchanged, but in a different order and with PARITY bits added.

blocky picture a fault in a DIGITAL TELEVISION picture that makes the picture appear to be built out of large blocks of colour. See also PIXELATION.

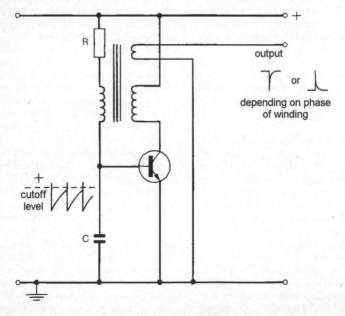

Fig. 12. **blocking oscillator**

blow EPROM   to program an EPROM with data.

blue laser   a SEMICONDUCTOR LASER using a zinc selenide JUNCTION (sense 2), producing an output wavelength of around 430 nm with a spot size typically half that of a red laser so that higher data packing for a DIGITAL VERSATILE DISC can be achieved.

bluetooth   a standardized method of short-range radio communication for computer PERIPHERALS, permitting items such as keyboards and mice to be used without connecting cables.

Blumlein, A. D.   (1903–1942) inventor of a vast number of electronic developments, including STEREO recording on disc.

BNC connector   a bayonet-fitting connector for RF cable terminations, usually matching 50Ω or 75Ω impedance.

BnZS code   a development of bipolar coding (see BIPOLAR CODE) that avoids long sequences of a single digit by adding bits to break up the sequence.

board (PC)   see CARD.

bobbin, transformer   the former on which the coils of a TRANSFORMER are wound before the CORE is inserted.

Bode diagram or **Bode plot**   a diagram in which logarithmic gain and phase shift are plotted against logarithmic frequency for an amplifier or control system. The diagram is used to assess frequency response and stability, particularly for control systems. For audio circuits, the NYQUIST DIAGRAM is more commonly used.

body capacitance   the CAPACITANCE of part of a circuit to a nearby human body. Body capacitance is particularly troublesome when variable capacitors are operated, because the setting that is obtained when the hand touches the adjuster may not be correct when the hand is removed.

Boella effect   the reduction of impedance for a CARBON RESISTOR for high-frequency signals, caused by STRAY CAPACITANCE between the carbon grains.

bolometer   a resistor for measuring radiated power, particularly infra-red radiation, that is blackened so as to absorb radiation. When the radiation is absorbed,

the resistor is heated, and its resistance value changes. The change in resistance value is then used to calculate the amount of power absorbed.

Boltzmann's constant   the factor that relates radiated power to ABSOLUTE TEMPERATURE per unit bandwidth of signal, used extensively in NOISE POWER calculations.

bond   to connect parts of a circuit so that they are at the same ELECTRIC POTENTIAL, usually earth potential. Bonding is reasonably straightforward for low-frequency circuits, but can be very difficult for high radio-frequency circuits, when the length of the bonding conductor can be an appreciable fraction of a wavelength.

bond wire   an internal connection to a semiconductor chip from the pins of the encapsulating PACKAGE.

bonding   see EARTH BONDING.

bonding pads   the metal contacts around a semiconductor chip. The connections to the chip from each bonding pad are made through fine gold wires, and the bonding pads are in turn connected with more substantial wires to the pins of the chip.

Boolean   (of a data quantity) taking one of only two values which can be described either as 1 and 0, or as TRUE and FALSE.

Boolean algebra   a system for dealing with logic problems, by writing the logic actions in the form of a set of mathematical equations. Boolean algebra is used in the design of circuits for computing purposes.

Boolean expression   a form of algebraic expression in which letters denote logical states and the signs + and × indicate the actions of OR and AND respectively. For example, the AND action on two inputs is written as A×B, and the OR action is written as A+B.

Boolean operation   an action carried out on data consisting of digits 0 and 1. The fundamental Boolean operations are NOT, OR and AND.

Boole, George   (1815–64) the mathematician who devised a form of algebra dealing with logical statements that has been extensively used in the design of logic circuits.

booster 1. any device used to increase the power of a signal. **2.** a transmitter that is installed to increase signal strength in an area of poor reception. **3.** a carrier-frequency amplifier located at or near a receiver aerial to improve signal-noise ratio. **4.** a local power-supply transformer that is used to maintain voltage in a remote area.

boost regulator a form of IC VOLTAGE REGULATOR circuit that can produce an output voltage level that is greater than its input level. See also BUCK CONVERTER.

bootstrapping a system of POSITIVE FEEDBACK across an amplifying stage whose gain is always less than unity, so that oscillation is not possible. Bootstrapping circuits are used to simulate constant current conditions in TIMEBASES, and to increase the INPUT IMPEDANCE of amplifiers. See Fig. 13.

borax one traditional type of solder FLUX (sense 2), now out of favour because of toxic fumes.

boresight the axis along which a PARABOLIC DISH aerial receives signals from a SATELLITE.

boresight error or **tilt angle** the incorrect alignment of an aerial so that the aim of the boresight is incorrect.

Bose-Chaudhuri-Hocquenghem (BCH) codes one of several developments of HAMMING CODE techniques for detecting and correcting errors in DIGITAL signals.

bottoming the DISTORTION of a signal because the signal voltage has reached earth level, or supply negative. An ACTIVE COMPONENT with a resistive load cannot provide an output voltage that rises above the level of the positive supply voltage or that falls below the level of the negative supply voltage, and distortion will be caused if the input signal is large enough to drive the output to (or near) these extremes.

boundary microphone or **PZM microphone** a small capsule element microphone, often an ELECTRET type, housed in a flat panel with the DIAPHRAGM very close to any surface on which the unit is placed. This provides an acoustic filtering effect that eliminates the irregular dips in frequency response that is common in other microphones.

boundary scan test a more rigorous test, using a dedicated test circuit, for complex circuits that cannot by automatically tested (see AUTOMATIC TEST EQUIPMENT) using such devices as the BED OF NAILS.

BPF see BAND-PASS FILTER.

BPI see BITS PER INCH.

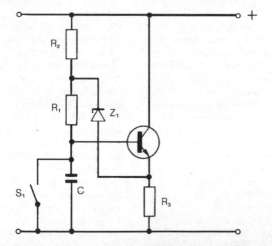

Fig. 13. **bootstrapping**

BPS see BITS PER SECOND.

braided cable a cable of woven construction used where high currents must be passed through a flexible connector.

braided ring network or **dual ring network** a form of RING NETWORK that uses two parallel rings to avoid interruption of data in the event of one ring being broken.

branch current the amount or fraction of current flowing in one branch of a parallel circuit.

branch-line coupler a MICROWAVE coupler that can be constructed in WAVEGUIDE, MICROSTRIP or DIELECTRIC form, providing two outputs at 90° phase difference.

branch point a point where three or more connections join in, for example, a NETWORK (sense 1) of components.

breadboard or **protoboard** a temporary assembly for testing purposes. Breadboard circuits are often constructed on purpose-built plug-in boards, so that circuits can be constructed simply by plugging in ICs, transistors and passive components, with the minimum of wiring. See also PATCHBOARD.

break an interruption in a circuit.

breakdown a failure of insulation or other electrical characteristics. Breakdown of an active component generally means either loss of gain, or a short circuit between electrodes.

breakdown diode see AVALANCHE DIODE.

breakdown power rating the power level at which a WAVEGUIDE will fail due to internal sparking.

breakdown voltage the reverse voltage at which the insulation of a JUNCTION (sense 2) fails, allowing uncontrolled reverse current to flow. See also AVALANCHE BREAKDOWN; ZENER BREAKDOWN.

breakdown, Zener see ZENER BREAKDOWN.

break frequency see 3DB FREQUENCY.

breakout box a JUNCTION (sense 4) box used on a connection to a SERIAL INTERFACE which allows connections to be transposed to suit the equipment being connected. It also allows signal values to be checked by instruments in the event of problems with interfacing.

breakover diode a FOUR-LAYER DIODE whose resistance becomes very low at some critical value of voltage so that the device is used mainly for TRANSIENT suppression on telephone or computer networking lines.

breakover voltage the minimum voltage level at which a DIAC will conduct.

breakthrough, image reception of an IMAGE FREQUENCY by a SUPERHETERODYNE RECEIVER because the MIXER stage cannot reject the image signals. The problem is overcome by use of the DOUBLE SUPERHET system.

breakup, cone see CONE BREAKUP.

breathing see PROGRAMME MODULATED NOISE.

brick wall filter a filter with a very STEEP CUT FILTER characteristic, typically the ANTI-ALIASING FILTER used in early CD players.

bridge a form of measuring circuit. The simplest form of bridge circuit is the Wheatstone bridge, that consists of two potential dividers across a common supply, Fig. 14. The condition for the potentials at the middle of the dividers to be identical is $R1/R2 = R3/R4$. This condition, the balance condition, is easy to identify if a sensitive current indicator is connected between the points, 'bridging' the gap. If three of the resistor values are known, then the fourth can be calculated. Alternatively, if one resistor in one arm is known, and the ratio of resistance values in the other arm is known, then the fourth resistance value can be calculated. The current indicator need not be calibrated, and the only requirement of it is that it should be sensitive. The bridge can, for example, be supplied with AC and headphones or an amplifier used as a detector.

Variations in the basic bridge, using various impedances, can be used for measuring capacitance, self-inductance, mutual inductance, and transformer ratios. For details of these other bridge circuits, consult a textbook of electrical measurements.

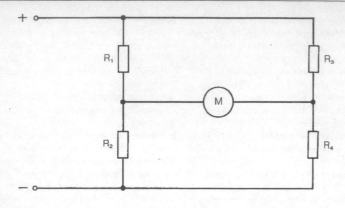

Fig. 14. **bridge**

bridge amplifier a circuit that uses two sets of output stages that provide signals, one of which is inverted. The load, usually a loudspeaker, is connected between the amplifier outputs. This is often used as a way of avoiding the use of an isolating capacitor between an amplifier output and a loudspeaker, since the steady voltage across the output terminals can be set to zero.

bridge balance conditions the conditions, in terms of equal ratios of impedances that lead to a BRIDGE being balanced.

bridge circuit, strain gauge see STRAIN GAUGE.

bridge measurement any form of measurement in which the electrical measuring device is part of a BRIDGE arranged so as to cancel the effects of AMBIENT conditions or cable connections.

bridge modulator a form of AM modulation circuit using diodes in a BRIDGE circuit that can be used to provide DOUBLE SIDEBAND SUPPRESSED CARRIER (DSBSC) modulation.

bridge package a set of four DIODES with identical characteristics arranged as a BRIDGE RECTIFIER and sold as a single component, often with a heat-sink attached.

bridge rectifier a FULL-WAVE RECTIFIER circuit in which the rectifiers are connected in a BRIDGE pattern, so that a different pair of rectifiers conducts for each direction of AC input.

bridge, resistance thermometer see RESISTANCE THERMOMETER bridge.

bridge, thermistor an arrangement of THERMISTORS and resistors in a BRIDGE circuit, with one thermistor mounted on a thermal conductor and used to detect temperature changes and the other maintained at AMBIENT TEMPERATURE. The bridge arrangement minimizes errors caused by ambient temperature changes.

bridging making connection between two different types of NETWORK (sense 2) so as to interchange information. See also BROUTER; ROUTING.

brightness the appearance of high LUMINANCE (light output level) of an image.

bright-up signal a signal, used particularly in an analogue CATHODE-RAY OSCILLOSCOPE, to brighten the trace on the screen by raising the beam current.

Brillouin scattering the modulation of a light CARRIER (sense 1) signal in a FIBRE OPTIC CABLE because of molecular vibrations due to temperature level.

British Telecom (BT) the major UK telecommunications provider which also offers INTERNET connection (*btinternet*).

British Telecom Lempel/Ziv algorithm (BTLZ) a digital data BIT REDUCTION technique for text that allocated shorter codes to the most frequently occurring letters such as the vowels.

broadband or **wideband** (of amplifiers and networks) capable of operation over a large range of frequencies. Typical broadband systems include VIDEO AMPLIFIERs for television, and the signal circuits of CATHODE-RAY OSCILLOSCOPES. The name is also used for data connections that offer higher bandwidth than a telephone line, though very much less than a TV channel.

broadcasting transmission of radio-frequency energy from an AERIAL so that the signals can be picked up by any suitable receiver. This distinguishes radiated signals from signals along cables that are delivered only to receivers that are connected to the cable.

broadcast network or **WiFi** a NETWORK (sense 2) on which a user can transmit a DATA PACKET that can be picked up and used by any other computer on the network. Normally, each packet carries an address code so that the packet can be intercepted by one other user.

broadcast quality or **broadcast standard** (of video equipment) conforming to the quality standards of broadcast TV, implying (in the UK) a rate of 25–30 frames per second at 525–625 lines per frame and with RESOLUTION of 800 × 640 pixels or more.

broadcast spectrum the complete range of radio frequencies that can be used for BROADCASTING.

broadcast standard see BROADCAST QUALITY.

broadcast storm severe interference to broadcast signals caused by electrical discharges from the Sun.

broadside array a set of AERIALS arranged to receive or transmit in a direction at right angles to the line of the aerials. See also AERIAL ARRAY.

brouter a network device that combines the actions of BRIDGING and ROUTING.

brownout the partial loss of data or services due to mains voltage fluctuations. See also BLACKOUT (sense 2).

BRR see BIT RATE REDUCTION.

brush a carbon or soft metal contact to a moving conductor, used on motors, servo-systems, selsyns and rotary transformers.

brush discharge a faint glow discharge surrounding a high-voltage conductor.

The brush discharge is particularly strong around points and sharp edges, and causes severe radio-frequency interference.

brushgear the connectors, often of carbon, used to bear against a revolving COMMUTATOR or SLIPRINGS of a MOTOR or GENERATOR (sense 1).

brushless AC motor a form of AC motor whose supply is generated from an OSCILLATOR so that the speed may be regulated by altering oscillator frequency.

brushless DC motor a motor using semiconductor devices in place of the usual COMMUTATOR and brush system to achieve longer life and lower interference than the conventional form of DC motor.

BS 1852 coding the system of writing values of resistance or capacitance using a letter reference in place of the decimal point, so that, for example, 2.7 kΩ is written as 2k7.

BS 4343 the British specification for electrical connectors for industrial use.

BSF see BAND-STOP FILTER.

BS gate symbols the set of rectangular symbols used as an alternative to the more familiar US MIL set. See Fig. 15.

BSI *abbrev. for* British Standards Institution, an association (founded in 1901) that establishes and maintains standards for units of measurement, technical terminology, etc.

BS/IEC plug the three-pin connector (Euroconnector) used along with a matching socket on electronic equipment. The (live) plug uses inaccessible sockets to prevent fingers touching a live lead; the (dead) socket uses pins.

BSRAM see BURST STATIC RANDOM ACCESS MEMORY.

BT see BRITISH TELECOM.

BTAM (Basic Telecommunications Access Method) any system for reading from and writing to a remote computer by way of telephone lines.

bubblejet™ a form of printer for computers in which a miniature heating element in a capillary tube boils ink to form a bubble that ejects a drop of ink on to paper.

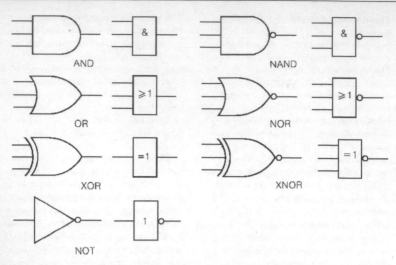

Fig. 15. **BS gate symbols along with MIL symbols**

bubble memory a form of magnetic memory for computers using microscopic zones (bubbles) of reversible field inside magnetic materials.

Buck converter a SWITCHING CIRCUIT used in a SWITCH-MODE POWER SUPPLY (SMPS).

bucket brigade see CHARGE-COUPLED DEVICE.

buffer 1. an isolating amplifier. 2. a temporary memory in a computer.

buffer memory a part of computer memory that is used to gather up data into convenient bundles. For example, data that is to be recorded on disk is gathered into units of 256 bytes before being recorded, and replay from a disk is also stored temporarily in a buffer.

buffer under-run a problem that can arise during recording on a CD-R or CD-RW (or corresponding DVD) disc, in which the stream of data being fed to the disc is slower than the writing speed of the laser on the disc.

bug a fault in a circuit or in a computer program.

build-up time the time needed for circuit current to reach its normal level.

bulk-erase to wipe all signals from the whole of a magnetic tape or disk by using

an intense AC MAGNETIC FIELD around the tape or disk.

bulk resistance the resistance of a sample of P- or N- DOPED SEMICONDUCTOR. The term 'bulk' implies that the sample is not of atomic dimensions.

buncher the electrode of a KLYSTRON that causes the steady electron stream to form into groups (bunches) of electrons separated by spaces.

bunching the effect of the differing electron velocities in a BEAM, causing electrons to gather into groups rather than to remain as a uniform stream.

buried diode a diode formed along with a heater element (to ensure a stable temperature level) in an IC REGULATOR.

buried layer a base layer of high-conductivity SEMICONDUCTOR. The layers of a transistor or IC are fabricated on top of this buried layer, that is then used for electrical and thermal connections.

burn to write data on a CD-R or CD-RW disc.

burn-in see AGEING.

burnproof drive a CD-ROM writing drive that is designed to maintain data in a BUFFER MEMORY, avoiding errors caused by writing ('burning') blank data to a disc.

This action is possible only if the software supports it.

burnt print   heat damage to a PRINTED CIRCUIT BOARD making it unusable.

burr   an irregularity in a metal surface, causing poor contact with any surface held against it.

Burrus diode   a form of LED designed for efficient coupling to an OPTICAL FIBRE.

burst   a few cycles of signal. See COLOUR BURST.

burst blanking   the removal of the COLOUR BURST signal from the CHROMINANCE SIGNAL stages of a COLOUR TELEVISION receiver to avoid interference with CLAMPING and other actions.

burst control or **burst firing** or **zero-voltage switching**   alteration of the average power controlled by a THYRISTOR or TRIAC by switching on for a number of complete cycles and then off for a number of complete cycles. Compare PHASE CONTROL.

burst EDO   burst extended data out: a variety of DIMM that achieves faster operation by using larger units of data, each unit providing access information to following units. The technology is unsuited to the faster BUS speeds now in use and has been superseded by DDR memory types such as DDR-SDRAM.

burst error   a DIGITAL signal error consisting of several BITs in one place, often due to contamination or scratching of a CD surface.

burst firing   see BURST CONTROL.

burst gate   a circuit, part of a TV COLOUR DECODER, that isolates the COLOUR BURST signal so that it can be used to correct the local subcarrier OSCILLATOR.

burst interference   electrical interference that occurs in short bursts and which can corrupt a DIGITAL signal.

burst isochronous transmission   the breaking up of a DIGITAL transmission into short bursts sent at intervals, used when the maximum rate for the channel is greater than the actual data rate.

burst noise or **popcorn noise**   a form of low-frequency noise caused by small changes in the BASE bias current of a semiconductor device.

burst static random access memory (BSRAM)   a form of fast STATIC RAM used for fast CACHE purposes.

bus   a set of connections to several devices. A power bus, for example, is a set of conductors that carries DC supply to several devices. In computing, a bus is a set of lines that connects to all the main components such as microprocessor, memory chips and ports.

bus cycle   the sequence of CLOCK PULSES that are used to complete a WRITE or READ action along a set of computer BUSes.

bus extension systems   a computer architecture that uses a MOTHERBOARD with slots for inserted cards that extend the computing actions, each slot being an extension of the computer main BUS.

bush   a form of bearing or insulator through which a shaft or cable is taken.

bus mastering   the software action of controlling the use of BUSes in a computer so as to avoid conflicts.

bus network   a form of NETWORK (sense 2) in which the signals are carried over a BUS and are available to all of the networked computers, but are used only by the computer that responds to a unique ADDRESS code. Failure of one computer does not necessarily disrupt the network action for the others, and it is easy to extend the network to include additional computers. See also RING NETWORK; STAR NETWORK.

bus speed   the rate of transmission along a BUS, usually in terms of megabytes (MB) per second.

bus timing diagram   a form of graph showing the CLOCK PULSE for a MICROPROCESSOR system and its time relationship to inputs, outputs and control signals.

bus width   the number of bits handled in one BUS action, typically 32 or 64 for modern processors.

Butler oscillator or **overtone oscillator** a form of CRYSTAL OSCILLATOR circuit in which the load circuit is tuned to an odd HARMONIC (usually 3rd or 5th) of the crystal frequency.

Butterworth response a form of FILTER response. The Butterworth type of filter provides a fairly uniform ATTENUATION over the stop-band, but with sloping sides. See also TCHEBYCHEV. (See Fig. 116.)

button cell a small cell of button shape, used to provide power for devices such as watches, hearing aids and other miniaturized equipment.

buzz on sound a noise on the SOUND CHANNEL of a TELEVISION RECEIVER, usually caused by a trace of the VIDEO SIGNAL due to mistuning.

BW see BANDWIDTH.

by-pass a component that provides a shunt for signals. A *by-pass capacitor*, for example, shunts unwanted signals to earth.

byte a group of eight BITS.

byte serial transmission sending bytes of data in natural sequence over a serial or parallel line system.

cabinet or **enclosure** a casing for one or more loudspeakers that will make the best possible acoustic matching between the loudspeaker CHARACTERISTICS and the open air outside the cabinet.

cable an insulated wire or a set of insulated (see INSULATOR) wires bound together. The individual wire CONDUCTORS in the cable are usually stranded, and the whole cable is reasonably flexible, so that it can be laid into ducts. The terms can denote a single signal conductor, such as the COAXIAL CABLE for a TV aerial, or for a complex set of conductors like the cable that links a TV camera to its control unit. Most cables incorporate some protection for the conductors, such as metal sheathing.

cable, aerial cable, mostly now of the coaxial type (see COAXIAL CABLE), used to connect a receiver to an aerial.

cable distribution the delivery of television or other signals through cables taken to individual houses rather than broadcasting by radio.

cable length compensation the use of circuit devices such as DUMMY LEADS in a bridge circuit to compensate for the resistance of cables for a RESISTANCE THERMOMETER, THERMOCOUPLE, or other remote sensing device.

cable loss the loss of signal power between an AERIAL and a receiver caused by the resistance of the aerial cable.

cable modem a MODEM that connects a computer to the INTERNET by way of a cable TV service. This can allow for faster transfer rates than are achieved with a conventional telephone line modem.

cable network a system for distributing TV, telephone, data and radio transmissions through a cable to any household. See also CABLE TV; TREE-AND-BRANCH; SWITCHED-STAR.

cable, RS-232 originally a 24-lead cable for full implementation of the RS-232

standard, but latterly manufactured with a 9-pin connector for computing uses.

cables, drive see DRIVE CABLES.

cables, thermocouple see CABLE LENGTH COMPENSATION.

cable TV distribution of TV signals by cables, using FIBRE OPTICS main lines and copper cable for house to house wiring. For DIGITAL TELEVISION, a multiphase modulation system such as QAM-64 is used.

cabling; IEEE 1394 the standard cable for the IEE 1394 ('firewire') connection system using dual shielded twisted pair data cable and two power lines.

cache a fast-acting MEMORY, usually of modest size compared to the main RAM memory and used as an intermediate store of data between the (fast) processor and the (slower) main memory, hard disk or other storage.

cache, hard drive a section of memory set aside to act as a CACHE for the HARD DRIVE(s) of a fast computer.

CAD see COMPUTER AIDED DESIGN.

caddy a holder for a CD-ROM disc in a CD-DRIVE, no longer widely used.

cadmium sulphide cell a PHOTOCONDUCTIVE CELL with peak response in the orange-red region, making it suitable as a flame detector. The cell is rugged and low-cost, but its response time is slow compared to semiconductor types.

CAE see COMPUTER AIDED ENGINEERING.

calibration the checking of a measuring instrument against a standard. The action is performed on instruments such as voltmeters and, particularly, CATHODE-RAY OSCILLOSCOPES whose characteristics may drift with time.

calibration pips a built-in form of timebase CALIBRATION for analogue CATHODE-RAY OSCILLOSCOPES, using short pulses generated by a crystal-controlled oscillator (see CRYSTAL CONTROL). By pressing a calibration switch, these calibration pips can be shown on the display, and used to check the accuracy of the timebase.

calibrator, CRO   a system of checking the AMPLITUDE and time precision of a CATHODE-RAY OSCILLOSCOPE display using a very stable square wave generator.

call-back   a NETWORK (sense 2) security method in which a user calls and provides a password. If this is accepted, the user terminates the call and the controller will then call the number assigned to the holder of the password.

call congestion ratio or **blocking ratio** the ratio of number of telephone calls blocked to the total number made in a given period.

caller ID   a method of displaying the number of a caller, either on an LCD screen at the receiver or at the telephone exchange (accessed using 1471). The ID is transmitted as a FREQUENCY SHIFT KEYING signal early in the ringing sequence.

calling devices   pull-cord or other emergency switches, part of a security system intended to summon help.

calling tone   a tone delivered along a telephone line that causes the receiver to indicate a call.

call point   the 'break glass in case of fire' box that is part of a fire alarm system.

call second   the unit of TRAFFIC volume for telephone calls. See also ERLANG.

call sign   a set of letters and numbers that is used to identify a TRANSMITTER. The system is used in the UK mainly by amateur operators, and by the users of radio links. In the US and many other countries, even entertainment radio stations are required to broadcast a call sign at intervals.

calorie   an old unit of (heat) energy content, now superseded by the JOULE.

CAM   1. computer-aided manufacture. 2. computer-aided management. The term is applied to the use of a computer as a management tool by providing information, forecasts, visual simulations and data retrieval. The most important action, however, is usually communication.

Cambridge Fast Ring   a later development of the CAMBRIDGE RING with a speed of 100 Mbit/second.

Cambridge Ring   a method of passing data round a set of computers. This is a form of LOCAL AREA NETWORK which as the full name suggests was developed in Cambridge, and which is widely used in educational applications. See also ETHERNET.

camcorder or **analogue camcorder** a VIDEO CAMERA and VIDEO CASSETTE RECORDER formed into one unit, using ANALOGUE methods to record the signals on tape. Compare DIGITAL CAMCORDER.

camcorder, digital   see DIGITAL CAMCORDER.

camera tube   a vacuum device that produces a VIDEO SIGNAL from an optical image. Camera tubes rely on either photoemissive or photoconductive effects to convert light intensity patterns into electrostatic charge patterns (see PHOTOELECTRIC EFFECT, PHOTOCONDUCTIVE CELL). A scanning electron beam then discharges these patterns, and the discharging current forms the output video signal as the beam scans. A camera-control unit provides the scanning signals for the camera, and also adds the correct BLACK LEVEL and the SYNCHRONIZING PULSES to the video output so that it can be used for studio monitors and ultimately transmitted. Camera tubes have now been superseded for most purposes by solid CCD devices. See also IMAGE ORTHICON; VIDICON.

CA module   see CONDITIONAL ACCESS.

Campbell Swinton, A. A.   (1863–1930) the first engineer to propose (in 1910) a system of electronic television that was remarkably close to that adopted in 1936, so that he can be said to be the true inventor of modern electronic TV even though the technology at the time was not adequate to make a working model. See also BAIRD.

cancellation circuit   a radar circuit technique to remove FIXED RETURNS. In a radar system that allows only moving objects to be noted, the pulses returned from fixed objects have to be cancelled.

This is done by using a DELAY LINE. The pulse from an object is compared with the pulse from the previous scan. If the pulses coincide, the object is non-moving, and the cancellation circuit removes it by adding an inverted signal.

canned 1. (of a portion of a circuit) protected against electrostatic or magnetic fields. A screening can around a coil reduces the chances of pickup of interfering signals, and also reduces the field around the coil that might affect other components. The can will, however, lower the Q-FACTOR of the coil. 2. a slang term for recorded, as in 'canned music'.

CAP carrierless amplitude and phase modulation: see SINGLE SIDEBAND SUPPRESSED CARRIER.

capacitance the property of a system that enables it to store electrostatic charge. The capacitance of an isolated conductor is defined as the slope of the graph of potential plotted against charge. Symbol: C; unit: Farad. An object is said to have capacitance (C) of one farad if it can store one COULOMB of charge (Q) at a potential of one volt. Capacitance can be written $C = Q/V$ and is measured in units of coulombs per volt. In practice, the farad is too large a unit, and microfarads (10^{-6}F), nanofarads (10^{-9}F) and picofarads (10^{-12}F) are used. See also CAPACITOR.

capacitance detector see CAPACITIVE PROXIMITY SWITCH.

capacitance meter any instrument used to measure capacitance, particularly the DIRECT READING CAPACITANCE METER.

capacitive coupling a circuit that transfers signal from one STAGE to another through a CAPACITOR.

capacitive crosstalk unwanted transfer of a signal (see CROSSTALK) by its electrostatic field affecting a conductor in another circuit. See also INDUCTIVE CROSSTALK.

capacitive load a load that behaves like a combination of resistor and capacitor. This implies that the PHASE of voltage lags the phase of current. If the load were purely capacitive, the phase angle would be 90°, but there would be no POWER DISSIPATION.

capacitive proximity switch a sensor that detects an earthed object by the change of capacitance between the body and a charged plate. See also DIFFUSE SCAN PHOTO DETECTOR; HALL-EFFECT PROXIMITY UNIT; INDUCTIVE PROXIMITY SWITCH; OPTICAL BEAM PROXIMITY DETECTOR.

capacitive reactance the ratio of signal voltage to current for a capacitor. This quantity decreases as the frequency is increased, with the relationship $X = 1/\omega C$, where X is reactance in ohms, ω is angular frequency (equal to $2\pi f$), and C is capacitance in farads. For a pure capacitor (with no series or parallel resistance and no inductance), the phase of current leads the phase of voltage by 90°. See also IMPEDANCE.

capacitive transducer any measuring device that can measure a quantity such as diaphragm movement or liquid level by changes in the capacitance between two conductors.

capacitive tuning the altering of the tuning of a RESONANT CIRCUIT by varying the capacitance. This involves using a variable capacitor or a variable inductor.

capacitor a passive circuit component with CAPACITANCE. A capacitor is formed from a pair of conducting surfaces separated by a layer of insulator. The capacitance value is proportional to the area of one plate (the smaller, if the two are not of identical area), and inversely proportional to the separation. The PERMITTIVITY of the insulator also contributes directly to the capacitance value. For parallel plates of area A m² separated by distance d metres by a dielectric with relative permittivity ε_r the capacitance is given by:

$$C = \frac{\varepsilon_r \varepsilon_0 A}{d}$$

where ε_0 is the permittivity of free space. The form of construction affects the amount of capacitance that can be achieved in a reasonable bulk, the stability of capacitance value, and the voltage that can be applied across the conductors (plates). The voltage-variable capacitance across a semiconductor JUNCTION (sense 2) can also be used in the form of a VARACTOR. See also CERAMIC CAPACITOR; ELECTROLYTIC CAPACITOR; FOIL CAPACITOR; MICA CAPACITOR; MOS CAPACITOR; PAPER CAPACITOR; PLASTIC-FILM CAPACITOR.

capacitor, backup see BACKUP CAPACITOR.

capacitor charging the action of connecting a capacitor to a voltage source so that the capacitor charges to that voltage level. If there is resistance in the circuit, a finite time is needed for charging, see TIME CONSTANT.

capacitor coupling the transfer of signals from one stage to another using a capacitor to block DC.

capacitor decoupling the use of a capacitor to provide a low-impedance path to earth for unwanted high-frequency signals.

capacitor discharging the action of connecting a conductor across the terminals of a capacitor so that current flows momentarily, discharging the capacitor. If there is resistance in the circuit, a finite time is needed for discharging, see TIME CONSTANT.

capacitor input filter the use of a large-value capacitor following a RECTIFIER stage and used as a RESERVOIR CAPACITOR and low-pass FILTER.

capacitor microphone a MICROPHONE in which the TRANSDUCER is a capacitor. The microphone consists of a metal backplate with a conducting DIAPHRAGM close-spaced from it. The diaphragm is electrostatically charged, so that when it vibrates, the voltage of the diaphragm will vary. This variation of voltage constitutes the output signal. The microphone tends to be bulky if reasonable sensitivity is required, and needs a polarizing voltage to supply the charge to the DIAPHRAGM. The ELECTRET microphone is a more modern version.

capacitor-resistor circuit a waveshaping or delay circuit formed from a capacitor and resistor.

capacitors, series see SERIES CAPACITORS.

capacitors, parallel see PARALLEL CAPACITORS.

capacitor substitution box a set of capacitors that can be selected and connected by a switch to terminals, used in testing by substitution.

capstan the rotating tape-drive spindle of a TAPE RECORDER. The capstan consists of an accurately ground cylindrical rod that rotates at a constant speed. The tape is sandwiched between the capstan and a rubber PINCHWHEEL, so that the constant speed rotation of the capstan causes a constant linear motion of the tape. Any irregularity of the capstan or its bearings will cause irregular tape speed that will in turn cause WOW or FLUTTER on musical notes recorded on the tape.

capstan motor a DC motor whose speed can be closely controlled, used to move tape past a TAPEHEAD at a steady rate.

capsule a container, often of liquid or gas, used to sense or measure quantities such as temperature.

caption generator a portion of a VIDEO editing system that will add text captions to video pictures.

capture band the range of input frequencies of signals to a PHASE-LOCKED LOOP circuit that will result in the output being locked to the input frequency and phase.

capture card a circuit CARD added to a computer in order to convert incoming data into digital form (see ANALOGUE TO DIGITAL CONVERTER) and store it on the hard drive.

capture effect, FM when two FM signals of the same frequency are received, an FM receiver will LOCK ON to the stronger signal and demodulate (see DEMODULATION) only that transmission.

capture range the frequency range for which a PHASE-LOCKED LOOP will detect an input signal and lock to it.

capture ratio the measure of the ability of an FM RECEIVER to lock into a more powerful transmission that is on the same frequency as a weaker one, expressed as the ratio of voltage strengths (in dB) that will ensure that the weaker transmission is ignored. A good figure is 1 dB, and 2 dB is acceptable.

capture time, DMM   the time needed for a DIGITAL MULTIMETER to achieve stability in making a reading.

carbon anode   the positive electrode of a CARBON-ZINC CELL.

carbon composition resistor   see CARBON RESISTOR.

carbon film resistor   a RESISTOR manufactured by evaporating carbon on to a ceramic rod, adding a connector at each end, and cutting the resulting film to obtain a precise resistance value.

carbon microphone   the type of microphone using carbon granules contained between a DIAPHRAGM and a metal backplate and used to modulate a current. The device was formerly used for telephones, but is now obsolete.

carbon monoxide detector   an indicator or measuring device for the presence of carbon monoxide in the air or in car exhaust. The electronic type uses a semiconductor whose properties alter in the presence of carbon monoxide, see also ORGANIC SEMICONDUCTOR FILM.

carbon moulded resistor   see CARBON RESISTOR.

carbon preset   a small adjustable POTENTIOMETER (sense 1) that is set to a suitable value during testing and then left undisturbed.

carbon resistor or **carbon-composition resistor** or **carbon moulded resistor**   once the most common and the cheapest construction of resistor. This uses a mixture of graphite and clay (the same mixture as is used for pencils), baked and moulded into a casing in contact with metal caps that are attached to the wire leads. The TOLERANCE range of resistance value for a batch is large, and the stability of resistance value is not high. For most purposes this type now been replaced by metal or carbon FILM RESISTORS.

carbon tetrachloride   a volatile solvent used for degreasing. Though not flammable, the vapour is toxic to breathe.

carbon-track potentiometer   a POTENTIOMETER (sense 1) that uses a carbon composition track (see CARBON RESISTOR).

carbon-zinc cell   the form of common CELL, widely used for various portable electrical appliances, but replaced by an ALKALINE CELL for more critical uses.

carcinotron or **crossed-field tube**   a form of TRAVELLING-WAVE TUBE that is used as a MICROWAVE oscillator. It is distinguished by the use of crossed electrostatic and magnetic fields, and a circular beam path. It is also classed as a form of BACKWARD-WAVE TUBE, because the electromagnetic wave motion is in the reverse direction as compared to the electron beam motion.

card or **plug-in card**   a PRINTED CIRCUIT BOARD with EDGE CONNECTORs that can be plugged into an EXPANSION SLOT of a computer in order to add new facilities.

card access   a security device, much used in hotels, that ensures that a door can be unlocked only by inserting a card containing information on a magnetic stripe.

cardioid microphone   a microphone constructed to provide a CARDIOID RESPONSE.

cardioid response or **cardioid pattern**   a heart-shaped response curve, providing a directional characteristic. See Fig. 16.

carriage servo or **sled servo** or **slider servo**   the SERVO system of a CD or DVD player that controls the movement of the whole optical assembly across the surface of the disc.

carrier   **1.** or **radio wave** a radio-frequency SINE WAVE or a light (or infra-red) wave that can be modulated (see MODULATION) and used to carry information. **2.** an electron, hole, or ion whose movement causes the flow of current.

carrier detect   a MODEM action used to sense the presence of an incoming signal.

carrier frequency   the frequency of an unmodulated CARRIER (sense 1).

carrier insertion oscillator (CIO)   see BEAT-FREQUENCY OSCILLATOR.

carrierless amplitude/phase modulation (CAP)   a form of BIT RATE REDUCTION of a digital data stream, followed by a DIGITAL TO ANALOGUE CONVERTER and LOW-PASS FILTER to give an analogue waveform that can be transmitted directly.

carrier sense multiple access (CSMA)   a NETWORK system in which each terminal

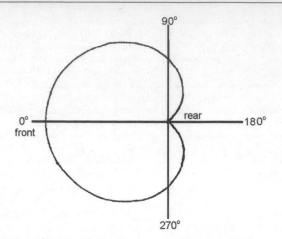

Fig. 16. **cardioid response**

can have exclusive access by allowing access only when a gap is data is detected.

carrier sense multiple access-collision detection (CSMA-CD) a variation of the CSMA system in which any COLLISION of data will cause each terminal to cease contact for a different length of time, so ensuring that no collision can occur when links are resumed.

carrier storage or **charge storage** the storage of charge in the form of excess CARRIERS (sense 2) near a semiconductor JUNCTION (sense 2). The significance of carrier storage is that when the bias across the junction is reversed, current will flow as a result of these carriers recombining. This means that a junction will continue to pass current until some (short) time after applying a reverse bias.

carrier suppression a form of radio MODULATION. The CARRIER (sense 1) is modulated (see MODULATION), giving a set of signals that consists of carrier and SIDEBANDS. The carrier is then suppressed by filtering or by adding an inverse carrier signal, leaving only the sideband(s). The effect of carrier suppression is to increase very greatly the power efficiency of the transmission. Another effect is to confine reception to receivers that are equipped to replace the missing carrier.

carrier to noise ratio (C/N) the ratio of radio CARRIER (sense 1) amplitude to NOISE amplitude prior to the demodulation of a signal. See also SIGNAL TO NOISE RATIO.

carrier wave see CARRIER (sense 1).

Carson's bandwidth the bandwidth of a frequency modulated signal (see FREQUENCY MODULATION), defined as $2[f_d + f_m]$ where f_d is FREQUENCY DEVIATION and f_m is the highest permitted modulating frequency.

cartesian coordinates numbers that fix a location along perpendicular axes such as the X and Y coordinates of a graph. See also POLAR COORDINATES. See Fig. 17.

cartridge **1.** a container for a medium such as ink (inkjet cartridge) or tape (tape cartridge). **2.** the TRANSDUCER for a VINYL DISC (pickup cartridge).

cartridge tape a CARTRIDGE (sense 1) containing digital TAPE, used for data backup.

cascade a set of STAGES in sequence, i.e. stages in which the output of one stage serves as the input of the next.

cascaded amplifier an amplifier of more than one STAGE in which the stages are CASCADEd.

cascode a form of amplifier circuit that has high output impedance and very large isolation between output and input. In BIPOLAR JUNCTION TRANSISTOR form, the

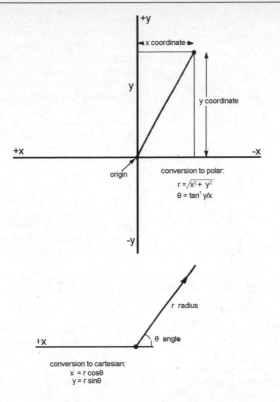

Fig. 17. **cartesian coordinates**

cascode consists of a COMMON EMITTER
stage directly coupled to a COMMON BASE
stage. See Fig. 18.

case or **casing** the enclosure around the
parts of a computer, often supplied along
with the POWER SUPPLY unit for the
computer.

Cassegrain reflector a hyperboloid convex
reflector used at the focus of a SATELLITE
DISH to pass a narrow beam through an
aperture at the centre of the dish.

cassette a plastic casing that contains two
tape reels with guides, using narrow tape
with a spring pad pressing the tape on to
a recording head when the cassette is
loaded into a player.

cassette counter the indicator, formerly
mechanical but now more likely to be

electronic, that indicates position on the
tape in a CASSETTE, either audio or video.

cassette end detection or **autostop** the
device that senses the approaching end
of tape in a cassette and stops the play,
wind or rewind action before the tape is
damaged.

cassette head see TAPEHEAD.

catalyst a material that will induce or
speed up a chemical reaction without itself
being affected. Metals of the platinum
group are often used as catalysts,
particularly in vehicle exhaust systems.

catcher the electron collecting electrode
of a KLYSTRON.

catching diode or **clipping diode** a diode
that is used to limit the amplitude of a
waveform.

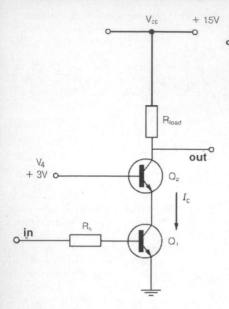

V_{cc} + 15V

R_{load}

out

V_4
+ 3V

Q_2

I_c

in

R_s

Q_1

Fig. 18. **cascode**

cathode or **hot emitter** 1. the electron-emitting part of a THERMIONIC VALVE. In transmitting valves, this consists of a winding of tungsten wire that is electrically heated to a very high temperature. The old-style receiving valves used a low-temperature cathode that consisted of a coating of oxides (calcium, strontium and barium oxides) deposited on a nickel tube. This was heated to a working temperature of around 1000K by a molybdenum filament inside the nickel tube. The filament was insulated by a coating of aluminium oxide (alumina). The cathode of a cathode-ray tube consists of a flat-topped nickel cylinder that is heated by an internal filament. The oxide coating is on the flat top of the cylinder. 2. the negative electrode of a DIODE or THYRISTOR. 3. the cell ELECTRODE that gains electrons from the electrolyte and is therefore negative.

cathode follower an obsolete form of THERMIONIC VALVE circuit with very high input impedance and low output impedance. The transistor equivalent is the EMITTER FOLLOWER or SOURCE FOLLOWER.

cathode-ray oscilloscope (CRO) or **oscilloscope** the instrument that is used for measurements on waveforms and pulses. The ANALOGUE oscilloscope is based on a CATHODE-RAY TUBE that uses ELECTROSTATIC DEFLECTION. The horizontal plates of the tube are supplied with a sawtooth TIMEBASE waveform that causes the electron beam to sweep across the face of the tube at a constant speed and return (flyback) very rapidly. The beam is automatically brightened during sweep, and blanked during flyback. The waveform that is to be measured is amplified and applied to the Y-deflection plates.

The combination of waveform and timebase produces a graph picture of the wave, showing the amplitude and time between wave peaks. By having both the timebase and the amplifier calibrated, the PEAK-TO-PEAK AMPLITUDE and the time between wave peaks can be measured for any wave that can be displayed. More advanced facilities include delayed triggering, second timebase, and multiple traces. See also DIGITAL CRO.

cathode-ray tube (CRT) an electron beam display device. Sometimes shortened to *tube* (but note that in the US, *tube* means any thermionic vacuum device). All cathode-ray tubes make use of the emission of electrons from a hot CATHODE (sense 1), the formation of emitted electrons into a beam by ELECTRON LENSES, and the emission of light from a material, the PHOSPHOR, that is struck by electrons. In addition, all cathode-ray tubes must provide for the beam to be deflected in any direction across the face of the tube.

The two main types of cathode-ray tubes are INSTRUMENT TUBES, used for CATHODE-RAY OSCILLOSCOPES, and PICTURE TUBES used for TV, computer monitors and radar.

cation a positively-charged ION. The name of cation is used because a positively-charged ion is attracted to a negatively-charged electrode, or CATHODE (sense 3). Contrast ANION.

cationic cocktail a solution of fabric softener used as an ANTISTATIC spray.

cat's whisker the sharpened wire contact to a lead-sulphide crystal as used in the early type of CRYSTAL RECEIVER. The detection of radio signals depended on the rectifying action of the metal point against a lead sulphide (*Galena*) crystal.

CATV see COMMUNAL AERIAL TV.

Cauer filter or **elliptic approximation** or **Zolotarev filter** a FILTER design with very sharp ROLL-OFF, but with ripple in both PASS-BAND and ATTENUATION-BAND.

causal (of a NETWORK, sense 2) not anticipating a signal, so that there is no output prior to an input.

CAV see CONSTANT ANGULAR VELOCITY.

cavity absorber a box resembling a LOUDSPEAKER casing, but with no loudspeaker, used to absorb a RESONANCE in a sound studio.

cavity resonator a MICROWAVE tuned circuit. The cylindrical cavity can be considered as a coil with one turn that is tuned by stray capacity, but it is more realistic to regard it in terms of the dimensions of a wavelength as related to the circumference of the cavity.

CAZAMP *acronym for* commutating auto-zeroing amplifier: a device consisting of a pair of MOSFET OPERATIONAL AMPLIFIERS and the number of FET switches (see FIELD EFFECT TRANSISTOR) contained within a single package. At any given time one amplifier is being zeroed (having its input–offset voltage removed) while the second amplifier behaves as a normal operational amplifier and provides gain. The operational amplifiers switch roles periodically by way of the FET switches and the effect is that drift due to INPUT OFFSETS is effectively cancelled out.

CB see CITIZENS' BAND.

C-band a range of frequencies (around 5GHz to 7GHz) used for satellite data links.

CBR constant BIT RATE.

CCD see CHARGE-COUPLED DEVICE.

CCIR Comité Consultatif International des Radiocommunications: the international standardizing committee for radio and television.

CCITT Comité Consultatif International Telegraphique et Telephonique: the international standardizing committee for telegraphs and telephones.

C-core transformer a form of TRANSFORMER whose core is C-shaped and encloses the windings to provide better magnetic efficiency. See E-I CORE.

CCTV see CLOSED-CIRCUIT TELEVISION.

CDA amplifier see NORTON AMPLIFIER.

CD burning see BURN.

CDDI see COPPER DATA DISTRIBUTED INTERFACE.

CD drive a computer drive for reading a CD-ROM. The drive fits into the standard 5-inch slot in the case of the computer and is connected by a data cable, a power cable and an audio cable (to the SOUND CARD).

CD drive speed the rotational speed of a CD is not constant (see CONSTANT LINEAR VELOCITY), so that CD drives fitted to computers are classed as ×10, ×20 and so on, according to how much faster they spin compared to an audio CD on the same track.

CDM see CODE DIVISION MULTIPLEX.

CDMA see CODE DIVISION MULTIPLE ACCESS.

CDPD see CELLULAR DIGITAL PACKET DATA.

CD player a standalone drive for playing a music CD, with an output to either a built-in or a separate amplifier and loudspeakers.

CD premium the additional price paid for a CD recording as compared to a tape recording of the same music, despite the fact that the CD is much cheaper to produce. The same effect maintains the price of a DVD higher than that of a videocassette.

CD quality the sound quality, typically of large BANDWIDTH and low NOISE and DISTORTION, typified by the specification of a COMPACT DISC.

CD-R a type of rewritable COMPACT DISC that can be written once only, though it can be erased. The action depends on altering the colour of a dye deposited on the disc, and such discs are used extensively for backing up computer data.

CD reader see CD DRIVE.

CD recorder see CD REWRITER.

CD rewriter or **CD writing drive** a form of CD DRIVE that can both read and write compact discs. The reading action is valid for all types of CDs, but writing can be carried out only on specially prepared blank discs described as CD-R or CD-RW.

CD ripping the action of extracting the music tracks of a CD to store in a computer for editing or re-assembly on another CD. The term 'ripping' is also used of the action of extracting movie data from a DVD.

CD ROM a CD, CD-R or CD-RW disc used for DIGITAL DATA, often for distribution of programs or for backup, as distinct from a CD used for recording sound or video.

CD-ROM drive a CD DRIVE in a computer, used mainly for data reading, but which can also be used to play music CDs if a SOUND CARD is fitted in the computer.

CD-R/RW the description of a CD WRITING DRIVE that can write to both CD-R and CD-RW discs.

CD-RW a form of blank disc for a CD WRITING DRIVE that can be erased and used for new data. Though such a disc can always be read in the drive that produced it, it may (if recorded with music) not play in a conventional music CD PLAYER.

CDTV see CONVENTIONAL DEFINITION TELEVISION.

CD-V see VIDEO COMPACT DISC.

CD writing drive see CD REWRITER.

CD-XA (compact disk-extended architecture) a CD-ROM system (including CD-R and CD-RW) that allows AUDIO and computer data to be mixed on the same disc.

Ceefax™ a form of TELETEXT service broadcast by the BBC, identical technically to the ITV ORACLE service.

CEI the French abbreviation of IEC.

Celeron™ the name used by Intel for their lower specification of processors (compared to **Pentium™**), used mainly in less-demanding consumer aimed computers.

cell any non-mechanical device that has an electric output. A *voltaic cell* is a generator of voltage from chemical effects, and such cells are used for low-voltage supplies, or when joined to make a BATTERY (sense 1), for higher voltages. Light-sensitive cells, or photocells, provide a voltage output when illuminated. Fuel cells generate power from the cold oxidation of a fuel.

cell relay or **cell switching** a form of PACKET SWITCHING in which the data is loaded into small units (cells) for asynchronous transmission.

cells in parallel see PARALLEL CELLS.

cells in series see SERIES CELLS.

cellular digital packet data (CDPD) a standard system for data transmission using cellular mobile telephones.

cellular MMDS a method of providing television signals to flat sparsely populated areas by using cellular mobile phone technology. See also MMDS.

cellular phone or **cellphone** a pocket telephone that uses UHF transmission and reception to a relay station from which it is routed by land line or microwave link.

cellular radio the use of multiplexing and low power transmission to allow the use of carriers for several transmissions, with CARRIER (sense 1) frequencies reused at separated places to provide a broadcast radio service. See also DIGITAL AUDIO BROADCASTING.

Celsius scale the temperature scale, named after its originator Anders Celsius (1701–1744) that uses the freezing point of water as its zero, and the temperature of steam above pure boiling water as its 100° mark. Celsius (not centigrade) temperatures are distinguished by the letter C following the degree sign, such as 100°C.

CE mark or **CE marking** the mark on electrical equipment that certified compliance with the Health & Safety low voltage directive (LVD) EN60950 and the emissions and immunity of EN50081/2.

CEN-CENELEC the European Committee for Standardization and European Committee for Electrotechnical Standardization.

centimetric wave a wave whose WAVELENGTH is less than a metre and more than a centimetre.

central processing unit (CPU)   the main data handling MICROPROCESSOR in a computer.

centre frequency   for a tuned circuit, the frequency for which response is maximum.

centre tap   a connection to the centre of a coil winding.

centre tapped transformer   a transformer whose output winding is centre tapped (see CENTRE TAP).

Centronics connector or **Centronics interface**   a 36-contact connector using flat contact faces, pioneered by the printer manufacturer, Centronics, and used as a standard connecting device on computer printers until the advent of USB.

ceramic capacitor   a CAPACITOR that is formed by METALLIZING two parallel surfaces of a ceramic slab. The range of capacitance can vary from a few picofarads to several nanofarads. The capacitance values of ceramic capacitors can change as the applied voltage is altered, and they can suffer from comparatively large energy losses. They are best used as BYPASS CAPACITORs for radio frequencies, and must never be used in the frequency-determining circuit of an oscillator.

ceramic cartridge   a transducer CARTRIDGE (sense 2) for a VINYL DISC that uses a ceramic type of PIEZOELECTRIC CRYSTAL material.

ceramic core resistor   a resistor, usually a METAL-FILM RESISTOR or CARBON-FILM RESISTOR, that is formed over a ceramic core that provided a SUBSTRATE with mechanical strength.

ceramic filter   see SAW FILTER.

ceramic pin grid array   a type of PIN GRID ARRAY package used by some microprocessor chips in the past.

ceramic resonator   a form of VARIABLE CAPACITOR used in the LOW NOISE BLOCK of a SATELLITE receiver.

ceramic tube capacitor   a low-value CAPACITOR formed by metallizing the inside and outside of a ceramic tube and making connections to each metal layer.

cermet   a ceramic-metal composite material. The cermet is very hard, but with a RESISTIVITY that makes it suitable for manufacturing POTENTIOMETERs (sense 1).

cermet potentiometer   a POTENTIOMETER (sense 1) that makes use of a CERMET material as its conductive track.

CFC   see CHLOROFLUOROCARBON.

change-line support   see DOOR SWITCH.

changeover or **CO**   a SWITCH action in which a contact is moved to either one of two static contacts, changing over the connection.

changeover microswitch   a MICROSWITCH whose contacts change over on actuation.

channel   **1.** in radio communication a specified frequency or frequency band used for signals. **2.** in a FIELD-EFFECT TRANSISTOR, the semiconducting path between the SOURCE and the DRAIN whose conductivity is controlled by the GATE (sense 1).

channel balance control   see BALANCE CONTROL.

channel capacity   the theoretical maximum amount of information that a CHANNEL (sense 1) can carry, given by SHANNON's equation: $C = B\log_2(1 + S/N)$ bits per second where B = bandwidth in Hz, C = channel capacity in BITS PER SECOND and S/N is the signal to noise ratio.

channel coding   the process of modulating (see MODULATION) serial digital data so as to make it self-clocking (see SELF-CLOCKING CODE) and with a SPECTRUM shape that ensures high efficiency and minimum interference with other units (such as servo systems in a CD PLAYER).

channel decoder   the circuitry within a SET-TOP BOX that separates the data of a single channel from the MULTIPLEX.

channelled substrate laser or **constricted heterojunction laser** or **plano-convex waveguide**   a semiconductor laser fabrication technique that buries a narrow active region by etching and deposition.

channel probing   see LINE PROBING.

channel separation control   see SEPARATION CONTROL.

channel sharing   the use of planned separation and different polarization (see POLARIZED, sense 1) for channels that use the same (UHF) frequency CARRIER (sense 1).

channel stopper a heavily doped layer in an IC that prevents the formation of unwanted FIELD-EFFECT TRANSISTOR channels.

channel, TV an allocation of frequency band, identified by number, for TV transmission and reception.

character-generator ROM a READ-ONLY MEMORY which contains the data for displaying alpha-numeric characters. Each item of data will be output from he ROM when a data number, usually the ASCII code for a character, is input.

character oriented protocol a communications protocol in which a minimum of one byte is used for control information.

character rounding a method of altering the PIXELS of a displayed character so as to round jagged edges.

characteristic a relationship or set of relationships among a number of quantities, usually between a pair. These are usually shown as a set of graphs in which one quantity is plotted against another, with a different graph line for each value of a third quantity. For example, a set of characteristics for a TRANSISTOR may show the output current plotted against input current for a range of different output voltages. See Fig. 19.

characteristic impedance the impedance of a correctly terminated line or any other network with two input and two output terminals. See ITERATIVE IMPEDANCE.

characteristic polynomial a mathematical expression used to program a SHIFT REGISTER so as to generate a PSEUDO-RANDOM number.

characters per inch (cpi) a measure of the density of printed characters in a line of evenly-spaced print.

characters per second (cps) a measure of the rate of transmission of data, usually in a SERIAL link or in a HARD DRIVE interface, or the rate of printing.

charge the fundamental property of the electron (negative charge) and proton (positive charge). The recognizable and measurable feature of charge is that one charge will exert force on any other charge. The relationship was discovered by Charles Augustin de Coulomb (1736–1806) after whom the modern unit of charge is named. The coulomb unit (equivalent to the charge of 6.24184×10^{18} electrons) is the charge which, placed one metre from an equal charge in a vacuum, repels it with a force of 8.9874×10^9 newtons.

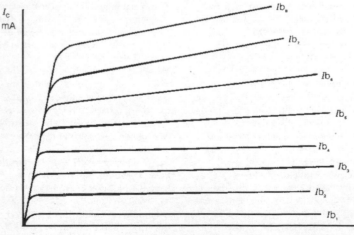

Fig. 19. **characteristic**

charge amplifier   a high INPUT IMPEDANCE amplifier using a capacitor in the NEGATIVE FEEDBACK path, used to amplify the signals from a CAPACITIVE TRANSDUCER.

charge carrier   any moving particle that is charged. The term denotes electrons, holes and ions that move under the influence of an electric field. The movement of a charge carrier constitutes CURRENT. Current is defined as rate of flow of charge in units of coulombs per second dQ/dt, otherwise known as amperes.

charge-coupled device (CCD) or **bucket brigade**   a charge-storage memory device. The CCD is based on a set of MOS capacitors formed in sequence on a chip, and with a common (earth) plate. By connecting adjacent groups of three capacitor plates to three-phase CLOCK signal lines, a charge that is placed on the first capacitor can be moved in sequence to each of the other plates on the chip. This forms a type of first-in, first-out memory that is used mainly as a SHIFT REGISTER, time-delay or serial memory. Another form of the circuit is the semiconductor photosensitive device used in CAMCORDERS which uses a photosensitive layer providing the charge in each cell, with the shift action providing the equivalent of a SCAN action.

charge density   a measure of the concentration of electric CHARGE. The surface density of charge is measured in terms of the number of coulombs of charge per square metre of surface. A more practical unit is microcoulombs per square metre. The volume density of charge is measured in terms of coulombs or microcoulombs of charge per cubic metre of volume.

charge/discharge curve   the graph of rise and fall of voltage across a capacitor as it is charged and discharged, see TIME CONSTANT.

charge pump circuit   see VOLTAGE DOUBLER CIRCUIT.

charger   a unit, nowadays often microprocessor controlled, for recharging a cell.

charge storage   see CARRIER STORAGE.

charge storage diode or **snap-off diode** or **step-recovery diode**   a DIODE that can be used as a PULSE generator. The STORED CHARGE allows the diode to conduct for a brief time after applying reverse voltage. This causes the reverse voltage across the diode to remain low until the carriers have been absorbed, following that the reverse voltage rise is very fast. This fast voltage rise, limited by the capacitance across the diode and the supply impedance, constitutes the leading edge of a pulse that is terminated when the diode conducts again.

charge-storage tube   see STORAGE TUBE.

charge transfer device (CTD)   any form of INTEGRATED CIRCUIT that operates by switching charge from one capacitor to another. See also CHARGE-COUPLED DEVICE.

charge unit   see COULOMB.

charging or **recharging**   the action of reversing the DISCHARGE of a CELL by applying a voltage higher than the output voltage and in the correct polarity.

chart recorder   an electromechanical signal WAVEFORM plotter. The recorder is used for signals that change too slowly to be analyzed with a CATHODE-RAY OSCILLOSCOPE. The signal AMPLITUDE operates a pen drive so that the height of the pen on a chart is related to signal amplitude. The chart is in the form of a roll that is driven past the pen at a steady slow rate. By using several separately controlled pens, a number of quantities can be plotted on one chart.

chassis   the metal base on which an electronic device is assembled.

chassis ground   the use of a CHASSIS as a common connecting point for earth leads. This will be truly earthed only if an earth connection is made to the chassis either though the mains connection or by way of a separate earthing wire.

Chebisheff or **Chebychev filter**   see TCHEBYCHEV RESPONSE.

check bit   a BIT added to a digital set of bits in order to act as an error check, see ERROR CORRECTION; CHECKSUM.

checksum   a method of detecting errors in a DIGITAL signal. At its simplest, the checksum is the sum (ignoring any carry beyond the limits of a register) of all the digital bits that have been transmitted, and is transmitted separately. If the transmitted checksum is not identical to a checksum made on the received data then an error must have occurred.

chemical cell a source of POTENTIAL DIFFERENCE that makes use of the electron-liberating chemical reaction between a metal CATHODE (sense 3) and an acid or alkali, with a conducting ANODE to complete a circuit.

chemical reaction, cell see CELL.

chemical tinning solution or **tinning solution** a liquid used to treat the surface of copper (usually on a PCB) to ensure that solder will flow over the copper and adhere to it.

chemical vapour deposition (CVD) or **vapour phase epitaxy (VPE)** growth of a SILICON crystal by the condensation of silicon atoms from a hot vapour. The vapour may contain DOPING atoms so that the deposited layers form a JUNCTION (sense 2) with the existing crystal structure.

child alert alarm an alarm triggered by the opening of a drawer or cupboard, intended to prevent a child reaching dangerous objects.

chime a form of security warning that is intended to inform rather than alarm, such as in a shop to indicate that a customer has entered.

chip 1. the small slice from a SEMICONDUCTOR wafer on which a transistor or integrated circuit is fabricated. 2. the unit of CLOCK CYCLE in a SPREAD SPECTRUM communications system.

chip count the number of INTEGRATED CIRCUIT (IC) chips used on a PRINTED CIRCUIT BOARD. A lower chip count can be achieved by using more complex chips and this can lower costs and improve reliability through the reduction in the number of interconnections between chips.

chip duration the time of a data unit, a set of CHIPS (sense 2), in a SPREAD SPECTRUM communications system.

chip select or **chip enable** an input pin for a DIGITAL IC. The chip-select pin allows the complete CHIP (sense 1) to be enabled or disabled according to the logic voltage

on the pin. This allows, for example, different banks of memory to be selected in a small computer.

chipset the ICs, other than the CPU, on a motherboard that provide the support functions for the CPU.

chirp filter or **dispersive filter** a form of ALL-PASS FILTER that will spread the energy of a pulse so as to reduce the peak load on a transmitter; the opposite action must be used at the receiver to reconstitute the pulse.

chirp radar a frequency-modulated (see FREQUENCY MODULATION) RADAR system in which the returning pulses will be closer spaced, giving the effect of increased power.

chirp system a SPREAD SPECTRUM technique in which the CARRIER (sense 1) frequency is swept over a large band of frequencies.

chirp-z transform a Laplace transform used in DIGITAL SIGNAL PROCESSING that gives a waveform similar to that of a CHIRP RADAR system.

chlorofluorocarbon (CFC) a family of volatile solvent liquids used for degreasing, now banned from use for removing FLUX (sense 2) residues from PCBs.

choke an obsolete term for INDUCTOR, particularly a large inductor with a magnetic core.

choke coupling the use of an INDUCTOR as the load for an amplifying stage.

choke input filter the use of a large-value INDUCTOR following a RECTIFIER in a POWER SUPPLY, used as a RESERVOIR CAPACITOR and low-pass FILTER.

cholesterol a fatty organic substance that is one type of LIQUID CRYSTAL, see LIQUID CRYSTAL DISPLAY.

chopped DC DC that has been converted into a signal, usually a square wave, by the action of a CHOPPER circuit.

chopped mode the use of a single-beam CATHODE-RAY OSCILLOSCOPE as a multi-beam instrument by switching the input signals alternately to the Y-AMPLIFIER.

chopper a circuit that converts a steady input voltage into a square wave by regular switching between the voltage source and earth. This was once done mechanically (using a vibrating switch), but is now achieved with MOS transistors or ICs. The chopped voltage can then be amplified using AC amplifier techniques. High-gain DC amplification (DC to DC conversion) can be achieved by using a chopper, amplifier and rectifier system.

chopper PSU see SWITCH-MODE SUPPLY.

chopper stabilized amplifier or **commutating auto-zero amplifier** an amplifier for low-frequency, low-amplitude signals by chopping (see CHOPPER) the input into AC and using an OPERATIONAL AMPLIFIER in a circuit that overcomes the problems of INPUT OFFSET.

chordal hop extension of propagation distance caused by signals becoming trapped in an ionized layer before being reflected back to Earth. See also SPORADIC-E.

chroma see CHROMINANCE SIGNAL.

chroma channel the portion of an analogue colour TV receiver that contains the CHROMINANCE AMPLIFIERS, AUTOMATIC COLOUR CONTROL, COLOUR KILLER, DELAY LINE and PAL MATRIX.

chroma keying or **blue screen** or **colour separation overlay** a television special effects system that uses the colour of a background as a trigger for replacing one signal by another. This allows a presenter standing in front of a blue screen, for example, to appear as if in an outdoor background. The presenter must not be wearing any item of clothing in the colour used for triggering the switch. See also LUMA KEYING.

chromaticity diagram a diagram that shows how various colours can be obtained from the three primary colours. See Fig. 20.

chrome tape see CHROMIUM DIOXIDE TAPE.

chrominance (chroma) amplifier the amplifier within an analogue TV receiver that amplifies the CHROMINANCE SIGNAL.

chrominance signal or **chroma** the portion of a TV signal that carries colour information. The analogue TV signal has to permit compatibility, meaning that the same signal can be used by both

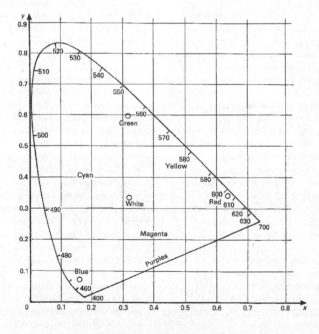

Fig. 20. **chromaticity diagram**

MONOCHROME (black/white) and COLOUR TV receivers. The monochrome signal, or LUMINANCE signal is transmitted normally, and the colour information is added in the form of a chrominance signal that is modulated onto a SUBCARRIER. A monochrome receiver does not demodulate (see DEMODULATION) this subcarrier, and thus uses only the luminance signal. The effect of the subcarrier on the monochrome receiver is to cause a fine bar pattern that is not visible at normal viewing distances. A colour receiver can demodulate the subcarrier, recover the chrominance signals and make use of them, mixed with the luminance signal, to provide three separate signals for the three ELECTRON GUNs of the COLOUR TUBE.

chromium dioxide tape or **chrome tape** recording tape using chromium dioxide in preference to iron oxide, providing higher performance than iron oxide tapes providing the correct BIAS and magnetizing levels are used.

cinch socket or **video CVBS socket** a connector used on videocassette and DVD recorders for COMPOSITE SIGNAL inputs.

cinema sound originally an optical system using a SOUNDTRACK image whose width or density conveyed the sound frequency and amplitude; now using magnetic tape on multiple tracks with noise-reducing systems for optimum quality.

CIO see CARRIER INSERTION OSCILLATOR.

cipher or **cypher** a form of coding in which each character in the CLEAR TEXT is replaced by a different character, usually in such a way that characters that are repeated in the plain text do not transform in the same way on each occurrence. Compare SCRAMBLER.

CIRC see CROSS INTERLEAVE REED-SOLOMON CODE.

circuit a path for electric current, consisting usually of a current path through both ACTIVE COMPONENTS and PASSIVE COMPONENTS. See also DEMODULATION; FILTER; GAIN; GATE (sense 2); MODULATION; OSCILLATION; SWITCH.

circuit board see PRINTED CIRCUIT BOARD.

circuit breaker a form of OVERLOAD switch. A circuit breaker is used in place of a FUSE to interrupt a circuit when excessive current flows or when a voltage surge occurs. The circuit breaker is magnetically operated, and can be manually reset.

circuit card see PRINTED CIRCUIT BOARD.

circuit diagram or **schematic (US)** a diagram that shows a circuit in symbolic form. There is a standard symbol for each type of component, showing the connections. In a circuit diagram, each current path is shown as a line that joins components. Some diagrams show input and output waveforms also at points in the circuit. Components in the diagram are labelled with an identifying letter and number (such as R234, C122) and sometimes also with their value. Compare WIRING DIAGRAM.

circuit diagrams by computer the use of a COMPUTER AIDED DESIGN (CAD) program to draw a CIRCUIT DIAGRAM, using computer-generated symbols and joining lines. The data of a diagram can be stored, modified, and printed and in some cases used to design a PRINTED CIRCUIT BOARD.

circuit element any one COMPONENT or unit in a circuit.

circuit junction a point in a circuit where COMPONENTs join, important in the manual or automatic layout of a practical circuit.

circuit layout the physical pattern of components on a PRINTED CIRCUIT BOARD, as distinct from a CIRCUIT DIAGRAM.

circuit magnification factor or **Q** for a REACTIVE CIRCUIT at RESONANCE, the ratio of signal voltage across a reactive component to the voltage across the whole circuit. This can be large (100 or more) for a tightly tuned circuit.

circuit switching altering the connections of a circuit through switch contacts.

circuit symbols the symbols for COMPONENTs that are used in a CIRCUIT DIAGRAM.

circular memory a memory addressed by a COUNTER that resets to zero after its maximum count, so that the memory is scanned continually, as if it were in a circular form.

circular polarization rotation of the plane of polarization (see POLARIZED, sense 1), but not the amount of polarization, for a wave. A wave approaching a receiver and rotating clockwise is taken as being left-hand circular polarized.

circulating memory see RING COUNTER.

circulator a MICROWAVE component used for separating incident and reflected signals. The circulator has three *ports* each spaced by 120°. A signal input at one port appears as an output at the next with the third port isolated from the signal. The behaviour of the ports can be changed by use of a bias magnet.

circumaural headphone or **closed headphone** a type of HEADPHONE that totally encloses the ears and seals against external sounds.

CISC see COMPLEX INSTRUCTION SET COMPUTER.

CIT see COMPUTER INTEGRATED TELEPHONY.

citizens' band (CB) a portion of the radio frequency range that is set aside for amateur users who do not hold an amateur licence. The main CB band is a part of the 28m band, though there are also UHF allocations. CB originated in the USA and became very popular with long-distance drivers in particular. A strong following in the UK was instrumental in obtaining allocation of bands, but the results were disappointing. The short range of permitted transmitters, together with the undisciplined behaviour of many users and the (later) availability of mobile phones killed off the original CB craze for all but a few genuine enthusiasts.

C-I-V-I-L mnemonic a method of remembering the effect of capacitors and inductors on PHASE, voiced as *C – I before V, V before I in I.*.

clamp, current meter a metal clamp placed over an AC power cable to measure current by using the clamp as a one-turn SECONDARY winding of what is effectively a current TRANSFORMER.

clamper or **compact disc clamper** the arm that holds a CD on to its turntable.

clamping to force a signal voltage level to a particular voltage at a selected time. Clamping is particularly important in a

VIDEO waveform, because the 30% voltage level of the video signal is the BLACK LEVEL. If this is not at the correct voltage when applied to the electron gun, correct black level will not be achieved. At the time when the signal is at black level, then, a clamp provides a low-resistance path to the correct voltage level. The clamp is then released for the remainder of the signal.

clamping diode or **clamp diode** a diode used to prevent a signal from exceeding preset voltage limits. The diode is connected between the signal and a reference voltage so that, if the signal exceeds the reference voltage, current flows through the diode and the signal voltage is *clamped*. More elaborate circuits can be devised using a BRIDGE connection of diodes with the connecting path opened by using pulses to bias the diodes.

Clapham Junction tone control a form of audio tone control that uses a large number of switch-selected FEEDBACK circuits containing capacitor and resistors in an operational amplifier circuit. The name derives from the appearance of the characteristics as a set of initially parallel lines that bend to a common convergence line. See Fig. 21.

Clapp oscillator an oscillator that uses a series resonant (see SERIES RESONANCE) tuned circuit between base (or gate) and earth, with FEEDBACK through a capacitive potential divider to the emitter (source) of a transistor operated in common collector (common DRAIN) mode. Used for its low drift CHARACTERISTICS as a stable VARIABLE-FREQUENCY OSCILLATOR.

clarity (of radio reception) freedom from unwanted INTERFERENCE or NOISE.

Clarke orbit see GEOSTATIONARY ORBIT.

class A the LINEAR operating mode of an amplifier. An amplifier is operating in class A if current flows in the amplifying device for each and any part of the input signal waveform. The amplifying device is never CUTOFF and never bottomed (see BOTTOMING). The mode is used in particular for audio voltage amplifiers, some audio output stages, and some RF amplifiers (for frequency-modulated signals).

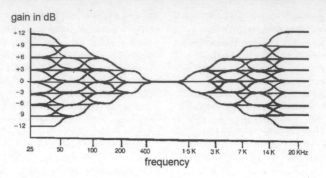

gain in dB

Fig. 21. **Clapham Junction tone control**

class AB the class of amplification in which the amplifying device can be CUTOFF or bottomed (see BOTTOMING) for a small part of the signal waveform. The mode is used for some audio output stages which use another amplifying device to deal with the remainder of the signal, and in RF amplifiers in which the tuned (tank) circuit supplies the missing part of the waveform.

class B the class of amplification in which the amplifying device passes no current for half of the signal input wave. This system can be used for audio output if a matching device is used to handle the other half of the wave. It can also be used for RF amplification with a tuned load, because the natural oscillation of the tuned circuit will provide the missing section of output signal.

class C the class of amplification in which the amplifying device is cut off for more than half of the signal waveform. The mode is used for high-efficiency RF amplifiers in transmitters, either CW or amplitude modulated. The load is always a tuned circuit whose resonance will supply the missing part of the waveform.

class D the class of amplification in which the amplifying device is based on a pulse-modulation amplification system. Pulses at high frequency have their width modulated by a low-frequency (usually audio) waveform. The pulses can be amplified with no regard to linearity,

and demodulation is achieved by any low-pass filter, even by direct coupling to a loudspeaker. The system requires good pulse handling, and early examples were not competitive with conventional analogue amplifiers.

class S a form of audio output stage in which a linear low-power stage drives a load and provides an input to a high-power FEEDBACK stage that can add current as required. See also CURRENT DUMPER ACTION.

classes, equipment the three classes of safety for electrical equipment based on potential hazards.

classes of error the three types of error that can affect a digital signal, classed as (1) detectable and correctable, (2) detectable but not correctable and (3) undetectable and so uncorrectable.

classification, frequency see FREQUENCY CLASSIFICATION.

C layer the lowest layer of the IONOSPHERE, approximately 40 to 60km above the surface of the Earth.

clean room a space in which dust has been excluded and air filtered so that materials that are susceptible to pollution can be handled. Clean rooms are used to work on SEMICONDUCTOR chips and other easily contaminated assemblies.

cleaner code an entry code for a security system intended to be used by a cleaner or other authorized personnel.

clear see RESET.

clear box testing see WHITE BOX TESTING.

clear text or **plain text** uncoded data, the original information that will be coded.

clear to send (CTS) a signal sent from a MODEM to indicate that a transmission can proceed.

click the perceived effect of a noise spike on an audio signal. See also SPARKLY.

client/server a form of NETWORK (sense 2) in which the *server* machine holds a large database and can transmit data simultaneously to several *client* computer systems.

clip-leads leads, usually to a measuring instrument, which can make contact with points in a circuit by way of clips. See also ALLIGATOR CLIP.

clip, logic see LOGIC CLIP.

clipped white/black a TV fault in which the LUMINANCE or CHROMINANCE signal can be clipped (see CLIPPING) at either PEAK, causing picture or colour distortion.

clipper or **clipping circuit** or **peak limiter** a circuit that removes part of a peak of a WAVEFORM. A peak clipper is typically a biased diode circuit that will conduct when a signal peak exceeds the bias level. This can be used for limiting the amplitude of the wave peaks. Clippers are extensively used in speech-quality radio transmitter circuits to prevent OVERMODULATION. Another application is to remove peaks caused by the effects of IMPULSE NOISE on FM or TV signals. See Fig. 22.

clipping the action of removing a portion of a PEAK of a WAVEFORM.

clipping circuit see CLIPPER.

clock a circuit that generates pulses at precisely controlled intervals. Used in connection with logic gates and counters of the SYNCHRONOUS type, and particularly in computer circuits. Clock circuits generally consist of QUARTZ CRYSTAL controlled oscillators along with pulse forming circuits.

clock back-up a battery or capacitor used to maintain power to the clock circuits of a VCR in the event of a main power failure. Battery backup offers the advantage of being able to maintain the clock for a much longer period.

clock circuit an OSCILLATOR, with CRYSTAL CONTROL, providing precisely timed CLOCK pulses.

clock cracker a test page for TELETEXT, consisting of 960 characters using the bytes 01111111 and 00000001 alternately, the most difficult pattern for maintaining clock synchronization.

clock cycle the time for one complete cycle of a CLOCK PULSE, used as the basic timing unit of a computer.

clocking the use of a CLOCK PULSE to synchronize the action of a digital device.

clock pulse a timing pulse of constant FREQUENCY and PHASE used to synchronize digital actions, particularly in a computer where several different clock pulse rates will be in use.

clock qualifier the use in a logic analyzer of a clock signal as the trigger for analysis.

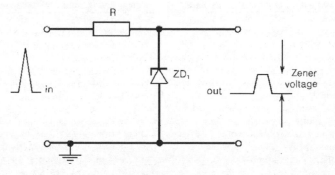

Fig. 22. **clipper**

clock rate or **clock speed** the frequency of a CLOCK PULSE generator, usually quoted in MHz or GHz.

clock run-in the two bytes of alternate 0 and 1 BITS used at the start of a TELETEXT code page.

clock skew the effect of differing path length on CLOCK signals, so that the clock pulse arrives at different parts of the circuit at slightly different times.

clock speed see CLOCK RATE.

closed box testing see BLACK BOX TESTING.

closed bus system an old system of computer ARCHITECTURE that does not allow circuit boards to be plugged into the main BUS. This greatly restricts expansion of the system.

closed caption transmission a form of TELETEXT specifically for viewers with impaired hearing.

closed circuit I. a complete electrical circuit through which current can flow when a voltage is applied. **2.** closed (non-broadcast) wire-transmitted TV and radio systems.

closed circuit television (CCTV) the direct connection of TV cameras and MONITORs to link two points without using broadcast signals.

closed headphone see CIRCUMAURAL HEADPHONE.

closed-loop control a control system that uses NEGATIVE FEEDBACK to monitor and guide the effect of the control action.

closed-loop gain the overall GAIN of a circuit to which NEGATIVE FEEDBACK has been applied. Contrast OPEN-LOOP GAIN.

clumping the uneven distribution of magnetic crystals on a tape, causing uneven response.

cluster a set of consecutive locations on a hard drive PLATTER, treated as one unit for the sake of simplified addressing (see ADDRESS).

clutter the unwanted signals in a radar system. Clutter consists of the signal echoes from such things as ocean waves, ploughed fields, buildings and other irregularities that are not radar targets. An anticlutter circuit is one that conceals such signals by making use of the fact the

signals always occur at the same times. By submitting a freshly received signal and a delayed signal to an ANTICOINCIDENCE CIRCUIT, the fixed signals of clutter can be removed, though this may also remove slowly changing signals from slow-moving targets.

CLV see CONSTANT LINEAR VELOCITY.

C-MAC see MAC.

CML (current mode logic) see EMITTER-COUPLED LOGIC.

CMOS (complementary metal oxide semiconductor) an IC structure that uses series combinations of N-channel and P-channel FIELD-EFFECT TRANSISTORS in each device. The important feature of CMOS construction is the very low power consumption, along with the ability to operate on low supply voltages. For computing purposes, the older CMOS ICs operate rather too slowly to be of use as processors, but CMOS memory with battery backup is sometimes used as a form of NON-VOLATILE memory, and modern CMOS designs are capable of higher speed operation. High-speed CMOS versions of microprocessors are available for small computers.

CMOS bilateral switch a switching IC that allows current to pass in either direction between source and DRAIN when a gate is enabled.

CMOS gate a low-power LOGIC GATE circuit formed using CMOS methods.

CMOS RAM a form of memory used in computers that is maintained by a backup battery and used to preserve essential data (such as memory size and hard drive PARAMETERS) while the computer is switched off.

CMY cyan, magenta, yellow, the three COMPLEMENTARY COLOURs that can be used to specify colour in a video image. See also RGB.

CNG see CALLING TONE.

CO see CHANGEOVER.

CO detector a SEMICONDUCTOR cell whose resistance changes in the presence of carbon monoxide.

coaxial (of conductors) having one enclosed within the other.

coaxial cable or **coax**   a type of shielded line for conducting signals. The signal conductor is stranded or single-core wire that is insulated. This insulated sleeve is surrounded by a braided wire covering, forming the outer earthed conductor of the cable. This braiding is in turn, covered by a tough outer insulator. Coaxial cable is used extensively in TV (RF and video) connections. The CHARACTERISTIC IMPEDANCE is normally around 50 to 75 ohms. By using solid inner wire, with insulating beads, the capacitance per meter and the loss per meter of the cable can be made very low. Compare TWIN CABLE.

coaxial connector   a form of connection in which there is an inner plug and socket completely surrounded by an outer shielding plug and socket, suitable for use with COAXIAL CABLE.

cobalt coating   a film of cobalt metal added to an iron-oxide tape surface to improve magnetic CHARACTERISTICS.

co-channel interference   moving lines or bars on a TV picture during times of high air pressure (increasing the propagation distance), caused by interference from distant transmitters using the same channel.

Cockcroft-Walton voltage multiplier   a circuit using a TRANSFORMER with RECTIFIER diodes and capacitor whose output is a DC voltage considerably higher than the PEAK voltage of the transformer. See also VOLTAGE MULTIPLIER. See Fig. 23 for the more common (parallel) form of this circuit.

codabar   a BAR CODE format that uses a 7-bit code including four start/stop characters.

code changing   altering the format of a digital code so as to suit the applications, see also DEMULTIPLEX; MULTIPLEX.

code converter   a device that converts one form of digital code into another.

code division multiple access (CDMA) a method of allowing several transmissions to occupy the same CHANNEL (sense 1) simultaneously, ensuring fair access to satellite frequencies with minimum interference.

code division multiplex (CDM)   a system for allowing several transmissions, particularly satellite transmissions, to use the same channel simultaneously using SPREAD SPECTRUM methods.

coded orthogonal frequency division multiplex (COFDM)   the method used in the UK for transmitting digital audio (see DIGITAL AUDIO BROADCASTING) and

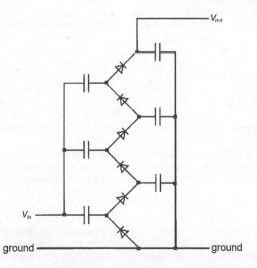

Fig. 23. **Cockroft-Walton voltage multiplier**

DIGITAL TELEVISION using existing aerials rather than cable or satellite techniques. This uses a large number (500–1000) of equally-spaced CARRIER (sense 1) frequencies, each digitally modulated with a portion of the signal, so that the transmission is effectively a parallel BUS.

code efficiency the ratio of the number of bits in the CLEAR TEXT to the number in ENCODED text (which will include REDUNDANT BITS used for error checking and correction).

code format a set of rules that unambiguously describes how a text character or digit will be represented in a digital code. Different code formats are used for different purposes.

Code-49 a form of BARCODE for extended amounts of data.

code key a set of digits that can be used to encipher and decipher plain text.

code level the number of BITS used in a code, usually 7 or 8.

code mark inversion (CMI) a TWO-LEVEL CODE in which 0 is represented by 01 and 1 is represented alternately as 00 and 11.

code rate the reduction of information due to the addition of REDUNDANT BITS, see also CODE EFFICIENCY.

code redundancy the ratio of REDUNDANT BITS to the total number of bits transmitted. This is equal to $1 - c$, where c is the CODE RATE.

coding **1.** converting an ANALOGUE quantity into a DIGITAL number. **2.** transforming a computer PROGRAM written in text into digital codes to be applied to the CPU. **3.** applying colours or symbols to a component for identification purposes.

coding, capacitor see COLOUR CODE.

coding, digital TV see DIGITAL TELEVISION.

coding, resistor see COLOUR CODE.

coding, transistor see TRANSISTOR CODING.

coefficient of coupling a number calculated from values of self- and mutual-inductance for two coils that expresses how closely two adjacent RESONANT CIRCUITS are coupled.

coercivity or **coercive force** the amount of magnetic field strength that has to be applied to a magnetized material in order

to reduce the flux density of the material to zero. Also called coercive force. When the field is removed, the magnetic material will have a remanent (see REMANENCE) flux density. See also MAGNETIC HYSTERESIS.

COFDM see CODED ORTHOGONAL FREQUENCY DIVISION MULTIPLEX.

cogging a fault of a SERVO rotor in which the ROTOR will stop in preferred positions that may not be precisely correct.

coherence remaining in phase, see COHERENT LIGHT.

coherence distance the average distance over which a pulse of light remains in PHASE, see also COHERENT LIGHT; LASER.

coherent demodulation see SYNCHRONOUS DEMODULATION.

coherent light light, as produced by a LASER, whose bursts of waves are all in phase, unlike light from other sources.

coherent oscillator an oscillator whose bursts of waves are all in PHASE, such as light and microwave oscillators of the LASER and MASER type respectively.

coherer an obsolete form of radio wave DEMODULATOR that made use of iron filings in a glass tube which stuck (cohered) together when a radio signal passed through them.

coil see INDUCTOR.

coincidence circuit a circuit that delivers an output when two inputs coincide. A pulse coincidence circuit will deliver an output pulse when two input pulses (to separate terminals) arrive at the same time. A voltage coincidence circuit (or VOLTAGE COMPARATOR) provides an output when the voltage levels at the two inputs are identical, or within a preset range of each other.

coincidence detector or **coincidence demodulator** see XNOR GATE.

coincident pair microphone a STEREO sound RECORDING method using two CARDIOID microphones set at 90° to each other, each at 45° to the audio signal path.

coincidental half-current switching a method, now obsolete, of using MAGNETIC CORES (sense 2) as computer memory elements. The magnetic characteristic graph shapes of the cores are approximately rectangular, and the magnetic state can be reversed by applying a known current. If each signal through one of a number of wires laced through the core consists of a current of about half the critical level, then one single signal cannot change the core magnetism. The magnetism will be changed only if two wires carry current signals in the same direction, hence the term 'coincidental half-current switching'.

cold cathode emitter an electron EMITTER (sense 2), operating in a vacuum, that requires no artificial heating. The emission of electrons is achieved by using a high value of electric field near the cathode. See also FIELD EMISSION.

cold-cathode fluorescent tube see COLD-CATHODE LAMP.

cold-cathode lamp or **cold-cathode fluorescent tube** a form of GAS DISCHARGE TUBE with a high light output and long life, used as a BACKLIGHT for an LCD display and also as the light source in a SCANNER (sense 2).

cold emission the emission of electrons from a surface that is not artificially heated. See also FIELD EMISSION.

cold-junction compensation a method of correcting the temperature readings from a THERMOCOUPLE to allow for the cold junction being at AMBIENT TEMPERATURE rather than 0°C.

cold pin the pin on a signal connector used for the return lead. See also HOT PIN.

cold-soldered joint a SOLDER joint that has been made using a soldering iron at too low a temperature, leading to an unreliable contact that sometimes is a RECTIFYING CONTACT.

collector the CARRIER (sense 2) collecting electrode of a transistor. Carriers that flow from the EMITTER (sense 1) through the BASE region end up in the collector region. The total rate of flow of charge into this region constitutes the collector current.

collector-base leakage noise a form of noise generated by a BIPOLAR JUNCTION TRANSISTOR and affected by operating temperature and DC supply voltage.

collector characteristic curve the graph of COLLECTOR current plotted against

collector voltage for constant BASE bias, for a BIPOLAR JUNCTION TRANSISTOR.

collet-fitting a method of fitting a knob to a potentiometer shaft using a split *collet*, without the use of a grub-screw.

collimator a lens, either optical or electron-beam, used to provide a parallel beam by placing the source at its focal point.

collinear array a set of DIPOLES arranged to be in PHASE and in line to produce an increase in gain (compared to a single dipole) equal to the number of dipoles.

collision or **data collision** the result of two transmitters of data on a network sending data at the same time, making it impossible for a receiver to separate the two.

collision window the time in a NETWORK (sense 2) between the start of a transmission and the signal reaching the other nodes of the network. This is the time in which a COLLISION can occur.

colophony see ROSIN.

Colossus the first programmable computer designed by Alan Turing and Tommy Flowers in 1943 for code-breaking at BLETCHLEY PARK.

colour the effect on the eye of the different frequencies of light.

colour balancing the adjustment of amplitude of colour signals in a television system so as to produce the best colour rendering of a scene.

colour-bar generator an instrument that generates COLOUR TELEVISION signals, used for testing and aligning an analogue colour TV receiver.

colour burst or **burst** the 10 cycles of SINE WAVE that are used to synchronize the colour oscillator in a TV receiver. These cycles of sine wave are at the colour SUBCARRIER frequency, and are placed in the BACK-PORCH of the line sync signal.

colour clock a form of colour description diagram for TV chrominance signals showing the amplitude and phase for any colour. See Fig. 24.

colour code the internationally standardized code that is used for marking resistors and, to a lesser extent, capacitor values. For details of the code, see the Appendix.

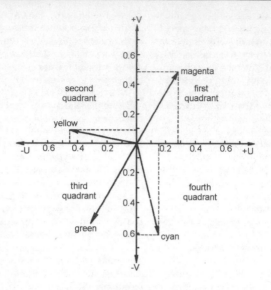

Fig. 24. **colour clock**

colour coding or **colour depth**   the number of colours that can be used for one screen PIXEL, often expressed as a number of bits per pixel. 4-bit colour is equivalent to $2^4 =$ 16 colours and 30-bit colour is equivalent to 2^{30} about 1,000,000,000 colours.

colour coding, wiring   a CODING (sense 3) of wiring, particularly of mains cables to indicate the functions such as live (brown), neutral (blue) and earth (striped green/yellow).

colour corrector   a circuit within a VIDEO editing device that converts a COMPOSITE SIGNAL to RGB format to make editing easier.

colour crosstalk   a colour patterning effect caused by unintentional mixing of the U AND V SIGNALS, often due to a fault in the DELAY LINE of a PAL receiver.

colour CRT   a CATHODE-RAY TUBE that can display a range of colours. The most familiar type uses a set of three colour-emitting PHOSPHORS that are laid down as fine vertical stripes on the face of the tube. Three separate electron guns are arranged in line, and a metal grille, the APERTURE GRILLE, is placed close to the screen. The effect of the apertures in the grille, one

aperture for each group of three colour phosphor stripes, is to shield each phosphor stripe from the electron beams of two of the electron guns. In this way, the beam from one gun can reach only the green phosphor, the beam from the second gun can reach only the red phosphor, and the beam from the third gun can reach only the blue phosphor. By controlling the relative beam currents of the three guns, any colour and any brightness that the system is capable of can be obtained. At the time of writing, colour CRTs are being replaced by digital flat-screen devices such as the LCD and the PLASMA SCREEN display.

colour decoder   the circuits within a colour television receiver that demodulate the colour subcarrier signals and combine the outputs (see PAL MATRIX) so as to produce three separate colour signals (see RGB).

colour depth   see COLOUR CODING.

colour diagonal patterning   a set of diagonal blue/yellow or green/magenta lines appearing in a replayed VCR picture, often due to interference from a nearby medium wave transmitter.

colour difference signals analogue colour TV signals obtained by a subtraction process, so that the result is a signal that is more suitable to modulate (see MODULATION) on to a CARRIER (sense 1). The standard PAL system uses the U and V colour difference signals in which U is derived from B – Y and V is derived from R – Y, where Y = amplitude of monochrome signal, B = amplitude of blue signal and R = amplitude of red signal. The amplitude of all three R, G, and B signals can be obtained from the U, V and Y signals.

colour flicker a flicker at 25 Hz of colour in a replayed VCR picture, a CHROMINANCE SIGNAL processing fault.

colour fringe a surrounding of unwanted colour at the edge of an image. This can be caused by MOIRÉ PATTERN effects (often called *strobing*) when a striped image is being viewed. It can also be caused by poor CONVERGENCE of electron guns, by undesired magnetization of tube electrodes, and other forms of faults. It is particularly undesirable around monochrome images on COLOUR TELEVISION tubes.

colour graduated filter a light filter, part clear and part tinted to emphasize a portion of a scene.

colour killer a SWITCHING CIRCUIT within a COLOUR TELEVISION receiver. The colour killer switches off the colour demodulator circuits when no colour burst is being received. This avoids the possibility of random noise signals being interpreted as colour signals and causing COLOUR FRINGES on monochrome images.

colour LCD a form of LCD that will show a coloured image, using TRANSMISSIVE, REFLECTIVE or TRANSFLECTIVE methods.

colour, LED the light wavelength that can be obtained by using a particular material as an LED. The most common colours are red and green, and these can be added to obtain yellow.

colour matrix a mixing circuit whose inputs are the COLOUR DIFFERENCE SIGNALS and LUMINANCE signal, with outputs of separate R, G and B signals.

colour misregistration colour blending in a replayed VCR picture, often caused by incorrect back tension of the tape.

colour modulation the amplitude modulation of a SUBCARRIER with the two COLOUR DIFFERENCE SIGNALS in the PAL colour TV system.

colour palette a range of possible colours for a display screen, not all of which may be immediately available.

colour peak sensitivity the wavelength of light for which a PHOTOCELL is most sensitive.

colour saturation a measurement of intensity of colour. A saturated colour primary would be 100% red, green or blue. Mixing white (itself a mixture of red, green and blue) with a saturated colour produces an unsaturated colour. For example, a 50% saturated blue would consist of 50% blue and 50% white light.

colour separation overlay see CHROMA KEYING.

colour signal a portion of a composite video signal (see COMPOSITE SIGNAL) that specifies the amplitude of one particular colour at a point.

colour signals, monitor the RGB or COMPOSITE signals fed to a monitor.

colour sub-carrier the carrier, 4.43361875 MHz in the UK PAL system, that is modulated in QUADRATURE with the COLOUR DIFFERENCE SIGNALS and in turn modulated on to the main UHF carrier.

colour sync interval see BACK PORCH.

colour television the production of coloured images on a TV screen. The older analogue COLOUR TV SYSTEM was designed to be compatible, i.e. capable of providing acceptable pictures on a monochrome receiver. This is done by adding the colour signals to the normal monochrome signal. The signals from the camera are processed into a LUMINANCE signal, the normal monochrome signal, and two COLOUR DIFFERENCE SIGNALS. These are (in the UK system), the R–Y and B–Y signals. In this nomenclature, Y means the luminance signal, and the negative sign implies inversion. These colour difference signals are modulated onto a subcarrier that in turn is modulated onto the main vision signal. At the receiver, the colour TV circuits will separate out the subcarrier signals, and generate a local subcarrier

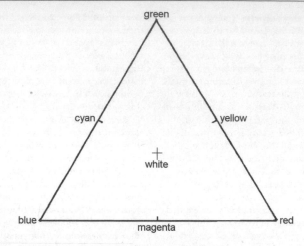

Fig. 25. **colour triangle**

from an oscillator that is synchronized to the COLOUR BURST in the BACK PORCH of the line sync pulse. By using two synchronous demodulators (see SYNCHRONOUS DEMODULATION), the colour difference signals are demodulated, and are then mixed with the luminance signal to provide three separate colour signals, red, green and blue. These are then used to operate the three electron beams of the colour TV tube. See also DIGITAL TELEVISION.

colour television system the method that is used to carry the COLOUR DIFFERENCE SIGNALS to an analogue COLOUR TV receiver. The main analogue systems are NTSC (US), PAL (most of Europe) and SECAM (France and Russia). The differences between the systems hinge on the methods of modulation of the subcarrier, and the way in which phase shift errors can be avoided. See also DIGITAL TELEVISION.

colour temperature a specification of light spectrum in terms of the temperature of a theoretical BLACK BODY that would produce an identical colour spectrum.

colour triangle a method of illustrating the relationship between SATURATED primary colours, COMPLEMENTARY COLOURS and LUMINANCE. See Fig. 25.

colour under frequency a VIDEO CASSETTE RECORDER system that converts the

CHROMINANCE SIGNAL to a comparatively low frequency of around 625 kHz for adding to the LUMINANCE signal.

Colpitts oscillator an oscillator circuit whose distinguishing feature is a POTENTIAL DIVIDER that uses capacitors. Contrast HARTLEY OSCILLATOR. See Fig. 26.

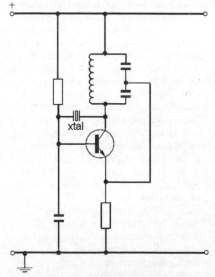

xtal

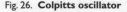

Fig. 26. **Colpitts oscillator**

column and row numbers the form of ADDRESS numbering used for DYNAMIC RAM to ensure rapid addressing along with REFRESH (sense 1) actions.

column loudspeaker or **line source** a set of loudspeaker units set in a vertical column in a slim enclosure.

comb filter a FILTER whose characteristic consists of a set of evenly spaced sharp peaks, like the teeth of a comb. See Fig. 27.

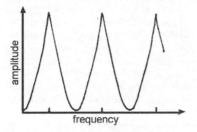

Fig. 27. **comb filter**

combi drive a combined CD DRIVE used in a computer to save space and cost. A typical combi drive will read or write a CD and will also play a DVD, requiring more than one laser source because of the differing requirements of these actions. Combi drives are gradually being phased out in favour of DVD RECORDER drives.

combination microphone a microphone designed to combine the CHARACTERISTICS of a PRESSURE OPERATED MICROPHONE and a VELOCITY OPERATED MICROPHONE to produce a CARDIOID pattern.

combination of capacitors see CAPACITORS, PARALLEL; CAPACITORS, SERIES.

combinational circuit a LOGIC CIRCUIT in which the combination of several inputs determines the output. Contrast SEQUENTIAL CIRCUIT.

combinational logic the action of GATE CIRCUITS which can have several simultaneous inputs whose values determine the output. Usually, one combination of inputs will yield a unique output, hence the name.

combiner a form of filter that allows two or more transmitters (or two or more receivers) to be coupled simultaneously to one AERIAL without mutual interference.

Comité Européen de Normalisation-Comité Européen de Normalisation Electrotechniques (CEN-CENELEC) European standards setting bodies.

Commission Electrotechnique Internationale (CEI) see IEC.

common-anode indicator an LED display in which the ANODES of each diode have been connected to one common positive point, and each display unit is controlled by the voltage applied to its CATHODE (sense 2). See also COMMON-CATHODE INDICATOR.

common-base connection or **grounded-base circuit** a form of transistor connection in which the BASE is maintained at signal earth. The signal input is to the emitter and the output is taken from the collector. The common-base connection offers unity current gain, moderate voltage gain, and good high-frequency CHARACTERISTICS. It is used mainly for impedance transformation (low input, high output impedances) and for radio frequency amplifier stages.

common-base stage an amplifier using a BIPOLAR JUNCTION TRANSISTOR (BJT) with the BASE held at signal earth, and input to the EMITTER (sense 1) terminal. The output is taken from the COLLECTOR and the circuit is best suited to moderate gain amounts for high-frequency signals.

common cathode amplifier a THERMIONIC VALVE circuit in which the input signal is taken to the CONTROL GRID and the output is taken from the ANODE.

common-cathode indicator or **common cathode display** an LED display in which the CATHODES of each diode have been connected to one common negative point, and each display unit is controlled by the voltage applied to its ANODE. See also COMMON-ANODE INDICATOR.

common-collector connection see EMITTER FOLLOWER.

common control block a non-rectangular symbol in the BSI set of symbols for logic devices that indicates an input that is combined with several other inputs.

common control switching a DIGITAL telephone exchange technique in which the dialled number is held in memory until the optimum route has been found.

common drain amplifier a MOSFET type of amplifier circuit, corresponding to the BJT COMMON-COLLECTOR AMPLIFIER, in which the signal input is to the GATE (sense 1) and the output is from the SOURCE.

common-emitter connection or **grounded-emitter circuit** a form of BIPOLAR JUNCTION TRANSISTOR connection in which the EMITTER (sense 1) is maintained at signal earth. This connection features very large current and voltage gain figures, with medium impedance input and output. It is the most common type of junction transistor circuit connection, and the corresponding common-source circuit is the most common connection for field-effect transistors. See Fig. 28.

common gate amplifier a MOSFET type of amplifier circuit, corresponding to the BJT COMMON BASE AMPLIFIER, in which the signal input is to the SOURCE and the output is from the DRAIN.

common image format (CIF) a video format of 288 lines, NON-INTERLACED, and 30 frames per second, used for transmitting video signals over telephone lines. The format allows relatively easy conversion to or from NTSC or PAL signals.

common-mode the application of identical signals (in the same phase) to both inputs of a DIFFERENTIAL AMPLIFIER, resulting ideally in zero signal output.

common-mode rejection ratio (CMRR) a measure of the usefulness of a DIFFERENTIAL AMPLIFIER circuit. The common-mode rejection ratio is the ratio, expressed in decibels, of the wanted balanced signal to the unwanted unbalanced signal when both are applied at equal amplitude. The rejection ratio can be very large, of the order of 100 dB, for some ICs.

common return the use of a single EARTH point in a circuit to avoid the effect of an EARTH LOOP.

common source amplifier a MOSFET type of amplifier circuit, corresponding to the BJT COMMON EMITTER AMPLIFIER, in which the signal input is to the GATE (sense 1) and the output is from the DRAIN.

communal aerial television or **community antenna television (CATV)** the use of a single aerial, or aerial array, and distribution

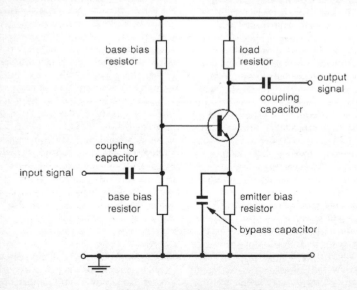

Fig. 28. **common-emitter connection**

amplifiers to serve a large number of users by way of a wired network.

communications   the transmission of data over distances using radio or cable links.

communications channel or **communications link**   a way of communicating electronics signals such as a radio band, a copper cable or a FIBRE OPTICS link.

communications port   a connection, usually the SERIAL PORT, used for communications.

communications satellite   a SATELLITE designed to act as a RELAY TRANSMITTER, accepting transmissions from one or more Earth stations and sending out signals to be received at other places.

communicator   see SPEECH DIALLER.

commutating auto-zero amplifier   see CHOPPER STABILIZED AMPLIFIER.

commutative law   the law of algebraic arrangement, expressed as A + B equals B + A and AB = BA. See also ASSOCIATIVE LAW; DISTRIBUTIVE LAW.

commutator   a form of POLARITY (sense 4) reversing switch, usually the mechanical rotary switch connected to coils in the ARMATURE of a motor.

compact disc   a method of sound or video RECORDING that uses a plastic disc and a laser. The signals are converted into DIGITAL form, and used to switch a laser beam on and off while the beam is being guided over the surface of a spinning metal disc. This produces a pattern of pitting on the surface that carries the information of the signals and this *master disc* can be used to print copies. These copies are compact discs, and their signals can be played back with a system that uses a low-power laser. Single copies can also be made with simple equipment (CD rewriter) using the laser beam to alter the colour of a dye on a plastic disc. See also DVD; SOUND REPRODUCTION.

compact disc clamper   see CLAMPER.

compact disc decoder   the circuitry in a COMPACT DISC player that receives the pulses from the photodiode stage and applies the decoding and error detection/correction actions followed by a DIGITAL TO ANALOGUE CONVERTER stage to obtain an audio signal.

compact disc traverse   see TRAVERSE SYSTEM.

compact disc video   see VIDEO COMPACT DISC.

compaction   see BIT REDUCTION.

compander   a combination of COMPRESSOR and EXPANDER circuits. Many audio systems, notably RECORDING systems, cannot cope with a large amplitude range, the DYNAMIC range of the signal. This can be remedied by using a NON-LINEAR AMPLIFIER to compress the volume range before recording or transmitting. The volume range is then restored later by another non-linear amplifier that expands the range again. The system is useful only if the compression and expansion can be very closely matched, and the systems developed by Dolby have dominated the market. The principle is slowly falling into disuse for domestic use because of the almost universal adoption of COMPACT DISC recording and other digital methods.

comparator or **comparator amplifier**   see DIFFERENTIAL AMPLIFIER.

comparator, logic   see LOGIC COMPARATOR.

comparator, phase   see PHASE COMPARATOR.

compatible colour TV   any COLOUR TELEVISION system whose signals will produce an acceptable monochrome image on a monochrome receiver. This requirement, once important, is now obsolescent with the advent of DIGITAL TELEVISION.

compatibility   the ability of a system to connect to, and operate with, others. The ability of software to run in a variety of different computer systems (*platforms*).

compensated attenuator   an ATTENUATOR that is designed to operate over a large frequency range. A resistive attenuator does not provide the correct ATTENUATION ratios for high-frequency signals. This is because of the STRAY CAPACITANCE across the resistors. By using low value resistors, and by wiring capacitors in parallel with the resistors (which also provide the correct division ratio), the attenuator can be compensated for strays, and so operate over a wide bandwidth.

compensating filter   a LIGHT FILTER used in front of a TV camera lens to make corrections for light colour or colour bias in RECORDING media.

compensating leads or **dummy leads**   a set of leads used as balancing RESISTORS, usually in a BRIDGE circuit. In measurements of small resistor values, or which involve small changes in resistance values, the behaviour of connecting leads may interfere with the measurement. The leads may, for example, interfere because their resistance changes with temperature. By using another pair of leads physically close, but electrically connected to the other part of the bridge, these changes can be compensated for.

complement   see NOT.

complementary circuit   a circuit that makes use of both PNP and NPN BIPOLAR JUNCTION TRANSISTORS or FIELD-EFFECT TRANSISTORS using oppositely doped channels, usually in a series circuit such as the LIN CIRCUIT.

complementary colour   the results of subtracting a primary colour from white light. The complementary colours are CYAN equal to white minus red (blue plus green), YELLOW equal to white minus blue (green plus red), and MAGENTA equal to white minus green (red plus blue).

complementary error function (erfc)   a number defined as 1–erf, see ERROR FUNCTION.

complementary noise reduction   any form of NOISE REDUCTION CIRCUITRY that requires signal filtering both on RECORDING (or transmission) and replay (or reception).

complementary push-pull or **totem-pole circuit**   see LIN CIRCUIT.

complementary stage   an AMPLIFIER stage that uses COMPLEMENTARY TRANSISTORS.

complementary symmetry   the use of matching COMPLEMENTARY TRANSISTORS in a circuit of the PUSH-PULL type.

complementary transistors   transistors of opposite (bipolar) type, one a PNP TRANSISTOR, the other an NPN TRANSISTOR, or opposite CHANNEL (sense 2) MOS types. The two are often used in series circuits, and require to be closely matched in their CHARACTERISTICS. The complementary bipolar pair is often used as an audio CLASS B output stage, and the MOS equivalent is the basis of CMOS ICs. See also LIN CIRCUIT.

complementer   see INVERTER (sense 1).

complex circuit   a circuit that contains a variety of resistive, capacitive and inductive components.

complex filter   a FILTER consisting of several sections with the aim of increasing the ATTENUATION of the STOP-BAND and steepen the ROLL-OFF.

complex instruction set computer (CISC)   a computer based on a MICROPROCESSOR that has a large and comprehensive set of instructions in code. The use of CISC can make software simpler and shorter, but at the expense of longer processing times for each instruction. Contrast REDUCED INSTRUCTION SET COMPUTER (RISC).

complex number   a number that consists of a real part and an imaginary part, in general of the form a + jb, where a and b are real numbers and $j = \sqrt{-1}$, an *imaginary number*. Mathematicians use i rather than j, but j is preferred in electronics use. Complex numbers are used in AC circuit theory to describe the magnitude and phase of voltage or current in an ARGAND DIAGRAM, showing the resistive component of a circuit as a real number around the component that is 90° out of phase as an imaginary number. The magnitude and phase of voltage or current can then be found from the a + jb form, since magnitude = $\sqrt{a^2 + b^2}$ and phase is arctan (b/a). See Fig. 29.

complex programmable logic device (CPLD)   a smaller-scale and less elaborate form of FIELD PROGRAMMABLE LOGIC ARRAY.

complex waveform   any waveform other than a SINE WAVE.

compliance   the inverse of stiffness, ability to bend, measured in μm/mN.

component   a term for any separately packaged unit of a CIRCUIT with its own connecting leads. See ACTIVE COMPONENT; PASSIVE COMPONENT.

component coding   see COLOUR CODE.

component density   the number of electronics components per unit area of a PRINTED CIRCUIT BOARD. High component densities require fan cooling to be used to

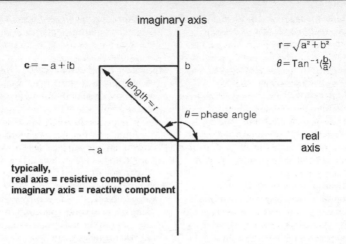

Fig. 29. **complex number**

keep the operating temperature low, and can make maintenance and repair difficult.

component jacks miniature connectors for components that are wired into a BREADBOARD.

component layout diagram see LAYOUT DIAGRAM.

component tolerance code the colour band or spot used to indicate TOLERANCE by COLOUR CODE.

component video a video signal set that uses the LUMINANCE signal and both COLOUR DIFFERENCE SIGNALS. See also COMPOSITE SIGNAL, RGB.

components any parts that can be connected together to make a working unit.

COM port any RS-232 SERIAL PORT in a small computer.

composite conductor a multiwire conductor, using different metals. One common type is a copper-steel composite that is used for suspended lines. The steel contributes little to the conductivity of the line, but most of its strength.

composite signal or **composite colour signal** or **composite video signal** an analogue VIDEO signal that contains all the necessary components for a COLOUR TELEVISON DISPLAY. A video signal from a camera very often consists only of the video portion from each colour pickup tube. The LUMINANCE signal has to be formed, and the COLOUR DIFFERENCE SIGNALS modulated on to the colour SUBCARRIER. The SYNCHRONIZING PULSES are then added, along with the COLOUR BURST to give the complete composite signal ready to be modulated on to the video CARRIER (sense 1).

compositing forming a VIDEO image from two sources, often using KEYING (sense 1).

composition resistor see CARBON RESISTOR.

compound semiconductor a semiconductor formed from compounds such as Gallium Arsenide rather than from elements such as Silicon.

compound transistor see DARLINGTON PAIR.

compressed (of DIGITAL DATA) reduced to a minimum by either LOSSY COMPRESSION or NON-LOSSY COMPRESSION so that it can be stored in minimum space and transmitted over a relatively narrow bandwidth.

compressed audio the compression of digital audio signals, using LOSSY methods and BIT REDUCTION, so that some eleven hours of music can be recorded on a single CD. See also MP3.

compressed serial data interface (CSDI) a SERIAL cable system for transmitting DIGITAL VIDEO signals at a high speed.

compressed video data consisting of
DIGITAL VIDEO signals that have been
subjected to compression, usually LOSSY
COMPRESSION, so that the bandwidth
needed to transmit them is reduced, and
they can be stored on a hard drive and
used for broadcast TV. See also MPEG.

compression see BIT REDUCTION.

compression, digital camera the BIT
REDUCTION in DIGITAL DATA carried out on
signals from a digital camera to allow the
signals to be stored on a memory or an
OPTICAL DISC.

compression on capture the process of
compressing (see BIT REDUCTION) signals
from a video camera or an ANALOGUE TO
DIGITAL CONVERTER as they are received;
this requires very fast processing,
normally using hardware methods.

compression ratio the ratio of the
amount of data in a non-compressed
DIGITAL VIDEO signal to the amount in
a compressed (see COMPRESSED VIDEO)
version. High compression ratios are
usually associated with poor quality,
but modern systems, notably MPEG, can
produce acceptable results with high
compression ratios.

compression, time the use of a high
reading rate for stored DIGITAL samples
so as to produce bursts of data, allowing
for actions to be carried out (such as
switching recording heads) in the
intervals between bursts.

compression trimmer a form of VARIABLE
CAPACITOR whose value is altered by
altering the pressure on a set of small
parallel plates; used for making small
changes (trimming) to a capacitance
value, particularly for TRACKING (sense 2)
in a SUPERHETERODYNE RECEIVER.

compressor an analogue circuit that
reduces the dynamic range of a signal.
The action is achieved by a nonlinear
stage whose gain reduces as the signal
amplitude increases. See also COMPANDER.

computational butterfly a diagram,
named because of its shape, showing
how a FAST FOURIER TRANSFORM can be
carried out with the minimum of signal
processing.

computer any device that operates on
data in accordance with a preset program
of instructions. See ANALOGUE COMPUTER;
DIGITAL COMPUTER.

computer aided design (CAD) the use
of a computer program that produces
precise technical drawings or diagrams
to scale, with lists of parts and quantities
calculated. The drawings can make use
of components that have previously been
drawn. Each drawing can be seen on the
SCREEN, and can be printed. These actions
are particularly useful for CIRCUIT DIAGRAMS.

computer-aided editing editing sound or
video signals in digital form by transferring
them to a hard drive and using computer
software to alter and re-record them.
See also NON-LINEAR EDITING.

computer-aided engineering (CAE)
the use of a program that is intended to
analyze a design (manual or computer-
generated) and simulate its action. This
is particularly useful for analyzing the
action of complex ANALOGUE circuits,
particularly where precise mathematical
methods are not available.

computer aided manufacturing (CAM)
the automation of manufacturing so that
a disk file of instructions can be used to
control automated production machines.

computer analysis, filter producing
graphs of the action of a FILTER circuit by
way of a computer program that has been
supplied with the details of the type of
filter circuit and the values of components.

computer diagnostic equipment
circuitry that can be connected to a faulty
device to provide diagnosis, aided by
computer control.

**computer integrated manufacturing
(CIM)** the use of a computer system for
all the actions of design, manufacturing,
and testing.

computer integrated telephony (CIT)
the use of computers to control ISDN
telephony, making the older type of
telephone system obsolete.

computer keyboard debouncing a
software system that debounces (see
DEBOUNCING CIRCUIT) the keys of a
computer keyboard by sampling the

state of a key over a small interval
following a delay in which the bouncing
action will have ceased.

computer monitor   see MONITOR.

computer system   a basic set of
COMPUTER, MONITOR and KEYBOARD along
with PERIPHERALS such as a MOUSE, MODEM,
SCANNER (sense 2), PRINTER, etc.

Computer Users Tape Standard   see
KANSAS CITY MODULATION.

computer user tape interface (CUTS)
see KANSAS CITY MODULATION.

computer vision   the use of a computer
to capture and process images, and to
recognise features. An example is the
recognition of the fingerprint, facial features
or eye iris pattern of an approved user.

concave screen   the curved reflective
screen often used for a FRONT-PROJECTION
TV display.

concealment, error   the use of an estimated
value in a digital stream to replace an
incorrect value. Compare CORRECTION, ERROR.

concentrator or **statistical multiplexer**
a system of dividing a data channel into
several streams, using as many time slots
as the data requires, on the basis that not
all need to transmit at the same time.

concurrency   (of a computer system) able to
deal with several operations simultaneously
rather than one following the other.

condensation damage   creasing of a VIDEO
CASSETTE RECORDER tape due to attempts to
use it while there is condensed water on
the tape DRUM (sense 1). Most VCRs are
designed so as not to operate while such
condensation is present.

condenser microphone   an old name for
CAPACITOR MICROPHONE.

conditional access (CA)   a system for
encrypted TV transmission (see SCRAMBLER)
that will block reception until a SMART CARD
has been inserted, read and decoded.

conditionally stable   (of an amplifier or
servo FEEDBACK circuit) being capable of
oscillating only under certain conditions.
This means that the circuit will not break
into oscillation unless some condition is
violated. A common condition is that the
load of an amplifier shall be resistive or
inductive, never capacitive. An amplifier

that can be used with any load without
any trace of oscillation is said to be
unconditionally stable.

conditions for oscillation   the requirement
of amplifier GAIN and the PHASE of
FEEDBACK that are required to make an
amplifier stage oscillate.

conductance   the inverse of RESISTANCE.
The unit of conductance is the SIEMENS
(inverse ohm) and the symbol is G.

conduction   the transmission of energy by
particle movement. Electrical conduction
in most metals is the result of free-electron
movement, but positive holes are present
in significant numbers in some metals and
are sometimes the main current carriers.
Conduction in gases and in liquids is by
movement of IONS. In liquids (mostly
water solutions), the ions are surrounded
by water molecules and are slow-moving.
In gases, the ions can be rapidly accelerated
so as to move fast enough to ionize any
molecules that they strike, causing total
IONIZATION. See also BREAKDOWN.

conduction angle   the fraction of a wave
cycle during which a device (usually
a transmitting THERMIONIC VALVE or
transistor operating in CLASS C) conducts.
One cycle is taken as an angle of 360°,
and the fraction of the cycle for which
the valve of transistor conducts is
multiplied by 360 to obtain the conduction
angle.

conduction angle control   a method
of using a THYRISTOR to regulate an
ALTERNATING CURRENT supply. In this
system, the point in the cycle at which
the thyristor fires can be controlled, and
the thyristor is switched off by the zero-
voltage part of each cycle. For a half-wave
of AC, then, the thyristor can be on for a
maximum of 180°, and a minimum of
zero. Full cycle control can be obtained
using more than one thyristor, or by the
use of a TRIAC. See also BURST CONTROL.

conduction band   the range of energy
levels for ELECTRONS in an ATOM that are
free to move so as to cause conduction.

conduction, electric   the action of
movement of charged particles, often
electrons, that results in an electric current.

conduction electrons the ELECTRONS in a solid that are free to move within the material, so providing CONDUCTIVITY.

conductive packing plastic plastic material that has a small degree of conductivity to prevent charge accumulating, used for packing MOS semiconductors

conductive plastic potentiometer a form of POTENTIOMETER (sense 1) that uses a conductive plastic for its TRACK.

conductivity the inverse of RESISTIVITY. Symbol: κ; unit: siemens per metre. The conductivity of a material measures the ease with which electric current will pass through the material.

conductor a material with good CONDUCTIVITY such as a metal or semiconductor that has a large density of free CARRIERS (sense 2).

cone the part of a loudspeaker that vibrates to produce sound waves. The cone is normally conical in shape, and is made of stiff material. Materials such as stiff paper, plastics, metal and composites have been used at various times, but stiffened paper remains the most widespread material. The cone is attached to the VOICE COIL and this in turn is held by the SPIDER in the gap of the magnet.

cone breakup a loudspeaker problem in which high frequency signals at the centre of the cone cause a standing wave over the cone surface, so that some parts of the cone can be moving in ANTIPHASE. See also TWEETER.

cone drive unit the unit, usually based on the MOVING-COIL PRINCIPLE, that is the TRANSDUCER for electrical signals to mechanical vibration for a LOUDSPEAKER.

confetti unwanted colour streaks on a COLOUR TELEVISION receiver during a monochrome transmission, caused by a fault in the COLOUR KILLER at the receiver.

configurations, transistor the three ways in which a transistor may be connected, classed according to which electrode is at signal earth. See COMMON-BASE; COMMON-COLLECTOR; COMMON-DRAIN; COMMON EMITTER; COMMON-GATE; COMMON-SOURCE.

conformal aerial (or antenna) or suppressed aerial (or antenna) an adaptation of a PLANAR ARRAY type of aerial in which the planar element is not flat but is part of the metal body of a vehicle.

conformity assessment an inspection of equipment made to assess the use of a CE MARK.

conjugate (of impedance values) for which the resistance portions are equal, and the reactive components are equal and opposite (one inductive, the other capacitive).

connecting up the wiring together of parts of a complete system to make the whole usable.

connector a plug or socket used to terminate a cable.

connector, keyboard the plug and socket, formerly a form of miniature DIN but more recently a USB connector, used to connect a keyboard to a computer.

connector, printer the 36-pin connector (see CENTRONICS CONNECTOR) used to connect a printer to a computer, now being replaced by a USB connection.

connectors, CD-ROM drive the power, data and audio cable connectors used to connect a CD DRIVE into a computer.

connector shell the outer casing for a CONNECTOR that protects the pins and often is used also to anchor the cable.

connectors, power connectors, many of which must be able to deal with large amounts of current (more than 50A) used to convey power to a computer MOTHERBOARD or to other units such as DRIVES.

connectors, USB the standardized form of four-pin connectors, with a square type used at the master or computer end of the cable, and a flat type used at the slave or peripheral end.

consistent failure a recurring problem that indicates a design fault rather than a random effect.

Constantan™ an alloy of nickel and copper used in manufacture of resistors that gets its name from having an almost constant resistance value as temperature changes. In other words, the TEMPERATURE COEFFICIENT of resistivity is unusually low. Since the resistivity value is fairly high for a metal alloy, fairly large value wire-wound resistors can be made of Constantan without the need to use very long lengths or impracticably small diameters of wire. Used also in conjunction with pure copper in THERMOCOUPLES.

constant angular velocity   rotation at a steady speed in terms of the amount of angle covered per second. For example, the old-style vinyl disk gramophone records revolved with a constant angular velocity equivalent to $33^{1}/_{3}$ revolutions per minute. Contrast CONSTANT LINEAR VELOCITY.

constant-current charging   a requirement for recharging NICAD CELLS which must not be used with the constant voltage type of charger intended for lead-acid cells.

constant-current circuit   a unit whose output is a constant stable current, usually obtained using an operational amplifier circuit. See also HOWLAND CIRCUIT.

constant-current source   a source of signal current or DC that remains constant despite fluctuations of load. The requirement of a constant current source is a high output impedance, so that the

current is determined by the source impedance rather than by the load impedance.

constant directivity horn   a design of loudspeaker intended for PUBLIC ADDRESS which has almost constant COVERAGE ANGLE at all frequencies.

constant failure rate   the low and steady failure rate for manufactured devices, forming the flat middle portion of a BATH TUB DIAGRAM.

constant k filter   a common form of filter in which the series and shunt impedances, Z_1 and Z_2 respectively are related by the equation $Z_1Z_2=R_0^2$. The value of R_0 is a constant resistance (k) that is independent of frequency and known as the *design impedance* of the filter. See Fig. 30. See also CHARACTERISTIC IMPEDANCE; M-DERIVED FILTER.

constant linear velocity or **constant-velocity scanning**   rotation of the type used for audio CD and CD-ROM, in which the disk spins faster when the inner part of the track is being read. The speed of the track past the reading beam is constant. Contrast CONSTANT ANGULAR VELOCITY.

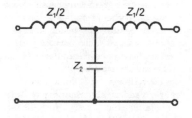

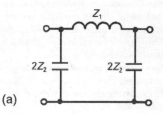

(a)

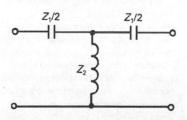

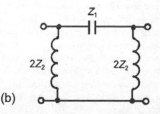

(b)

Fig. 30. **constant k filter**

constant luminance the effect of deriving the LUMINANCE signal in an analogue TV receiver from the gamma-corrected (see GAMMA CORRECTION) R, G and B signals, resulting in loss of resolution because of the limited bandwidths of the colour signals.

constant-velocity scanning see CONSTANT LINEAR VELOCITY.

constant-voltage source a very low impedance source that can maintain a constant voltage across a varying load.

constellation analyzer an instrument that can distinguish the differing causes of BIT ERRORS in MULTIPHASE MODULATION systems such as QAM.

constricted double heterojunction laser see CHANNELLED SUBSTRATE LASER.

constructive interference addition of two waves that are in PHASE, so that the AMPLITUDE of the sum is greater than the amplitude of either component. Contrast DESTRUCTIVE INTERFERENCE.

consumer electronics standard the IEC60065:1998 which sets the test standards for the CE MARK system.

consumer semiconductor types the semiconductor types used in domestic radio, TV, video, computing and other 'domestic' electronics products, as distinct from semiconductors for industrial or military applications which are more closely specified.

contact a point or area where two materials touch. When the materials are both conductors, current can be made to flow across the contact. Unless the conductors are joined by high pressure, welding or soldering, the resistance at this point, the CONTACT RESISTANCE, may be high. See also CONTACT POTENTIAL.

contact bounce the mechanical effect due to the elasticity of switch CONTACTs, leading to closing contacts bouncing open again before closing finally.

contact bounce suppression any system, such as the use of a diode or an R-C circuit connected across CONTACTs to prevent the multiple pulse effects of CONTACT BOUNCE.

contact breaker an electro-mechanical protective device for circuits. The action of the contact breaker is to interrupt a supply when a fault condition, usually excessive current flow, arises. Once the contact breaker has operated, it will have to be reset by hand to allow resumption of supply. See also OVERCURRENT TRIP.

contact configuration, relay the arrangement of the contacts of an unenergized relay, classed as NO (normally open), NC (normally closed) or CO (changeover).

contact noise, tape a form of noise in MAGNETIC TAPE replay machines caused by fluctuations in the tape thickness.

contactor a form of RELAY for switching large currents, often also at high voltage levels. A contactor is designed with a larger mechanical movement than a relay, and with a parallel movement of contacts rather than the normal hinged-arm movement of a relay.

contact potential or **contact voltage** a potential difference of a few tenths of a volt DC that is present when two different metals are in contact. This contact potential is temperature variable, so the contact can be used as a THERMOCOUPLE.

contact resistance the resistance between conducting materials that are in contact with each other.

contacts, printhead the set of contacts that link the (detachable) printhead of a computer printer to the electronic control systems of the printer.

contact voltage see CONTACT POTENTIAL.

content addressable memory (CAM) a data search system in which the search WORD is stored and compared with the contents of a set of memory locations. When a match is found, the memory ADDRESS is loaded into a REGISTER (the *snapshot register*).

contention sharing of a NETWORK (sense 2) so that each TERMINAL (sense 2) can have exclusive use of the network, but only if no other terminal is using the network.

contiguous literally touching, applied to units of MEMORY or of PIXELS in a character.

continuous interference interference from a steady source, as distinct from TRANSIENT interference, such as from a SWITCH-MODE POWER SUPPLY.

continuous phase modulation (CPM) a
form of FREQUENCY SHIFT KEYING or PHASE
SHIFT KEYING in which a single oscillator is
used so that the change from one phase
or frequency to the other is less sharp.

continuous tone coded squelch system
or **sub-audible tones** a selective calling
system for mobile radios in which an
inaudible tone is transmitted in addition
to voice signals. A receiver will start its
SQUELCH action only if the correct tone is
received.

continuous wave (CW) a radio wave of
constant frequency and amplitude, not
carrying information. See also CARRIER
(sense 1).

continuous wave laser a laser, usually of
the semiconductor HETEROJUNCTION type,
in which laser light is maintained for as
long as the current exceeds some
threshold amount.

continuous wave radar a form of RADAR
used for speed determination rather than
range, with a continuous rather than a
pulsed beam.

contoured beam aerial an AERIAL or
aerial array designed to deliver the
optimum signal power to a specific area.

contouring an image process that
produces the effect of a relief map,
typically by discarding the lowest order
bits in pixel information.

contrast the ratio of intensities of lit and
unlit parts of a picture. The contrast of a
TV signal is determined, within limits,
by the amplitude of the video signal.
The contrast control of a TV receiver or
monitor is the video GAIN control.

contrast ratio the ratio of the brightest
TV screen area to the darkest that can be
discerned. The value of contrast ratio for
an average picture depends on room
illumination, but is often taken to be
about 50:1.

control bus a bus set of lines in a
computer or other digital system that
carries control signals as distinct from
DATA or ADDRESS signals.

control chip or **syscon** see SYSTEM CONTROL.

control electrode the electrode that
controls current flow between other

electrodes of an active device. The control
electrode of a BIPOLAR JUNCTION TRANSISTOR
is the BASE, which controls current flow
between emitter and collector. The
controlling PARAMETER in this example is
base current. For a MOSFET, the controlling
electrode is the GATE (sense 1), and its
voltage controls the current between
SOURCE and DRAIN. For a transmitting
THERMIONIC VALVE, the controlling
electrode is the GRID, the voltage of which
controls current between CATHODE (sense 1)
and ANODE. The grid voltage can be positive
or negative with respect to the cathode
voltage, and when the grid voltage is
positive, current (*grid current*) will flow
between the grid and the cathode will flow.

control gear electrical or electronic circuit
for controlling a GAS DISCHARGE TUBE so as
to allow for a high starting voltage, a
reduced running voltage, and current
control to avoid excessive current due
to the NEGATIVE RESISTANCE characteristic.

control grid the electrode next to the
CATHODE (sense 1) of a THERMIONIC VALVE
that regulates the flow of electrons to the
ANODE.

control grid, crt the electrode, basically
a cup with a small aperture surrounding
the cathode, used to control the electron
beam current in a CATHODE-RAY TUBE.

control head the TAPEHEAD on a VCR that
reads the timing pulses from the CONTROL
TRACK.

control key one of three keys used to
encrypt satellite broadcasts using the MAC
system. For unrestricted broadcasts the
control key is fixed and the receiver can
descramble such programmes. For
controlled access, the control key is
encrypted by two other keys, the
authorization key and the *distribution key*.

controlled carrier modulation or
floating carrier modulation or **Hapug**
a complex AMPLITUDE MODULATION system
in which a CARRIER (sense 1) is modulated
by a signal, and this modulated carrier is
further modulated by a wave that is the
(short-term) average of the signal. The
result is a modulated wave with almost
constant DEPTH OF MODULATION.

controller or **controller device** the control type of device used in the IEEE-488 BUS design, see also TALKER; LISTENER.

control panel a flat panel that contains a set of related controls and readouts for a system or sub-system.

control section, microprocessor the portion of a MICROPROCESSOR that deals with timing and synchronization.

control system an assembly of components designed to control a process.

control track a set of timing pulses recorded along one edge of a VIDEO CASSETTE RECORDER tape and used for synchronization.

control word the 8-bit word added to a CD to provide disc identification.

convection transfer of HEAT energy by a gas or liquid, making use of the principle that a hot gas or liquid will be less dense and will rise above a cooler layer.

conventional current flow the conventional flow of current from positive to negative, established before it was known that the more usual flow is of electrons in the opposite direction. See ELECTRON; ION; HOLE.

conventional definition television (CDTV) the ANALOGUE television system using the 4:3 ASPECT RATIO picture as provided in the UK by analogue transmitters using the PAL system.

conventions, circuit diagram the agreed principles for circuit drawing, for example that lines shown crossing do not indicate a join.

convergence the meeting of the three electron beams of a COLOUR TELEVISION tube. The three beams should converge and cross over at the APERTURE GRILLE.

conversion analogue/digital see ANALOGUE TO DIGITAL CONVERTER.

conversion digital/analogue see DIGITAL TO ANALOGUE CONVERTER.

conversion efficiency the percentage of energy output/energy input for any energy converting device.

conversion efficiency, microphone the figure of output voltage for a standardized input sound pressure.

conversion gain ratio a figure of merit for a FREQUENCY CHANGER, equal to the ratio of output power at the changed frequency to input power at the original frequency. The figure is usually expressed in decibels.

conversion loss for a MIXER stage, the ratio of the output IF signal level to the CARRIER (sense 1) input signal level, usually expressed in dB.

converter any device that converts electrical energy from one form to another. A power INVERTER (sense 2) changes DC into AC. The circuit that changes from AC to DC is normally known as a POWER PACK. The term can also denote a *frequency converter*. This is a circuit that beats signals together to form a new signal frequency, see also BEAT NOTE MIXER. An *impedance converter* allows signal impedance to be better matched to load impedance. See also TRANSDUCER.

convolution the digital equivalent of filtering (see FILTER), a weighted averaging process used to smooth out pulse signals.

convolutional coding or **Viterbi coding** a system used on SATELLITE digital transmissions that uses 100% redundancy to achieve almost perfect ERROR CORRECTION.

convolutional interleaving rearrangement of the positions of DATA PACKETs so that a fault (such as a scratch on a COMPACT DISC track or a burst of interference on a radio frequency) will not affect packets of data that are placed together after having their positions restored (being *deinterleaved*).

convolution code or **recurrent code** or **Hargelbarger code** a coding system that uses CONVOLUTION techniques to deal with BURST ERRORS in a digital signal.

cook-book a set of diagrams for circuits of reliable character, intended for a constructor.

cooling the dissipation of heat energy. For solid materials such as TRANSISTORS, cooling relies firstly on conduction to transfer heat energy from the semiconductor to external materials such as cooling fins or metal blocks. The fins then convect heat (with a small amount of radiation), and blocks can be water-cooled. Cooling for transmitting THERMIONIC VALVES can be by radiation or convection. Radiation-cooled valves use a glass envelope, and the heat of the ANODE is allowed to radiate away. Larger valves use metal envelopes that can be water cooled, steam cooled, or forced-air cooled. ICs and transistors use metal cooling fins, but more recently vapour cooling systems (*heat-pipes*) with cooling radiators have been developed for microprocessors.

coplanar transistor   a form of TRANSISTOR construction in which the electrodes are all on the surface of the SEMICONDUCTOR.

coplanar waveguide   a form of WAVEGUIDE formed as a set of three metal strips on a flat insulating SUBSTRATE. The inner strip is the signal strip and the outer strips are earthed.

co-polar signal   a signal at a POLARIZED (sense 1) aerial that is polarized in the correct direction for optimum reception.

copper   a metal element universally used for low-resistance connections. Copper is used for wire, cable, and printed-circuit tracks.

copper-clad material   blank PCB board with its copper coating.

copper data distributed interface   a data cable intended for high-speed transmission, using copper cable rather than FIBRE OPTIC CABLE.

copper loss   see resistive loss, transformer.

copper-oxide rectifier   a type of RECTIFIER, now obsolete, that used copper/copper-oxide JUNCTIONS. Formerly used in low-voltage supplies (particularly chargers for secondary cells) until replaced by silicon. Copper-oxide rectifiers have a low forward voltage drop, and were until recently still used as ANALOGUE METER-movement protection devices.

copper tail   the final wire link of a CABLE TV system into a house.

copying losses   the degradation of quality when an ANALOGUE video signal is copied from one VIDEO CASSETTE RECORDER to another. Copying a DIGITAL VIDEO signal is usually free from such degradation unless the signal has been decoded and then re-encoded in a LOSSY way.

cordless audio   a radio or infra-red link used for distributing audio signals within

a home without the need for cables. The radio links use the 863–864 MHz band.

cordless telephone   a telephone system in which a BASE UNIT is connected to the fixed line (or long-range radio link) and handsets are linked to the base unit, using 1800 to 1900 MHz digital transmitters and receivers.

core   the magnetic mass around which TRANSFORMERS and other INDUCTORS are wound.

core loss   the loss of energy from an INDUCTOR or TRANSFORMER caused by the CORE. The two main factors that cause loss are EDDY CURRENTS and MAGNETIC HYSTERESIS. Eddy currents are caused by induction of voltages across parts of the core, and can be minimized by shaping the core, particularly with air gaps. Hysteresis loss is caused when the magnetism of the core is changed, and can be minimized only by careful choice of material and operating conditions.

core, magnetic   see MAGNETIC CORE.

core memory   see CORE STORE.

core saturation   see MAGNETIC SATURATION.

core store   an obsolete form of computer MEMORY system that used magnetic cores. Each core, about 2mm diameter, was threaded by wires that magnetized the core in one direction or the other. The two directions of magnetization correspond to logic states 0 and 1. See also COINCIDENTAL HALF-CURRENT SWITCHING.

core supply   see CORE VOLTAGE.

core-type transformer   a TRANSFORMER that is wound on to a core so that the core is surrounded by the winding. The alternative is the *shell-type transformer* in which the magnetic material surrounds the windings.

core voltage or **core supply**   the operating voltage for a CPU, nowadays of the order of 1.6V or less.

corner frequency   a frequency, usually the HALF-POWER POINT frequency, found by making straight line approximations to the RESPONSE CURVE and taking the intersection of lines as indicating the 3dB points.

corona or **corona discharge**   an electric discharge through ionized air (see

IONIZATION), used to charge or discharge materials, particularly in ELECTROSTATIC COPIER and in LASER PRINTER technology.

correction, error the use of any method of re-establishing a faulty digit in a data stream, such as by re-transmission or the use of PARITY checks. See also CONCEALMENT, ERROR.

correlation the degree of similarity between signals that are not identical.

correlation decoding or **maximum likelihood** or **minimum distance** an error-reducing method of checking each received signal word against the known CODE-SET to find the most likely code word.

correlation detection a system of using a digital CODE KEY to separate out a wanted digital signal in a CODE DIVISION MULTIPLE ACCESS SYSTEM.

correlation detector part of the CHROMINANCE SIGNAL circuits of a VIDEO-8 recorder which detects large changes in hue and cuts the chrominance DELAY LINE out when such changes occur.

correlation of noise sources the increase in correlation between noise signals when two signals have been passed through the same circuits.

correlator a circuit with which a WAVEFORM can be detected amid surrounding noise because of the predictable periodic nature of the waveform.

corridor a shape of VOLUMETRIC DETECTION coverage for a security system that has a narrow width but considerable length, as much as 40 metres.

corruption distortion, particularly of DIGITAL DATA, that destroys the meaning of data or makes it unavailable.

co-siting using the same sites for transmitters for BBC, ITV, Channel 4 and Five transmissions.

cosmic noise the noise frequencies that have their origin outside the solar system, in outer space.

Costas loop a SPREAD SPECTRUM method for DEMODULATION using a PHASE-LOCKED LOOP and three multipliers.

coulomb the unit of electric charge. Symbol: C. The coulomb is defined as that charge which, when displaced one metre

from an equal charge in a vacuum, repels it with a force of 8.9874×10^9 newtons. The unit itself is much too large for practical use, and the submultiples microcoulomb (10^{-6}C), nanocoulomb (10^{-9}C) and picocoulomb (10^{-12}C) are more often found.

Coulomb, Charles Augustin de (1736–1806) French physicist who investigated the properties of electric CHARGE.

Coulomb's law the law relating the force between two charges at a given separation in a vacuum. For charges Q_1 and Q_2 at a separation of d metres, the force **F** is given by:

$$\mathbf{F} = \frac{Q_1 Q_2}{4\pi\varepsilon_0 d^2}$$

newtons, where ε_0 is the permittivity of free space.

countdown see DOWNWARD COUNT.

count input a pulse or set of pulses used as the input to operate a COUNTER circuit.

count rate the rate of arrival of pulses, in terms of pulses per second. See COUNTER.

counter any circuit that gives an output that is the total of the number of pulses that have been applied to the input. A digital counter may indicate the count on a digital display, an analogue counter may present it as a meter reading. Many counters display the COUNT RATE, that is the number of pulses per second. Counters are used as frequency meters, and also to count the conduction pulses for detectors of radioactivity such as the GEIGER-MÜLLER TUBE.

counter, asynchronous see ASYNCHRONOUS COUNTER.

countermeasure any electronic method of combating enemy RADAR or communications. Also used of methods for counteracting JAMMING.

counterpoise or **earth mat** a set of radial wires close to the earth but insulated from earth, substituting for a good earth connection for transmissions at the lower frequencies (below 30 MHz).

counter, synchronous see SYNCHRONOUS COUNTER.

counting A/D converter or **voltage to time A/D converter** a relatively slow form of

ANALOGUE TO DIGITAL CONVERTER that counts the number of CLOCK pulses required into an INTEGRATOR to provide a voltage level equal to the applied (signal) level. Used mainly in DIGITAL VOLTMETERS.

coupled tuned circuits tuned circuits placed so close that they have appreciable mutual inductance, so that signals will be passed from one to the other. See also COEFFICIENT OF COUPLING.

coupler/multiplexer or **T-coupler** a device that will split optical signals using optical fibres connected to waveguides formed in a glass block.

coupling the passing of a signal from one stage of a system to another. *Direct coupling* implies that the signal and its DC level are passed. *AC coupling* means that the DC is blocked, and only the alternating part of the signal is passed. A *tuned coupling* (see TUNED TRANSFORMER) is used to pass one particular frequency or band of frequencies; the opposite is *broadband, wideband* or APERIODIC COUPLING. See also CRITICAL COUPLING; STAGE COUPLING.

coupling bits three extra BITS inserted between 14-bit SYMBOLS in a COMPACT DISC RECORDING so as to ensure that there is not a run of identical digits because one symbol starts with the same bit as has ended the previous symbol. These coupling bits are inserted under computer control and are discarded in the playing process.

coupling coefficient a measure of the effectiveness of coupling of a TUNED TRANSFORMER. The coefficient is defined as the ratio of coupling impedance to the geometrical average of impedances on each side of the coupling. The quantity is measured rather than calculated in most cases.

coupling loop a small inductor that is used to pick up a sample of a signal.

coupling, stage see STAGE COUPLING.

covalent bond a form of chemical bond, weaker than the electrostatic bond, created by electron sharing and common in the materials we class as organic (mainly carbon compounds).

coverage angle the angle over which the sound from a loudspeaker is at significantly the same volume as along the axis of the loudspeaker.

CPI see CHARACTERS PER INCH.

CPLD see COMPLEX PROGRAMMABLE LOGIC DEVICE.

CPM see CONTINUOUS PHASE MODULATION.

CPS see CYCLES PER SECOND.

CPU see CENTRAL PROCESSING UNIT.

C-R (or **CR** or **R-C** or **RC) network** a combination in a NETWORK (sense 1) of capacitors and resistors, forming a FILTER or used for INTEGRATION or DIFFERENTIATION.

cradle a holder with connections for a handheld computer (personal digital assistant or PDA), allowing information to be exchanged with a desktop or laptop computer.

cradle, cartridge a receptacle for the PRINTHEAD and ink cartridge of a computer printer, containing the connectors for the printhead.

CRC see CYCLIC REDUNDANCY CHECK.

CRCC see CYCLIC REDUNDANCY CHECK CODE.

creep zone the lowest part of a room space that might not be covered by a security PASSIVE INFRA-RED device.

crest factor for NOISE or other intermittent pulses, the ratio of PEAK AMPLITUDE to RMS amplitude, usually 5:1 or more.

crimping the fastening of a wire to a connecting point by compression, often more reliable than SOLDERING.

crispening the addition of a differentiated (see DIFFERENTIATING CIRCUIT) portion of signal to the edge of an analogue VIDEO signal to improve sharpness at boundaries, particularly useful to improve the appearance of a replayed VIDEO CASSETTE RECORDER tape.

critical angle the angle, measured to a radius from the Earth, of incidence of a wave that will no longer be reflected back to Earth but will escape into space.

critical coupling the amount of coupling that provides maximum transfer of signal between two tuned circuits. As the coupling between two tuned circuits is increased, the graph of amplitude plotted against frequency for the output rises in a steep peak at the RESONANT FREQUENCY. This PEAK is at its maximum at the point of critical coupling. See also OVERCOUPLING; UNDERCOUPLING. See Fig. 31.

critical damping a measure of circuit loading that is just sufficient to prevent OSCILLATION in a RESONANT CIRCUIT. If a resonant circuit is loaded by a resistor in parallel or in series, the resistor will dissipate energy and discourage oscillation. The effectiveness of this resistor can be seen if the circuit is briefly pulsed and the output viewed on an oscilloscope screen. If the damping is low, the circuit will oscillate freely, or *ring*. As the damping is increased (lower value of parallel resistance or higher value of series resistance), the oscillations die away more quickly. Eventually, the shape of the output is of the form of an exponential decrease, with no oscillation. This is the point of *critical damping*.

critical frequency the frequency of wave for which the CRITICAL ANGLE becomes zero, so that no waves, of that frequency or above that frequency, can be reflected back.

CRO see CATHODE-RAY OSCILLOSCOPE.

cross colour false colours in an ANALOGUE COLOUR TELEVISION display due to LUMINANCE signals reaching the CHROMINANCE SIGNAL channels. See also CROSS LUMINANCE.

cross correlation function a mathematical function that indicates the degree of similarity between two signals.

cross-coupling an undesired coupling between circuits, usually inductive circuits. Cross-coupling can be reduced by shielding and good earthing. See also EARTH LOOP.

crossed-field tube see CARCINOTRON.

cross interleave Reed-Solomon code an error detection and correction system for DIGITAL systems used for COMPACT DISC recording and replay. This form of code is particularly suited to LONG-BURST ERRORS, and can cope with errors of up to 4000 bits, corresponding to a fault 2.5 mm long on a CD track.

cross luminance fine pattern effects in a displayed analogue COLOUR TV picture caused by CHROMINANCE signals reaching the LUMINANCE amplifier.

cross-modulation or **intermodulation** the unwanted modulation of one frequency by another. The effect occurs mainly in audio circuits and in wideband circuits in which a range of signal frequencies will be present. In audio circuits, cross-modulation causes noticeable distortion when the signal contains both a BASS note and a treble note. Nonlinearity in an amplifier stage causes the bass note to modulate the treble note, so that the sound from the loudspeaker gives the effect of a treble note whose loudness is rising and falling at the rate of the bass frequency.

crossover distortion the result of a bias problem in a CLASS A-B power output stage that leaves low-amplitude input signals completely or partially cut off.

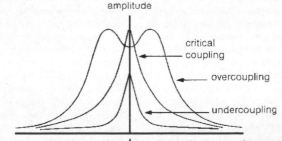

Fig. 31. **critical coupling**

crossover frequency   a value of frequency that represents the transition between the PASSBAND and the STOPBAND of a FILTER, usually taken as the 3dB level.

crossover network or **crossover**   a network used in loudspeaker systems. It is very difficult to design a magnetic type of loudspeaker that will cover the whole audio frequency range satisfactorily. Because of this, high-quality loudspeaker systems contain a unit, the WOOFER, that is designed to give optimum reproduction of the lower notes, and another unit or units (TWEETER) that works best at high frequencies. The output from the amplifier then has to be divided so that the lower notes are fed to the woofer, not to the tweeter, and the higher notes are fed to the tweeter and not to the woofer. The filter network that carries out this action is called the *crossover network*. At its simplest (which regrettably, it often is) it consists of a capacitor and a large-value iron-cored inductor. See also BIAMPING.

cross polar signal   a signal at a POLARIZED AERIAL that is in the wrong polarization (90° to the aerial polarization). Contrast CO-POLAR SIGNAL.

crosstalk   interference between communications so that each channel receives some signal from the other. This can be due to unwanted coupling between telephone lines, between nearby amplifier circuits, or between different CARRIER (sense 1) frequencies. Crosstalk between different radio channels is often due to nonlinearity in some stage. This can occur when one transmitter is very close and is overloading the first stage of a receiver. The amount of crosstalk is usually specified in decibels.

crowbar circuit   see CROWBAR PRINCIPLE.

crowbar principle or **crowbar circuit**   the use of a device such as a THYRISTOR to short a power supply when an overload occurs in order to trigger a fuse or other shutdown system. The importance of a crowbar device is that it can act much faster than any fuse or contact-breaker.

crowbar thyristor   a THYRISTOR used in a crowbar circuit, see CROWBAR PRINCIPLE.

CRT   see CATHODE-RAY TUBE.

cryogenic   (of a device) operated at a very low temperature, near 0°K, such as a JOSEPHSON JUNCTION.

crystal   a solid material in which the units, usually ions (see IONIZATION), are arranged in a precise geometrical pattern to create rigidity and hardness, the ability to be cleaned easily along certain preferred directions (see ANISOTROPIC) leading a perfectly plane surface and, in many cases useful electrical properties. QUARTZ CRYSTALS are used in OSCILLATORS, crystals of silicon for the manufacture of TRANSISTORS and INTEGRATED CIRCUITS, and crystals of materials such as BARIUM TITANATE in transducers.

crystal control   the use of a vibrating QUARTZ CRYSTAL to control the frequency of a sine wave OSCILLATOR. The crystal acts as a form of RESONANT CIRCUIT with an exceptionally high Q-FACTOR (30000 or more). This stabilizes the frequency of the oscillator, and can also be used to produce a very pure sine wave, free from HARMONICS. For highest stability, the crystal must be cut in a certain way, and contained in a thermostatically-controlled enclosure, the CRYSTAL OVEN.

crystal counter   a device for detecting IONIZING RADIATION. Several types of crystalline substances are affected when they are struck by radioactive particles. Some crystals emit a flash of light for each particle, and this light can be detected by a photocell, giving an electrical pulse. Another method is to separate an electron from a hole in a semiconducting crystal, that will make the material momentarily conductive. In either case, the resulting electrical pulse can be amplified and applied to a counter.

crystal cut   the directions of cutting a QUARTZ CRYSTAL, defined by their relationship to the X and Y axes of the crystal. These cuts are designated by letters X, Y, AT, BT, CT, DT or FT.

crystal equivalent circuit   a representation of the action of a QUARTZ CRYSTAL in terms of L, C and R values, usually with impractical values of these quantities.

crystal filter a form of filter that uses a QUARTZ CRYSTAL in place of a tuned circuit. This allows a very narrow band of frequencies to be accepted or rejected.

crystal microphone a form of microphone, seldom used now, that employs a PIEZOELECTRIC CRYSTAL. The sound waves vibrate the crystal, either directly or by way of a DIAPHRAGM, causing a voltage waveform to be generated between conducting electrodes on the surface.

crystal oscillator an oscillator circuit that uses a quartz or other CRYSTAL as its frequency determining component.

crystal oven a small temperature controlled container for a CRYSTAL OSCILLATOR that assists frequency stability by maintaining the crystal at a constant temperature.

crystal, quartz see QUARTZ CRYSTAL.

crystal receiver or **crystal set** a primitive form of radio receiver using a RESONANT CIRCUIT with a CAT'S WHISKER and CRYSTAL for detection, with no form of amplification.

crystal set see CRYSTAL RECEIVER.

CSDI see COMPRESSED SERIAL DATA INTERFACE.

CSMA see CARRIER SENSE MULTIPLE ACCESS.

CTC see CARBON TETRACHLORIDE.

CTCSS see CONTINUOUS TONE CODED SQUELCH SYSTEM.

CTL head see CONTROL HEAD.

CTS see CLEAR TO SEND.

Curie point the temperature above which a magnetized material will lose all retained magnetism.

current the rate of flow of electric CHARGE. Symbol: I. Current is usually measured in AMPERES (amps) and submultiple units such as milliamperes (milliamps, 10^{-3}A) and microamperes (microamps, 10^{-6}A). The ampere is equivalent to the rate of flow of one coulomb per second.

current adding converter a form of DIGITAL TO ANALOGUE CONVERTER working with currents that are added, as distinct to the PLASSCHE CONVERTER.

current addition integrator a DIGITAL TO ANALOGUE CONVERTER system in which a current is generated for each digit, and the currents are summed to provide a current analogue signal.

current amplifier an amplifier whose output signal current is much greater than its input signal current. If the voltage signal levels are unchanged, or if there is also voltage gain, the current amplifier acts also as a POWER AMPLIFIER (sense 1).

current checker see CURRENT TRACER.

current conveyor a form of voltage or current-controlled amplifier with a frequency-dependent negative resistance characteristic, used in voltage-controlled oscillator, filter, differentiator and integrator applications.

current density 1. the amount of current flow per unit area of cross section of a conductor. 2. a measure of radiated energy, such as a radio beam.

current-derived feedback see CURRENT FEEDBACK.

current differencing amplifier (CDA) or **Norton amplifier** an amplifier device with very high input resistance whose output depends on the difference between two current inputs.

current divider see CURRENT DIVIDER CONVERTER.

current divider converter a circuit using parallel resistors in which current is divided between the resistors, usually fabricated as an INTEGRATED CIRCUIT and used in the Plassche DIGITAL TO ANALOGUE CONVERTER.

current dumper action the use of a POWER TRANSISTOR to pass a large current under the control of a transistor that passes a very small current.

current dumping circuit see CURRENT DUMPER ACTION.

current feedback or **current-derived feedback** the FEEDBACK of a signal whose amplitude is proportional to the current output.

current gain the ratio of output current to input current for an amplifying device.

current law see KIRCHOFF'S LAW.

current limiter any device that will not permit the current in a circuit to exceed some fixed value. A resistor forms a simple form of current limiter, but the term is usually reserved for a circuit that is part of a constant voltage power supply. The function of the circuit is to limit the current to a safe level in the event of the load becoming a short circuit.

current-limiting resistor a resistor placed in a circuit for the purpose of preventing excessive current flowing.

current loop a standard system for serial data devices, using standardized current levels of 20 mA or 60 mA, with zero current signifying logic 0.

current map a circuit diagram with 'normal' current values marked to serve as a servicing guide.

current mirror or **current reflector** an IC circuit, much used in OPERATIONAL AMPLIFIER designs, with a very low INPUT IMPEDANCE and very high output impedance, in which the output current is almost exactly equal to the input current.

current mode logic (CML) see EMITTER-COUPLED LOGIC.

current nulling a form of current measuring system for a PRINTED CIRCUIT BOARD in which the voltage drop between probes is used to generate an equal and opposite current that is then measured.

current probe a form of oscilloscope probe that detects current flow, particularly useful for servicing a SWITCH MODE POWER SUPPLY (SMPS).

current reflector see CURRENT MIRROR.

current regulation an electronic system of controlling current, particularly for charging NiCd cells.

current shunt resistor a resistor used to extend the current range of an analogue MULTIMETER.

current sinking the (load) action of taking current from a source, contrast CURRENT SOURCING.

current source a circuit that provides a steady and precise value of current.

current sourcing the action of passing current to a load, contrast CURRENT SINKING.

current surge a pulse of current that can be destructive to a semiconductor. A short-term current surge will not

necessarily blow a FUSE, so that fast-acting surge detectors are required to protect circuits. See also VOLTAGE SURGE.

current switching the action of switching a current from one circuit path to another.

current-time characteristics graphs that define how quickly a FUSE will blow.

current tracer or **current checker** a handheld device with two pin contacts that can be used to indicate the direction and approximate amplitude of current along a PRINTED CIRCUIT BOARD track.

current transformer or **instrument transformer** a step-up TRANSFORMER whose low-impedance primary winding is connected in series with an AC supply line. The secondary voltage of the transformer is then proportional to the primary current. This secondary voltage can be rectified and used to drive a meter that is scaled in terms of primary current. A development of the idea uses a clamp as the primary winding. When the clamp is placed over an insulated cable, the meter reading shows the current passing. This is one of the few methods of measuring current without breaking the circuit.

current unit see AMPERE.

current/voltage graph a plot of current flowing against applied voltage that will reveal whether a substance is OHMIC or NON-OHMIC.

curtain a shape of VOLUMETRIC DETECTION coverage for a security system that has a vertical pattern running parallel with the area to be protected.

curvature deviation from a straight line graph that indicates NONLINEARITY.

curve-matched thermistor a thermistor which is guaranteed to have a temperature-resistance characteristic that is precisely maintained in manufacture, so that any two thermistors will match each other.

curve tracer an instrument that will plot the CHARACTERISTIC of a TRANSISTOR, particularly useful for selecting matching characteristics.

cut and splice editing the form of editing used for ANALOGUE audio tapes in which an undesired section is cut out and the ends of the cut tape rejoined by splicing.

Cutler feed a form of WAVEGUIDE feed to a microwave DISH in which the waveguide is split and turned to face the reflector.

cutoff the BIAS point at which current just ceases in control devices such as a CATHODE-RAY TUBE, TRANSISTORS and THERMIONIC VALVES. The cutoff voltage of a CRT is the (negative) value of voltage between grid and cathode that will *just* cause the electron beam to disappear.

cutoff frequency 1. a value of signal frequency at which the gain of an amplifying device is noticeably reduced, conventionally by –3dB. 2. a frequency at the edge of a filter PASS BAND at which the ATTENUATION noticeably increases, usually taken as the point where the signal is attenuated by –3dB. 3. the frequency beyond which the gain of a transistor rapidly drops because of its construction. Once again, the –3dB point is usually selected.

cutoff region the region of operation of an ACTIVE COMPONENT in which no current flows.

cutoff voltage the voltage that is applied as BIAS in order to achieve CUTOFF of current.

cutout an automatic overload switch that will open under excess current or dissipation conditions. The cutout may reset automatically after a time delay, or have to be reset manually. TV receivers often contain thermal cutouts that have to be reset by resoldering two spring-loaded contacts. See also CONTACT BREAKER.

cutter or **disc cutter** a device used in the preparation of a master RECORDING on vinyl disc. The sound signals from the master tape are applied to an electromagnetic cutter head that carries a stylus. The vibrations of the stylus cut a groove of modulated width in the material of the master disc. This disc is then used to prepare a number of moulds, and these are in turn used in stamping vinyl copies, the old-style audio records. The process is now obsolescent, having been superseded by COMPACT DISC recording.

CVBS signal colour, video, blanking and syncs: the video COMPOSITE SIGNAL that is modulated on to a CARRIER (sense 1) to form the transmitted analogue colour broadcast.

CW see CONTINUOUS WAVE.

CW laser a LASER that emits light continuously rather than in pulses.

CW RADAR see CONTINUOUS WAVE RADAR.

cyan a COMPLEMENTARY COLOUR, equivalent to white minus red (or blue plus green).

cycle a complete alternation of voltage or current. Typically, this may start at zero, rise to a positive maximum, reverse, pass through zero and fall to a negative minimum followed by a return to zero again. A complete cycle is often represented by 360° or 2π radians.

cycles per second (CPS) the measure of FREQUENCY, now named HERTZ.

cyclic code code units that are related so that any code shifted round one place will result in another valid code (such as 1011, 0111, 1110, 1101). Using such codes makes it easier to detect and correct BURST ERRORS.

cyclic redundancy check an elaborate method of checking and correcting errors based on CYCLIC CODES, and incorporated into many digital devices, such as the CD.

cylindrical lens a glass lens with one flat surface and the other cylindrical, used with a LASER to increase the effective power output.

cylindrical winding or **solenoidal winding** a coil wound on a cylindrical former. The coil can be single-layer or multilayer, and if the length is much greater than the diameter it is fairly easy to calculate the SELF-INDUCTANCE value if no magnetic core is used. NOMOGRAMS are available for finding the number of turns of wire of a given diameter to achieve a target inductance value. Such wound inductors are now rarely used in electronic circuits.

cymo-motive force the product of electric field strength of a wave and distance (in a specified direction) from a transmitter.

D/A   see DIGITAL TO ANALOGUE CONVERTER.

DA   see DEMAND ASSIGNMENT.

DAB   see DIGITAL AUDIO BROADCASTING.

DABS   direct addressed beacon system: see ADDRESS SELECTED SYSTEM (ADSEL).

DAC   see DIGITAL TO ANALOGUE CONVERTER.

daisychain   to connect (digital) devices so that a pulse will affect the first device in a series string that is enabled (see ENABLING), and that device in turn will affect the next in line. An example is leading-zero suppression in a digital display. The zero-suppression pair of connections in each display unit are daisychained. When a number is displayed, a zero in the first display (the most-significant digit) will be suppressed, and a pulse will be sent to the next display. This process will continue until a display is reached which is not displaying a zero. The daisychain ends there, and no other zeros will be suppressed.

DAM   see DYNAMIC AMPLITUDE MODULATION.

DAM CD   a CD containing *digital automatic music*, meaning some tracks of MP3 coded sound along with others of conventionally recorded CD sound.

damped   (of a resonant circuit) being prevented from OSCILLATION. A resonant circuit is damped by a load of any type, such as a PARALLEL (sense 1) resistor. A completely undamped resonant circuit (which never exists in practice) would oscillate indefinitely after any stimulus. In practice, quartz crystals with no external damping can execute several thousand oscillations after being pulsed. Increased damping (a smaller value of parallel resistor) causes the amplitude of oscillations to decrease. At critical damping, a pulse input produces a single cycle of output with no subsequent oscillation. Damping can also be applied to mechanical oscillations, either mechanically, using dashpots and oil,

or electromagnetically. See also CRITICAL DAMPING; OVERDAMPED; UNDERDAMPED.

damp-heat change   the percentage change in value of a COMPONENT when subjected to a standardized test of high temperature and high humidity.

damping   reduction of OSCILLATION by dissipation of power, such as the action of a shock-absorber in a mechanical springing system, or the use of a resistor connected across a tuned circuit.

damping factor   a measurement of the effectiveness of damping (see DAMPED) i.e. the ratio of the amplitude of one oscillation to the amplitude of the next. The logarithm of this quantity is also used, and is known as the LOGARITHMIC DECREMENT or logdec.

damping resistor   a resistor connected across a RESONANT CIRCUIT in order to flatten and broaden the BANDWIDTH.

DAO   see DISC AT ONCE.

dark clip   the action of clipping a video signal at BLACK LEVEL to avoid OVERMODULATION during the processing of a LUMINANCE signal for video cassette recording (see VIDEO CASSETTE RECORDER). See also WHITE CLIP.

dark current   the current that flows in an un-illuminated PHOTOCELL. This current can arise from defects in the material or structure, and it limits the usefulness of the photocell at low light levels.

dark spot   a point on the PHOSPHOR of a CATHODE-RAY TUBE that is insensitive, and does not shine when struck by electrons. A dark spot may be due to poisoning of the phosphor, to ion bombardment, or to having beam current steadily on the spot over a long period. A dark spot on an LCD screen arises from the failure of a PIXEL unit, possibly because of pressure at that point on the screen.

Darlington pair   a form of compound EMITTER FOLLOWER circuit for transistors.

The circuit has very high current gain, but its voltage gain is limited by the finite value of resistance between the collector and the base of the first transistor. See Fig. 32.

Darlington push-pull a form of LIN CIRCUIT using complementary transistors in DARLINGTON PAIRS.

DASH (digital audio stationary head) see DIGITAL MULTI-TRACK.

dashpot a mechanical damping device that consists of a small pot filled with oil. A cylinder floating in the oil is connected to the mechanical system whose motion is to be DAMPED.

DASS see DATA ACCESS SIGNALLING SYSTEM.

DAT see DIGITAL AUDIO TAPE.

data information in electronic form, usually DIGITAL, which can refer to sound, picture, text or other information.

data access signalling system or **digital access signalling system** an implementation of the OPEN SYSTEMS INTERCONNECT (OSI) standard for message-based communications.

data analyzer an instrument that connects to a set of data cables and presents the data content in the form of a display, see DATA DOMAIN ANALYSIS, TIMING DOMAIN ANALYSIS.

data broadcasting a form of TELETEXT service for business users.

data buffer a portion of MEMORY within a computer that is allocated for use by data that is in the course of being transferred to or from a printer, DISK DRIVE or other device.

data bus a set of lines (see BUS) used to carry data to or from a microprocessor. A data bus is normally BI-DIRECTIONAL, unlike an ADDRESS BUS.

data cable a multistranded cable, usually flat, used to connect a drive to the motherboard of a computer. Serial data cables of fewer strands, are now being used.

data capture any method that converts raw (not recorded) data into the form of digital numbers that the computer can use, and includes keyboards, voice input, and OPTICAL CHARACTER READER devices. In computers that are used to control manufacturing processes, the data may be obtained from measuring instruments, using DIGITIZERS to convert to BINARY (sense 1) form. Data capture in such a case is entirely automatic and does not depend on a human operator.

data collection platform (DCP) an automatic sensing unit, land- (sea- or air-) based usually for environmental measurements, that transmits its data to satellites for worldwide broadcasting.

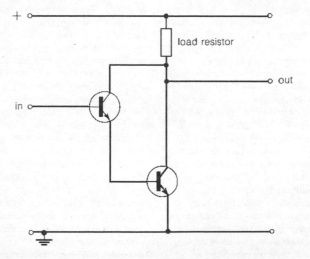

Fig. 32. **Darlington pair**

data collision　see COLLISION.

data communication equipment (DCE)
a device, typically a MODEM, used to
establish, maintain and finally terminate a
data transmission. Contrast DATA TERMINAL
EQUIPMENT (DTE).

data communications　the collection,
organization, transmission and use of
electronic data.

data compression　reduction in the number
of BITS or rate of DIGITAL DATA, either
reversibly (NON-LOSSY) or irreversibly
(LOSSY) so as to reduce the requirements
for transmitting and storing the data. See
also COMPRESSED AUDIO; COMPRESSED VIDEO.

data domain analysis or **word display**　an
output from a data analyzer that shows
the signals on the data cables at each
clock edge in the form of a data word
rather than in the form of a waveform,
see also TIMING DOMAIN ANALYSIS.

data downloading　see DOWNLOADING.

data encryption standard (DES)
algorithm　a method of encoding blocks
of 64 bits of CLEAR TEXT into CIPHER, using
a 56-bit KEY (sense 1), standardized by the
US National Bureau of Standards.

data glove　a device used with VIRTUAL
REALITY programs. The user wears a glove
that can detect finger movements that are
transmitted to the computer and used to
control the image of the glove on the screen
together with effects of pushing or pulling.

data matrix　a two-dimensional coding
system, allied to bar-coding, of black
and white squares used to store larger
amounts of data, typically 2 kB in an area
33 mm square.

data packet or **packet**　a set of BYTES
of data together with start, stop and
identification bits or bytes. See also START
BIT; STOP BIT.

data rate　the rate of transmitting or
processing data, usually expressed in BITS
PER SECOND (b/s) or bytes per second
(B/s), or multiples such as kb/s, Mb/s.

data recorder　a recorder, disk or tape,
specifically designed for RECORDING and
replaying data signals, and using error
detection and correction systems to
ensure INTEGRITY of data.

data reduction　the use of compression
(see COMPRESSING) techniques to reduce
the amount of DIGITAL DATA for a given
transmission.

data set ready (DSR)　a code that is
transmitted on a SERIAL link to indicate
that a MODEM is ready for signals.

data sheet　an information leaflet on a
component, particularly on a complex
component such as a semiconductor chip.

data sink　a receiving terminal for data,
contrast DATA SOURCE.

data size　the data handling unit size for
a MICROPROCESSOR, such as 32-bit, 64-bit,
128-bit etc.

data source　a terminal that originates
data for transmission, contrast DATA SINK.

data storage device　any unit, such as
MEMORY, DISK DRIVES, CD-ROM or data TAPE,
that will retain DIGITAL DATA, either for a
short time (see VOLATILE) or a long time.

data terminal equipment (DTE)　a
HARDWARE device that is a source or
destination of data as distinct from an
intermediate device such as a MODEM.

DATATRAK　an automatic vehicle location
system using a low frequency receiver, high
frequency transmitter and microprocessor.
Locating signals from fixed locations are
picked up and position calculated from
their PHASE difference; the position
information for the vehicle is then
broadcast.

data transfer rate　the speed at which
data is moved from one system to
another, such as from a computer to a
HARD DRIVE. Measured in units of BITS PER
SECOND (b/s) or bytes per second (B/s),
or multiples such as kb/s, Mb/s, Gb/s.

data unit　see WORD.

DATV　see DIGITAL ASSISTANCE SIGNAL.

daughterboard　a PRINTED CIRCUIT BOARD,
particularly in a computer, that can be
plugged into an existing MOTHERBOARD
to add new functions.

daylight sensor　a PHOTOCELL used to detect
daylight and thus switch off security
systems that are used only at night.

dB or **db**　see DECIBEL.

dBA level　a measurement of comparative
sound pressure level, weighted to the 'A'

scale to correspond as closely as possible to the effect on the human ear.

DBPSK see DIFFERENTIAL BINARY PHASE SHIFT KEYING.

DBS see DIRECT BROADCASTING BY SATELLITE.

dbx™ a very effective COMPANDER system. The system has been used for tape-hiss suppression on domestic cassette recorders and for increasing the signal to noise ratio for FM receivers (not in the UK).

DC see DIRECT CURRENT.

DC amplifier an amplifier whose signal inputs and outputs are DC levels. See also CHOPPER AMPLIFIER; DIRECT COUPLING.

DCC dynamic carrier control: see DYNAMIC AMPLITUDE MODULATION.

DC component the voltage difference between earth voltage and the average voltage of a wave.

DC erase the use of a steady current through an ERASE HEAD of a TAPE RECORDER. This will erase the tape, but makes subsequent recordings noisy. See also AC ERASE; PERMANENT MAGNET ERASE.

DC feedback FEEDBACK of signals of zero frequency, requiring the use of DC COUPLING through the LOOP (sense 1).

DC load line a line drawn in a graph of voltage plotted against current for an amplifier to show the effect of using a specified value of LOAD resistor.

DC motor a motor that operates with a DC input, using either a mechanical or an electronic commutator (see BRUSHLESS DC MOTOR). The use of DC motors is favoured because of the ease with which they can be controlled.

DC offset the input voltage required to an OPERATIONAL AMPLIFIER to produce a zero output voltage when no signal is applied to the amplifier. See also CHOPPER.

D-connector a multiple-pin connector shaped as an elongated 'D'.

DCP see DATA COLLECTION PLATFORM.

DC power supply see POWER PACK.

DC restoration the recovery of the correct DC level in a signal that has been transmitted by radio, or passed through a capacitor. A VIDEO signal, for example, that has been passed through a capacitor, will not have its BLACK LEVEL at zero volts, and the voltage of the black level will vary with the ratio of light to dark in the signal. The DC position of the black level can be restored by CLAMPING, or more simply by a DC restoration circuit.

DC restoring diode a diode used in a DC RESTORATION circuit along with a capacitor to establish the correct BLACK LEVEL of a VIDEO signal. See Fig. 33.

DC shift a steady voltage applied between the plates of a CATHODE-RAY TUBE using ELECTROSTATIC DEFLECTION to position the beam at a specific part of the screen.

DCS 1800 a digital CELLULAR PHONE system operating at 1800 MHz.

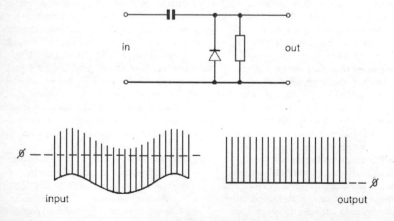

Fig. 33. **DC restoring diode**

DCT see DISCRETE COSINE TRANSFORM, DIGITAL CORDLESS TELEPHONE.

DC to DC or **DC-DC converter** a method of converting DC voltage up or down with high efficiency, basically using an OSCILLATOR, TRANSFORMER and RECTIFIER system.

DC value see ROOT MEAN SQUARE (sense 2).

DDC digital data channel.

DDR memory see DOUBLE DATA RATE MEMORY.

DDS see DIRECT DIGITAL SYNTHESIZER.

dead (of electronic equipment) totally non-functioning, with no indication of any action.

dead-beat (of a mechanical meter movement) being critically DAMPED to avoid oscillation. This means that when the meter movement is connected in a circuit, the needle will not oscillate around a steady value, but move steadily to that value. If the movement is OVERDAMPED, the needle may take an irritatingly long time to reach its final value.

deadlock or **deadly embrace** a stalemate situation in a MULTIPROCESSOR computer in which two tasks are interlocked because each task contains a reference to the other.

deadly embrace see DEADLOCK.

dead room a space with high absorption and almost negligible reverberation, so that sound is almost inaudible at a distance from the source.

dead short an unintended connection of very low resistance. A dead short across a power supply will blow a FUSE.

dead space see SKIP DISTANCE.

dead time the time for which a device is disabled following some event. Many detectors of radioactivity are unable to detect another particle for a short time following the arrival of a particle, and this time is the 'dead time' for the detector. Some electronic circuits exhibit a dead time following an overload.

dead zone or **skip zone** or **silent zone** the area between the furthest limit of a GROUND WAVE (sense 1) and the first reflection of a SKY WAVE in which no signal can be received. See also SKIP DISTANCE.

debouncing circuit a circuit that is used to suppress multiple pulses from a switch. When a mechanical switch is closed, the contacts will bounce open again, and may bounce several times. This causes the closure of a switch to generate a set of voltage pulses. If the switch is part of a counter circuit, the excess pulses have to be suppressed, and this is done by a circuit connected across the switch. A typical circuit uses the RS FLIP-FLOP.

debugging the process of removing faults (BUGS) from a computer program.

debunching the separation, due to mutual repulsion, of bunched (SEE BUNCHING) electrons in a beam because of their CHARGE. Debunching affects dense electron beams and particularly 'packets' of electrons in KLYSTRONS.

deca- or **dec** a prefix denoting ten or tenfold.

decade literally ten years, but used to mean ten as in phrases such as DECADE COUNTER.

decade counter a counter that displays in the familiar scale of ten, as distinct from a BINARY CODE or HEXADECIMAL CODE display.

decamired filter a light filter that is used for COLOUR BALANCING because it shifts COLOUR TEMPERATURES uniformly.

decay the latter portion of the waveform for a musical note in which the amplitude reduces comparatively slowly towards zero. See also ATTACK; RELEASE; SUSTAIN.

decay time the time needed for the AMPLITUDE of a voltage to reduce below a threshold. The decay time for a back edge of a pulse is often measured from the 90% to the 10% amplitude levels.

Decca navigator an old-established DIRECTION FINDING system using a set of four transmitters to convey positional information, particularly for ships.

decibel (dB or **db)** the unit of comparative power, one tenth of a BEL. For power levels P1 and P2, the decibel ratio is defined as $10\log_{10}(P_2/P_1)$. It can (often incorrectly) be taken in the form of a voltage ratio, using $20\log_{10}(V_2/V_1)$ but this is correct only if these voltages are measured across the same level of impedance.

decibel variants extensions of the definition of the decibel used for specific purposes, such as dBA (sound pressure levels weighted to the 'A' scale) dBW (decibels relative to 1 watt), dBm (decibels relative to one milliwatt), dBV (decibels relative to 1 volt), dBµ (decibels relative to one microvolt), and dBc (decibels relative to a CARRIER (sense 1) level).

decimal strictly speaking, a fractional number expressed as figures showing tenths, hundredths, thousandths, etc. Often used to mean DENARY.

decimation filter or **decimator** a form of digital filter which, in spite of its name, usually accepts every *other* value in a data stream, used typically as a DEMULTIPLEXER where two 4-bit channels have been multiplexed into one 8-bit stream.

decimator see DECIMATION FILTER.

decit or **Hartley** a unit of information based on the logarithm to base 10 of probability of occurrence of a symbol. See also BINIT; NAT; SHANNON.

declination angle an additional amount of tilt relative to the INCLINATION angle for a SATELLITE DISH in a POLAR MOUNT so that it can track a GEOSTATIONARY ORBIT of a satellite.

decoder any circuit that converts data from coded form into data that can be used directly as an audio, video or other readable signal. See also DIGIBOX.

decoder, BCD see BCD DECODER.

decoder, PCM a demodulator for PULSE CODED MODULATION transmissions.

decoder, seven-segment see SEVEN-SEGMENT DECODER.

decoding the action of converting coded material into CLEAR TEXT, or encoded digital signals into analogue form.

de-correlation an operation on digital signals that increases the differences between signals, making methods such as HUFFMAN CODING more effective. See also DIFFERENTIAL PULSE CODE MODULATION.

decoupling the process of shorting unwanted signals to earth. A decoupling CAPACITOR is used to short out unwanted high frequencies, and an INDUCTOR can be used to decouple unwanted low frequencies.

decrement 1. the reduction of a count by one. 2. a measurement of damping in the form of *logarithmic decrement* (see DAMPING FACTOR).

decremented (of a count or measurement) decreased by one step. Compare INCREMENTED.

decryption the action of producing CLEAR TEXT from encoded text, usually by inverting the ENCRYPTION process.

decryption, DTV the set of actions that convert a DIGITAL TELEVISION signal (from satellite, cable or terrestrial transmitter) into a usable RGB and AUDIO signals for use in a MONITOR.

decryption key a set of digits (see KEY, sense 1) used to convert coded text or signals into plain form.

dedicated line a communications line, such as a telephone cable, that is not shared; it is for one user and/or one purpose.

dedicated port a computer input/output connector that is intended for one purpose only (such as a printer port) as distinct from a general-purpose port such as a SERIAL or USB port.

de-emphasis a method of reducing noise or maintaining correct response (where PRE-EMPHASIS has been used on transmission or RECORDING) by reducing the amplitudes again, using a LOW-PASS FILTER, at reception or playback. Used in particular in FM broadcasting and in cassette recording.

deep discharge a problem that affects a LEAD-ACID CELL that has been left on load or discharged for a long time, causing permanent damage. Such a cell must be scrapped.

de-esser a circuit used in PUBLIC ADDRESS equipment to reduce sibilance, the exaggeration of the letter 's'.

defects, square waves see SQUARE WAVE DEFECTS.

definition see RESOLUTION.

deflection angle the maximum angle, measured to the axis of a CATHODE-RAY TUBE, to which the ELECTRON BEAM has to be deflected to touch each corner of the screen. This angle can be as low as 50° for miniature colour tubes, and as high as 114°

for large tubes. Picture distortion is higher when large deflection angles are used.

deflection, beam the use of electrostatic or magnetic fields to bend the electron beam of a CATHODE-RAY TUBE.

deflection centre the point at which deflection of an ELECTRON BEAM in a colour CATHODE-RAY TUBE should start, which should be the point from which phosphors were deposited during manufacture of the tube.

deflection coils coils used to supply magnetic fields for the beam deflection of a TV or radar CATHODE-RAY TUBE. The coils are shaped to wrap tightly around the neck of the tube, and are fed with a sawtooth *current* waveform to cause beam deflection. The voltage waveform across the coils takes the form of a large pulse at the moment when current is switched off, and this is utilized in an energy-recovery circuit, returning power to the supply and also generating the EHT voltage for the FINAL ANODE of the tube.

deflection defocusing a fault of an electron optical system (see ELECTRON OPTICS) that results from the fact that a beam that is focused when aimed at the centre of the screen or target will be out of focus at the edge. The cure is DYNAMIC FOCUSING, in which part of the deflection waveform is added to a focus current in a coil.

deflection plates a method of applying ELECTROSTATIC DEFLECTION to an instrument CATHODE-RAY TUBE. The plates are usually shaped in a diverging pattern to avoid being struck by the beam. The sensitivity of the tube will be proportional to the length of the plates.

deflection sensitivity a measure of the effectiveness of a deflection system. For ELECTROSTATIC DEFLECTION, this is measured as the amount of beam deflection at the screen per volt applied between the deflection plates at a given acceleration voltage. The deflection sensitivity is inversely proportional to the accelerating potential between CATHODE (sense 1) and FINAL ANODE. For a tube that uses MAGNETIC DEFLECTION, the deflection

sensitivity is not internally fixed, because the deflection coils are external. The tube manufacturer may quote deflection sensitivity in terms of millimetres of deflection per unit flux density. In this case, deflection sensitivity is inversely proportional to the square root of accelerating potential.

deflection yoke the set of coils used for beam deflection in a magnetically deflected (see MAGNETIC DEFLECTION) CATHODE-RAY TUBE.

deflector plates the metal plates within a CATHODE-RAY TUBE using electrostatic deflection (see DEFLECTION, BEAM) by applying voltages to each plate.

defluxer a demagnetizing device. Most defluxers consist of a magnetic core with a large air gap and a coil that is connected to AC mains. The large AC field can be applied to a magnetized material to force the material to undergo the MAGNETIC HYSTERESIS cycle. If the material is then pulled slowly away from the defluxing coils, or the current slowly reduced, the magnetism will go through ever-decreasing peaks until it reaches zero.

De Forest, Lee (1873–1961) inventor of the first amplifying radio valve (see THERMIONIC VALVE) and of the *Phonofilm* system that made it possible to use a sound track on a film.

deformation voltage the voltage between the electrodes of a PIEZOLECTRIC crystal when a force is applied to the crystal.

degaussing the demagnetization action on a metal, carried out by using a defluxer. This action is carried out automatically on a colour CATHODE-RAY TUBE each time a receiver is switched on. Named for Karl Friedrich Gauss (1777–1855), German mathematician and physicist whose name was also formerly used for a unit of magnetic field strength.

degenerative feedback see NEGATIVE FEEDBACK.

de-glitcher a circuit used to eliminate RACE HAZARD problems on a DIGITAL TO ANALOGUE CONVERTER if SYNCHRONOUS operation does not eliminate the problems. See also GLITCH.

degreasing agent a solvent, many of which are flammable, toxic, or both, used to remove grease and FLUX (sense 2) from components and PRINTED CIRCUIT BOARDS.

degree a unit of ANGLE or of TEMPERATURE; symbol: °.

de-interleaving the action of assembling interleaved (see INTERLEAVING) digital DATA PACKETS into their correct order.

delay a time interval, or a voltage bias. The delay time for a pulse circuit is the time that is needed for an input pulse to produce an output. Voltage bias delays the effect of a rising voltage until it reaches a preset level, see DELAYED AGC.

delay distortion the distortion of an ANALOGUE waveform caused by change in the relative PHASES of its (SINE WAVE) components as the waveform passes through a network.

delayed AGC an AUTOMATIC GAIN CONTROL voltage that is applied against a bias. This causes the AGC to be ineffective until the signal strength has reached some preset level. In this way, small signals will benefit from the full gain of the RF and IF stages of the receiver.

delay equalizer a network that corrects the distortion of wideband signals that have passed through a DELAY LINE.

delay line a circuit or system that causes a deliberate time delay to a signal. Delay lines may be made from COAXIAL or TWIN CABLES. An alternative is to use a LUMPED PARAMETER line, consisting of a capacitor-inductor ladder network. For delays of more than a fraction of a microsecond, ACOUSTIC DELAY LINES are more practical. For digital circuits, CHARGE COUPLED DEVICE delay lines are used.

delay line, SAW see SURFACE ACOUSTIC WAVE DEVICE.

delay modulation see MILLER CODING.

Dellinger fade out an ionospheric (see IONOSPHERE) effect that results in the total disappearance of reflected signals in the range 1 to 30 MHz for several hours during daylight, particularly near to the equator.

delta connection the connection of three phase AC signals as three lines with no neutral line, see STAR CONNECTION; STAR-DELTA TRANSFORMATION.

delta match a method of matching a DIPOLE AERIAL to 600 OHM LINE by making connections one eighth of a wavelength apart.

delta modulation an old form of ANALOGUE TO DIGITAL CONVERTER that converts the *difference* between consecutive samples into binary data rather than the absolute values of the samples.

delta pulse code modulation (DPCM) see DIFFERENTIAL PULSE CODE MODULATION.

delta-sigma modulation (DSM) a form of DIFFERENTIAL PULSE CODE MODULATION in which an INTEGRATOR is placed ahead of the modulator, so that the resulting signal represents signal amplitude rather than variations in amplitude.

delta-star transformer a form of transformer for AC power circuits. A three-phase supply network with no NEUTRAL (sense 3) line may be transformed in this type of system to a three-phase and neutral supply. See also STAR-DELTA TRANSFORMATION.

demagnetizing the action of reducing the magnetic field strength of a magnetic material to zero. This usually requires the application of a steadily decreasing alternating magnetic field using a DEFLUXER.

demand assignment (DA) a DIGITAL transmission system in which a connection is made available only when required.

demand assignment multiple access (DAMA) a variation of demand assignment that caters for multiple users.

demand multiplexing a form of MULTIPLEXING in which the percentage of time allocated to one type of signal is not fixed but can be altered to suit the demand.

demand paging a form of memory addressing (see ADDRESS) into units called PAGES that can be held in a CACHE for rapid loading.

demineralized water water that is free from dissolved salts, preferably distilled water, used as a final cleaning wash on PRINTED CIRCUIT BOARDS and for other electronic assemblies.

democratic network a NETWORK (sense 2) in which each connected computer has equal priority on data and resources. Compare DESPOTIC NETWORK.

demodulation or **detection** the recovery of a modulating waveform from a modulated CARRIER (sense 1). For AMPLITUDE MODULATION, this can be achieved by using a diode and capacitor to rectify the carrier. For frequency modulation, the FOSTER-SEELEY DISCRIMINATOR or RATIO DETECTOR has been used, but PHASE LOCKED LOOPs and ICs that use pulse counting techniques are now more common. Phase-sensitive SYNCHRONOUS DEMODULATION is used for analogue colour TV CHROMINANCE SIGNALs, and various methods are used for the many forms of pulse modulation, ranging from a simple low-pass filter to elaborate decoders.

demodulator or **detector** any circuit that accomplishes DEMODULATION.

demodulator, FM a circuit whose output is dependent on the frequency at the input so that a frequency modulated input will result in a demodulated (see DEMODULATION) output. See also FOSTER-SEELEY DISCRIMINATOR; PHASE LOCKED LOOP; RATIO DETECTOR.

De Morgan's theorem a useful connection between logic actions of AND and OR, stated in the two forms: $\overline{A+B} = \overline{A} \cdot \overline{B}$ and $\overline{A \cdot B} = \overline{A} + \overline{B}$. First enunciated by the mathematician Augustus de Morgan (1806–1871) a colleague of George Boole.

demultiplexer or **demux** a circuit that separates signals that have been transmitted in combined form by a MULTIPLEXER (sense 1).

demux see DEMULTIPLEXER.

denary scale of ten, the ordinary counting scale, as distinct from BINARY (sense 1) or other scales using a NUMBER BASE other than ten.

denominator the portion of a fraction that is below the bar. Contrast NUMERATOR.

depletion layer or **depletion region** the region in a SEMICONDUCTOR around a JUNCTION (sense 2). In the region close to a junction, the number of free carriers is lower than in the remainder of the material because they combine and eliminate each other. This is the *depletion layer*. Its size can be increased by reverse biasing the junction, and decreased by forward biasing. See also VARACTOR.

depletion mode the operation of a FIELD EFFECT TRANSISTOR with reverse bias. A depletion mode FET will pass maximum current at zero bias, and the effect of bias is to reduce the channel current. Compare ENHANCEMENT MODE.

depletion region see DEPLETION LAYER.

depolarizer a chemical oxidizing agent, used to remove bubbles of hydrogen that form on the ANODE of a CELL and so raise the INTERNAL RESISTANCE.

deposition the laying down of a material on another layer. Typical deposition methods include electroplating, vacuum metallization, sputtering and chemical plating.

depth-multiplex audio a method of using the rotating heads of a VIDEO CASSETTE recorder to record AUDIO signals as well as VIDEO, by RECORDING the audio with a larger head gap, so penetrating the magnetic material further. The replay is carried out using the same heads, with filters to separate the signals. See also FREQUENCY MULTIPLEX AUDIO.

depth of field or **depth of focus** the range of distances between a camera lens and a scene over which an image appears to be in focus. The depth of focus is large if the lens is STOPPED DOWN to a small APERTURE.

depth of modulation or **modulation factor** a factor (for AMPLITUDE MODULATION of a CARRIER, sense 1) equal to amplitude of modulating signal divided by amplitude of unmodulated signal expressed as a percentage. When the depth of modulation approaches 100%, the distortion of the signal will be very large, but when the depth of modulation is low, 20% or less, the SIGNAL-TO-NOISE RATIO will be poor.

derating a deliberate reduction in operating RATINGS under some conditions. For example, the maximum voltage that can be applied to a TRANSISTOR may have to be reduced when the temperature is increased or when high-frequency signals are used.

DES see DATA ENCRYPTION STANDARD ALGORITHM.

design impedance the quantity R_0 for a filter, a resistance, defined by the equation: $Z_1 Z_2 = R_0^2$ where Z_1 = series impedance and Z_2 = shunt impedance for a filter section. See also CONSTANT K.

desoldering the removal of soldered connections. This can be done using solder-braid, that removes SOLDER by capillary effect. A more suitable method for extensive use is a DESOLDERING GUN (*desoldering pump*) which sucks up molten solder, using either a built-in or a separate hot iron to melt the solder. Desoldering is particularly important if working ICs are to be removed. For faulty ICs, it is easier to cut all the pins and then remove them with a soldering iron and pliers. Because of the cost of reliable sockets, very few ICs (mainly microprocessor chips with a large number of pins) are mounted in sockets.

desoldering gun or **desoldering pump** a combination of soldering iron and suction pump that will melt solder and suck the liquid away.

desoldering pump see DESOLDERING GUN.

despotic network a NETWORK (sense 2) in which one computer synchronizes all connections and controls the access of all the others to data and other resources.

despun aerial (or **antenna)** a device used in a communications SATELLITE to ensure that the aerials are pointing always towards the Earth station.

destructive interference the summation of two waves that are in ANTIPHASE, so that the amplitude of the resultant wave is lower than the amplitude of either component. See also CONSTRUCTIVE INTERFERENCE.

destructive read an action of reading memory that destroys the contents of the memory, now obsolete. Magnetic core stores were subject to destructive read because the reading was carried out by pulses that set the direction of

magnetization to the logic 0 direction. This caused no effect on a read wire when the core was already at the 0 condition, but induced a pulse when the core was at logic 1 and was changed to logic 0. The core then had to be rewritten to logic 1 by another circuit if the content of the memory was not to be lost.

detached contact system a method of indicating RELAY action in circuit diagrams. The coil of the relay is shown in the part of the circuit where it is wired. The contacts are then shown in whatever circuit they switch, and these may be illustrated on a separate page of the circuit. The correspondence of the coil and its contacts is shown by label numbers.

detection bandwidth the range of frequencies for which a PHASE-LOCKED LOOP will detect and lock into an input signal.

detectivity for a TRANSDUCER, the ratio of S/N (see SIGNAL TO NOISE RATIO) of output signal to size of input signal.

detector 1. see DEMODULATOR. 2. a device that detects subatomic particles.

detector, average see AVERAGE DETECTOR.

detector, peak see PEAK DETECTOR.

deterministic network a network in which each user is guaranteed a time slot at regular intervals.

detune to adjust a RESONANT CIRCUIT so that it is not in resonance with an input signal.

Deutsches Institut für Normung (DIN) a German standardizing body, well known for the DiN plug and socket standards.

deviation 1. the difference from a standard value in error measurement and assessment. 2. in FREQUENCY MODULATION, the difference between the modulated frequency and the CARRIER (sense 1) centre frequency at any instant.

deviation distortion demodulated FM signal distortion caused by NONLINEARITY in the DEMODULATOR.

deviation ratio a figure of limiting MODULATION for an FM broadcast, defined as maximum allowed CARRIER (sense 1) frequency change/maximum allowed modulating frequency.

deviation sensitivity   a measure of sensitivity of an FM demodulator, measured as the number of volts of output signal per hertz of DEVIATION (sense 2).

device   a component or small group of components (see ASSEMBLY) that carries out an action, electrical or mechanical.

dew   condensed vapour, usually water.

dew-point   the temperature at which water vapour will condense on to a surface. This is not a fixed temperature; it varies with the relative humidity of the air, but it is possible to heat a surface to such a temperature that there will be no condensation even if the air humidity is high.

dew sensor   a high-resistance sensor on the DRUM (sense 1) of a VIDEO CASSETTE RECORDER, used to detect water vapour (by the resistance change) that would cause tape sticking and tearing if the machine were used.

DFB laser   see DISTRIBUTED FEEDBACK LASER.

DFT   see DISCRETE FOURIER TRANSFORM.

DGPS   see DIFFERENTIAL GLOBAL POSITIONING SYSTEM.

DHDTV   see DIGITAL HIGH DEFINITION TELEVISION.

diac™   a form of DIODE that conducts in either direction. The diac is an insulator for low voltages in either direction, but it will break down for a critical voltage and can pass currents in either direction. Diacs are used mainly in the triggering circuits of TRIACS and THYRISTORS.

diagnostic equipment, computer   see COMPUTER DIAGNOSTIC EQUIPMENT.

diagnostic program   a program that can be run on a computer and by indicating answers to questions can be used to help locate a fault.

dial drive   a mechanical system using a belt, string or gear set to move a pointer along a dial to indicate a quantity such as tuned frequency.

diaphragm   a thin vibrating sheet used in MICROPHONES to convert the wave of sound into a mechanical movement that will then be converted into an electrical signal.

diaphragm, loudspeaker   see LOUDSPEAKER DIAPHRAGM.

dibit   a two-bit group representing the four states of 00, 01, 10, 11.

dichroic filter   see DICHROIC MIRROR.

dichroic lens   a lens, used in LCD PROJECTOR displays that will pass two-thirds of the spectrum, but reflect the remainder, so separating, for example, red from blue and green signals.

dichroic mirror or **dichroic filter**   a colour-selective mirror consisting of a thin film of material on a flat glass plate. The material must have a refractive index very different from that of glass. The thickness of the film is arranged to make use of lightwave INTERFERENCE effects so the film acts as a mirror for only a selected range of light wavelengths.

Dicke's radiometer   a TRANSDUCER for measuring microwave power by using the heating effect on a small resistive element.

dicode   a format for coding digital signals using pulses that are obtained by differentiating (see DIFFERENTIATION) the original signal pulses into half-width pulses.

DID   direct inward dialling.

dielectric   an insulator, particularly one that separates the plates of a CAPACITOR. The RELATIVE PERMITTIVITY of an insulating material was formerly known as the *dielectric constant*.

dielectric absorption   see SOAKAGE.

dielectric breakdown   a failure of insulation in a capacitor, which can cause permanent damage to some types of capacitor, though others are SELF-HEALING.

dielectric constant   see RELATIVE PERMITTIVITY.

dielectric heating   the heating of an insulator by making it the dielectric in a capacitor that is supplied with high-frequency signals. Heat is generated because of a form of electric HYSTERESIS. See also INDUCTION FURNACE.

dielectric isolation   the deposition of an insulating layer such as silicon monoxide or silicon dioxide surrounding groups of components on an INTEGRATED CIRCUIT, so reducing leakage.

dielectric lens aerial (or **antenna)**   a lens formed from a dielectric material used to form the radiation from a dipole or a waveguide into a beam.

dielectric loss the loss of energy in a capacitor due to a PHASE SHIFT that is not exactly 90°, usually measured by POWER FACTOR. Typical power factors for capacitors (other than electrolytic) range from 2×10^{-4} to 600×10^{-4}.

dielectric resonator a small disc of PIEZOELECTRIC CRYSTAL material, typically barium or zirconium titanate, used like a QUARTZ CRYSTAL in a FILTER circuit, but capable of use at much higher frequencies, up to 20 GHz.

dielectric strength for a DIELECTRIC material, the maximum ELECTRIC FIELD strength, often measured in kV/m, that can be applied across a specimen of the material without causing BREAKDOWN.

difference frame a frame of DIGITAL TELEVISION that consists only of differences between the current frame and the previous frame. See also B-FRAME; GROUP OF PICTURES; MPEG-3; P-FRAME.

difference signal, stereo the ANALOGUE L–R audio signal derived from the separate L and R channel signals, usually of a low amplitude compared with the MONOPHONIC (L+R) signal.

differential amplifier or **long-tailed pair** or **emitter-coupled circuit** an amplifier that has two inputs. The output of a differential amplifier is proportional to the voltage or current difference between the inputs. See also COMMON-MODE REJECTION.

differential binary phase shift keying (DBPSK) a data encoding system using PHASE shifting of the CARRIER (sense 1) to indicate a bit value. See also FREQUENCY SHIFT KEYING.

differential capacitor a capacitor with two sets of static plates and one set of moving plates. The moving plates can be adjusted so that their capacitance to either set of fixed plates is increased or decreased.

differential encoding or **differential modulation** a digital coding system in which logic 0 is represented as a change in level and logic 1 by no change.

differential gain an effect of NONLINEARITY in an analogue COLOUR TELEVISION system,

causing the amplitude of a colour SUBCARRIER to be different when it is superimposed on different parts of a LUMINANCE waveform.

differential global positioning system (DGPS) a modification to the GLOBAL POSITIONING SYSTEM that uses a receiver at a known point to transmit information that will correct the readings of other receivers.

differential group delay the variation in GROUP DELAY for a range of frequencies.

differential mode the application of signals in ANTIPHASE to a DIFFERENTIAL AMPLIFIER to obtain maximum gain, contrast COMMON MODE.

differential modulation see DIFFERENTIAL ENCODING.

differential nonlinearity the random unevenness of each QUANTIZATION level of a sampled signal.

differential phase detection demodulation of a phase-modulated (see PHASE MODULATION) signal by comparing each received bit symbol with the previous one.

differential phase distortion a problem in NTSC colour TV receivers in which PHASE changes affect LUMINANCE and CHROMINANCE signals differently, leading to hue changes and so requiring a manual HUE ADJUSTMENT on the receiver. See also PAL; SECAM.

differential phase shift keying (DPSK) a variation of PHASE SHIFT KEYING in which the phase of one bit is used as the reference phase for the next following bit.

differential pulse code modulation (DPCM) a predictive form of modulation used when an ANALOGUE SIGNAL is being sampled. For each sample, a predicted value is also taken, and the coded signal is the difference between sampled and predicted value. This produces a very small signal where the input is slowly changing and a large signal when there are steep transitions. See also DE-CORRELATION.

differential quadrature phase shift keying (DQPSK) a form of DIFFERENTIAL PHASE SHIFT KEYING in which the carrier is modulated in four phases, representing two bits per cycle.

differential resistance see INCREMENTAL RESISTANCE.

differential winding a winding on a TRANSFORMER that can be used as a form of control by passing a current that opposes the current in the main coil.

differentiating circuit a circuit, usually based on an OPERATIONAL AMPLIFIER, with capacitive input and resistive FEEDBACK, that carries out the mathematical operation of differentiation, so that $V_{out} = dV_{in}/dt$. When a VOLTAGE STEP is applied to a differentiating circuit, the output of the circuit is waveform that is the differential of the unit step, a unit pulse or impulse. The effect of a differentiating circuit on any waveform apart from a sine wave is to produce a signal with sharp spikes where the waveform voltage has changed rapidly. The effect on a sine wave is to produce a cosine wave which is of the same shape but phase-shifted by 90°. An approximation to differentiation can be obtained from a simple series C-R circuit, with the input across both components and the output across the resistor, see Fig. 34.

differentiation the action of a DIFFERENTIATING CIRCUIT to emphasize waveform edges.

diffraction the bending of electromagnetic waves as they pass an edge, causing the range to extend beyond the optical horizon. See also RADIO HORIZON.

diffraction grating, CD player a set of finely-ruled lines that act as a form of lens, used in a CD player to split the reading laser beam into three parts, one for reading and the side beams for tracking.

diffused junction a semiconductor JUNCTION (sense 2) that has been produced by DIFFUSION.

diffuse scan photo detector a form of optical beam PROXIMITY DETECTION in which the light source and detector are in a single unit, making use of diffusely reflected light from the object being sensed.

diffusion a method of creating a semiconductor JUNCTION (sense 2) by heating the pure semiconductor material in contact with a DOPING impurity. The doping impurity is in the form of a gaseous compound, and the semiconductor is heated to a temperature just below the melting point. At this temperature, atoms of the doping material that strike the surface of the semiconductor are able to travel (*diffuse*) into the semiconductor, forming a junction.

diffusion filter a light filter that is polished on one side but slightly rough on the other, causing light to become scattered and diffuse.

diffusion isolation a semiconductor manufacturing technique in which devices are formed in N-type layers that are separated by heavily doped P-type layers.

diglbox or **decoder** a digital conversion or decoding box for domestic use whose input is a signal from an aerial, a cable, or satellite dish, and whose output is an analogue signal to a television receiver.

DigiCrypt™ one of several SCRAMBLER systems that uses line shuffling and displacement to make the signal unusable until decrypted.

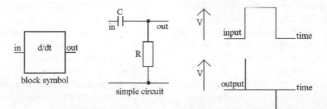

Fig. 34. **differentiating circuit**

DigiCypher™ a US terrestrial DIGITAL TELEVISION system.

digital (of an electronic component or circuit) operating with a small number of voltage levels, usually two. When two levels only are used, they are described, no matter to what voltage they correspond, as level 0 (FALSE) and level 1 (TRUE). Because only two easily distinguished voltage levels are used, most of the forms of distortion that affect analogue waveforms become irrelevant to a digital system.

digital access signalling system (DASS) see DATA ACCESS SIGNALLING SYSTEM.

digital assistance signal (DATV) a method of regenerating lost lines in a compressed analogue HIGH-DEFINITION TV system, HD-MAC, that was demonstrated but never entered service.

digital audio an audio signal that has been digitized (see DIGITIZER) and that can be subsequently compressed. The signals stored on COMPACT DISC are uncompressed, but other formats such as Minidisc™ and MP3 are compressed (see COMPRESSION) using MPEG techniques.

digital audio broadcasting (DAB) the European standardized scheme for digital radio broadcasting intended to produce CD quality and using CODED ORTHOGONAL FREQUENCY DIVISION MULTIPLEX methods.

digital audio interfaces the standardized two-channel serial interfaces for digital audio signals. These are the balanced (professional) AES/EBU or IEC958 type 1 or the unbalanced (consumer) SPDIF or IEC958 type 2.

digital audio tape (DAT) a sound RECORDING system using an ANALOGUE TO DIGITAL CONVERTER followed by recording using a helical scan system (see video tape recorder). Development was hindered by the insistence of the recording industry that copy-protection was essential, so that DAT never became established, particularly after the introduction of CD REWRITER drives (which the recording industry did not seem to anticipate).

digital audio workstation a computer system used to edit digital audio recordings.

digital broadcasting see DIGITAL AUDIO BROADCASTING; DIGITAL TELEVISION.

digital camcorder a combination of DIGITAL VIDEO camera and DIGITAL TAPE RECORDER, allowing COMPRESSED VIDEO pictures to be stored on tape for editing in a computer. Later types have used DVD discs or HARD DRIVES for storage. Connection to the computer is usually by IEEE-488 BUS.

digital camera a still camera, though often with some movie capabilities, that uses a CCD device as a light-sensitive detector to record an image on a static memory in the form of a thin card. The image files, which are usually COMPRESSED can be downloaded (see DOWNLOADING) to a computer, processed and printed using a colour INK-JET PRINTER of photographic quality.

digital carrier any method of transmitting digital signals that can be classed as BASEBAND or BROADBAND. A baseband carrier can have a frequency range from DC upwards, but broadband carriers are modulated by the signals and do not convey DC.

Digital Cellular System (DCS) see DCS 1800.

digital circuit a circuit whose inputs and outputs can take only two levels, referred to as (logic) 0 and (logic) 1. The word logic is often omitted.

digital circuit blocks shapes, mainly rectangular, used in a BLOCK DIAGRAM for a digital circuit.

digital circuit simulation the use of a computer to analyze the action of a LOGIC CIRCUIT and show what outputs will be obtained for any given set of inputs.

digital clock a circuit that consists of a CRYSTAL OSCILLATOR driving a set of DIVIDER circuits to produce an output of hours, minutes and seconds on a display. Note that the term *real-time clock* is applied to such circuits in a computer to avoid confusion with the CLOCK PULSE generator.

digital coding the conversion of information in ANALOGUE form into digital signals, usually involving an ANALOGUE TO DIGITAL CONVERTER.

digital communicator a circuit used in a security system to dial up and communicate with an emergency service in the event of an alarm.

digital compression the reduction in the number of bits needed to represent an audio or video signal, typically by discarding bits that do not make a detectable contribution to the signal.

digital computer a computer that acts on numbers in BINARY CODE. Any type of information can be coded into number form, and the digital computer can carry out actions of selecting, storing, retrieving and arranging the coded information. A particular advantage of the digital computer is that the programming can also be in number codes, whereas ANALOGUE COMPUTERS require HARDWARE alteration. See also BLETCHLEY PARK; COLOSSUS.

digital cordless telephone (DCT) a European standard for cordless telephones using the 1880MHz to 1900 MHz band.

digital counter a circuit that counts the number of pulses that arrive at its input. The counting is achieved using digital circuits, and may be displayed in BINARY (sense 1) or DENARY figures, or even as a meter reading. The input pulse must be of a level that will operate the counter.

digital CRO see DIGITAL STORAGE OSCILLOSCOPE.

digital data data in the form of BINARY (sense 1) 0 or 1 signals.

digital delay a form of signal delay system using digital registers of the SERIAL-IN SERIAL-OUT type.

digital demodulation recovery of a sound, video or text signal from a digitally modulated CARRIER (sense 1). Demodulation methods can be SYNCHRONOUS or ASYNCHRONOUS, but synchronous methods predominate because of a lower BIT ERROR RATE.

digital disk recorder a VIDEO recorder based on the use of a HARD DRIVE to record and replay DIGITAL VIDEO signals.

digital display the readout of a digital meter as a set of numerals, indicating the position of a decimal point or of any multipliers.

digital distortion the degradation of a digital pulse into a sine wave due to the removal of high-frequency components, causing mistiming in digital circuit. See also EYE DIAGRAM.

digital editing the processes of cutting and splicing actions carried out on digital files either ON LINE or OFF LINE.

digital effects cinematic effects such as mix, fade, wipe, mosaic, still, zoom, CHROMA KEYING and LUMA KEYING that can be carried out using DIGITAL VIDEO files manipulated by a computer.

Digital-8™ a hybrid digital tape format, due to Sony, that can be used along with video-8 and HI-8 analogue recorders and players.

digital filling see BIT STUFFING.

digital filter a digital circuit that can carry out the equivalent of an analogue FILTER action, often with more precision and using an IC. Digital filters can also be devised to carry out actions that are impossible using analogue filters.

digital high definition television (DHDTV) any of a number of schemes that use existing bands to carry digital broadcasts with much higher definition (as high as 2000 lines) than currently used. Only digital systems are capable of this extension, but agreement is needed on a worldwide standard.

digital IC an IC in which the signals are pulses and the semiconductor devices are being switched on and off, so that POWER DISSIPATION can be low, allowing millions of semiconductor devices to be used on one CHIP (sense 1).

digital keying a form of CHROMA KEYING method for digital television that is more precise than analogue chroma keying. The three digital TV signal components (Y, B–Y, R–Y) are checked and a key generated for each. These are then combined into a composite key that is used to match the colour.

digital light processor (DLP) a method of displaying large-screen VIDEO by using a MATRIX of half a million or more tiny mirrors, each one corresponding to a PIXEL, that can be moved by piezoelectric (see PIEZOELECTRIC CRYSTAL) methods to reflect a beam of red, blue or green light. The mirrors and their associated controllers are all created on a microchip. See also BEAMER; PLASMA SCREEN.

digital line-up level the standardized digital signal level, either for audio or for video signals, used in order to make interconnection of equipment simple.

digital logic the use of the AND, NAND, OR, NOR functions on pairs of BITS and the NOT function on single bits so as to produce a result in accordance with the rules for these LOGIC actions. See also BOOLEAN ALGEBRA.

digital mastering the use of digital signals as a source for RECORDING, usually for digital recording.

digital meter see DIGITAL MULTIMETER; DIGITAL VOLTMETER.

digital mixing the addition of digital signals to perform the same function as analogue mixing (see MIXER). This can reduce distortion, but a complex circuit must be used to avoid overflow if adding two numbers produces a result that is too large to hold.

digital modulation any system of representing information in a BINARY (sense 1) code suitable for imposing on a CARRIER (sense 1). See AMPLITUDE SHIFT KEYING; DELTA MODULATION; DELTA-SIGMA MODULATION; FREQUENCY SHIFT KEYING; PHASE SHIFT KEYING; PULSE MODULATION; QUADRATURE AMPLITUDE MODULATION; QUADRATURE PHASE SHIFT KEYING; SPREAD SPECTRUM.

digital monitor a monitor which operates with analogue video signals (usually RGB) but whose controls are push-buttons connected to a digital control system rather than the less reliable POTENTIOMETERS (sense 1).

digital multimeter (DMM) a measuring instrument for voltage, current and resistance that uses digital methods of measurement and display. See also DIGITAL VOLTMETER.

digital multiplexer a MULTIPLEXER (sense 1) for digital signals that takes bits in sequence from several sources and combines them into a single BITSTREAM.

digital multi-track a form of digital tape RECORDING system that uses stationary heads and multiple tape tracks, now obsolescent.

digital noise generator a circuit that uses digital signals to generate analogue noise, allowing the noise pattern to be closely controlled. Used for audio equipment testing and sound masking. See also PINK NOISE; WHITE NOISE.

digital noise reduction the use of digital filtering methods to reduce the effect of noise either in audio or video applications. Sound engineers use digital noise reduction when transcribing old recordings from vinyl or shellac discs, and similar filtering methods can be used on digital still or video recordings to enhance picture quality.

digital oscilloscope see DIGITAL STORAGE OSCILLOSCOPE.

digital phosphor the memory unit used in a DIGITAL OSCILLOSCOPE to store signal data.

digital pulser see LOGIC PULSER.

digital quadrature phase shift keying (DQPSK) a CARRIER (sense 1) MODULATION system for NICAM digital sound using a carrier of constant amplitude and four possible PHASE values, so providing two bit information in each cycle.

digital radio see DIGITAL AUDIO BROADCASTING.

digital readout the output of a number directly in readable form on an LCD display, SCREEN, or other display.

digital recording any recording process, tape or disc, that uses modified (see MODIFIED FREQUENCY MODULATION; RUN LENGTH LIMITED) digital signals at two levels. On MAGNETIC MEDIA these signals will saturate (see SATURATION, sense 1) the magnetic material in one direction or the other.

digital resistance meter a form of resistance meter that makes use of a constant-current supply passed through the resistor under measurement and measures the voltage across the resistor digitally. The advantages are that the scale is linear and the reading can be more precise than that obtained from an analogue resistance meter.

digital reverb the use of a DIGITAL DELAY LINE to produce artificial reverberation for a SYNTHESIZER.

digital signal any signal that consists of only two levels representing the BINARY (sense 1) digits 0 and 1.

digital signal processing (DSP) the techniques of SAMPLING, digitizing (see DIGITIZE), ERROR DETECTION and ERROR CORRECTION that provide the advantages of noise-immunity, wide dynamic range, precision copying and low distortion as compared to analogue methods.

digital signal processor (DSP) a chip used in sound and video cards that contains an ANALOGUE TO DIGITAL CONVERTER to convert incoming analogue signals into digital form.

digital speech interpolation (DSI) the use of a MULTIPLEXED digital channel to carry speech of more than one user, because the gaps between words and sentences can be used to carry another speech signal.

digital storage oscilloscope (DSO) a form of CATHODE-RAY OSCILLOSCOPE designed to capture TRANSIENT events or repetitive signals. Sampling rates as high as 5 GHz can be used, capable of capturing a 200 ps pulse. Such an instrument is essential for detecting a GLITCH.

digital subscriber line (DSL) a system that uses conventional copper telephone lines to carry high-speed digital signals. See also ADSL; LOCAL LOOP.

digital subscriber line access multiplexer a circuit used to separate voice signals from data signals over copper telephone lines.

digital sum a measure of DC level in a digitally coded signal, obtained by summing pulse values in a system where a positive pulse represents logic 1 and a negative pulse represents logic 0. If no DC level is present, the digital sum should be zero.

digital switching the connection of digital telephone lines, see SPACE SWITCHING.

digital tape magnetic tape whose characteristics are particularly suitable for SATURATION RECORDING rather than for analogue use.

digital tape recorder a tape recorder used along with compressed (see BIT REDUCTION) digital audio signals. The (obsolescent) SDAT type of recorder uses a multitrack head, recording part of the data on each track of the tape, allowing the tape speed to be comparatively low. The more successful RDAT type uses a rotating head drum, similar to that of a video cassette recorder, but with only 90° of wrapping because the signals are time compressed. RDAT was expected to replace analogue tape recorders for domestic use, but delays due to objections from the recording industry about copying music delayed its acceptance, and its place in domestic recording was taken by the recordable CD. The RDAT recorders are, however, widely used for professional recording work.

digital television the use of digitizing (see DIGITIZE) techniques on the Y, U, V and audio components of a TV camera output and the processing of a combined digital signal so that it can be transmitted using a MULTIPLEX system that allows six channels to occupy the space of a single analogue channel. The propagation methods can be by terrestrial transmitters (see CODED ORTHOGONAL DIGITAL FREQUENCY MULTIPLEX), cable or satellite, and the received signal can be of a higher standard (with the future possibility of higher definition) than that received by analogue methods. See also GROUP OF PICTURES; MPEG-2.

digital to analogue (D/A) converter or **DAC** a circuit whose input is a digital signal, either single-bit (see BITSTREAM) or multi-bit, and whose output is an analogue wave, an exact copy of the wave that was digitized (see DIGITIZE) to provide the digital signal. See also BINARY WEIGHTED RESISTOR NETWORK; CURRENT DRIVEN CONVERTER; MULTIPLYING D/A CONVERTER; R/2R LADDER.

digital transistor a semiconductor indicated on a servicing circuit diagram by using transistor symbols in a square box as a warning that voltage readings will not be normal as compared to a linear device.

digital tuner the portion of a digital receiver that converts the coded signal into analogue signal(s).

digital TV see DIGITAL TELEVISION.

digital TV receiver a TV receiver that consists of the display circuits of a monitor together with tuners for either satellite or conventional aerial (see FREEVIEW) reception of digital signals. At the start of DIGITAL TELEVISION transmissions, most viewers were using a set-top box (cable, Freeview or satellite) for conversion, with the TV receiver used as a monitor and fed with RGB signals.

digital TV sound systems such as NICAM (terrestrial broadcasts) and MAC (satellite broadcasts) that add a digital sound signal to an analogue TV signal.

digital versatile disc (DVD) a development of the CD system, using a laser with a shorter wavelength so that a higher density of data can be obtained on the same size of disc. In addition, it is possible to use separate layers on a single side of a disc to record or play another set of tracks by refocusing the laser. By using compression methods (see MPEG) on the DIGITAL VIDEO signals, a complete 1–6 hours of playing can be obtained on one side of a disc, and this playing time can be increased by using both sides of the disc. The disc was originally intended for video only and was termed *digital video disc*, but the name changed when it was applied also to backup storage of digital computer data.

digital video the use of analogue Y, V and U signals (see COLOUR DIFFERENCE SIGNALS) converted into digital form by SAMPLING and digitizing (see DIGITIZE), usually interleaved into 8 bits of Y signals, 2 bits of U and 2 bits of V to provide a 12-bit signal free of noise and other problems of analogue signals.

digital video broadcasting (DVB) the transmission of DIGITAL TELEVISION picture data by cable, satellite or through conventional TV transmitters (see FREEVIEW).

digital video cassette (DVC) the first common standard for a digital camcorder,

introduced in 1995, but challenged by the Sony DIGITAL-8 and JVC D-VHS systems.

digital voltmeter (DVM) a voltmeter that measures a voltage level by counting the number of small voltage steps needed to reach that level. The digital voltmeter generates a waveform that consists of a staircase wave of (typically) one millivolt steps. The steps are counted in a COUNTER, and the count stops and is displayed when the staircase waveform voltage becomes equal to the applied voltage. The sequence automatically repeats several times per second so that varying voltages can be tracked.

digital weighing machine an assembly of springs and LOAD CELLs along with an ANALOGUE TO DIGITAL CONVERTER that will produce a digital output when a mass is placed on the weighing pan.

digital zoom a form of zoom, used in still digital cameras or camcorders, that creates a picture from a small selected number of pixels in part of a complete picture, so that the effect is similar to that of zooming a lens. The resolution is inferior to that produced by an OPTICAL ZOOM, because the picture is effectively created from a smaller number of larger pixels.

digit counting see PARITY.

digitize to change ANALOGUE data into BINARY (sense 1) coded form. Any type of signal can be digitized by measuring the AMPLITUDE of the signal and converting this number into binary form. The process may have to be repeated at frequent intervals if the signal changes amplitude. Digitization is comparatively simple for signals that change comparatively slowly, but needs a very high SAMPLING RATE if the signal is a rapidly-changing one, such as an AUDIO or VIDEO signal.

digitized image an image represented in digital form, using any of the large number of formats ranging from the (uncompressed) BITMAP to (highly COMPRESSED) JPG.

digitizer any device that can convert a measurement into the form of a BINARY (sense 1) number. The easiest methods usually involve a TRANSDUCER to convert the quantity being measured into a voltage, and then an ANALOGUE TO DIGITAL CONVERTER to obtain a binary number count.

digitizing the action of converting an analogue signal into digital form.

digitizing pad or **tablet** a device that can be used to provide data inputs to a computer. The pad contains a MATRIX of connections which will sense the position of a pen on the surface and translate this position into X-Y co-ordinates in digital form. This is a useful way of tracing graphics information into the machine.

DIL (dual-in-line) package a method of packaging an INTEGRATED CIRCUIT by attaching the chip to a plastic or ceramic slab that has a set of pins at 0.1 inch spacings along each side. The standard widths between the lines of pins are 0.3" for the smaller packages and 0.6" for the larger types (such as microprocessors).

DIMM see DUAL IN LINE MEMORY MODULE.

DiN see DEUTSCHES INSTITUT FÜR NORMUNG.

din plug/socket a standardized connection system for domestic use that uses a common shell size for a large range of connectors ranging from 2-way to 8-way.

diode a component that allows current to pass in only one direction between its two connectors. The direction in which current passes is the forward direction, and the voltage that causes current flow is the forward voltage. A reverse voltage does not cause current to flow unless the voltage is high enough to cause diode BREAKDOWN. Virtually all of the diodes in use nowadays are semiconductor diodes, using either point contact or JUNCTION (sense 2) construction. See also GUNN DEVICE; IMPATT DIODE; LIGHT-EMITTING DIODE; PHOTODIODE; TUNNEL DIODE; ZENER DIODE.

diode-bridge gate a type of simple analogue GATE (sense 2) circuit using a BRIDGE connection of four diodes.

diode demodulator or **diode detector** a simple form of DEMODULATOR for AM signals that acts as a HALF-WAVE RECTIFIER, followed by SMOOTHING (sense 2) to remove the CARRIER (sense 1) from the signal.

diode drop see DIODE FORWARD VOLTAGE.

diode forward voltage or **diode drop** the voltage across a DIODE when it is conducting in the normal forward direction. This voltage is decided mainly by the SEMICONDUCTOR material from which the diode is constructed. Typical figures are 0.55V for a silicon diode, and 0.15V for a germanium diode.

diode mixer see DIODE MODULATOR.

diode modulator or **diode mixer** a MODULATOR circuit that uses the NON-LINEAR action of a DIODE to produce signals mixing, usually in a BRIDGE form of circuit, see DIODE RING MIXER.

diode protection the use of a diode to protect against a reverse voltage, such as for cell charging, relay contacts, or ELECTROSTATIC voltages on an FET.

diode pump a form of pulse counting circuit that produces an output voltage that is proportional to the number of input pulses.

diode pump multiplier a VOLTAGE DOUBLER circuit, similar to the COCKCROFT-WALTON multiplier.

diode reverse voltage a voltage applied across a DIODE in the reverse, nonconducting, direction.

diode ring mixer a MIXER circuit using four diodes inductively connected to an RF input and a LOCAL OSCILLATOR. See Fig. 35.

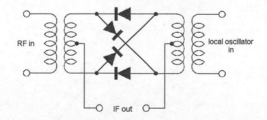

Fig. 35. **diode ring mixer**

diode-split transformer a type of LINE-OUTPUT TRANSFORMER in which diodes are wired in series as part of the EHT windings. This reduces the PEAK INVERSE VOLTAGE on each diode to safer levels and allows the self-capacitance of the windings to be used for smoothing.

diode suppression the connection of a diode across the contacts of a switch or relay in a DC circuit to avoid damage to the contacts (see ARCING) caused by the BACK EMF when the switch opens.

diode-transistor logic (DTL) a method once used to implement logic devices in IC form using diodes and transistors.

diode valve a THERMIONIC VALVE using a CATHODE (sense 1) and ANODE only, constituting a diode. Now obsolete except for applications requiring very high voltages.

DIP see DUAL-INLINE PACKAGE.

dip soldering a mass-production soldering method. PRINTED CIRCUIT BOARDS have their components inserted, and the SOLDER side of the board is coated with flux. The whole surface of the board is then dipped into a bath of molten solder. The level of the solder is maintained so that solder does not run onto the component side of the board, but comes in contact with all the joints on the underside. Where dense packing of printed circuit lines is used, solder-repelling varnish is coated between lines to prevent solder 'bridges' from causing unwanted short circuits.

diplexer a circuit that allows the transmission of two signals along one wire or channel without interference. See also MULTIPLEXER (sense 1).

dipole 1. any system of two equal and opposite elements, such as a pair of equal and opposite electrical charges. 2. see DIPOLE AERIAL.

dipole aerial (or antenna) or dipole an aerial that consists of two conducting rods arranged in line but electrically separate. The rods are of equal length, cut to a definite fraction of the wavelength of the signal that is to be received or transmitted. A very common size is half a wavelength, meaning half of the wavelength on the conductor rather than half of the free-space wavelength. For the lower range of frequencies, the dipole is more likely to consist of wires, possibly parallel sets of wires, rather than rods. The signals are applied to, or received from, the dipole halves in ANTIPHASE. See Fig. 36.

dipulse a pulse of one polarity followed closely by a pulse of the opposite polarity.

dipulse code a three-level binary coding system in which zero signal level represents one logic digit, and a DIPULSE represents the other.

direct broadcasting by satellite (DBS) the use of small satellite dishes for domestic reception of broadcast audio and TV signals from a satellite in a GEOSTATIONARY ORBIT.

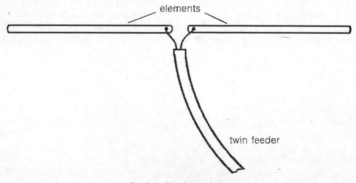

Fig. 36. **dipole aerial**

direct conversion receiver or **autodyne receiver** or **homodyne receiver** or **zero-IF receiver**   a form of SUPERHETERODYNE receiver in which the OSCILLATOR frequency is equal to that of the input CARRIER (sense 1) signal, and only SIDEBANDS are taken from the mixing stage.

direct coupling   the connecting of the output of one amplifier STAGE directly to the input of another. Direct coupling implies no DC blocking components such as CAPACITORS or TRANSFORMERS, so the DC level is also being amplified. Some designs attenuate the DC level by using resistors or ZENER DIODES in the coupling.

direct current (DC)   a steady current in one direction as is provided by a CELL, a DYNAMO, or the smoothed output of a RECTIFIER circuit.

direct digital synthesizer   a circuit that generates a waveform of a specified frequency from digital information, as distinct from the use of an analogue PHASE-LOCKED LOOP.

direct drive motor   the type of DC MOTOR used for tape drives, in which the motor spindle is also the tape CAPSTAN, eliminating the need for gearing or drive belts.

direct drive turntable   a turntable for a VINYL DISC that is driven directly by a low-speed motor as distinct from using belts or stepped pulley wheels.

direct memory access (DMA)   a method of accelerating the processing in a computer by using a separate MICROPROCESSOR to control all disc inputs and outputs.

direct reading capacitance meter   a method of measuring capacitance by rapidly and repetitively switching a voltage to a capacitor and then measuring the integrated current flowing as the capacitor discharges. This makes use of the relationship Q=CV in the form $I = Q/t = CV/t$, so that with I, V and t all known the value of C can be calculated and displayed.

direct sequence spread spectrum   a form of SPREAD SPECTRUM modulation that uses digital codes to determine the way the transmission is spread over the bandwidth.

direct to home (DTH)   see DIRECT BROADCASTING BY SATELLITE.

direct voice input   a form of computer software that allows voice commands to control computer programs, or the dictation of text into a word processor with a high degree of fidelity.

direct wave   the straight line wave path from transmitter to receiver along the Earth's surface. A direct wave is possible only if the transmitter and receiver are reasonably close, approximating to *line of sight* conditions. The wave that is received as a result of reflection from the ionosphere is known as the SKY WAVE.

directed measurement technique   a simple test method for a COMMUNICATIONS system in which the response to a specified input signal is measured.

directional   having a specified direction.

directional aerial   an aerial that transmits or receives signals in one preferred direction. A simple DIPOLE AERIAL is not strongly directional, but it can be made so by adding REFLECTOR and DIRECTOR elements. See also YAGI. See Fig. 37.

directional coupler   a three-port MICROWAVE device in which a portion of the signal flowing from input to output(1) will be diverted to output(2). If the flow is reversed (from output(1) to input), then no output(2) signal is available.

directional microphone   a MICROPHONE that is more sensitive in one particular direction than in others, see CARDIOID.

direction finding   the finding of the direction of the transmitter of a radio frequency SIGNAL. The oldest method (*loop direction finding*) involves the use of two aerials in combination, one VERTICAL WHIP and one rotating loop (see LOOP AERIAL). A rotating loop aerial will give maximum signal when its axis points to the source of signal, but this occurs at two positions of the loop. By comparing the phase of the loop signal with a signal from a fixed aerial, the correct direction of the two can be found. Modern direction finding methods make use of precisely timed signals sent to and from satellites and do not require a geometric arrangement of aerials.

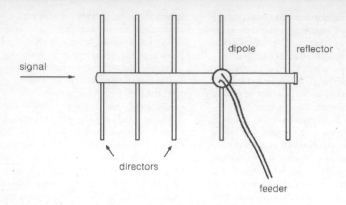

Fig. 37. **directional receiving aerial**

direction-finding aerial an aerial, such as a LOOP AERIAL, that can be used to find the direction of a received signal.

direction of current the conventional direction of current is taken as from positive to negative. See also ANODE CURRENT.

directivity the ability of an AERIAL system to transmit or receive in one particular direction, or the ability of a microphone to pick up sound from one particular direction.

director a rod element added to a DIPOLE AERIAL. Director rods are placed in the desired direction of transmission or reception. They consist of conducting rods, but are not electrically connected to the dipole, or to any signal. The distance of each director from the dipole, or from the previous director, and the overall length of the director, must be theoretically calculated from a formula.

dirty waveform an analogue waveform with poor WAVESHAPE, or a digital signal with GLITCHes; either of which can cause equipment malfunction.

disabling (of a circuit or device) switching off or otherwise preventing action. A circuit can be disabled by, for example, removing or reversing BIAS so that an input signal is ineffective. Digital devices are often provided with an input to activate or deactivate them as required. Contrast ENABLING.

disc 1. a flat plastic disc for the RECORDING of sound or video signals. The obsolescent LP disc is made of vinyl, and hot-stamped with an impression of the sound pattern. The COMPACT DISC uses a form of digital recording and requires a laser reading system and the DVD uses a more advanced form of digital recording to store several hours of video on a disc the same size as the CD. See also RECORDING OF SOUND. **2.** an alternative spelling of DISK.

disc at once or **DAO** a method of RECORDING a COMPACT DISC, particularly one that is to be used as a master for several copies. In this system the LEAD-IN (sense 1) is written followed by data or audio tracks and the LEAD-OUT recorded. The recording laser is never turned off so that no blocks are written to link the tracks as distinct from the method used for TRACK AT ONCE.

discharge the removal or neutralization of electric charge. An electrostatic charge on a material may be discharged by connection to earth or by IONIZATION of the surrounding air. An ionized gas passes current by movement of oppositely charged ions in opposite directions, and this is known as a GAS DISCHARGE or CORONA. A capacitor or a cell will be discharged by passing current from the capacitor or cell.

discone aerial (or **antenna)** an OMNIDIRECTIONAL AERIAL that uses an insulated disc or set of horizontal rods arranged in a circle at the top, with a skirt section of angled rods of quarter wavelength.

discontinuous (of the AMPLITUDE of a WAVEFORM) changing level very rapidly.

discontinuous transmission a system used with CELLULAR PHONES in which the transmitter is turned off when there is no voice input.

discrete 5.1 audio a system used in home cinema systems along with a DVD player. The five main channels are classed by loudspeaker position as left, centre, right, left rear and right rear, and the 0.1 portion refers to a non-directional bass loudspeaker (SUB-WOOFER). See also DOLBY DIGITAL.

discrete access a feature of a STAR NETWORK in which a TERMINAL (sense 2) has direct access to the switching controls.

discrete circuit a circuit using DISCRETE COMPONENTS rather than ICs.

discrete components separate components, such as resistors, capacitors, inductors and transistors arranged on a PRINTED CIRCUIT BOARD. Contrast IC.

discrete cosine transform a processing system for DIGITAL VIDEO signals that analyzes the signals and prepares for the use of LOSSY COMPRESSION methods such as MPEG.

discrete Fourier transform (DFT) a mathematical transformation method used in signal processing theory. A FOURIER TRANSFORM is a method of analyzing the frequencies in a continuous signal, and the discrete form of the Fourier transform is used for sampled (see SAMPLING) signals, which are not continuous. This makes the transform amenable to being calculated by computer software.

discrete multi tone modulation (DMT) a proposed VIDEO ON DEMAND system resembling CODED ORTHOGONAL FREQUENCY DIVISION MULTIPLEX.

discrete wavelet multi tone modulation (DWMT) a variation of DISCRETE MULTI TONE MODULATION that is claimed to be more immune to interference.

discrimination, capture see CAPTURE RATIO.

discriminator 1. a circuit that demodulates a frequency modulated or phase modulated signal (see MODULATION). 2. a circuit that selectively passes pulse inputs of some particular amplitude range.

disc winding a method, now obsolete, of coil winding in which the coil is wound as a flat disk. Such coils can be seen on radios of the later 1920s and early 1930s.

dish or **microwave dish** see PARABOLIC REFLECTOR.

dish overrun excessive movement of a SATELLITE DISH whose position can be altered by remotely-controlled electric motors.

disk or **disc** a thin flat circular plate (of plastic, glass, or metal) coated with magnetic material for the storage of computer data. See also COMPACT DISC; DIGITAL VERSATILE DISC; FLOPPY DISK; HARD DRIVE.

disk controller or **drive controller** a set of circuits on a printed circuit card that will control the selection of disk TRACKS and SECTORS, so that the DISK ACCESS commands of the computer operating system can be used. On modern computers these circuits are incorporated with a hard drive under the scheme called INTEGRATED DEVICE ELECTRONICS (IDE).

disk drive or **drive** an assembly that contains the mechanisms for spinning a disk and moving a READ/WRITE HEAD over the surface. Hard drives usually contain a DISK CONTROLLER with a MICROPROCESSOR controller chip of its own that will ensure that the disk spins at the correct speed, the head locates the correct part of the surface, and the required TRACKS and SECTORS are used. Drives for COMPACT DISCS or DIGITAL VERSATILE DISCS need to be able to locate the correct position on the spiral track by using information held in a table of contents.

diskless workstation a computer that has no DISK DRIVES, and is fed from a NETWORK (sense 2).

disparity the difference between the number of 1s and the number of 0s in a binary WORD. The disparity is 1 if there is an excess of 1s, otherwise the disparity is zero. See also PARITY.

dispersion or **pulse spreading** the effect of different speeds of electromagnetic waves through media, causing a PULSE to be broadened out.

dispersive (of a transmitting medium) carrying waves of different frequency values at different speeds.

dispersive filter see CHIRP FILTER.

dispersive power a measure of the ability of a medium to disperse waves, calculated from refractive indices n_1 and n_2 for two different wavelengths. If n_0 is the average of n_1 and n_2, then the dispersive power is $(n_1 - n_2)/(n_0 - 1)$.

displaced frame difference (DFD) a DIGITAL TELEVISION technique that codes the difference between two successive FRAMES (sense 1) of a picture.

displacement current the current that flows as a result of charge displacement in an INSULATOR. Displacement current is responsible for the REACTANCE of a capacitor and for the TRANSMISSION of electromagnetic waves in space.

displacement vector a digital signal derived from the differences between digital FRAMES (sense 2), using either PIXEL, area or complete frame information for a signal.

display any device that presents information as an image. Thus CATHODE-RAY TUBES and digital SEVEN-SEGMENT DISPLAY devices are displays, but meter scales are not.

display adapter or **graphics adapter** a CIRCUIT CARD used in a computer to provide display actions, often at high speed, using a separate MICROPROCESSOR and a form of MEMORY (VRAM) that can be written and read at the same time.

dissipated power power lost as heat, as distinct from being stored in an inductor or a capacitor.

dissipation the loss of POWER from a system, either in the form of HEAT, or as ELECTROMAGNETIC RADIATION.

dissipation factor a number expressing losses in a DIELECTRIC, calculated by dividing the resistive part of the IMPEDANCE by the reactive part.

distance, code the differences between two digital codes in terms of a comparison of the BIT POSITIONS of the two codes.

distortion an unwanted change of signal waveshape, as for example on received radio sound or a TV picture. See also CROSSOVER NETWORK; DELAY; DEVIATION; FREQUENCY; HARMONIC; INTERMODULATION; NON-LINEAR; PHASE DISTORTION.

distortion, digital see DIGITAL DISTORTION.

distortion figure a number expressing the deviation from LINEAR operation, usually as a percentage, of an electronic ANALOGUE device.

distortion, harmonic see HARMONIC DISTORTION.

distortion, intermodulation see INTERMODULATION.

distortion meter a device for measuring distortion of an AMPLIFIER by applying a pure SINE WAVE as an input and measuring the amplitude of each HARMONIC in the output signal.

distributed architecture (of a communications system) having the transmission medium shared among several services.

distributed capacitance the CAPACITANCE that exists between conductors rather than contained in a discrete (see DISCRETE COMPONENTS) capacitor. For example, two lines of a TRANSMISSION LINE will have capacitance to each other. This value is not located in one place or as one component, but is present distributed along the length of the line (the value of capacitance is usually quoted per metre of line length). Similarly the windings of a coil have capacitance to each other that is distributed rather than lumped (see LUMPED PARAMETER).

distributed feedback (DFB) laser a form of SEMICONDUCTOR LASER in which the need for a reflective end is eliminated by a corrugated structure.

distributed inductance a SELF-INDUCTANCE or MUTUAL INDUCTANCE that cannot be localized in DISCRETE COMPONENTS. A TRANSMISSION LINE will have a value of inductance, for example, that is distributed along the whole length of the line. Distributed inductance is usually quoted per metre of line length.

distribution key   the third KEY (sense 1) used in scrambling (see SCRAMBLER) a satellite TV signal. The distribution key encrypts the AUTHORIZATION KEY which in turn encrypts the CONTROL KEY.

distributive law   the algebraic and arithmetic law, stated as A(B + C)=AB + AC. See also ASSOCIATIVE LAW; COMMUTATIVE LAW.

disturbed-sun noise   the additional radio frequency NOISE that is the result of sunspot or other eruptions in the sun.

dither   noise deliberately added to a very low level digital signal so as to reduce digital noise. This is possible because the dither breaks the CORRELATION between QUANTIZATION NOISE and signal level.

divergence angle   the angle between the sides of a diverging BEAM. A beam of electrons that ought to have parallel sides will diverge because of the repulsion between electrons. A LASER beam can have almost zero angle of divergence, hence the use of laser beams for signalling and as pointing beams.

diversity reception or **barrage reception** a system of reception that uses several aerials or channels to carry the same information. The principle is to overcome interference or FADING by making use of the strongest of the signals at any given time. The most common form is in the form of a multiple DIVERSITY RECEPTION aerial system, using many aerials spread over a large area. The receiver then automatically selects the aerial that provides the largest signal at the desired frequency. Another form of diversity is *frequency diversity* which uses transmissions on several different frequency bands, with the receiver switched to the strongest signal at any time.

divide and conquer   see HALF-SPLIT METHOD.

divider   a circuit that carries out a reduction of a circuit quantity. A POTENTIAL DIVIDER uses (typically) two resistors to reduce a voltage by a calculable amount. A FREQUENCY DIVIDER changes an input frequency to a lower value that is an exact submultiple of the

original (half, third, tenth, etc.). Modern frequency divider circuits make use of digital systems.

divider-chain oscillator   see PHASE SHIFT OSCILLATOR.

divider stage   one unit of a FREQUENCY DIVIDER, normally a FLIP-FLOP.

dividing network   a form of DIVIDER that separates signals on the basis of frequency. This will use potential divider circuits that contain reactances rather than pure resistors. See also CROSSOVER NETWORK.

division ratio   the ratio of output signal to input signal for an ATTENUATOR or POTENTIOMETER (sense 1).

D layer   the layer in the IONOSPHERE that is located approximately between 60 and 90km above the earth's surface. This layer reflects mainly the lower radio frequency signals.

DLP   see DIGITAL LIGHT PROCESSOR.

DMA   see DIRECT MEMORY ACCESS.

D-MAC/packet   one of the many systems proposed for analogue satellite TV broadcasting. See MAC.

dmm   see DIGITAL MULTIMETER.

D-MOS   double-diffused MOS, a MOSFET structure used for power devices that has high packing density with good isolation between components.

D MOSFET   a form of power MOSFET construction that uses a narrow CHANNEL (sense 2) and a GATE (sense 1) constructed from polycrystalline silicon rather than aluminium. See also U MOSFET; V MOSFET.

DMT   see DISCRETE MULTI TONE MODULATION.

DNR   see DIGITAL NOISE REDUCTION.

DOC   see DROPOUT COMPENSATION.

DocFax   a system for transmitting photographic and text information over radio and satellite links.

docking station   an attachment to a LAPTOP computer that provides connection to a desktop machine and/or options such as a CD-ROM drive, ports, loudspeaker, etc.

dog bark   an electronic security alarm that produces a simulated barking sound when activated.

Doherty modulation   an AMPLITUDE MODULATION system, originating in the

1930s, that uses two or more POWER AMPLIFIER (sense 2) stages in a transmitter, each unit handling a different power level.

Dolby AC-3™ a NOISE REDUCTION CIRCUITRY system for home use developed from the professional Dolby SR-D system, using a 5.1 coding of left, centre, right, two surround and bass channels.

Dolby™ **adaptive delta modulation (ADM)** a system of modified DELTA MODULATION developed for use with B-MAC (see MAC) and other analogue satellite TV systems.

Dolby A system a form of NOISE REDUCTION CIRCUITRY for professional use, first developed in 1966, and still in use by recording studios. The system splits the audio signal in several frequency bands, using separate COMPANDERS for each band.

Dolby B system a noise reduction system initially developed in 1967 for slow tape, and then revised in 1969 for compact cassette. This is a simplified system using only a single audio band COMPANDER.

Dolby C system a noise reduction system for domestic use, launched in 1983, that uses two separate stages of COMPANDERS and achieves better results.

Dolby digital™ a compression system (see COMPRESSING) for digital sound, used on DVD players to provide output to loudspeakers and catering for 1 to 5.1 (see DISCRETE 5.1 AUDIO) loudspeakers.

Dolby HX Pro a NOISE REDUCTION CIRCUITRY system used in high-quality analogue tape recorders which allows up to six dB more HF signal to be recorded without tape saturation.

Dolby Pro-Logic™ an audio digital decoder and processor system for home cinema applications.

Dolby S™ a refined NOISE REDUCTION CIRCUITRY system for consumer analogue tape equipment, introduced in 1990 and incorporating most of the features of SR but with fewer COMPANDERS.

Dolby SR a professional NOISE REDUCTION CIRCUITRY system using SPECTRAL SKEWING and ANTI-SATURATION.

Dolby surround™ a passive audio decoder system for MULTICHANNEL AUDIO reproduction, used for home cinema applications.

domain or **magnetic domain** a group of atoms forming an unit of permanent magnetism on a molecular scale.

dominance vector the signal in a DOLBY PRO-LOGIC system that indicates where the most significant sound is to be located.

domino plug another name for the 5-way DIN PLUG that uses the connectors in a symmetrical layout.

donor an impurity material that provides free ELECTRONS to a SEMICONDUCTOR. See also ACCEPTOR.

don't care state a variable in a BOOLEAN EXPRESSION that can take either value (0 or 1) without affecting the output.

door release a magnetic latch for fire doors that keeps the doors open in normal service but allows them to be shut when a fire alarm is activated.

door switch or **change-line support** a switch used in a FLOPPY DRIVE to detect when a disk has been inserted and the drive door shut.

doped crystal a crystal which has been created of a pure material, and has subsequently had atoms added that modify its characteristics. See ACCEPTOR; DONOR.

doping the adding of a DONOR or ACCEPTOR impurity to a pure semiconductor.

Doppler effect (originally) the change of sound frequency when either the source of sound, the receiver, or both are in motion. In sound, Doppler effect can be due to an increase of sound wave velocity when the source is moving. Electromagnetic waves travel at a constant rate in free space, and the Doppler effect for electromagnetic waves is due to changes in the wavelength of the signal caused by movement of source or receiver.

Doppler radar a RADAR system that relies on the change of echo frequency caused by a moving target. This is a system that is used for low-level navigation, and also in speed meters for such diverse actions as measuring the speed of a tennis serve or that of a moving vehicle.

Doppler radar proximity unit a proximity detector that uses X-BAND radar, usually consisting of a GUNN DEVICE transmitter and a simple diode mixer receiver, intended for sensing human movement in the range 1m to 15m.

Doppler range see DORAN.

Doppler shift the change of frequency of a wave that has been reflected by a moving object, used to measure the speed of the moving object in the beam direction.

DORAN (Doppler range) a DOPPLER RADAR system designed for tracking missile paths.

dot clock the rate at which DIGITAL DATA is transmitted in a TELETEXT form of display.

dot crawl a MONITOR or TV picture problem that appears as a set of moving dots along any vertical line in a picture where there is a colour contrast.

dot generator a form of signal generator used for COLOUR TELEVISION. The correct adjustment of a CATHODE-RAY TUBE, particularly a colour tube, is checked by connecting a dot generator to the receiver. This produces a pattern of dots that should be white and evenly spaced. Any irregularity in the spacing of the dots points to timebase or deflection coil faults, and any trace of colour fringes indicates gun CONVERGENCE faults.

dot matrix a method of displaying letters or digits as a pattern of dots. The method is used mainly in computers both for CATHODE-RAY TUBE and LCD screen displays and for printing on paper.

dot-matrix printer any printer that deposits ink as a pattern of fine dots. The term is mostly used of the impact dot-matrix printer in which a set of needles hits an inked ribbon that in turn strikes the surface of paper. An ink-jet printer, however, also uses a set of ink nozzles and operates as a matrix printer.

dot pattern an undesired effect on a TV picture that can be caused by insufficient SOUND CARRIER filtering.

dot pitch the distance between dots, typically the PIXELS of a display unit.

dot size the factor that determines the resolution of a display or printed output by setting the minimum size of a PIXEL.

dot size, monitor the average size of the smallest possible dot (see PIXEL) that can be displayed on a CRT or LCD screen.

dots per inch a measure of RESOLUTION of a MONITOR display, a PRINTER or a SCANNER (sense 2). Monitor manufacturers often prefer to quote the overall number of dots, such as 800×600 because the same dot structure can be used on MONITOR screens of very different size.

double-base diode see UNIJUNCTION.

double-beam CRT an analogue CATHODE-RAY TUBE that has two independent electron guns, producing two traces on the screen. The guns are usually interconnected so that the same TIMEBASE is applied to both guns, which also share focus and brightness circuits. The Y-PLATES are independent so that the two traces can display different signals. The double-beam tube is particularly useful for displaying phase differences between sine waves and time differences between pulses. At one time, some split-beam guns were made that used a single gun, but split the beam after the focus electrode. This provided two-beam operation, but with the disadvantage that one signal was displayed in inverted form. Some oscilloscopes simulate double (or multiple) beam action by BEAM SWITCHING.

double-beam oscilloscope or **dual-trace oscilloscope** a CATHODE-RAY OSCILLOSCOPE that can display two input traces, usually on the same timebase.

double cassette deck a cassette deck with two independent units connected to allow a tape to be copied from one to the other either at normal speed or at higher speeds.

double conversion see DOUBLE SUPERHET.

double data rate memory (DDR) a form of DYNAMIC RAM memory, currently in widespread use, in which both the rise and fall of the CLOCK pulse are used for timing, enabling the memory to operate at twice the clock rate.

double diffused MOS see D-MOS.

double-gate MOSFET a form of MOSFET with two separate GATES (sense 1), used particularly as a signal mixer because there is very little CROSSTALK between the gates.

double insulation the use of two layers of insulation between a live point and a user of equipment that has no EARTH connection.

double knock a security scheme that will sound alarms only if a detector is activated twice in five minutes (or other set period).

double modulation the use of a modulated SUBCARRIER that is in turn modulated on to a main carrier, as in analogue COLOUR TV systems.

double-pole changeover (DPCO) a form of SWITCH that has two switched contacts (poles) that both change connection when the switch is operated.

double-pole single-throw an on/off switch with two moving contacts (poles).

double-pole switch a form of SWITCH that has two unconnected contact sets so that two separate circuits can be switched.

double-sideband suppressed carrier (DSBSC) a DOUBLE-SIDEBAND TRANSMISSION signal which has had the CARRIER (sense 1) filtered out, leaving only the SIDEBANDS which contain all the information. See also SINGLE-SIDEBAND SUPPRESSED CARRIER.

double-sideband transmission the TRANSMISSION of both of the SIDEBANDs that are generated by conventional AMPLITUDE MODULATION along with the CARRIER (sense 1). Broadcast radio transmissions other than FM use double-sideband transmission with full carrier amplitude.

double-sided PCB a PRINTED CIRCUIT BOARD with tracks on each side, using PLATED-THROUGH CONNECTIONS to make connections between tracks on opposite sides.

double superhet or **triple detection receiver** a SUPERHETERODYNE RECEIVER with two conversion stages. The system is often used for receivers that have to cover a very wide range of input frequencies, such as a 'communications' receiver. One IF will be a high-frequency one, 10MHz to 30MHz, and the second IF will be at the conventional 470kHz. The system allows narrowband reception, good selectivity, and no risk of FREQUENCY PULLING of the local oscillators.

doublet see DIPOLE (sense 1).

double-tuned circuit a CIRCUIT that contains two inductors that have MUTUAL INDUCTANCE and that are each part of a tuned circuit.

down-converter a frequency changer circuit whose output is at a lower frequency than its input. The term usually denotes a converter from SHF or MICROWAVE frequencies to normal TV frequencies, as, for example, direct reception through a dish from a satellite.

down-counter a digital COUNTER circuit whose output count number decreases for each input pulse.

downforce see PLAYING WEIGHT.

downlead the cable connecting an AERIAL to a receiver.

downloading the reception of DIGITAL DATA from a remote source to any system, such as of an updated operating system to a DIGIBOX.

down sampling taking a sample of a digital signal at intervals, the action of a DECIMATOR.

downstream any part of a communications system that is nearer the user (receiver) than another section.

down time time for which equipment is not working, either because of repairs being carried out or planned maintenance. See also MEAN TIME TO REPAIR.

down-to-air (of a CATHODE-RAY TUBE or THERMIONIC VALVE) leaky, allowing air to enter and make operation impossible.

downward count or **countdown** a count that starts with a fixed number and decrements the count at each input pulse until zero is reached.

DPCM see DIFFERENTIAL PULSE CODE MODULATION.

DPCO see DOUBLE-POLE CHANGEOVER.

DPI see DOTS PER INCH.

DPSK see DIFFERENTIAL PHASE SHIFT KEYING.

DPST see DOUBLE-POLE SINGLE THROW.

DQPSK see DIFFERENTIAL QUADRATURE PHASE SHIFT KEYING.

drain the charge-collecting electrode of a FIELD EFFECT TRANSISTOR.

DRAM dynamic random-access memory: see DYNAMIC RAM.

drift **1.** a free movement of a beam of electrons that is not being acted on by an accelerating field. Such electrons will drift with a steady velocity, see DRIFT SPACE; KLYSTRON. **2.** an unwanted change in quantities such as the frequency of an oscillator or the voltage output of a supply. Drift often occurs in the first few minutes after switching on, and is mainly due to heating of components.

drift-cancelling oscillator see BARLOW-WADLEY LOOP.

drift space a part of an electron beam tube, particularly a KLYSTRON. There are no accelerating fields in this region, so each electron in a beam will continue with the velocity that it had as it entered this space. This allows bunching to occur (see BUNCHER).

drive a mechanical system for spinning a disc or moving a tape and reading or writing information used as part of a COMPUTER. See also FLOPPY DRIVE; HARD DRIVE.

drive bay the shelf within a computer casing that is used to retain DRIVES, such as hard drive, floppy drive, and CD-ROM drive or DVD ROM drive.

drive cables the cables, once parallel but now predominantly serial, that are used to connect the motherboard of a computer to the various drives.

drive capacity the number of bytes (or MB or GB) that a computer HARD DRIVE can store.

drive coil a coil located around a magnet whose input is a fluctuating signal and whose output is mechanical movements, as used for a LOUDSPEAKER or to move the heads of a HARD DRIVE.

drive controller see DISK CONTROLLER.

drive, loudspeaker see MOTOR UNIT.

driven aerial an aerial that is directly connected to a transmitter or receiver. An example is the dipole of a YAGI.

driver a CIRCUIT that provides power. A *line driver* provides output signal power at an IMPEDANCE that matches a line, so power can be transmitted along the line. A *bus driver* is a digital circuit that provides current amplification for the data or ADDRESS signal outputs of a MICROPROCESSOR, so allowing a large number of connections to be made to the bus (see FANOUT). A *driver stage* in an AUDIO AMPLIFIER is the STAGE that supplies signal to the output stage.

driver transformer a TRANSFORMER that is connected to act as a DRIVER. The term usually denotes a transformer that allows a SINGLE-ENDED transistor stage in an audio amplifier to provide signals to a COMPLEMENTARY STAGE, or to a more complex SINGLE-ENDED PUSH-PULL CIRCUIT.

driving impedance the IMPEDANCE of a driven CIRCUIT, usually a line, or a power-absorbing electromechanical system. A loudspeaker, for example, has a driving impedance that is composed of its coil resistance and its MOTIONAL IMPEDANCE.

droop or **sag** the reduction of voltage level of a pulse top. A square pulse ought to have a pulse top that is of constant voltage. If this voltage decays towards zero, it is said to droop, and the amount of droop is the difference between the ideal voltage level and the true level at the end of the top section. See Fig. 38. See also FALL TIME; OVERSHOOT; RIPPLE (sense 2); RISE TIME.

drop cable or **final loop** or **last mile** the connection between a telephone exchange and a subscriber, usually copper cable with a narrow bandwidth.

dropin a piece of nonmagnetic material on a MAGNETIC TAPE. A dropin is caused by contamination, and will result in loss of signal when the tape is replayed.

dropout a piece of tape with missing magnetic coating. Signal cannot be recorded on a dropout section, so this also results in loss of recorded signal.

dropout compensation (DOC) an analogue VIDEO RECORDING technique that detects a DROPOUT in the signal and fills it in with the signals from a previous line of picture.

dropout, picture missing portions of a picture from a worn VIDEOTAPE, caused by tape DROPOUT.

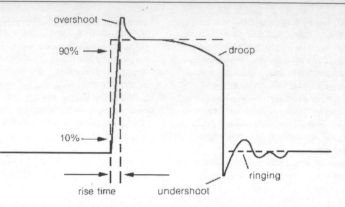

Fig. 38. **droop** or **sag**

dropout, regulator the minimum voltage difference that must exist between input and output voltages for REGULATOR action to operate.

dropper or **dropping resistor** a resistor that dissipates power by heating, and reduces circuit voltage. The term usually denotes a resistor in a circuit that is fed by DC mains.

drum 1. the revolving container used on a VIDEO CASSETTE RECORDER to carry the heads. 2. the central working part of a LASER PRINTER or a photocopier. The drum is made from a photoconductive (see PHOTOCONDUCTIVITY) material, one that conducts electricity when exposed to light. In operation, the revolving drum is charged overall, and then selectively discharged by scanning its surface with a LASER beam, making the drum conduct away the charge. The charge pattern remaining will pick up powdered ink (called toner) from a CARTRIDGE (sense 1), and this is transferred to paper when the paper is fed through. The toner is then melted on to the paper to fix it in place, the drum is scraped clean, and another page can be printed.

dry cell a PRIMARY CELL that uses a jelly ELECTROLYTE rather than a liquid. The name is unfortunate because a truly dry cell would have no output since IONS cannot move freely in a solid.

dry electrolytic an ELECTROLYTIC CAPACITOR that has suffered loss of fluid and which is no longer useful.

dry joint a faulty soldered connection. A dry joint occurs when the SOLDER has not been hot enough, has not been applied to the joint for long enough, or when FLUX (sense 2) has burned off completely. In a dry joint, there is a high resistance between each metal and the solder, and the joint may also be a RECTIFYING CONTACT. See also COLD JOINT.

DSB see DOUBLE-SIDEBAND TRANSMISSION.

DSBSC see DOUBLE-SIDEBAND SUPPRESSED CARRIER.

DSI see DIGITAL SPEECH INTERPOLATION.

DSL see DIGITAL SUBSCRIBER LINE.

DSLAM see DIGITAL SUBSCRIBER LINE ACCESS MULTIPLEXER.

DSM see DELTA-SIGMA MODULATION.

DSO see DIGITAL STORAGE OSCILLOSCOPE.

DSP see DIGITAL SIGNAL PROCESSING.

DSR see DATA SET READY.

DSSS see DIRECT SEQUENCE SPREAD SPECTRUM.

DSU data switching unit.

DTE see DATA TERMINAL EQUIPMENT.

DTF see DYNAMIC TRACK FOLLOWING.

DTH (direct to home) see DIRECT BROADCASTING BY SATELLITE.

DTL see DIODE-TRANSISTOR LOGIC.

DTM data terrain mapping.

DTMF see DUAL TONE MULTI-FREQUENCY DIALLING.

DTV   see DIGITAL TELEVISION.

D2-MAC   see MAC.

DTX   see DISCONTINUOUS TRANSMISSION.

D-type (or **D type**) **connector**   a form of D-shaped multiway connector that was devised originally in 25-pin format for SERIAL connections to a teleprinter or other communications equipment. Other connectors of the same shape have been manufactured with 15-pin or 9-pin connections.

D-type flip-flop or **D-type latch**   a form of IC FLIP-FLOP that has a CLOCK input and a data input. The data input (the D of the title) is normally disabled until the clock pulse arrives. When a clock pulse arrives, data present at the D input is transferred to the device output, and is held until the next clock pulse. Some types of D-type flip-flop will LATCH at the leading edge of the clock, some at the trailing edge, some on the top according to the design. See also EDGE-TRIGGERED.

dual capstan   a cassette tape technique that uses a separate CAPSTAN drive on each side of the record-play head to achieve better tape tension and speed stability without the use of TAPE PRESSURE PADS.

dual-converter   a form of ANALOGUE TO DIGITAL CONVERTER that uses a two-stage action with one unit handling values in the range 0 to 255, and the other handling the range 256 to 65280, so that the output is two 8-bit numbers that can be combined as a 16-bit number. The advantage is that this split action is faster than can be obtained using a single 16-bit conversion.

dual feed   a SATELLITE DISH system that allows reception from two satellites, using a single dish with two LOW-NOISE BOXes and DOWNLEADS.

dual gap head   an ERASE HEAD for use in an audio CASSETTE recorder that uses two gaps to give more erasure without requiring excessive current.

dual-gate FET   a form of signal mixer device. The FIELD EFFECT TRANSISTOR channel is controlled by two GATES (sense 1), so that signal on either or both gates will affect the channel current. This forms

an excellent mixing circuit for high-frequency receivers, because there is virtually no connection between the two gates. The device is used to a very large extent in FM and TV receivers.

dual-in-line (DIL)   see DUAL-INLINE PACKAGE.

dual-inline memory module (DIMM)   a RAM memory board for computers, using 168 pins, replacing the older single units that had to be used in pairs.

dual-inline package (DIP)   a form of packaging used for IC chips, in which the casing is connected to a PCB by way of two parallel lines of pins.

dual processor   (of a computer) using two MICROPROCESSORS working in parallel to allow much higher processing speeds to be achieved, given suitable software.

dual ring network   a network using two rings so that the data flow is not affected when one ring is broken.

dual slope ADC or **dual slope A/D**   a form of integrating ANALOGUE TO DIGITAL CONVERTER in which an input current charges a capacitor for a fixed time and the capacitor then discharges at a constant current. The discharge time is digitized and the count number is used to represent the value of input current.

dual technology detector   the use in a security system of both infra-red and microwave detectors, resulting in a very low rate of false alarms.

dual tone multi-frequency dialling (DTMF)   the telephone dialling system that replaced PULSE DIALLING by using combinations of frequencies for each dialled digit.

dual trace oscilloscope   see DOUBLE-BEAM OSCILLOSCOPE.

dubbing   the mixing of recorded sound or video SIGNALS to form a single signal. The process of sound dubbing is commonly used with multi-track RECORDING methods, in which each instrument has its own microphone and provides a separate recording track. Dubbing allows the sound engineers more control over the sound of a recorded performance, but may produce results that are quite unlike any live performance.

Video dubbing can edit the video and add sound to a video that is silent or has a different sound track. See also LINEAR EDITING; NONLINEAR EDITING.

Dummer, G.R. the scientist working at the Radar Research Establishment who first suggested that complete circuits could be made out of semiconductor material, so anticipating the INTEGRATED CIRCUIT.

dummy aerial (or antenna) see ARTIFICIAL AERIAL.

dummy driver a device for servicing digital circuit faults by providing a set of simulated inputs.

dummy leads see COMPENSATING LEADS.

dummy load a power-absorbing circuit that acts like a LOAD and is used for test purposes. A loudspeaker, for example, can be replaced by a resistor of the correct value (about 8 ohms) and power rating. This will not allow the effects of MOTIONAL IMPEDANCE to be simulated, but does allow testing of such features as the power-frequency characteristics.

dummy pad see VIA.

duo-binary code a form of code in which a logic 0 is represented by no transition, and a logic 1 by alternate positive and negative pulses, producing a code with no DC COMPONENT.

duplex a two-way simultaneous signalling operation such as a telegraph system in which messages can be sent over the lines in both directions at the same time. Compare HALF-DUPLEX; SIMPLEX.

duplex operation the use of a single digital line for simultaneous two-way traffic.

duplexer a WAVEGUIDE arrangement that permits the same HORN AERIAL to be used for both transmitting and receiving. See also ATR; TR.

duress code a security action in which a silent alarm is sent to a remote location when an incorrect code has been tapped on a control panel.

dust core or powdered-iron core a form of magnetic core for an inductor. A dust core is made from powdered magnetic material bound by a resin. The dust is itself an insulator so that EDDY CURRENTS

cannot flow, and the main source of losses is MAGNETIC HYSTERESIS. Dust cores are used in coils for frequencies in the range 100kHz to 100MHz, but the materials that are used for high-frequency signals need to be carefully selected.

duty cycle a unit of repeated on and off operations, such as a SYSTEM that is pulsed on and off (see PULSE).

duty factor or duty ratio the ratio of on-time to total DUTY CYCLE time for a pulse.

DV see DIGITAL VIDEO.

DVB see DIGITAL VIDEO BROADCASTING.

DVB-S digital video broadcasting by satellite.

DVC see DIGITAL VIDEO CASSETTE.

DVD see DIGITAL VERSATILE DISC.

DVD compatibility the problem posed by the existence of three competing systems for DVD RECORDING for domestic use. The DVD +R/+RW and the DVD –R/–RW types require different media, but can be replayed by either type of recorder, or by any DVD player. The DVD-RAM system uses a different system that is not compatible with the others, but has some advantages for users, such as the ability to record and play simultaneously. All three compete with the use of hard drive recorders for the domestic digital recording market.

DVD –R one of the competing forms of DIGITAL VERSATILE DISC that can be written once and replayed many times, but not re-written. It can be read by any normal DVD-ROM drive. See also DVD COMPATIBILITY; DVD–RW; DVD+RW; DVD+R; DVD-RAM.

DVD –RW one of the competing rewritable forms of DVD that creates discs that are compatible with normal DVD players, and can read CD audio, CD-ROM, and DVD video discs. See also DVD COMPATIBILITY; DVD+RW; DVD-R; DVD+R; DVD-RAM.

DVD +R one of the competing forms of DIGITAL VERSATILE DISC that can be written once and replayed many times, but not re-written. It can be read by any normal DVD-ROM drive. See also DVD COMPATIBILITY; DVD–RW; DVD+RW; DVD-R; DVD-RAM.

DVD +RW   one of the competing
rewritable forms of DIGITAL VERSATILE DISC
that creates discs that are compatible
with normal DVD players, and can read
CD audio, CD-ROM, and DVD video discs.
See also DVD COMPATIBILITY; DVD +R; DVD –R;
DVD –RW; DVD-RAM.

DVD-RAM a form of DIGITAL VERSATILE DISC
housed in a container (*cartridge*) that can
be written, erased and re-written many
times, so that it can be used like a RAM
system. DVD-RAM can be written and
read almost simultaneously, like a hard
drive, and allows video editing. The disc
life is long, around 100,000 record/rewrite
sessions. DVD-RAM cannot be read by a
DVD player, nor by drives intended for
DVD-R/RW or DVD+R/RW. See also DVD
COMPATIBILITY; DVD–RW; DVD+RW; DVD-R;
DVD+R.

DVD recorder or **DVD rewriter**   a device
that can record DIGITAL VIDEO on a blank
DVD, usually with facilities to convert an
ANALOGUE input to digital and a digital
output to analogue.

D-VHS   the JVC digital camcorder cassette
RECORDING system that maintains
compatibility with the older analogue
VHS standards, allowing physically
similar cassettes, tape mechanism, and
the use of cheaper ferric-oxide tape.

DVM   see DIGITAL VOLTMETER.

Dword   a digital unit of four BYTES, 32 BITS.

dye polymer technology   the use of
dyestuffs that change their reflection
characteristics on being struck by a laser
beam, used for fabricating recordable CD
and DVD discs.

dynamic   (of a SYSTEM) used under
working conditions with signals applied.
A dynamic measurement, for example,
means a measurement on a circuit that is
operating with power on and a signal
input, as distinct from a measurement
made with no signals, or with power
switched off.

dynamic amplitude modulation (DAM)
a power-saving modulation system in
which the CARRIER (sense 1) is operated
at reduced amplitude up to the 40%
modulation level, but increased levels of

carrier amplitude are used for higher
modulation levels.

dynamic carrier control (DCC)   see
DYNAMIC AMPLITUDE MODULATION.

dynamic characteristic   a graph of input
and output voltages or currents taken
under working conditions for a device.

dynamic convergence   the CONVERGENCE
of a set of electron beams when scanned.
For a COLOUR TELEVISION tube, the STATIC
CONVERGENCE means that the three
electron beams of the guns strike the
correct phosphor stripes at the centre
of the tube. When the tube is scanned,
however, the convergence may not be
correct at the edges. This is a dynamic
convergence problem, and is solved by
applying correcting signals, derived from
the timebase waveforms, to the
convergence coils.

dynamic drum   a VIDEO CASSETTE RECORDER
mechanism, invented by JVC, that allows
the drum to be tilted to achieve STILL-
FRAME action, previously obtainable only
with the Sony Betamax™ recorders.

dynamic error   measurement error caused
by loading of the measuring instrument.
See also STATIC ERROR.

dynamic impedance   the slope of a graph
of current plotted against voltage for a
device that has no constant value of
impedance.

dynamiciser   a circuit that converts
parallel digital signals into a single
BITSTREAM.

dynamic memory   see DYNAMIC RAM.

dynamic microphone   see MOVING-IRON
MICROPHONE.

dynamic noise filter   a form of noise
FILTER whose high frequency cutoff is
varied according to the signal level,
linked to the response of the human ear.

dynamic RAM (DRAM)   a form of
computer MEMORY in which each BIT is
stored as CHARGE on a semiconductor
CAPACITOR. The charge leaks away unless
regenerated by special refresh circuits, but
the principle can be used to construct
single chips with very large memory
storage. Most of the memory of a modern
computer is of this type.

dynamic range the available range of output signal from a device. The lower limit of output is set by the noise level, and the upper limit by BOTTOMING or SATURATION (sense 1). The dynamic range is usually quoted in dB.

dynamic range the range of recorded sound from the softest audible tones to the loudest that can be handled.

dynamic resistance 1. the resistance of a PARALLEL RESONANT CIRCUIT at the RESONANT FREQUENCY. 2. the resistance of any device measured with AC of a stated frequency.

dynamic routing strategy a NETWORK (sense 2) system that will direct messages using a different route if the shortest route is busy or faulty.

dynamic track following or **dynamic tracking** a method of improving VIDEO CASSETTE recording. Conventional video recorders use revolving heads that scan across the moving tape at high speed. Because of mechanical tolerances, there must be a 'guard band' of unrecorded tape between recorded bands. If the recording and replay head is mounted on a PIEZOELECTRIC CRYSTAL transducer, it is possible to lay down much more closely spaced tracks, and to follow any track by tiny adjustments of the head position, achieved by a servo-FEEDBACK system. This was pioneered by Philips for their 8-hour play VIDEO CASSETTE system, now abandoned.

dynamic tracking filter demodulation a circuit for FM DEMODULATION that has a narrow bandwidth and a centre frequency that follows the frequency changes of the FM CARRIER (sense 1). This produces a very useful increase in SIGNAL-TO-NOISE RATIO.

dynamo an electrical generator that uses a rotating coil (*rotor*) and a magnetic field (*stator*). By convention, a dynamo picks up current from the coils by using a COMMUTATOR and brushes. This gives an output that is, for a single coil, the same as that from a full-wave rectifier. If slip rings are used for making connections, the machine is described as an ALTERNATOR.

Nowadays, it is more common to use a magnetic rotor fed with DC, and take the AC from the stator to a RECTIFIER system to obtain DC. Such a system is easier to control by electronic methods, using the electronic system to control the current to the rotor.

dynamo principle the generation of a POTENTIAL DIFFERENCE between the ends of a wire that moves in a magnetic field.

dynode an ELECTRODE that acts as a multiplier of electrons. When a fast-moving electron strikes a material, it may be reflected, absorbed, or cause SECONDARY EMISSION. If the accelerating potential is in the region of 200V to 2000V, then secondary emission is more common. This means that for each electron incident on the surface, more than one electron will be emitted. For some materials, notably elements such as caesium that are also photoelectric emitters the number of secondary electrons per primary electron is high, of the order of three to seven.

A dynode consists of a metal mesh or perforated plate that is coated with a material that has a high secondary emission ratio. When an electron beam strikes this dynode, the beam leaving the dynode is much denser in electrons than the beam striking. In other words, the beam current has been amplified. This form of amplification is virtually noiseless, and so is used extensively in photoelectric devices as a way of obtaining very great sensitivity.

dynode chain a series chain of resistors with a DYNODE fed from each junction of two resistors. This chain ensures that the correct relative accelerating voltages are applied to each dynode in a chain of, typically, four to eight dynodes.

e and i sections see E-CORE.

EAPROM see ELECTRICALLY ALTERABLE PROGRAMMABLE READ-ONLY MEMORY.

Early effect the effect of collector-emitter voltage changes in a BIPOLAR JUNCTION TRANSISTOR on the BASE junction, making the gain dependent on signal amplitude.

early warning RADAR any radar system designed to give warning of hostile aircraft or missiles at the greatest possible distance.

EAROM (electrically alterable read-only memory) a type of programmable memory that can be erased and reprogrammed without removing it from its circuit. The EAROM is now widely used for computer BIOS chips to allow updating without the need to remove or replace the chip.

earphone a miniature electrical to sound TRANSDUCER. The earphone is designed to be used in contact with the ear, so comparatively good sound quality can be achieved with none of the complications of loudspeaker enclosures, and with much lower power levels.

earth or **ground** any zero-voltage point. The earth itself is taken as being of zero voltage because its potential is not greatly affected by small changes of charge.

earth bond resistance the allowable resistance of an earth lead in a consumer appliance, usually around 0R1, never exceeding 0R5.

earth bonding the making of a connection to EARTH. This is typically done by burying a metal plate in the earth and connecting to this. An alternative is to use metal waterpipes but care must be taken to connect to a pipe that passes through the ground. Pipes for central heating and hot water supply must not be used. The use nowadays of plastics for water and other pipes means that very great care is needed in earthing equipment,

particularly transmitters. Electrical circuits are now 'multiple-earthed', meaning that all pipework and other metal is bonded to a common earth that is also used for the AC supply earth.

earth capacitance the CAPACITANCE of any point in a circuit to the EARTH. If this capacitance is variable, it may lead to tuning errors in RF receivers.

earth current a CURRENT flowing to or through the EARTH. A current will flow to the earth if an insulation fault develops in earthed equipment. This type of fault should cause fuses to blow, or EARTH-LEAKAGE CONTACT BREAKERS to open. Currents that flow through the earth may cause electrolytic corrosion of metals, including EARTH BONDING plates.

earth fault a BREAKDOWN of insulation that causes current to flow to earth.

Earth footprint the area on the Earth that receives a usable signal from a SATELLITE.

earth loop or **ground loop** a cause of unwanted FEEDBACK of signal that is caused by using separated earth connections in a circuit. The currents flowing between the two earth points result in a potential difference that provides the unwanted feedback signal.

earth loop impedance the total IMPEDANCE of an EARTH connection (not simply resistance).

earth mat a set of metal conductors buried in the earth under an AERIAL, used to improve the conductivity of the earth in the region of the aerial. See also COUNTERPOISE.

earth node a point where a number of circuits are connected to Earth (ground).

earth plane or **ground plane** a sheet of metal that is earthed or (particularly in a battery-operated circuit) used as an EARTH. The surrounding metal on a PRINTED CIRCUIT BOARD is often used as a form of earth plane.

earth potential or **zero potential**   the zero point of potential (see ELECTRIC POTENTIAL). All potentials on earth are measured relative to the potential of the earth, which does not change rapidly.

earth radius factor   the ratio of apparent radius to true radius of the Earth (approximately 4:3) caused by the effects of refraction. See also RADIO HORIZON.

earth return   the return half of a CIRCUIT in which a wire is used for the first half. An earth return was used in early Morse-code telegraphy.

earthing   the connection of any conducting object to EARTH.

earthing strap   a metal strap earthed through a 1M resistor and connected to the wrist of anyone handling MOSFETs or other electrostatically sensitive devices. This ensures that any electrostatic voltages developed by movement are harmlessly discharged. The resistor ensures that large currents cannot flow if the operator comes into contact with a high voltage.

earth-leakage contact breaker (ELCB) a safety device that has largely replaced the use of fuses in domestic AC supply systems. The ELCB operates by balancing the live line current and the return (neutral) line current. Any imbalance must be due to EARTH current, and causes the breaker to trip, opening the circuits. The ELCB can be manually reset after the fault is cleared. An ELCB should be used in conjunction with any mains-operated equipment that is used out of doors.

EBCDIC   see EXTENDED BINARY CODED DECIMAL INTERCHANGE CODE.

E-beam   an electron-beam pattern writing system for the design of ASICs.

EBU   see EUROPEAN BROADCASTING UNION.

ECA   exchangeable card architecture: see PLUG AND PLAY.

ECC   1. emitter-coupled circuit, see DIFFERENTIAL AMPLIFIER. 2. see ERROR-CORRECTION CODING.

eccentric line   a COAXIAL CABLE type of line in which the inner electrode is not central.

E-cell   an ELECTROLYTIC timer that is cheap to construct and can be used to indicate service intervals. The principle of the device is based on the deposition of metal in a needle-shape from a solution, and the length of the metal needle indicates the time for which current has flowed.

ECG   see ELECTROCARDIOGRAPH.

ECH   see EDDY CURRENT HEATER.

echo   a reflected wave of sound or electromagnetism. The return beam of a RADAR system is called an echo. TV signals, particularly on UHF can be reflected by objects, and cause disturbing effects. For example, if an echo is strong, and not too far out of line from the main signal direction, it will cause a second image on the TV receiver screen. This is particularly noticeable if the echo signal is delayed, because this causes the second image to be displaced. An echo image of this type is termed a *ghost*. Ghosting is dealt with by using more DIRECTIONAL AERIALS, or by shifting the aerial position. Ghosting can also be caused by a long and incorrectly terminated transmission line (see TERMINATION).

echo cancelling or **echo suppression**   a method used to avoid echo interference in digital DUPLEX communications by adding the echo signals (usually an echo of the transmitted signal) in ANTIPHASE.

echoplex   a signalling system in which the integrity of a message is checked by returning it to the sender.

echo sounding   the location of underwater objects by using RADAR methods with sound waves in water.

echo suppression   see ECHO CANCELLING.

ECL   see EMITTER-COUPLED LOGIC.

eclipse shutdown   the shutdown for about an hour in transmissions from high-power satellites because of the effect of the shadow of the earth in an eclipse on the solar cells. The effect persists for periods of about four weeks.

E-core   one of a pair of core shapes (the other being I-CORE) for a conventional transformer, allowing the core to be built up. See also C-CORE.

EDA   see ELECTRONIC DESIGN AUTOMATION.

eddy current   an unwanted current flowing within the iron core of a TRANSFORMER, causing energy loss. Eddy currents in metals are the result of voltages induced by the varying magnetic field around a transformer. They can be reduced by dividing the transformer core into a number of thin plates or LAMINATIONS. See also EDDY CURRENT HEATER.

eddy current heater (ECH) or **induction heater**   a method of heating metal objects without making physical connections. The object is surrounded by or placed near a coil in which a large current of high-frequency signal is flowing. The induced eddy currents will then heat the metal. Metals can be heated in a vacuum in order to remove absorbed gas, or melted by using an ECH. Eddy current heating can occur in a TRANSFORMER as an unwanted effect.

edge   the sharp rise or fall at the start or end of a PULSE. The LEADING EDGE is at the start of the pulse and the TRAILING EDGE at the end.

edge card   a CIRCUIT CARD that is fitted with an EDGE CONNECTOR. An edge card offers a cheap, simple and convenient way of adding facilities (such as additional graphics capabilities, extra memory, communications facilities) to a computer. A computer that can use extra edge cards, is almost infinitely expandable, and does not readily become out of date. See also MOTHERBOARD.

edge connector   a connector that is formed as part of a PRINTED CIRCUIT BOARD. The metal at the edge of the board is shaped into a set of strips, each strip connected to some part of the circuit. Connections are made by a plug that grips the board and uses metal springs to make contact to each strip.

edge effect   any disturbance of a field by an edge of material, such as the non-uniform rapidly changing ELECTRIC FIELD at the edge of a CAPACITOR plate.

edge emitter   a type of LIGHT-EMITTING DIODE whose structure is similar to that of a SEMICONDUCTOR LASER, used as an optical transmitter.

edge triggered   (of a flip-flop) whose transition is initiated by the EDGE of a pulse. Contrast LEVEL TRIGGERED.

edge triggered logic   a sequential logic circuit that is triggered by a pulse edge.

edge triggered flip-flop   a form of FLIP-FLOP, such as the D-TYPE FLIP-FLOP, that is triggered by one edge, usually the LEADING EDGE, of a CLOCK PULSE. Contrast MASTER-SLAVE FLIP-FLOP.

EDI   see ELECTRONIC DATA INTERCHANGE.

EDP   see ELECTRONIC DATA PROCESSING.

EDTV   see EXTENDED DEFINITION TELEVISION.

EEPLD™   electrically erasable programmable logic device: a reusable type of PROGRAMMABLE LOGIC DEVICE.

EEPROM   electrically erasable programmable read-only memory: a form of PROM that can be erased by an electrical signal rather than by UV light.

effective aperture   the equivalent diameter of a MICROWAVE DISH that contributes to the signal handling, excluding the portion masked by the FEED HORN and its supports. See also BLOCKING LOSS.

effective electrical length   the length of an AERIAL ELEMENT that is electrically active, usually larger than the physical length because the end of the aerial rod or wire is not the end of the field around it.

effective height   a figure for height of a vertical RECEIVING AERIAL, derived from the ratio of voltage delivered to FIELD STRENGTH.

effective permittivity   a value of PERMITTIVITY for a microwave STRIP LINE formed on an insulator. The effective value is lower than the measured value for the same dielectric used in a conventional capacitor.

effective radiated power (ERP)   the equivalent power figure for a TRANSMITTING AERIAL, obtained by assuming that the radiation is from a simple DIPOLE AERIAL. The ERP is often much higher than the actual power if the signal is beamed.

effective resistance   the resistance to AC, measured by the dissipated power. By measuring power and dividing by the square of current, or by dividing the square of voltage by power, a figure of resistance is obtained. This may not correspond to DC resistance value, because it includes a resistance equivalent for power lost by EDDY CURRENTS, HYSTERESIS, etc.

effective series resistance (ESR) the resistance of an ELECTROLYTIC CAPACITOR measured as loss of power when a current flows.

effective value 1. a value of some quantity measured under operating conditions. 2. the ROOT MEAN SQUARE (sense 2) value of an alternating quantity.

effects of current electric current flowing in any medium will cause effects of heating and magnetic field, and flowing through a molten or dissolved salt will cause chemical separation of the constituents of the salt.

efficiency the percentage conversion of energy, usually to another form. The efficiency of a radio transmitter power amplifier stage is the output power as a percentage of the DC supply power (also known as the *input power*) to the stage.

EFM see EIGHT TO FOURTEEN MODULATION.

EHF see EXTREMELY HIGH FREQUENCY.

EHT (extra high tension) or **EHV (extra high voltage)** a very high voltage supply for a CATHODE-RAY TUBE, CAMERA TUBE, DYNODE CHAIN, or radio transmitter. Any voltage higher than 1000 V (1kV) is in the EHT range.

EHT supply a source of EHT, formerly supplied from the mains using a transformer and rectifiers but now more usually obtained from an oscillator. See also VOLTAGE MULTIPLIER.

EHV (extra high voltage) see EHT.

EIA see ELECTRONIC INDUSTRIES ASSOCIATION.

EIAJ Electronic Industries Association of Japan.

E-I core see E-CORE; I-CORE.

EIDE (extended integrated device electronics) a set of interfacing circuits that are a development of the IDE system, and now incorporated as part of the ATA-2 standard and other interfacing circuits needed for the drive.

Eidophor™ an early form of LIGHT-VALVE used in PROJECTION TV displays, now obsolete.

eigentones or **room modes** the acoustic room RESONANCES caused by groups of reflections that travel to and fro in phase within a space between walls or between floor and ceiling.

eight to fourteen modulation or **EFM** the transformation of an 8-bit data word into a 14-bit SYMBOL so as to avoid an excessive number of identical bits or a set of alternating bits such as a 101010…

eight track a tape medium using wide tape in an auto-reversing cartridge with eight tracks. This was popular at one time for car audio, but is now obsolete.

8-4-2-1 binary the conventional system of BINARY (sense 1) code with the position of a digit indicating its weighting, unlike GRAY CODE.

EIS see ELECTRONIC IMAGE STABILIZER.

EISA 1. see ELECTRONICS INDUSTRY STANDARDS ASSOCIATION. 2. extended ISA: an enhanced version of the old AT BUS design for personal computers, later known as industry standard architecture (ISA).

elastoresistance the change of electrical resistance with stress. Stretching a film of a conductor will lengthen the specimen and also cause its cross section to decrease. Both of these effects will also cause the resistance to rise. The effect is used for strain measurements in STRAIN GAUGES.

E-layer or **Heaviside layer** or **Kennelly-Heaviside layer** the layer in the IONOSPHERE that lies approximately between 90 and 150km above the Earth's surface. It reflects the medium frequency range, and was one of the first of the ionospheric layers to be identified. Oliver Heaviside (1850–1925) predicted the possibility of the ionosphere, and Arthur Kennelly (1861–1939) proved the existence of the layers and measured their heights by using RADAR techniques.

ELCB see EARTH LEAKAGE CONTACT BREAKER.

electret a permanently-charged insulating material. Electrets are made by allowing molten plastics to solidify in a large electric field, and have been used in the construction of capacitor microphones and (VINYL DISC) gramophone pickups.

electrical latching a LATCHING action (such as in a latching relay) carried out by electrical methods rather than by mechanical methods.

electrically alterable programmable read-only memory (EAPROM) a form of PROM that can be re-written by altering the electrical voltage applied to a pin, and then writing data.

electrically alterable read-only memory see EAROM.

electrically erasable programmable read-only memory see EEPROM.

electrical recording on disc the system formerly used for sound recording (see RECORDING OF SOUND), in which an amplified audio signal was used to vibrate a cutting stylus that was touching a metal, wax or plastic disc. The stylus was carried on a set of arms that were driven so as to cut a spiral groove. See also COMPACT DISC; VINYL DISC.

electrical rotation the maximum angle through which the shaft of a POTENTIOMETER (sense 1) can be turned while altering the resistance ratio. This is always less than the mechanical rotation because of end-connections.

electric axis the direction in which the maximum potential difference is developed when a PIEZOELECTRIC CRYSTAL is stressed.

electric charge see CHARGE.

electric circuit a complete path for electric current.

electric eye see PHOTOCELL.

electric field a field of force surrounding a charged particle within which another charged particle will experience a force of attraction or repulsion, depending on the sign of its charge. The intensity (*strength*) of the electric field at a point is equal to the force per unit change at that point. The symbol, for electric field is E, where $E = F/Q$, with Q = charge in coulombs and F = force in newtons. The unit of electric field is therefore newtons per coulomb. An electric field can also be caused by a varying MAGNETIC FLUX. The strength of an electric field at any point is equal to the POTENTIAL GRADIENT.

electric flux the 'flow' of an electric field through a surface, equal to the integral of (field × area) for a surface at right angles to the field direction. Compare MAGNETIC FLUX.

electric lockset an electrically operated lock, cylindrical or mortise, that can be electronically controlled as part of a security system.

electric polarization the separation of charge on an object so that one end is positive and the opposite end negative.

electric potential or **voltage** a measurement of the electrical equivalent of height. Symbol: V; unit: volt. The potential at a point is measured as the POTENTIAL DIFFERENCE from EARTH POTENTIAL, and is defined as the amount of work done per unit CHARGE when a charge is moved from that point to infinity. The unit is the VOLT, equal to one joule per coulomb, and the symbol is V. Potential and particularly POTENTIAL DIFFERENCE is easily measurable, unlike charge.

electric shock paralysis and burning caused by a flow of current through the body; fatal if the current flows through the heart.

electroacoustics the study of devices that work with electric and sound signals, including MICROPHONES, LOUDSPEAKERS and all forms of sound TRANSDUCERS, including ULTRASONIC transducers.

electroacoustic transducer any TRANSDUCER that converts electric waveforms into sound or vice versa.

electrocardiograph (ECG) an instrument for displaying and RECORDING heart currents. The operation of the heart, like any other muscle, is controlled by small electrical signals that can be picked up on probes and displayed on a CATHODE-RAY TUBE or on a chart recorder. An electrocardiograph normally uses BALANCED AMPLIFIERS because of the very small voltages that are being picked up. Earthing (see EARTH) is very important, because any fault current transmitted to the probe electrodes would be fatal.

electrode a conductor in an electronic device that is at some ELECTRIC POTENTIAL and which can collect or emit charged particles.

electrodynamic (of an electrical device) operated by the mechanical forces between wires carrying CURRENTS, particularly in coil form.

electroencephalograph   an instrument that detects and displays the voltage waveforms of the brain, using the same general techniques as the ELECTROCARDIOGRAPH.

electroluminescence   the giving out of light from a material when an ELECTRIC FIELD is applied. Materials that are electroluminescent will give out light when subjected to an alternating electric field, using a construction like a CAPACITOR with one transparent plate.

electroluminescent lamp   a light source that makes use of ELECTROLUMINESCENCE.

electrolysis   the effect of the flow of IONS in a molten or dissolved solid. By immersing conducting plates into the material, one positive (the ANODE), the other negative (the CATHODE, sense 3), the ions can be collected. The combination of ion collection with chemical changes can be a very valuable source of pure materials, including some elements that cannot be prepared in any other way (aluminium, for example).

electrolyte   a liquid that conducts because of the presence of IONS. Conducting liquids include molten salts, and water solutions of acids, salts and alkalis. Some ionic materials such as liquid ammonia also form ionic solutions.

electrolyte, cell   the conducting liquid or jelly, usually acidic or alkaline, that is in contact with the negative ELECTRODE of a CELL.

electrolyte leakage   a common cause of trouble in miniaturized equipment using batteries or ELECTROLYTIC CAPACITORS, particularly CAMCORDERS, because the leaking electrolyte not only affects the performance of the battery or capacitor but will corrode printed circuit board tracks and components leads as well as mechanical components.

electrolytic capacitor   a type of capacitor that provides very large capacitance values in a small volume. The simplest electrolytic capacitor consists of aluminium sheets sandwiching a piece of blotting paper that has been soaked in aluminium perborate. Applying a voltage

to this arrangement causes a thin film of insulating oxide to form on one sheet, and it is the large capacitance across this film that is utilized. The capacitance value can be increased by increasing the area of one plate by perforating it and folding it. The capacitor is sealed to avoid evaporation of the electrolyte liquid.

Though high values of capacitance can be achieved, there is always a comparatively large leakage current. The capacitor is POLARIZED (sense 2), which means that the voltage must always be applied to it in the same polarity as was originally used to form the insulating layer. Failure to observe this can lead to explosive failure. The voltage that can be permitted across the capacitor is also low, and very few electrolytic capacitors can be used at DC voltage levels of over 500V. The capacitors are also temperature sensitive, and the voltage rating must be drastically reduced when high AMBIENT TEMPERATURES are present. Many specifications for military equipment, or equipment that is to be used under a wide range of environmental conditions, do not permit the use of electrolytic capacitors or permit only the TANTALUM ELECTROLYTIC type to be used.

electrolytic corrosion   the corrosion of metals that are damp and which can form one ELECTRODE of a CELL.

electrolytic polishing   a method of obtaining a very high polish by removing irregularities from the surface of a metal. The metal is used as the ANODE in an electrolytic cell.

electrolytic recording   a very old system of marking paper for FACSIMILE reception, using impregnated conducting paper that will change colour when a current flows through it from a metal stylus.

electrolytic, tantalum   see TANTALYTIC.

electromagnet   a magnet that has a high FLUX DENSITY value only when current flows through coils. Any coil of wire will act as an electromagnet, but the effect is greatly enhanced when a core of FERROMAGNETIC material such as soft iron (see SOFT MAGNETIC MATERIAL) is used.

electromagnetic communication the use of electromagnetic waves for communicating signals usually by way of a CARRIER (sense 1) wave.

electromagnetic compatibility (EMC) the requirement that an electronic device should neither interfere with other equipment, nor suffer from interference from other equipment. A European standard for tolerable interference exists, and equipment that has passed the compatibility tests is marked with a CE symbol.

electromagnetic damping the reduction of oscillation of a moving coil in a magnetic field by short-circuiting the ends of the coil so that an opposing force is generated, see LENZ'S LAW.

electromagnetic deflection the deflection of an electron beam, such as in a CATHODE-RAY TUBE by electromagnets. The neck of the tube is surrounded by a set of coils. When a current of SAWTOOTH WAVEFORM flows in the coils, the beam is deflected to form a linear TIMEBASE. Two pairs of coils are used to form a TV RASTER scan. For RADAR use, a radial scan is used, and this is usually done using three coils at 120° angles. The phase of the sawtooth current in the three coils is controlled so as to alter the position of the end of each scan.

electromagnetic field the combined electric and magnetic field radiated by any conductor carrying an alternating current. The fields are polarized at 90° to each other, and the rate of propagation in free space is 3×10^8 m/s.

electromagnetic focusing the focusing of an ELECTRON BEAM by electromagnets. This is now unusual, because modern TV receiver tubes use electrostatic focusing. Electromagnetic focusing was used on early designs, and for some radar tubes.

electromagnetic induction the production of a POTENTIAL DIFFERENCE by changing MAGNETIC FLUX. A potential difference will be produced between two points if the magnetic flux at right angles to a line drawn between the points changes. If the two points are joined by a conductor, the potential difference can be used to produce a current. This is the basis of generators; alternators or dynamos. The size of potential difference is equal to the rate of change of flux (Faraday's law), and its polarity is such that if current flowed, it would set up a flux change in the reverse direction (Lenz's law). If no conductor is present, the changing magnetic flux causes an ELECTRIC FIELD.

electromagnetic interference (EMI) unwanted signals that can enter through mains cables, connecting leads or by EARTH LOOPS.

electromagnetic lens a lens for ELECTRON BEAMS produced by using coils to form a magnetic field that will focus the electron beams. An electromagnetic lens is easier to work with than an ELECTROSTATIC LENS when very high energy electron beams are used, as in electron microscopes and some electron beam tubes.

electromagnetic pickup any TRANSDUCER for VINYL DISCS based on moving coil, moving magnet or variable reluctance principles.

electromagnetic pulse (EMP) a large surge of electromagnetic energy that can damage semiconductors, due to lightning, inductive BACK-EMF, or a nuclear explosion.

electromagnetic radiation the radiation of energy in the form of varying electric and magnetic fields (static fields do not cause wave radiation). Radiation is a consequence of the laws of electrostatics and of electromagnetism that are gathered together in MAXWELL'S EQUATIONS. The fundamental cause of electromagnetic radiation is the acceleration of charged particles, so that any alternating current is capable of causing radiation. In practice, radiation is achieved efficiently only for frequencies that are of the order of 100kHz upwards. Light is one (high frequency) form of electromagnetic radiation. See ELECTROMAGNETIC SPECTRUM.

electromagnetic relay see RELAY.

electromagnetic screening earthed casings made from metals that will shield equipment from electromagnetic wave interference.

electromagnetic spectrum the range of known and possible ELECTROMAGNETIC RADIATION. This range extends from very long waves, low frequency, at 100kHz or even less, up to very short wavelengths (high frequencies) such as x-rays and gamma radiation. The spectrum includes all known radio waves, including many that cannot at present be easily generated or detected, infra-red, light, ultra-violet and all of the wave frequencies that arrive from outer space.

electromagnetic wave a complex wave for electric and magnetic FIELDS, with the field directions always at right angles to each other. Such a wave can be propagated in air, in free space or along TRANSMISSION LINES or WAVEGUIDES.

electromagnetism MAGNETISM caused by electric currents. The term is commonly used to denote magnetism caused by the passage of electric currents through coils of wire, but magnetism produced by any moving charge such as in a radiated wave, or even permanent magnetism, is electromagnetism.

electromechanical generator a dynamo or alternator that generates an electrical supply from mechanical rotation, usually powered by a petrol or diesel engine but also from wind or water turbines.

electromechanical sequencer a switching device operated by an electric motor, such as the programmer of old-fashioned washing máchines.

electromechanical transducer any device that produces a mechanical output for an electrical input, such as a MOTOR or SOLENOID.

electrometer a form of voltmeter with a very high input resistance. The term was once used to denote electrostatic voltmeters, but is now applied to FET and valve voltmeters that can be used to measure potential differences across very high resistances.

electromigration the displacement movement of atoms within a crystal due to temperature. This can cause damage to IC chips when they are operated at temperatures exceeding 100°C.

electromotive force (EMF) the voltage of a source of electrical energy. The term POTENTIAL DIFFERENCE (PD) should be reserved for the voltage across a device that is dissipating electrical energy.

electron a stable, negatively charged particle that forms the outer 'layer' of any atom, best imagined as orbiting the positive nucleus. The number of electrons in a NEUTRAL (sense 4) atom is equal to the number of positive PROTONs in the central nucleus (the atomic number of the element). The amount of charge of an electron is 1.6022×10^{-19} coulomb; this charge is of equal magnitude but opposite sign to that of a proton. Electrons have very small rest mass (9.1096×10^{-31} kilogram, 1836 times smaller than that of a proton), and can easily be detached from atoms (leaving IONs) in a vacuum and accelerated to high speeds. The movement of electrons (as for any charged particles) is what we call electric CURRENT. Solid conductors are materials in which some electrons (the valence or conduction electrons) are only very loosely attached to atoms and will move readily through the solid material.

electron beam or (formerly) **beta ray** a large number of ELECTRONs flowing in the same direction in a confined path. An electron beam is achieved by using ELECTROSTATIC FIELDS to accelerate electrons away from a source, and either electrostatic or magnetic fields to form the scattering electrons into a beam. See also ELECTRON LENS.

electron beam accessed memory a form of memory, now obsolete, that uses a CATHODE-RAY TUBE structure with a screen made from MOS elements, each accessed for reading or writing by the electron beam. The technique dates back to the first types of TV camera tubes.

electron cloud see SPACE CHARGE.

electron gun an arrangement of an electron-emitting CATHODE (sense 1) and ELECTRON LENS set that forms an ELECTRON BEAM in a CATHODE-RAY TUBE. The direction and speed of the beam is determined by the potential difference between the cathode and the accelerating anode (sense 1).

electron-hole pair the charged particles produced by heating or DOPING a SEMICONDUCTOR. The pure (INTRINSIC, sense 2) state of semiconductors is almost free of charged particles that can move. By heating, or by the addition of doping impurities, electrons can be released, leaving gaps (HOLES) in the structure of the materials. These holes behave like charged particles, with positive charge and an apparent mass that is rather more than the mass of the electron. Since there must be a hole for each free electron, these particles always exist in pairs in a semiconductor.

electronically resettable fuse or **multifuse** a semiconductor device with a positive TEMPERATURE COEFFICIENT, so that the resistance can increase considerably when excess current flows, resetting automatically when the current drops.

electronically variable resistor (EVR) a resistor, part of a complex circuit, whose value can be adjusted electronically in servicing, using computer-controlled equipment provided by the manufacturer.

electronic compass a precise form of magnetic compass in which a Hall (see HALL EFFECT) element is rotated by a servomotor to find the position of maximum magnetic flux, and the amount of rotation is electronically measured and displayed. Later developments have used laser gyroscopes for true compass directions, and the system has been overtaken by the development of GLOBAL POSITIONING SATELLITE technology.

electronic data interchange (EDI) a standardized system for exchanging documents in electronic form between computer systems, using telephone or other lines.

electronic data processing the main action of all digital COMPUTERS. It consists of the fundamental actions of data entry, storage, rearrangement and display.

electronic design automation (EDA) see COMPUTER AIDED DESIGN, COMPUTER AIDED ENGINEERING, COMPUTER AIDED MANUFACTURING.

electronic device any device that achieves its effect by directly controlling the movement of ELECTRONS or HOLES. The electrons may be moving in a vacuum, in a solid or in a gas, and their movement can be accompanied by the movement of holes or ions.

electronic hour meter a form of QUARTZ digital clock used to determine the number of hours for which a device has been operated.

electronic image stabilizer a system used in some small CAMCORDERS to ensure that an image is not affected by camera shake when the camera is handheld.

Electronic Industries Association (EIA) a trade association formed in 1924 for the North American electronics industry.

electronic memory a form of MEMORY in which writing, storage and reading are electronic. The storage action can include CHARGE storage (electrostatic memory), switching of an electron flow between devices (FLIP-FLOP static memory) or magnetization of a magnetic material (as on the obsolete CORE STORE).

electronic news gathering (ENG) the use of small TV cameras and microwave links that enable a news item to be captured using only a commentator and a camera operator rather than by a large team of specialists.

electronic noise absorber a method of reducing acoustic noise by using a microphone, amplifier, and loudspeaker to cancel out the noise by reproducing it in ANTIPHASE.

electronic point of sale (EPOS) the use of BAR CODES and other electronic methods to record sales and ensure continuous adjustment of stock control.

electronic program guide (EPG) a facility in DIGITAL TELEVISION programmes to see a listing on screen of the time and contents of programs being viewed or appearing shortly.

electronics 1. the science and technology concerned with the development, behaviour and application of devices that use moving electrons, ions or holes. **2.** the circuits and devices of a piece of electronic equipment.

electronic security the application of electronic methods to security systems that warn of intrusion, fire, smoke and theft.

electronic sequencer a counting and SWITCHING CIRCUIT, often using a microprocessor, which has replaced the older type of ELECTROMECHANICAL SEQUENCER. Any electronic sequencer should provide backup power in the event of mains failure.

Electronics Industry Standards Association (EISA) a body that promotes standardization for electronics products in the U.K.

electronic switch a SWITCH with no moving parts. The switching is carried out by acting on the electrons (or other CARRIERS, sense 2) with FIELDS (sense 1), electric or magnetic. This makes the switching very fast, with no problems of contact corrosion or wear.

electronic tuning the changing of the FREQUENCY of a tuned circuit without mechanical movement. Electronic tuning by means of VARACTOR diodes is extensively used for FM radio and TV receivers.

electronic viewfinder a miniature TV display used in TV cameras to display the signal picture, as distinct from an optical viewfinder that shows the picture formed by the lens.

electron lens a set of ELECTRODES or coils that can form and focus an ELECTRON BEAM. The electrons from a CATHODE (sense 1) are attracted through a hole at the end of a GRID CYLINDER that is at a negative potential. The shape of the fields at this aperture cause the electron paths to cross over, with a point of minimum diameter. This is the start of a beam, and the diverging paths of the electrons from this point are then controlled either by using ELECTROSTATIC FIELDS or MAGNETIC FIELDS.

electron microscope an instrument for viewing images of very small objects. The microscope is based on the principle that a fast-moving particle will exhibit the properties of a short-wavelength wave, so that an ELECTRON BEAM behaves like a

short-wavelength light beam. The electron beam can be arranged to pass through the specimen or to be reflected from it. Greater resolution is achieved by this means than is possible optically because the wavelength of an electron beam is much shorter than that of light.

The *transmission electron microscope* (*TEM*) allows the electrons to pass through the specimen, and the resulting image is viewed on a fluorescent screen. Considerable experience is needed if the images are to be correctly interpreted.

The *scanning electron microscope* (*SEM*) uses TELEVISION techniques, scanning the electron beam across the object and picking up the scattered, reflected and secondary electrons from the surface. These returned electrons are then used as a TV-type of output signal. Microscopes of this type yield an image that is much easier to interpret, and which looks like the image seen through an optical microscope.

electron multiplier a set of DYNODES arranged to multiply the number of electrons in a beam at each dynode stage. The principle is used particularly in photoelectric devices as a way of achieving noiseless amplification.

electron optics the study of the control of ELECTRON BEAMS. Electron optics includes the production, focusing, deflection and use of electron beams.

electronvolt the amount of energy acquired by an electron accelerated by one volt. Symbol: eV. A useful unit for measuring small energy changes, equal to 1.6×10^{-19} joules. See also WORK FUNCTION.

electroplating the deposition of metals from a solution onto a conductor. The object that is to be coated is suspended from wires in a bath of an acid or alkaline solution that contains salts of the metal that is to be used for coating. A bar or sheet of the coating metal (the ANODE) is also connected into the solution, not touching the object that is to be coated. The two are then connected to a DC supply, the anode to the positive pole, using a low voltage, typically four to eight volts. By movement of ions and chemical actions, metal is dissolved from the anode and deposited onto the object that is to be coated. Electroplating is used extensively for coating metal objects with gold, silver, chromium, nickel and other metals.

electrostatic of, concerned with, producing, or caused by electric charges and fields at rest.

electrostatic copier a document copying system that scans a page with a light beam and uses the reflected light to alter the conductivity of an electrically-charged DRUM (sense 2). The drum is then coated with an ink (known as *toner*), which drops off in uncharged regions, and this is transferred to paper and melted into place to make an exact copy. The same principles are used in the LASER PRINTER.

electrostatic damage BREAKDOWN, usually of SEMICONDUCTOR materials, caused by high electrostatic voltages applied across a very high resistance circuit, such as the GATE (sense 1) circuit of a MOSFET. See also PROTECTING DIODE.

electrostatic deflection the deflection of an ELECTRON BEAM that results when ELECTRIC FIELDS are applied between metal plates. The beam is deflected in the direction of the more positive plate. See DEFLECTION SENSITIVITY.

electrostatic discharge unwanted current through a high-resistance material, caused by high electrostatic voltages and causing ELECTROSTATIC DAMAGE.

electrostatic effects the effects of ELECTROSTATIC FIELD and force on another charge or on an insulator that are caused by a charge at rest.

electrostatic field the ELECTRIC FIELD that acts with force on an electron or ion. An electrostatic field exists around any charged particle, around any conductor that is connected to a potential, and in a region where the magnetic field is changing.

electrostatic focusing the focusing of an ELECTRON BEAM by passing it through shaped metal electrodes at different potentials. The aim is to create a SADDLE-SHAPED FIELD to converge a diverging

beam so that it will focus on some target, such as a PHOSPHOR screen.

electrostatic hum interference with AUDIO equipment caused by the alternating ELECTROSTATIC FIELD produced by the AC mains.

electrostatic induction the production of electric CHARGE on an object, conductor or non-conductor, because of another charge. Electrostatic induction is caused by the separation of electrons from atoms under the influence of an electrostatic field from another charge or potential.

electrostatic lens an assembly of metal electrodes at different ELECTRIC POTENTIALS. The fields that are set up will cause an electron beam to be converged or diverged, just as an arrangement of glass lenses will affect a beam of light. Compare ELECTROMAGNETIC LENS; see also SADDLE-SHAPED FIELD.

electrostatic loudspeaker a loudspeaker whose operating principle is the deflection of a charged membrane by electrostatic forces. The device is used for very high quality sound reproduction, as in the famous QUAD ESL units.

electrostatic precipitator a method of removing dust in, for example, an air-conditioning system. Air is forced through a metal mesh that is maintained at a very high DC potential (several kV). Dust particles, which are usually charged, are attracted to the mesh, which can be cleaned at intervals by switching off the potential. Precipitators of this type also generate ions, which some people believe affect the well-being of users of the conditioned air either adversely (positive ions) or beneficially (negative ions).

electrostatic printer an obsolete system of printing for computer data output that uses black paper coated with a thin metal film. The printing head is of the DOT-MATRIX type, using a set of sharp needles. When a high voltage is placed between the metal coating and a needle, the resulting spark will vaporize the metal, leaving the black paper exposed. The system is simple, but suffers from the disadvantages that special paper is needed, only one copy is made, and the paper retains fingerprints and will mark other papers.

electrostatic recording the use in a FACSIMILE receiver of an electrostatic system of printing similar to the mechanism of a LASER PRINTER but using a metal stylus in place of a laser beam. The stylus leaves a charge pattern on the paper which then has a black (toner) powder deposited on the charged areas. The toner is fixed in place by melting it using an infra-red heater.

electrostatic screen an earthed metal or metal-gauze casing around a circuit that will ensure no penetration of an ELECTRIC FIELD into the casing.

electrostatic sensitivity the liability of a MOSFET to damage caused by an ELECTROSTATIC FIELD in terms of the minimum field strength that will damage the device.

electrostatic separator a method of separating powders of insulating materials that are falling or moving along a belt. The principle is to apply a very strong ELECTRIC FIELD so that materials with different PERMITTIVITY values experience different amounts of force, and take different paths.

electrostatic voltage a high voltage on an insulating material caused by rubbing against another insulator. Though the voltage can be high enough to damage semiconductors, the current that flows when the voltage is discharged is very small.

electrostriction the movement of the atoms of a material caused by ELECTROSTATIC FIELDS. This means that the materials will expand or shrink by a very small amount when the field is applied or removed.

element a material made up entirely of identical ATOMS.

elevation the angle of a satellite position measured from the horizontal.

ELF see EXTREMELY LOW FREQUENCY.

e-line package a form of miniature transistor package that uses a plastic encapsulation that is flat on one side and rounded on the other.

elliptic approximation filter see CAUER FILTER.

elliptical polarization a form of polarization for a wave in which the electric field strength in one direction is of a different amplitude compared to the field strength in a direction at 90°.

email an electronic mail system that allows for interchange of messages between computers connected over lines of radio links to a central provider.

embedded diodes see DIODE-SPLIT TRANSFORMER.

embedded thermistor a THERMISTOR contained inside an electronic assembly and used as a temperature SENSOR to protect against overheating.

EMC see ELECTROMAGNETIC COMPATIBILITY.

EMF see ELECTROMOTIVE FORCE.

EMF constant the figure of BACK-EMF per 1000 r.p.m. for a SERVOMOTOR.

EMI see ELECTROMAGNETIC INTERFERENCE.

EMI filter a filter constructed from INDUCTORS and CAPACITORS and designed to reflect unwanted interfering energy but pass the desired signal bands with low ATTENUATION.

emission the release of electrons from a material. The term usually denotes the release of electrons into a vacuum from a metal under the influence of heat (THERMIONIC EMISSION), light (PHOTOEMISSION) or electric fields (FIELD EMISSION). For emission to be achieved, each electron must acquire an amount of energy greater than the binding energy that holds it in place. Electrons in SEMICONDUCTORS are not emitted from the material, only displaced.

emitter 1. the electrode in a SEMICONDUCTOR device from which electrons or holes pass to another layer of the material. 2. another term for CATHODE (sense 1).

emitter-coupled circuit see DIFFERENTIAL AMPLIFIER.

emitter-coupled logic (ECL) or **current-mode logic (CML)** a fast-acting form of logic circuit used in computing. The ECL circuit makes use of TRANSISTORS that are connected at the emitters to a common LOAD. The load is such that the current through it is constant. Small changes of

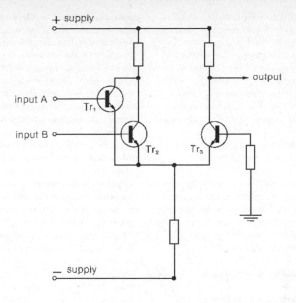

Fig. 39. **emitter-coupled logic (ECL)**

bias voltage at the bases of the transistors will cause current to be switched from one transistor to the other. The voltage that is needed for switching can be very small, and the amount of current that is switched can be comparatively large, allowing STRAY CAPACITANCES to be rapidly charged or discharged. A modern ECL device can be switched at rates of several GHz. See Fig. 39.

emitter follower or **common-collector connection** or **grounded collector connection**   a circuit that has high INPUT IMPEDANCE and low output impedance. The load is placed in the emitter circuit, and the input signal is applied to the base. Because the base-emitter voltage of a BIPOLAR JUNCTION TRANSISTOR varies only very slightly when a small signal is applied, the emitter voltage follows the base voltage very closely, hence the name. The circuit is used extensively as a BUFFER (sense 1) and a DRIVER for loads with high stray capacitance. The use of emitter followers as buffers has largely been superseded by

the introduction of OPERATIONAL AMPLIFIER follower circuits. See Fig. 40.

EMP   see ELECTROMAGNETIC PULSE.

empty slot   a networking system in which DATA PACKETS circulate and a terminal loads data into an empty packet and marks it as used.

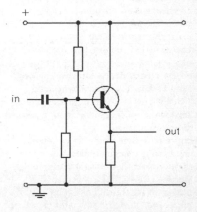

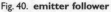

Fig. 40. **emitter follower**

enabling (of a circuit or device) allowing to act normally. A circuit can be disabled by, for example, removing or reversing BIAS so that an input signal is ineffective. Digital devices are often provided with an enable input to activate or deactivate them as required. Contrast DISABLING.

enclosed coil an INDUCTOR construction in which the CORE completely encloses the coils.

enclosure see CABINET.

encoded in code form as distinct from plain form (see CLEAR TEXT).

encoder a device that produces an output in electronic form corresponding to some measurement. The output is nowadays usually in digital signal form. For example, a shaft position encoder is a form of TRANSDUCER that produces different digital number signals corresponding to different angular positions as a shaft rotates.

encrypted text text whose characters have been substituted by another code pattern (cypher). See also CLEAR TEXT.

encryption the substitution of a coded pattern for the original CLEAR TEXT. Contrast the action of a SCRAMBLER.

encryption key a digital pattern (see KEY, sense 1) that can be used to encrypt text or other digital data.

encryption, TV see SCRAMBLER.

endaround shift see ROTATION.

end effect the difference between the physical end of a conductor and the end of the field pattern over it, requiring an AERIAL rod to be cut shorter than theory would suggest. See also EFFECTIVE LENGTH.

end fed wire aerial (or **antenna) or long-wire aerial** a horizontal wire aerial, usually quarter wavelength or longer at the lowest frequency of operation and fed from one end.

endfire array an AERIAL array in which the aiming direction is along the line of aerials rather than at right angles to the line.

end flag a BIT or set of bits at the end of a signal DATA PACKET that is used to indicate the end of data.

endless loop tape a piece of tape that has had its ends spliced together and which will return to any position simply by winding in one direction.

end of discharge voltage (EODV) or **end-point** the voltage at which a CELL can be considered discharged. At this voltage, a RECHARGEABLE CELL must be recharged, and a non-rechargeable cell must be discarded.

end point see END OF DISCHARGE VOLTAGE.

end sensor a TAPE drive mechanism that detects the approaching end of a tape and applies brakes before the tape is stretched by being violently stopped.

energized (of a circuit) provided with power.

energy the capability for doing useful work. All forms of energy can be converted into mechanical work, making use of TRANSDUCERS.

energy band a permitted range of energy values for particles in a solid. An energy value within this range is called the *band energy*. In single atoms, each electron has a definite amount of energy, its energy level, and no intermediate levels of energy are found. When atoms are closely spaced, as in solids, these permitted energy levels merge into bands, so that electrons can take any of a range of energy values. The arrangement of energy bands in a material, and whether bands are full (with one electron taking each possible level of energy), empty (no electrons with any of the permitted levels of energy), or part-filled, determine whether a material is an insulator, semiconductor or conductor.

energy/bit per watt a measure of NOISE POWER for a digital signal, roughly equivalent to the SIGNAL TO NOISE RATIO for an analogue signal.

energy content, battery the total available energy that can be drawn from a battery, defined as EMF × average CURRENT × active life in hours.

energy dispersal waveform a 25 Hz waveform added to the VIDEO signal of an analogue TV satellite broadcast to reduce the appearance of fixed patterns that could disrupt other communications. The 25 Hz signal is removed at the receiver prior to DEMODULATION.

energy level the average amount of energy of electrons in a particular electron orbit (*shell*) of an atom.

Energystar specification an environmental requirement for MONITORS using a CATHODE-RAY TUBE that specifies maximum energy consumption and provides for lower power for standby operation.

ENG see ELECTRONIC NEWS GATHERING.

engine the electronic and mechanical parts of a computer printer. Printers sold under different names may use the same engine.

enhanced other networks (or EON) a feature of car radio that allows the set to be tuned to a national network but interrupted by travel news on a local station.

enhanced television system an ANALOGUE TV system that retains existing transmission standards but offers improvements in image quality. Such schemes are obsolescent due to the changeover to DIGITAL TELEVISION.

enhancement mode a BIAS that is required for correct operation of some types of FIELD EFFECT TRANSISTORS. A FET that needs enhancement mode biasing will pass little or no current in the absence of bias voltage, and a bias voltage has to be applied in order to pass working current. Compare DEPLETION MODE.

enhancer a circuit or software action of sharpening the focus of a stored picture.

Enigma a mechanical ENCRYPTION machine developed in Germany and used for secret communications during World War II, later using the Lorenz machine. The team working at BLETCHLEY PARK in the UK found ways of deciphering these messages, first manually and subsequently by mechanical and, ultimately, electronic computers. See also COLOSSUS; FLOWERS.

ensemble averaging or **averaging** a method of signal processing used for a noisy communications channel. Sample points from a set of input data are averaged to produce the signal output with a considerably better signal to noise ratio.

entropy in classical physics, a measure of disorder; so that the term is often used to mean NOISE in a digital communications system.

envelope the outline of the AMPLITUDE peaks of a modulated radio wave. This envelope shape should be of the same shape as the wave that is being used to modulate the radio frequency.

envelope demodulation DEMODULATION of a wave using a RECTIFIER so that the outer shape (envelope) of the wave, which is the modulation pattern, is recovered.

envelope distortion see GROUP DELAY DISTORTION.

envelope elimination and restoration a method of improving the power efficiency of a HF transmitter by using a SINGLE-SIDEBAND technique that amplifies separate components of the signal in different amplifier paths before recombining them.

envelope signal the appearance on a CATHODE-RAY OSCILLOSCOPE of the replayed RF video signal from a video recorder (see RECORDING OF VIDEO). A good envelope will be of almost constant amplitude with no sharp peaks or dips.

environmental tests tests of reliability of electronic equipment in conditions of extreme temperature, humidity, pressure, shock, vibration and pollution.

EODV see END OF DISCHARGE VOLTAGE.

EON see ENHANCED OTHER NETWORKS.

E1 rate the rate of 2.048 Mb/s used for European DIGITAL telephone communications.

EOS Earth observing system (satellite).

EPIC explicitly PARALLEL (sense 3) instruction chip (processor).

epitaxial transistor a PLANAR transistor that has been formed by EPITAXY. This means that a layer of lightly doped material has been deposited on to a heavily doped main collector region. The use of this extra layer allows better collector-base BREAKDOWN characteristics, while the heavily doped region permits a low-resistance collector connection, and good THERMAL CONDUCTIVITY.

epitaxy   the growth of other layers on the surface of a SEMICONDUCTOR crystal, usually from a gas or vapour. The layers will be of doped or INTRINSIC (sense 2) material, and the importance of the process is that the added layers maintain the same crystal structure as the underlying crystal, so that the whole structure behaves as one crystal. Epitaxy has been the main process for creating transistors and ICs for many years. However, it is being superseded by ION IMPLANTATION for some specialized purposes.

E-plane horn or **E-plane sectoral horn** a form of microwave tapering HORN with a pair of parallel sides that are at right angles to the direction of ELECTRIC FIELD.

E-plane lens   a form of aerial structure that contains a set of metal parallel plates that are aligned in the direction of the electric field, acting as a lens to converge the waves.

EPLD   see ERASABLE PROGRAMMABLE LOGIC DEVICE.

EPOS   see ELECTRONIC POINT OF SALE.

epoxy resin   a plastics resin with exceptionally good insulating characteristics. The value of epoxy resins is that many of them are particularly easy to use in coating or moulding applications. Most of these resins can be obtained as 'two-pack' types, consisting of a viscous resin and a liquid setting agent. The two are mixed just before use, and the setting time depends on the mixture ratios and on temperature.

EPROM (erasable programmable read-only memory)   a form of ROM chip that can be erased using ultra-violet light and subsequently programmed with data by writing the data repeatedly while higher than normal electrical voltages are applied to the chip. See also EEPROM; PROM.

EPX connector   a form of heavy-duty signal connector for professional audio equipment.

equalization   a form of controlled DISTORTION of an analogue signal. The best example is the treatment of audio signals for vinyl disc RECORDING. The bass signals are reduced in amplitude, because

otherwise the amplitude of the groove wave would be too great. Similarly, the amplitudes of high-frequency signals are boosted, because the disc noise is mainly in this region. After transcribing (converting back into electrical signals), the bass amplitude has to be boosted and the treble attenuated in order to recover the correct signal balance.

equalizer   any circuit that carries out EQUALIZATION. The term is used also to denote circuits that will selectively boost or attenuate parts of the audio spectrum. Equalizers are used in professional applications to overcome studio problems of 'boom' or 'deadness'. The device is sometimes called a *graphics equalizer*, particularly when the control panel shows the effect of the controls on a frequency response graph.

equalizing pulses   a set of five pulses placed before and after a FIELD SYNC pulse in the analogue TV system in order to provide time for synchronizing circuits (see SYNCHRONIZING PULSE) to adjust to the differences between an odd-numbered line and an even-numbered line. See also INTERLACE.

equal loudness contours   a set of graphs showing how the sensitivity of the human ear varies with both frequency and intensity of sound.

equatorial orbit   a satellite orbit over the Earth's equator. Contrast ELLIPTICAL ORBIT; GEOSTATIONARY ORBIT; POLAR ORBIT.

equivalent capacitance   a single value of capacitance equivalent to a set of capacitors wired in any combination of SERIES and PARALLEL (sense 1).

equivalent circuit   an arrangement of simple electrical COMPONENTS that is electrically equivalent to a complex CIRCUIT. The equivalent circuit is used for calculation purposes, and makes use of simple real components (like resistors, inductors and capacitors) along with idealized components (signal voltage or current generators). By representing a complex device such as a transistor voltage amplifier as an equivalent circuit which might, for example, contain a voltage generator and a few resistors, it is possible to calculate gain and other features closely enough for practical purposes. See also NORTON'S THEOREM; THEVENIN'S THEOREM.

equivalent noise resistance a theoretical resistance value that would produce the same noise level as that in a COMMUNICATIONS link at the same temperature and using the same BANDWIDTH.

equivalent noise temperature the theoretical temperature of a NOISE source that would provide the same NOISE POWER and spectrum as that of noise received by an aerial.

equivalent resistance a single resistance value that has the same effect as a number of other RESISTORS or power-dissipating components. A circuit may, for example, contain RESISTANCE and inductance. Its equivalent resistance value will allow calculation of total power dissipated in all the parts of the circuit, including the resistance of the inductor, and the effect of any effects like motional impedances. The use of an equivalent resistance is particularly suited to the treatment of the inputs and outputs of ACTIVE COMPONENTS.

erasable programmable logic device (EPLD) an assembly of identical gate and inverter circuits whose interconnections can be established by programming and can be reprogrammed. An EPLD is a form of UNCOMMITTED LOGIC ARRAY.

erasable programmable read-only memory see EPROM.

erasable storage any form of data storage that can be erased and overwritten (see OVERWRITE). RAM, for example, will store data for as long as power is applied to the memory, or until other data is written in to the memory. A disk will similarly store data until it is full, after which data can be added only by overwriting older data. Digital tape recorders can overwrite tape, though it is usual to erase a BACKUP tape completely before using it again.

erase to remove data from a MEMORY store, usually semiconductor or magnetic memory, but also magnetic media such as

disks or tapes, or rewritable media such as CD-RW or rewritable DVD.

erase head a tape recorder head that is used to erase tape immediately prior to RECORDING. The erase head uses a comparatively large magnetic GAP and is fed by a high-amplitude high-frequency signal. The effect is to take each part of the tape through a large number of MAGNETIC HYSTERESIS cycles, gradually reducing the PEAK AMPLITUDE so that the magnetic particles are left unmagnetized.

E-rating, resistor a European standard that uses the letter E along with a number (a multiple of six) to indicate TOLERANCE of value.

erbium-doped fibre amplifier or **Raman amplifier** an amplifier for optical signals that uses a LASER form of action in an erbium-doped fibre to increase the power of a signal using an injected unmodulated signal of higher power.

Erlang a unit of traffic flow in a DIGITAL telephone system.

ERMES see EUROPEAN RADIO MESSAGE SYSTEM.

ERP see EFFECTIVE RADIATED POWER.

erratic start-up a problem of a switch-mode power supply which manifests itself as random refusal to switch on.

error checking the action of checking digital codes to ascertain that they have not been corrupted. See CRC; PARITY.

error classes see CLASSES OF ERROR.

error control see ERROR DETECTION AND CORRECTION.

error correction the action of correcting digital codes that have been corrupted, generally by using redundant bits in a signal to carry checking information. See CRC; HUFFMAN; LZW; PARITY.

error correction coding (ECC) a form of REED-SOLOMON CODE used in a DIGITAL VIDEO CASSETTE RECORDER to detect and correct errors.

error correction routine a type of program routine used in COMMUNICATIONS. In a communications link, a detected error in a BLOCK (sense 2) of data will cause the error correction routine to clear the data and request a re-transmission.

error detection and correction or **error control** or **error-reduction methods** any ALGORITHM that will detect and correct errors, ranging from PARITY methods or CYCLIC REDUNDANCY CHECK to more elaborate methods that can correct all but gross errors.

errored second one second of a digital communication that contains at least one error.

error extension or **error multiplication** a problem of SCRAMBLER circuits or CODE CONVERTERS in which one bit of error in a signal can cause up to four errors in the decoded data, particularly if the error arises in a FEEDBACK signal.

error function a calculation of probability of digital BIT ERROR RATE made assuming GAUSSIAN NOISE.

error rate see BIT ERROR RATE.

error-reduction methods see ERROR DETECTION AND CORRECTION.

error signal or **error voltage** or **system deviation** in a control system, the difference between a set level (e.g. of temperature) and the achieved level.

error spread a set of errors caused by a single bit error (see BIT ERROR RATE) and ERROR EXTENSION.

error voltage see ERROR SIGNAL.

Esaki diode see TUNNEL DIODE.

escape ray an electromagnetic wave that strikes the IONOSPHERE at more than the CRITICAL ANGLE, so that it escapes into space and is not reflected.

ESD see ELECTROSTATIC DISCHARGE.

ESR see EFFECTIVE SERIES RESISTANCE.

etched PCB a PRINTED CIRCUIT BOARD created by etching rather than by drawing with a conductive ink.

etching the dissolving of material by a chemical process, particularly with acids. Etching is used to produce PRINTED CIRCUIT BOARDS (using solutions of materials such as ferric chloride), and in the production of TRANSISTORS and INTEGRATED CIRCUITS.

etch-resistant ink a type of ink used to mark out PRINTED CIRCUIT BOARDS. The areas of copper covered by the ink will not be etched (see ETCHING) away.

ETF see ELEVEN TO FOURTEEN MODULATION.

ethanol or **ethyl alcohol** a cleaning agent that absorbs water. Ethanol is toxic, particularly to the liver, and highly flammable.

Ethernet a widely used HALF-DUPLEX computer network using 5-ohm coaxial cable, maximum length 2.5 km. The data rate is 10 Mb/s, using a MANCHESTER CODE format.

ethyl alcohol see ETHANOL.

ETSI see EUROPEAN TELECOMMUNICATIONS STANDARDS INSTITUTE.

EU directives regulations that affect many aspects of electronics, particularly CE MARK and the LOW VOLTAGE DIRECTIVE.

Euro AV connector see SCART CONNECTOR.

Eurocard any of a set of standard PRINTED CIRCUIT BOARD sizes, used for experimental work.

Eurocard prototyping boards a set of standardized printed circuit BREADBOARDS that are intended for testing construction of digital circuits.

euroconnector see IEC CONNECTOR.

Eurocrypt the SCRAMBLER system used for D-MAC (see MAC) analogue satellite transmissions in Europe.

Eurocypher a form of scrambler system for MAC broadcasts.

Euronet the European Union data communications system, using PACKET SWITCHING and linked to the public system.

European broadcasting union (EBU) an organization founded in 1950 to promote international cooperation in broadcasting.

European radio messaging system (ERMES) a standard for radio messaging using sixteen channels in the 169.425 MHz to 169.80 MHz band for digital communications at 6.25 Kb/s with ERROR CORRECTION. Receivers are designed to scan all the sixteen channels.

Eurosocket or **IEC connector** a three-contact plug and socket arrangement used to connect small electronic equipment to the mains and designed so as to minimize the risk of shock if the connection is parted while still live. See Fig. 41.

eutectic alloy a SOLDER alloy of tin and lead which has the lowest melting point (183°C) of all the possible tin/lead alloy compositions.

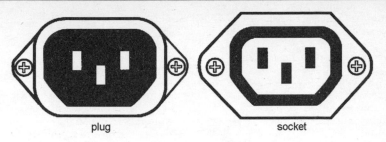

plug　　　　socket

Fig. 41. **Eurosocket**

evaporated coating a film of metal
produced by evaporating the metal in
a vacuum, typically used to metallize
an insulator in the construction of a
CAPACITOR.

even function a waveform that can be
analyzed in terms of cosine terms (see
FOURIER SERIES) only, with an amplitude
that is not zero at time zero. Contrast
ODD FUNCTION.

even parity a PARITY scheme in which the
number of 1 bits in a byte must be even,
otherwise an error is signalled.

EVF see ELECTRONIC VIEWFINDER.

EVR see ELECTRONICALLY VARIABLE RESISTOR.

exalted carrier reception a method of
minimizing distortion in a transmission
that uses reduced carrier power, in which
the remaining CARRIER (sense 1) is used
to generate a larger modulated signal in
phase, and this is then demodulated.
See also REDUCED CARRIER TRANSMISSION;
SINGLE-SIDEBAND.

excess current protection a circuit that
will cut off or reduce a supply voltage
when excessive current flows. See also
CROWBAR CIRCUIT.

excess noise the difference between the
NOISE generated in a component or system
and the theoretical noise that would be
emitted from an object (BLACK BODY) at a
temperature of 290K.

excess noise temperature a figure
calculated from the ratio of NOISE
TEMPERATURES of transmitter and receiver.

excess-3 code a form of BCD code in
which 3 is added to each denary digit
before coding to 8-4-2-1 BINARY (sense 1).

In such a code any code below 0011 or
above 1100 must be an error, making error
detection easy.

excess voltage protection a circuit that
will reduce or cut-off a voltage supply if
the output voltage exceeds a preset level.
See also CROWBAR CIRCUIT.

exchangeable card architecture (ECA)
see PLUG AND PLAY.

excitation the addition of energy to a
system, for example signals that form an
input for a system such as an AMPLIFIER or
OSCILLATOR.

exclusive OR (XOR) gate a form of LOGIC
GATE giving a logic comparison. The OR
gate produces an output if any or all of
its inputs are at logic 1. The XOR gate
excludes the case where more than one
input is at logic 1. See Fig. 42.

exosphere the low-density region of the
atmosphere lying beyond 400 km.

exotic supply a source of electrical power
that does not use conventional mechanical
or chemical cell actions, such as fuel cells,
nuclear cells, PHOTOCELLS and thermal
cells. The fuel cell is in such large-scale
production now as almost to be classed
as conventional.

expanded sweep a TIMEBASE for a
CATHODE-RAY OSCILLOSCOPE in which the
timebase amplitude can be greatly
increased. This allows the effect of time-
magnification, so that a small part of a
waveform can be examined in greater
detail without the need to switch to another
timebase speed and resynchronize.

expander a circuit that increases the
DYNAMIC RANGE of an audio signal. This is

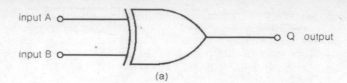

(a)

A	B	Q
0	0	0
0	1	1
1	0	1
1	1	0

(b)

Fig. 42. **exclusive OR (XOR) gate**

achieved by a nonlinear stage whose gain increases as the signal amplitude increases. See also COMPANDER; COMPRESSER.

expansion bus a set of BUS connections on a MOTHERBOARD that allows the computer to be expanded and updated by plugging in cards to a connector, the EXPANSION SLOT.

expansion card or **expansion board** a PRINTED CIRCUIT BOARD with an edge connector, plugged into the MOTHERBOARD of a computer in order to add new facilities.

expansion slot or **slot** a socket fastened to the MOTHERBOARD of a computer, used to hold and connect an EXPANSION CARD.

explicit access a network system in which a terminal is allowed to connect with full control of the network but only at specified times. See also CARRIER SENSE MULTIPLE ACCESS.

exponent a power of 10, see STANDARD FORM.

exponential amplifier or **logarithmic amplifier** an OPERATIONAL AMPLIFIER with NEGATIVE FEEDBACK through a DIODE so that the output signal is proportional to the logarithm of the input signal over a limited range.

exponential curve or **exponential graph** a graph shape in which the variable quantity (plotted on a y-axis) changes by the same multiple or fraction in each unit

of time. For example, a population graph might show doubling in each 25-year period, or the voltage change on a charging capacitor might halve in each 20 μs interval. See Fig. 43.

exponential graph see EXPONENTIAL CURVE.

exponential horn a horn shape in which the cross-sectional area increases exponentially (see EXPONENTIAL CURVE) with length of sound path. This shape can be used for loudspeakers or microwave aerials, and provides very high efficiency of wave transfer.

exponential rise a form of exponential curve in which the slope of the graph increases in an exponential way. Any such rise, continued indefinitely would end up at infinity.

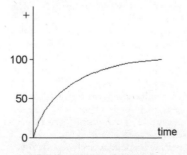

Fig. 43. **exponential curve**

exponentiation the action of raising of a number to a power. For instance, 5 raised to the power 4 equals $5 \times 5 \times 5 \times 5 = 125$. On hand-calculators, 5E4 is shorthand for 5 multiplied by 10 raised to the power 4, or $5 \times 10,000$, equal to 50,000. The letter E or exp is used to indicate this action, so that 5E3 or 5exp3 would mean 5 raised to the third power, five cubed, equal to 125.

exponent-mantissa form see STANDARD FORM.

expression a collection of symbols or symbolic equation that illustrates a mathematical fact or relationship.

expression, Boolean see BOOLEAN EXPRESSION.

extended binary coded decimal interchange code (EBCDIC) a code that uses all 8 BITs in each byte, unlike ASCII which uses only 7 bits. The EBCDIC code can be used for transmitting data from one computer to another. It is not in general use for small computers, but is used in some communications equipment.

extended definition television (EDTV) the use of a standard ANALOGUE TV system to produce higher image quality without changes to the transmission standards. Such systems are obsolescent because of the adoption of DIGITAL TELEVISION.

extended integrated device electronics see EIDE.

extended PAL a proposed method of enhancing analogue PAL transmissions by reducing the CHROMINANCE SIGNAL bandwidth and extending the LUMINANCE bandwidth.

external trigger, CRO the use of a pulse to trigger the TIMEBASE of a CATHODE-RAY OSCILLOSCOPE applied from an external source rather than derived from the input signal to the Y-AMPLIFIER.

extra high tension see EHT.

extractor hood a cowl with an extractor fan placed over a bench on which processes that develop toxic fumes are carried out.

extrapolation the action of finding a quantity by extending a graph line beyond its measured points, or by using proportionality. Extrapolation is justified if the graph line is straight, but can be dubious in other circumstances, sometimes amounting to no more than an educated guess.

extremely high frequency (EHF) millimetric waves in the wavelength range 1mm to 10mm.

extremely low frequency (ELF) the FREQUENCY range of about 100 Hz or lower, radiated from all mains-operated electrical equipment.

eye height display or **eye display** or **eye diagram** a method using a CATHODE-RAY OSCILLOSCOPE fed with a digital signal and a sinusoidal timebase that will produce a pattern similar in shape to a human eye. The extent to which the 'eye' appears open is an indication of the BIT ERROR RATE of the data, with a wide opening indicating a low bit error rate.

Eyring formula a formula used to find the reverberation time of acoustically dead rooms from the volume of the room and air absorption constant.

faceplate the viewing screen of a CATHODE-RAY TUBE. INSTRUMENT TUBES have always used a flat faceplate, and the TV type of tube has over the years become steadily flatter, due to improved design to withstand the enormous force of atmospheric pressure on the surface.

facsimile or **fax** the TRANSMISSION of text or diagrams on paper by line or radio. Formerly done by electro-mechanical methods, but nowadays achieved by using microcomputing techniques. The material to be transmitted is scanned and each unit area shape generates a BINARY CODE which is transmitted. At the receiver, each code operates a printer, producing the same pattern that existed in the transmitted material.

factor of cooperation (FOC) or **index of cooperation (IOC)** a measure of ASPECT RATIO of document pages in a FACSIMILE machine. Using machines with the same FOC ensures that document shapes will remain unchanged even when working with documents of different sizes.

fader a form of ganged ATTENUATOR, normally using one single control. A fader allows one signal to be reduced to zero amplitude smoothly while another signal is increased from zero to normal amplitude.

fading the reduction of CARRIER (sense 1) signal strength at a receiver. Fading is usually caused by interference between waves that arrive at the receiver by different routes. At least one such path must be caused by reflection of a wave by the IONOSPHERE, and the reflecting height of the ionosphere is continually shifting. Because of this, waves meeting at the receiver combine to produce a resultant wave which can be of low or high amplitude according to the phase angle between the arriving waves. Fading is counteracted by DIVERSITY reception and by the use of AUTOMATIC GAIN CONTROL. See Fig. 44.

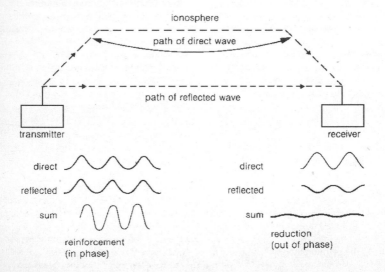

Fig. 44. **fading**

failure in time (FIT) a measure of FAILURE RATE for very reliable devices, expressed usually as the number of failures in 10^9 device-hours.

failure rate a measure of the unreliability of a component or system. The failure rate is measured in terms of the number of failures per thousand hours operation, or thousands of on/off cycles, whichever is more appropriate. For some systems using ICs, the failure rate may be immeasurably small (for example, no system may have failed during testing), so failure rates then have to be computed on the basis of ACCELERATED LIFE TESTS under unnatural conditions. Compare RELIABILITY; see also MEAN LIFE.

fall time the time for the amplitude of a pulse to change from a high value to almost zero, usually measured as the time from 90% of PEAK AMPLITUDE to 10% of peak. (See Fig. 38.) Contrast RISE TIME.

family, logic circuit a set of IC devices that follow a common pattern, such as standards for input and output signals. See also CMOS; TTL.

fan-in the number of inputs provided for a GATE (sense 2).

Fano's algorithm or **Fano trellis** an encoding ALGORITHM that assigns codes based on the probability of use for each symbol. See also HUFFMAN ALGORITHM.

fan-out the maximum number of LOGIC CIRCUIT inputs of the same family that the output of a logic device can drive. This quantity is decided by the current that is available at the output, and by the capacitance at each input. Fan-out can be increased by the use of BUFFERS (sense 1). Compare FAN-IN.

farad see CAPACITANCE.

Faraday cage a metal box or mesh screen that is earthed to prevent ELECTROSTATIC interference between circuits inside the cage and circuits outside. Large Faraday cages are used in testing transmitters or, conversely, to test equipment that might be affected by interference.

Faraday effect the rotation of the plane of polarization (plane of vibration) of a light beam by a magnetic field. This is used in

some types of optical storage media. See also KERR CELL.

Faraday, Michael (1791–1867) intuitive discoverer of electromagnetism and pioneer of electricity generation.

Faraday rotation the change of direction of a MICROWAVE signal in a CIRCULATOR due to the application of a field from a permanent magnet.

Faraday's laws the defining relationships between magnetic field strength, speed of cutting MAGNETIC FLUX and area of coil for INDUCTION of voltage in a coil moving in a magnetic field.

far end cross talk (FEXT) coupling of signals between lines carrying different signals in a cable.

far field or **Fraunhofer region** the distance from a long TRANSMITTING AERIAL beyond which the field is not disturbed by the aerial; usually taken as $2D^2/\lambda$ where D is the aerial length (several wavelengths) and λ is the wavelength, both in metres.

fast cache memory memory, usually static RAM, employed close to the MICROPROCESSOR in a computer and used as a CACHE for processor commands to speed up processing since the cache is much faster than the main RAM.

fast diode a diode intended for a SWITCHING CIRCUIT, with a recovery time of 2 ns or less following the reversal of the applied voltage.

fast Fourier transform (FFT) an ALGORITHM for fast conversion of a sampled signal into digital form by discarding values that will not contribute much to the result.

fast frequency shift keying (FFSK) a FREQUENCY SHIFT KEYING system that uses two OSCILLATORS, connecting one or other to the output as required.

fast half wave rectifier a diode and OP-AMP circuit that operates as a RECTIFIER for high-frequency signals, subject to the SLEW RATE of the op-amp.

fast packet network see ASYNCHRONOUS TRANSFER MODE.

fast picture search a facility provided in VIDEO CASSETTE RECORDERS and DVD players and recorders to search quickly for a particular portion of the recording. The search is much more rapid in a DVD player or recorder than in a video cassette recorder.

fast-recovery diode a diode in which current shuts off very rapidly following the reversal of BIAS. Ordinary diodes suffer from CARRIER STORAGE effects, which make the shut-off comparatively slow. For use with microwave signals, SCHOTTKY DIODES or diodes fabricated from compound semiconductors such as GALLIUM ARSENIDE, must be used.

fast shutter a CAMCORDER facility that allows the response time to light for each 20 ms field period to be very short so as to reduce blurring of a moving target.

fastext a teletext decoder system that uses a large memory so that eight pages of text are stored in one operation, allowing for fast progress from one page to the next when required.

fatigue failure failure of a component due to age rather than from overloading; often a cause of a fuse blowing when no overload has occurred.

fault current a current, usually large, that flows because of a circuit fault, usually a failure of insulation.

fault finding the art of locating a fault in a circuit, using a combination of experience, expertise and trial-and-error.

fault tolerant (of a system, generally a software system) capable of dealing with minor faults and providing a suitable output.

fault, intermittent see INTERMITTENT.

FAW see FRAME ALIGNMENT WORD.

fax see FACSIMILE.

fax modem a computer MODEM that can deal with FACSIMILE signals, with the computer providing for sending and receiving fax by use of software.

FC fibre channel: see FIBRE OPTICS.

FC cut crystal a cut of QUARTZ CRYSTAL used for crystals that will be encased in a CRYSTAL OVEN, particularly for global positioning satellite systems.

FCC see FEDERAL COMMUNICATIONS COMMISSION.

FDD see FREQUENCY DIVISION DUPLEX.

FDDI see FIBRE DISTRIBUTED DATA INTERFACE.

FDM see FREQUENCY DIVISION MULTIPLEX.

FDMA see FREQUENCY DIVISION MULTIPLE ACCESS.

F/D ratio the ratio of focal length to diameter for a SATELLITE DISH, typically 0.35 to 0.45.

FDVDI see FIBRE DISTRIBUTED VIDEO/VOICE DATA INTERFACE.

FEC see FORWARD ERROR CONTROL.

Federal Communications Commission (FCC) the regulating body for radio broadcasting in the USA.

feedback the return as part of the INPUT (sense 1) to an AMPLIFIER of a signal that is obtained from the output. If the signal that is fed back is in phase the amplifier is supplying part of its own input. This makes the effective GAIN very much higher, and will cause oscillation if the gain of the amplifier is greater than the loss in the network that connects the output with the input. If the fed-back signal is in ANTIPHASE, the feedback is negative. This lowers gain, but also reduces noise and distortion caused by the amplifier. An amplifier that has NEGATIVE FEEDBACK is also stabilized against changes caused by alterations in the characteristics of components such as transistors or resistors. When the amount of negative feedback is very large, the only components that noticeably affect the gain are the resistors or other components in the FEEDBACK LOOP itself. The use of negative feedback is a very important feature of the design of linear amplifiers. See also POSITIVE FEEDBACK.

feedback amplifier an amplifier whose characteristics are controlled by the use of NEGATIVE FEEDBACK.

feedback balance a form of electronic weighing balance in which no springs are used, because the counterbalancing force is provided electromagnetically, with a FEEDBACK AMPLIFIER system controlling the current in the ELECTROMAGNET.

feedback control loop a FEEDBACK LOOP used in a control system. The control system may contain mechanical, thermal, or optical components, and these are therefore included as part of the feedback loop.

feedback equalization   the use of a circuit with WAVE SHAPING components in the FEEDBACK LOOP to carry out EQUALIZATION.

feedback factor   for a FEEDBACK amplifier, the ratio (CLOSED-LOOP GAIN)/(OPEN-LOOP GAIN).

feedback loop   the connection from output back to input that constitutes the FEEDBACK path for signals in an AMPLIFIER.

feedback loop stability   the factor that determines the ability of a FEEDBACK AMPLIFIER to remain stable under all normal operating conditions. See also BODE DIAGRAM; NYQUIST CRITERION.

feedback network oscillator   a form of oscillator that uses an INVERTING AMPLIFIER with a network in the FEEDBACK LOOP that reverses PHASE at one frequency only.

feedback, positive   see POSITIVE FEEDBACK.

feedback, series current   see SERIES CURRENT FEEDBACK.

feedback, series voltage   see SERIES VOLTAGE FEEDBACK.

feedback, shunt current   see SHUNT CURRENT FEEDBACK.

feedback, shunt voltage   see SHUNT VOLTAGE FEEDBACK.

feeder   a line or set of lines that carries radio power from a transmitter to an AERIAL system.

feed forward   an error correction circuit for an analogue POWER AMPLIFIER (sense 1). A portion of the input signal is compared with the output signal and the result used to add a correction signal to the output.

feedforward circuit   a circuit in which signal is fed from an early stage to a comparator to be compared with signal from a later stage, with the result used to correct the voltage applied to a load.

feed horn   a tapering horn shape used to match a waveguide to free space.

feed point   the physical position on an AERIAL at which the FEEDER from a transmitter or to a receiver is connected.

feed-through   a form of connection that passes through a material. The device is often used as a type of component, such

as a feed-through CAPACITOR. A feed-through capacitor consists of a pin that is surrounded by a coaxial capacitor, creating a comparatively large capacitance between the pin and the body of the capacitor. The device is used to decouple (see DECOUPLING) connections that pass out of or into a circuit through a metal panel.

feed-through capacitor   see LEAD-THROUGH CAPACITOR.

feed-through port connector   a connector for a port that allows a second connector to be plugged into place for another piece of equipment using that port.

feed unit   the waveguide or inductor that is placed at the focus of a SATELLITE DISH so as to receive or transmit signals.

female connector   the socket portion of a plug and socket system. See also MALE CONNECTOR; JACK PLUG; JILL.

femto-   a submultiple equal to 10^{-15}.

femtosecond   unit of time equal to 10^{-15} seconds.

FEP   see FRONT END PROCESSOR.

FEPROM   see FLASH ERASABLE PROGRAMMABLE READ-ONLY MEMORY.

Fermi-Dirac statistics   the mathematical relationship between ELECTRON energy in an ATOM and the number of electrons with that given energy.

Fermi level   the maximum energy levels of electrons at a temperature of ABSOLUTE ZERO.

ferric oxide   the red oxide of iron (Fe_3O_4), which is fairly strongly magnetic and extensively used for magnetic tape coatings. See also CHROMIUM DIOXIDE; GAMMA FERRIC OXIDE.

ferrite   a brittle crystalline material made from oxides of iron and other metals, used as an electrically-insulating magnetic material.

ferrite bead   a pierced ball of FERRITE material that can be threaded on to a connecting lead in order to increase inductance and so block unwanted high-frequency signals.

ferrite core or **ferrite dust core**   a core for an inductor using FERRITE material to increase the inductance.

ferrite-core inductor an inductor wound on a FERRITE core or contained within a ferrite enclosure.

ferrite memory an old-established form of MAGNETIC CORE (sense 2) memory using small FERRITE beads threaded over pairs of wires that are used for reading and writing each unit. The size and cost of a ferrite memory prohibits its use except in conditions that are impossible for semiconductors.

ferrite rod or **ferrite slab** a rectangular block of FERRITE material with a coil wound on it, often used as an AERIAL in a MW RADIO receiver.

ferro-chrome tape a tape for cassette recorders in which a thin layer of chromium oxide is applied over a thicker layer of ferric oxide.

ferroelectric (of a DIELECTRIC material) capable of being IONIZED in one of two directions depending on the surrounding electric field.

ferroelectric memory a form of random access memory that uses a capacitor cell construction, but with a FERROELECTRIC MATERIAL, typically lead zirconate titanate, as a dielectric.

ferromagnetic (of a material) exhibiting the same type of magnetic behaviour as iron, a characteristic of magnetic materials that have high PERMEABILITY. See also HYSTERESIS LOOP.

FET see FIELD EFFECT TRANSISTOR.

fetch-execute cycle the MICROPROCESSOR cycle of fetching an instruction code, decoding it and then carrying out the instruction.

FEXT see FAR END CROSS TALK.

F fuse or **normal blo fuse** a fuse that will rupture in 10 ms or less for a tenfold overload and in about 20 seconds for a twofold overload See also FF FUSE; M FUSE; SLO-BLO FUSE; T FUSE; TT FUSE.

FF fuse the fastest category of FUSE that will rupture in 1 millisecond for a tenfold overload.

FFSK see FAST FREQUENCY SHIFT KEYING.

FFT see FAST FOURIER TRANSFORM.

FG *abbrev. for* frequency generator, see SIGNAL GENERATOR.

fibre channel a data transmission system using optical fibre, designed initially for FULL DUPLEX connection at up to 100 Mb/s for video editing uses.

fibre dispersion the effect of broadening and flattening the shape of a PULSE carried over a FIBRE OPTIC CABLE, caused by DISPERSION.

fibre distributed data interface (FDDI) a TOKEN RING network system that uses OPTICAL FIBRE interconnections, with a typical bit rate of 100Mb/s.

fibre distributed video/voice data interface (FDVDI) a more recent development of the FDDI network with a data rate of 2.48 Gb/s.

fibre jointing connection of two ends of OPTICAL FIBRE so as to achieve low signal loss, usually by FUSION SPLICING.

fibre optic cable a cable of optical fibre (see FIBRE OPTICS) covered with protective sheathing and used for carrying WIDEBAND signals over large distances with minimum ATTENUATION.

fibre optics the use of highly transparent glass fibres to carry light signals. The fibres are of coaxial structure, using a core of material that has a higher REFRACTIVE INDEX than the surrounding material. This causes total internal reflection and so prevents light beams from escaping from the material. Because a light beam is an electromagnetic wave with a frequency in the range of 10^{14}–10^{15} Hz, huge amounts of information can be carried on one beam.

field **1.** a part of space in which a force effect acts. In an ELECTRIC FIELD, a force can be detected on any charge. In a MAGNETIC FIELD, a force will be detected on any magnetic material, or on a wire that carries current. **2.** (in TV) a half-frame of a picture, see RASTER.

field coil a coil that is used to generate a MAGNETIC FIELD by passing current through the coil.

field control the adjustment of MAGNETIC FIELD in an electric motor or AC generator. Field control is used to adjust DC motor speed or AC generator output voltage.

field effect transistor (FET) a form of transistor in which current flow through a conducting CHANNEL (sense 2) is controlled by voltage applied to a GATE (sense 1). Considering the older junction field effect transistor (JFET or JUGFET), contacts are made to the two end faces of a bar of doped silicon which is called the *channel* (the *n-channel* if doped using N-TYPE impurities, and the *p-channel* if doped using P-TYPE impurities). The contacts to the channel are called the *source* and the *drain* respectively. Supposing that the channel is of the n-type, a p-type region will be diffused into the centre of the silicon bar. If a voltage is applied between the source and the drain, electrons will be injected into the channel at the source and collected at the drain, constituting channel current. See Fig. 45.

Around the p-n junction formed between the gate and the channel, a DEPLETION LAYER will form. The presence of this depletion layer narrows the effective width of the channel as far as current carriers (electrons in this example) are concerned. If the gate is made negative with respect to the source, the width of the depletion layer increases, reducing the drain-source current. Thus voltage on the gate controls the current through the device. If the FET uses a p-channel, the action is the same but with the voltages and currents reversed. The gate must never be operated at a voltage that allows current to flow between the gate and the channel; it is used only in DEPLETION MODE.

If a thin layer of silicon oxide is placed between the channel and the gate regions, the gate may be made positive (for n-channel devices) without current flowing between gate and channel, but the effect is to widen the effective conducting area of the channel and so reduce the channel resistance. This type of FET is known as a *metal-oxide semiconductor FET (MOSFET)* (the older name was *insulated gate FET,* or *IGFET*) after the form of construction used. A MOSFET can be used in either depletion or ENHANCEMENT MODE, and the amount of insulation resistance at the gate is very high so that gate current is almost immeasurably small. The gate is, however, very susceptible to electrostatic damage.

field emission the emission of electrons in a vacuum due to a very large ELECTRIC FIELD. Any sharp point at a high potential can cause field emission, and this can be a cause of failure or flashover, particularly in large THERMIONIC VALVES.

field force any force, such as gravity or magnetism, that can be exerted without any visible physical contact between objects.

field frequency the rate of repetition of the complete screen scan in a TV system. See RASTER.

field magnet a permanent magnet that is used to obtain a magnetic field. The field can be used in a small DC motor or for deflecting an electron beam. An electromagnet is more controllable, so a FIELD COIL is more often used.

field programmable logic array (FPLA) a type of PROGRAMMABLE LOGIC DEVICE (OR and AND gates) whose interconnections can be carried out on the completed chip.

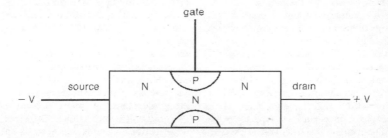

Fig. 45. **field effect transister**

field scan the vertical SCANNING action in a TV receiver, covering half of the lines of a FRAME (sense 1) in each scan action.

field-strength contour a map of ELECTROMAGNETIC FIELD strength plotted against geographic position to indicate the quality of radio reception at various places.

field strength meter or **intensity of field meter** an instrument used to measure received signal strengths. The meter typically uses tuning circuits, followed by a rectifier to obtain a DC voltage proportional to the amplitude of the radio frequency signal. The meter is used in conjunction with an AERIAL to plot the strength of CARRIER (sense 1) signal at various places remote from a transmitter. This allows maps of field strengths to be drawn up to assess the effective SERVICE AREA of a transmitter.

field sync the synchronizing of each FIELD (sense 2) of a TV FRAME (sense 1). Because of the differences between odd and even fields, this requires EQUALIZING PULSES to be added to the waveform. See also RASTER.

field timebase the circuit that generates and controls the VERTICAL SCAN in a TV receiver or a TV camera device.

field winding the set of coils in the YOKE of a TV RECEIVER that carry the FIELD SCAN current and so deflect the electron beams in a vertical direction.

FIFO memory or **FIFO register** see FIRST IN FIRST OUT.

figure of eight response see CARDIOID.

figure-of-merit (FOM) 1. see OHM PER VOLT FIGURE. 2. an amplifier factor for efficiency calculated from (peak AC power output)/(DC power input) × 100%. This factor can produce figures greater than 100%.

filament a thin metal wire heated by passing CURRENT through it, used in THERMIONIC VALVES to provide CATHODE (sense 1) heating or electron emission. For indirect heating, molybdenum wire is used. For direct emission, tungsten is the most common filament material, though platinum is used in some x-ray tubes and x-ray rectifiers.

filament display an ALPHANUMERIC display that is manufactured using tiny metal filaments set into a figure eight pattern. This allows the normal form of SEVEN-SEGMENT DISPLAY decoder to drive the filaments.

filament lamp a lamp that uses a hot filament in a non-oxidizing gas to produce heat and light.

film a thin coating of any material.

film resistor a resistor that is manufactured by coating a FILM of metal, metal oxides, or carbon onto a ceramic cylinder. A spiral is then cut into the film to adjust the resistor to its nominal value. Film resistors have now replaced most of the older resistor types for use in electronics.

filter or **wave filter** a network that can select signals of a required frequency range. Any filter will have a PASS BAND, meaning the range of frequencies that it will pass with low attenuation, and a STOP BAND of frequencies that are greatly attenuated (see ATTENUATION). The main filter types are LOW-PASS FILTERS, HIGH-PASS FILTERS, BAND-PASS FILTERS and BAND-STOP FILTERS. Filters may contain only PASSIVE COMPONENTs such as resistors, capacitors and inductors, or use ACTIVE COMPONENTS such as transistors and ICs. Modern ACTIVE FILTERS are much easier to design than passive filters, though computer-aided design systems make either type reasonably easy to deal with. Contrast ALL-PASS NETWORK.

filter, active see ACTIVE FILTER.

filtering mains see MAINS FILTERING.

filtering, SAW see SAW FILTER.

filter method the system for achieving a SINGLE SIDEBAND signal by filtering off the unwanted sideband. See also PHASING METHOD.

filter, optical see OPTICAL FILTER.

filter, rectifier the circuit that reduces the amplitude of RIPPLE (sense 1) following RECTIFICATION of an AC voltage into DC.

filter, Sallen and Key see SALLEN AND KEY FILTER.

filter section a portion of a LADDER FILTER, usually of the constant-k type, that can be either of the T or Pi form. See Fig. 46.

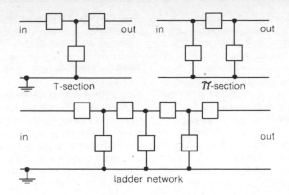

Fig. 46. **filter section**

filter synthesis the use of computer methods to design FILTERs of various types by specifying the required performance.

filter, twin-T notch see TWIN-T NOTCH FILTER.

fin a metal surface in an air stream, used for cooling a SEMICONDUCTOR either directly or as part of a HEATSINK.

final anode the anode in a CATHODE-RAY TUBE design that collects most of the emitted electrons. The final anode will be a conducting layer either on the screen (see ALUMINIZED SCREEN) or immediately surrounding the screen.

finalized disc a CD-R, CD-RW or DVD writable disc that has had its overall LEAD-IN (sense 1) and LEAD-OUT information written so that nothing further can be recorded. An unfinalized disc can usually be read by the computer that created it, but may not play on an ordinary music CD (or film DVD) player.

final loop see DROP CABLE.

final setting switch an external switch that arms a security system manually, as distinct from a time-delay system that will arm all systems at a fixed time after a setting switch is used.

fine-matrix tube a colour CATHODE-RAY TUBE with a larger number of picture elements (see TRIAD) on the screen, providing higher RESOLUTION if the CONVERGENCE system is adequate.

fingerprint a recognizable SPECTRUM of noise that remains following a noise reduction process, an undesirable feature.

finite impulse response filter or **FIR** or **non-recursive filter** or **transversal filter** a form of filter based on SHIFT REGISTERS that sums the result of amplified and delayed signals to produce a PHASE-LINEAR stable filter used mainly for LOW-PASS FILTERing and equalizing.

finline a form of MICROWAVE INTEGRATED STRUCTURE that uses metallized glass-fibre reinforced PTFE inserted into a WAVEGUIDE so as to couple with the ELECTRIC FIELD. Losses are low, and operation up to 100 GHz is usual. See also COPLANAR WAVEGUIDE; MICROSTRIP; SLOTLINE.

FIR see FINITE RESPONSE FILTER.

Fire code a form of correcting CYCLIC CODE (invented by P. Fire) that will detect and correct a single BURST OF ERRORS in a BLOCK (sense 2) of digits with minimal REDUNDANCY.

fire detector any form of device that detects flame by temperature, light or smoke.

firewall a guard against intrusion into a computer that is connected into a network, particularly into the Internet. A firewall can be implemented by SOFTWARE, but for a large installation it is usually a separate computer through which all external communications must pass, and which performs checks on all such signals.

Firewire see IEEE 1394-1995 BUS.

firing pulse a pulse applied to the gate of a THYRISTOR or similar device in order to make the ANODE to CATHODE (sense 2) path conductive.

firmware any program for a computer that is built into the system by being held in a PROM so that it can be altered if necessary but is not easily altered accidentally. Firmware is also used extensively on devices such as DVD recorders and set-top boxes, and can be altered by downloading new code either directly (as for a set-top box) or via the internet and a computer (for a DVD recorder).

first anode see ACCELERATING ANODE.

first detector the FREQUENCY CHANGER of a SUPERHETERODYNE RECEIVER.

first in first out (FIFO) memory or **FIFO register** a data storage REGISTER for computers that operates as a queue, so that the first bit written into the register becomes the first bit to be retrieved. Compare LAST IN FIRST OUT (LIFO).

first in last out (FILO) memory or **FILO register** a data storage REGISTER for computers that operates as a stack, so that the first bit written into the register becomes the last bit to be retrieved. Compare FIRST IN FIRST OUT (FIFO).

FIT see FAILURE IN TIME.

five unit code a five bit TELEPRINTER code of 32 characters that can be extended by using case shift codes for letter and figure shift.

fixation the act of finalizing (see FINALIZED DISC) a CD-R, CD-RW or DVD writable disc.

fixed pattern noise noise that remains of the same spectrum, and hence more noticeable to the ear or eye, irrespective of the data content of the signal.

fixed resistor a RESISTOR whose value is not variable by any mechanism.

fixed return a RADAR wave echo from a fixed object such as a building or a mountain. The problem posed by fixed returns is that they can make it difficult to detect moving objects. See also CANCELLATION CIRCUIT; RADAR.

fixed-voltage regulator or **fixed-voltage stabilizer** a REGULATOR integrated circuit whose output regulated voltage cannot be adjusted.

fixed-voltage stabilizer see FIXED-VOLTAGE REGULATOR.

flag one or more bits used in a DIGITAL SIGNAL to carry other information and indications such as start of data, end of data, PARITY, etc.

flame detector a photocell, usually of the CADMIUM-SULPHIDE LDR type, used to detect flame in boiler controls because of its high sensitivity in a red and infra-red region.

flame electrode a flame used to make an electrical connection by way of the conductivity of the hot gases in the flame, see PLASMA. The flame electrode is used to measure the PD at points in the air to calculate ELECTROSTATIC FIELD strength and the amount of CHARGE causing the fields.

flameproof switch a switch enclosed in a gas-tight casing so that any sparking at the switch contacts cannot ignite FLAMMABLE GAS or vapour outside the switch.

flammable gas any type of gas that will ignite if mixed with air and exposed to a spark, flame or high temperature.

flammable gas sensor a device, based on a form of CELL or on the effect of contamination on a SEMICONDUCTOR surface, that will provide an electrical output in the presence of some specified FLAMMABLE GAS.

flanger an analogue delay line circuit used to provide frequency-sweeping effects for a SYNTHESIZER. See also PHASER.

flash to apply a voltage PULSE to a COMPONENT. Flashing can be used to burn away tiny sharp points, because of intense FIELD EMISSION, and is often used in the AGEING of THERMIONIC VALVES.

flash ADC see FLASH CONVERTER.

flash BIOS a form of BIOS for a computer that can be rewritten with data by using a combination of software and hardware. This allows for easy updating of the BIOS, but is a potential entry point for a VIRUS.

flash converter a very fast form of ANALOGUE TO DIGITAL CONVERTER, using a set of 256 converters linked to a

256-resistor chain, each converter operating over a limited range of signal and producing a bit for one signal level.

flash erasable programmable read-only memory (FEPROM) a form of low-cost PROM that can be erased in one second or less by a pulse applied to a pin. Such devices have large capacity, years of data retention and relatively low access times (sense 1).

flash memory a form of read-write memory that remains read-only until operated under higher voltage conditions.

flashover a temporary BREAKDOWN of insulation, allowing a spark or discharge.

flash test a test of a component that involves applying higher than normal voltage and/or current for a short period.

flat line a signal TRANSMISSION LINE that is perfectly matched, with no trace of STANDING WAVES.

flatpack a thin package that contains an INTEGRATED CIRCUIT. The IC is connected to leads that emerge from the edges of the pack. Compare DIL PACKAGE.

flat panel display a MONITOR display, usually LCD or PLASMA, that is in the form of a flat panel, as distinct from any type of CATHODE-RAY TUBE.

flat plate battery a form of rechargeable LEAD-ACID CELL, often in a transparent case with visible ELECTROLYTE indicators.

flat response a horizontal line on a graph of AMPLITUDE plotted against FREQUENCY.

flat tuning a tuning position at which a variation of the tuning control produces very little change of signal strength at the DEMODULATOR.

F layer or **Appleton layer** the main reflecting layer in the IONOSPHERE, extending from about 150km to 1000km above the Earth's surface. The layer is very strongly ionized and will reflect waves with wavelengths of between 6mm and 20m.

Fleming's rules a method of remembering directional relationship between current, magnetic field and force; used in motor and dynamo principles. See Fig. 47.

flexible lead or **flexible cable** a conducting wire that can be flexed without breaking, used to connect a stationary circuit to one that is moved, such as a printer carriage.

flicker the small variations in brightness that are obvious to the eye. Because the eye stores an image for a short time, about a tenth of a second, variations in brightness that are not too large are not noticed if they occur fast enough, 16 to 24 times per second. For bright pictures, however, a much higher repetition rate must be used if the eye is not to notice flicker, hence the use of a field rate of 50 fields per second for TV.

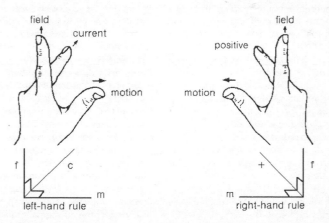

Fig. 47. **Fleming's rules**

flicker effect the irregular emission of current carriers, causing FLICKER NOISE.

flicker noise a type of noise signal caused by tiny irregular variations in CURRENT. This type of noise exists because current carriers (ELECTRONS or HOLES) are not emitted at a perfectly uniform rate, either into a vacuum or into semiconductor material.

flickering colour a VIDEO CASSETTE RECORDER problem caused by a large difference in the CHROMINANCE SIGNAL response between the two heads or from a fault in the phase SWITCHING CIRCUITS.

flip chip an INTEGRATED CIRCUIT chip connected directly to a circuit. The flip-chip uses thick bonding pads that can be welded to circuit connections when the chip is inverted.

flip-flop or **binary** (sense 2) a BISTABLE device used in digital circuits. The output of a flip-flop changes state from 1 to 0 or vice versa each time an input pulse is applied. Some flip-flops are triggered by the rising or falling edge of a pulse (*edge-clocked devices*), and some by the flat top of the pulse (*level-clocked devices*). The action can be described by a STATE TABLE that shows the inputs and the various outputs that they produce at or just following the clock pulse. See also D-TYPE FLIP-FLOP; J-K FLIP-FLOP; MASTER-SLAVE FLIP-FLOP; R-S FLIP-FLOP; TOGGLING.

float charge the continuous charging of a LEAD-ACID CELL, particularly when used in an UNINTERRUPTABLE POWER SUPPLY (UPS). The float charge voltage must not exceed 2.25V per cell, otherwise hydrogen release ('gassing') becomes excessive.

floating (of an electronic device or connection) unconnected to any voltage or signal.

floating carrier modulation see CONTROLLED CARRIER MODULATION.

floating earth or **floating ground** a point in a circuit that provides a current return path but is not connected to a true EARTH (ground).

floating input an input to a circuit that is left unconnected.

floating line a connecting line that can be isolated so that any voltage on the line does not affect devices connected to it. See also THREE-STATE LOGIC.

floating point converter or **flying comma converter** a form of ANALOGUE TO DIGITAL CONVERTER in which the input signal range has been adjusted so that it makes use of the whole possible range of converter number outputs. The gain adjustment has to be coded along with the output.

floating point operation an arithmetical action performed on a number that is represented in MANTISSA-EXPONENT FORM. The time taken for a typical floating point operation is used as a unit to compare MICROPROCESSOR speed in Mflop/s, millions of floating point operations per second.

floating regulator or **floating stabilizer** a circuit in which the three connections of an IC REGULATOR are returned to a common line that is not connected to EARTH, such as in a current regulator (see CURRENT REGULATION) circuit.

float switch a switch operated by a float and arm mechanism, used to detect the level of a liquid.

FLOF full level-one features: see FASTEXT.

flood-gun an ELECTRON GUN that produces a wide parallel beam of electrons. This type of gun was used in the direct view STORAGE TUBE.

floppy disk a thin plastic disk, now obsolescent, coated with magnetic material and used as a method of data storage and interchange for small computers. See also CD-ROM.

floppy drive or **floppy disk drive** a computer drive that is used along with a FLOPPY DISK.

flow soldering a technique used in large scale assembly of PRINTED CIRCUIT BOARDS to solder all the connections in one operation by moving the board over a wave of molten solder.

Flowers, Tommy see BLETCHLEY PARK; COLOSSUS.

fluctuating sound a VIDEO CASSETTE RECORDER problem caused usually by tape speed variations, often due to CAPSTAN or PINCH-WHEEL faults.

fluorescence the emission of light without heating. A fluorescent substance emits light when it is struck by electrons or by high-energy radiation such as ultra-violet radiation.

fluorescent display a form of bright ALPHANUMERIC display using gas IONIZATION and a fluorescent PHOSPHOR to produce illumination rather than the LED or LCD principles.

fluorescent screen see FLUORESCENCE; PHOSPHOR.

fluorescent tube a light source that uses a gas discharge in mercury vapour to generate ultra-violet, and converts this to visible light using a PHOSPHOR coating on the inside of the tube.

flutter a rapid variation of the pitch of an audio note that should be constant. Flutter is a fault of an analogue RECORDING or playback system that is usually caused by poor speed control of a tape drive or turntable. See also WOW.

flux 1. or **lines of force** a quantity that represents the effect of a field over an area. 2. see SOLDER FLUX.

flux cored solder SOLDER formed into tiny tubes that are filled with resin FLUX (sense 2), making the soldering action easier provided that the metal surfaces are clean.

flux density the concentration of ELECTRIC FLUX or MAGNETIC FLUX per unit area, measuring the strength of a FIELD (sense 1).

flux gradient a progressive change of FLUX (sense 1) spacing over a distance or area, used to provide better CONVERGENCE in a colour CATHODE-RAY TUBE.

flux, magnetic see MAGNETIC FLUX.

fluxmeter a meter for measuring MAGNETIC FLUX. The most common modern type is the HALL EFFECT fluxmeter, which uses the effect of the magnetic field on a tiny semiconductor slab. The slab carries current, and applying a magnetic flux causes a potential difference to be generated across the slab. This potential difference is amplified and used to drive a meter that is calibrated in terms of flux or flux density.

flux pattern the shape of an area or volume of FLUX (sense 1) in the form of a graph of flux strength plotted against position.

flux reversal the condition of maximum rate of change of FLUX (sense 1) for a magnetic signal, causing a maximum output from an INDUCTIVE HEAD.

flyback the part of a TIMEBASE waveform in which voltage or current returns to its starting state. Contrast SWEEP. See Fig. 48.

flyback converter or **flyback regulator** or **ringing choke converter** a form of SWITCH MODE POWER SUPPLY (SMPS) that uses a SWITCHING TRANSISTOR and INDUCTOR to generate a stable output with a high RIPPLE (sense 1) frequency that is easily smoothed. This form of SMPS is not suitable if high peak currents are likely to be drawn.

flyback lines, visible a TV receiver problem that can indicate a failing CATHODE-RAY TUBE, but which can also be due to excessive FIRST ANODE voltage or to problems in the BLANKING circuits.

fly-by memory a form of error detection and correction applied to words read from a MEMORY. When a BIT ERROR is detected it is corrected in the memory before the word is placed on the DATA BUS.

flying comma converter see FLOATING POINT CONVERTER.

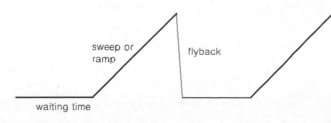

sweep or ramp

flyback

waiting time

Fig. 48. **flyback**

flying spot scanner a device that allows films, either still or cine, to be televized. The scanner consists of a high-brightness CATHODE-RAY TUBE whose moving SPOT (sense 1) is focused onto the film. The light that passes through the film is picked up by a photocell and used to produce the output signal. After addition of BLANKING pulses, sync pulses and colour sync, this can be used as a standard TV signal.

fly-through memory a slower form of error detection and correction applied to words read from memory that applies detection and correction to all of the words before placing them on the DATA BUS.

flywheel 1. a rotating wheel that makes use of inertia to store KINETIC ENERGY. 2. (of a synchronizing circuit in a TV receiver) making use of a sine wave oscillator for generating the line timebase frequency. This oscillator uses a relatively HIGH-Q resonant circuit, so that the oscillation frequency will continue unchanged even if the synchronization is irregular.

flywheel diode or **freewheel diode** a diode used in a THYRISTOR motor control circuit to allow current to flow while the thyristor is not conducting. See Fig. 49.

flywheel effect the use of a RESONANT CIRCUIT, either L/C or crystal, to sustain oscillations with only a minimum of drive power, sometimes on a brief SYNCHRONIZING PULSE.

flywheel sync the use of a long TIME CONSTANT in a synchronizing circuit (see SYNCHRONIZING PULSE) so that the average effect of synchronizing pulses is used rather than the disrupting effects of IMPULSE NOISE.

FM see FREQUENCY MODULATION.

FM front end a unit consisting of RF AMPLIFIER, LOCAL OSCILLATOR and MIXER stages for an FM RECEIVER.

FM generator or **FM stereo generator** a form of specialized signal generator for testing and servicing FM stereo audio equipment.

FM modulator the circuitry in a VIDEO CASSETTE RECORDER that uses frequency modulation of the luminance signal at constant amplitude, so as to avoid problems of tape response. The CARRIER (sense 1) frequency is usually in the range 3 to 5 MHz.

FM RADAR a CONTINUOUS WAVE frequency modulated radar used particularly for radar altimeters. The reflected signal beats with the transmitted signal to form a frequency that is proportional to range.

FM stereo the system of transmitting the STEREO difference signal (L – R) on a suppressed SUBCARRIER along with the normal MONOPHONIC (L + R) signal frequency modulated on a carrier so as to provide for stereo transmission and reception.

FM stereo decoder the circuit portion of an audio stereo FM receiver in which the

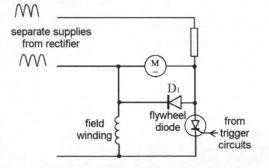

Fig. 49. **flywheel diode**

MULTIPLEX signal SIDEBANDS are separated from the mono sidebands, and the PILOT TONE is used to regenerate the CARRIER (sense 1) so that a PHASE-SENSITIVE DEMODULATOR can be carried out to recovered the L–R and L+R signals.

focal length   for a lens, the distance between the geometrical centre of the lens and the main FOCAL POINT.

focal point   for a perfect lens, the point on one side of the axis of a lens at which parallel rays entering the opposite side of the lens will all converge.

focus   a point through which a set of refracted or reflected rays or beams all pass, intensifying the power in the beam.

focus coil   1. the coil, part of a YOKE, used to focus the beams in a CATHODE-RAY TUBE that uses magnetic focusing. 2. the coil used to move the lens assembly of a CD PLAYER so that focus is maintained on the CD surface.

focus electrode   the metal cylinder within a CATHODE-RAY TUBE using electrostatic focusing whose voltage determines the point of focus of the electron beam on the screen.

focusing   the effect of making a beam of light or of electrons converge to a point, using a glass lens or a concave mirror for light and an electrostatic or magnetic lens for electrons.

focus servo   the servo mechanism and circuitry in a CD PLAYER that uses the FOCUS COIL (sense 2) and the TRACKING COIL to ensure correct focusing of the laser beam on the surface of a CD.

foil capacitor   a CAPACITOR that makes use of metal foil as its conducting electrodes. The term usually denotes paper capacitors that consist of thin oiled paper sandwiched between metal foils. The term can also denote some types of electrolytic capacitor in which the plate is of foil, such as the tantalum foil capacitor, see TANTALYTIC.

foil-shielded twisted pair (FTP)   a pair of BALANCED LINES in which the lines are twisted and contained in a metallic foil so as to improve their rejection of interference.

FOIRL   fibre optics inter-repeater link.

foldback protection   part of the circuitry of a REGULATOR IC that ensures that the output voltage and current will drop to a safe level if the output current rating is exceeded.

folded binary code or **symmetrical binary code**   any BINARY CODE in which the MOST SIGNIFICANT BIT is used to denote polarity, usually 0 for positive and 1 for negative.

folded dipole   a DIPOLE AERIAL in which the rod has been folded twice. This leaves the two connections at the centre as before, but reduces the IMPEDANCE of the aerial.

folded sideband or **ghost sideband**   a SIDEBAND that extends beyond zero frequency, caused by using a low frequency CARRIER (sense 1). Typically, a folded sideband is caused if (carrier frequency – modulation frequency) for a harmonic is a negative quantity.

foldover distortion   the effect of a folded sideband generating unwanted frequencies.

foldover, picture top   a TV receiver problem caused by a defect in the circuit that triggers FLYBACK.

follower circuit   a circuit arrangement, a form of BUFFER (sense 1), in which the output signal is in phase with the input circuit with a gain of less than unity. See also EMITTER FOLLOWER; FOLLOWER WITH GAIN; SOURCE FOLLOWER.

follower with gain   a circuit, usually implemented using an operational amplifier, that provides an output that is in phase with the input and of greater amplitude. Compare EMITTER FOLLOWER. See Fig. 50.

FOM   see FIGURE OF MERIT.

footprint   the ground area covered by a signal of given strength from a SATELLITE, usually displayed as contour lines on a map.

forbidden state   a combination of inputs, particularly to an R-S FLIP-FLOP, that results in an indeterminate or undesirable output.

force cube   a force sensor that uses a cube of deformable material with a STRAIN GAUGE on each axis, so that any force applied to the cube will cause deformation that will in turn cause an output from each strain gauge.

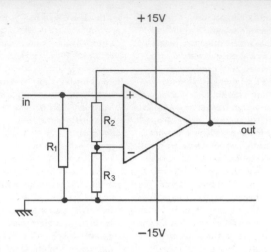

+15V

in

R_2

R_1

R_3

out

−15V

Fig. 50. **follower with gain**

forced-air cooling the cooling of a
component, such as transmitting
THERMIONIC VALVES or computer processor
chip, by passing air from a fan over the
hot material or over fins on a heatsink
attached to the hot device.

format wars marketing battles for
supremacy in consumer acceptance for
recording formats, such as Beta v. VHS,
and more recently the three DVD formats
of +R/+RW, −R/−RW and DVD-ROM.

form factor 1. a conversion factor for
calculating RECTIFIER output. The form
factor for a wave is the ratio of ROOT MEAN
SQUARE (sense 2) value to the rectified
DC value (average value) for a half-cycle.
2. the ratio of length to diameter for a coil;
used in NOMOGRAMS for calculating
inductance.

forming electrolytic the action of
establishing the film of hydrogen gas over
the electrodes of an ELECTROLYTIC
CAPACITOR, done by applying a voltage in
the correct polarity after manufacturing.

Forney formula a form of INTERLEAVING
used to reduce BURST ERRORS on digital
signals transmitted by SATELLITE.

forward AGC a system of AUTOMATIC GAIN
CONTROL that is used with modern

transistors. These transistors are operated
with a resistive load so that an increase of
bias will reduce the collector voltage, and
the characteristics of the transistors are
such that this will reduce the gain. The
steady voltage at the demodulator is
therefore used to add to the voltage bias.
Compare REVERSE AGC.

forward bias a voltage BIAS in the
direction that causes current to flow
easily. The term is used mainly of
semiconductor junctions and other types
of diodes. Compare REVERSE BIAS.

forward-biased junction a SEMICONDUCTOR
JUNCTION in which a voltage BIAS is
applied in the direction that will cause
current to flow.

forward converter a form of SWITCH MODE
POWER SUPPLY (SMPS) in which a transformer,
controlled by a switching transistor, is used
to supply the diode and inductor arrangement of a FLYBACK CONVERTER. This provides
isolation, higher efficiency and the ability
to cope with high peak current demand.

forward current the amount of current
flowing in the forward (freely conducting)
direction.

forward current transfer ratio (h_{fe}) the
ratio of COLLECTOR current to BASE current

for a BIPOLAR JUNCTION TRANSISTOR at constant collector voltage.

forward direction   the direction of normal current flow in a semiconductor JUNCTION (sense 2).

forward drop   the potential difference across a forward biased (see FORWARD BIAS) device such as a semiconductor diode.

forward echo   see ROUND THE WORLD ECHO.

forward error control (FEC) or **forward error correction**   an error detection and correction method for DIGITAL SIGNALs in which REDUNDANT BITS are used to provide checking and correcting information.

forward error correction   see FORWARD ERROR CONTROL.

forward resistance, diode   the resistance of a conducting DIODE; which is not a constant quantity but depends on the FORWARD CURRENT value.

forward scatter   a change of direction of a radio wave caused by small particles that are large compared to the wavelength but small compared with the diameter of the beam. The amount of deflection is less than 90° so that the direction of the radio wave is still forwards with respect to the transmitter rather than backwards as it would be if the beam had been reflected. See also BACK SCATTER.

forward voltage   the amount of bias required to make a semiconductor JUNCTION (sense 2) conduct.

forward wave   a wave travelling in the intended direction. For example, when a transmitter is connected to an AERIAL system, the forward wave travels from transmitter to aerial. There may be a reflected backward wave from aerial to transmitter, that will then result in STANDING WAVEs being set up. The term also denotes the input wave in a TRAVELLING WAVE TUBE.

Foster-Seeley discriminator   a form of DEMODULATOR circuit that was formerly used in FM receivers of high quality.

four binary-three ternary code (4B3T) a system of BINARY CODING in which the message is divided into groups of four bits and each group is converted into TERNARY CODE following a conversion

table. The signal has almost zero DC component, it is easy to detect errors and it requires a lower bandwidth.

four-head drum   a drum for a VIDEO CASSETTE RECORDER that uses four heads evenly spaced around the drum. This allows for a much less extensive tape wrap and better transition from one head to another, permitting a much better quality of still or slow motion picture.

Fourier analysis   a mathematical method of determining the frequency content of a signal. Any NON-SINUSOIDAL waveform can be shown to consist of a set of sine wave frequencies of various amplitudes and phases. The lowest frequency is the FUNDAMENTAL FREQUENCY and the others are harmonics. Fourier analysis allows the amplitude and phase of each component of the signal to be calculated. Computer programs can be used for this analysis.

Fourier representation   the analysis of a signal WAVEFORM into a set of sine or cosine waves with different AMPLITUDE and PHASE characteristics.

Fourier series   a set of sine or cosine wave terms that can be summed to provide the equation for a complex wave.

Fourier transform   the relationship between a WAVESHAPE and the SPECTRUM of the wave.

four-layer diode   see THYRISTOR.

four quadrant multiplier   a type of MULTIPLYING D/A CONVERTER that uses a binary signal input along with an AC REFERENCE VOLTAGE.

four-terminal resistor   a form of standard resistor for use with POTENTIOMETER (sense 2) measurements. Two thick connectors are provided for passing current through the resistor. Two thin connectors are then used for connecting the resistor to the potentiometer for PD measurements. This greatly reduces any errors that would be caused by the resistance of contacts.

FPLA   see FIELD PROGRAMMABLE LOGIC ARRAY.

FPU   floating point unit: a standard arithmetical action used as a comparison of processing speed of computers.

fractal transform coding   a method of coding an image using pattern matching and an AFFINE TRANSFORM to compress the data very efficiently, though at a slow rate.

frame 1. a set of two television fields, see RASTER. 2. a unit of DATA containing several data WORDS along with bits used for error detection and correction, commonly used for digital radio and television signals.

frame aerial an AERIAL wound in the form of a large loop, used in early types of direction finding equipment and also in very old portable radio receivers.

frame alignment word (FAW) an 8-bit sequence used at the start of each BLOCK (sense 2) of 728 bits in a NICAM stereo signal DATA PACKET.

frame check BITS in a DATA PACKET used for FORWARD ERROR CONTROL purposes.

frame compression the removal of redundant information from the frames of a DIGITAL VIDEO picture.

frame interline transfer (FIT) a form of CCD for image sensing in which a variable speed shutter is used to maximize exposure, with an intermediate gate layer to avoid over-exposure.

frame, relay metal supports for the coil and contacts of a RELAY.

frame sequential an early form of COLOUR TELEVISION system in which FRAMES (sense 1) were transmitted in sets of three, one in each primary colour. This required a faster rate of frame, and was not compatible with existing monochrome systems.

frame store a memory used in a HIGH DEFINITION TV display system that allows frame speeds higher than 50 Hz to be used because the display speed need not be linked to the arrival speed of picture frames.

frame structure the assembly of data BITS into a set (frame), usually of 125µs duration, that provides a unit for transmission. See also DATA PACKET.

frame transfer (FT) a form of CCD for image sensing in which charge accumulates over a field period, following which the shutter closes and the charge pattern is moved to a storage memory from which the bits are read out line by line.

framing code part of the signal sent out by a remote control handset to identify type of handset and prepare the receiver for data.

framing signal or **timing signal** a signal of constant PHASE that accompanies a phase code modulated (see PHASE CODE MODULATION) digital signal to provide a demodulation phase standard.

Franklin aerial (or antenna) an aerial that uses three DIPOLE (sense 2) elements connected in series with a quarter-wavelength coupling between sections, providing high gain with all-round coverage. A folded version can also be used with little loss of gain.

Franklin oscillator a form of OSCILLATOR that makes use of a two-stage amplifier, with inversion in each stage, and one RESONANT CIRCUIT.

Fraunhofer region see FAR FIELD.

free-air condition the oscillation of a DIAPHRAGM in air without any form of enclosure.

free electron see CONDUCTION ELECTRON.

free-field calibration the CALIBRATION of a MICROPHONE in terms of output per unit sound-pressure. The calibration has to be carried out so that the presence of the microphone itself does not disturb the sound-wave pattern (the free field). If this is not possible, then the results have to be adjusted to allow for the field disturbance.

free oscillation an OSCILLATION that is not supplied with energy after an original impetus. Free oscillations will die away at a rate that depends on the amount of damping (see DAMPED) in the circuit.

free running multivibrator a MULTIVIBRATOR circuit that is not synchronized (see SYNCHRONIZATION) to any input, so that its frequency can vary due to changes in component values as temperature changes.

free space any space, such as a vacuum, that has unity values of RELATIVE PERMITTIVITY and RELATIVE PERMEABILITY. In practical terms, the air approximates to free-space conditions.

free space attenuation a measure of ATTENUATION dependent on WAVELENGTH that can be calculated for any transmitted wave at distance d from the transmitter as $\lambda/(4\pi d)^2$ where λ is the wavelength.

Freeview a DIGITAL TELEVISION standard used in the UK to transmit signals using CODED ORTHOGONAL FREQUENCY DIVISION MULTIPLEX (COFDM) format to existing TV aerials. See also SET-TOP BOX.

freezer spray or **freeze-mist** an aerosol that will rapidly lower the temperature of a component on which it is used, so as to check for faulty operation when the device is cooled.

frequency the rate at which a waveform action repeats, measured in HERTZ.

frequency agile system see SPREAD SPECTRUM.

frequency analyzer a measuring device that can detect the frequencies present in a signal, including FUNDAMENTALS and HARMONICS. See FOURIER ANALYSIS.

frequency band a range of frequencies (usually RF) used for a particular purpose in telecommunications. There are, for example, frequency bands allocated by international agreement (usually violated by at least one country and by innumerable 'pirate' broadcasters) for medium wave broadcasting, television, mobile radio, etc.

frequency changer the important mixer stage in a SUPERHETERODYNE receiver. In this stage, the incoming (variable) signal frequency is converted to a fixed INTERMEDIATE FREQUENCY for subsequent amplification.

frequency classification the listing of radio frequencies in convenient groups that are named, such as LF, HF, VHF, etc. Microwave frequencies are classed by letters, but the European set of letters are not identical to the US set. See Table 2.

Frequency	Wavelength	Name
<30 kHz	>10km	VLF
30kHz – 300kHz	10km – 1km	LF
300kHz – 3MHz	1km – 100m	MF
3MHz – 30MHz	100m – 10m	HF
30MHz – 300MHz	10m – 1m	VHF
300MHz – 3GHz	1m – 10cm	UHF
3GHz – 30GHz	10cm – 1cm	SHF
30GHz – 300GHz	1cm – 1mm	EHF

Table 2(a). **Frequency band classification**

Band	European lettering	US lettering
P	0.2 – 0.375GHz	0.2 – 1.0GHz
L	0.375 – 1.5GHz	1 – 2GHz
S	1.5 – 3.75GHz	2 – 4GHz
C	3.75 – 6GHz	4 – 8GHz
X	6 – 11.5GHz	8 – 12.5GHz
J	11.5 – 18GHz	–
Ku	–	12.5 – 18GHz
K	18 – 30GHz	18 – 26.5GHz
Ka	–	26.5 – 40GHz
Q	30 – 47GHz	–

Table 2(b). **Microwave sub-band classifications**

frequency compensation the design of a circuit to allow it to be used for wideband purposes. See COMPENSATED ATTENUATOR.

frequency control the determination of the frequency of an OSCILLATOR using such components as INDUCTORS, CAPACITORS, CRYSTALS, DIELECTRIC RESONATORS, and SURFACE ACOUSTIC WAVE devices.

frequency counter an instrument for precisely measuring frequency by counting the number of complete cycles in a unit of time.

frequency demodulation the extraction of the signal from a frequency modulated CARRIER (sense 1) using a FREQUENCY DISCRIMINATOR.

frequency deviation the change of CARRIER (sense 1) frequency caused by FREQUENCY MODULATION.

frequency discriminator a circuit that produces an output voltage proportional to input frequency over a limited range. Discriminators are used in FM demodulation, and in frequency controllers. Circuits such as the RATIO DETECTOR and the FOSTER-SEELEY DISCRIMINATOR have now been almost completely replaced by pulse-counting ICs, such as the PHASE-LOCKED LOOP.

frequency dispersion differences in the transmission time of signals of different frequencies along a line.

frequency distortion the distortion of a signal due to passing through circuits whose graph of GAIN plotted against frequency is not LINEAR over the BANDWIDTH of the signal.

frequency divider a circuit whose output is a lower frequency than that of the input, equal to the input frequency divided by an integer. Dividers generally make use of high-speed COUNTER INTEGRATED CIRCUITS.

frequency division duplex (FDD) the use of two channels at different frequencies to achieve analogue DUPLEX communication.

frequency division multiple access (FDMA) a system for multiple analogue broadcasts, particularly for analogue satellite transmissions, that allocates a separate frequency for each CHANNEL (sense 1) within a large band.

frequency division multiplex a SATELLITE broadcasting system in which each amplitude-modulated channel is allocated one of a set of contiguous channels in a large frequency band. See also CODE DIVISION MULTIPLEX; TIME DIVISION MULTIPLEX.

frequency division multiplexing (FDM) The use of two or more frequencies for a transmission by assigning a channel to each frequency.

frequency domain the use of frequency as the x-axis of a graph, as for a SPECTRUM ANALYZER display.

frequency-domain analysis the representation of a waveform by plotting its amplitude against frequency. See also TIME-DOMAIN ANALYSIS.

frequency doubler a circuit whose output is at exactly twice the frequency of the input. See FREQUENCY MULTIPLIER.

frequency hopping see SPREAD SPECTRUM.

frequency interleaving the use of the gaps in a SPECTRUM to carry additional information, as in the analogue colour TV system in which the gaps in the LUMINANCE spectrum are used to house the CHROMINANCE SIGNAL subcarrier with minimal interference.

frequency meter an instrument used to measure wave FREQUENCY. Nowadays, this consists of a counter and time standard, which effectively counts the number of cycles of wave in one second. For microwave frequencies, wavelength rather than frequency is measured, using calibrated CAVITY RESONATORS.

frequency modulated feedback demodulator a type of DEMODULATOR for FM signals in which the demodulated output passes through a LOW-PASS FILTER back to the VOLTAGE-CONTROLLED OSCILLATOR that is applied to the MIXER.

frequency modulation (FM) the MODULATION of a wave by the alteration of its FREQUENCY rather than its AMPLITUDE. The amplitude of the modulating wave corresponds to the frequency of the CARRIER (sense 1). The maximum change of frequency that is permitted by the specification for the system is called the FREQUENCY DEVIATION. The main advantage of the system is that fluctuations of carrier amplitude caused by FADING or interference should not affect the demodulated output at the receiver. See also PHASE MODULATION.

frequency multiplex audio a method of recording a digital audio portion of a video signal on a VIDEO CASSETTE RECORDER by frequency modulating (see FREQUENCY MODULATION) the audio on to a SUBCARRIER at 1.5 MHz and recording this at a low amplitude level along with the LUMINANCE signals. This is particularly useful for NICAM stereo sound signals.

frequency multiplier a stage whose output is at a FREQUENCY that is an integer multiple of the input frequency. Frequency multiplication is used in transmitters, particularly as a way of allowing one CRYSTAL OSCILLATOR to control frequencies in a number of different bands. The basis of frequency multiplication is an underbiased stage, whose output is rich in harmonics. The required harmonic is picked out by making the load a resonant circuit at the desired frequency. The most common multiplication ratios are two (FREQUENCY DOUBLER) and three (frequency tripler), because the amplitude of the harmonics for higher ratios is generally insufficient for reliable use.

frequency pulling the alteration in the FREQUENCY of an OSCILLATOR because of the electrical loading effect of a circuit connected to it. Applies to alteration of frequency caused by loading, because the frequency of oscillation is affected by the dynamic resistance, so reducing the overall resistance value. Frequency pulling is a particular problem in BEAT FREQUENCY oscillators that are intended to produce low frequency outputs, because the oscillator frequencies are very close to each other.

frequency range the set of frequencies over which a device or circuit is intended to operate.

frequency range, ear the limits of response of the human ear to sound of a constant amplitude. This response is not linear, and extends from 20 Hz to about 20 kHz, though the upper limit reduces with age.

frequency response or **frequency response graph** a graph of amplifier GAIN or filter ATTENUATION plotted against frequency.

frequency re-use extension of the usefulness of a radio band by using the same frequency for differently POLARIZED (sense 1) signals.

frequency selective surface a technique that allows a REFLECTOR dish to be used for two different frequencies by coating the surface with a pattern of conductors that operates as a reflector for a different feeder horn.

frequency shift keying (FSK) a method of coding DIGITAL information using one frequency to represent logic 1 and another frequency to represent logic 0.

frequency shift keying demodulation the methods COHERENT or NON-COHERENT of demodulating a FREQUENCY SHIFT KEYING signal, involving the use of two demodulator stages, one for each separate frequency.

frequency standard 1. a very stable oscillator whose output is used to calibrate other instruments. Nowadays, low cost rubidium MASERs can be bought for this purpose. 2. the standard transmissions from the Rugby transmitter that are used to check oscillator frequencies in the UK.

frequency synthesizer a circuit, usually based around a PHASE-LOCKED LOOP, that can generate a wide range of frequencies all under CRYSTAL CONTROL, used extensively as a LOCAL OSCILLATOR.

frequency synthesis a method of generating a stable frequency using a CRYSTAL OSCILLATOR, phase comparator, and VOLTAGE CONTROLLED OSCILLATOR. Using a programmable divider, a wide range of stable frequencies can be obtained from a single crystal.

frequency-synthesis tuning tuning a SUPERHETERODYNE receiver by making use of a FREQUENCY SYNTHESIZER to provide a LOCAL OSCILLATOR signal. This makes actions such as SEARCH TUNING and precise tuning control much easier.

frequency synthesizer, programmable see PROGRAMMABLE FREQUENCY SYNTHESIZER.

Fresnel lens or **zone plate** or **stepped lens** a form of lens fabricated by cutting, etching or printing a circular pattern into a transparent material. The effect is to alter the PHASE of a light beam so that in-phase light is directed to a point, the FOCUS of the Fresnel lens.

Fresnel zone plate aerial (or **antenna)** an aerial system consisting of a dielectric printed with concentric rings of wave reflective or absorbing ink, providing a gain figure proportional to the number of rings.

Frii's equation an equation for calculating the total NOISE FACTOR of a system, given the individual noise factors and gain figures for the component stages of the system.

fringe or **fringe reception area** an area at a long distance from a transmitter in which signal reception is only just usable.

front end processor a rudimentary computer used to operate on raw data before it is fed to a main machine. See also BACK END PROCESSOR.

front porch a part of a TV SYNCHRONIZING PULSE, consisting of a short interval of BLACK LEVEL that immediately precedes the line synchronizing pulse.

front projection a form of PROJECTION TV in which the projector unit faces the screen, like a photographic slide projector arrangement. Compare REAR PROJECTION. See also BEAMER; DIGITAL LIGHT PROCESSOR; PLASMA SCREEN.

front side bus the bus line in a computer that determines the speed of the processor and also the speed of access to memory.

For modern computers values of 133 MHz to more than 400 MHz are commonly used.

front to back ratio the ratio of radiated power in the intended direction of a DIRECTIONAL AERIAL to the power emitted in the reverse direction.

fruit false signals due to secondary interrogation in a SECONDARY SURVEILLANCE RADAR system.

frying 1. the sizzling sound that usually indicates ARCING in a high voltage circuit. 2. noise in an audio circuit caused by poor contacts.

FSB see FRONT SIDE BUS.

FSD or **f.s.d.** see FULL SCALE DEFLECTION.

FSK see FREQUENCY SHIFT KEYING.

FT see FRAME TRANSFER.

FTP see FOIL-SHIELDED TWISTED PAIR.

F2 layer the higher part of the F layer of the IONOSPHERE which is the result of the split in the F layer during daylight. The F2 layer peaks between 350 and 500 kilometres during summer daylight.

fudging the electronic adjustment of recorded sound, often providing an artificial effect.

fuel cell a form of cell in which a fuel, gaseous or liquid, is oxidized to provide electrons that move to provide a current. This is an action that is much more difficult to achieve than the normal type of CELL reaction in which a metal is dissolved by an acid or alkali.

full adder a LOGIC CIRCUIT that carries out the complete addition action. For two bits, a full adder needs three inputs that consist of the two bits to be added, plus any carry from a previous stage. The output consists of the sum digit and the

carry to a further full adder stage. See also ADDER; HALF-ADDER. See Fig. 51.

full cosine roll-off a form of LOW-PASS FILTER used in a data stream to reduce the effects of INTER-SYMBOL INTERFERENCE.

full duplex (of a channel) able to carry data in both directions at the same time.

full level one features (FLOF) see FASTEXT.

full motion video (FMV) any system for digitally coding fast-moving video pictures with a large amount of COMPRESSION. See MPEG.

full power response bandwidth the BANDWIDTH of an amplifier at full power, usually lower than the bandwidth for low-power because of the effects of SLEW-RATE limiting.

full scale deflection (FSD) the deflection of the needle of a meter movement to the last figure on the dial.

full subtractor a logic circuit that performs the action of subtraction with a carry in digit and a carry out digit. Compare HALF SUBTRACTOR.

full-wave bridge see BRIDGE RECTIFIER.

full-wave dipole a DIPOLE AERIAL whose total length is equal to a full WAVELENGTH of the signal frequency.

full-wave rectifier a rectifier circuit that produces a half wave peak in one direction for each half of an AC wave. This is nowadays carried out by using a transformer and a BRIDGE RECTIFIER circuit. See Fig. 52.

fumes, flux toxic gases emitted when a FLUX (sense 2) is heated during SOLDERING.

function generator a type of SIGNAL GENERATOR that can produce a set of different waveforms.

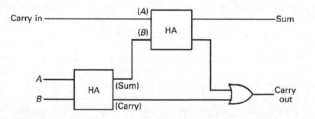

Fig. 51. **full adder**

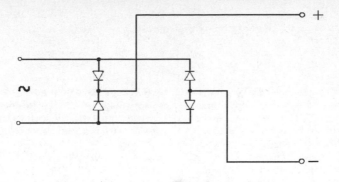

Fig. 52. **full-wave rectifier**

functional testing   see BLACK BOX TESTING.

fundamental frequency or **basic frequency** the lowest frequency of repetition in a wave that can consist also of HARMONICS. See also FOURIER ANALYSIS.

fundamental resonance   the lowest frequency at which an electronic circuit or a diaphragm can resonate (see RESONANCE).

fuse or **fuze**   a short piece of metal wire made from material that has a low melting point. Excessive current flowing through the fuse will melt the metal, so interrupting the circuit. The fuse then has to be replaced after the fault that caused the excessive current has been located and repaired. See also CIRCUIT BREAKER; CROWBAR PRINCIPLE; ELECTRONICALLY RESETTABLE FUSE; F FUSE; FF FUSE; M FUSE; T FUSE; TT FUSE.

fuse group   one of a set of five categories into which FUSE characteristics are grouped, mainly concerning the speed at which a fuse will blow under given overload conditions. See also F FUSE; FF FUSE; M FUSE; T FUSE; TT FUSE.

fuse holder   a clip that holds a FUSE and makes electrical connection to the ends of the fuse.

fusible link PROM   a form of PROGRAMMABLE READ-ONLY MEMORY in which the units are fusible threads which initially are all intact, representing logic 1. The programming action consists of addressing each link that is to be set to logic 0 and rupturing each using a high current.

fusible resistor   a resistor, often of nominal 10R or lower value, fitted into a circuit for safety reasons. These resistors will go open circuit or to a high resistance value to prevent an excessive current starting a fire and are often identified by special symbols on the circuit diagram.

fusion splicing   a method of connecting FIBRE OPTIC cables by aligning, melting and pushing glass strands together.

Futurebus   a design of MOTHERBOARD architecture for programs requiring fast processing, designed for up to 128-bit processors.

fuzzy logic   a system of processing imprecise data to provide the most likely outcome.

FYI   for your information.

G

GaAs FET a form of FET using GALLIUM ARSENIDE and capable of amplification at SHF, typically 15 dB gain with a low noise figure of 0.5 dB. A GaAs FET is used in a satellite receiving LOW-NOISE BOX.

gadolinium gallium garnet a non-magnetic alloy that is deposited on magnetic garnet to form a BUBBLE MEMORY.

gain or **amplification** the ratio of signal output to signal input for an amplifier. The ratio is often quoted in DECIBELS, using 10log(out/in) for power ratios and 20log(out/in) for voltage ratios. The gain of an AERIAL is the ratio of the signal power transmitted or received in the intended direction compared with the signal from or received by a simple DIPOLE AERIAL. Compare ATTENUATION.

gain, aerial see AERIAL GAIN.

gain bandwidth product a figure of merit for an OP-AMP, obtained by multiplying the gain in an amplifier circuit by the bandwidth. This does not allow for SLEW-RATE effects, but is useful for calculating bandwidth for small signals when the gain is fixed by FEEDBACK.

gain compression the effect of loss of gain as a LINEAR amplifier approaches SATURATION (sense 1).

gain control a POTENTIOMETER (sense 1) or switch for varying signal amplitude.

gain-frequency response the graph of GAIN plotted against FREQUENCY for a LINEAR CIRCUIT such as an AMPLIFIER. Ideally, this should be a straight line for the band of frequencies handled by the circuit.

gain riding a system of channel BALANCE and GAIN control for multichannel audio in which the lowest and largest amplitudes in any channel are sampled to maintain the correct levels.

gain, TV screen the reinforcement in light output from a reflective screen of a FRONT-PROJECTION TV display seen from a head-on direction.

gain, voltage see VOLTAGE GAIN.

galactic noise electrical noise originating in outer space which reaches its lowest levels in the frequency range of 1 GHz to 10 GHz.

galena a lead sulphide crystal that can form an unreliable SEMICONDUCTOR point contact with a steel wire (see CAT'S WHISKER); formerly used in a CRYSTAL RECEIVER as a detector.

gallium arsenide a compound SEMICONDUCTOR. Unlike silicon or germanium, gallium arsenide is not an element. It is almost impossible to dope by diffusion, and modern methods rely on ION IMPLANTATION. The doped material has very low resistivity, but its reversed biased junctions are of very high resistance. Gallium arsenide is used mainly for microwave diodes, and for FETs that can be used at UHF and SHF.

gallium arsenide transistor a form of low-noise high-frequency transistor used mainly in satellite reception, see LOW-NOISE BOX.

galloping pattern or **galpat** a form of MEMORY test in which the first memory cell has a logic 0 stored and all remaining cells are tested for corruption, and this is applied to each cell in turn. The whole sequence is then repeated with a logic 1 stored.

Galvani, Luigi (1737–1798) discovered that the leg of a dead frog would twitch when touched by dissimilar metals (a form of CELL) and when an electrostatic generator was being used nearby (effect of ELECTROMAGNETIC RADIATION). His name has been perpetuated in the *galvanometer* (a sensitive current meter), and *galvanizing* (coating iron with zinc as a rust-prevention system).

gamepad a small handset connected to the computer and used for controlling games.

games paddle see PADDLE.

games port a connection to a computer, often to the SOUND CARD, that allows games JOYSTICKS or PADDLES to be plugged in and used by games software.

gamma a constant for a colour or monochrome MONITOR that expresses the relationship of light intensity to signal voltage. The usual value is around 2.5, depending on which primary colour is being used and the design of the monitor.

gamma correction a compensating system that allows for the value of GAMMA for a MONITOR so that the light output will be proportional to the signal voltage. Gamma correction is usually handled by the GRAPHICS ADAPTER.

gamma ferric oxide a crystalline form of FERRIC OXIDE used for tape recording.

gamma ray a highly penetrating ELECTROMAGNETIC WAVE emitted from some radioactive materials. IONIZING POWER is low but the effect of deep penetration of gamma rays is lethal.

ganged capacitors a set, usually two but sometimes more, of variable capacitors on a common shaft so that their capacitance can be altered together by rotating the shaft. This was once the main method of varying incoming signal and OSCILLATOR tuning in a SUPERHETERODYNE receiver. See also PADDER; TRIMMER.

ganged circuits a set of CIRCUITS in which VARIABLE CAPACITORS, INDUCTORS or POTENTIOMETERS (sense 1) are mechanically linked and are operated with a single control. The ganging of variable capacitors in a SUPERHETERODYNE receiver, for example, allows the tuning of the oscillator and AERIAL frequency circuits to be altered together in step.

ganging the mechanical connection of adjustable COMPONENTS so that several can be operated by a single control.

gap a narrow break in a circuit. A *magnetic gap* consists of a narrow piece of non-magnetic material placed in a magnetic circuit. This is put in to prevent MAGNETIC SATURATION of the material. A SPARK GAP is often included in high voltage circuits. This consists of two metal conductors

close together, one at high voltage and the other earthed. The principle is that a voltage surge will cause a spark rather than damage components. See also BAND GAP.

gap, head a small gap of non-magnetic material, of the order of microns wide, across which an intense flux is developed in a tape recording head, or at which the movement of recorded tape will induce a voltage signal in a replay head.

gas breakdown see AVALANCHE.

gas discharge the flow of current in an ionized gas (see IONIZATION). Gases do not conduct current unless ionized, and a high enough field must be used to start ionization. The voltage that is required to start ionization will be higher in the absence of light, unless the gas in the tube is slightly radioactive. One former use of gas-discharge tubes was as voltage reference standards, since the voltage drop across a conducting gas is fairly constant. During the action of a gas-filled tube, the gas can be seen to glow, and this leads to applications of the effect as display devices.

gas discharge tube or **gas discharge lamp** a light-emitting tube that uses an IONIZED GAS at low pressure as its light source, see GAS DISCHARGE. See also FLUORESCENT TUBE.

gas-filled tube any type of valve that contains low-pressure gas rather than a vacuum. GEIGER-MÜLLER TUBES are gas-filled, as were the old THYRATRONS and IGNITRONS that were used as electronic relays. Gas-filled tubes were also used as voltage reference devices and for display devices.

gas-flame torch a miniature blowlamp, used as an alternative to the use of an electric soldering iron, particularly for work on highly conductive materials.

gas laser a type of LASER using a GAS DISCHARGE TUBE with precisely parallel and steadily reflecting ends, used as a source of coherent high power light for industrial or military purposes.

gas plasma display see PLASMA SCREEN.

gate **1.** the controlling electrode of a FIELD EFFECT TRANSISTOR or a THYRISTOR. **2.** a circuit that uses one WAVEFORM to control the passage of another. In analogue circuits, a gate will pass an input signal for a time that is determined by a gating signal, usually a square wave. Digital circuits use gates to carry out logic actions, see AND GATE; EXCLUSIVE OR GATE; NOT GATE; OR GATE.

gate array   a form of INTEGRATED CIRCUIT that consists of many separate gates. If these gates are not connected to each other, the array is described as uncommitted, see ERASEABLE PROGRAMMABLE LOGIC DEVICE; UNCOMMITTED LOGIC ARRAY.

gate expander   a CIRCUIT that is connected to the INPUT (sense 2) of a LOGIC GATE so as to allow further inputs to be connected.

gate insulation resistance   the very high resistance of a MOSFET gate that can allow electrostatic damage to occur unless diodes are used to prevent high voltages accumulating.

gate-turn-off (GTO)-thyristor   a form of THYRISTOR that can be turned on by a high current positive pulse to the GATE (sense 1) electrode and turned off by a negative pulse of lower current.

gating   the switching of a signal, on or off, by another (usually square wave or pulse) signal. See also LOGIC GATE.

gauge factor   the quantity defined by fractional change of the measurable quantity divided by the change of the quantity being gauged. For example, the gauge factor for a RESISTIVE STRAIN GAUGE is fractional change in resistance divided by change of strain.

Gaussian distribution or **normal distribution**   the graph of distribution for random numbers, which takes a bell-shape if the numbers are truly random.

Gaussian minimum frequency shift keying (GMFSK) or **Gaussian minimum shift keying (GMSK)** or **Gaussian filtered minimum shift keying**   a system of FREQUENCY SHIFT KEYING in which the input binary PULSES are filtered to the shape of a GAUSSIAN DISTRIBUTION. This results in a signal that uses the SPECTRUM more efficiently and is less liable to CO-CHANNEL INTERFERENCE.

Gaussian noise   see WHITE NOISE.

Gauss, Karl Friedrich   (1777–1855) German mathematician who developed the theory of MAGNETIC FIELDS and worked extensively on statistics. The name lives on in the name of a DEGAUSSING coil, and in the GAUSSIAN DISTRIBUTION.

GB or **Gbyte**   a unit of data equal to 10^9 (one thousand million) BYTES.

gbps   gigabits per second, a fast rate of data transfer of 10^9 BITS PER SECOND.

Geiger-Müller counter   a radiation detector for IONIZING PARTICLES, using a GEIGER-MÜLLER TUBE and a digital counter to indicate a count-rate.

Geiger-Müller tube   a form of GAS-FILLED TUBE used to detect IONIZING RADIATION. The tube contains a low-pressure gas, and a trace of a de-ionizing material such as bromine. Two electrodes in the tube are kept at a potential difference that is lower than is needed to start a discharge. When an ionizing particle enters the tube, gas is ionized, but the effect of the de-ionizing material is to cause RECOMBINATION of these ions when the particle passes out of the tube. The tube therefore passes current only for a brief interval, one pulse for each particle. See also DEAD TIME.

gender mender or **sex changer**   a connector for RS-232 serial cables to allow either two plugs or two sockets to be joined.

general packet radio system (GPRS)   the CELLULAR PHONE system developed from GSM (2G), also termed 2.5G, using PACKET SWITCHING and bit rates up to 115 kb/s.

general-purpose interface bus (GPIB)   see IEEE-448 BUS.

general-purpose port   an IC that has two sets of DATA pins along with CONTROL pins that allow data to be passed in either direction.

generator   **1.** a device that can supply electrical power, such as a DYNAMO or ALTERNATOR, both of which convert mechanical energy into electrical energy. **2.** any signal source that can be represented as a generator of signals in an EQUIVALENT CIRCUIT.

generator, audio   see AUDIO SIGNAL GENERATOR.

generator code   a set of digital bits that can be combined with the bits of data to produce a code either for security purposes or for error detection and correction, see FORWARD ERROR CONTROL.

generator polynomial   an equation of several terms that is used to generate a code. The generator POLYNOMIAL will be selected from a set of polynomials known as *primitive polynomials*.

generator, RF   see SIGNAL GENERATOR.

genlock   a system for synchronizing VIDEO signals so that images from different sources can be edited and combined.

geometric distortion   distortion of a TV image due to the screen not being an arc of a sphere with a radius equal to the distance between the ELECTRON GUN and the SCREEN. Flatter screens would display a very distorted image if corrections were not applied by modulating the LINE-SCANning waveform with a parabolic voltage shape at field and modulating the FIELD (sense 2) scanning current with a SAWTOOTH at line frequency.

geostationary orbit or **geosynchronous orbit** or **Clarke orbit**   the orbit of a SATELLITE that takes exactly one day to complete, so that the satellite always appears to be in the same position as seen from Earth. The use of satellites in such an orbit was predicted by Arthur C. Clarke in 1945.

Gerber™ machine   a plotting machine used for making PRINTED CIRCUIT BOARDS under computer control.

germanium   an element that was the first to be used for manufacturing transistors. Its use has now been almost completely superseded by that of SILICON.

getter   a material for removing the last traces of gas from a THERMIONIC VALVE or CATHODE-RAY TUBE. A getter consists of a thin film of a metal such as barium. This is a reactive metal that will absorb any traces of gas that may be produced as the tube is used. The use of getters is confined to the smaller receiving valves and cathode-ray tubes, because transmitting valves run at a temperature that would vaporize the getter. See also OUTGASSING.

Gflop   see GIGAFLOP.

ghost   see GHOSTING.

ghost cancelling   a system used to cancel the effect of GHOSTING by inserting, at the transmitter, a frequency sweep into one line in the vertical blanking time. At the receiver, the portion of line following this sweep is checked for a ghost signal, whose delay time can then be determined. Using this delay time, a ghost cancelling signal can be added to each line of the picture.

ghosting   the appearance of faint displaced images on a TV screen, usually caused by MULTIPATH RECEPTION of weak signals reflected from trees, buildings, etc.

GHz   see GIGAHERTZ.

Gibb's phenomenon   the OVERSHOOT and OSCILLATION effects on a pulse caused by filtering with a sharp cutoff. See also WINDOW FUNCTION.

giga   a multiple equal to 10^9.

gigabyte   a data unit of one thousand million bytes.

gigaflop   a unit of processing speed of one thousand million FLOATING POINT operations per second.

gigahertz or **GHz**   a unit of frequency equal to 10^9 (one thousand million) Hertz.

gimbal   a framework used to keep a small surface level despite movements of its surroundings, originally use for suspending ships' compasses.

glass-bar effect   the appearance of a band of distortion moving slowly up or down a SCREEN during the replay of a video cassette (see VIDEO CASSETTE RECORDER), caused by faulty changeover from one head to the other.

glass-box testing   see WHITE BOX TESTING.

glass delay line   a form of ACOUSTIC DELAY LINE formerly used in PAL TV receivers to delay the CHROMINANCE SIGNAL by the time of one line. Digital delays have superseded this electro-acoustical system.

glass electrode   a device for measuring the acidity (pH) of solutions, consisting of a wire connection to a conducting liquid inside a thin glass bulb. The voltage from a glass electrode needs to be amplified by an ELECTROMETER circuit (an amplifier with very high input resistance) before it can be measured.

glass fibre board   the insulating base for a PRINTED CIRCUIT BOARD with superior insulation and strength as compared to the usual SYNTHETIC RESIN BONDED PAPER (SRBP).

glitch   a TRANSIENT voltage spike that causes problems in a digital circuit because it is often indistinguishable from a PULSE. One common cause is a RACE HAZARD.

global positioning satellite or **global positioning system** or **GPS**   a method of defining position on Earth by making use of signals from at least three of the twenty-four SATELLITES orbiting the Earth at a height of 11,000 miles.

global register   a CACHE register for general use.

glow lamp   a GAS-FILLED TUBE used as an indicator or voltage regulator.

glue logic   the logic circuits that form interconnections between a MICROPROCESSOR or MICROCONTROLLER and the circuits that are controlled.

g_m or G_m   see MUTUAL CONDUCTANCE.

GMFSK   see GAUSSIAN MINIMUM FREQUENCY SHIFT KEYING.

GMSK   see GAUSSIAN MINIMUM FREQUENCY SHIFT KEYING.

GNN   global network navigator.

go/no go   a form of testing in which the standards are very strict, with low tolerance.

Golay code   a form of CYCLIC ERROR DETECTION AND CORRECTION code following the pattern of HAMMING CODE.

gold-bonding   a method of making a conducting connection between n-type germanium and a gold leadout wire.

Gold codes   a set of BINARY NUMBER codes generating ALGORITHMS devised by R. Gold to provide PSEUDO-RANDOM keys for encoding data. Gold codes are used in GLOBAL POSITIONING SATELLITE transmissions.

golden ratios   sets of values for relative height, width and length of rooms intended for optimum reproduction of sound or for recording-studio use. Typical H:W:L set of values are 1.0:1.14:1.39; 1.0:1.28:1.54; and 1.0:1.60:2.33.

good system   a CONTROL SYSTEM that is stable, responds quickly and works with a very low level of ERROR SIGNAL.

GOP   see GROUP OF PICTURES.

GPIB   general purpose instrumentation bus: see IEEE488 BUS.

GPRS   see GENERAL PACKET RADIO SERVICE.

GPS   see GLOBAL POSITIONING SATELLITE.

GPU   see GRAPHICS PROCESSING UNIT.

graceful degradation   the performance of an ANALOGUE channel under increasingly noisy conditions, steadily becoming of poorer quality, unlike the sudden failure of a digital link, known to digital TV viewers as *disgraceful degradation*.

graded index fibre   a form of construction for OPTICAL FIBRE in which the REFRACTIVE INDEX of the glass is varied more smoothly from core centre to outer layer, resulting in a lower reflection loss.

graded junction diode   a PN junction diode in which the CARRIER (sense 2) concentration varies linearly across the junction width, making the junction capacitance less dependent on applied reverse voltage. Contrast VARICAP DIODE.

grainy colour   a colour TV fault caused by a weak CHROMINANCE SIGNAL.

gramophone   a general name for the traditional audio VINYL DISC player. The term *compact disc player* is used for the modern successor. See also REPRODUCTION OF SOUND.

granular   (of a picture) composed of grains or visible PIXELS.

graph   a pictorial representation of how one quantity (the independent variable) varies as another (the dependent variable) is deliberately changed; usually drawn on squared paper. See INTERCEPT; SLOPE; X-AXIS; Y-AXIS.

graphic equalizer   a form of control used in some audio systems that consists of a set of FILTERS, allowing the user to tailor the amplitude-frequency response to suit his/her taste.

graphics   illustrations, as distinct from text, particularly in digital form.

graphics processing unit (GPU)   a single chip fast-acting computing processor for video signals corresponding to three-dimensional images, used in a GRAPHICS CARD.

graphic symbol   a symbol used to represent a component in a CIRCUIT DIAGRAM.

graphics accelerator board an add-on
BOARD for a computer that uses a GRAPHICS
COPROCESSOR to speed up the handling of
GRAPHICS by relieving the main processor
of this task. See also ACCELERATED
GRAPHICS PORT.

graphics adapter or **display adapter** or
graphics card a BOARD used in a small
computer to convert digital signals into
the outputs that will drive a CATHODE-RAY
TUBE or LCD display to provide graphics
display actions. For fast graphics actions,
a graphics card should be connected to a
LOCAL BUS such as AGP.

graphics card memory fast memory,
often of a type that allows simultaneous
input and output, for a GRAPHICS CARD
capable of high-speed animation displays.

graphics connector the fifteen-pin D-TYPE
CONNECTOR used for connecting the
computer to a MONITOR.

graphics coprocessor a separate
microprocessor used entirely to generate
signals for driving a MONITOR with still
and moving images.

graphics tablet a computer INPUT DEVICE
consisting of a rectangular plastic sheet
over which a STYLUS can be moved. The
movement of the stylus moves the cursor
on the computer screen and pressure on
the stylus will leave a mark on the screen,
so that drawing on the stylus produces
a digitized (see DIGITIZE) screen image of
the drawing.

graph recorder a form of CHART
RECORDER.

grass see GROUND CLUTTER.

graticule a set of horizontal and vertical
lines on a transparent plastic rectangle,
usually scaled in centimetre units and
placed on the screen of a CATHODE-RAY
TUBE for measuring TRACE amplitude and
timescales.

Gray code a four-bit BINARY CODE in which
only one bit will change when the number
is INCREMENTED or DECREMENTED. Table 3
shows the Gray code and (8-4-2-1) binary
codes compared for four-bit numbers.

Gray/XS3 code a combination of GRAY
CODE and EXCESS-3 CODE.

grazing losses signal losses caused by
REFLECTION and REFRACTION when a signal
is propagated parallel to the surface of the
Earth.

green monitor any MONITOR that uses
a power management system so that it
operates on reduced consumption when
not being actively used.

Gregorian reflector a small concave
reflector, a portion of an ellipse, used to
reflect beams entering a dish towards the
centre of the DISH where they can enter
the feed system. Contrast CASSEGRAIN
REFLECTOR. which uses a convex reflector.

grey scale the number of discernible
shades of grey between black and white
on the screen of a monitor. The larger the
grey scale, the better the picture quality.
A good grey scale is important in
computer use if graphics are to be used
on a monochrome screen or printed in
monochrome.

Denary	Gray code	8-4-2-1 binary	Denary	Gray code	8-4-2-1 binary
0	0000	0000	8	1100	1000
1	0001	0001	9	1101	1001
2	0011	0010	10	1111	1010
3	0010	0011	11	1110	1011
4	0110	0100	12	1010	1100
5	0111	0101	13	1011	1101
6	0101	0110	14	1001	1110
7	0100	0111	15	1000	1111

Table 3. **Gray code and binary compared**

grey scale image an image that represents colours by shades of grey.

grey scale monitor a MONITOR that will display shades of grey rather than colours.

grey scale tracking the adjustment of electron gun characteristics in a colour TV CATHODE-RAY TUBE so as to ensure that all three beams effectively have the same brightness/current curve shape.

grid an ELECTRODE that controls electron flow in a vacuum THERMIONIC VALVE or CATHODE-RAY TUBE. The type used in a cathode-ray tube consists of a small aperture in a top-hat shaped electrode. In a transmitting THERMIONIC VALVE, the grid is a winding of molybdenum wire surrounding the hot FILAMENT.

grid bias the voltage applied between CATHODE (sense 1) and GRID of a THERMIONIC VALVE or CATHODE-RAY TUBE to control electron flow. The bias is normally applied with the grid negative, and at a sufficiently large negative potential the electron stream will be cut off.

grid cylinder a cup-shaped electrode with a small hole to allow the passage of a beam of electrons from the CATHODE (sense 1) of the CATHODE-RAY TUBE. The voltage between grid cylinder and cathode controls the amount of beam current.

grid dip a form of passive TELEMETRY in which inductive COUPLING is used to transmit information over distances of up to 50cm. The name arises from a now obsolete circuit used to detect the frequency of a passive circuit by its effect on the grid current of a THERMIONIC VALVE oscillator tuned to the same frequency. Grid-dip telemetry is extensively used for biomedical work in which measurements have to be made by sensors implanted within a patient, where no physical connections are possible.

grid emission the emission of electrons from an overheated GRID, usually in a transmitting THERMIONIC VALVE used near its maximum ratings. The electrons from the grid will be accelerated to the ANODE, and will not be controlled by the grid

bias. This can result in more overheating, causing failure of the valve. Grids are commonly coated with graphite to reduce the emission of electrons and to help dissipation of heat by radiation.

grid modulation one method of achieving AMPLITUDE MODULATION at a transmitter. The final power amplifier THERMIONIC VALVE has its bias applied through a transformer winding to which is applied the modulating frequency. The advantage of this form of modulation is that the power that is required is relatively low. The disadvantage is that the power output stage has to be reasonably linear in operation, as distinct from the more usual CLASS C design.

groove packing density the number of grooves per inch in a VINYL DISC, typically 180–360.

groove pitch the distance between adjacent grooves in a VINYL DISC RECORDING.

gross information content the total content of a digital signal, consisting of both data and REDUNDANT BITS, needed for transmission with a specified BIT ERROR RATE.

ground see EARTH.

ground absorption or **ground attenuation** the loss of radiated signal power to EARTH. If the ground wave is absorbed rather than reflected, the range of the transmitter will be fairly short.

ground clutter RADAR reflections from irregular ground. These cause a fuzzy screen display that looks like grass.

grounded-base connection see COMMON-BASE CONNECTION.

grounded-collector connection see COMMON-COLLECTOR CONNECTION.

grounded-emitter connection see COMMON-EMITTER CONNECTION.

ground loop see EARTH LOOP.

ground plane see EARTH PLANE.

ground reflection a wave that has been reflected from the ground. If this happens to a radar echo, the distance measurements for the signal will be incorrect.

ground return ground echoes that cause GROUND CLUTTER.

ground wave or **surface wave** 1. an electromagnetic wave that travels close to the surface of the Earth, below the lower IONOSPHERE. This method of propagation is most useful for low-frequency waves. 2. a RADAR return wave that has been reflected from the ground causing an incorrect reading for distance.

group delay the characteristic of PHASE change per unit FREQUENCY for a transmission medium. If a transmission line has a fairly constant group delay it can transmit pulses with little distortion even if high frequencies are severely attenuated.

group delay distortion change of shape of the ENVELOPE of a wave due to a non-constant GROUP DELAY.

group of pictures (GOP) a set of IMAGE FRAMEs in an MPEG set, consisting of one I-FRAME and a set of DIFFERENCE FRAMES (P-FRAME and B-FRAME). The frames in a set of twelve are arranged as I B B P B B P B B P B B.

group velocity the velocity of a group of electromagnetic waves in a medium other than a vacuum. This velocity is always less than the velocity of the waves in a vacuum. Individual waves within the group *appear* to travel with a PHASE VELOCITY that is greater than the velocity of the waves in a vacuum.

grow back corruption of data in a FUSE-LINK PROM due to metal migration in electric fields causing broken links to be re-made.

grown junction an old method of producing a semiconductor JUNCTION (sense 2) by adding DOPING impurities to the molten material from which a crystal is being pulled.

grub-screw a miniature headless screw, usually with a pointed end, used typically to secure a control knob to a shaft.

grumbling a low-pitched irregular noise from an audio system, usually caused by a noisy coupling capacitor or a resistor.

GSM the first European standard for digital cellular phones, using a 900 MHz CARRIER (sense 1) with 200 kHz channel spacing and TIME DIVISION MULTIPLE ACCESS.

GTO see GATE TURN-OFF THYRISTOR.

G/T ratio the ratio of GAIN to NOISE TEMPERATURE for a satellite signal.

guard band 1. an unused frequency band. The purpose of this is to avoid the chance of cross-talk between two adjacent bands. 2. (or GUARD RING) An earthed metal strip that avoids the spread of an electric field, used in standard capacitors.

Gunn device or **Gunn diode** a two-terminal MICROWAVE device that is used as an OSCILLATOR, and has replaced KLYSTRONs for many microwave applications. The Gunn device is made from GALLIUM ARSENIDE, and emits low-power microwave radiation when a large electric field is placed across the material. The name 'diode' was used because it is a two-terminal device but its action is not primarily one of rectification.

Gunn effect the generation of microwave oscillations from a GALLIUM ARSENIDE semiconductor diode.

gyration resistance the quantity $R = \sqrt{Z_i Z_L}$ for an op-amp GYRATOR filter circuit in which Z_i = input impedance and Z_L = load impedance. The effect of FEEDBACK is that Z_i and Z_L are always opposite impedances, so that if Z_i is capacitive, Z_L is inductive.

gyrator a MICROWAVE circuit COMPONENT. Its action is to pass signals in one direction, but reverse the phase of signals travelling in the other direction.

gyro frequency or **gyro-magnetic frequency** the RESONANT FREQUENCY generated by an electron orbiting in the weak magnetic field of the Earth. This frequency is around 1.25–1.4 MHz, making wave propagation difficult in this range.

Haas effect the delayed echo effect used in sound reinforcement systems. If a listener in a large hall can hear a speaker directly and also by way of a loudspeaker, the combined sound is often unintelligible unless the signal to the loudspeaker is delayed by about 5 to 25 ms following the direct sound.

HAD see HOLE ACCUMULATION DIODE.

hairline cracks very narrow cracks in the conducting strips of a PRINTED CIRCUIT BOARD, causing an open circuit to occur, particularly when the board is flexed.

hairline shorts very narrow strips of conducting material across two lines in a PRINTED CIRCUIT BOARD, shorting two points that ought to be separated.

HAL see HARD ARRAY LOGIC.

halation a fuzzy glow around the SPOT (sense 1) on a CATHODE-RAY TUBE. The effect is noticeable on CATHODE-RAY OSCILLOSCOPE and RADAR tubes and is caused by light being reflected several times in the thick glass at the front of the screen.

half-adder a simple adding circuit for two BINARY (sense 1) bits. Only two inputs are needed, because no CARRY input is provided for, though a carry out must be provided. The half-adder can be constructed from any standard GATE (sense 2) type, such as NAND or NOR. See also ADDER; FULL ADDER. See Fig. 53.

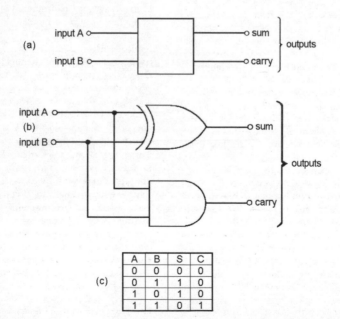

Fig. 53. **half-adder**

half-duplex   a line communication system that allows signals to pass in either direction, but not at the same time. Compare DUPLEX; SIMPLEX.

half filter section or **half section**   a connection of two impedances that form half of a T or PI filter, used to ensure matching at the input and output of a filter. See Fig. 54.

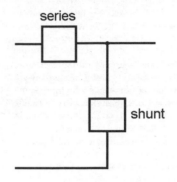

series

shunt

Fig. 54. **half filter section**

half-power bandwidth   see HALF-POWER POINT.

half-power point or **–3dB point**   a graph point used in determining the useful frequency range of an amplifier. The BANDWIDTH is measured between the frequency limits at which the output power is equal to half of the midrange power output. This corresponds to the 3dB voltage points.

half-split method or **divide and conquer**   a fault-finding method in which a circuit is divided arbitrarily into two portions so that the portion containing the fault can be identified. This portion is once again divided into two and the fault more closely located. The process continues until the precise location of the fault is found.

half-subtractor   a logic circuit that allows subtraction of two binary bits with a borrow output but no borrow input. Compare HALF-ADDER.

half-track   a tape recording (see RECORDING OF SOUND) system that uses one half of the tape for a recording channel, now less common.

half-wave dipole   a DIPOLE AERIAL (or antenna) whose total length is half of the desired WAVELENGTH so that each section of the dipole is a quarter wavelength long.

half-wave rectifier   a RECTIFER that passes one half of an AC voltage and blocks the other half (which has opposite polarity); for example, a single DIODE.

Hall effect   a VOLTAGE that is generated by the effect of a MAGNETIC FIELD on a material that is carrying current. SEMICONDUCTORS give particularly large Hall effect voltages, and the effect is used to measure magnetic fields (see FLUXMETER).

Hall-effect proximity unit   a magnetic detector using a HALL-EFFECT SENSOR in a PROXIMITY SWITCH operated by a magnet.

Hall-effect sensor   a sensor for magnetic field strength and direction, used as a form of compass.

Hall-effect switch   a system used for switching a circuit on and off without using mechanical contacts. A HALL EFFECT semiconductor is made to change conduction as a magnet approaches it.

Hall probe   the probe of a HALL EFFECT fluxmeter, containing the semiconductor slab in which the Hall effect occurs.

Hall voltage   the EMF across a conducting material that is carrying current in a magnetic field, see HALL EFFECT.

ham   an old slang term for amateur radio enthusiast.

Hamming code   a complex and very useful error correcting code, invented by R.W. Hamming, that is used for DIGITAL DATA transmission. Hamming showed how to calculate the number of PARITY bits needed to correct a single error for a code word of any given number of bits, and many ERROR DETECTION AND CORRECTION codes have been devised working on Hamming's principles.

Hamming distance   see DISTANCE, CODE.

Hamming window function   one of a set of WINDOW FUNCTIONs that can be used to reduce the effect (see GIBB'S PHENOMENON) of a SHARP-CUT FILTER.

Hammond organ a pioneering form of electronic organ that initially used rotating cogged wheels (known as *tone wheels*) but in 1939 the Hammond company introduced a model using THERMIONIC VALVES.

hand off or **hand over** the changeover of mobile telephone service from one BASE STATION to another where signal strength is higher.

hand scanner 1. a handheld unit for DIGITIZING text or pictures. 2. a handheld unit for reading BAR CODES.

hands free access control a security method that reads information from a miniature transmitter carried by approved personnel and will unlock a door only for such personnel.

handshaking any method used in a communication system to signal that data can be exchanged. See CLEAR TO SEND (CTS); DATA SET READY (DSR); DATA TERMINAL READY (DTR); READY TO SEND (RTS); HARDWARE HANDSHAKE; SOFTWARE HANDSHAKE.

hang or **hangup** or **lockup** the state in which a computer or other data system ceases to respond to a keyboard or mouse, and sometimes displays no further information on the screen.

hang-over a DAMPED oscillation, usually of a loudspeaker CONE, following a TRANSIENT.

hang-up 1. an effect of clipping on an AUDIO waveform at the POWER OUTPUT STAGE that introduces a sharp transition that emphasizes the unpleasant effect of the clipping. 2. see HANG.

Hanning window a form of WINDOW FUNCTION similar to a HAMMING WINDOW.

Hanover bars a fault condition of the PAL type colour TV system in which the picture appears broken into coloured horizontal bars.

Hapug modulation see CONTROLLED CARRIER MODULATION.

hard (of a magnetic material) needing a large amount of MAGNETIZING FORCE, but retaining magnetism after the magnetizing force is reduced to zero. Compare SOFT.

hard array logic (HAL) a type of PROGRAMMABLE ARRAY LOGIC device in which all the interconnections are made permanently during manufacture.

hard breakdown see AVALANCHE BREAKDOWN.

hard disc recorder the alternative to CD or DVD recording for AUDIO or VIDEO signals, with the advantages of rapid access and high capacity.

hard drive or **hard disk drive (HDD)** a high-capacity magnetic data storage device for computers and data recorders. The hard drive consists of a set of PLATTERS coated with magnetic material on each side and spinning at up to 10,000 rpm, using two HEADS per platter for reading and writing. The heads 'float' over the platter surface on an air cushion, so achieving a very small gap between head and magnetic surface with minimum risk of scraping the surface. ACCESS TIMES (sense 2) are much faster than those of FLOPPY DISKS, but much longer than memory access so that a memory CACHE is usually incorporated as part of a hard drive.

hard drive interface standards the various standardized systems, such as SMALL COMPUTER SYSTEM INTERFACE (SCSI) and EXTENDED INTEGRATED DEVICE ELECTRONICS (EIDE), used for passing parallel data signals to and from a HARD DRIVE. All are currently being superseded by fast serial methods, see SERIAL ATA.

hard echo an echo effect caused by pickup at a receiver of signals from the adjacent transmitter. Contrast NETWORK ECHO.

hard error an error in transmitted data that cannot be corrected even if the data is re-read several times. Contrast SOFT ERROR.

hard failure equipment failure caused by ELECTROSTATIC DAMAGE (ESD) or by ELECTROMAGNETIC INTERFERENCE (EMI).

hard magnetic material a magnetic material that requires a large amount of FIELD STRENGTH to magnetize but which retains some FLUX DENSITY when there is no applied field. Such a material is suitable for making PERMANENT MAGNETS.

hard valve a THERMIONIC VALVE that uses a vacuum, as distinct from a (*soft*) GAS-FILLED TUBE.

hardware the electronics components of a computer system, as distinct from program instructions. Contrast SOFTWARE.

hardware-dependent (of a computer program) able to be used only on the computer system it was designed for.

hardware handshaking the use of HANDSHAKING signals over separate lines rather than by using codes over a single data line.

hardware interrupt an INTERRUPT signal that is delivered to a processor by way of wiring, usually from a PERIPHERAL, as distinct from an interrupt generated by SOFTWARE.

hardware, MIDI see MIDI.

hardware platform a particular form of computer design. In general, programs designed for one hardware platform will not run on another.

hardware reset a button or switch on the case of a computer that will completely reset and restart the system.

hardwire to assemble a circuit by wiring from component to component rather than by using a PRINTED CIRCUIT BOARD.

hard wiring connection with wires rather than by using metal strips on PRINTED CIRCUIT BOARDS. Hard wiring implies that the connections are made by hand, though in fact automated methods are normally used. Hard wiring may also be needed to carry out modifications to a circuit.

Hargelbarger code see CONVOLUTION CODE.

harmonic a part of a signal whose frequency is an integer multiple of the FUNDAMENTAL FREQUENCY of the signal. Any periodic waveform other than a sine wave will contain harmonics. Compare SUBHARMONIC.

harmonic distortion a form of NON-LINEAR AMPLIFIER distortion whose effect is to generate HARMONICS of any input frequency.

harmonic generator a circuit that deliberately generates HARMONICS. This can use reverse-biased transistors, diodes or other NONLINEAR elements. The aim is to steepen the sides of any sine wave and so result in the generation of harmonics.

HARP see HIGH-GAIN AVALANCHE-RUSHING AMORPHOUS PHOTOCONDUCTOR.

HART see HIGHWAY ADDRESSABLE REMOTE TRANSDUCER.

Hartley see DECIT.

Hartley oscillator or **tapped-coil oscillator** a very old form of oscillator circuit that uses a tapped inductor to obtain a FEEDBACK signal. See Fig. 55. See also COLPITTS OSCILLATOR.

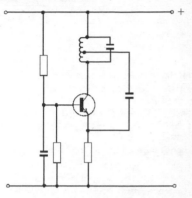

Fig. 55. **Hartley oscillator**

Hartley-Shannon law the law for DIGITAL transmissions that links the amount of information transferred to channel BANDWIDTH, transmission time, and SIGNAL TO NOISE RATIO.

Harvard architecture the use in a computer of separate BUS lines for program and data bytes.

hash electrical noise from sparking at a rotary COMMUTATOR.

H-attenuator an attenuator of symmetrical construction intended for use with balanced circuits. See BALANCED AMPLIFIER. See Fig. 56.

Hayes AT command set a set of software signals for controlling modem actions originally devised by the Hayes Corporation and now universally adopted.

Hayes standards the standard MODEM commands established by the Hayes corporation and used almost universally. See also AT COMMAND.

HBT-HEMT device a high-gain low-noise MICROWAVE amplifier device that uses both HETEROJUNCTION bipolar transistors and HIGH ELECTRON MOBILITY TRANSISTORS on the same chip.

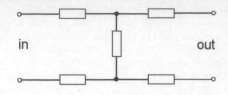

Fig. 56. **H-attenuator**

HCFCs   see HYDROFLUOROCARBONS.

HDCD   see HIGH DEFINITION COMPATIBLE DIGITAL.

HDD   see HARD DRIVE.

HDSL   see HIGH DATA-RATE SUBSCRIBER'S LINE.

HDTV   see HIGH DEFINITION TELEVISION.

head   a magnetic reading or writing RECORDING device, applied mainly to magnetic read/write heads for tape recorders and for computer floppy or hard drives. See READ/WRITE HEAD; RECORDING OF SOUND; SOUND REPRODUCTION.

head actuator   the mechanism that moves the READ/WRITE HEAD of a DISK DRIVE across the tracks. See also STEPPER MOTOR; VOICE-COIL DRIVE.

head arm   a rigid rod that holds each READ/WRITE HEAD of a computer DISK DRIVE.

head crash   the contact of disk HEAD and rotating disk surface on a HARD DRIVE, causing the disk surfaces to be scratched and made useless. A head crash is usually due to a violent movement of the drive while data is being read or written, because the head is located over an unused track at other times. See also VOICE-COIL DRIVE.

head demagnetizer   a device, usually a solenoid fed with mains AC, that can be used to demagnetize a tape recorder head by switching on the current with the solenoid placed close to the head and gradually pulling the solenoid away to a distance of more than one foot, or by gradually reducing the current.

head drum   the rotating drum of a VIDEO CASSETTE RECORDER in which the recording HEADS (two at least, often four) are embedded. The drum is tilted with

respect to the tape so that the head writes and reads tracks that are at a small angle to the tape direction.

head gap   the gap between magnetic materials at a magnetic HEAD, where the flux is concentrated. The smaller the gap, the shorter the wavelength (hence higher frequency) the head can deal with. For a VIDEO CASSETTE RECORDER, head gaps of the order of 0.5 microns are used.

head loss   loss of signal due to the imperfections of a tape REPLAY HEAD.

head-mounted display   a pair of miniature CRT or LCD displays that are arranged to be worn like goggles, used to provide 3-D effects (*stereoscopy*) in connection with VIRTUAL REALITY displays. See also DATA GLOVE.

headphones   miniature transducers for electrical signal to audio output worn directly over the ears.

headroom   allowance for signal PEAKS in the estimates for amplitude of signals prior to transmission or recording.

head switch   the electronic switch that is used in a VIDEO CASSETTE RECORDER to switch connections from one record/play HEAD to another. There is a short overlap during which both heads are active.

heat   the energy that an object possesses because of its temperature.

heat conduction   the transfer of heat energy through a material such as a metal, due to oscillating molecules in one part of the material starting an oscillation in the adjacent molecules.

heat detector   any device that senses temperature change. Examples include THERMOCOUPLES, THERMISTORS, and PYROELECTRIC generating materials.

heat dissipation   the removal of HEAT energy to prevent overheating.

heater   1. a THERMIONIC VALVE filament or other heating element. 2. the molybdenum spiral that is placed inside the CATHODE (sense 1) of an indirectly heated valve, and insulated from it. 3. a wire-wound resistor in a CRYSTAL OVEN or a THERMOSTAT accelerating heater.

heat flow   the movement of HEAT energy from a high temperature to a lower temperature by way of conduction, convection or radiation.

heating effect   the effect of current passing through a resistance. The heat dissipation rate in watts is found by multiplying current (in amperes) through the resistor by voltage (in volts) across the resistor.

heating time   the time needed for a hot CATHODE (sense 1) device to reach operating temperature.

heat sensitive technology   a method of making REWRITABLE CD discs, using a layer of tellurium and selenium alloy (doped with arsenic). During writing, the LASER beam will burn a microscopic hole for each LOGIC 1 bit, but the written portions can be erased by using a lower power beam to melt the material without punching a hole.

heat shunt   a metal object clamped to an electronic component, usually a SEMICONDUCTOR, to prevent excess heating during soldering by providing a lower-resistance path to HEAT.

heat sink or **sink**   a massive metal slab to which power transistors can be bolted. The purpose of a heat sink is to spread the conducted HEAT from the collector of a transistor over a large mass and a large area, and so ultimately to the air. The transistor will still have to be operated in such a way that the rate of POWER DISSIPATION does not exceed the rate of heat dissipation. Computer processors dissipating 20W or more will need a fan in addition to a heat sink for cooling, and vapour cooling is being used in some designs.

heat-sink grease   a form of silicone grease that is a good electrical insulator but also a good HEAT conductor, used to make a more effective thermal connection between a SEMICONDUCTOR and a HEAT SINK.

heat slug   a soft metal plate placed between a MICROPROCESSOR and its HEAT SINK to assist in conducting HEAT away from the processor. The use of silicon grease or other thermal materials is much more common now.

Heaviside layer   see E LAYER.

Heaviside, Oliver   (1850–1925) a brilliant engineer who predicted the reflection of radio waves at a time when long-distance radio was thought impossible. He also devised a mathematical system for analyzing pulse waveforms that was totally neglected until the later use of Laplace transformations showed that Heaviside's methods were totally justified.

height control   the TELEVISION RECEIVER control for amplitude of FRAME SCAN. This has the effect of altering the picture height. Modern receivers either dispense with this control or use a preset POTENTIOMETER (sense 1).

height gain   the amount of gain in FIELD STRENGTH (at a specified distance) that can be obtained by raising the height of an AERIAL above ground level.

helical aerial (or **antenna)**   an AERIAL that consists of a wire in a corkscrew shape. The radiated wave is elliptically POLARIZED (sense 1).

helical beam aerial (or **antenna)**   an AERIAL in the shape of a helix of rod or wire emerging from a DISH reflector, having a circumference for each loop of the helix equal to the wavelength of the CARRIER (sense 1).

helical potentiometer or **helipot**   a POTENTIOMETER (sense 1) in which the element is in helical form. This means that several turns of the actuating shaft are needed to wind the contact from one end of the element to the other. Such a potentiometer, using anything from 3 to 50 turns from one stop to the other, has very high resolution (see RESOLUTION OF POTENTIOMETER), and is used in measuring instruments.

helical scan   the action of a tape HEAD on a sloping DRUM (sense 1) scanning strips along a magnetic tape, as used in a VIDEO CASSETTE RECORDER.

helipot see HELICAL POTENTIOMETER.

Helmholtz coils a pair of identical coils placed on the same axis and separated by a distance equal to coil radius. The MAGNETIC FIELD in the space between the coils is fairly uniform.

HEMT see HIGH ELECTRON MOBILITY TRANSISTOR.

henry the unit of INDUCTANCE, self or mutual. Symbol: H. The henry is the unit equivalent to volt-seconds per ampere. Named after Joseph Henry (1797–1878), US physicist.

herringbone a pattern produced on a TV SCREEN usually because of ADJACENT CHANNEL INTERFERENCE or RF interference from a VIDEO CASSETTE RECORDER.

hertz (Hz) the unit of FREQUENCY, equal to one complete cycle per second. Symbol: Hz. Named after Heinrich Hertz (1857–1894), German physicist who first reported radio transmission and reception.

Hertzian dipole a theoretical pair of equal and opposite charges at infinitesimal spacing, used as a mathematical ideal model for a source of radiation.

heterochronous (of digital signals) that have TRANSITIONs that are not simultaneous.

heterodyne a circuit technique that produces a BEAT FREQUENCY by mixing two higher frequencies.

heterodyne action the mixing of waves to create two new frequencies, one the sum of the original frequencies and the other the difference. See SUPERHETERODYNE.

heterodyne wavemeter a form of FREQUENCY METER that operates with a calibrated oscillator. The oscillator frequency is varied until beats (see BEAT FREQUENCY) of a particular frequency (often zero) are detected. The input frequency is then read from the calibrated scale.

heterogeneous multiplex a MULTIPLEX formed from digital signals whose BIT RATEs are different. Contrast HOMOGENEOUS MULTIPLEX.

heterojunction a JUNCTION (sense 2) between different semiconductor materials, or between a SEMICONDUCTOR and a metal.

heuristic (of a device or software) able to learn so that it is self-adapting to altering circumstances.

Hewlett-Packard interface bus (HPIB) or **general purpose interface bus (GPIB)** see IEEE-488 BUS.

Hewlett-Packard interface loop a two-wire SERIAL loop connection standard for portable instruments.

hex see HEXADECIMAL SCALE.

hexadecimal scale the number scale that uses 16 digits. The letters A to F are used to represent the denary numbers 10 to 15 in this scale. For example, the hexadecimal number A5 is the denary number 165.

hex coding the use of HEXADECIMAL notation for BINARY NUMBERS, making the numbers shorter and reducing errors in entering numbers into a keypad.

hex pad or **hexadecimal keypad** a keyboard that contains digits 0 to 9 and letters A to F for entering numbers in hexadecimal form. This would be used to enter short code sequences into a MICROCONTROLLER or PROGRAMMABLE LOGIC ARRAY.

HF see HIGH FREQUENCY.

HF bias see TAPE BIAS.

HF bias rejection the attenuation of TAPE BIAS frequency in the signal circuits of a tape recorder.

h$_{fe}$ see FORWARD CURRENT TRANSFER RATIO.

HF saturation MAGNETIC SATURATION of tape for signals of high frequency.

HF stabilization circuitry designed to prevent high frequency OSCILLATION in an AUDIO AMPLIFIER.

Hickman voltage multiplier a modification of the COCKCROFT-WALTON VOLTAGE MULTIPLIER that uses fewer components but requires dual oppositely-phased square wave drives.

Hi-8 a variation of the analogue VIDEO-8 CAMCORDER tape format, using METAL TAPE and higher FM RECORDING frequencies to achieve almost 400-line resolution under favourable conditions.

hi-fi   see HIGH-FIDELITY SOUND.

hi-fi headphones   miniature LOUDSPEAKERS in headphone casings providing a large audio bandwidth and striking audible effects.

high data-rate subscriber's line (HDSL) a fast telephone link for data, facsimile, video or voice communication.

high definition compatible digital (HDCD)   a development of the compact disc that use a faster SAMPLING RATE, but retains BANDWIDTH by using COMPRESSION.

high definition television (HDTV)   any system of TELEVISION that uses more than 1000 lines per picture height and an ASPECT RATIO of 16:9, requiring considerable COMPRESSION of the signal in order to achieve a realistic BANDWIDTH.

high density bipolar code (HDB-code) a form of digital code that uses a positive or negative voltage for logic 1 and 0V for logic 0, and avoids using long strings of zeros by applying a substitution law for such strings. See also BIPOLAR CODE.

high-dissipation resistors   resistors, usually of WIREWOUND construction on ceramic cores with vitreous or silicone resin coating. Some resistors can be obtained that have aluminium fins built in for added dissipation.

high electron mobility transistor (HEMT) a device that uses a JUNCTION (sense 2) of gallium arsenide and gallium aluminium arsenide, a few atoms thick. The high electron MOBILITY in this structure allows the device to be used as an amplifier at frequencies exceeding 60 GHz.

higher speed slot   an EXPANSION SLOT on a computer MOTHERBOARD that is connected to a high speed BUS for fast data transfers. See also ACCELERATED GRAPHICS PORT.

high-fidelity sound or **hi-fi**   a speciality that covers all aspects of RECORDING and reproduction of sound with the aim of securing the most realistic possible reproduction. The term is often used indiscriminately to denote stereo audio systems that are of noticeably low fidelity.

high frequency (HF)   1. the radio FREQUENCY BAND that covers the frequencies between 3 and 30 megahertz approximately.

2. any frequency higher than mid-range audio frequency.

high-frequency beaming   the effect of directional high-frequency sound, a problem of early horn loudspeakers used for PUBLIC ADDRESS until the CONSTANT DIRECTIVITY horn was invented in 1971.

high-gain avalanche-rushing amorphous photoconductor (HARP)   a light sensitive semiconductor that is used in imaging systems, and likely to become a high-sensitivity high-resolution replacement for CCD image-sensing devices in TV cameras.

high-impedance distribution   the use of lines with a nominal 100V signal amplitude (and comparatively low current) to distribute power to a set of loudspeakers for PUBLIC ADDRESS systems.

high logic level   the actual voltage level that is taken to represent the logic 1. For most modern logic circuits, this means any voltage between +3.5 and +5.0 volts, but lower voltage levels, typically 1.6V, are used within microprocessor chips to reduce heat dissipation.

high-pass filter (HPF)   a FILTER whose PASS BAND starts at a high frequency and continues indefinitely.

high performance serial bus (HPSB) see IEEE 1394-1995 BUS.

high-permittivity ceramic   a ceramic material, usually with a high titanium content, that has a very high value of RELATIVE PERMITTIVITY. Capacitors made with such material often show a considerable variation of capacitance value as applied voltage changes, making them unsuitable for frequency-determining circuits such as filters or oscillators.

high polymer headphone   a HEADPHONE design based on plastics that have ELECTRET qualities.

high-Q   (of an inductor or tuned circuit) having a large ratio (100 or more) of IMPEDANCE to resistance at the RESONANT FREQUENCY.

high tension (HT)   an obsolete for high voltage, usually taken to mean voltages in the range of 100 to 500V. See also EHT.

high-voltage test a method of testing INSULATION. The test consists of applying higher than normal voltages across the insulation, often in the form of pulses. The quality of the insulation is measured by the current that passed during each pulse.

highway addressable remote transducer (HART) a system that uses input TRANSDUCERS each connected to the same BUS but separately controllable.

hiss the particularly obtrusive form of audio NOISE from analogue recorded tape, caused by random magnetization of particles on the tape. Tape hiss is particularly noticeable on tapes of narrow width operated at low speeds. This makes some form of COMPANDER system, such as DOLBY or DBX, essential for analogue

cassette systems if reasonably good reproduction is needed.

historical reliability the record of problems encountered with equipment; a useful guidance for maintenance engineers.

hit a success in reading data from a CACHE rather than from a slower DISK DRIVE.

hit rate the percentage of HITS made in a CACHE.

h_oe see OUTPUT RESISTANCE; TRANSISTOR.

hogging excessive use of a NETWORK (sense 2) by one NODE (sense 1) at the expense of other users, a problem of networks that use POLLING.

hoghorn aerial (or antenna) a combination of FEED HORN and reflector, similar in shape to a ship's ventilator, used in terrestrial microwave links. See Fig. 57.

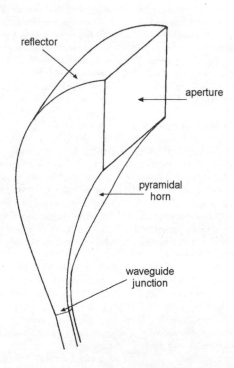

reflector

aperture

pyramidal horn

waveguide junction

Fig. 57. **hoghorn aerial**

holding current the minimum CURRENT needed to maintain conduction of a THYRISTOR. The current that flows between the ANODE and CATHODE (sense 2) of a thyristor serves also to keep the thyristor switched on. If this current falls below a minimum holding level, the thyristor will switch off. Too low a voltage in the forward direction will also allow the thyristor to switch off.

holding current, Zener the minimum current that will ensure a stable voltage across a ZENER DIODE.

holding power, relay the minimum power that must be dissipated in the coil of a relay to keep the contacts in their changed over state.

hold mode the state of a J-K FLIP-FLOP in which both J and K inputs are at logic 0, so that the output does not change at a CLOCK pulse.

hold range or **lock range** or **tracking range** the range of frequencies around the central frequency for which a VOLTAGE CONTROLLED OSCILLATOR will remain synchronized to the input signal.

hole the space that is left in the atomic arrangement of a crystal when an ELECTRON is removed. This space is mobile and behaves as if it carried positive charge and had a mass rather greater than electron mass.

hole accumulation diode (HAD) a form of PHOTODIODE, devised by Sony, in which electrons that would contribute to DARK CURRENT are trapped by heavily doped P-layer. A further development is the *Hyper-HAD*.

hole conduction the CONDUCTION in a metal or a semiconductor caused by HOLE movement in the direction of a positive ELECTRIC FIELD.

hole current the amount of CURRENT that is due to HOLE movement. In several metals, a substantial amount of the current that can flow is conducted by hole movement. In p-type semiconductors, almost all of the current is conducted by hole movement.

hole in the middle the audible effect in a two-channel STEREO system of using

loudspeakers or microphones that are spaced too far apart.

hole storage a problem of BIPOLAR JUNCTION TRANSISTORs that are driven into SATURATION (sense 1), causing the saturated region to conduct uncontrollably. This has caused the adoption of T-MOS and VERTICAL FET power output stages for hi-fi (see HIGH-FIDELITY SOUND) amplifiers.

hole trap a fault in a SEMICONDUCTOR crystal that can stop the movement of holes by allowing RECOMBINATION with an electron.

hologram a pattern formed on a screen or a photographic film when an object is illuminated with light from a LASER. The hologram is due to light waves reinforcing or cancelling depending on their path, and the hologram can be used to reconstruct a three-dimensional image.

holography the production of images by way of HOLOGRAMS, a possible way to three-dimensional TV images.

home channel the channel in a digital MULTIPLEX for TERRESTRIAL DIGITAL BROADCASTING that contains the ELECTRONIC PROGRAM GUIDE.

home cinema a domestic system consisting of a wide-screen TV receiver with digital access, SURROUND-SOUND system, multiple loudspeakers and a DVD player or recorder.

home recordable DVD see RECORDABLE DVD.

HomeRF one of several short-range radio communications systems intended for use within a home or other confined spaces. See also BLUETOOTH, IEEE802.11.

homing beacon see BEACON.

homodyne receiver see DIRECT CONVERSION RECEIVER.

homogeneous multiplex a MULTIPLEX formed from digital signals whose BIT RATES are equal. Contrast HETEROGENEOUS MULTIPLEX.

homojunction a traditional form of JUNCTION (sense 2) formed on one single crystal of semiconductor material.

homopolar generator a GENERATOR (sense 1) that uses a rotating metal disc between magnet poles, rather than a coil. The homopolar generator delivers low-voltage DC without the use of any form of COMMUTATOR.

honeycomb coil an obsolete type of coil construction that reduces STRAY CAPACITANCE between the turns of the coil.

hook-up or **lash-up** a temporary CIRCUIT for assessment or measurement. See also BREADBOARD.

hop any computer site that is an intermediate between an INTERNET user and the SERVER source.

horizontal blanking a signal applied to the grid of a receiver CATHODE-RAY TUBE to cut off the beam and so avoid signals being displayed during the LINE FLYBACK period.

horizontal deflection the action of sweeping an ELECTRON BEAM from side to side of a CATHODE-RAY TUBE.

horizontal hold the control over SYNCHRONIZATION of the HORIZONTAL TIMEBASE of a TELEVISION RECEIVER.

horizontally polarized aerial an AERIAL whose DIPOLE (sense 2) rods are arranged horizontally and at right angles to the direction of transmission or reception.

horizontally polarized wave a wave whose ELECTRIC FIELD direction (electric vector) is POLARIZED (sense 1) in a horizontal plane.

horizontal polarization a property of an electromagnetic wave in which the direction of the ELECTRIC FIELD is horizontal. A wave transmitted from a horizontal wire or rod AERIAL will be horizontally polarized.

horizontal resolution the RESOLUTION in terms of lines per horizontal inch for a TV display, or in terms of PIXELS per screen width for a monitor.

horizontal scan or **horizontal sweep** the movement of an electron beam horizontally across the face of a CATHODE-RAY TUBE. This is the result of applying a ramp waveform of voltage to horizontal deflection plates of an INSTRUMENT TUBE, or a ramp waveform of current to the horizontal deflection coils of a PICTURE TUBE.

horizontal scan rate the speed at which a horizontal line is scanned on the face of a screen.

horizontal sync the SYNCHRONIZATION signal sent at the start of each line of TV picture information in the HORIZONTAL BLANKING interval.

horizontal timebase the circuit that generates the horizontal TIMEBASE ramp waveform.

horn aerial (or **antenna)** or **horn** a MICROWAVE aerial consisting of a horn shape that starts with the waveguide and flares out in each direction.

horn feed the use of a flared end on a WAVEGUIDE to distribute MICROWAVES to a reflecting dish.

horn loudspeaker or **horn-loaded loudspeaker** the most efficient form of LOUDSPEAKER, used as a comparison standard. The horn loudspeaker consists of a *drive unit* that can be a conventional electromagnetic unit with a small cone. The speaker walls then follow the pattern of an exponential curve, increasing in area. This loudspeaker is a relatively efficient converter of electrical energy into sound energy (4% typically), but requires a large amount of space. The material that is used for the walls of the horn must not resonate within the audible frequency range.

horse power an old unit of POWER based on a mechanical definition and equivalent to 746 watts.

horseshoe magnet a magnet whose shape is like that of a horseshoe. This means that the poles of the magnet are close, causing an intense field across the air gap.

Hosiden socket a mini-DiN socket used on video cassette or DVD recorders for an S-VHS signal input.

host or **host computer** the central or server computer in a communications system.

hostile surroundings the presence of corrosive or flammable gases or liquids surrounding electronic equipment.

host, strain gauge the material to which a strain gauge is fastened and whose strain is to be measured.

hot live, at a dangerous voltage.

hot-box reference a heated solid aluminium box used to house one JUNCTION (sense 3) of a thermocouple at a stable temperature.

hot-carrier diode see SCHOTTKY DIODE.

hot cathode a cathode that emits electrons into a vacuum when heated. See also COLD CATHODE EMITTER.

hot-coil system a TV receiver design that uses a SWITCH MODE POWER SUPPLY without isolation so that LINE-SCAN COILS and other TIMEBASE components are live to mains, presenting servicing hazards.

hot dip or **tinning bath** a method of coating metals with other metals by dipping them into a bath of molten metal. The method is used to coat printed circuit boards with solder.

hot doming the buckling of the APERTURE GRILLE of a CATHODE-RAY TUBE for COLOUR TELEVISION due to excess temperature that can be caused by using excessive levels of brightness.

hot electron a high energy electron.

hot pin the pin in a three-pin XLR AUDIO CONNECTOR that carries the in-phase signal. Contrast COLD PIN.

hot-plugged connection or **hot swapping** a connection, usually to a computer, that can be made or broken with the machine running. When a hot-plugged connection is made this causes suitable software to run.

hot resistance the resistance of a heating coil when at high temperature, considerably greater than the cold resistance.

hot spot a part of an electrode that is overheated. Hot spots become particularly troublesome in THERMIONIC VALVE vacuum devices if they start to emit electrons as a result of their high temperature. A hot spot in a SEMICONDUCTOR can cause diffusion of impurity, so altering the characteristics of the material.

hot-wire gas flow detector a detector based on the principle that a hot wire will be cooled by a gas flow over it, and the change in the resistance of the wire can be used as a measure of the gas flow.

hot-wire meter an old type of measuring instrument that operates on the hot-wire principle. In a typical hot-wire meter, a

wire is held between supports, and a tensioning spring is attached to the centre of the wire. The attachment to the needle movement is also made at the centre. When the wire is heated by passing current it will expand. The resulting sag at the centre of the wire is mechanically amplified by levers and used to drive the needle. Hot-wire instruments, though not very accurate, are particularly useful for indicating true ROOT MEAN SQUARE (sense 2) values of high-frequency currents.

Hough transform a method used in IMAGE ANALYSIS to find straight edges in an image.

hour meter a form of timer used to determine the working time of an electronic circuit so that preventative maintenance can be carried out at scheduled times.

housekeeping bit an extra bit inserted into a data stream to carry out some signal action at the receiver.

howl an unwanted audio OSCILLATION. Howl is caused by unwanted POSITIVE FEEDBACK, and this can be in audio amplifier stages, in radio frequency stages, or as a result of acoustic feedback (from a loudspeaker to a microphone or gramophone pickup, for example).

Howland constant current source an OPERATIONAL AMPLIFIER circuit with both positive and negative FEEDBACK that supplies a precisely constant current to a load.

h parameter see HYBRID PARAMETER.

HPIL see HEWLETT PACKARD INTERFACE LOOP.

H-plane the direction of the MAGNETIC FIELD portion of a MICROWAVE signal. See WAVEGUIDE.

H-plane sectoral horn a HORN AERIAL of rectangular cross section, flared in one dimension only, whose ELECTRIC FIELD is parallel to the parallel metal sides.

H RADAR a form of navigation system for aircraft in which the aircraft interrogates and receives information from two ground stations.

HSSI high speed serial interface.

HT see HIGH TENSION.

hub a form of distribution point for data. A USB hub plugs into one USB port on a computer and allows a number of USB peripherals to be plugged into the hub. A network hub is a computer that links networks.

hue the spectral colour of a portion of a picture. In COLOUR TELEVISION applications, a given colour has two measurable quantities, *hue* and *saturation*. Hue refers to the colour itself, saturation to the ratio of pure colour to white, so that pastel shades are highly unsaturated.

hue adjustment a control included on a COLOUR TELEVISION receiver using NTSC so that changes in HUE can be corrected. Hue adjustment is not required on PAL or SECAM receivers.

hue error a problem of NTSC TV receivers in which PHASE changes in the signal have a drastic effect on picture HUE, requiring manual adjustments in the early receivers.

hue, saturation, brightness (HSB) one of the ways that a colour can be defined in terms of light wavelength (HUE), percentage of colour (SATURATION, sense 2) and BRIGHTNESS. See also CMY; RGB.

Huffman algorithm a message coding ALGORITHM for NON-LOSSY COMPRESSION in which the most likely messages are allocated the shortest code words. See also FANO'S ALGORITHM.

Huffman coding a form of non-lossy coding for compressing digital signals using the HUFFMAN ALGORITHM.

hum or **mains hum** a low frequency signal, usually picked up from AC mains supplies. The picking up of hum is a problem for designers of high-gain audio equipment. It cannot be eliminated by using simple FILTERS, because the action of a rectifier generates HARMONICS of the hum frequency, and these harmonics radiate.

human eye characteristics the factors of image retention, different response to different colours and inability to see fine detail in colour that all combine to make colour television possible.

hum-bar a TV picture fault in the form of a wide black horizontal bar, usually due to failure of SMOOTHING (sense 1) components in the power supply.

humbucker coil an old method of reducing mains HUM pickup on a microphone by using a coil that adds an ANTIPHASE hum signal. See also ANTINOISE.

humidity or **absolute humidity** the amount of water vapour in a specified sample of air. A more useful figure is the RELATIVE HUMIDITY.

hum modulation the MODULATION of signal AMPLITUDE by low-frequency hum.

hunting an OSCILLATION in a CONTROL SYSTEM, i.e. any system in which electronic circuits control mechanical or other non-electronic actions and in which a FEEDBACK CONTROL LOOP is used. Hunting is the consequence of poor design in which a NEGATIVE FEEDBACK loop with insufficient damping has been applied to an unsuitable system. The result is that the feedback overcorrects, so that the system never becomes stable.

hunting, dish unwanted oscillation of a satellite DISH that can be moved from one position to another, often due to an actuator that is not secured correctly.

hybrid circuit see THICK FILM CIRCUIT.

hybrid IC a form of INTEGRATED CIRCUIT that mixes COMPONENTs on the chip with components separately connected. The added components are welded to bonding pads, and are components that cannot easily be manufactured in IC form, such as capacitors, inductors and quartz crystals. Hybrid ICs are used mainly in military applications.

hybrid junction or **rat-race** or **Magic-T** a method of connecting WAVEGUIDES so as to change signal direction and avoid reflected signals.

hybrid parameter any of a set of CHARACTERISTIC figures that have different units. When graphs are drawn of component or circuit characteristics, the slope of each graph will yield a parameter figure that will have units such as resistance, conductance, gain, etc. Hybrid parameters form sets whose units are not consistent, i.e. not all resistances, nor all ratios, but a mixture of different types.

hybrid-pi equivalent   an old form of EQUIVALENT CIRCUIT for a TRANSISTOR. This has seldom been used since silicon transistors became predominant, because simpler equivalents can now be used.

hybrid ring or **rat-race**   a MICROWAVE device composed of a ring 1.5 wavelengths in circumference with four equally spaced PORTS. This can be used to divide a signal into two, or to form the sum and difference of two input signals.

hybrid spread spectrum system   a SPREAD SPECTRUM system that uses both DIRECT SEQUENCE SPREAD SPECTRUM and FREQUENCY HOPPING methods.

hydrofluorocarbons   non-destructive and non-flammable cleaning agents that have replaced chlorofluorocarbons for degreasing and general cleaning of electronic components. The main storage precaution is to avoid high temperatures which can break them down into highly toxic residues.

hyperbolic horn, loudspeaker   a very efficient but very large loudspeaker enclosure.

Hyper-HAD   see HOLE ACCUMULATION DIODE.

hysteresis   an effect in which the direction of change of a quantity must be considered as well as size of change. See HYSTERESIS LOOP.

hysteresis distortion   a form of signal distortion that is caused by HYSTERESIS.

hysteresis loop   the shape of a graph for any quantities that exhibit HYSTERESIS. The best-known examples are MAGNETIC HYSTERESIS, the SCHMITT TRIGGER characteristic, and the behaviour of a bimetal thermostat. Such a graph has a loop shape, because the path taken as one plotted quantity is increased is not the same as the path taken when the quantity is decreased. Only the ends of the loop are common to the two paths. The area of the loop usually indicates the amount of energy that will be dissipated during each cycle. See Fig. 58.

hysteresis loss   the loss of energy that is the result of tracing out a graph that contains a HYSTERESIS LOOP. The amount of energy lost is represented by the area of the hysteresis loop.

hysteresis, magnetic   see MAGNETIC HYSTERESIS.

hysteresis, thermostat   see THERMOSTAT HYSTERESIS.

Hz   see HERTZ.

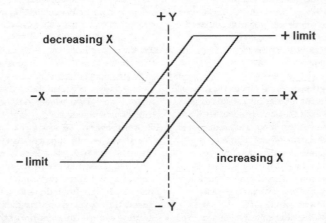

Fig. 58. **hysteresis loop**

IBM compatible computer any personal computer that follows the basic design principles, known as industry standard architecture (ISA), of the IBM PC-AT machine of 1982, now extended and known as EXTENDED INDUSTRY STANDARD ARCHITECTURE (EISA).

IC see INTEGRATED CIRCUIT.

I-core the I-shaped section of magnetic sheet that forms part of the conventional laminated transformer core along with the E-core.

IC package the plastic or ceramic container for an IC, containing the connecting pins.

IC power amplifier a POWER AMPLIFIER (sense 1), usually for AUDIO, in IC form, often in a package that allows for a HEAT SINK to be attached.

IC regulator a VOLTAGE REGULATOR, usually for a fixed voltage, in an IC package that allows for a HEAT SINK to be attached.

IC stabilizer see IC REGULATOR.

IC tuner a TV or RADIO TUNER stage that uses only an IC, so that all control inputs are electrical with no need for components such as VARIABLE CAPACITORS.

IC voltage regulator see IC REGULATOR.

ICW transmission see INTERRUPTED CONTINUOUS WAVE TRANSMISSION.

IDC connector see INSULATION DISPLACEMENT CONNECTOR.

IDE (integrated device electronics) a set of circuits for interfacing a HARD DRIVE that is part of the hard drive rather than contained in a separate card on the computer MOTHERBOARD. This allows a simple connection to be used at the motherboard irrespective of the coding and other interfacing circuits needed for the drive. See also EXTENDED INTEGRATED DEVICE ELECTRONICS (EIDE).

ideal bunching the gathering of moving electrons into tightly packed groups, with no electrons between the groups. See BUNCHER; KLYSTRON.

ideal crystal see PERFECT CRYSTAL.

ideal diode characteristic a graph that shows a straight line shape for the forward current/voltage characteristic, with no curvature and no intercept on the voltage axis.

ideal opamp a perfect operational amplifier with very high INPUT RESISTANCE, very low OUTPUT RESISTANCE, very high OPEN-LOOP GAIN and very wide BANDWIDTH.

ideal transformer see PERFECT TRANSFORMER.

ident signal a PHASE identifying signal in the PAL colour TV standard. The ident signal enables the receiver to recognise the correct phase of the V component of the colour signal that is inverted in alternate lines.

identification friend or foe (IFF) a form of RADAR in which a coded radar signal will be decoded and correctly returned by a friendly aircraft. See INTERROGATING SIGNAL; SECONDARY RADAR; TRANSPONDER.

identifying mark, cable a marker such as a coloured or spotted edge used to identify a particular connection in a RIBBON CABLE, usually the connection to pin 1 at the plug.

idle character a 'do nothing' code denoting a byte that is sent repeatedly down a connecting line in a SYNCHRONOUS TRANSMISSION to inform the receiver that there is no data to be sent, but that contact must be maintained.

idle component see REACTIVE CURRENT.

idler signal an input to a PARAMETRIC AMPLIFIER for MICROWAVE frequencies, set to a frequency midway between that of the input signal and the pump circuit.

idler wheel a form of drive for a turntable, using a rubber rimmed wheel bearing against the inner rim of the turntable and in turn driven by the motor.

IEC see INTERNATIONAL ELECTROTECHNICAL COMMISSION.

IEC casing standards   the set of IEC standards for casings for electronic equipment, such as the IEC297, which defines the successor to the old 19-inch rack system.

IEC connector or **euroconnector**   a mains connector that uses shrouded rectangular pins. The mains cable uses the IEC socket so that live pins cannot be touched, and the same form of plug and socket is used to allow a MONITOR to be powered from the main computer, so that a separate mains switch is not needed.

IEC qualifying symbols   the symbols standardized for LOGIC DEVICE diagrams to indicate such features as SCHMITT TRIGGER input or THREE-STATE LOGIC output.

IEE   see INSTITUTION OF ELECTRICAL ENGINEERS.

IEEE   see INSTITUTE OF ELECTRICAL AND ELECTRONIC ENGINEERS.

IEEE-488 bus   a PARALLEL TRANSMISSION data connection BUS for connecting complete systems, due largely to Hewlett-Packard. Devices connected to the bus can be classed as TALKERS, LISTENERS or CONTROLLERS according to their function. The bus consists of eight BI-DIRECTIONAL data lines, five bus control lines, and three HANDSHAKING lines.

IEEE 1394 bus or **firewire** or **i-link** or **high performance serial bus (HPSB)**   This is a connecting serial link similar in action to the UNIVERSAL SERIAL BUS, but operates at speeds up to 2 Gb/s using a 6-wire cable. Firewire connectors are fitted on several digital camcorders and other devices that make use of video data. The firewire system supports PLUG AND PLAY, and devices can be connected or disconnected (see HOT PLUGGED CONNECTION) without the need to switch the computer off.

IEE wiring regulations   the regulations that govern correct practice in domestic and industrial electrical wiring in the UK.

IF   see INTERMEDIATE FREQUENCY.

IF amplifier or **IF strip**   the part of a SUPERHETERODYNE RECEIVER that operates at the INTERMEDIATE FREQUENCY. This consists of all the stages from the MIXER to the demodulator (see DEMODULATION), along with the AGC connections.

IF breakthrough   interference with RADIO (sense 1) reception due to a strong signal at the SUPERHETERODYNE IF passing through the tuner stage and being amplified by the IF stages.

IFF   see IDENTIFICATION FRIEND OR FOE.

IF filter   the RESONANT CIRCUIT or other frequency selective circuit used in an IF stage of a SUPERHETERODYNE receiver.

IF instability   oscillation of an IF stage, causing effects such as whistling noises on sound, often caused by failure of a DECOUPLING capacitor.

IFL   see INTEGRATED FUSE LOGIC.

I-frame   one lightly-compressed FRAME (sense 2) in a set of twelve DIGITAL VIDEO frames in a digital TV MPEG-2 coding. The I-frame contains a complete set of data for a digitized picture, unlike the B-frame and P-frame, so that a splice can be executed on an I-frame. See also GROUP OF PICTURES.

IF strip   see IF AMPLIFIER.

IGBT   see INSULATED GATE BIPOLAR TRANSISTOR.

IGFET   see INSULATED GATE FIELD EFFECT TRANSISTOR.

ignition interference   impulse interference generated by car ignition components, and particularly a problem for car radios operating with short AERIALS.

ignition voltage   the voltage that has to be applied across a GAS DISCHARGE TUBE to start current flowing. This is always higher than the voltage needed to sustain current, so that some form of CONTROL GEAR is required.

ignitron   an old form of mercury-vapour controlled RECTIFIER for very high voltages and large currents.

i-link   see IEEE 1394-1995.

illuminant D   a standard of daylight illumination corresponding to a COLOUR TEMPERATURE of 6500K.

illumination efficiency   a figure of efficiency for a transmitting REFLECTOR AERIAL, in terms of the percentage of energy from a HORN FEED that strikes the reflector.

ILR   Independent Local Radio.

IM2   second order INTERMODULATION.

IM3   third order INTERMODULATION.

image analysis a computerized method for medical diagnosis of interpreting data such as from an ultrasonic or magnetic resonance scanner and producing a recognizable picture image from the data.

image channel see IMAGE FREQUENCY.

image channel interference or **image breakthrough** unwanted signals caused by a transmission on the IMAGE CHANNEL for a SUPERHETERODYNE RECEIVER.

image compression the reduction in size of a DIGITAL set of signals for an image, based on LOSSY COMPRESSION or LOSSLESS COMPRESSION, or a combination of both.

image converter or **image intensifier** a device that achieves light amplification or frequency changing by the use of a PHOTOCATHODE and a PHOSPHOR screen operated in a vacuum with a large potential difference between them. An image that may be of ordinary visible light, or ultra-violet or infra-red light, striking the photocathode causes electrons to be emitted. These electrons are accelerated by the electrodes, and their relative positions maintained until they strike the phosphor. The electrons that strike the phosphor form a bright image. This image will be a (visible) light image, a copy of the original image that might be too dim to see, or may be composed of invisible wavelengths. Image converters and intensifiers are used with x-ray systems, allowing x-ray dosage to be greatly reduced; and in infra-red night-sights.

image frame (MPEG) a set of the digital bits that describes an image taking up a full screen on a DIGITAL TELEVISION receiver. Because of the redundancy of an image, only one complete set of the bits is required in a set of 12 frames unless there is a very large change of scene. See also B-FRAME; GROUP OF PICTURES; I-FRAME; P-FRAME.

image frequency the frequency of a signal into a SUPERHETERODYNE RECEIVER that will provide the same INTERMEDIATE FREQUENCY as the correct frequency to which the receiver is tuned. For example, if the receiver is tuned to 98MHz, using a 10.7MHz IF, then the oscillator frequency will be 108.7MHz. An input frequency of 119.4MHz, however, will also produce an IF of 10.7MHz (by subtracting the oscillator frequency), and this is the image frequency. If the IF is suitably chosen, the image frequency should be spaced sufficiently far from the desired frequency to be rejected by the RF tuning circuits. When a low frequency IF is needed, the DOUBLE SUPERHET principle will avoid image frequency problems.

image impedance a value of IMPEDANCE measured at the terminals of a FILTER network, i.e. the values of INPUT IMPEDANCE (with output open circuit) and output impedance (with input open circuit).

image intensifier a device that can increase the brightness and contrast of an image electronically. Originally, this consisted of a photoemitting plate in an evacuated tube, with the emitted electrons being accelerated to a PHOSPHOR screen to form a bright image. Modern intensifiers use low-light level CCD sensors with an output to a backlit LCD screen.

image line a form of MICROWAVE INTEGRATED STRUCTURE formed from a rectangular strip of DIELECTRIC on an earthed metal plane.

image orthicon a form of TV CAMERA TUBE that was used until the start of colour TV broadcasting, when it was largely replaced by the VIDICON type of tube. Solid-state image sensors have now almost completely replaced all the older electron-beam devices.

image processing the manipulation of the DIGITAL information for a picture to produce effects that can range from enhancement of brightness, contrast or colour to warping, wrapping and colour distortions.

image recognition a branch of ARTIFICIAL INTELLIGENCE that deals with using computer software to interpret shapes in a digitized (see DIGITIZE) image. An example is fingerprint analysis by computer.

image rejection a SUPERHETERODYNE tuner action that uses a filter to reject the IMAGE FREQUENCY

image response the response of the input circuits of a SUPERHETERODYNE RECEIVER to an IMAGE FREQUENCY signal.

image sensor any device that will convert an image into a digitized signal, now usually a CCD camera chip.

image stabilizer see ELECTRONIC IMAGE STABILIZER.

image transducer a device that will transform an optical image into electronic signals. See CCD; PHOTOCELL.

imaginary axis the axis, usually the y-axis, of a graph that is used to represent the *imaginary* or 90° phase component of a signal. The term 'imaginary' arises because the 90° phase shift can be represented mathematically using the square root of −1 (j), an imaginary number. See COMPLEX NUMBER.

imaginary part the portion of a COMPLEX NUMBER that is imaginary, multiplied by j (or i), the square root of −1 ($\sqrt{-1}$).

IMEI see INTERNATIONAL MOBILE EQUIPMENT IDENTITY.

immobilizer a circuit that will open-circuit or cross couple electronic circuits in the management system of a car, making it impossible to start without a key that contains a coded CHIP (sense 1).

impact avalanche and transit time (IMPATT) diode or **READ diode** a microwave semiconductor device using heavily doped (see DOPING) SILICON or GALLIUM ARSENIDE separated by an INTRINSIC (sense 2) or lightly doped region. The diode is operated close to avalanche conditions with a DC bias of around 120V, so that an input microwave signal will drive the diode in and out of avalanche, producing a signal of up to 1W power at a typical frequency of 20 GHz. The tuning action is obtained by operating the diode in a RESONANT CAVITY.

impact dot-matrix see IMPACT PRINTER.

impact printer any type of printer whose action involves mechanically striking the paper. The ELECTROSTATIC PRINTER and THERMAL PRINTER (now obsolete) both use special papers, and do not strike the paper. Similarly, the INKJET PRINTER and LASER PRINTER rely on depositing material on the paper without direct contact. Impact printers, however, rely on the principle of needles or type shapes being hammered against inked ribbons that strike the paper. These dot-matrix printer types are comparatively noisy and slow, but they have the considerable advantage that they can be used with ordinary paper, and also with several sheets of interleaved carbons if copies are needed.

impact vibration detector a PIEZOELECTRIC CRYSTAL detector used to sense vibration caused by attempted burglary.

IMPATT diode see IMPACT AVALANCHE AND TRANSIT TIME DIODE.

impedance the ratio of signal POTENTIAL DIFFERENCE to signal current for a device that has both REACTANCE and RESISTANCE. Symbol: **Z**; unit: ohm. If an AC signal is applied to a circuit containing reactive components, the phase of output current will not necessarily be the same as the phase of output voltage. The relationship between V and I cannot be described by a simple (scalar) quantity like resistance, and requires the use of a complex number, impedance. The impedance for a series circuit containing reactance X and resistance R is given by **Z** = R + jX where j = $\sqrt{-1}$. See Fig. 59.

impedance coupling the use of an impedance, as distinct from a resistance, as a load in an amplifying stage.

impedance, LS the IMPEDANCE of a loudspeaker, due not only to the INDUCTANCE, RESISTANCE and CAPACITANCE of the DRIVE COIL but to the MOTIONAL IMPEDANCE of the mechanical parts such as the cone and its suspension.

impedance matching a method of ensuring that the IMPEDANCES of circuits that are to be connected are equal. Impedance matching is particularly important for RF power circuits and TRANSMISSION LINES. The maximum transfer of power from an amplifier to a load occurs when the two are matched, meaning that the output impedance of the amplifier equals the INPUT IMPEDANCE of the load. In a transmission line, MATCHING impedances prevent reflections that

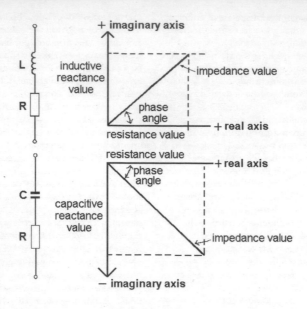

Fig. 59. **impedance**

would otherwise occur at the point where unequal impedances were connected. FILTER SECTIONS that are to be connected together will operate correctly only if the impedances are matched.

impedance scaling the conversion of calculated values of CHARACTERISTIC IMPEDANCE for a filter into practical values.

impedance transformation the action of a TRANSFORMER and of some active circuits, such as the EMITTER FOLLOWER, having different MATCHING impedance at the output as compared to the input, so providing efficient power transfer from a circuit at one impedance level to a circuit at a different impedance level.

impedance transformer or **quarter-wave transformer** a portion of TRANSMISSION LINE that is a quarter wavelength long, used to match lines with different impedance levels. If the impedance of the quarter wave section is Z_3, and the lines to be matched have impedances of Z_1 and Z_2, then matching is achieved if $Z_3 = \sqrt{Z_1 \times Z_2}$.

implosion a hazard of all vacuum devices because of the huge pressure of the atmosphere, but particularly hazardous for large CATHODE-RAY TUBES.

impregnated cable a cable that uses paper or cloth insulation impregnated with oil.

impulse I. a sudden rise and fall of voltage or current. Impulses are generated by switching, particularly in inductive circuits, and also by spark discharges.
2. or **unit impulse**, a theoretical pulse of infinite height and zero width.

impulse amplitude limiter a form of NOISE LIMITER for AM receivers based on detection of rate of change of AMPLITUDE.

impulse generator a SIGNAL GENERATOR that provides an IMPULSE (sense 1) voltage or current. Impulse generators are used for testing insulation.

impulse invariant transform the design system for a DIGITAL FILTER that will respond to a pulse in the same way as a given analogue FILTER.

impulse noise or **impulsive noise**   a form of RF NOISE that arises from SPARKS. The spark ignition system of petrol engines is one common source of impulse noise. Another source is sparking contacts in thermostats (refrigerators, central heating systems). Impulse noise is particularly troublesome to VHF transmissions, particularly FM and TV transmissions that have a broad bandwidth.

impulse signal   a single isolated PULSE used for test purposes.

impurity   the atoms contained in a semiconductor CRYSTAL that are not of the semiconductor element or compound. Impurity may exist because it cannot be removed, or because it has been deliberately added, in which case it is referred to as a DOPING impurity.

impurity elements   elements that are used to dope SEMICONDUCTORS, usually TRIVALENT ELEMENTS such as aluminium, gallium and indium, or PENTAVALENT ELEMENTS such as phosphorus, arsenic and antimony.

IMSI   see INTERNATIONAL MOBILE SUBSCRIBER IDENTITY.

incandescent lamp   a lamp whose light is generated by a hot object, usually a metal filament.

inches per second (ips)   the measure of tape speed on a tape recording (see RECORDING OF SOUND) system.

incidental modulation   an additional unwanted MODULATION of a modulated CARRIER (sense 1) caused by a NONLINEAR process. For example, an FM signal passing through a nonlinear amplifier can gain an AM component.

inclination   the angle of elevation of a DISH aerial with respect to the horizontal.

incoming traffic   the signals received by a computer communications link and directed to the computer.

incremental resistance or **slope resistance** or **differential resistance**   the value of slope of the graph of voltage plotted against current for a component or circuit. This corresponds to the EQUIVALENT RESISTANCE for a small signal applied with the bias set to the same voltage and current levels.

incremental writing   a method used for recording on CD-R or CD-RW discs that allows data to be added in more than one recording session. The disc cannot be read by a conventional CD player until the disc has been finalized, see FINALIZED DISC.

incremented   (of a count or measurement) increased by one step. Compare DECREMENTED.

independent sideband signal (ISB) the use of two differently modulated SIDEBANDS of the same (suppressed) CARRIER (sense 1) frequency. See also SINGLE SIDEBAND; SUPPRESSED CARRIER.

index of cooperation   see FACTOR OF COOPERATION.

index of directivity   a factor usually symbolized as Q, for directional properties of a sound, taking OMNIDIRECTIONAL radiation of sound as giving a Q-value or unity.

index search   a search action for an item on a video cassette tape (see VIDEO CASSETTE RECORDER), using index marks recorded on the tape.

indicating instrument   an instrument that indicates only that a current or voltage exists, but does not measure the value. See also INDICATOR.

indicator or **indicator lamp** or **indicator light**   a lamp that is illuminated to provide a warning or signal a condition (such as power on) in a circuit.

indicator, recording level   see RECORDING LEVEL INDICATOR.

indicator tube   a form of miniature CATHODE-RAY TUBE. Typically, indicator tubes are built into equipment so that waveforms can be checked without the need to connect up a separate CATHODE-RAY OSCILLOSCOPE.

indirect wave   a radio wave that reaches a RECEIVER by reflection from, for example, the IONOSPHERE.

induce   to produce an electrical effect at a distance. An electrostatic CHARGE can be induced in any object by bringing up another charge. A MAGNETIC FLUX can be induced in a magnetic material by bringing up a magnet or a coil that is carrying current.

induced AC voltage or **induced voltage**
the signal voltage induced in a metal by
an alternating MAGNETIC FIELD.

induced current the CURRENT that flows
in a CONDUCTOR because the conductor
is cutting through lines of magnetic flux.
This can be achieved by moving the
conductor across a magnetic field or by
changing the size of the magnetic field
around the conductor.

induced noise the NOISE that is induced
from another circuit. For example, HUM
in an audio circuit may be induced from
a mains transformer by way of an EARTH
LOOP.

inductance the quantity that relates
MAGNETIC FLUX to the CURRENT that causes
it. Symbol: L; unit henry. Inductance of
two types exists, SELF-INDUCTANCE as
applied to a single inductor (coil) and
MUTUAL INDUCTANCE between two coils
as in a TRANSFORMER.

inductance, electrolytic the SELF-
INDUCTANCE of an ELECTROLYTIC CAPACITOR
due to the foil winding construction, so
that an electrolytic cannot be relied on to
provide a low-impedance path for high-
frequency signals.

inductance, wire-wound the SELF-
INDUCTANCE of a resistor that has been
wire-wound, usually reduced by reversing
the direction of winding at intervals.

induction the process of inducing
MAGNETISM or CHARGE.

induction compass a miniature AC
GENERATOR (sense 1) that acts as a
magnetic compass. A coil rotates, and
the peak output is obtained when the axis
of the coil (at right angles to the axis of
rotation) faces along the Earth's magnetic
north-south axis.

induction flowmeter a method of
measuring the flow rate for a conducting
liquid. The flow of the liquid is at right
angles to a MAGNETIC FIELD, and a small
voltage is generated or induced across
the liquid, and can be measured. The
importance of the method is that there
need be no interference with the flow
of the liquid, and the method is equally
applicable to very hot or very cold liquids

or to ionized gases (see IONIZATION).
The principle is also used as a method
of generating power, the magnetohydrodynamic generator.

induction furnace or **induction heater**
a method of melting metals by making
the metal the secondary 'winding' of a
TRANSFORMER. This is used for large scale
heating; for small samples an EDDY
CURRENT HEATER is more useful.

induction heating see EDDY CURRENT
HEATER; INDUCTION FURNACE.

induction instrument a form of MOVING-
IRON meter. The STATOR coil is supplied
with alternating current to be measured.
The EDDY CURRENTs that are induced in a
movable conductor cause force effects that
move the conductor, and a needle, against
the restoring force of a spring.

induction microphone see RIBBON
MICROPHONE.

induction motor a type of electric MOTOR
that depends on INDUCTION effects. The
FIELD COILs are fed with AC, and induce
currents in the ROTOR coils (these may be
metal bars). The forces between the two
fields cause the rotor to rotate. Many
types of induction motors are not self-
starting, and have to be spun to operating
speed by an auxiliary motor.

inductive circuit a circuit that is
predominantly inductive, so that the phase
of voltage leads the phase of current.

inductive crosstalk unwanted transfer
of a signal (see CROSSTALK) by its magnetic
field affecting a conductor in another
circuit. See also CAPACITIVE CROSSTALK.

inductive distance sensor a TRANSDUCER
in which the position of a magnetic
core between coils is sensed by the
TRANSFORMER action of the coils and core.
See also LINEAR VARIABLE DIFFERENTIAL
TRANSFORMER (LVDT).

inductive head a TAPE HEAD that consists
of an inductive winding over a core and
therefore generates a voltage output
proportional to the rate of change of
magnetic flux caused by the moving tape.
Contrast MAGNETO-RESISTIVE HEAD.

inductive load a LOAD in which the PHASE
of voltage leads the phase of current.

inductive output tube (IOT) a microwave amplifier similar in principles to the KLYSTRON but designed for high power output, typically more than 60 kW over a frequency range of 450 MHz to 1GHz, used extensively for UHF TV broadcasting.

inductive proximity switch a TRANSDUCER that detects the nearness of metal objects by the change of INDUCTANCE of a coil.

inductive reactance the reactance of an INDUCTOR, symbol X_L, equal to $2\pi f L$ where L is the inductance in HENRIES.

inductive reservoir the use of an INDUCTOR as an energy store, particularly in the use of a CHOKE INPUT FILTER in a power supply.

inductive source a source of signals that is predominantly inductive such as a MOVING-COIL MICROPHONE or guitar pickup.

inductor a coil, loop or wire that is used for its INDUCTANCE value.

inductor, stripline see STRIPLINE INDUCTOR.

industry standard architecture see ISA.

infant mortality the failure of any device early in a LIFE TEST.

infinite baffle a form of LOUDSPEAKER mounting system in which the sound path from the front of the cone to the rear is infinitely long compared to the WAVELENGTH. This is impracticable for the lowest wavelengths, but forms a good theoretical standard for comparing other enclosures.

infinite impedance demodulator a simple AM demodulator that uses a source-follower circuit with high INPUT IMPEDANCE, with the demodulated (see DEMODULATION) signal taken from the source electrode.

infinite impulse response (IIF) filter a form of DIGITAL FILTER that uses delay stages with both FEEDFORWARD CIRCUITS and FEEDBACK of signals from one stage to the adjacent stages. These filters are used in telephony, reverberation units, noise reduction units or video special effects generators.

information content for a DIGITAL SIGNAL a figure for content calculated from the probability of occurrence of a SYMBOL. See INFORMATION THEORY.

information rate the product of average information content per symbol and the number of symbols transmitted per second. See INFORMATION THEORY.

information theory a system of theory based on the work (in the 1920s to 1940s) of Hartley and Shannon, concerning the transmission of data, particularly applicable to DIGITAL DATA transmission.

infra-red the range of radiated waves with WAVELENGTHS of about 700nm to 1mm. These are the wavelengths that are longer than that of the red colour in the visible spectrum, hence the name. The main effect of these waves on any object that they strike is heating, and they are emitted strongly by hot objects.

infra-red (IR) beam or **active infra-red** the use as a security device of beams of INFRA-RED light that will reflect from an intruder and can be used to form an image using a TV camera that is sensitive to infra-red.

infra-red detector passive see PASSIVE INFRA-RED (PIR).

infra-red remote control a controller for audio or video equipment using a coded infra-red beam. Each controller is usually specific to one device or a set of devices of one make, but universal controllers that are programmable are a useful and practical solution to the problem of a lost remote control or too many controls.

infra-red tester a testing device for an INFRA-RED REMOTE CONTROL that acknowledges a working remote control by flashing an LED or sounding a tone.

infrasonic see SUBSONIC.

inhibit to suppress an OUTPUT, or prevent an INPUT (sense 1) from having any effect.

inhibit pin a connection to an IC that will carry out the action of preventing or reversing the effect of a signal at another pin.

inhibit pulse a PULSE applied to a MAGNETIC CORE to prevent writing. See also COINCIDENT HALF-CURRENT SWITCHING.

initialization the action of preparing a circuit or device for use.

injection 1. the applying of a SIGNAL, particularly a test signal, to a CIRCUIT.

2. the supply of a signal from an OSCILLATOR into a MIXER. **3.** the introduction of CARRIERS (sense 2) into a SEMICONDUCTOR.

inkjet printer a form of non-impact printer that uses a MATRIX of fine jets to squirt ink at the paper. The ink cartridge and the set of jets can be made as one unit so that clogging of the jets is avoided by changing the jets along with the ink-cartridge. The advantages include fairly high speed, silent operation, high resolution (600–1200 or more dots per inch) and the ability to form any character shape and to execute high-resolution graphics. In addition, colour ink-jet printers can be made at little more initial cost than the monochrome version, though running costs are higher. Two main types use different principles to control the ink flow. The bubblejet™ system, devised by Canon, uses heating elements in a microscopically fine tube to evaporate ink, creating a bubble that then displaces ink through the jet. The Stylus™ system, devised by Epson, uses a piezoelectric (see PIEZOELECTRIC CRYSTAL) tube that constricts, squirting ink, when acted on by an applied voltage.

inner coding a digital television process that uses modulation and transmission of two separate data streams to ensure redundancy for error correction before other (*outer*) coding methods are applied. See also CONVOLUTIONAL CODING; VITERBI CODING.

in-phase component I. the portion of a signal VOLTAGE that is in PHASE with current, or the portion of a signal CURRENT that is in phase with voltage. **2.** or **I component** the CHROMINANCE SIGNAL component in the NTSC colour TV system that is in PHASE with its SUBCARRIER. See also QUADRATURE COMPONENT (Q component).

input I. a SIGNAL taken into a component or system. Contrast OUTPUT. **2.** the connections to which the input signal is applied.

input attenuator, cro the switched POTENTIOMETER (sense 1) at the input of the Y-AMPLIFIER of a CATHODE-RAY OSCILLOSCOPE that is used to prevent a large signal overloading the amplifier.

input capacitance the capacitance, usually STRAY CAPACITANCE, at the input of a circuit which will have an attenuating effect on high-frequency signals.

input characteristic the graph of current plotted against voltage (or *vice-versa*) at the input of an electronic component, particularly a SEMICONDUCTOR device.

input current the DC or signal current at the input of a device, which for a logic device can be a DC SINK (sense 1) or SOURCE (sense 3) current.

input impedance the IMPEDANCE at the input terminals of a device, generally expressed by a COMPLEX NUMBER.

input node a point where signals enter an electronics circuit.

input offset the very small difference between DC levels at the two inputs of an OPERATIONAL AMPLIFIER with a BALANCED POWER SUPPLY, that will result in the output being at zero potential.

input/output (I/O) the parts of a computer circuit that deal with the INPUT (sense 1) or OUTPUT of signals.

input/output controller a form of INTERFACE found on the larger computers, that controls the paths between the computer and its peripherals. This allows the peripherals to be used more efficiently, and speeds up the action of the main computer. Some types of input/output controller incorporate both memory and a separate MICROPROCESSOR. They can therefore free the main processor from carrying out input or output steps. See also DMA.

input resistance the ratio of voltage to IN-PHASE current (for AC or DC) at the input of an electronic device.

inrush rating the current rating for a changeover action on a heavy-duty RELAY.

insertion gain the GAIN of an amplifier when it is placed between a source of SIGNAL and a LOAD. The figure is usually expressed in decibels.

insertion loss the loss of SIGNAL power due to a NETWORK (sense 1) placed between a source of signal and a LOAD. The figure is usually expressed in decibels.

insertion test signals (ITS) signals added to transmitted ANALOGUE or DIGITAL broadcasts that are not apparent to the listener or viewer but can be used by service engineers for signal quality test purposes.

insertion tool a device for fitting an IC into a PRINTED CIRCUIT BOARD for soldering.

in service testing checks of performance carried out on a DIGITAL transmission channel while normal TRAFFIC is flowing. Contrast OUT OF SERVICE TESTING.

instantaneous current the value of CURRENT in an AC circuit at some instant of a signal cycle.

instantaneous failure rate a quality control PARAMETER equal to the number of devices failing per hour of testing divided by the number that are still active at a particular instant.

instantaneous frequency the FREQUENCY of a SIGNAL at any instant, applied mainly to a frequency modulated signal, see FREQUENCY MODULATION.

instantaneous power the power transferred or dissipated in a CIRCUIT or a COMPONENT at an instant of sampling.

Institute of Electrical and Electronic Engineers (IEEE) the US society formed in 1963 by amalgamation of the institutes of Electrical Engineers and Radio Engineers in the US.

Institution of Electrical Engineers (IEE) the senior electrical and electronic engineering institution in the UK.

instruction cycle the cycle of actions involved in one MICROPROCESSOR action, consisting of putting out an address on the ADDRESS BUS, sending a READ pulse, reading DATA from the data bus, and then decoding and acting on the instruction.

instrumentation the equipping of a system with instruments that measure and monitor the state of the system.

instrumentation amplifier an amplifier intended for precise DC amplification and featuring high INPUT IMPEDANCE, high COMMON-MODE REJECTION RATIO and a precise value of high GAIN.

instrumentation tape recorder a tape recorder, usually for DIGITAL signals, used to record instrument readings on a system over a long period.

instrument rating the limit of current or voltage that can be applied to a measuring instrument without causing damage. If no rating is known, a figure of 1.5 times FULL SCALE DEFLECTION is often assumed.

instrument sensitivity the ratio of the number of dial scale divisions to the unit that is being measured. Examples are divisions per volt, per milliamp, per watt, etc.

instrument transformer a form of CURRENT TRANSFORMER used for measuring large alternating currents in conjunction with an AC current meter operating with lower currents.

instrument tube a form of CATHODE-RAY TUBE intended as a measuring device rather than for picture display. Instrument tubes need to be operated with beam deflection times that may range from seconds to fractions of a microsecond. Their size need not be large, but the sensitivity in terms of millimetres of deflection per volt of deflection waveform must be high. Electrostatic deflection is used, and the leads to the deflection plates are often taken through the sides of the tube neck to avoid excessive STRAY CAPACITANCE. The deflection is carried out at a point where the beam is comparatively slow-moving (hence easier to deflect) and the beam is then accelerated (see POST-DEFLECTION ACCELERATION) to its final velocity. The face of the tube will be flat so that measurements of distance between points on the face can easily be made.

insulate to prevent flow of CURRENT to or from a conductor.

insulated gate bipolar transistor (IGBT) a hybrid structure consisting of a BIPOLAR transistor whose base is controlled by an insulated GATE (sense 1), used as power devices at output levels of typically 100W.

insulated gate FET (IGFET) see FIELD EFFECT TRANSISTOR.

insulated system an electrical supply system with no EARTH. The system is used mainly when DOUBLE INSULATION is possible, with no metal parts accessible to the user.

insulating resistance the value of RESISTANCE between points that are insulated. The value can be used to calculate the amount of leakage current, but it is important to remember that insulating resistance is nonlinear (i.e. can change with applied voltage), and can be greatly affected by the presence of moisture.

insulation material with very high RESISTIVITY used as insulation to separate conductors so that no current flows from one conductor to the other.

insulation displacement connector (IDC) a connector system for ribbon cables, widely used in computer connections, in which the connector pins at the cable side are shaped into V-grooves, so that forcing the cable against the connector and clamping it causes each V to slice the insulation and make contact with the metal strand.

insulation, heater-cathode the high resistance between HEATER (sense 2) and CATHODE (sense 1) connections to a cathode-ray tube.

insulation resistance, mains the high resistance between the live or NEUTRAL (sense 3) and earth leads of a mains operated device. This should be at least 2MΩ for earthed devices and 7MΩ or more for DOUBLE-INSULATED devices.

insulation tester an instrument that generates and applies a high voltage to points that are insulated from each other and measures any small current that flows. One very well-known example is the Megger™.

insulator any material used to separate conductors and prevent CURRENT flow between them.

integer a whole number, with no fractional content.

integrated circuit (IC) a CIRCUIT that is constructed entirely on a SILICON CHIP though other semiconductor materials are now in use. The silicon is used to form TRANSISTORS (usually FET types), RESISTORS, and, less commonly, CAPACITORS. This is made possible by using doped silicon as a conductor and silicon oxide as an insulator. The main advantages in the use of ICs are reliability and low cost. A conventional circuit makes use of a number of components that have to be electrically connected. In such conventional circuits, the reliability greatly decreases as the number of components is increased, partly because each component contributes another source of failure, and partly because each interconnection is unreliable.

The IC is manufactured as a single COMPONENT, and has the reliability of a single semiconductor component, despite the fact that it may carry out the actions of a circuit with thousands of components and interconnections. In addition, the actions required to manufacture an IC with millions of components are not significantly more (other than initial design and tooling) than are needed for a simple semiconductor.

integrated circuit power amplifier an amplifier that provides both voltage and power amplification, with low output impedance. Such IC power amplifiers must provide for heat dissipation, usually by being mounted on a HEAT SINK.

integrated device electronics see IDE.

integrated digital receiver a TV or radio receiver that has a TUNER and DECODER for digital services (particularly for terrestrial digital transmissions) built in, as distinct from an analogue receiver with a converter (SET-TOP BOX).

integrated fuse logic (IFL) a form of PROGRAMMABLE LOGIC DEVICE that uses links that can be blown like fuses to separate connections, leaving others intact.

integrated injection logic or **I²L** a form of INTEGRATED CIRCUIT construction for digital circuits using BIPOLAR JUNCTION TRANSISTORS.

integrated services digital network see ISDN.

integrating ADC see INTEGRATOR A-D CONVERTER.

integrating circuit see INTEGRATOR.

integration the mathematical operation that sums the effect of a set of changes, applied in electronics to mean a smoothing action. The output wave from an integrator is represented by an expression that is the time integral of the expression for the input signal.

integrator or **integrating circuit** a CIRCUIT that smooths out a PULSE into a half-wave of longer duration and lower amplitude. The application of repeated pulses to an integrator will have the effect of creating a steadily increasing voltage level. The term arises from the mathematical operation of integration. The output wave from an integrator is represented by a mathematical expression that is the time integral of the expression for the input waveform. See Fig. 60.

integrator A-D converter or **integrating ADC** a form of ANALOGUE TO DIGITAL CONVERTER that counts CLOCK pulses into an INTEGRATOR until the integrated level is the same as the level of the signal that has been sampled. The count is then the digital representation of that signal level.

integrator, opamp an INTEGRATING CIRCUIT consisting of an OPERATIONAL AMPLIFIER with FEEDBACK through a DIFFERENTIATING CIRCUIT to the INVERTING INPUT.

intelligent terminal or **smart terminal** an assembly of keyboard and MONITOR that also includes some computing circuits. An intelligent terminal can download (see DOWNLOADING) data from a main computer, and carry out some processing work, thus decreasing the load on the main system.

intelligent time division multiplex see CONCENTRATOR.

intelligibility a measure of the utility of a communication system derived from the percentage of correctly received meaningless words in a sample transmission.

Intelsat see INTERNATIONAL SATELLITE AGENCY.

intensity 1. an alternative term for strength of an electric or magnetic field (see FIELD-STRENGTH METER). 2. the brightness of the SPOT (sense 1) on a CATHODE-RAY TUBE.

intensity, led the light brightness of an LED, which depends fairly linearly on current.

intensity modulation the variation of brightness of the light spot (sense 1) on the face of a CATHODE-RAY TUBE. Intensity modulation is essential to TV reception, and is an option in most CATHODE-RAY OSCILLOSCOPES.

intensity of field meter see FIELD STRENGTH METER.

interactive service a feature of CABLE TV networks that permits viewers to communicate with the central control system and so participate in interactive programs.

interactive video any video service that allows the viewer to communicate with the broadcaster.

interactive voice response see IVR.

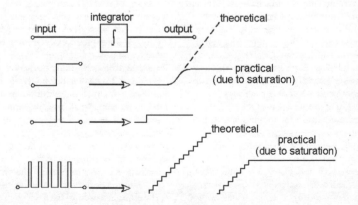

Fig. 60. **integrator**

interblock gap a space between groups of data. Usually applied to tape backup systems in which the data is grouped into BLOCKs (sense 2). Each block starts with a HEADER that contains the filename and some information on the block, such as the number of bytes in the block. A short part of the tape is then left unrecorded between blocks, and this is referred to as the *gap*, or *interblock gap*. The presence of this gap allows time for the computer to check the block data, and to stop the tape if an error is found. The tape can then be rewound to the previous gap so that another read can be attempted.

intercarrier sound a system of sound IF used in analogue COLOUR TELEVISION receivers. The sound signal is frequency-modulated and transmitted on a frequency that is 6MHz higher than the video signal CARRIER (sense 1). The RF and IF stages of a receiver deal with the whole band of frequencies. At the VIDEO DEMODULATOR, the nonlinear action of the diode mixes the sound and vision carriers (at their IF frequencies) to produce a 6MHz intercarrier frequency. This signal is still frequency-modulated with the sound signal, and is filtered off to be further amplified and then frequency-demodulated. See also NICAM.

intercept the point on a GRAPH where the line crosses one AXIS. Often this is the ORIGIN but some graphs have an intercept on one or both axes. For example, the graph of a cell voltage plotted against cell current has a voltage intercept at zero current which is the open-circuit EMF value. See also SLOPE and Fig. 109.

interchangeability the ability to replace COMPONENTS in a CIRCUIT without detriment to the action of the circuit.

interconnection the making of CURRENT paths between systems or devices, e.g. between different circuit boards in a SYSTEM.

interdigital transducer a metallic comb-like structure used to apply an ELECTRIC FIELD to, typically, a PIEZOELECTRIC CRYSTAL substrate. See also SURFACE ACOUSTIC WAVE TRANSDUCER.

interelectrode capacitance the CAPACITANCE between the separate ELECTRODES of a device. Capacitance of this type, such as the capacitance between the BASE and COLLECTOR of a BIPOLAR JUNCTION TRANSISTOR, may adversely affect operation. For example, the capacitance will affect the phase of high-frequency signals, and will also have to be charged and discharged when pulse signals are being used.

interface a circuit that allows SIGNALS to be passed between two otherwise incompatible systems.

interference any form of unwanted signal that may be NOISE, natural or man-made, or a transmitted signal on the same frequency or on an adjacent frequency.

interference rejection ratio a measure of INTERFERENCE based on the ratio of DEMODULATOR output due to interference to demodulator output due to wanted signal, expressed in DECIBELS.

interferometry a form of measurement for very small displacements that depends on the interference between (LASER) light waves. A basic interferometer produces a pattern of dark and bright bands, and a movement equal to that from a dark to a bright band corresponds to a displacement by one half of a wavelength of the light used, typically 10^{-4} mm.

interframe comparison the DIGITAL TELEVISION action of comparing information between successive frames (see FRAME, sense 1) of a video and coding only the differences between these frames.

inter-IC bus see I^2C BUS.

interlace the deliberate interweaving of lines on a TV RASTER, originally used as a way of reducing bandwidth. Interlace is used on analogue TV transmissions, but is not used on computer displays or on DIGITAL TELEVISION pictures.

interleaved code see INTERLEAVING.

interleaved memory a method of using DYNAMIC RAM that overcomes the problem of the time needed for REFRESH (sense 1). The chips are used in banks with consecutive bytes of data stored in different banks. This allows for refreshing one bank while another is being used and it also allows the use of memory with a comparatively slow ACCESS TIME (sense 1) to be used.

interleaving or **interlacing** a data shifting system that minimizes the effect of INTERFERENCE. If a set of data WORDS that belong together are transmitted on different FRAMES (sense 2), then only the worst interference would have affected all of them when they are reassembled, and an error in one word could be corrected relatively easily. Interleaving is used for data on a CD to minimize the effect of a scratch on the surface, and on DIGITAL TELEVISION pictures to minimize the effects of interference.

interline flicker or **interline crawl** a flickering effect due to the use of an interlaced (see INTERLACE) RASTER on a TV picture, absent on digital pictures displayed on LCD or PLASMA screens.

interline transfer (IT) a form of CCD device in which the vertical columns of PIXEL cells perform both sensing and storage actions alternately. See also FRAME INTERLINE TRANSFER; FRAME TRANSFER; HOLE ACCUMULATION DIODE.

interlock a form of safety SWITCH that allows power to be applied only when doors of cabinets are shut, and all live points covered. In ROBOTICS, interlocks are used to ensure that a robot cannot move if a human is in the operating area.

intermediate frequency (IF) the FREQUENCY used for the main amplifying stages in a SUPERHETERODYNE RECEIVER. The term arose because the frequency is intermediate between audio (or video) frequency and the incoming signal frequency.

intermediate frequency amplifier the amplifying stages in a SUPERHETERODYNE RECEIVER that deal with the signal at intermediate frequency.

intermittent or **intermittent fault** the most difficult type of electronics fault to diagnose and repair, because there is no certainty that the fault can be reproduced or its source found.

intermodulation the unwanted MODULATION of one frequency by another, caused by a NONLINEAR stage.

internal (of a computer component) mounted in the same casing as the MOTHERBOARD.

internal resistance the RESISTANCE of the internal circuits of a BATTERY or GENERATOR (either sense). Any source of signal (or DC) can be represented as a voltage supply in series with an internal resistance. The size of the internal resistance is found by measuring the change of output voltage per change of supplied current.

International Electrotechnical Commission (IEC) an organization set up in 1904 in St. Louis to promote cooperation in international standards for electrical equipment.

international mobile equipment identity (IMEI) an identification code contained within a MOBILE PHONE, independent of the SIM card.

international mobile subscriber identity (IMSI) a personal identification code contained in the SIM card of a MOBILE PHONE.

International Satellite Agency (Intelsat) an organization set up in 1964 by more than 100 countries to own and manage a global satellite system for consumer use.

International Standards Organization (ISO) a specialized standardizing agency, centred in Geneva, working on definitions, performance requirements, specifications, testing methods and symbols used in technical work

Internet a global network of large computers, linked by satellites, that can be accessed by a home user from a computer connected through a MODEM to an INTERNET SERVICE PROVIDER (ISP).

internet service provider (ISP) an organization that provides access to the INTERNET using a computer that can be accessed through telephone lines. The ISP is an intermediate between the user and the main internet, and many ISPs provide a free service financed by advertizing.

interoperability the ability of a system to work with others, such as the ability of a MPEG-2 digital television MULTIPLEX to be transmitted over networks that were originally designed for ANALOGUE transmissions.

interpolated value a value that is read off from a graph rather than measured directly.

interpolation the use of reliable values that are deduced rather than measured, often by using a graph line. Contrast EXTRAPOLATION.

interrogating signal a PULSE signal that triggers a coded reply from a matching device, the TRANSPONDER. The system is used to identify friendly aircraft, or aircraft that belong to one group. See also IFF; SECONDARY RADAR.

interrupt a PULSE signal applied to a MICROPROCESSOR at an interrupt INPUT (sense 2). This signal will cause normal processing to be suspended while a special routine, the *interrupt service routine*, is run.

interrupted continuous wave transmission a radio signal in which the CARRIER (sense 1) is interrupted, either in a DIGITAL code or in MORSE CODE.

interrupted count a method of obtaining any desired count number from a set of flip-flops (sufficient to perform a count to the next higher power of two) by interrupting the count at the desired end figure.

interrupter a DEVICE that switches a CURRENT on and off at set intervals.

interrupt rating, fuse the specified excess current and time needed to blow a FUSE.

interrupt request (IRQ) a signal to a microprocessor that will initiate an INTERRUPT.

intersection the means by which two or more DIRECTION FINDING stations locate a transmitter sending a distress signal, using a DIRECTIONAL FIX from each station and finding the point where these lines intersect.

interstage coupling see STAGE COUPLING.

interstation noise the noise that is heard when tuning a radio receiver between stations. The increase in noise is due to the increase in sensitivity of the receiver because of the action of the AGC line when no strong signal is present. Some receiver designs incorporate a MUTING circuit that suppresses this noise.

inter-symbol interference (ISI) or **phase shift distortion** a form of distortion of digital signals in which a signal pulse affects an adjacent pulse, such as occurs when two adjacent pulses are recorded on magnetic media.

intra-aural headphone a HEADPHONE whose TRANSDUCER fits inside the ear rather than being clamped over the ear.

intra frame see I FRAME.

intranet a NETWORK (sense 2) that operates in a way similar to the INTERNET but which is confined to a single organization or set of organizations. An intranet need not be connected to the Internet, but when such a connection is made it is through a FIREWALL so that a *virus* cannot be transmitted from the Internet to the intranet.

intrinsic **1.** of, or relating to, a specific quality of a material. **2.** (of a SEMICONDUCTOR) consisting of pure undoped (see DOPING) material.

intrinsic impedance the theoretical IMPEDANCE of an AERIAL with lossless elements and located over a perfect EARTH PLANE.

intrinsic noise the level of NOISE in a COMMUNICATIONS CHANNEL when all transmissions are halted.

intrinsic noise level the noise level of a semiconductor device under perfect operating conditions.

intrinsic semiconductor or **i-type semiconductor** a semiconductor consisting of pure undoped (see DOPING) material.

intrinsic stand-off ratio the ratio of triggering voltage to applied voltage in a UNIJUNCTION.

intro search a VIDEO CASSETTE RECORDER system in which a tape with INDEX SEARCH marks will play at normal speed around each index mark, before performing a fast forward or reverse wind to the next.

inverse gain the GAIN figure for a TRANSISTOR operated with COLLECTOR and EMITTER (sense 1) circuit connections reversed.

inverse square law the law relating signal strength to distance for any non-beamed radiation, stating that received signal amplitude is inversely proportional to transmitted distance.

inverse video or **reverse video** a display that uses black text on white background when the normal display consists of white text on a black background. The name denotes any display that interchanges the normal background and foreground colours.

inversion the action of an inverting AMPLIFIER on a SIGNAL. High and low voltages in the parts of the signal are interchanged, producing a waveform that is the mirror image of the INPUT (sense 1).

inverted L aerial (or antenna) an aerial used for low frequency transmission where a quarter length vertical wire would be impossible to achieve, so that some of the length of the aerial is used horizontally to form an inverted L shape. See also INVERTED T AERIAL.

inverted microstrip a form of MICROWAVE INTEGRATED STRUCTURE in which a conductor laid on a DIELECTRIC is spaced close to a GROUND PLANE with the conductor facing the ground.

inverted output a signal output from a device that is in ANTIPHASE with the input.

inverted strip line see INVERTED MICROSTRIP.

inverted T aerial (or antenna) an aerial used for low frequency transmission where a quarter length vertical wire would be impossible to achieve, so that a shorter vertical section is used with a horizontal section to form an inverted T shape. See also INVERTED L AERIAL.

inverted V aerial (or antenna) a DIRECTIONAL form of LONG-WIRE AERIAL that uses an inverted V shape with legs of 2 to 4 wavelengths long.

inverted wave a waveshape that is the mirror image (around the time axis) of another wave. An inverted wave is sometimes referred to as a 180° PHASE shift, but this is true only for a sine wave.

inverter 1. an ANALOGUE or DIGITAL CIRCUIT or device that inverts a signal. The digital inverter is also called a *NOT gate*. The digital inverter converts a 0 to a 1, and a 1 to a 0. **2.** or **power converter** a circuit that converts DC into AC (a power oscillator).

inverting amplifier an AMPLIFIER whose OUTPUT is inverted with respect to the INPUT (sense 1). Any single stage transistor amplifier with input to the base and output from the collector load will therefore be an inverting amplifier.

inverting input the input to an OPERATIONAL AMPLIFIER that will result in an output that is in ANTIPHASE. Feedback from the output to the inverting input will be NEGATIVE FEEDBACK.

inverting regulator an IC that converts a positive supply to form a negative supply, using SWITCH-MODE principles.

inverting signal the action of creating an inverse signal wave by using an inverting amplifier or a transformer.

inverting word the interchanging of bits 0 and 1. Inverting the byte 11110000, for example, would give the byte 00001111.

I/O see INPUT/OUTPUT.

ion the particle with CHARGE that is the result of an ELECTRON being added to or taken from a neutral (sense 4) atom. For a few materials, two electrons can sometimes be added or removed. See NEGATIVE ION; POSITIVE ION.

ion burn or **ion spot** a form of damage to the PHOSPHOR screen of a CATHODE-RAY TUBE. The damage is caused by NEGATIVE ION bombardment, and results in the phosphor becoming deactivated, so that it no longer emits light when struck by electrons. The negative ions result from remaining gas atoms that have been struck by electrons. See also ION TRAP; SCREEN BURN.

ionic conduction a form of CONDUCTION by the movement of positive or negative ions.

ion implantation a method of DOPING a semiconductor by bombarding the surface with IONs of the doping material. The technique can be more closely controlled than other doping methods, and is particularly useful for making GALLIUM ARSENIDE FETs.

ion spot see ION BURN.

ion trap a method of preventing ION BURN in a CATHODE-RAY TUBE. The electron gun of a monochrome TV cathode-ray tube is tilted sideways so that any particle emerging straight along the axis of the electron gun will strike the neck of the tube. The ELECTRON BEAM is deflected back onto its correct path by a small magnet, but the heavier ions are not measurably affected and strike the tube neck. Ion traps are used on monochrome TV tubes; neither oscilloscope nor colour TV tubes are affected greatly by ion problems.

ionization the formation of IONs from NEUTRAL (sense 4) atoms. High energy particles or radiation are needed to form ions in a gas at normal temperature. In the absence of such particles or radiation, a gas can be ionized by strong electric fields (particularly when the gas is at low pressure) or by very high temperatures of the order of several thousand Kelvin. A completely ionized gas is called a PLASMA.

ionization chamber a space in which the production of IONs can be detected. An ionization chamber contains gas, which may be air (a mixture of the gases nitrogen and oxygen), and two ELECTRODES with a POTENTIAL DIFFERENCE between them. If ions are produced in the gas, the movement of the ions between the electrodes produces a brief current that can be detected. This is the basis of most methods of measuring radiation from outer space or from radioactive materials. See also GEIGER-MÜLLER TUBE.

ionization current the current that flows in an IONIZATION CHAMBER as the result of ionization of the gas.

ionization gauge a method of measuring low gas pressures. A stream of electrons is used to ionize the gas within the gauge, and the IONs that are produced are attracted to a positive electrode. The ion current is related to the pressure over a wide range of low pressures.

ionization smoke detector a form of smoke detector that uses a radioactive source to ionize (see IONIZATION) air and measures the resulting current. In the presence of smoke, the ionizing particles

cling to the smoke and the current is greatly reduced, triggering an alarm. See also OPTICAL SMOKE DETECTOR.

ionized (of a material) able to conduct electricity because of charged particles created by IONIZATION.

ionizing particle an atomic particle which is charged and rapidly moving so that collision with any atom or nucleus will result in IONIZATION.

ionizing power the ability of a charged particle to cause IONIZATION, depending on its charge and mass.

ionizing radiation the charged particles or waves from outer space or from radioactive materials that will cause IONIZATION of any gas through which they travel.

ionosonde the instrument used for IONOSPHERIC SOUNDING.

ionosphere the outer layers of the atmosphere. These consist of air at low pressure that is ionized by the bombardment of particles from the sun. The IONIZATION is most intense when the sun shines directly on the layer, and the lower regions revert to a normal less-ionized state when the sun is shielded from them by the Earth. Several distinct layers have been identified. These shift in size and position according to the time of day, the season, and the state of the sun. The ionosphere layers will reflect radio waves whose wavelength is more than 20m or less than 6mm. The layers were known at one time as the Appleton or Heaviside-Kennelly layers. See also C-LAYER; D-LAYER; E-LAYER; F-LAYER.

ionospheric absorption ATTENUATION of radio waves in a layer of the IONOSPHERE due to the interaction with molecules of oxygen and nitrogen.

ionospheric cross modulation or **Luxembourg effect** the effect of the NONLINEARITY of the IONOSPHERE causing a weak CARRIER (sense 1) being modulated (see MODULATION) by the signal on a stronger carrier, first observed on broadcasts from Radio Luxembourg.

ionospheric disturbance changes in ionospheric layers caused by sun flares that send out a stream of IONIZING PARTICLES.

ionospheric focusing the increasing of signal strength at a RECEIVER because of the effect of the curvature of layers of the IONOSPHERE. The curved layers act as a concave mirror for radio signals.

ionospheric propagation the long-distance radio propagation due to radio waves being reflected from layers in the IONOSPHERE.

ionospheric sounding the use of RADAR type signals sent vertically to find the heights of various layers, changing the CARRIER (sense 1) frequency according to the reflective layer being investigated.

ionospheric storm electrical discharges in the upper atmospheric, one important source of radio interference.

IOT see INDUCTIVE OUTPUT TUBE.

IPA see ISOPROPYL ALCOHOL (isopropanol).

IPS see INCHES PER SECOND.

IQ modulator a digital signal system that uses 2-phase modulation, with signals at 90-phase difference. See also GAUSSIAN FILTERED MINIMUM SHIFT KEYING.

IR see INFRA-RED.

IR control extension a method of using an INFRA-RED REMOTE CONTROL when the device being controlled is out of sight. The extension consists of a small unit with an infra-red receiver, linked by cable to the device being controlled.

IrDA INFRA-RED data association.

IRE unit the unit of measurement for a video signal defined (by the Institute of Radio Engineers at the time) as 1% of the video range from BLANKING level to peak white. This was taken as 7.14 mV when the video range was standardized at 1V, with 0.714V between blanking level and peak white.

iris the light-controlling variable opening that is part of the lens structure of a CAMCORDER, automatically controlled to maintain as constant a picture brightness as possible.

iron loss the loss of energy because of MAGNETIC HYSTERESIS in a magnetic core in an inductor. See also CORE; EDDY CURRENT.

IRQ see INTERRUPT REQUEST.

irradiance a measure of illumination of a photocell as the radiated power per cm^2 of sensitive area striking the cell.

irradiation the act or process of exposure of a material to IONIZING RADIATION or NEUTRAL (sense 4) nuclear particles.

ISA (industry standard architecture) the use of design and construction methods that are based on the IBM PC-AT and were followed by virtually all personal computer manufacturers until superseded by later and faster, but compatible, systems. See also IBM COMPATIBLE, EISA (sense 2).

ISB see INDEPENDENT SIDEBAND.

ISDN integrated services digital network: a digital telephony service that, compared to older analogue systems, features greater reliability, faster access, computer access and the possibility of new services such as video delivery and high-speed facsimile.

ISI see INTER-SYMBOL INTERFERENCE.

ISM industrial, scientific and medical (equipment).

ISO see INTERNATIONAL STANDARDS ORGANIZATION.

isochronous transmission a DIGITAL transmission in which signals are transmitted as a continuous stream and are all of the same duration.

isolate to disconnect from a supply, or to make only an indirect connection (such as through an ISOLATING TRANSFORMER).

isolating diode a DIODE that is used to allow DC or PULSES to pass in one direction only. One common application is in battery chargers to prevent damage caused by incorrect connection of a cell.

isolating transformer a double wound TRANSFORMER that is used to supply power to a system. Because of the insulation between the windings, there is no direct connection between the system and the mains supply. Isolating transformers are extensively used in servicing workshops to ensure that no equipment can be dangerous because of a direct connection to the mains.

isolation amplifier a type of INSTRUMENTATION amplifier used in medical applications where a very high degree of isolation is required to prevent dangerous voltages being developed due to large radio-frequency fields.

isolation, winding the RESISTANCE between PRIMARY and SECONDARY windings of a TRANSFORMER, particularly important for mains transformers.

isolator a MICROWAVE device made from FERRITE that allows a wave to travel along the waveguide in one direction, but absorbs any reverse wave.

isopropyl alcohol or **isopropanol** a flammable but non-toxic cleaning agent for electronics components, used also for glass cleaning (including lenses).

isotropic (of a material) having measured quantities unaffected by direction. Many quantities, particularly magnetic quantities, are affected by the direction of metal CRYSTALS, and thus are ANISOTROPIC, having different values when measured along different crystal axes.

isotropic radiator or **isotropic source** a theoretical perfect AERIAL with a perfectly spherical RADIATION PATTERN.

isotropic source see ISOTROPIC RADIATOR.

I²C bus a standard form of two-wire BUS arranged as a short range ring NETWORK (sense 2) for small-scale systems control. Later developments allow data rates up to 3.4Mb/s.

I²L see INTEGRATED INJECTION LOGIC.

I²R loss see JOULE LOSS.

IT information technology.

iterated coding a system for correction of an error in a single bit in which data WORDS are loaded into a MATRIX and row/column PARITY bits calculated and added in to the matrix for transmission.

iterative impedance the value of impedance measured in a NETWORK (sense 1), where the impedance can be connected at one end of a network, thus making the network impedance at the other end identical. If a network has the same value of iterative impedance at both ends, then that value is equal to the CHARACTERISTIC IMPEDANCE. See also IMAGE IMPEDANCE.

iterative measurement a measuring method in which a system's input is steadily changed until some prearranged output is achieved. See also BOUNDARY SCAN TESTING; CURRENT NULLING TECHNIQUE; DIRECTED MEASUREMENT TECHNIQUE; INSERTION TEST SIGNAL.

ITI data the portion of data recorded on a digital video tape recorder that keeps reference data on track height and position.

ITS see INSERTION TEST SIGNAL.

IVR interactive voice response: a telephone system that uses a set of recorded messages to present options to a user, so that pressing keys will select one option. The system also makes it possible to store and retrieve messages like a TELEPHONE ANSWERING system.

I-type semiconductor see INTRINSIC SEMICONDUCTOR.

jabber a continuous stream of meaningless DATA from a faulty TERMINAL (sense 2).

jack plug a type of plug originally used for telephone connectors. Jack plugs of several sizes are used in audio circuits, mostly stereo versions. See also JILL.

jamming the deliberate interference with TRANSMISSIONS using signals on the same or a very close frequency.

JAN Japanese Article Numbering.

JANET see JOINT ACADEMIC NETWORK.

JEDEC see JOINT ELECTRON DEVICE ENGINEERING COUNCIL.

Jerusalem cross a form of pattern used on a FREQUENCY SELECTIVE SURFACE.

JETEC see JOINT ELECTRON TUBE ENGINEERING COUNCIL.

JFET see FIELD-EFFECT TRANSISTOR.

J-hook a crook-shaped portion of WAVEGUIDE used to couple signals from a DISH.

jill or **jill socket** a term sometimes used to mean a socket for a JACK PLUG.

jitter an instability of DC or SIGNAL level resulting in small variations in amplitude or phase, particularly of a PULSE signal. Phase jitter on a pulse appears on an oscilloscope display as an irregular oscillation in the horizontal direction, and will cause timing faults in equipment using the pulse as a CLOCK. Jitter can also cause problems in SAMPLING circuits.

jittering HT voltage a problem encountered in SWITCH MODE POWER SUPPLY units in which the output voltage varies slightly in amplitude.

J-K flip-flop a clocked FLIP-FLOP, with two data inputs, labelled J and K The operation is summarized in the state table in Fig. 61. If J and K are complements (see NOT), Q takes the value of J at the next clock pulse. If J and K are both low (0) the output does not change. If J and K are both high (1) the output Q will toggle, changing state after each clock pulse. The $\overline{Q}$ (NOT Q) output is always the complement of Q.

JKFF see J-K FLIP-FLOP.

J-leg a form of connection to a SURFACE MOUNT COMPONENT in which the soldered connection to the PRINTED CIRCUIT BOARD is inaccessibly mounted underneath the component.

Johnson counter or **twisted-ring counter** a counting circuit using FLIP-FLOPS in a serial chain with FEEDBACK from the last unit to the first, producing a maximum count figure equal to twice the number of flip-flops. The feedback is twisted in the sense that the Q output of the last flip-flop is connected to the K input of the first, and the $\overline{Q}$ output of the last flip-flop is connected to the J input of the first.

Johnson noise see THERMAL NOISE.

Joint Academic Network (JANET) a computer NETWORK (sense 2) linking academic and research institutes.

Joint Electron Device Engineering Council (JEDEC) the standardizing body in the UK that allocates transistor and other ACTIVE COMPONENT reference numbers.

Joint Electron Tube Engineering Council (JETEC) the standardizing body in the UK that controls development of valves and electron beam devices.

Joint Photographic Expert Group (JPEG) a study group that sets standards for DIGITAL IMAGE processing methods.

Josephson effect the current flow in an insulating gap, the JOSEPHSON JUNCTION, between superconductors (see SUPERCONDUCTIVITY) at very low temperatures.

Josephson junction a fast switching device that operates only at temperatures of 4.2K or lower, using layers of Niobium separated by a thin insulator. The junction works with very low values of voltage and current and is capable of switching current in a time measured in picoseconds when a magnetic field is applied.

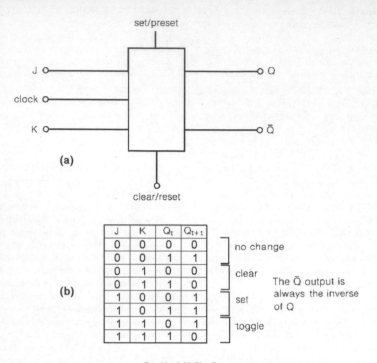

(a)

(b)

J	K	Q_t	Q_{t+1}
0	0	0	0
0	0	1	1
0	1	0	0
0	1	1	0
1	0	0	1
1	0	1	1
1	1	0	1
1	1	1	0

no change

clear

set

toggle

The $\bar{Q}$ output is always the inverse of Q

Fig. 61. **J-K flip-flop**

Josephson junction memory a computer memory using JOSEPHSON JUNCTION devices, in which the voltage across a junction is read to determine the state of a magnetic field across the junction.

joule the unit of energy, equal to the watt-second. The kilowatt-hour unit is equivalent to 3.6 megajoules (MJ).

joule effect the heating effect of a current through a RESISTOR.

joule loss or I^2R **loss** the loss of electrical energy as heat when current flows through a RESISTOR or any material with resistance.

Joule's law the law relating POWER dissipated in a RESISTOR to current, voltage, and resistance. The law can be expressed in three forms: $P=V\times I$, $P = I^2\times R$, and $P = V^2/R$ where P = power in watts, V = voltage in volts and I = current in amperes.

joystick a pivoted vertical arm that can be moved in two dimensions, using two POTENTIOMETERS (sense 1) to convert the movements into electrical signals, and used for controlling actions such as ROBOTICS, aircraft control or computer games.

JPEG see JOINT PHOTOGRAPHIC EXPERT GROUP.

jumper a connection, often temporary, between two points. A jumper connection is made by wires or plugs, and is not part of a printed circuit.

jumperless motherboard a computer MOTHERBOARD for which all important settings are made by software rather then by JUMPERS.

junction 1. a contact between two materials. 2. the connection between differently doped pieces of semiconductor. 3. the contact between two metals in a thermocouple. **4.** a point where metallic conductors or waveguides are joined.

junction box   a box that contains circuit JUNCTIONS (sense 4).

junction capacitance   the capacitance across a DEPLETION LAYER at a semiconductor P-N junction, which varies with the amount of bias on the junction. See VARICAP DIODE.

junction coupling   a method of tapping a COAXIAL line into a cavity so as to pick up or inject MICROWAVE signals.

junction diode   a DIODE formed by a P-N JUNCTION (sense 2) in a SEMICONDUCTOR crystal. See also POINT CONTACT.

junction FET   a form of FET in which the current flow between SOURCE and DRAIN is controlled by the voltage at a junction (GATE (sense 1) terminal), usually reverse-biased, see DEPLETION MODE. Junction FETs are not now so common as MOSFETs.

junction potential   the ELECTRICAL POTENTIAL between two materials that are in contact.

junction, thermocouple   see JUNCTION (sense 3).

junction transistor   a BIPOLAR TRANSISTOR that makes use of two close-spaced JUNCTIONS (sense 2).

justification   see BIT STUFFING.

Kalman filter a predictive design of CIRCUIT that uses summation of signals, delay, and FEEDBACK to process sampled data and allow for the effects of noise and uncertainty. The filter is used mainly in air-traffic control and navigational radar applications.

Kansas city modulation an early form of FREQUENCY SHIFT KEYING used by early microcomputers for storing DIGITAL DATA on AUDIO TAPE, using eight cycles of 2400 Hz to represent logic 1 and eight cycles of 1200 Hz to represent logic 0.

Karnaugh map a tabular method of designing a given LOGICAL FUNCTION that allows the most simple implementation to be quickly picked out. The implementation of many logic functions using NOT, AND and OR gates is not unique; for example there are at least two ways to connect up these gates to provide the XOR action. For logical functions requiring more than four inputs Karnaugh mapping cannot be carried out manually and requires computer-aided techniques.

K-band the MICROWAVE band covering approximately wavelengths of 8 to 27mm.

kbps or **kb/s** see KILO BITS PER SECOND.

kbyte or **KB** see KILOBYTE.

keep-alive electrode a small discharge ELECTRODE in a gas-filled device that keeps enough IONS present to allow the main discharge to start quickly. See also TRANSMIT-RECEIVE SWITCH.

keeper a piece of FERROMAGNETIC material placed across the poles of a permanent magnet. The purpose of the keeper is to complete the MAGNETIC CIRCUIT and so avoid the progressive demagnetization that occurs if the magnetic circuit is left open.

Kell factor an empirical factor of about 0:7, used to find effective RESOLUTION for a scanned display. If a SCAN uses 500 active lines per picture height, the Kell factor reduces the practical resolution to about 350 lines per picture height.

kelvin the unit of temperature based on the ABSOLUTE SCALE. Symbol: K. The size of the kelvin is identical to the size of the Celsius degree, but the zero of the Kelvin scale is ABSOLUTE ZERO. Named after William Thomson, Lord Kelvin (1824–1907), Scottish physicist.

Kelvin connection a connection method used for precise measurements in which two wires are used to carry current and two others to sense voltage. This ensures that the measurement does not include any losses due to long connecting cables.

Kelvin scale see ABSOLUTE SCALE.

Kelvin temperature a temperature measured on the absolute scale, on which 0°C is 273.16K.

Kendall effect or **sideband folding** a form of modulation distortion in which the lower SIDEBAND overlaps the highest modulating frequencies. See also OVERLAPPING SIDEBANDS.

Kennelly-Heaviside layer see E-LAYER.

Kerr cell a method of controlling light by means of ELECTRIC FIELDS. Liquid in a Kerr cell will rotate the plane of polarization in POLARIZED (sense 1) light according to the size of the electric field applied across the liquid.

Kerr effect the change from plane polarization to elliptical polarization of light on reflection from a polished magnetized surface, used in MAGNETO-OPTICAL storage discs.

key 1. a set of digits used to encode digital data. 2. a miniature switch as used on a keyboard or keypad.

keyboard a set of KEYS (sense 2) bearing alphanumeric characters and symbols and usually laid out in the conventional typewriter (QWERTY) pattern, used to communicate to a computer or to send text signals digitally.

keyboard buffer a portion of memory used to hold the codes generated from pressing keys. This allows the computer to suspend reading the keyboard for short periods (such as when access to a DISK DRIVE is needed) without losing typed information.

keyboard connector the connector used for the serial cable that links a keyboard to a computer, using either a DIN PLUG, a PS/2 CONNECTOR, a SERIAL plug or a USB plug.

keyboard port a SERIAL PORT on a computer used only for keyboard connection.

keyboard processor a MICROPROCESSOR that is part of the KEYBOARD circuits of a computer, used to detect key closure and generate the appropriate codes. This relieves the main processor of the work and therefore speeds computing actions.

key distribution system or **key system** any secure method of conveying a CODE KEY to a user.

keying 1. the substitution of one area of a picture by an area clipped from another picture. See also CHROMA KEYING; DIGITAL KEYING; LINEAR KEYING. 2. the action of using a keyboard to enter data. 3. any modulation system for digital signals (see FREQUENCY SHIFT KEYING; PHASE SHIFT KEYING).

keyless delay alarm a car security system that automatically activates at a time after the ignition is switched off, and detects the voltage drop due to the interior light when a door is opened.

key-matrix a set of connections arranged into rows and columns with key switches at each crossing of a row and column, allowing the use of a number of keys equal to row number × column number.

keypad an auxiliary set of keys, usually numeric and used for entry of numbers for control purposes, such as is used on an INFRA-RED REMOTE CONTROL.

key scanning a method for detecting a key press on a KEY MATRIX, using pulses (the scanning pulses) in sequence to each column line and detecting output pulses from a row line in which a key is pressed. For any one column pulse, only one key will deliver an output pulse. See Fig. 62.

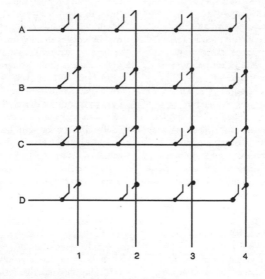

Fig. 62. **key scanning**

keystone distortion a form of picture shape DISTORTION in which the upper and lower borders are not of equal length. In optical projection, keystone distortion is caused by projecting a picture to a screen that is not on the same axis. In early TV cameras, the effect was caused by the geometry of early camera tubes that used an off-centre beam. It can also be caused if the amplitude of the horizontal timebase is affected by the amplitude of the vertical timebase.

keystream the PRIVATE KEY in a PUBLIC KEY ENCRYPTION system.

keyway a strip of metal or plastic in a plug that ensures the plug can be connected only one way into a socket.

K factor see TANGENTIAL ERROR.

K56flex™ a standard system for fast MODEMS (56,000 BITS PER SECOND) developed by Rockwell. This and the rival X2™ system were merged into a single V90 standard, since developed to V92.

kHz see KILOHERTZ.

kilo- prefix denoting 10^3 (1000); symbol: k.

kilobaud a transmission speed for data of one thousand BAUD.

kilo bits per second a unit of speed of TRANSMISSION of data in terms of thousands of BITS PER SECOND.

kilobyte or **kB** or **KB** a unit of data size equal to 1000 bytes.

kilohertz unit of frequency equal to 1000 cycles or pulses per second.

Kilostream™ a point-to-point communications line for speech or data provided by BT. Kilostream offers transmission speeds of 2.4 kilobits per second to 64 kilobits per second, and no MODEM is needed to make use of the line. See also MEGASTREAM.

kilovolt the unit of 1000 volts, used in high-voltage engineering.

kilovolt-ampere a unit of electrical power equal to 1000 watts.

kilowatt-hour an energy unit used for domestic electricity meters and equal to 3.6 megajoules (MJ).

kinetic energy the energy of a moving object, contrast POTENTIAL ENERGY.

Kirchoff's laws the two laws describing the flow of CURRENTs and summation of VOLTAGEs in steady state circuits. The first law states that the algebraic sum of currents at a point in a circuit must be zero. This is true only if no changing magnetic fields are present. The second law states that in any closed circuit, the algebraic sum of the ELECTROMOTIVE FORCEs and of POTENTIAL DIFFERENCEs must also be zero. See also SUPERPOSITION THEOREM.

kluge an unsatisfactory temporary solution to a problem.

klystron an electron beam tube, formerly widely used in MICROWAVE transmitters and receivers. For low-power applications, such as local oscillators in microwave receivers, reflex klystrons (see below) have been replaced by GUNN DEVICES, but the tubes are still used for higher power applications. The basis of the klystron is an electron beam that passes through a cavity in which the electrons can be affected by resonant microwaves. Following this cavity, the BUNCHER, the electrons move through the DRIFT SPACE, in which no accelerating fields are applied. The movements of the electrons that were started by the fields in the buncher make the electrons gather into groups or bunches as they pass through the drift space. When the bunched electrons pass into another cavity, the CATCHER, they can give up their energy to the cavity. This energy will be considerably greater than the energy that was used in the buncher.

For very high power gains, klystrons with several cavities can be used, with each cavity bunching the electrons tighter. The tendency for debunching, caused by electrostatic repulsion of electrons, can be counteracted by magnetic focusing. The REFLEX KLYSTRON is an oscillator that operated by reflecting the bunched electrons back to the buncher.

knee voltage a voltage level at which a graph of voltage plotted against another variable suddenly changes direction.

knife edge refraction or **mountain edge scattering** the REFRACTION and scattering of a wave, particularly in the band 100 MHz to 300 MHz, as it passes over an edge, causing signals to be usable despite the shadowing of a mountain.

knife switch a form of switch used now only for high voltage and high current supplies. The switch contacts are metal blades, that make a wiping contact with springy holders as the switch is closed.

Ku band the range of MICROWAVE frequencies for SATELLITE use of 11.7GHz to 12.7GHz.

KVA see KILOVOLT AMPERE.

labyrinth a type of LOUDSPEAKER enclosure. The sound wave from the rear of the loudspeaker cone is dispersed in a long heavily DAMPED path.

lacing see THREADING.

LADAR or **LOPPLER** a form of DOPPLER RADAR that uses a LASER beam in place of a radio beam.

ladder filter a network that is made by connecting alternate T SECTIONS and PI SECTIONS of FILTERS. See Fig. 63.

ladder oscillator see PHASE SHIFT OSCILLATOR.

lag 1. a signal or phase delay. 2. an image signal that is retained in a CAMERA TUBE for several frames after the image has been removed from the face of the tube.

lagging current or **leading voltage** a CURRENT that lags in PHASE behind voltage.

lagging load a LOAD, such as an inductive load, in which the current PHASE lags behind the voltage phase. See also LEADING LOAD.

laminated core a TRANSFORMER core that is made by clamping together a set of thin metal laminations. The high resistance between laminations deters the flow of EDDY CURRENTS. See C-CORE; E-CORE; I-CORE.

laminations thin strips of a soft magnetic material that can be used as the core of a TRANSFORMER.

LAN see LOCAL AREA NETWORK.

LANC see LOCAL AREA NETWORK CONTROL.

Lange coupler a form of TRANSFORMER coupling for WAVEGUIDES, transferring power with a 90° PHASE shift.

LAN server or **file server** a computer, usually possessing a fast processor, large memory and large-capacity HARD DRIVE, used in a NETWORK (sense 2) to pass files to other machines on the network.

LAP-B or **LAP-D** or **LAP-M** see LINK ACCESS PROTOCOL.

Laplace transform a method of transforming a set of equations using a variable (usually time) into a form using a different variable that makes solution simpler.

Laplacean distribution see GAUSSIAN DISTRIBUTION.

lapped transform a form of DIGITAL FILTER system that allows blocks of data to overlap before applying a digital transform.

laptop a small battery operated computer with most of the facilities of a larger machine.

large area flicker the appearance of flicker in the left and right edges of a TV picture, related to the peripheral vision of the eye.

large optical cavity laser a form of SEMICONDUCTOR LASER that obtains power outputs of 25 mW or more by using a large OPTICAL CAVITY.

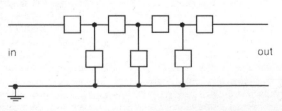

Fig. 63. **ladder filter**

large scale integration the SCALE OF
INTEGRATION in which the number of
ACTIVE COMPONENTS on one chip is of
the order of ten thousand.

laser *acronym for* Light Amplification
by Stimulated Emission of Radiation:
a generator of monochromatic coherent
light (see COHERENT OSCILLATOR). Normal
sources emit PHOTONs of light in 'packets',
with the phase changing in each group.
This lack of phase stability is called *non-coherence*. It is impossible, for example,
to set up any light interference experiment
in which light of one group of waves can
interfere with light in another group.
This is because the phases of the waves
from a conventional source are continually
changing, cancelling out any interference
effects.

The laser generates light by allowing
one group of waves to stimulate the
emission of the next in a form of RESONANT
CAVITY. This ensures that the waves are
synchronized, and in phase. Laser light is
termed *coherent light*. The synchronization
can extend over a very large number of
groups, so much so that waves that are
separated by as much as a metre of space
can still be in phase. Gas lasers use gas
discharges as the source of light, and
diode lasers use the LIGHT EMITTING DIODE
principle. The main applications for lasers
in electronics are in optical transmission,
using glass fibres, and in CD and DVD
recorders and players. See also MASER.

laser diode a form of LED that uses
reflecting surfaces to force LASER action
to occur at some threshold value of
applied current. This is the form of laser
that is used in consumer laser equipment
such as CD or DVD players and recorders.

laser gyroscope a very stable form of
gyroscope using rotating LASER beams.

laser printer a form of printer that
depends on the use of LASER light.
The laser printer uses the laser to scan
over a photosensitive DRUM (sense 2),
releasing charge, and then picking up
a powdered ink (*toner*) on the charged
portions. The ink powder is then
transferred to paper by discharging

the drum, and the powder is heated to
fuse it to the paper. This principle is
known as *xerography*, and was discovered
by the Xerox Corp.

laser scanner a method of reading a BAR
CODE. The scanner moves a LASER beam
to and fro over the bar codes, reading the
reflected light pulses and converting into
digital form. Since the codes are read
many times and only the most frequently
obtained answer is used, this gives more
reliable readings than hand scanners.

Laservision™ the original OPTICAL
RECORDING disc system launched by
Philips in 1972, forerunner of the present-day DVD.

lash-up see HOOK-UP.

last in first out (LIFO) or **pushdown list**
or **stack** a data memory list in which
the last item that was added is at the top
of the list and is the first to be retrieved.

last mile see FINAL LOOP.

latch the storage action of a FLIP-FLOP
circuit. The output of a flip-flop is said
to be latched if it remains constant
despite any changes in the input.

latching the use of FLIP-FLOPS or a REGISTER
for short-term storage of data.

latching relay a RELAY that can be
switched on by a pulse of current through
the coil and which will remain in that
state until it is unlatched by a pulse of
current in the opposite direction.

latch-up or **lock-up** or **hang-up** (of a
software controlled system) not
responding to any input.

late-arriving sounds see HAAS EFFECT.

latency the response time for a device,
particularly in a computer.

lateral chromatic aberration a lens
defect that causes misregistration of red,
blue and green light beams because the
magnification of the lens is different for
different colours. See also LONGITUDINAL
CHROMATIC ABERRATION.

lateral device a MOSFET that is constructed
on the plane surface of a semiconductor,
as distinct from vertical types.

lateral recording the system of lateral
movement of a stylus used first by
Emile Berliner for recording, superseding

the earlier vertical (hill and groove) Edison system.

lathe the turntable and stylus arrangement used to cut a master disc for the old vinyl disc RECORDING process.

lattice filter a form of FILTER in which the impedances are arranged in a BRIDGE network.

law, potentiometer see POTENTIOMETER LAW.

layer, MPEG the numbers used to denote increasing complexity of MPEG coding, the higher number for the more complex system.

layering, MIDI the use of MIDI to connect two keyboards to produce effects that would normally be produced only by several instruments.

layout diagram or **component layout diagram** a diagram showing component positions and PRINTED CIRCUIT BOARD connections, as distinct from a symbolic CIRCUIT DIAGRAM.

lazy-H aerial (or antenna) a high-impedance aerial structure consisting of two full-wave DIPOLES separated by a half wavelength, and with the feed to one dipole the inverse of the feed to the other.

L band the MICROWAVE band covering about 19 to 77cm wavelength; about 15GHz to 3.9GHz.

LCD see LIQUID CRYSTAL DISPLAY.

LCD monitor a computer MONITOR using a THIN-FILM TRANSISTOR controlled display, providing a slim, low-power consumption, flicker-free display which can be viewed over a wide viewing angle.

LCD projector a system of (usually) three separate LCD panels (one red, one green, one blue) each with a powerful backlight, with an optical system that combines the separate coloured beams onto a single projected beam. This can be used to project a TV picture onto a flat screen with typical resolution of 350 lines or more.

L-C network a RESONANT CIRCUIT that contains CAPACITANCE and INDUCTANCE. The tuned frequency is inversely proportional to the square root of the product of capacitance and inductance values.

LCR circuits circuits that contain INDUCTORS, CAPACITORS and RESISTORS.

LDR see LIGHT DEPENDENT RESISTOR.

lead 1. an electrical wire. 2. the advance in phase of one wave as compared to another. 3. the soft metallic element used in secondary cells and as a component of solder.

lead-acid cell a form of secondary RECHARGEABLE CELL, or ACCUMULATOR, (sense 2) that uses LEAD (sense 3) plates in sulphuric acid. The lead plates are treated so that one (spongy lead) acts as a CATHODE (sense 3) and the other (packed with lead(IV) oxide) as an ANODE (sense 3).

lead content the percentage of metallic lead in SOLDER, now being reduced on health grounds.

leader the first piece of a RECORDING TAPE that carries no coating. This part is used only for THREADING and cannot be recorded on.

lead-free alloys soldering alloys that are completely free from lead.

lead-in 1. a portion of a CD that contains information on music tracks, recorded preceding the music tracks. 2. a connector through which an AERIAL lead enters a building or a receiver.

leading current or **lagging voltage** a current whose PHASE is earlier than the phase of VOLTAGE.

leading edge a rapid voltage change that is the start of a PULSE.

leading load a LOAD in which the PHASE of CURRENT is earlier than the phase of VOLTAGE, such as a capacitive load. See also LAGGING LOAD.

leadless chip carrier a square package for a CHIP (sense 1) using flat contacts on each side. This is inserted into a socket and clamped into place.

lead-out a portion at the end of a CD that signals the end of all RECORDING. A disc with no lead-out may not be playable on music CD players, but computer CD drives can ignore this portion.

lead oxide vidicon a form of VIDICON developed in the 1950s, using lead oxide in place of the antimony trisulphide previously used as a photoconductor.

lead-through capacitor or **feed-through capacitor**   a capacitor with one connection made to a metal plate and the other passing through both capacitor and plate, used mainly for DECOUPLING a cable link that passes into or out of a metal shielded space.

leakage   any loss either of substance, such as electrolyte from a cell, or of FLUX (sense 1) from a circuit.

leakage current   the unwanted CURRENT caused by BREAKDOWN of insulation.

leakage current, electrolytic   the DC current flowing through an ELECTROLYTIC CAPACITOR as a result of imperfect insulation.

leakage flux   the MAGNETIC FLUX that is generated by the primary winding of a transformer, but not coupled to or used by the secondary. Leakage flux is one source of loss in a transformer. See also EDDY CURRENT; HYSTERESIS.

leakage inductance   a figure of inductance corresponding to, and calculated from, the amount of LEAKAGE FLUX in a transformer.

leakage reactance   the amount of REACTANCE in a TRANSFORMER that would correspond to the quantity of LEAKAGE FLUX.

leakage resistance   an unwanted resistance in a circuit caused by imperfect insulation.

leakproof cell   a CELL with an outer casing of steel so that the gradual dissolving of

the CATHODE (sense 3) metal does not cause leakage of corrosive ELECTROLYTE.

leaky feeder aerial (or **antenna)** or **leaky wave aerial (**or **antenna)**   a perforated WAVEGUIDE or poorly shielded coaxial cable structure that will dissipate energy throughout its length, so acting as a radiating aerial, (antenna).

learn mode   a method of using AUTOMATED TEST EQUIPMENT in which good systems are analyzed so that the test equipment can establish the normal values of measurable quantities.

least-significant   (of an item) carrying least importance in a group.

least-significant bit (lsb)   the lowest order bit in a BINARY NUMBER, signifying 0 or 1 in the total.

least-significant byte (LSB)   the BYTE in a multi-byte WORD that is in the LEAST-SIGNIFICANT position.

least-significant digit   the units digit in a denary number, such as the '1' in the number 2561.

Lecher lines   an obsolescent method of measuring WAVELENGTH. A wave is coupled to a pair of parallel lines, and ANTINODES are found by using a small DIPOLE (sense 2) placed across the lines and connected to a lamp or a diode/meter arrangement. The distance between consecutive antinodes is equal to half a wavelength. A form of Lecher line can also be used for matching lines of different impedances. See Fig. 64.

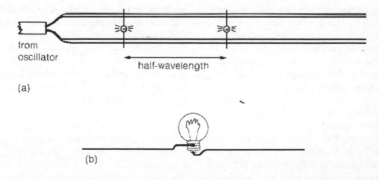

from
oscillator

half-wavelength

(a)

(b)

Fig. 64. **Lecher lines**

Leclanché cell the original type of zinc-carbon CELL using an ELECTROLYTE of ammonium chloride. This was the basis of the zinc-carbon dry cell.

LED see LIGHT-EMITTING DIODE.

LED indicator a small INDICATOR LAMP using an LED rather than a FILAMENT light.

LED printer a low-cost form of LASER PRINTER that uses a row of tiny LED light sources in place of a LASER.

left-hand rule see FLEMING'S RULES.

Lempel-Ziv algorithm coding a form of NON-LOSSY COMPRESSION for DIGITAL DATA by using short codes for the most frequently used pieces of data.

lengthened dipole a form of DIPOLE AERIAL in which the rods have been moved apart to make the overall length greater than normal.

lens aerial (or antenna) an aerial that treats radio waves as if they were light waves, using lenses constructed from dielectric materials, metal plates or FRESNEL LENS patterns. The aim is to focus the radio wave into a beam. See also DIELECTRIC LENS AERIAL; FRESNEL ZONE PLATE AERIAL; METAL PLATE LENS AERIAL.

lens aperture see APERTURE.

lens coating or **lens blooming** a thin layer of magnesium fluoride applied to a glass lens to reduce reflections and improve the light transmission through the lens.

Lenz's law a law of ELECTROMAGNETIC INDUCTION. The induced voltage is in such a polarity as to oppose the change of MAGNETIC FLUX that causes it. For example, if the applied POTENTIAL DIFFERENCE across an inductor is increased, the increase of current through the inductor causes an increase of flux, and the voltage induced by this change of flux will be in a direction opposite to the applied potential difference, so opposing the change. The practical effect is to reduce the rate at which the change can be made. When current through an inductor is abruptly switched off, the induced voltage can be large enough to cause a spark across the switch contacts.

LEO see LOW EARTH ORBIT.

letterbox image the description applied to the 16:9 ASPECT RATIO standardized for DIGITAL TELEVISION displays in Europe.

level detector an OPERATIONAL AMPLIFIER circuit comparator circuit whose output indicates which of two inputs is the higher.

level of heat see TEMPERATURE.

level triggered (of a flip-flop) whose state is changed when the voltage input level changes beyond a predetermined level. See also EDGE TRIGGERED.

level, teletext a number used to differentiate various improvements in graphical TELETEXT displays, from the basic monochrome level 1 symbols used on most receivers to a proposed level 5 that can display photographic quality colour images.

lever solenoid a SOLENOID transducer arranged with a lever action like that of a RELAY.

lever switch the conventional form of switch using a toggle and spring construction.

Leyden jar the earliest form of (18th century) capacitor, fabricated from a glass jar and layers of metal foil. The name persisted until 1939 in the Navy, where the unit of capacitance was termed a *jar*.

LF see LOW FREQUENCY.

LF signal generator a SIGNAL GENERATOR for frequencies below 20 kHz, used for AUDIO equipment testing.

LIDAR see LIGHT DETECTION AND RANGING.

lie detector or **polygraph** a circuit that detects small changes in skin resistance that can indicate a change in human emotional state when a false statement is made.

life test a timed use of COMPONENTs in a circuit to determine the time before failure. For very reliable components such as SEMICONDUCTORS, an ACCELERATED LIFE TEST may have to be used.

lifetime the average time for which a current CARRIER (sense 2) exists in a SEMICONDUCTOR. This is the average time between electron-hole separation and RECOMBINATION.

LIFO   see LAST IN FIRST OUT.

light   the ELECTROMAGNETIC RADIATION in the range of approximately 10 THz to 10^4 THz, of which the range 4×10^8 MHz to 7.9×10^8 MHz is visible light.

light-dependent resistor (LDR)   a RESISTOR fabricated from a material whose resistance reduces when struck by light. Typical materials include selenium, cadmium sulphide, cadmium selenide and lead sulphide. LDRs are rugged devices that can be used at relatively high voltage levels, and are often applied to such tasks as flame detection in boilers.

light detection and ranging (LIDAR)   a method of using LASER beams to detect wind speed and airborne pollution.

light-emitting diode (LED)   a DIODE that emits light while CURRENT passes. The diode materials are compounds such as gallium arsenide or antimony phosphide. The material around the JUNCTION (sense 2) must be transparent so that the light can escape. LEDs are used as voltage indicators in electronic equipment. They are also used in ALPHANUMERIC displays for mains-operated equipment. The amount of current that is needed rules out the use of LEDs for most battery-operated applications, though they were at one time used for calculators and watches. For these low-energy applications, LIQUID-CRYSTAL DISPLAYS are now preferred.

light filter   a semi-transparent coloured material, often glass or plastic, that will pass only a small range of frequencies (colours) when illuminated with white light.

light flux   the amount of illumination, particularly illumination measured in units of lux falling on a photosensitive cell. See also IRRADIANCE.

light guide   an application of FIBRE OPTICS in which the glass fibre allows a light at one place to be seen elsewhere. For example, in a meter a fixed light source can be placed at one end of a fibre. The other end of the fibre can then be used to illuminate the scale needle, moving with the needle.

light management system   an electronic control system that will switch off artificial lighting when the level of daylight is adequate.

light pen   a miniature PHOTOCELL mounted at the end of a pen-holder. This is used along with a computer program to 'write' on the computer monitor screen, or select items by holding the pen at the correct place on the screen.

light pipe   see FIBRE OPTICS.

light ray   the straight line path of a narrow beam of light.

light threshold frequency   the minimum frequency of light that will release ELECTRONS from a PHOTOEMITTER. See also QUANTUM THEORY.

light transducer   any device whose input or output is light, usually with a corresponding output or input that is electrical.

light valve   the electronic equivalent of a camera shutter, passing light for a brief instant controlled by an electrical pulse. The earliest types used the same principle as the IMAGE INTENSIFIER, and other versions have used KERR EFFECT or FARADAY EFFECT.

light valve projector   any large-screen image projector that uses a light bulb (as distinct from a CATHODE-RAY TUBE) as the light source. The light colour and intensity is modified by a LIGHT VALVE, and the beam is deflected horizontally and vertically so that an image is seen on the screen. See also BEAMER; DIGITAL LIGHT PROCESSOR.

lightning   a high-energy electrical discharge through the air from a charged cloud.

lightning conductor   a pointed metal rod facing upwards on the top of a building. Under conditions of high CHARGE, the air around the point ionizes (see IONIZATION) and allows a quiet controlled discharge to take place, averting a lightning strike.

limb   a part of a TRANSFORMER core on which a winding is centred.

limit mask a transparent surface placed over the screen of a CATHODE-RAY OSCILLOSCOPE used for testing to indicate the limits of AMPLITUDE or time for an acceptable waveform.

limiter a CIRCUIT that prevents the AMPLITUDE of a signal from exceeding a preset level. See also CLAMPING DIODE; CLIPPER.

limiting an amplifier fault in which the output signal AMPLITUDE does not increase when the input amplitude increases beyond a certain level. All amplifiers will limit if OVERDRIVEN, but if the level of the input signal is correctly regulated, limiting should not occur.

Lin circuit or **quasi-complementary circuit** or **totem-pole circuit** a SINGLE-ENDED push-pull circuit used extensively as an audio power output stage or an output stage for digital devices. In its simplest form, it uses two series-connected COMPLEMENTARY TRANSISTORS driven from the same signal source and driving in turn two power transistors that are of the same type. The same signal is taken to both bases, with a steady bias voltage superimposed. Each transistor then deals with one half of the output signal. Since each transistor is being used in CLASS B, the stage is very efficient, and with NEGATIVE FEEDBACK and some care about biasing, can produce good-quality audio output. See Fig. 65.

lincompex a form of COMPANDER system used to counter the effects of FADING and NOISE on long-distance radio links.

line 1. see TRANSMISSION LINE.
2. a horizontal SCAN of a TV screen.

linear of, in, along, or relating to a straight line. The term is generally applied to a relationship between quantities that produces a straight line graph.

linear amplifier an AMPLIFIER with low distortion. The graph of output plotted against input for such an amplifier is substantially a straight line. For the region of the graph that is a straight line, ᵗʰᵉ DISTORTION will be minimal.

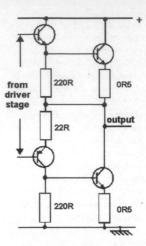

Fig. 65. **Lin circuit**

linear array any AERIAL (antenna) system in which all the elements are arranged in a straight line.

linear circuit a CIRCUIT for which the output/input graph is a straight line. For such a system, the output is related to the input by an expression of the form $S_{out} = CS_{in} + B$ where C and B are constants.

linear circuit analysis the calculation of the GAIN and PHASE characteristics for a linear circuit from knowledge of the CIRCUIT DIAGRAM and the values of components. This type of action is now most easily done using computer software.

linear code a BINARY CODE whose set of CODE WORDs is a portion of all the possible codes that can be formed with a given number of bits.

linear control system a system in which a device is regulated by a FEEDBACK mechanism aimed at keeping a measured quantity constant. As an example, if a heating system is designed so that the heat output is steadily reduced to zero as the difference between the measured temperature and the set temperature is reduced, this provides linear control. Contrast BANG-BANG CONTROL.

linear detector a DEMODULATOR for which the demodulated output is linearly proportional to the amount of MODULATION of the CARRIER (sense 1).

linear digital encoder any device whose output is a BINARY (sense 1) number corresponding to a distance moved. The most common types are OPTICAL ENCODERS using a glass slide and a set of photocells, but for more precise readings an INTERFEROMETER combined with a pulse counter is preferred.

linear editing the slow form of editing that is used for ANALOGUE videotape, in which the final version has to be assembled from start to end, using insertions and other effects in the correct sequence, re-recording the edited material on another tape. See also NON-LINEAR EDITING.

linear function an algebraic function whose graph is a straight line, typically a function of the form $y = mx + c$ where m and c are constants, the SLOPE and INTERCEPT respectively.

linear graph a graph whose shape is a straight line whose SLOPE and INTERCEPT can be determined.

linear IC an IC intended for use as a LINEAR AMPLIFIER or for use in other analogue circuits.

linear interpolation see INTERPOLATION.

linearity, instrument the ability to measure using a linear reading scale that makes interpolation much simpler.

linear keying a method of mixing one VIDEO signal with another so that transparent KEYING (sense 2) can be achieved.

linear law or **linear taper** the response of a POTENTIOMETER (sense 1) measured as a linear change of resistance per unit of shaft rotation.

linear mixing the mixing of signals in a linear device, such as an audio mixer, so that no INTERMODULATION frequencies are generated.

linear network a network of components in which the graph of voltage plotted against current is always a straight line.

linear phase system a system in which the PHASE of a signal varies linearly with FREQUENCY.

linear potentiometer a POTENTIOMETER (sense 1) whose graph of change of resistance plotted against shaft rotation is reasonably linear. See also LOGARITHMIC POTENTIOMETER.

linear predictive coding a set of ALGORITHMs that produce realistic voice sounds with a minimum of memory use.

linear scan or **linear sweep** a SCAN across the face of a CATHODE-RAY TUBE at a constant speed. This is not necessarily produced by a LINEAR TIMEBASE, because the shape of the tube face and the characteristics of the deflection system can cause nonlinearity.

linear solenoid a SOLENOID transducer whose graph of displacement plotted against current is mainly linear.

linear sweep see LINEAR SCAN.

linear timebase a timebase whose waveform is a SAWTOOTH with a straight line sweep portion.

linear variable differential transformer (LVDT) an inductive distance sensor for distance ranges of millimetres to centimetres, using three INDUCTOR windings on a moveable CORE. The two outer windings feed a DIFFERENTIAL AMPLIFIER, and the central winding is energized with AC, so that movement of the core alters the amplitude and phase of the signal into the differential amplifier, and a PHASE-SENSITIVE DETECTOR can be used to provide an output proportional to the movement of the core. See Fig. 66.

line communication the sending of SIGNALS by wire as distinct from using radiated waves.

line concentrator a telephone exchange multiplexing circuit that uses a small number of output lines to serve a greater number of subscribers.

line conditioner a form of mains voltage FILTER, based on inductors, that removes mains surges and interference.

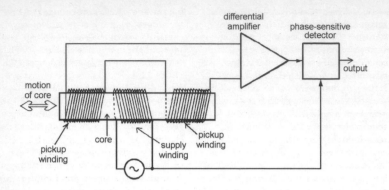

Fig. 66. **LVDT**

line crawl an appearance of TV picture line vertical movement due to an incorrect relationship between COLOUR SUB-CARRIER frequency and LINE FREQUENCY.

line driver a circuit, usually in IC form, that is used to transmit pulses down a long transmission line.

line filter a LOW-PASS FILTER in a power supply to prevent interference reaching equipment along the power supply lines.

line flyback the part of a TV line TIMEBASE waveform in which the voltage or current returns to its starting value. See also RASTER.

line frequency the frequency of line (horizontal) SCAN in TV. In the US the term is also used to mean the mains supply frequency of 60Hz.

line hold see LINE SYNCHRONIZATION.

line-matching transformer a step-up transformer used along with a PUBLIC ADDRESS amplifier to match the low output impedance of the amplifier to the higher impedance of a public address line (100V line) feeder.

line noise meaningless electrical interference on a LINE (sense 1) that causes unwanted characters to appear, or other CORRUPTION of messages.

line of flux a line in a diagram that shows the direction of magnetic FLUX ...TY. See also LINE OF FORCE.

line of force a term that is sometimes used to denote ELECTRIC FIELD direction, with LINE OF FLUX used to denote MAGNETIC FIELD direction. The two are more often used interchangeably.

line oscillator the circuit in a TV RECEIVER or MONITOR that provides the HORIZONTAL SCAN for the cathode-ray tube.

line output stage the power output circuit that applies the scanning current to the DEFLECTION COILS of a TV CATHODE-RAY TUBE.

line output transformer (LOT or LOPT) the transformer used in a TELEVISION RECEIVER using a CATHODE-RAY TUBE to couple the LINE OUTPUT STAGE to the low impedance of the line scan coils. An additional winding provides a large-amplitude pulse that is rectified to provide EHT. See also DIODE-SPLIT TRANSFORMER; OVERWIND.

line probing or **channel probing** a MODEM action carried out during HANDSHAKING that checks the quality of the connection and sets an optimum data rate to suit.

line reflection the reflection of a signal from the far end of a TRANSMISSION LINE. This will cause a STANDING WAVE pattern if a steady signal is being sent continually down the line.

line regulation the allowable percentage change in power line supply voltage.

line scan the action of sweeping an ELECTRON BEAM horizontally across the screen of a TV CATHODE-RAY TUBE.

line segmentation a system for scrambling (see SCRAMBLER) a video transmission in which each LINE (sense 2) is divided into segments and the segments interchanged, with the division points varying in a PSEUDO-RANDOM sequence.

line sequential a method of transmitting COLOUR TELEVISION signals in which each line is transmitted three times, with the information for each of the three primary colours. This type of system is not compatible with broadcast television, but has been used for low bandwidth slow scan systems.

line shuffle a method of scrambling (see SCRAMBLER) a DIGITAL VIDEO transmission in which the lines of a frame are transmitted in a different order, with the order changed in each frame following a PSEUDO-RANDOM pattern.

line source see COLUMN LOUDSPEAKER.

line sync see LINE SYNCHRONIZATION.

line synchronization or **line sync** or **line hold** the use of a SYNCHRONIZING PULSE to ensure that a scanned line on a TV display is correctly timed in relation to the video signals for that line.

line timebase the circuit that develops a WAVEFORM (voltage or current) of SAWTOOTH shape in order to effect the LINE SCAN of a CATHODE-RAY TUBE.

line translation a method of scrambling (see SCRAMBLER) a TV transmission in which the line BLANKING time is changed following a PSEUDO-RANDOM pattern over several frames.

line voltage the VOLTAGE between the wires of a TRANSMISSION LINE. In the US, line voltage is the AC supply voltage of 115 volts.

link **I.** a system of TRANSMITTERS and RECEIVERS that connects two points by means of radio signals. **2.** a mechanical connection between SWITCHes that results from GANGING the switches. **3.** a wire connection between points on a circuit board.

link (or **line) access procedure (LAP)** a protocol for INTEGRATED SERVICES DIGITAL NETWORK (sense 2) use. The older LAP-B has now been replaced by the LAP-D system that incorporates error detection. The LAP-M protocol refers to modems with error correction.

lin-log response a specialized AMPLIFIER circuit characteristic. The circuit gives a linear response for small signals, but logarithmic for larger signals. This enables a very large signal amplitude range to be used without overloading, a feature that is particularly important for RADAR receivers and also used in cassette tape NOISE-REDUCTION systems.

lip microphone a form of MICROPHONE case construction for outdoor use, designed to be used very close to the lips, often as part of a headphone/microphone assembly. The advantage is that wind noise and other external noises are greatly reduced because the sensitivity does not need to be high.

lip-sync a very close synchronization of sound and picture. This is a problem of film, in which sound is separately recorded, rather than of TV. If true lip-sync is achieved in a film, the lip movement of speakers corresponds with the sounds.

liquid crystal a liquid whose (long) molecules can be aligned like the atoms of a CRYSTAL under the influence of an ELECTRIC FIELD. The ALIGNMENT of these molecules causes transmitted light to be POLARIZED (sense 1), and can be carried out by a small electric field. Many types of liquid-crystal materials are based on cholesterol, a fatty-acid.

liquid-crystal display (LCD) a form of ALPHANUMERIC display that uses a POLARIZED (sense 1) filter fitted over a LIQUID CRYSTAL cell or set of cells, and a reflector. With no ELECTRIC FIELD applied to any cell, light passes through the filter and is reflected back from the rear of each cell. When an electric field is applied to a cell, the change in polarization of the cell makes it opaque, and with no reflected light the cell looks black from the outside. The cells are often arranged in the form of a SEVEN-SEGMENT display, but can take the form of words, diagrams or any other shape that is required. Displays for use in dark conditions dispense with reflective backing and use a BACKLIGHT. See also TFT.

Lissajou figure a pattern that is traced out by 2 objects vibrating in two directions at right angles to each other. The term is used in electronics to describe a technique that was once used for very precise FREQUENCY comparison. One frequency, a standard, is applied to one pair of deflection plates (or amplifier) of an OSCILLOSOPE. An unknown frequency is then applied to the other plates. If the signals are identical in amplitude and frequency, the resulting shape will be a straight line (frequencies in phase), a circle (90° phase difference), or an ellipse if the phases are of a different value. If the frequencies are not equal, the ellipse will rotate. For frequencies that are harmonically related (twice, three times, etc.), the display shows patterns in which a count of the peaks gives the ratio of frequencies. The slightest change of phase will cause a rotation of a pattern.

listener or **listener device** a device on a IEEE-488 BUS that receives DATA but does not place data on the bus. See also CONTROLLER; TALKER.

lithium cell a cell using metallic lithium with a carbon ANODE and a water-free electrolyte, providing the very high output EMF of around 3.0V. This type of lithium call is normally made in button form for use in cameras and on computer MOTHERBOARDS. Such cells must be disposed of carefully and never broken open. See also LITHIUM-ION CELL.

lithium chloride hygrometer a method of measuring RELATIVE HUMIDITY using the principle that the resistance of lithium chloride varies reasonably linearly with variations of relative humidity.

lithium-ion cell a rechargeable form of the LITHIUM CELL with an EMF of around 3.6V when fully charged.

lithography the PHOTORESIST, exposure and etching set of operations used to make a PRINTED CIRCUIT BOARD or an INTEGRATED CIRCUIT.

Litz wire multistranded wire, reducing EDDY CURRENT effects, used to wind coils for RF inductors.

live (of an electrical device) at high voltage or with signal present.

live chassis circuit a circuit in which the metal chassis is connected to one pole of the mains supply. This is the NEUTRAL (sense 3) pole, but there can be a voltage difference between earth and neutral, and miswiring of a plug can cause the chassis to be connected to the live lead. A live chassis circuit being serviced should be connected through an isolating transformer.

live insertion see HOT-PLUGGED CONNECTION.

live wire any conductor not at EARTH potential, particularly a conductor at a voltage that would be harmful if touched.

live working servicing actions carried out on equipment that is mains-connected and working, presenting an electric shock hazard if any parts are at high voltages.

LNB see LOW NOISE BLOCK.

load a COMPONENT or DEVICE that dissipates power from a CIRCUIT. The output of most electronic circuits is delivered to a load such as a heater, motor, AERIAL, loudspeaker, etc. All of these loads require power to be converted, so the circuits that supply loads need to be capable of delivering the required power.

load cell an arrangement of strain TRANSDUCERS on a cubic block, used to measure pressure or force.

load current the current, usually signal current, flowing in a load which can be a RESISTOR, a motor, a loudspeaker coil or an AERIAL, etc.

loading dissipating power by using a resistive load. Loading an OSCILLATOR circuit can have the effect of changing the oscillation frequency.

loading coil or **loading inductor** an INDUCTOR that is added to a CIRCUIT. For a TRANSMISSION LINE, loading coils are connected at intervals to correct the value of CHARACTERISTIC IMPEDANCE. For the oscillator of a SUPERHETERODYNE RECEIVER loading coils are switched into circuit to change the frequency band to a lower band, typically from medium wave to long wave.

load impedance the IMPEDANCE of a LOAD as it appears to the output circuit. Few loads are purely resistive, and many loads have MOTIONAL IMPEDANCE that will cause their apparent impedance value to vary with frequency or with time.

loading effect the change of frequency of an OSCILLATOR due to connecting a load to the output.

loading inductor see LOADING COIL.

load line a line drawn on a graph to represent the behaviour of a LOAD. The usual load line is drawn on a graph of output current against output voltage. The line then represents the conductance of the load, and allows the signal output voltage to be read off against signal current values. See Fig. 67.

load line, register the input to a REGISTER that enables DATA inputs to the register.

load matching the adjusting of a LOAD impedance to maximize the transfer of power.

lobe the elliptical shape that is the contour line of constant field strength from a TRANSMITTING AERIAL. The term is also applied to a RECEIVING AERIAL to show the contour line of equal values of sensitivity. The radiation pattern of an aerial shows lobes of different field values. See Fig. 68.

lobe switching an electronic method of altering the direction of peak sensitivity of an AERIAL by using several driven elements and varying the phase of signals to each.

local action a CELL problem in which the CATHODE (sense 3) metal is steadily dissolved by the ELECTROLYTE even when no current is flowing, usually caused by impurities in the cathode.

local area network (LAN) a small scale NETWORK (sense 2) for data exchange.

local area network control (LANC) a system for editing video signals that allows both reading of source video and writing of edited video to be controlled together.

local bus a fast internal computer BUS that connects the MICROPROCESSOR to other parts of the computer.

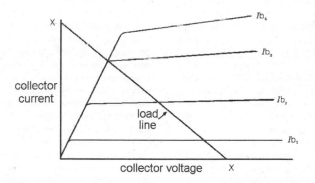

Fig. 67. **load line**

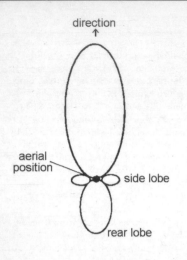

direction
↑

aerial
position

side lobe

rear lobe

Fig. 68. **lobe**

local loop the telephone cables between a local exchange and a subscriber. These are normally the slowest part of a link, and the main obstacle to the widespread use of BROADBAND Internet supply in the UK.

local oscillator (LO) the oscillator within a SUPERHETERODYNE RECEIVER. The signal from the local oscillator beats with the incoming signal to form the INTERMEDIATE FREQUENCY.

lock-angle error an error in a DIGITAL signal stream caused by PHASE differences between the data stream and the decoder CLOCK.

lock in to synchronize the frequency of an OSCILLATOR. One oscillator is said to be locked-in to another if it oscillates with the same FREQUENCY and (usually) with the same PHASE.

lock-in amplifier a SENSOR amplifier that uses, along with the sensor circuit, an AC supply whose frequency is high compared with the expected signal variation rate. This has the effect of greatly reducing the effect of noise.

locking-on 1. the establishing of automatic control over a varying quantity such as range, direction, frequency, etc. 2. an AUTOMATIC FREQUENCY CONTROL circuit that will lock-on when the (manual) tuning is almost correct, and will from then on maintain that tuning automatically. 3. the action of electro-mechanical tracking systems, such as RADAR aerials, that lock on to a target and from then on follow it as long as it is within range.

lock on to follow a moving target or synchronize to an input frequency.

lock out a failure of a MICROPROCESSOR control system which results in loss of control, usually cured by switching off power and then starting again.

lock range see HOLD RANGE.

locking relay a RELAY that can be mechanically or electrically locked in one position. The relay may be latched, meaning that the current to the coil can be supplied through the relay contacts. Once such a relay has been operated by another circuit (using a push button, for example), it will remain energized until power is removed.

lockup see HANG.

log law or **log taper** see LOGARITHMIC POTENTIOMETER.

logarithm a number transformation relative to a base number. For base-ten logarithms (sometimes indicated as $\log_{10}$), x is the logarithm of y if $y = 10^x$. The value of logarithms is that the adding of logarithms is equivalent to the multiplication of the plain numbers, and the subtraction of logarithms is equivalent to the division of the plain numbers. In electronics, some functions use natural logarithms (often written as ln), for which the base number is the irrational number e.

logarithmic amplifier see EXPONENTIAL AMPLIFIER.

logarithmic decrement or **log dec** the logarithm of the ratio of the PEAK AMPLITUDES of two successive OSCILLATIONS of a system, a measure of the damping (see DAMPED) of oscillation.

logarithmic potentiometer a form of POTENTIOMETER (sense 1) in which the division ratio follows a logarithmic rather than a linear law.

logarithmic scale a scale used for a graph in which equal distances represent equal multiples of a quantity, so that a large range of quantities can be plotted. For example a logarithmic scale of frequency might use equally spaced points for frequencies of 100Hz, 1kHz, 10kHz, 100kHz and 1MHz.

logic a method of deducing a result (OUTPUT) from data (INPUT, sense 1). George Boole showed in 1832 that all human logical processes could be described in terms of three simple steps or operations, AND, OR and NOT.

logical function any of the logical actions such as AND, OR etc.

logical product see AND FUNCTION.

logical sum see OR FUNCTION.

logical testing see WHITE BOX TESTING.

logic analyzer an instrument that can be connected to BUS lines and which will give a display of WAVEFORMS (see TIMING DOMAIN ANALYSIS) or of DIGITAL bits (see DATA DOMAIN ANALYSIS).

logic circuit a DIGITAL circuit that compares INPUTS (sense 1) and gives an OUTPUT that follows a logic rule or set of rules. The elementary logic actions are carried out by LOGIC GATES, whose actions are described in TRUTH TABLES or STATE TABLES.

logic clip or **logic comparator** or **logic monitor** a fastener that makes a set of connections to a CHIP (sense 1) so that the logic STATES of a set of points can be read, usually as 0, 1 or pulsing. See also LOGIC ANALYZER; LOGIC PROBE.

logic comparator see LOGIC CLIP.

logic diagram a diagram for a LOGIC CIRCUIT that shows LOGIC GATES in symbol form. This is not the same as an electronics CIRCUIT DIAGRAM, because it ignores power supplies, the internal circuitry of gates, and any connections that are not logic signal connections. The positions of gates in the diagram may not correspond to their physical position on a circuit diagram.

logic element a single LOGIC GATE or FLIP-FLOP.

logic gate a circuit that carries out a single logic action. The output of a logic gate is determined completely by the combination of inputs to that gate at that instant. The fundamental actions are AND, OR and NOT, but the main logic gates that are manufactured in IC form are NAND and NOR. This is because any other gate action, such as XOR, can be obtained by appropriate connections of NAND gates, or by (different) connections of NOR gates. The diagram, Fig. 69, shows the truth tables for the NAND and NOR gates, and illustrates how some other gate actions can be obtained by the use of NAND gates.

logic level the VOLTAGE range that is represented by a BINARY DIGIT, 0 or 1.

logic minimization see MINIMIZATION.

logic monitor see LOGIC CLIP.

logic one the voltage that corresponds to the BINARY DIGIT 1. For 5V logic circuits, this can be any voltage between 3.5V and 5.0V.

logic operations see LOGIC.

logic probe an instrument for reading LOGIC LEVELS. A flying lead is earthed, and the probe tip is placed on some connection in the logic circuit. The probe will then signal whether the logic voltage is 0, 1, or an oscillating voltage.

logic pulser or **digital pulser** a device that can be connected to BUS lines and which will force pulses on to the lines so that the effects of the pulses can be traced through the circuit.

logic symbol a shape on a diagram that represents a fundamental logic action. The shapes that originated in the US have been used by manufacturers of ICs and most users for a considerable time. Several attempts have been made to establish different shapes as a British Standard, and these shapes are used for teaching and in public examinations, but are seldom encountered elsewhere. See Fig. 15.

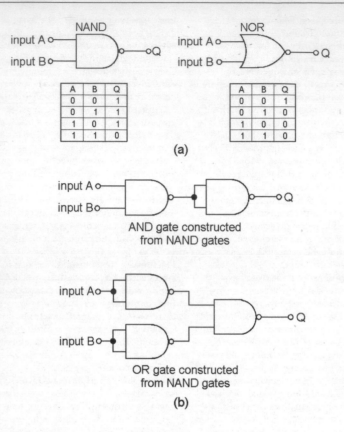

Fig. 69. logic gate

logic zero the BINARY (sense 1) 0 level of voltage. This is usually any voltage in the range 0 to +0.8V. See LOGIC LEVEL.

log-periodic aerial (or antenna) a development of the YAGI aerial using dipole elements mounted on two parallel bars that act as a TRANSMISSION LINE. The gain is lower than that of acorresponding yagi, but the BANDWIDTH is considerably greater.

long burst error an error that can affect up to 4000 digital bits on a CD, corrected by using CROSS INTERLEAVE REED-SOLOMON CODE (CIRC).

long haul network (LHN) a computer NETWORK (sense 2) that consists of NODES that are at least several kilometres apart, requiring the use of MODEMS.

longitudinal chromatic aberration a lens defect that causes coloured fringes on images because different colours focus at different points along the axis.

longitudinal timecode the time signals, recorded like an AUDIO track along one edge of an analogue VIDEOTAPE and phased to the video signal.

longitudinal track either edge track of a VIDEO TAPE, recorded and replayed using a fixed head, used for the sound track and/or the control or LONGITUDINAL TIMECODE track.

longitudinal wave   a wave, such as a sound wave, whose direction of OSCILLATION is in the direction of travel of the wave. Contrast TRANSVERSE WAVE.

long-line pull   a change of OSCILLATOR FREQUENCY when its output is fed to a long TRANSMISSION LINE.

long-persistence screen   a form of PHOSPHOR screen once used for RADAR displays. A long-persistence screen gives a bright glow when the ELECTRON BEAM strikes a SPOT (sense 1), and the glow continues at lower brightness, often in another colour, for a considerable time afterwards. This allows changes in the position of a radar target to be seen as a *trail*, gradually fading at the end. The tube must be viewed in darkness, and the operator has no control over persistence, so that the tube cannot easily be 'erased'.

At one time, the direct-view STORAGE TUBE was seen as a replacement for the long-persistence tube, but these were replaced in turn by computer-operated systems in which the retention of information is in a computer memory, and the displays are TV type displays. This allows the displays to be viewed in more normal illumination, the persistence time to be controlled, and the screen cleared if the trails become confusing.

long-playing record (LP)   the vinyl disc 33$\frac{1}{3}$ r.p.m. RECORDING system that replaced the older 78 r.p.m. shellac records and was itself replaced by the compact disc.

long-tailed pair   see DIFFERENTIAL AMPLIFIER.

long-tailed pair gate   a form of ANALOGUE gating circuit using the DIFFERENTIAL AMPLIFIER circuit with one input fed with a switching square wave.

long throw   (of a loudspeaker cone) vibrating with a large amplitude; often causing distortion.

long wave   a range of WAVELENGTHs that are measured in kilometres rather than in metres.

long wavelength cut-off   the longest wavelength (lowest frequency) of signal that a PHOTODETECTOR can respond to, determined by the BANDGAP of the semiconductor.

long-wire aerial (or antenna)   an aerial, usually horizontal, that consists of a length of wire greater than the wavelength of the transmission and not resonant for the frequency being used.

look angles   see AZIMUTH ANGLE (sense 2), ELEVATION.

look-up table   a table of matching values that can be used in a microprocessor system to specify a response.

loop   **1.** a connection of the output of a circuit or SYSTEM to its input, so causing FEEDBACK. **2.** the connection of one end of a wire or cable to the other so forming an endless closed path for current.

loop aerial   an AERIAL in the form of a flat coil with a strongly directional response. See also FRAME AERIAL.

loop back test   see LOOP CHECK.

loop check or loop-back test   a method of checking the action of a communications link using a MODEM by having the remote terminal return messages that can be compared with the original to detect CORRUPTION.

loop direction finding   see DIRECTION FINDING.

loop disconnect   see PULSE DIALLING.

loop gain   see CLOSED LOOP GAIN; OPEN LOOP GAIN.

loop inductance   the INDUCTANCE per unit length of a TRANSMISSION LINE. See also LOOP RESISTANCE; SHUNT CAPACITANCE; SHUNT CONDUCTANCE.

loop resistance   the RESISTANCE per unit length of a TRANSMISSION LINE. See also LOOP INDUCTANCE; SHUNT CAPACITANCE; SHUNT CONDUCTANCE.

loop-through   a connection made to a device that also provides an unaltered output, such as the aerial input and output terminals of a VIDEO CASSETTE RECORDER.

loose coupled   (of a pair of coupled resonant circuits) whose coupling is loose, see LOOSE COUPLING. Contrast TIGHT COUPLED.

loose coupling a form of TUNED TRANSFORMER coupling in which the COUPLING COEFFICIENT is low so that only a small fraction of the input signal is transferred to the output. A loose coupling is inefficient in terms of signal transfer but it reduces the loading on the signal source. Compare TIGHT COUPLING.

LOPPLER see LADAR.

LOPT see LINE OUTPUT TRANSFORMER.

LORAN system the long range navigation system developed before radar and satellite systems to establish position at sea, using three widely spaced powerful pulsed transmitters so that differences in arrival of pulses from the transmitters can provide positional information accurate to about 300 metres.

Lorentz force the force on an ELECTRON or ION that is moving in a MAGNETIC FIELD.

loss a dissipation of power.

loss angle a measurement of LOSS from a CAPACITOR. A perfect capacitor would have a phase angle of 90°, current leading voltage. In practice, the angle is very slightly less (as little as a thousandth of a degree) because of the loss of energy caused by slight electric leakage. The difference is the loss angle. See also POWER FACTOR.

loss factor, capacitor a number, usually very small, that represents the dissipative AC resistance of a capacitor.

loss of consonants method or **percent Alcons method** a way of measuring the intelligibility of an announcement over a PUBLIC ADDRESS system based on how many consonants can be distinguished.

lossless compression any method of reducing the size of a digital signal without loss of information, such as eliminating redundancy and using short codes for frequently used symbols. Examples are HUFFMAN CODING, RUN-LENGTH ENCODING, and LZW CODING. Contrast LOSSY COMPRESSION.

lossless DPCM a theoretical DIFFERENTIAL PULSE CODE MODULATION system in which the next set of signals could be predicted from the previous set, so requiring no information to be transmitted. Contrast LOSSY DPCM.

lossless line an imaginary TRANSMISSION LINE with no resistance, hence no loss. A real line can be imagined as a length of theoretically perfect lossless line with a series resistor in which all the loss of signal occurs. See also EQUIVALENT CIRCUIT.

lossy (of a material) dissipating energy, used, for example, of an insulator that has current leakage.

lossy action dissipation caused by the use of a CERAMIC CAPACITOR in a circuit.

lossy compression any BIT-REDUCTION system that irreversibly reduces the information, often by omitting bits that contribute little to the total information.

lossy DPCM any DIFFERENTIAL PULSE CODE MODULATION system in which perfect prediction of signals is impossible, and the range of possible error signals is limited. This introduces errors that can be reduced by further processing, but some information loss is inevitable.

lossy line a TRANSMISSION LINE that dissipates signal power.

lossy term, resonance the term R^2/L^2 in the PARALLEL RESONANCE equation that indicates the losses in the circuit, and which should be small for a good resonant circuit. See also Q FACTOR.

loudness level a subjective judgement of loudness of sound as compared to a standard 100 Hz note.

loudspeaker or **speaker** a TRANSDUCER that converts electrical signal energy into sound (acoustic) energy sufficient to be heard by occupants in a room. See also ELECTROSTATIC LOUDSPEAKER; HEADPHONES; SPIDER; VOICE-COIL.

loudspeaker diaphragm the surface, usually cone-shaped, that is connected to the VOICE-COIL of the loudspeaker and suspended in the SPIDER so that it can vibrate and so reproduce sound. See also CONE.

loudspeaker driver the electromagnetic part of a loudspeaker, consisting of voice coil and magnet.

low-bandwidth (of a COMMUNICATIONS link, a lecture or a document) carrying little information.

low-capacitance probe a CATHODE-RAY OSCILLOSCOPE lead that uses a COMPENSATED ATTENUATOR circuit to attenuate the input signal and reduce losses due to the STRAY CAPACITANCE of the probe.

low contrast filter an OPTICAL FILTER that reduces CONTRAST by spreading light from highlights into shadows.

low dimensional structure see HIGH ELECTRON MOBILITY TRANSISTOR.

low-dropout regulator or **low-dropout stabilizer** a VOLTAGE REGULATOR IC in which the difference between (unregulated) input voltage and (regulated) output voltage can be small, typically less than 1.0V.

low earth orbit the path of a satellite used for COMMUNICATIONS. A low earth orbit satellite constantly circles the Earth (unlike the GEOSTATIONARY ORBIT type), so that several low earth orbit satellites are needed to cover the whole Earth.

low-emission a problem of THERMIONIC devices in which the emission of electrons from the cathode is greatly reduced. Emission can be restored for some time by running the HEATER (sense 2) at a higher output, but replacement of the device is the only long-term solution. Low emission in a CATHODE-RAY TUBE manifests itself as dull low-contrast pictures and inability to obtain high brightness.

low energy lighting lights using miniature fluorescent tubes that provide a high light output for a very low electrical input, typically less than 25 watts.

lower sideband the FREQUENCY RANGE that is obtained by subtracting each modulating frequency from the CARRIER FREQUENCY. See also DOUBLE SIDEBAND; SINGLE SIDEBAND; UPPER SIDEBAND.

lowest usable frequency (LUF) the lowest FREQUENCY in the HF band that a given communications link can use, depending on ionospheric conditions.

low frequency (LF) or **long-wave band** the band that covers the frequencies of approximately 30kHz to 300kHz, corresponding to wavelengths of 100 kilometres to 10 kilometres.

low frequency compensation the AMPLITUDE and phase correction of a low-frequency signal (see PHASE-CORRECTION CIRCUIT). A signal containing low frequencies will have these frequencies attenuated and phase shifted by the coupling time constants of an amplifier. The low-frequency compensating circuits are designed to restore normal amplitude and phase.

low insertion force (LIF) socket a socket for a small MICROPROCESSOR or other chip that has no clamping handle, so that the chip is simply pushed in and levered out. Now replaced by the ZIF socket for large chips.

low level language the symbolic programming language used to program a microprocessor. Converted into binary code by an ASSEMBLER program.

low-level modulation the MODULATION of a CARRIER (sense 1) while it is at a low AMPLITUDE. The modulated carrier is then amplified. Amplitude modulation is usually carried out at high level and frequency modulation at low level (on the oscillator). The use of low-level modulation means that subsequent radio frequency amplification must use fairly LINEAR stages.

low logic level the level 0 voltage, usually in the range of 0 to 0.8V.

low-noise amplifier see LOW-NOISE BLOCK.

low-noise bias a tape recorder oscillator circuit which develops a pure SINE WAVE with a very low NOISE level for optimum TAPE BIAS.

low-noise block or **low-noise box (LNB)** the unit that is constructed as part of a MICROWAVE receiving DISH for SATELLITE TV, converting a block of microwave signals in KU BAND and converting them to TV UHF signal frequencies using the SUPERHETERODYNE principle

low-noise box (LNB) see LOW-NOISE BLOCK.

low-noise temperature aerial (or antenna) a highly directional RECEIVING AERIAL for satellite communications with minimal sensitivity to noise signals originating at Earth level.

low-pass filter a FILTER whose PASS BAND extends from DC up to the cut-off frequency of the filter.

low-power Schottky (LS) a family of LOGIC CIRCUITS that uses SCHOTTKY devices for high operating speed and low power operation.

low resolution (of an image) constructed with a low number of PIXELS per inch. A RESOLUTION of, for example, 15 dots per inch can be classed as low, just as 1000 dots per inch is high, but the terms are relative, and the boundary between low and high resolution is flexible.

low voltage directive the EU directive that governs the electrical standards for equipment using voltages in the range 50V to 1000V AC and 75V to 1500V DC, so that it covers all domestic electrical and electronic equipment.

low voltage operation the use of a 3.3V supply for computer components such as memory chips. Microprocessors operating at 1.6V or less are also in use, reducing power requirements.

LP see LONG-PLAYING RECORD.

L–R signal the STEREO information signal that is modulated on to a SUBCARRIER in the FM stereo system and combined with the mono L+R SIGNAL to produce separate L and R channel signals.

L+R signal the MONOPHONIC signal in an FM STEREO broadcast. This is used by mono receivers, and the L–R SIGNAL on its SUBCARRIER is used along with the L+R signal in a stereo receiver to obtain the separate L and R signals.

LP video the use of lower tape speeds in a VIDEO CASSETTE RECORDER in order to prolong playing time at the expense of picture and sound quality.

LS see LOW-POWER SCHOTTKY.

LS protection circuitry circuits in the OUTPUT STAGE of an AUDIO AMPLIFIER that act to protect a loudspeaker from excessive current or voltage.

lsb see LEAST-SIGNIFICANT BIT.

LSB see LEAST-SIGNIFICANT BYTE.

LSI see LARGE SCALE INTEGRATION.

LSTTL the LOW-POWER SCHOTTKY version of TRANSISTOR-TRANSISTOR LOGIC circuit.

LUF see LOWEST USABLE FREQUENCY.

luma keying the use of the brightness of a televized scene as a method of inserting another picture. See also CHROMA KEYING; DIGITAL KEYING.

luma signal see LUMINANCE.

luminance or luma or luminance signal the part of a VIDEO signal that carries light/shade information, the monochrome signal. See also COLOUR TELEVISION.

luminance amplifier the amplifier in a COLOUR TELEVISION receiver that deals with the LUMINANCE signal.

luminescence the illumination of a material because of bombardment with electrons or other radiation.

luminous flux the rate of flow of light energy. Unit: lumen.

lumped components model a simplified circuit for a TRANSMISSION LINE or other connection, imagining it as a set of series inductors and shunt capacitors.

lumped parameter a 'spread-out' value that is treated as a single COMPONENT. A TRANSMISSION LINE, for example, will have a value of inductance per metre and capacitance per metre. A length of line can therefore be simulated by using inductors and capacitors of the appropriate values, which are the lumped parameters.

Luneberg lens aerial (or antenna) a form of focusing lens aerial that uses a set of partly spherical shells of materials of differing permittivity, so that a beam striking the surface will come to a focus on the other side of the lens.

lux a unit of illumination. Unit: lumens per square metre.

Luxembourg effect   see IONOSPHERIC CROSS MODULATION.

LVD   see LOW VOLTAGE DIRECTIVE.

LVDT   see LINEAR VARIABLE DIFFERENTIAL TRANSFORMER.

LZW coding   see LEMPEL-ZIV ALGORITHM CODING.

MAC the multiplexed analogue
component system used for analogue
satellite broadcasting before the change
to digital broadcasting by satellite. This
is one of many proposed systems
collectively using the MAC (multiplexed
analogue component) name for analogue
multiplexing of TV signals identified by
letter (A-MAC, B-MAC, C-MAC etc.).

machine code or **machine language**
BINARY CODE for programming a
MICROPROCESSOR, or a program written
in binary code.

machine cycle one cycle of a
microprocessor CLOCK. The processing
speed of the MICROPROCESSOR is governed
primarily by the clock pulses. The time
between two clock pulses is referred to
as a machine cycle, because any of the
actions of the microprocessor can be
timed in terms of an integral number of
machine cycles. An instruction set for a
microprocessor will contain timings for all
of the microprocessor actions in terms of
the machine cycle. In this way, if the clock
pulse timing is known, the time required
for any instruction or set of instructions
can be calculated.

machine language see MACHINE CODE.

machine-readable or **machineable**
capable of being read directly by a
computer, such as a FLOPPY DISK or CD-ROM.

macroblock a set of DIGITAL VIDEO data
codes grouped as 16 lines of 16 PIXELS.
Data compression (see BIT REDUCTION)
is applied to these units.

macrocell a large area of cell (see
CELLULAR PHONE) for telephone use in
remote areas.

macrovision a coding system for DVD
discs intended to prevent copying and
ensure that a disc intended for one region
cannot be played in another. The system
has not proved effective because many
DVD players allow for multi-region use

and others can be modified (by software)
so as to allow multi-region use.

magamp see MAGNETIC AMPLIFIER.

magenta a COMPLEMENTARY COLOUR equal
to white minus green (or red plus blue).

magic T see HYBRID JUNCTION.

magnet see ELECTROMAGNET; PERMANENT
MAGNET.

magnetic amplifier or **magamp** a form
of AC power AMPLIFIER with very high
power GAIN. A control winding on a
MAGNETIC CORE (sense 1) is used to control
the magnetic characteristics of the core,
and so vary the REACTANCE of another
winding. The power supply to the
magnetic amplifier is AC, and the signals
are DC or slowly-changing signals.

magnetic card a storage system for small
amounts of data. The magnetic card, as
exemplified by credit cards and cash
cards, uses a stripe of magnetic material
to store data. The card is written by
automatic processes that can control the
rate at which the magnetic stripe is pulled
past the head of a recorder.

magnetic cell the unit of magnetic
storage, meaning a particle of magnetic
material that can be magnetized in one
direction or the other.

magnetic circuit a closed path in a
magnetic material. The magnetic circuit
'conducts' MAGNETIC FLUX in an analogous
way to a metal circuit conducting current.

magnetic circuit breaker a CIRCUIT
BREAKER that uses current through an
electromagnet to operate a switch that
breaks the circuit.

magnetic clutch an arrangement of two
FERROMAGNETIC discs with a magnetic
liquid or powder between them. When
one disc rotates very little power is
transmitted to the other plate until a coil
surrounding the assembly is activated,
so 'freezing' the liquid or powder into a
solid mass and transmitting the rotation.

magnetic core 1. a piece of magnetic material on which an INDUCTOR can be wound. 2. in computing, the miniature magnetic rings formerly used for constructing memory for large computers. The principle is that a binary 1 is stored in the form of one direction of magnetic flux, and a binary 0 as the opposite direction. The cores are read and written by passing current through wires that thread through each core. Modern computers use SEMICONDUCTOR memory. See also COINCIDENT HALF-CURRENT SWITCHING.

magnetic coupled interference unwanted signals picked up because of the MAGNETIC FIELD round a wire affecting adjacent wiring.

magnetic damping a method of damping (see DAMPED) mechanical oscillations by using induced currents. The oscillating object is attached to a piece of metal that moves between the poles of a magnet. The EDDY CURRENTs induced in the metal set up forces that oppose the motion (Lenz's law), thus damping the motion. The advantage of magnetic damping is that the damping force is proportional to speed. This means that the maximum damping is achieved when the movement is a maximum, and there is practically no damping when the object is almost at rest.

magnetic deflection the DEFLECTION of an ELECTRON BEAM by a MAGNETIC FIELD.

magnetic dependent resistor or **magneto-dependent resistor (MDR)** any resistive material (mainly SEMICONDUCTOR) whose RESISTANCE value is altered by the presence of a MAGNETIC FIELD. See also MAGNETORESISTANCE.

magnetic disk a disk which may be plastic, metal or other material, coated with magnetic powder that is used as a storage medium for computers. The storage method is based on direction of magnetism (see MAGNETIC CORES, sense 2) and the disk is spun while a READ/WRITE HEAD is put into contact or near-contact with its surface. This allows access to any part of the disk in a short time. See FLOPPY DISK; HARD DRIVE; PLATTER.

magnetic domain the smallest possible MAGNETIC CELL (of atomic dimensions) in a magnetic material, corresponding to the minimum possible amount that can be magnetized. A material is fully magnetized when all of its domains are aligned in the same direction.

magnetic effect, current the MAGNETIC FIELD that is created when current flows in a conductor.

magnetic elements the magnetic constants for the Earth, in terms of strength and direction of the MAGNETIC FIELD at various points.

magnetic field the space around any form of magnet in which force effects on FERROMAGNETIC materials can be detected.

magnetic field strength the magnetic field generated by a current, unaffected by magnetic material. Symbol: H. Unit: ampere-turn. This is a VECTOR quantity.

magnetic flux a 'flow' or FLUX (sense 1) of magnetism. This is most easily measured in terms of the ELECTROMOTIVE FORCE that is generated when a circuit surrounding the flux is removed from the flux.

magnetic flux density a measure of the strength of MAGNETIC FIELD in a material. Symbol: B; unit: weber/sq. metre. See also FLUX DENSITY.

magnetic focusing a method of focusing an ELECTRON BEAM by using MAGNETIC FIELDS.

magnetic force on conductor the force on a current-carrying conductor in a MAGNETIC FIELD, whose direction is given by the LEFT-HAND LAW and whose size is $B.I.l$ where B is the flux density, in tesla, of the field, I is the current in amperes, and l is the length (in metres) of the conductor in the field.

magnetic head see READ/WRITE HEAD.

magnetic history the number of cycles of MAGNETIZATION and DEMAGNETIZATION of a magnetic material.

magnetic hysteresis the NONLINEAR relationship between FLUX DENSITY in a material and the MAGNETIC FIELD that produces it. In the diagram, Fig. 70, the initial part of the graph that starts at the origin is traced out when a magnetic field is applied to a material that is not initially magnetized. Increasing field strength

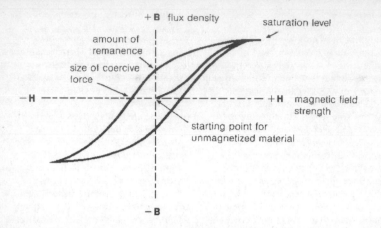

+**B** flux density

saturation level

amount of
remanence

size of coercive
force

−**H** — — — — — — — — — — — — — +**H** magnetic field
strength

starting point for
unmagnetized material

−**B**

Fig. 70. **magnetic hysteresis**

leads to the condition of MAGNETIC
SATURATION, at which increases of field
strength cause only comparatively small
changes in flux density.

If the field is then reduced, the shape
of the graph from the saturation point
downwards is not the same as the shape
when the field was being increased.
There will be a flux density remaining
in the material even when the external
field is zero. This value of flux density is
called the REMANENCE.

If the field is now reversed, and its
strength increased, it now opposes the flux
density direction, and the flux density
decreases. The field value that is needed to
reduce the flux density to zero is called the
COERCIVITY (or *coercive force*), and is a measure
of the permanence of the magnetism.

Increasing the field again now reverses
the direction of the flux density until
saturation is reached in the opposite
direction. Reduction of field strength from
this point now causes another path to be
traced, making the trace symmetrical.
The area that is enclosed by the path of
this HYSTERESIS LOOP represents the amount
of energy lost in the whole cycle. Note
that in hysteresis diagrams, the units are
always chosen so as to produce diagrams
of reasonable scale.

magnetic leakage a loss of FLUX (sense 1)
from a MAGNETIC CIRCUIT. Unlike current
in a metallic circuit, flux is not totally
confined to magnetic material, and the
amount of flux that strays from the
intended path is the LEAKAGE FLUX.

magnetic lens a lens for focusing an
electron beam produced by using magnets
to form a magnetic field. The magnetic
lens may utilize permanent magnets, but
it is more common to use electromagnets
to form an ELECTROMAGNETIC LENS whose
focus can be easily adjusted by varying
the current through the electromagnet(s).

magnetic medium any form of storage
system based on magnetic materials, such
as MAGNETIC TAPE, FLOPPY DISK, HARD DRIVE
or the (obsolete) CORE STORE.

magnetic memory a MEMORY system in
which data is represented as direction or
intensity of magnetization of a material.
The advantage of any such system is that
it is NONVOLATILE, i.e. the data is not
erased when power is removed from
the system. Compare VOLATILE.

magnetic moment a quantity that is
sometimes used to measure the strength
of a magnet. The torque acting on a bar
magnet in a field is the vector (cross)
product of magnetic moment and the
FLUX DENSITY of the surrounding field.

magnetic pickup a type of gramophone PICKUP for VINYL DISCs that makes use of electromagnetic induction. See MOVING-COIL PICKUP; MOVING-IRON PICKUP.

magnetic pole a point around which magnetism is concentrated. Any magnet that has an air gap will have a pole on each side of the air gap.

magnetic recording a method of recording electrical signals as variations of the MAGNETISM of a material. For analogue AUDIO recording, the material is a finely powdered metal oxide (iron oxide, chromium oxide) or metal (usually iron) coated on plastic tape. The tape is fed past a recording head at a steady speed. The head consists of a MAGNETIC FLUX path that is almost totally closed, but with a tiny gap that touches the tape. This causes an intense MAGNETIC FIELD to cross the tape and so magnetize the particles on the tape. The signal to the tape head takes the form of audio current signals on a winding around the magnetic material. On playback, the tape is again drawn at the same constant speed past a similar head, often the same head. This time, the variations in magnetization of the tape cause a varying flux in the magnetic circuit of the head, and so induce varying voltages in the winding. See also MAGNETIC TAPE.

Because the graph of tape magnetism plotted against head coil current is a nonlinear (HYSTERESIS) shape, some form of BIAS is needed to achieve acceptable results. This is achieved by using high-frequency signals. See also AZIMUTH ANGLE (sense 1).

The recording of analogue video, or of digital signals requires more elaborate methods in which revolving read/write heads are mounted on a revolving DRUM (sense 1) around which the tape is wrapped, see VIDEO CASSETTE RECORDER.

magnetic reed switch see REED SWITCH.

magnetic saturation the point at which the magnetic FLUX DENSITY of a material ceases to increase perceptibly when the magnetizing force is increased. At this point, the PERMEABILITY of the material is

virtually the same as the permeability of the air around it.

magnetic screening or **magnetic shielding** the protecting of COMPONENTs against the unwanted effect of MAGNETIC FIELDS. This is necessary if unwanted fields are present near CATHODE-RAY TUBES, TRANSISTORS, INTEGRATED CIRCUITS, or INDUCTORS. The 'magnetic screening' is a closed box that is made from material of very high PERMEABILITY so that MAGNETIC FLUX passes through the screening material in preference to any other path.

magnetic shunt an alternative path for MAGNETIC FLUX consisting of a piece of high-PERMEABILITY material whose position on a magnetic path can be varied so as to control the amount of flux in another path. This is the principle of the permanent magnet whose magnetization can be switched on and off.

magnetic tape a plastic tape coated with magnetic material for the purpose of recording. Iron oxide is the most usual coating, but Chromium (IV) oxide and metallic iron have also been used for high-quality recording. See MAGNETIC RECORDING.

magnetic tape drive or **streamer** or **tape drive** a tape mechanism using DIGITAL tape intended for large scale data storage. See also DATA.

magnetic tuning a tuning method for MICROWAVE cavities. Part of the RESONANT CAVITY is made of FERRITE, whose PERMEABILITY can be altered by the steady field from an electromagnet.

magnetism a field effect that produces strong forces on FERROMAGNETIC and paramagnetic materials such as iron and a group of elements with similar atomic structures. MAGNETIC FIELDs are produced by circulating currents. These can be currents in wire conductors, or the atomic-scale circulation of electrons that have spins in the same directions.

All materials are affected to *some* extent by magnetism, though the effect is very small with most non-metals. *Paramagnetic* materials will line up in a magnetic field with their axes in line with the field, *diamagnetic* materials will line up at right angles to the field. Ferromagnetic materials are a form of paramagnetic materials, like iron, on which very strong forces act. Many ferromagnetic materials can be permanently magnetized.

magnetization the effect of creating a magnetic FLUX DENSITY in the space around a material. Magnetization may be due to the presence of a PERMANENT MAGNET, or to the MAGNETOMOTIVE FORCE caused by electric current.

magnetize to make a material permanently or temporarily magnetic.

magnetizing current the current flowing through the windings of a coil so that a MAGNETIC FIELD is created round the coil.

magnetizing force or **magnetic field strength** the measure of magnetic field of a coil carrying current or a permanent magnet. Symbol: H; unit: ampere-turn per metre.

magnetohydrodynamic generation the generation of electricity from the movement of charged particles, such as IONs, in a MAGNETIC FIELD.

magnetohydrodynamic sensor a sensor for movement of IONIZED particles, making use of MAGNETOHYDRODYNAMIC GENERATION.

magneto-ionic double refraction the effect on linearly POLARIZED (sense 1) waves of the Earth's magnetic field and the ionization of the IONOSPHERE, causing the waves to separate into two components with opposite directions of ELLIPTICAL POLARIZATION. This will cause MULTIPATH PROPAGATION interference effects at a receiver.

magnetomotive force the cause of magnetization. Symbol: F_m. Unit ampere-turn. The magnetomotive force of a coil, which is the product of the number of turns and the current flowing, causes MAGNETIC FLUX in a MAGNETIC CIRCUIT.

magneto-optical (of a data storage system) using a combination of magnetic and optical effects, see FARADAY EFFECT.

magneto-optical drive (MOD) a form of writable CD-ROM drive that makes use of a laser beam to affect a magnetic layer.

The resulting data can be read using the same methods as are used for CD-ROM, and the disk can be erased and re-used, making the system very useful for large scale data storage, typically 1.5 Gbyte and more. The system has been overshadowed by the development of CD-R, CD-RW, and DVD discs.

magnetoresistance a change of resistance caused by magnetism. See MAGNETIC DEPENDENT RESISTOR.

magneto-resistive head or **MR head** a tape REPLAY HEAD based on MAGNETORESISTANCE, and used on tape players that have low tape speeds.

magneto-resistor see MAGNETIC DEPENDENT RESISTOR.

magnetostatic surface wave filter (MSSWF) the microwave equivalent of a surface ACOUSTIC WAVE filter, using a thin film of yttrium iron garnet (YIG) on a gadolinium gallium garnet (G^3) substrate to form a FILTER that can be used at MICROWAVE frequencies up to about 20 GHz.

magnetostriction a stress caused in a material by MAGNETIZATION. The forces between atoms in a magnetized material cause stresses that can affect the dimensions of the material. *Positive magnetostriction* causes an increase in length of a material when it is magnetized. *Negative magnetostriction* means that the length of a sample will decrease when it is magnetized. Alternating magnetic fields applied to either type of material will cause mechanical vibrations that are commercially used in ULTRASONIC generators. The whistling sound from an old 405-line TV receiver was caused by magnetostrictive vibrations of the core of the LINE-OUTPUT TRANSFORMER.

magnetostrictive transducer a transducer for electrical signals into mechanical vibrations, using the principle of MAGNETOSTRICTION and used mainly for ultrasonic cleaning baths.

magnetron the earliest type of high-power MICROWAVE oscillator. The principle is based on the creation of pulsed beams of electrons that travel in circular paths in a vacuum. By making the ELECTRON BEAM travel across the mouth of each of several identical tuned cavities, the cavities are set into resonance at a microwave frequency. The OSCILLATION reaches a peak when the speed of circulation of the electrons is such that one cycle of the electrons round the beam path takes the same time as one cycle of the microwave frequency. Stability of frequency is achieved by making connections (see STRAPPING) between alternate cavities. The microwave signal energy is tapped by a loop in one cavity that is coupled to an external WAVEGUIDE. See Fig. 71.

magnitude   the ABSOLUTE VALUE or amplitude of a signal expressed as a positive quantity.

mainboard   see MOTHERBOARD.

main fan   the fan incorporated into the POWER SUPPLY unit of a computer.

mainframe   the largest type of computer.

mains or **mains supply**   see ALTERNATING CURRENT.

mains-borne interference   noise or other interference introduced into electronic equipment through the mains supply; usually reduced by a MAINS PLUG FILTER.

mains filter or **conditioner**   electronic equipment that will remove SURGES or SPIKES from a MAINS supply, so protecting computer systems connected through the filter.

mains filter capacitor   a polyester or polypropylene film type of SELF-HEALING capacitor intended for MAINS FILTER use, specified as class X or Y. Class X can be used when failure would not cause a danger, but Class Y has to be specified if failure could cause danger of shock.

mains filtering   the action of removing SPIKES and high frequency interference from a mains supply so that this does not cause interference to enter a circuit from its power supply.

mains hum   see HUM.

mains isolation   the use of an ISOLATING TRANSFORMER to supply mains to equipment so as to allow working on a LIVE CHASSIS CIRCUIT without the risk of a direct connection to the mains.

mains monitor   a metering device that senses changes in the mains supply (see ALTERNATING CURRENT). This can, for example, be used to cause a computer to record vital data on to MAGNETIC DISKS in the event of any sign of a supply interruption.

mains plug filter   a LOW-PASS FILTER circuit incorporated into a mains plug to remove interfering signals.

mains ripple   a trace of AC at mains or double-mains frequency on a DC supply line, due to insufficient SMOOTHING (sense 1) or excessive loading.

mains supply   see MAINS.

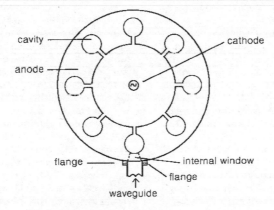

cavity

cathode

anode

flange

internal window

flange

waveguide

Fig. 71. **magnetron**

mains surge a sudden and usually short-lived increase in AC MAINS voltage that can cause damage or disruption of electronic equipment. See also SPIKE.

mains switch the switch that controls the mains supply to equipment.

mains transformer a transformer powered from the mains and used to supply (normally) lower voltages to rectifier circuits to feed electronic components.

majority carrier the charged CARRIER (sense 2) (electron or hole) that is responsible for more than 50% of the current flow in a SEMICONDUCTOR.

majority voting logic a LOGIC system in which several checks for integrity of data are made, and the most frequently obtained result is used.

major lobe the longest LOBE in an AERIAL (antenna) radiation pattern. This corresponds to the direction of transmission or reception for a DIRECTIONAL AERIAL.

make to close a CIRCUIT.

make-and-break circuit a form of mechanical circuit INTERRUPTER that converts steady current into pulses. See also CHOPPER.

make before break (MBB) a switch construction that makes a new connection before breaking the original connection. This is used mainly for signal switching from lines at the same DC level.

make/break time the time needed for a RELAY to pull in (make contacts) or release (break contacts). The release time is usually longer.

male connector the plug portion of a plug and socket system. See also FEMALE CONNECTOR; JACK PLUG; JILL.

MAN see METROPOLITAN AREA NETWORK.

Manchester code a BIPHASE digital code in which each DIGITAL DATA bit is represented by two code bits, using 01 to represent binary 0 and 10 to represent binary 1. This ensures that there will never be more than two consecutive identical bits in a data stream, making RECORDING easier.

manganese alkaline cell the original cell invented by Sam Ruben in 1939, using a steel ANODE coated with manganese dioxide and zinc cathode, with potassium hydroxide electrolyte.

manganese silver chloride cell a non-rechargeable CELL that is activated by contact with water and used in marine search and rescue applications. The cell has an indefinite storage life when dry, and delivers a large energy content when wet.

manganin a copper-manganese alloy that is used for constructing WIRE-WOUND RESISTORS. It is particularly suitable because of comparatively large RESISTIVITY, low TEMPERATURE COEFFICIENT of resistivity and small CONTACT POTENTIAL with copper.

man-made noise the electrical NOISE that is caused by man-made DEVICES such as car ignition systems, thermostats, light switches, fluorescent lights, etc.

mantissa the number that forms the multiplier in STANDARD FORM, so that in $A \times 10^n$ the number represented by A, which will be greater than 1 and less than 10, is the mantissa. See also EXPONENT.

mantissa-exponent form see STANDARD FORM.

mapping memory the use of ADDRESS numbers to locate data in memory.

Marconi aerial (or antenna) a simple vertical wire AERIAL.

Marconi, Guielmo (1874–1937) the Italian pioneer of radio who demonstrated not only that radio waves could be transmitted and received but that they could be used for long-distance communications, as HEAVISIDE had predicted.

marginal circuit a circuit whose correct working depends on maintaining precise values of components, so that component replacement, ageing, temperature change can all affect the operation of the circuit.

mark the part of an on/off cycle of voltage or current that is the on-time. If a voltage is switched on for 2ms and is off for 3ms, then the mark is the 2ms time for which the voltage is on. The off-time is called the *space*, and in this example the MARK-SPACE RATIO is 2:3.

marker pulse a pulse that is used as a time reference in PULSE-TIME MODULATION and MULTIPLEXER (sense 1) systems.

marking amplifier the AMPLIFIER in a FACSIMILE terminal that drives the printing mechanism.

mark-space ratio the ratio of on-time (during which voltage is applied or current flows) to off-time for a rectangular pulse. The mark-space ratio for a perfectly square pulse is 1:1. See also DUTY CYCLE; MARK. See Fig. 72.

maser *acronym for* Microwave Amplification by the Stimulated Emission of Radiation: a form of microwave amplifier that uses the electron energies in a gas or in a solid crystal. The electrons in the material are excited to a high energy level and the incoming signal is used to trigger the return to normal level, releasing energy. Solid crystal masers run at very low temperatures (liquid helium temperatures of around 4K) and offer very high power gain with very low noise. Gas masers are used as very precise microwave oscillators. Similar principles are used for LASERS.

MASH™ **circuit** see MULTISTAGE NOISE SHAPING.

mask to shield areas of a CHIP (sense 1) in order to make a process such as ETCHING or DIFFUSION follow a shape pattern.

maskable interrupt an INTERRUPT signal to a MICROPROCESSOR that can be ignored (masked) by either hardware or software.

masked ROM a form of permanent read-only memory that consists of electrical connections. Each unit of memory consists of a permanent connection either to earth (0) or to the positive supply terminal (1), so that the data is fixed when the memory IC chip is manufactured by a process called *masking*. This type of memory is NON-VOLATILE because the retention of data does not depend on the power supply being maintained.

masking the AUDIO effect in which a loud sound at low frequency masks a softer sound at a slightly higher frequency, allowing the data of the quieter sound to be discarded when the data bytes are compressed (see BIT REDUCTION).

masking losses see BLOCKING LOSSES.

mass-plate cell a form of NICKEL-CADMIUM CELL that uses solid plates, so achieving a low discharge rate. Contrast SINTERED PLATE CELL.

master clock the main source of timing CLOCK pulses in a computer to which all the units are synchronized and from which all other clock pulses are derived.

master copy an ANALOGUE videotape made by copying selected portions of the original tape(s), to which an edited sound

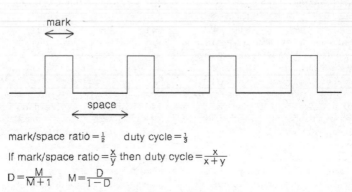

mark/space ratio $= \frac{1}{2}$ duty cycle $= \frac{1}{3}$

If mark/space ratio $= \frac{x}{y}$ then duty cycle $= \frac{x}{x+y}$

$$D = \frac{M}{M+1} \qquad M = \frac{D}{1-D}$$

where M = mark/space ratio and D = duty cycle

Fig. 72. **mark-space ratio**

track can be added. The master copy is then used to make the distribution copies.

master oscillator a high-stability OSCILLATOR that is used as the source of a CARRIER (sense 1) signal or as a timing reference for digital circuits. The master oscillator output is to a BUFFER (sense 1) stage (or stages), to ensure that the effect of connecting a LOAD to the master oscillator is negligible.

master-slave flip-flop a form of double FLIP-FLOP in which the first unit, the master, drives the second (slave), allowing isolation between inputs and outputs. See J-K FLIP-FLOP; MASTER-SLAVE LOGIC.

master-slave logic a triggering system in which both edges of the CLOCK pulse are used, the first changing the state of a primary (master) flip-flop, the second transferring the change to the secondary (slave) flip-flop.

master tape or **production master** the analogue tape, usually edited from multi-track sources, that is used as the source of audio for a disc cutter for VINYL DISC recordings, or nowadays, the DIGITAL TAPE that is the source for CDs.

masthead amplifier a small WIDEBAND RF amplifier connected close to a receiving DIPOLE AERIAL in order to boost the amplitude of the signal fed to the down cable. The cable is also used to supply DC to the masthead amplifier.

matched filter a DIGITAL FILTER used to minimize BIT ERROR RATE in a DECODER.

matched load a LOAD whose IMPEDANCE is equal to that of the driving output stage.

matched termination a cable or line termination at which no signal REFLECTION occurs. The termination is the load at the end of a TRANSMISSION LINE or WAVEGUIDE, and if correctly matched produces no STANDING WAVES in the line.

matching obtaining equality of the magnitude of LOAD and OUTPUT impedance. This ensures maximum power transfer in the case of a fixed output resistance (see MAXIMUM POWER THEOREM).

matching network a form of FILTER for signal frequencies intended for impedance MATCHING so as to ensure maximum power transfer.

matching transformer a TRANSFORMER used as an IMPEDANCE MATCHING device between two circuits or between a circuit output and a load or between a source and a circuit input.

MATE modular automated test equipment.

mathematically compensated oscillator a form of CRYSTAL OSCILLATOR controlled by a MICROPROCESSOR that uses data on crystal characteristics to correct for the effects of temperature changes.

maths coprocessor or **floating-point unit** or **floating point accelerator** or **number cruncher** a processor chip designed to work along with a main microprocessor so as to speed up the handling of FLOATING-POINT calculations by early microprocessor designs. Later processor types have included a floating-point unit on the same chip.

matrices plural of MATRIX.

matrix a set of points arranged in rows and columns, so that two numbers can be used to define any point.

matrix board see MATRIX STRIPBOARD.

matrix circuit, FM the adding circuit that is used to produce separate L and R signals from the L+R SIGNAL and L−R SIGNAL that are transmitted.

matrix display any image display that uses a set of dots set into a matrix, usually rectangular, to form letter, number or image shapes when the appropriate PIXELS are activated. See also LCD; PLASMA SCREEN.

matrixing the action of obtaining separate R, G, and B signals from the LUMINANCE signals and the two CHROMINANCE signals.

matrix keyboard a keyboard in which each key switch makes a connection between a line and a column of conductors. See KEY-MATRIX.

matrix stripboard or **matrix board** a pre-printed PRINTED CIRCUIT BOARD that consists of a set of conducting strips drilled at 2.5 mm intervals and used for temporary circuit construction. See also BREADBOARD.

matrix transform the process in DIGITAL TELEVISION transmission in which each data BLOCK (sense 2) is rearranged to produce runs of zero values, which can then be discarded to compress (see BIT REDUCTION) the signal further.

matte a plain background for a scene, used for overlaying a VIDEO image.

maximum available noise power the NOISE POWER from a source whose IMPEDANCE is matched to a load, see MATCHED LOAD.

maximum dissipation the rating of maximum power for an electronic device, depending on surrounding (ambient) temperature.

maximum likelihood decoding or **minimum distance decoding** or **correlation decoding** a method of DECODING a digital signal that compares a signal word with each code word used until a match with the lowest BIT ERROR is found.

maximum output level (MOL) the maximum acceptable remanent flux density (see REMANENCE) on analogue recorded tape, usually quoted as the value that will result in 3% of THIRD-HARMONIC DISTORTION at a frequency of 315 Hz.

maximum power theorem a theorem for finding matching LOAD value. For a given output impedance, the maximum power theorem shows that the maximum power is developed in a load whose resistance is exactly equal to the output resistance, and whose reactance is exactly equal and opposite to the reactance of the output. The converse is not true – if the load is fixed, then the maximum power in the load is achieved when the output resistance of the driving stage is as low as possible.

maximum usable frequency (MUF) the highest frequency in the HF band that can be reliably used, depending on range and SUNSPOT conditions.

maxterm a BOOLEAN EXPRESSION for a LOGIC GATE system that is a sum of products, such as $A \cdot B \cdot C + A \cdot D \cdot F + B \cdot C \cdot F$. Contrast MINTERM.

Maxwellian distribution a mathematical function that describes the distribution of electron energy within a semiconductor.

Maxwell, James Clark (1831–1879) Scottish physicist whose analysis of electric and magnetic fields showed that radio waves could exist and that they were of the same family of waves as light.

Maxwell's equations the equations of electromagnetic waves that link magnetic field strength (**H**), the electric displacement (**D**), the magnetic flux density (**B**) and the electric field strength (**E**). The solution of the equations takes the form of a wave whose velocity is dependent on the PERMEABILITY and PERMITTIVITY of the medium in which the wave travels.

MB or **Mbyte** see MEGABYTE.

MBB see MAKE BEFORE BREAK.

MBE molecular beam epitaxy: a form of VAPOUR PHASE EPITAXY.

Mbyte see MEGABYTE.

MD see MINI-DISC.

mdas rule or **My Dear Aunt Sally** the rule for remembering priority in arithmetic, which is multiplication, division, addition, subtraction.

M-derived filter a filter that has a reactive component in one arm and a RESONANT CIRCUIT in the other. See Fig. 73.

MDS see MINIMUM DISCERNIBLE SIGNAL.

Mealy machine a LOGIC circuit, usually for SEQUENTIAL LOGIC, in which the output(s) depend on the present state and also on present input(s). Contrast MOORE MACHINE.

mean holding time the average time in a telephone system during which calls use the system.

mean life or **mean time between failures (MTBF)** the average working life of a COMPONENT that can be repaired or replaced. This may be measured under working conditions, or calculated from ACCELERATED LIFE TESTS taken under abnormal conditions. See also MEAN TIME TO FAILURE.

mean square the average value of the sum of the squares of a set of numbers. See also ROOT-MEAN-SQUARE (sense 1).

mean time between failures (MTBF) see MEAN LIFE.

mean time to failure (MTTF) the average time to fail for a device that cannot be repaired.

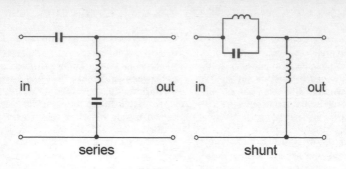

in   out   in   out

series   shunt

Fig. 73. **M-derived filter**

mean time to recovery a measure of how quickly a self-resetting device can be expected to return to service after (non-fatal) failure.

mean time to repair (MTTR) or **down time** the average time for which a device or system will be out of use between failure and repair.

mechanical hysteresis the principle of the snap-over action of a lever switch.

mechanical impedance see MOTIONAL IMPEDANCE.

mechanical latching a switch action that will hold a switch in position after it has been actuated electrically. See also LATCHING.

mechanical resonance a forced mechanical OSCILLATION at RESONANT FREQUENCY. Mechanical resonance can be a cause of failure of mechanical parts, but it can be turned to good use as in a pendulum or a tuning-fork. It is also responsible for resonant peaks in MOTIONAL IMPEDANCE, but this can be turned to advantage if a large amount of power needs to be converted to mechanical form at one particular frequency.

median filter a form of DIGITAL FILTER that uses a DELAY LINE to select and gate out the median data number (the middle term in a sorted sequence). A median filter is used mainly to remove IMPULSE NOISE from video signals.

medium frequency (MF) or **medium wave (MW)** the band that covers the

(approximate) FREQUENCY range of 300kHz to 3MHz, wavelengths of 10km to 1km.

medium scale integration the SCALE OF INTEGRATION in which the number of ACTIVE COMPONENTS on one chip is in the range 100 to 1000.

mega- prefix denoting one million, 10^6. Symbol: M.

megabits per second (Mb/s) a measure of rate of flow of data.

megabyte or **MB** a data unit of one million bytes, usually taken as 8 million bits.

megabytes per second (MB/s) a measure of the rate of flow of data.

megaflop or **Mflop** a rate of computer processing equal to one million floating-point (arithmetic) actions per second.

megahertz or **MHz** a unit of frequency equal to one million HERTZ.

mega instructions per second (MIPS) a measure of the rate of processing, see also MEGAFLOP.

megapixel camera a DIGITAL CAMERA whose CCD imaging device consists of a million or more units.

Megastream™ a British Telecom data line service that provides for communication at rates between 2 and 8 megabits per second, using interfacing equipment obtained from B.T. See also KILOSTREAM.

Megger™ an instrument for measuring INSULATING RESISTANCE. The original trade name denoted an instrument that combined a hand-wound high-voltage generator with a sensitive current meter. Modern versions use a DC INVERTER (sense 2) and an electrometer.

Meissner oscillator   a form of oscillator in which the tuned circuit is DC isolated from the amplifier portion and coupled inductively to it.

membrane keyboard   a form of KEYBOARD in which the contacts are made through metallized strips on plastic sheets. The term is also (incorrectly) used to mean keyboards that are covered by clear plastic sheeting to allow use in wet or dirty environments.

memory   a method of storing data in BINARY CODE, particularly for a computer. This applies to storage as current in one of a pair of transistors (STATIC RAM), charge in a capacitor (DYNAMIC RAM) or connections within an IC (MASKED ROM). Memory systems can also be constructed using magnetic effects, such as BUBBLE MEMORY, MAGNETIC CORE (sense 2), MAGNETIC DISK, and MAGNETIC TAPE.

The types of memory that depend on current or charge are generally VOLATILE, because the data is lost when power is switched off. Magnetic and masked ROM memories are nonvolatile, because the stored data remains in store until replaced by other data. See also PROM; ROM.

memory access time   the time that elapses between sending out the pulses that address the memory and receiving the data from the memory, now usually of the order of 30 ns (see NANOSECOND) or less.

memory backup capacitor   a high-value low-voltage electrolytic capacitor used to provide a temporary voltage supply to low-consumption equipment in the event of power failure. Values of around 1 farad at 3V are typical.

memory bank   a set of memory chips connected together so as to make a memory unit. Memory chips are usually organized so as to store one bit (sometimes 4 bits) per chip, so that for a 32 megabyte memory bank, a set of 8 4-megabyte chips would be used.

memory board or **memory card** or **memory strip**   a board or card added

to a computer to increase the total memory. See DUAL INLINE MEMORY MODULE; SINGLE INLINE MEMORY MODULE.

memory buffering   see BUFFER (sense 2).

memory cache   see CACHE.

memory card   see MEMORY BOARD.

memory cell   the unit of BIT memory, that is a small capacitor for a DYNAMIC RAM (DRAM) or a flip-flop circuit for a STATIC RAM.

memory chip   a single IC that contains a large number of memory units.

memory controller   a portion of a computer that determines how memory is used.

memory effect   a problem, particularly of NICKEL-CADMIUM rechargeable cells, in which recharging a cell before it becomes exhausted causes an apparent loss of capacity of the cell and the inability to discharge beyond the stage at which it has been recharged.

memory location   the binary number ADDRESS signal that is required to gain access to a set of memory units. This is usually written as a HEXADECIMAL number which is shorter and less likely to be miscopied than a binary number.

memory management unit (MMU)   a chip used to control data transfer between a RISC processor and the MEMORY.

memory-mapped screen   a system in which the position of each PIXEL in a screen display corresponds to an ADDRESS in memory, so that altering the data in that unit of memory will alter the colour and brightness of the pixel. See also LCD; PLASMA SCREEN.

memory strip   see MEMORY BOARD.

mercuric oxide cell   a cell, often of button size and shape, using a steel or nickel casing (ANODE) with a zinc CATHODE (sense 3) containing potassium hydroxide and zinc oxide mixture, and an ELECTROLYTE of potassium hydroxide and mercuric oxide.

mercury-arc rectifier or **mercury rectifier** an old method of RECTIFICATION using current flowing between electrodes in mercury vapour at low pressure. This method persisted mainly because for many decades it was the only way of handling high-voltage high-current rectification.

mercury cell a PRIMARY CELL with a very stable voltage, formerly used as a standard voltage source.

mercury lamp a GAS DISCHARGE TUBE using mercury vapour at low pressure whose light is mainly in the violet and ultra-violet region.

mercury tilt-switch a switch consisting of a curved glass tube with two contacts that can pass current when a drop of mercury provides a conducting path as the tube is tilted.

mercury-wetted contact a system often used to reduce contact resistance of a relay by using a mercury coating on each contact.

mesa transistor a form of silicon BIPOLAR JUNCTION TRANSISTOR construction. The BASE of the transistor is formed on a portion that is raised above the level of the COLLECTOR and EMITTER (sense 1), like the small flat-topped hill called a 'mesa' (Spanish: table).

mesh a NETWORK (sense 1) of CURRENT paths.

mesh current the CURRENT in a network MESH. This can be used to form equations of network action, using KIRCHOFF'S LAWS or NORTON'S THEOREM.

mesh-PDA tube a specialized form of POST-DEFLECTION ACCELERATION for INSTRUMENT TUBES. The DEFLECTION SENSITIVITY of an electrostatically deflected cathode-ray tube is very low if the accelerating voltage is high, of the order of 10kV or more. Modern oscilloscopes demand tubes that have very high deflection sensitivity. At the same time the trace must be bright so that high-speed traces are visible, and this demands large accelerating potentials. The mesh-PDA tube solves the dilemma by placing a wire mesh of high transparency between the end of the DEFLECTION PLATES and the FINAL ANODE. The mesh serves to separate the fields, so that the region of the deflection plates can use low velocity electrons, that are then accelerated after passing through the mesh.

mesochronous signal a DIGITAL signal whose CLOCK rate can vary within limits, with the average value constant.

mesosphere an intermediate region, either the lower mesosphere between 40 and 80 km above the Earth's surface, or the upper mesosphere between 400 and 1000 km.

message polynomial the POLYNOMIAL FORM of a digital WORD that is to be used as part of a message as distinct from GENERATOR POLYNOMIAL and PARITY CHECK POLYNOMIAL.

message switching or **store and forward** a method of improving the efficiency of transmission of digital messages by transmitting stored messages in sequence rather than allocating space for messages on arrival.

metal film a thin layer of metal, usually on an insulator, obtained by using a METALLIZING process.

metal film resistor a form of FILM RESISTOR that makes use of a thin metal film as its conductor.

metal fuse regrowth the re-establishment of a connection between blown points on a PROGRAMMABLE FUSE DEVICE, caused by the migration of a thin film of metal.

metal-glaze see CERMET.

metal insulator semiconductor FET (MISFET) a form of FET with a NEGATIVE RESISTANCE characteristic, used in microwave FREQUENCY MULTIPLIER circuits.

metal nitride oxide semiconductor (MNOS) a variation of MOS construction using a metal nitride layer and an oxide layer as insulator, along with dual-gate construction. The advantages are higher speed and lower power consumption.

metal oxide resistor a resistor that uses a metal oxide, usually tin oxide in the form of a film onto a ceramic substrate.

metal plate lens aerial (or antenna) a form of aerial that uses a set of parallel metal plates of different lengths arranged so that their outline has a lens shape, used to focus radiated power from a point source into a parallel beam.

metal rectifier a RECTIFIER that makes use of a metal-semiconductor contact. Copper-oxide and selenium rectifiers were used to a considerable extent at one time.

metal tape recording tape, usually for analogue RECORDING, using a coating of powdered pure iron as the magnetic medium.

metallized paper capacitor a form of PAPER CAPACITOR that makes use of a METALLIZING coating on the paper, rather than on the use of metal strips.

metallizing the process of coating a material with metal. This can be done chemically, by ELECTROPLATING (on metals), or by chemical reduction (on other surfaces). Another method is to evaporate the metal in a vacuum, as used for depositing thin films of aluminium. SPUTTERING is a third method in which the material to be coated is placed in a low-pressure gas in which a GAS DISCHARGE is operating with the metal that forms the coating material being used as one electrode. Sputtering is more suitable for depositing powdery films of metals. Combinations of methods can be used, so that it is fairly common to find an insulating material coated with a thin conducting film by sputtering, and then electroplated.

metal-oxide-semiconductor field effect transistor (MOSFET) see FIELD EFFECT TRANSISTOR.

metal-resistance thermometer a temperature SENSOR working on the principle that the resistance of a metal rises reasonably linearly with rising temperature. See TEMPERATURE COEFFICIENT.

metamerism the optical effect that allows any colour to be synthesized from three primary colours.

meteor burst communication or **meteor scatter communication** communications using frequencies above 100 MHz over long distances, typically up to 2000 km, using the IONIZATION produced by the (estimated) 75 million meteors that enter the upper atmosphere daily.

meteor scatter signal reflection and scattering from the ionized (see IONIZATION) trails left by meteors.

meter an analogue measuring instrument whose reading is usually in the form of a needle positioned on a scale.

meter errors the errors involved in using a meter, either inherent in the meter and its reading system, or caused by the alterations to the circuit caused by the resistance of the meter.

meter FSD the amount of current that will cause a meter to indicate full-scale, its maximum reading.

meter overload a condition in which the voltage or current applied to a meter is excessive and likely to cause meter failure.

meter-protection diode a DIODE used in pairs wired across the movement of an ANALOGUE METER. The principle is that the diodes form a high-resistance path for voltages up to and exceeding the normal voltage across the meter terminals. For a large overload voltage, however, one or both diodes will conduct, thus preventing damage to the meter. The protection diodes are particularly effective in preventing damage from TRANSIENT pulses.

meter ranges the different values of VOLTAGE and CURRENT corresponding to FULL SCALE DEFLECTION for each setting of the meter range switch.

meter resistance the INTERNAL RESISTANCE of a METER movement, including any internal SHUNT (sense 1) resistors.

meter RF damage damage to a meter caused by high RF currents that do not cause a meter indication but can overheat the meter circuits.

metre the basic SI unit of length. Symbol: m. Originally defined as a fraction of the diameter of the Earth, the length of the metre is now specified in terms of the number of wavelengths of light from a specified source.

metre-ampere a unit used to assess a ship's radio, based on the product of maximum height of the AERIAL (antenna) above sea level and the RMS drive current into the aerial.

metropolitan area network (MAN) a medium-range computer NETWORK (sense 2) system of diameter up to 50 km.

Metrosil™ a type of nonlinear RESISTOR, seldom used nowadays. The Metrosil has a very NONLINEAR current-voltage characteristic, with current proportional to about the fourth power of voltage. This made the device very useful as a protection against voltage surges, and it was also used as a crude form of high-voltage regulator. See also VARISTOR.

MF   see MEDIUM FREQUENCY.

MFLOPS   see MEGAFLOP.

MFM   see MODIFIED FREQUENCY MODULATION.

M-fold interpolator   a circuit that will replace missing samples (see DECIMATOR) in a stream in which M is the sample number. For example, if $M = 3$ then every third sample is transmitted, and the interpolator must replace 2 samples $(M - 1)$ at the receiver.

M fuse   the medium time-lag type of FUSE that will rupture in 30 ms on a tenfold overload.

MHz   see MEGAHERTZ.

MIC   see MICROWAVE INTEGRATED CIRCUIT.

mica   a natural INSULATOR, related to asbestos, that can be split into very thin sheets. The silver form is preferable to the ruby form for electronics use.

mica capacitor   a capacitor made by METALLIZING mica plates. Mica capacitors have low losses, low TEMPERATURE COEFFICIENTS and good stability of characteristics.

MICR   magnetic ink character recognition.

micro-   prefix denoting one millionth. Symbol: μ or mu.

microamp or **microampere**   a current unit, symbol μA, of one millionth of an ampere.

microcell   a small cell (see CELLULAR PHONE) with a typical diameter of 1 km, used in an urban area.

microcontroller   a single IC consisting of a MICROPROCESSOR, memory and associated functions for controlling a system with the minimum of interfacing.

microelectronics   the design and construction of electronic devices using INTEGRATED CIRCUITs.

microfarad   the practical unit of CAPACITANCE, one millionth of a FARAD. Symbol: μF.

micron   one-millionth of a metre, i.e. a micrometre.

microphone or **mike**   a sound to electrical wave TRANSDUCER. Many types of microphone have been devised, starting

with the carbon-granule type that was used in early telephones. Most modern types are ELECTRODYNAMIC. CAPACITOR MICROPHONEs, which once seemed to be obsolescent, were revived when ELECTRETs became available commercially.

The main features of a microphone that might affect choice are sensitivity, directionality, size, quality and price. The sensitivity is measured in terms of peak-to-peak output for a given sound pressure wave, and is usually very low, particularly when compared to the human ear. Many microphone types are directional, and the way in which a microphone is housed can enhance the main lobe of sensitivity. Size varies considerably, but ribbon microphones tend to be larger than the other types.

The highest quality is obtained from ribbon microphones, mainly because the MECHANICAL RESONANCEs can be at frequencies well above the audio range. As often happens, ribbon microphones are generally the most expensive, and capacitor microphones the cheapest. The enclosure in which the microphone is housed is at least as significant acoustically as the construction of the microphone itself. See MOVING-COIL MICROPHONE; MOVING-IRON MICROPHONE; RIBBON MICROPHONE.

microphone transformer   a MATCHING TRANSFORMER used to connect a low-impedance microphone such as a moving-coil type, to an amplifier input.

microphonic effects   see MICROPHONY.

microphony or **microphonic effects**   an unwanted electrical signal generated in response to sound waves. Some electronic components, particularly plates of air-spaced variable capacitors, can vibrate when struck by sound waves, and cause MODULATION of electrical signals. THERMIONIC VALVEs were particularly prone to this problem, which is seldom encountered in receivers or studio equipment nowadays.

microprocessor   a VLSI integrated circuit that carries out computing actions. The microprocessor is an assembly of interconnected REGISTERS and GATES (sense 2) whose connections are PROGRAMMABLE. A master CLOCK determines the speed of execution, and the program is in the form of number codes stored in consecutive locations in memory. The microprocessor can then, given the correct starting location in memory, load in the instruction codes one by one and execute them. The processes that can be carried out include simple arithmetic (addition and subtraction of small numbers), LOGIC actions such as AND GATE, OR GATE, XOR GATE and NOT, and SHIFTING and ROTATION. All the operations of a computer are obtained from these few logic actions by suitable programming.

microprocessor accumulator see ACCUMULATOR (sense 1).

microprocessor fetch-execute cycle see FETCH-EXECUTE CYCLE.

microprocessor interrupt see INTERRUPT.

microprocessor interrupt service routine see INTERRUPT.

microprocessor program counter see PROGRAM COUNTER.

microprogram the instructions that are built into a MICROPROCESSOR by the manufacturer. These instructions allow the microprocessor to carry out only the fixed set of actions under external program instruction that are described in the manufacturer's specification.

microsecond (μs) a unit of time equal to one millionth of a second.

microstrip a form of TRANSMISSION LINE consisting of a metal ribbon that acts as a ground plane, separated by a ribbon of insulator from a narrower ribbon of conductor, the signal conductor. The CHARACTERISTIC IMPEDANCE depends on the width, and is typically between 10 and 50 ohms.

microswitch a switch that needs a very small actuating effort over a short distance, used to detect small movements or to mark an end point of movement. For example, a microswitch is used to control the light in a refrigerator.

microwave the range of wavelengths that are from approximately 135cm down to a fraction of a millimetre. These cannot

easily be generated or amplified by the conventional devices that are used for lower frequencies, and are transmitted more readily through a WAVEGUIDE than along an open line.

microwave band frequencies in the range 0.2 GHz to 47 GHz, separated into sub-bands and indicated by letters, so that, for example, X-band covers 6 GHz to 11.5 GHz. There are different letter ranges for US and European use, but the band frequencies are broadly similar (see Table 2).

microwave beam fence a form of invisible security fencing using MICROWAVE beams arranged to sound an alarm if a beam is broken.

microwave cooker or **microwave oven** a cooker in which food is the target of a microwave beam from a MAGNETRON. The frequency is 2.45GHz, because this corresponds to a resonance of the hydrogen atoms in water. Any water present in food will therefore be rapidly heated internally. Objects with a very low water content are not heated. Metal objects must not be present because they can damage the magnetron by reflecting power back into the system.

microwave detector 1. a security system that operates by 'lighting' an area with a pattern of microwaves and detecting any change in the pattern caused by an intruder. 2. a car-contained microwave aerial and amplifier unit for detecting DOPPLER RADAR signals sent out by a speed checking unit.

microwave dish aerial or **microwave dish** see DISH.

microwave generator a DEVICE, vacuum or semiconductor, that is used as an OSCILLATOR at MICROWAVE frequencies. This includes the CARCINOTRON, GUNN DEVICE, JOSEPHSON JUNCTION, KLYSTRON and MAGNETRON.

microwave integrated circuit (MIC) the use of metal conductors deposited on an insulator to perform the action of INDUCTORS, CAPACITORS, FILTERS or TRANSFORMERS for MICROWAVE signals.

microwave integrated structure a planar form of transmission line for MICROWAVES, resembling a PRINTED CIRCUIT BOARD. Typical SUBSTRATES include alumina, sapphire or quartz, along with synthetic materials, and the metallic conductors are formed from copper or gold on chromium. See also FINLINE; IMAGE LINE; INVERTED MICROSTRIP; SLOT LINE; SUSPENDED STRIP LINE.

microwave tube any vacuum thermionic microwave device, including the KLYSTRON, MAGNETRON, and TRAVELLING-WAVE TUBE.

midband gain or **mid-range gain** or **mid-band response** the value of GAIN for an AMPLIFIER taken at a frequency that is in the middle of the band between the 3DB POINTS.

middle-side (M-S) arrangement a method of microphone placement for STEREO recording using one OMNIDIRECTIONAL MICROPHONE to provide an (L + R) signal and a BI-DIRECTIONAL MICROPHONE mounted at right angles to provide an (L − R) signal.

MIDI see MUSICAL INSTRUMENT DIGITAL INTERFACE.

MIDI interface the 15-pin D-connector used on a computer to connect MIDI equipment.

MIDI layering see LAYERING.

MIDI time code a timing system used in MIDI signals to ensure SYNCHRONIZATION of instruments or matching sound to video.

mid-point bias the amount of BIAS that will set an AMPLIFIER to conditions at the middle of its LOAD LINE.

Mie scattering losses in a FIBRE OPTICS line due to variations in reflection or flattening of the fibre over a distance comparable to the wavelength of the light. Contrast RAYLEIGH SCATTERING.

mike see MICROPHONE.

mil a unit of length equal to one thousandth of an inch, about 0.0254mm.

Miller code or **delay modulation** a form of code used for recording DIGITAL DATA on magnetic media. A logic 1 is represented by a TRANSITION in either direction at the centre point of the logic level, and a 0 by no transition, though two zeros in sequence are represented by a transition timed at the end of the first zero. One disadvantage of the system is that a DC component is produced when an even number of 1s occurs between two 0s. A variation is Miller[2] code which omits a level 1 transition when an even number of logic 1 bits occurs between two 0 bits.

Miller effect the effect of NEGATIVE FEEDBACK from output to input of an amplifying device through stray or internal CAPACITANCE. The capacitance is the total of inter-electrode capacitance and stray capacitance. For inverting amplifiers, the Miller effect makes this capacitance value appear to be multiplied by the voltage gain.

Miller integrator a wide-range INTEGRATOR circuit that depends for its action on a CAPACITANCE connected between the input and the output of an INVERTING AMPLIFIER. See Fig. 74.

Miller oscillator an OSCILLATOR circuit that uses the drain-gate capacitance of a MOSFET, amplified by MILLER EFFECT, to provide POSITIVE FEEDBACK.

Miller's theorem the representation of a CAPACITOR in a NEGATIVE FEEDBACK loop as the equivalent input or output capacitance.

Miller timebase a TIMEBASE circuit that consists of a square-wave generator combined with a MILLER INTEGRATOR.

milli- prefix denoting one thousandth, 10^{-3}. Symbol: m.

milliamp unit of current, equal to one thousandth of an ampere. Symbol: mA.

millimetres of mercury an old unit of pressure, still used for barometers, in terms of the pressure needed to maintain a column of mercury.

millimetric waves or **millimetre waves** the wavelengths in the range 1mm to 9mm.

millions of instructions per second (MIPS) a fairly simple measure of computing speed. See also MEGAFLOP.

millisecond a time unit equal to one thousandth of a second.

millivoltmeter a sensitive form of AC voltmeter intended for measuring the AMPLITUDE of small AUDIO signals for servicing purposes.

MIL specification a specification drawn up for equipment that is to be used by (US) armed forces, either as original equipment or as spares.

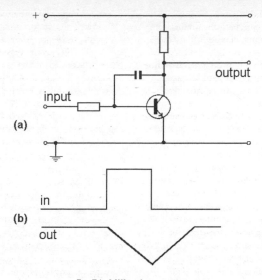

Fig. 74. **Miller integrator**

miniature circuit breakers (MCBs)
a replacement for FUSES in electrical
distribution boards, providing easier
resetting and also the facility to detect
earth leakage if required.

minicomputer   formerly an intermediate
stage between the mainframe and the
microcomputer that makes use of the
electronics technology of the micro, but
has memory capacity and speed that takes
it closer to the mainframe in capability.
A mini will consist of several cabinets
of equipment, but these will not take up
nearly so much space, nor require the
elaborate cooling that is needed by a
mainframe. Fast-acting SEMICONDUCTOR
memory will be used as the main store,
and several HARD DRIVES as the backing
store. The keyboard and video monitor
units will generally be remote from the
main processor unit, often connected by
serial links. There is often provision for
multi-user connections and NETWORK
(sense 2) use. The distinction between
minicomputer and microcomputer is
rapidly disappearing.

Mini disc™   a Sony designed RECORDING
system using 3.5-inch discs recorded in the
same way as a CD, with the capability of
using re-writable discs also. Audio input is
digitized and compressed using ADAPTIVE
TRANSFORM ACOUSTIC CODING (ADTRAC),
a system essentially similar to MUSICAM.

mini-DVD   a DVD disc of small diameter
designed to be recorded by a CAMCORDER
and intended to be replayed on later
designs of DVD player.

minimization   the application of LOGIC
theory to a LOGIC GATE circuit. Minimization
applies theory to find redundant gates, and
often allows a logic action to be carried out
in a much simpler form. See KARNAUGH MAP.

MiniMoog™   a simple music SYNTHESIZER
system based on the principles laid down
by Dr. Robert Moog (b. 1934).

minimum (frequency) shift keying   a form
of FREQUENCY SHIFT KEYING that minimizes
PHASE discontinuities by changing the
frequency at the point where the signal
amplitude is momentarily zero (the
crossing point).

minimum discernible signal   the smallest
amplitude of received signal that can
provide a usable message output.

minimum distance decoding   see
MAXIMUM LIKELIHOOD DECODING.

minimum radial distance a RADAR system measurement that determines whether targets on the same bearing can be distinguished.

mini tower case a vertical main case for a small computer, with a restricted number of DRIVE BAYS and a small base area (*desk footprint*).

minority carrier the CARRIER (sense 2), electron or hole, in a SEMICONDUCTOR that carries less than 50% of the current. Contrast MAJORITY CARRIER.

minterm a BOOLEAN EXPRESSION for a LOGIC GATE system that consists of the product of sums, such as $(A+B+C)\cdot(A+D+E)\cdot(B+C+E)$.

MIPS see MEGA INSTRUCTIONS PER SECOND.

mirror amplifier an amplifier used to indicate mistracking in the tracking system for replaying a CD.

MISFET see METAL INSULATOR SEMICONDUCTOR FET.

mismatch the inequality of OUTPUT IMPEDANCE and LOAD IMPEDANCE. Mismatch can cause loss of power, and REFLECTION along a line.

mismatching units an audio problem arising where units of a system have been bought from different manufacturers and though compatible on paper are not so in practice.

mission critical (of a component or software) completely essential to operation.

mistracking failure to locate the correct track on a CD, usually caused by failure of the PHOTODETECTORS that sense reflections from tracks.

mixer or **mixer stage** the frequency changer stage of a SUPERHETERODYNE RECEIVER. The mixer has two inputs, one at received signal frequency, which is modulated, and one from the local oscillator. The result of mixing is a signal at INTERMEDIATE FREQUENCY that carries the original modulation.

mixer amplifier an adder for ANALOGUE signals, formed usually from an OPERATIONAL AMPLIFIER with NEGATIVE FEEDBACK and multiple inputs to the – terminal. See Fig. 75.

mixer, diode ring see DIODE RING MIXER.

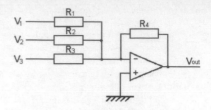

Fig. 75. **mixer amplifier**

mixer noise noise generated in the MIXER stage of a SUPERHETERODYNE receiver, usually the predominant internal noise source affecting reception.

mixer stage see MIXER.

M-JPEG see MOTION JPEG.

MKS system a system of units used in modern electronics theory, based on the metre, second and kilogram as fundamental mechanical units, supplemented by the ampere for electrical work and the candela for light measurement. Later developed into the SI UNIT system.

MMDS see MULTIPOINT MICROWAVE DISTRIBUTION SYSTEM.

MMIC see MONOLITHIC MICROWAVE INTEGRATED CIRCUIT.

MMU see MEMORY MANAGEMENT UNIT.

mnemonics a set of simple words that are used to write MACHINE CODE programs for a MICROPROCESSOR. The term derives ultimately from the Greek for 'to remember', and the words are intended to remind the user of the action that is required.

MNOS see METAL NITRIDE OXIDE SEMICONDUCTOR.

mobile equipment ID or **MEID** the code that identifies an individual call phone (see CELLULAR PHONE).

mobile phone see CELLULAR PHONE.

mobility, carrier see CARRIER MOBILITY.

mode I. the frequency and waveform of a resonating system. **2.** the classification of a wave in terms of its polarization (see POLARIZED, sense 1). The three modes are TEM wave, TE wave and TM wave.

mode switch a VIDEO CASSETTE RECORDER system used to check that the THREADING of a tape is complete so that the CAPSTAN drive can be enabled.

modem   *acronym for* MOdulator-
DEModulator, a device used to convert
digital signals into a tone form suitable for
long-distance transmission, and to reconvert
received tone signals into digital form.

The modem is widely used for linking
computers over telephone lines and via
radio links (where this is permitted). The
modulator section translates the data bits
of 0 and 1 into phase-modulated tone
signals at different frequencies. The data
is then transmitted as a set of tones, using
rates of transmission that are slow by
computing standards. At the receiving
end, the demodulator converts the
received tones into data signals again.
See also SERIAL TRANSMISSION.

modem data compression   the use of
NON-LOSSY COMPRESSION, notably the
LEMPEL/ZIF ALGORITHM, for modem data
so as to maximize the signal rate.

**modified alternate mark inversion code
(MAMI)**   a variation of the ALTERNATE
MARK INVERSION CODE.

modified chemical vapour deposition
a method of manufacturing FIBRE OPTICS
threads by depositing the glass from a
vapour inside a silicon tube.

modified frequency modulation (MFM)
a well-established method of coding digital
signals into magnetic signals that can be
recorded on a HARD DRIVE or FLOPPY DISK.

modified Huffman code   a variation of
HUFFMAN CODE used for FACSIMILE links.

modified refraction index   a correction
factor for the REFRACTIVE INDEX of air that
takes the effect of the curvature of the
Earth into account.

MO drive   see MAGNETO-OPTICAL DRIVE.

modulation   the alteration of a CARRIER
(sense 1) wave so that it bears
information. The most elementary form of
modulation (often regarded as not being a
form of modulation at all) is Morse code,
in which the carrier is switched on and
off. For carrying analogue audio or video
signals, AMPLITUDE MODULATION or
FREQUENCY MODULATION is used. Any of
these modulation methods will produce a
signal that consists of a carrier and a set of
SIDEBANDS, in which the sidebands carry

the information. The most common forms
of modulation are wasteful of transmitted
energy, because only a fraction of the total
radiated power is in the form of the
sidebands that carry the information.

Several systems exist that suppress one
sideband and/or the carrier in order to
use the transmitter power more
effectively. These SINGLE SIDEBAND systems
require special MODULATION circuits. The
carrier frequency must be considerably
higher than the highest frequency that
will be modulated on to it. For MICROWAVE
transmissions, it is generally easier to
pulse the carrier on and off, and modulate
the pulsing system. At the receiver,
various types of demodulator are needed
to recover the form of the original signal.

Digital signal transmission makes use of
several specialized systems of modulation
of one or more carriers, see CODED
ORTHOGONAL FREQUENCY DIVISION MULTIPLEX.

modulation, COFDM   see CODED
ORTHOGONAL FREQUENCY DIVISION MULTIPLEX.

modulation control   a feature of Dolby SR™
analogue tape NOISE REDUCTION CIRCUITRY
that provides more effective noise
reduction as compared to simpler systems.

modulation efficiency systems   systems of
MODULATION that make the most efficient
use of transmitter power. See DIGITAL
MODULATION; DOHERTY MODULATION;
DYNAMIC AMPLITUDE MODULATION;
DYNAMIC CARRIER LEVEL; ENVELOPE
ELIMINATION AND RESTORATION; PULSAM
SYSTEM; PULSE DURATION MODULATION;
PULSE STEP MODULATION.

modulation factor   see DEPTH OF
MODULATION.

modulation Index   a figure used in
calculating BANDWIDTH for frequency-
modulated signals (see FREQUENCY
MODULATION). The modulation index is
obtained by dividing the maximum
frequency change of the CARRIER (sense 1)
by the maximum frequency of the
modulated signal. The modulation index
should be a small fraction.

modulation noise or **bias noise**   a form
of analogue TAPE NOISE caused by using a
TAPE BIAS signal that is not a pure sine wave.

modulation, QAM see QAM.

modulator any CIRCUIT that modulates a CARRIER (sense 1) or otherwise converts a signal into a form suitable for transmission.

modulator, IQ see I-Q MODULATOR.

modulo-n counter a COUNTER made from FLIP-FLOP units whose count is to the number n-1, where n is any integer. For example, a modulo-9 counter will count 0 to 8 and then reset.

Moebius counter see JOHNSON COUNTER.

moiré pattern an image formed by light passing through two or more grids. Moiré patterns are a problem in TV pictures, because of the use of scanning in lines, and the vertical bar structure of the APERTURE GRILLE. The effect is that pictures that contain horizontal or vertical stripes appear to contain elaborate moving patterns, often coloured. These moiré patterns are sometimes referred to by camera operators as *strobing*.

molecular beam epitaxy (MBE) see VAPOUR PHASE EPITAXY.

molecule the smallest possible unit of a compound, composed of a set of linked atoms.

monaural see MONOPHONIC.

monitor a VISUAL DISPLAY UNIT based on a CATHODE-RAY TUBE or LCD screen and used along with a computer or for checking the quality of studio TV pictures.

monochromatic radiation radiation consisting of one single frequency, or a very small range of frequencies. An unmodulated CARRIER (sense 1) that is a perfect SINE WAVE is a monochromatic radiation.

monochrome (of an image) of one colour, meaning usually black and white.

monochrome monitor a MONITOR, often for CCTV use, that displays only monochrome pictures.

mono-crystalline (of a material) consisting of a single crystal, used of a semiconductor material on which transistors will be formed.

monolithic circuit a CIRCUIT made in one piece, i.e. an INTEGRATED CIRCUIT that is fabricated from a single piece (see CHIP, sense 1) of silicon.

monolithic microwave integrated circuit (MMIC) a MICROWAVE INTEGRATED CIRCUIT fabricated on GALLIUM ARSENIDE and including ACTIVE COMPONENTS such as DIODES and TRANSISTORS in addition to PASSIVE COMPONENTS, all working at frequencies up to 30 GHz.

monomode propagation the use of a glass FIBRE OPTIC CABLE with a very small diameter core so that reflections are reduced and paths as long as 30 km can be used without the need for a REPEATER amplifier.

monomode step index fibre a form of OPTICAL FIBRE construction using an inner core of less than 10 μm diameter and an outer sheath of more than 100 μm diameter, used for wide bandwidth long-haul transmissions.

monophonic or **monaural** or **mono** (of a sound reproducing system) using one sound channel only. Compare STEREOPHONIC.

monopole aerial or **whip aerial** the upper half of a DIPOLE AERIAL, often made physically shorter than a quarter wave by connecting a LOADING COIL in series with the lower part of the aerial.

monopulse RADAR a form of RADAR that makes use of a single PULSE repeated randomly, so making detection less likely.

monoscope an obsolete form of TV SIGNAL GENERATOR tube that is used to provide a pattern such as a test chart. Simple dot and bar patterns can be generated by signal generators, but the monoscope used camera-tube techniques to generate a more elaborate picture signal. Monoscopes have been replaced by the use of computer-generated test patterns.

monostable or **monostable multivibrator** or **one-shot** or **single-shot** a type of MULTIVIBRATOR with one stable state. A TRIGGER pulse is used to switch the monostable to its unstable state, and, after a short time, the circuit switches back to its original state. The time is determined by a capacitor-resistor TIME CONSTANT. The circuit is used to generate a pulse of known width from a trigger pulse. See Fig. 76.

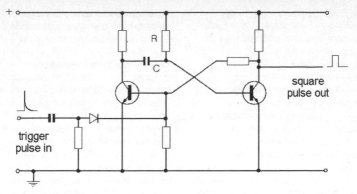

Fig. 76. **monostable**

monostatic RADAR   a radar system, very
commonly used, that employs the same
AERIAL (antenna) for both transmitting and
receiving, along with ATR and TR cells
(see ANTI-TRANSMIT/RECEIVE SWITCH;
TRANSMIT/RECEIVE SWITCH).

Moog, Dr. Robert   (b. 1934) inventor in
1964 of the modern music SYNTHESIZER
using devices such as VOLTAGE-
CONTROLLED OSCILLATOR, VOLTAGE-
CONTROLLED AMPLIFIER and VOLTAGE-
CONTROLLED FILTER.

Moore machine   a logic circuit, usually a
combinational circuit, in which the output
state of a unit depends solely and entirely
on the present state of the unit.

Moore's law   the empirical law due to
Dr. Gordon Moore (Intel) that the number
of TRANSISTORS that can be fabricated on a
given area of SILICON doubles each year.

morphing   a gradual change of an image
into another image by altering each pixel
in an image to the average value of that
PIXEL and the corresponding pixel in the
final image. See also WARPING.

Morse code   an old-established system
of communication. Morse code uses two
signals, the short dot and the long dash,
to code letters of the alphabet and digits.
Morse can be used for communication
along very long lines, and for radio
signalling by switching a CARRIER (sense 1)
on and off. The advantage of Morse is that
it makes very efficient use of a low-power

carrier and is highly immune to noise.
It is nowadays mainly used for emergency
systems only, but its influence on radio
practice still lingers on in the requirement
for radio amateurs to take a test in Morse.

Morse demodulator   a method of making
the CARRIER (sense 1) switching of a Morse
signal audible, see BEAT-FREQUENCY
OSCILLATOR.

MOS   acronym for Metal-Oxide-
Semiconductor, see FIELD-EFFECT TRANSISTOR.

mosaic   a set of insulated conducting dots
on an insulating (see INSULATOR) surface.
The mosaic was a feature of early types of
TV camera tubes in which the dots acted
as CAPACITORS, storing CHARGE quantities
that formed a charge image corresponding
to the light image.

MOS capacitor   a metal-oxide-
semiconductor capacitor formed on a chip
by using doped (see DOPING) silicon for
plates and silicon oxide as the INSULATOR.
MOS capacitors are the basis of CHARGE-
COUPLED DEVICES and of BUCKET-BRIGADE
and DYNAMIC RAM devices.

MOSFET   see FIELD-EFFECT TRANSISTOR.

MOS IC   an INTEGRATED CIRCUIT that is
constructed using MOSFETs as the active
components. See FIELD-EFFECT TRANSISTOR.

MOS transistor   see FIELD-EFFECT TRANSISTOR.

most significant bit (MSB)   the BIT in a
BYTE or WORD that represents the highest
power of two, conventionally the bit at
the left hand side. For example, in the

binary number 1101, the left-hand 1 represents 2^3, denary 8, and is the most significant bit of this half-byte or *nibble*.

most significant byte (MSB) the BYTE in a set of bytes that represents the lowest part of a multi-byte binary number, conventionally the byte at the left-hand side.

motherboard or **mainboard** a baseboard for a COMPUTER circuit used in small computers. The main parts of the computer are on a single board, called the 'motherboard'. This board is fitted with sets of sockets or slots, each of which can connect to another (extension) board. All the computer signals are made available at each socket, so that the facilities of the computer can be greatly extended by plugging in extension boards.

The system is often referred to as having open architecture, in the sense that the computer can be extended by using boards made by suppliers other than the original manufacturer. Computers of this design type, such as the IBM PC, can have very long working lives because it is usually possible to upgrade the design rather than replace the whole machine.

motion compensation the relocation of large parts of a DIGITAL picture, typically when a camera has been panned across a scene, achieved by a few codes as distinct from the effort of relocating each pixel separately.

motion detector any device that will detect a moving object in a confined area.

motion estimation a method of predicting the position of PIXELS in a set (*block*) as the result of motion, so reducing the amount of data that needs to be provided to update a FRAME (sense 1) of a digital video.

motion JPEG (MJPEG) the coding of TV pictures by applying JPEG coding to each frame. This does not apply enough compression (see BIT REDUCTION) for transmitted DIGITAL TELEVISION, but is suitable for studio work. Motion JPEG compression is used by a TV CAPTURE CARD in a computer to produce a compressed AVI file from an analogue source such as a CAMCORDER.

motion picture expert group (MPEG) a committee that has set standards for digital compression of video and sound information.

motion prediction the use of computation based on existing data to predict the path for a moving object in a digital picture, so that very little change is needed to place the PIXELS correctly.

motion vector see DISPLACEMENT VECTOR.

motional impedance or **mechanical impedance** a form of IMPEDANCE found in an electro-mechanical TRANSDUCER. A transducer such as a LOUDSPEAKER converts electrical signals into mechanical motion. The current that a signal of constant voltage can pass will be greatest if mechanical motion is prevented, least if the motion is completely unimpeded. This means that the electrical impedance will also vary with the resistance to mechanical motion, particularly if there is mechanical resonance. Compare BLOCKED IMPEDANCE.

motional induction the induction of an EMF by moving a magnet relative to a conductor. Contrast TRANSFORMER INDUCTION.

motor a device that converts electrical energy into motion. Most motors convert to rotation, but linear motors convert AC energy directly into linear motion. See also INDUCTION MOTOR; SYNCHRONOUS MOTOR; UNIVERSAL MOTOR.

motorboating a form of PARASITIC OSCILLATION at low frequencies. Motorboating in audio amplifiers produces a noise like a motorboat engine, hence the term. The cause is usually BREAKDOWN of a DECOUPLING capacitor, or sometimes ACOUSTIC FEEDBACK.

motorized dish a completely moveable SATELLITE DISH that can scan all available satellites, using a motor drive under computer control.

motor unit or **drive unit** the electro-mechanical drive unit of a LOUDSPEAKER, usually a moving-coil device, as distinct from the DIAPHRAGM.

MOTT diode a diode using a thick GALLIUM ARSENIDE SUBSTRATE, used as a MIXER for MICROWAVE frequencies up to 110 GHz.

mountain edge scattering   see KNIFE EDGE REFRACTION.

mountain hopping   the use of HF signals directed almost vertically so as to produce a signal on the other side of a mountain.

mouse   the small trolley that is used along with the computer. Movement of the mouse will move a pointer on the SCREEN, allowing selection by pointing and then clicking a button on the mouse.

mouth size   the dimensions of the output area of a horn, particularly as applied to a HORN LOUDSPEAKER.

movement, damping   the use of a short circuit across the terminals of a sensitive meter to create ELECTROMAGNETIC DAMPING that will prevent excessive movement of the meter coil.

moving-coil   see MOVING-COIL PRINCIPLE.

moving-coil cartridge   a form of TRANSDUCER for VINYL gramophone records that uses a coil vibrated by the movement of the stylus in the field of a fixed magnet. The OUTPUT IMPEDANCE is very low, and the signal amplitude is also low, but distortion is also minimal.

moving-coil head amplifier   a LOW-NOISE AMPLIFIER unit placed close to a MOVING-COIL CARTRIDGE to increase the signal amplitude.

moving-coil headphones   high-quality headphones that use a moving-coil and DIAPHRAGM assembly, like a miniature loudspeaker, for each ear.

moving-coil loudspeaker   a loudspeaker that uses the MOVING COIL PRINCIPLE, with the coil mechanically connected to the cone of the loudspeaker to move air when the coil is actuated.

moving-coil meter   the basic DIRECT CURRENT analogue measuring movement. A coil, attached to an indicating needle, is suspended from springs or from a taut fibre in the field of a permanent magnet. The shape of the field is radial over a large part of its area, because of the presence of a cylindrical magnetic core. Current flowing through the coil will cause torque that rotates the coil against the restoring torque of the springs or suspension. The angle of rotation is proportional to the current through the coil over a wide range of angle. The current range can be extended by using shunts, voltage ranges can be read using series resistors, and ALTERNATING CURRENT can be measured by adding a RECTIFIER bridge.

moving-coil microphone   a MICROPHONE in which the sound waves affect a moving COIL. The sound waves strike a DIAPHRAGM to which the coil is attached. The vibration of the coil then generates a signal voltage because the coil is placed.

in the field of a permanent magnet.

moving-coil pickup   see MOVING-COIL CARTRIDGE.

moving-coil principle   the interaction between a MAGNETIC FIELD and a coil that can be moved in the field. This can operate in either direction, so that mechanical movement of the coil in the magnetic field will generate an EMF, and passing a current though the coil will cause the coil to move.

moving-iron   see MOVING-IRON PRINCIPLE.

moving-iron headphone   a form of headphone using a soft iron DIAPHRAGM between the poles of an electromagnet that is energized by the audio signals. This type of headphone, for a long time used on telephones, is of low quality, but has a high amplitude sound output and fairly high impedance.

moving-iron meter   an ANALOGUE METER that makes use of the movement of a SOFT MAGNETIC MATERIAL. The magnetic material, called the ARMATURE, usually forms part of a MAGNETIC FLUX path in a soft MAGNETIC core, and is suspended from springs and attached to an indicating needle. A coil is wound around the magnetic core, and current in this coil will cause flux. The flux will cause a force to act on the armature, pulling it into line with the flux. This force is opposed by the spring suspension, so that the angle of the turning of the armature is related to the amount of current. The instrument is non-linear unless the armature is suitably shaped. The advantage of a moving-iron instrument is that it measures true RMS values of signals whose frequencies are within its range. The instrument cannot be used for high-frequency signals because of the high inductance of the coil. See also HOT-WIRE INSTRUMENT; MOVING-COIL METER.

moving-iron microphone a MICROPHONE that uses the MOVING-IRON PRINCIPLE. The vibrations of a DIAPHRAGM affect a soft magnetic ARMATURE that is placed in a MAGNETIC FLUX gap of a permanent magnet. A coil wound round the magnet body converts variations of flux into signals.

moving-iron pickup a very popular form of gramophone pickup at one time, using the vibration of a stylus to move an ARMATURE that is part of a MAGNETIC FLUX circuit for a permanent magnet. A coil wound around the magnet has a signal induced by the flux variations. The output is reasonably large, a few millivolts, and the IMPEDANCE low enough to avoid interference problems. The LINEARITY depends greatly on the design of the magnetic circuit.

moving-iron principle the interaction between MAGNETIC FLUX and a coil of wire in which the movement of a piece of SOFT magnetic material (such as iron) in the flux field causes a change in the flux that induces a voltage in the coil.

moving magnet cartridge or **variable reluctance cartridge** a form of TRANSDUCER for VINYL gramophone records that uses a fixed coil and a magnet vibrated by the movement of the stylus. The OUTPUT IMPEDANCE is fairly high, as is signal amplitude.

moving-target indicator (MTI) a form of RADAR using a PHASE SENSITIVE DETECTOR that allows moving targets to be distinguished from fixed targets. Modern MTI systems use computer techniques to carry out the cancellation and display. See also CANCELLATION CIRCUIT.

MP3 a form of MPEG coding for sound and music, allowing a large amount of compression (see BIT REDUCTION), typically of the order of 10:1 or more, so that music can be transmitted over Internet links, and CDs can be made that will play for ten hours or more.

MPEG see MOVING PICTURE EXPERTS GROUP.

MPEG-IV a proposed system for DIGITAL TELEVISION transmission based on the concept, originally developed for computing, of *object-oriented* software.

MPEG layer I audio or **PASC** a coding system for DIGITAL AUDIO in which the incoming digital signal is divided into 32 sub-bands, each of which is QUANTIZED at 1/32 of the original sampling rate, and each is then COMPRESSED.

MPEG layer II audio coding or **MUSICAM** a digital audio coding system that uses larger groups of data than MPEG LAYER I AUDIO, and achieves higher compression, used in digital audio broadcasting The name is an acronym of **M**asking pattern-adapted **U**niversal **S**ub-band **I**ntegrated **C**oding **a**nd **M**ultiplexing.

MPEG layer III audio or **mp3** a very highly COMPRESSED coding system for DIGITAL AUDIO used for transmitting sound by way of the INTERNET, and for making ultra-long playing (10 hours or more) CDs.

MPEG-1 the older MPEG compression system for video signals that operates at 1.2 Mb/s, the same as the CD-ROM data rate. This allows CD-R or CD-RW discs to be used to store video which, while not of BROADCAST STANDARD, is adequate for camcorder recordings. See also VIDEO COMPACT DISC.

MPEG sound see MPEG LAYER II AUDIO CODING.

MPEG-2 the more advanced MPEG specification used for DIGITAL TELEVISION broadcast pictures. This uses coded FRAMES (sense 1) in sets of twelve, of which one, see I-FRAME, contains a complete set of picture bits, and the others (see B-FRAME, P-FRAME) contain block-matched or predicted information. See also GROUP OF PICTURES.

MPEG-2 packet the set of 204 bytes containing 184 bytes of data for a video signal, constituting, with header, sync and data correction bytes, a unit of MPEG-2 broadcast signal.

MPEG video decoder the most complex portion of a DIGITAL TELEVISION receiver, carrying out the actions of expanding the

COMPRESSED VIDEO, reversing the DISCRETE COSINE TRANSFORM, interpolating (see INTERPOLATION) missing data, and ERROR CORRECTION.

MR magnetoresistor, see MAGNETORESISTANCE.

MRAM magnetic random access memory.

msb see MOST SIGNIFICANT BIT.

MSB see MOST SIGNIFICANT BYTE.

MS43 code a form of 4-BINARY TO 3-TERNARY code (see 4B3T) with a better spectral frequency distribution.

MSI see MEDIUM SCALE INTEGRATION.

MSK or MFSK see MINIMUM FREQUENCY SHIFT KEYING.

MSSWF see MAGNETOSTATIC SURFACE WAVE FILTER.

MTBF mean time between failures: see MEAN LIFE.

MTI see MOVING-TARGET INDICATOR.

MTSO mobile telephone switching office.

MTTF see MEAN TIME TO FAILURE.

MTTR see MEAN TIME TO REPAIR.

MUF see MAXIMUM USABLE FREQUENCY.

muffled sound a problem on audio or video tape players caused usually by a build-up of dirt on the REPLAY HEAD.

mu-law see POTENTIOMETER LAW.

multichannel audio the use of more than a single channel of sound signal to loudspeakers. Conventional stereo systems use two channels, but systems designed to produce cinema sound effects use at least four channels. See also DISCRETE 5.1 AUDIO.

multi-chip module an IC mounting technique in which the bare IC has a set of contact pads that press against corresponding mounting pads on a silicon or ceramic substrate.

MultiCrypt a SCRAMBLER system for DIGITAL TELEVISION signals.

multi-drop a connection system for a set of slave computers connected to a master, with software to ensure correct addressing of each slave.

multi-frequency dialling the system of telephone tone dialling that has replaced the older pulse system. See DUAL TONE MULTI-FREQUENCY; PULSE DIALLING.

multifuse see ELECTRONICALLY RESETTABLE FUSE.

multi-head drum the use of more than two heads on the revolving drum of a VIDEO CASSETTE RECORDER, allowing effects such as 'freeze-frame' to be achieved without too much loss of picture quality.

multi-level signal a form of DIGITAL signal in which different levels of voltage carry the coding of numbers. For example a four-level signal could carry the two-bit numbers 00, 01, 10, and 11.

multilingual teletext the development of the TELETEXT standards to incorporate additional characters (a total of 192 characters) to cope with the languages in the 35 countries that use the UK form of teletext.

multimeter a meter with several ranges, usually of current, voltage and resistance, that can be selected by a switch.

multi-miking the use of a large number of MICROPHONES to record sound from different positions, each microphone RECORDING on a separate tape or digital track, with the various tracks edited later into a MASTER TAPE.

multi-mode graded index fibre a form of OPTICAL FIBRE in which the REFRACTIVE INDEX of the glass core varies with radial distance from the centre, resulting in very low loss transmissions and therefore ideal for long-haul use.

multi-mode laser a SEMICONDUCTOR LASER that emits a set of spectral lines. differing by a few tenths of a NANOMETRE.

multi-mode step index fibre a form of OPTICAL FIBRE using a 50μm core and 125μm cladding, suitable only for short haul uses.

multipath immunity the ability of a COFDM digital sound broadcast system to ignore reception problems caused by several signals reaching the receiver using the same frequency.

multipath propagation reception of the same transmitted signals at different times due to reflections from objects (such as mountains, towers or buildings) and the IONOSPHERE.

multipath reception interference with AM or FM radio because of signals on the same frequency arriving in or out of phase, usually because of reflections. See DIVERSITY RECEPTION; FADING; LINCOMPEX; SERVICE AREA.

multiphase drive the set of signals to a STEPPER MOTOR so that rotation through any number of steps can be achieved.

multiphase PSK a form of PHASE SHIFT KEYING in which more than two phases are used, so that more than one bit can be indicated by a particular phase. See also QUADRATURE PHASE SHIFT KEYING.

multiple reflections signal reflections that occur both at an IONOSPHERE layer and at Earth, so that a signal can travel farther than the (approx.) 4000 km that is possible using a single ionospheric reflection from the F2 layer.

multiplex a digitally coded set of signals on one single CARRIER (sense 1), each carrying identification so that a receiver can gather signals relating to one selected channel. One domestic example is the set of compressed DIGITAL VIDEO channels transmitted as one stream and separated at the SET-TOP BOX. This is the main reason for the difficulty of RECORDING one program while viewing another on a DIGITAL TELEVISION system.

multiplexed analogue components (MAC) the basic system for MULTIPLEXED ANALOGUE TV broadcasting by satellite, now superseded by DIGITAL broadcasting methods. There have been many versions and variants of MAC over its lifetime.

multiplexed display a display of several digits of letters in which the signals are time-multiplexed so that only one digit is activated at any one time, but fast cycling from one to another makes the display appear to be continuous.

multiplexer or **MUX** I. a CIRCUIT that allows the TRANSMISSION of several signals at once over a single channel communication system (a *multiplex* system). This can denote a CARRIER (sense 1) that is modulated in two ways, but more commonly denotes a DIGITAL circuit using PULSE methods. The original signals can be recovered by a DEMULTIPLEXER circuit. A single-channel system is sometimes called a *simplex system*.

2. (in instrumentation systems) a hybrid digital/analogue device in which one of a number of analogue signals is selected by means of a binary ADDRESS and routed to a single output. **3.** (in logic circuits) a device in which one of a number of digital inputs is selected by means of a binary address and connected to a single output.

multiplexing the action of using a MULTIPLEXER (sense 1) to carry several signals at once over a single channel.

multiplexing, digital the use of a single CARRIER (sense 1) band to send several transmissions by sending a DATA PACKET from each transmission in turn.

multiplicative mixing the multiplication of two ANALOGUE signals to produce sum and difference frequencies.

multiplier a CIRCUIT or DEVICE that carries out a multiplying action. An ELECTRON MULTIPLIER multiplies the number of electrons in a beam (see DYNODE). A FREQUENCY MULTIPLIER produces a HARMONIC of its input signal. An *analogue multiplier* produces an output whose amplitude is proportional to the product of the amplitudes of the inputs. A *digital multiplier* carries out the arithmetical operation of multiplication on a pair of binary numbers.

multiplier resistor a resistor, usually one of a chain, that is used to extend the range of a voltmeter.

multiplier, universal see UNIVERSAL MULTIPLIER.

multiplying amplifier a form of OPERATIONAL AMPLIFIER that can be used as an analogue MULTIPLIER.

multiplying D/A converter or **programmable attenuator** a form of DIGITAL TO ANALOGUE CONVERTER using both a binary signal and an analogue input.

multipoint microwave distribution system (MMDS) a short-range distribution system for radio signals that is used where copper cable connection is uneconomic.

multi-pole (of a SWITCH) able to open or close more than one circuit when it is actuated.

multi-satellite reception the ability to receive signals from several satellites, either by using a large DISH with several LOW NOISE BLOCKS, or by moving the dish using a motor, see MOTORIZED DISH.

multiscan monitor see MULTISYNC MONITOR.

multisegment display a display for letters and numbers that consists of a set of units that can be individually controlled, such as the 7-segment numerical display.

multi-session CD a recordable CD organized so that a RECORDING can be made, and others added later until the disc is fully recorded.

multistable (of an electronic DEVICE or CIRCUIT) possessing more than one stable state, like the old gas-filled counter tubes (Dekatrons) and more modern RING COUNTER circuits.

multistage (of an electronic CIRCUIT) possessing more than one unit, particularly of amplification.

multistage depressed collector klystron a form of KLYSTRON that uses several collector electrodes run at different voltages to obtain higher power efficiency.

multistage noise shaping (MASH™) a form of digital NOISE SHAPER circuit, used in conjunction with INTERPOLATION of a 16-bit audio signal to 28-bit, and removal of lower order bits that contain noise.

multistandard decoder IC a COLOUR DECODER IC that can deal with more than one type of COLOUR SIGNAL, often with PAL and NTSC, sometimes all three (NTSC, PAL and SECAM).

multisync monitor or **multiscan monitor** a monitor, following the layout of a design by NEC, that allows a variety of high-resolution graphics cards to be used with various line and frame rates and will automatically adapt to the type of signal from each card.

multitasking the ability of a computer system to run several tasks simultaneously, or apparently simultaneously.

multithreading a form of MULTITASKING applied to a single task, so that different parts of a task are carried out simultaneously.

multi-trace CRO a CATHODE-RAY TUBE for use in a CATHODE-RAY OSCILLOSCOPE in which more than one electron beam can be used, so that several traces, all using the same TIMEBASE, can be displayed.

multi-track recorder a recorder, usually a TAPE RECORDER, that can record and play several tracks simultaneously, allowing for stereo or other multi-channel effects, or MULTI-MIKING recordings.

multi-turn dial or **multi-turn knob** a dial or adjustment unit fitted with gearing so that several turns of the dial or control knob are required to make one turn of the main shaft that is usually fitted to a POTENTIOMETER (sense 1).

multi-turn potentiometer a POTENTIOMETER (sense 1) with a MULTI-TURN DIAL system built in.

multi-unit steerable array an AERIAL system consisting of several elements, whose directional axis (see BORESIGHT) can be changed as required.

multivibrator a form of OSCILLATOR circuit for non-sine waves. The oscillator uses two INVERTING AMPLIFIERS that are cross-coupled. This means that the output of each amplifier is connected to the input of the other, providing POSITIVE FEEDBACK. If both connections are made through capacitors, the multivibrator is free-running or ASTABLE, and will generate a square wave for as long as power is applied. If one connection is direct, and the other through a capacitor, then the circuit is MONOSTABLE. With two direct couplings, the circuit becomes a FLIP-FLOP. See Fig. 77.

multivibrator, astable see ASTABLE.

multivibrator, bistable see FLIP-FLOP.

multivibrator, monostable see MONOSTABLE.

multi-way (of a SWITCH) able to connect a circuit to several others in sequence when actuated.

mu-metal a nickel-iron alloy that has very high PERMEABILITY. Mu-metal is used for MAGNETIC SCREENING.

Murphy's law anything that can go wrong, will. Now supplemented by Finagle's addendum: "Murphy was an optimist".

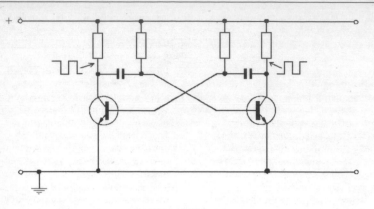

Fig. 77. **multivibrator**

Murray code   a five-BIT code used in early
TELEPRINTER systems.

MUSA   see MULTI-UNIT STEERABLE ARRAY.

MUSA connector   a specialized form of
COAXIAL CONNECTOR for professional use.

mush   the NOISE in a radio receiver that is
being operated with too weak a CARRIER
(sense 1) signal.

**musical instrument digital interface
(MIDI)**   a system for connecting
electronic musical instruments to each
other and to a computer so as to allow
the computer or one instrument to control
all of the others.

MUSICAM   see MPEG LAYER 2 AUDIO CODING.

music centre   a combined radio, cassette
recorder and gramophone, with
amplifiers and loudspeakers, once
popular. The modern equivalent is the
radio/CD/cassette player.

music chip   a specialized IC, used on a
SOUND BOARD, that can be programmed
to synthesize analogue signals that when
amplified and fed to a loudspeaker will
produce sound.

musician's amplifier   an audio amplifier
with very high distortion figures designed
to produce a more impressive sound from
a single source such as a guitar pickup.

music power   a calculated figure for
power output of an audio AMPLIFIER.
The figure attempts to take into account
the non-sinusoidal nature of music, and

is always much greater than the true
power figure for sine wave output. The
term has fallen into disrepute because of
its use in advertising to suggest that an
amplifier has much more power output
than is truly the case.

muting   the suppression of a SIGNAL by
any DEVICE or CIRCUIT that shuts off
unwanted signals. One application is
automatic muting of inter-station noise in
FM receivers. The muting circuit comes
into operation when the CARRIER (sense 1)
strength falls below a preset limit, and
this is used to suppress the audio output,
thus eliminating the loud rushing noise
that is otherwise heard before a signal is
tuned in.

mutual characteristic   the graph of
output current plotted against input
voltage for an ACTIVE COMPONENT.

mutual conductance or **transconductance**
the ratio of change of output current to
change of input voltage for an ACTIVE
COMPONENT. Symbol: g_m. Units usually
milliamperes per volt, or siemens. See also
CONDUCTANCE.

mutual inductance   see INDUCTANCE.

MUX   see MULTIPLEXER.

M-wrap   the form of tape THREADING used
in a VIDEO CASSETTE RECORDER, named from
the shape of the tape during LACING.

Mylar™   a form of polyester plastic, used
as an insulator, particularly in capacitors.

NAC network adapter card: see NETWORK CARD.

NAK see NEGATIVE ACKNOWLEDGE.

NAND a logical operation in which a TRUE (1) output is obtained unless all of the inputs are at the TRUE (1) level. See also AND; BOOLEAN LOGIC; OR; NOT.

NAND gate a type of LOGIC GATE equivalent to an AND gate followed by an INVERTER (sense 1). The NAND gate is easy to manufacture, and is extensively used in small-scale integrated circuits. The advantage of using NAND gates is that any gate circuit can be built up from NAND gates alone. The same is true of NOR gates. See also AND GATE; INVERTER (sense 1); KARNAUGH MAP; NOR GATE; OR GATE; XOR GATE. See Fig. 78.

nano- prefix a submultiple denoting 10^{-9}. Symbol: n.

nanoamp a current unit of 10^{-9} amperes. Symbol nA.

nanometre a unit of length equal to 10^{-9} metres, used for measurement of wavelengths of light.

nanosecond the unit of 10^{-9} seconds. Symbol ns.

nanotechnology a construction technology that works with individual atoms to create objects smaller than has previously been possible. This would make it possible to fabricate extremely small electronics units, particularly simple robots or computers.

narrowband frequency modulation (NBFM) a FREQUENCY MODULATION system with a very low MODULATION INDEX (below 0.5) so that only one or two pairs of SIDEBANDS are generated, giving a bandwidth comparable with an AM transmission.

narrowband noise the result of passing WHITE NOISE through a BAND-PASS FILTER with a narrow response.

narrow-beam aerial an aerial with a very narrow RADIATION PATTERN and negligible SIDE LOBES. A narrow-beam aerial has a large GAIN in its aimed direction, as compared to a simple DIPOLE AERIAL. This can permit good reception even in noisy conditions.

National Television Standards Committee (NTSC) The (US) committee that decides on technical standards for TV broadcasting in the US, notable for the

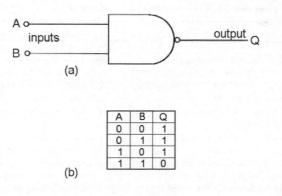

Fig. 78. **NAND gate**

1951 colour TV standard that is named NTSC after the committee.

nats see NATURAL UNITS.

natural frequency see RESONANT FREQUENCY.

natural interference interference with radio signals from natural causes such as lightning, or meteor showers or sunspots causing changes in ionization of the upper atmosphere.

natural units or **nats** a unit for information in which a natural logarithm is used in the formula. See also BINIT; HARTLEY.

NBFM see NARROW BAND FREQUENCY MODULATION.

nBmB code any form of DIGITAL CODE that converts n bits of original code into m bits of new code, where m is greater than n, so adding REDUNDANCY that can be used for error detection and correction.

NBS National Bureau of Standards (US).

nc (normally closed) (of a SWITCH) having contacts that are closed until the switch is actuated.

n-channel a path for current constructed from an N-TYPE doped semiconductor. This is applied to FIELD-EFFECT TRANSISTOR construction in which the conducting width of the channel is controlled by altering the BIAS on the surrounding material by means of a GATE (sense 1) electrode. See also P-CHANNEL.

n-channel MOS see NMOS.

near end cross talk (NEXT) interference between signals on a set of lines in a cable, occurring at the receiver end of the cable. Contrast FAR END CROSS TALK (FEXT).

near field or **Rayleigh region** the space close to an AERIAL (antenna) in which the field pattern is disturbed by the structure of the aerial. Contrast FAR FIELD.

near instantaneous companded audio multiplex see NICAM.

near vertical incidence propagation the use of HF signals radiated almost vertically to be reflected at the same angle, used for MOUNTAIN HOPPING.

near video on demand the use of multiple TV channels, typically ten, to send out the same program, with the starting time

staggered, so that a viewer needs to wait only a short time, typically five minutes, to catch the start of a program.

negative (of a material) possessing an excess of ELECTRONS. The term is applied to any material in which there is a surplus of electrons over protons, whether these are free or bound. Note that an n-type semiconductor is not negative in this sense, because the number of electrons is exactly balanced by the number of HOLES. The distinguishing feature of an n-type semiconductor is that many of the electrons are free to move but the holes are not. Contrast POSITIVE.

negative acknowledge (NAK) a signal sent by a receiver on a serial transmission line to indicate that a DATA PACKET has not been correctly received and must be re-transmitted.

negative bias the application of a steady negative potential to a circuit or ACTIVE COMPONENT, e.g. the GATE (sense 1) of a FET, the base of a TRANSISTOR or the GRID of a THERMIONIC VALVE or CATHODE-RAY TUBE to which a negative potential is applied in order to control the flow of electrons. A sufficiently large negative bias will prevent electron flow, and this amount of bias is called CUTOFF. Contrast POSITIVE BIAS.

negative charge the result of having more electrons than protons in a material.

negative earth or **negative ground** connection of the negative terminal of a circuit to the metal chassis and usually also to a conductor buried in the earth.

negative feedback or **degenerative feedback** the process by which a portion of the output of an AMPLIFIER is fed back to the input in such a way as to diminish the total input signal. This reduces the effective GAIN of the amplifier, but markedly increases its INPUT IMPEDANCE and reduces its output impedance. In addition, linearity (see LINEAR CIRCUIT) is greatly improved. See Fig. 79.

Negative feedback takes several forms. The feedback may be proportional to either the output voltage or the output current, and it may be added to the input

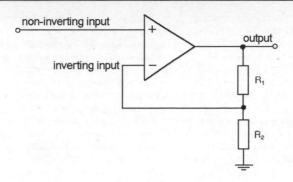

Fig. 79. **Negative feedback**

either in series or in parallel with the signal being amplified. There are therefore four basic types of negative feedback: *series voltage feedback*, *parallel voltage feedback*, *series current feedback*, and *parallel current feedback*.

A further advantage of using negative feedback is that for an amplifier with high OPEN-LOOP GAIN (such as an OPERATIONAL AMPLIFIER), the use of negative feedback ensures that the circuit gain is determined solely by the external (feedback) component values. Contrast POSITIVE FEEDBACK.

negative ion   an atom that has gained one or (sometimes) more ELECTRONs and is therefore negatively charged. Because of the charge, the ion will experience force in an ELECTRIC FIELD, and if free to move will do so. Contrast POSITIVE ION. An ion should not be confused with a HOLE, which cannot exist independently of a crystal structure.

negative logic   a logic voltage system in which the more negative voltage represents LOGIC ONE. Negative logic is seldom used nowadays. See also POSITIVE LOGIC.

negative modulation   the standard form of modulation for AM TV carriers, in which the most negative part of the waveform (the tip of the SYNC PULSE) is represented by maximum CARRIER (sense 1) level. This ensures that any impulse interference does not appear on the picture.

negative resistance   an unstable condition in which an increase of voltage across two points is accompanied by a decrease of current between the points. The term 'negative' is used because this is the opposite of the normal OHMIC resistance. Any device that can produce negative resistance over a range of voltage levels can be used as an OSCILLATOR. If negative resistance can occur in an AMPLIFIER under certain circumstances, the amplifier will be unstable under these conditions.

negative resistance oscillator   an oscillator constructed by connecting a RESONANT CIRCUIT to a device, such as a TUNNEL DIODE, that has a NEGATIVE RESISTANCE portion of CHARACTERISTIC.

negative temperature coefficient (NTC)   a figure that expresses by how much a quantity decreases as its temperature increases. NTC capacitors are used to stabilize RF oscillator frequency, and NTC resistors are used for similar purposes in RC oscillators. Compare POSITIVE TEMPERATURE COEFFICIENT.

nematic crystal   a type of LIQUID CRYSTAL with long thin molecules, used for LCD displays.

neon   a gas used in display devices. The neon signal lamp consists of two small parallel ELECTRODES surrounded by low-pressure neon. The lamp glows orange-red at a POTENTIAL DIFFERENCE of around 70V only after the gas has been ionized (see IONIZATION) by a higher potential difference called the STRIKING POTENTIAL. When the gas is ionized, an increase of current through the gas causes a drop in the potential difference across the electrodes so that the characteristic is that of a NEGATIVE RESISTANCE.

neper a unit of ATTENUATION for TRANSMISSION LINES equivalent to 8.686 dB.

net information content the amount of useful information in a message to be transmitted over a noise-free channel.

net loss the overall loss of SIGNAL, usually expressed in DECIBELS, in any device or network, active or passive.

network 1. a circuit that consists of PASSIVE COMPONENTS, such as resistors, capacitors and inductors. Most types of electronic circuits can be divided into ACTIVE COMPONENTS, such as transistors, and passive networks. 2. a set of interconnected computers that can exchange information.

network architecture the arrangement of each NODE (sense 1) and the connections between nodes in a NETWORK (sense 2) system. There are five main architectures used, with names that are descriptive of the arrangement. The *fully connected network architecture* (or *mesh*) contains links between each pair of nodes, so that the number of links is very large for a large number of nodes. The *partially connected architecture* contains links only between selected nodes. The *tree architecture* has one root node linked to two others, each of which is in turn linked to two others. *Star architecture* uses a central node linked to each other node, and *ring architecture* has all of the nodes linked in a chain that is joined at the ends to form a ring.

network card or **networking card** or **network adapter card** or **network interface card** a card or board inserted into a computer so that connections can be made to a NETWORK (sense 2).

network echo a signal echo in a TRANSMISSION LINE caused by incorrect MATCHING of devices connected to the line. Contrast HARD ECHO.

network hogging excessive use of a digital NETWORK (sense 2), usually by a slow device as a result of using POLLING control.

networking card see NETWORK CARD.

network node an interface between two main NETWORKS.

network protocol a set of rules governing the use of a NETWORK (sense 2) by a MODEM.

network time delay the time needed for a message to reach its correct destination on a NETWORK (sense 2).

network topology the geometrical design of a NETWORK (sense 2) in terms of NODES and connections. The network topology can be centralized, such as the *star network,* or de-centralized like a *ring network.* See NETWORK ARCHITECTURE.

Neuman, John Van (1903–1957) the originator in the 1940s of Van Neuman architecture for computers, using stored program control and serial processing.

neural network a software or hardware system that is capable of learning. Inputs and outputs are subjected to a learning process with known data so as to teach the system some rules. This is then used to request outputs from new sets of inputs. The idea is to emulate part of the process that the brain uses in learning. The system thus, effectively, develops its own method of solving problems, with no software program written for the solution, which simply 'exists' in the neural network. A program must, however, be written to allow the network to carry out inputs, process data, and provide outputs.

neutral 1. being earthed, or connected neither to positive nor to negative potential. 2. unconnected. 3. the return line of an AC mains supply. 4. uncharged.

neutral atom an atom that contains the same number of ELECTRONS as its NUCLEUS contains PROTONS so that it is in a stable uncharged state. See also ION.

neutral–earth voltage the small and fluctuating AC voltage between the EARTH and NEUTRAL WIRES of a MAINS power supply, arising because the earth is local, but the neutral has been earthed at some distance so that voltage can be induced on the line.

neutralization a form of connection or set of connections made in an amplifier

STAGE in order to prevent OSCILLATION. A neutralizing connection generally consists of a capacitor connected between two stages of amplification, and is intended to counteract the effects of STRAY CAPACITANCE by shifting the signal phase in the opposite direction. Neutralization is particularly needed when a TRANSISTOR is being used for tuned radio-frequency amplification at a frequency near to the limit of its frequency response. See also UNILATERAL NETWORK.

neutral wire the connection to a MAINS supply that is the return for current from the LIVE WIRE.

neutron an uncharged elementary particle found in the nucleus of an atom. The nucleus also contains positively charged particles called protons. The neutron has about the same rest mass as the PROTON, 1.67482×10^{-27} kg, 1839 times that of an electron.

newton the SI and MKS unit of force. Symbol: N. A newton is defined as the force required to produce an acceleration of 1 metre per second per second to a body of mass 1kg. In the earth's gravitational field the downward force on a 1kg mass is approximately 9.81N.

Newton's rings the coloured rings that appear when a convex glass surface is in contact with a plane glass or metal surface, caused by light WAVE INTERFERENCE effects.

nibble or **nybble** one half of a DIGITAL BYTE, equal to four BITS.

NIC network interface card, see NETWORK CARD.

nicad or **nicad cell** a NICKEL-CADMIUM CELL or battery, a rechargeable form of alkaline electrolyte cell, used as a power-source in portable equipment.

NICAM near-instantaneous companded audio multiplex: a system devised for adding STEREO sound to ANALOGUE PAL TV in the UK. This uses a digitally DKQPS coded SUBCARRIER at 6.552 MHz above the vision CARRIER (sense 1) frequency, with BIT REDUCTION to reduce bandwidth.

Nichrome™ an alloy of nickel and chromium that has fairly high RESISTIVITY,

and can be used at fairly high temperatures. It is extensively applied in heating elements, and can be used for WIRE-WOUND resistors that will be operated with high DISSIPATION.

nickel-cadmium or **NiCd** or **Nicad cell** a RECHARGEABLE CELL with an EMF of 1.2 V, used extensively in portable equipment, but subject to the MEMORY EFFECT and hence now being replaced by the NICKEL METAL HYDRIDE CELL and NICKEL COBALT CELL.

nickel-cobalt or **Ni-Co cell** a RECHARGEABLE CELL using cobalt, nickel hydroxide and water with an EMF of 1.28 V. No GASSING is produced if the cell is recharged from a 1.5 V source, and the cell is often used as a store for PHOTOVOLTAIC EFFECT devices.

nickel-metal hydride or **NiMH** or **nickel hydride cell** a sealed RECHARGEABLE CELL using nickel metal and nickel hydride with no cadmium content. The energy capacity is some 40% higher than that of a NICKEL-CADMIUM CELL, with longer life and faster charge and discharge rates. The MEMORY EFFECT is also less, though the cell needs to be completely discharged before recharging at intervals.

Ni-Co see NICKEL-COBALT CELL.

Nife™ a nickel-iron CELL or battery. This was an early (1901) design of rechargeable alkaline electrolyte cell, now mainly used for electric traction.

nightfall detector a light sensor that will switch on security lighting when the level of natural illumination becomes low.

NIMH see NICKEL METAL HYDRIDE CELL.

Nipkow, Paul (1860–1940) the German inventor of a mechanical system of TELEVISION around 1886 whose drawings and principles were used by John Logie BAIRD to construct his Televisor machines, the first public displays of television, in the late 1920s. See also CAMPBELL-SWINTON; ROSING.

NLR see NONLINEAR RESISTOR.

NMOS or **N-channel MOS** a digital circuit constructed using N-CHANNEL FETs only.

NNI network to network interface.

NO normally open, referring to a switch contact that is closed when the switch is operated.

noble metals the group of metals that includes platinum and rhodium, named because of their resistance to acids and used in THERMOCOUPLES.

nodal drive a method of connecting the MOVING COIL portion of a LOUDSPEAKER to the cone at the annular distance for the nodes (see NODE, sense 2) of the first RESONANCE.

node 1. a joining point in a NETWORK (sense 1 or 2), particularly a FILTER network, at which components are connected.
2. A point in a STANDING WAVE pattern at which there is no wave motion. The position of maximum wave motion is called the ANTINODE. Nodes and antinodes are particularly important in AERIAL design, and in TRANSMISSION LINES. See Fig. 80.

noise any form of unwanted electronic SIGNAL, usually signals of random frequency, phase and amplitude but also including mains HUM. See also IMPULSE NOISE; MAN-MADE NOISE; SCHOTTKY NOISE; SOLAR NOISE; THERMAL NOISE; WHITE NOISE.

noise, aliasing see ALIASING NOISE.

noise band a band of disturbance on a replayed picture from a simple VIDEO CASSETTE RECORDER, usually when a picture is paused. This can be reduced by using a FOUR-HEAD DRUM design.

noise bars dark bars on a picture from a VIDEO CASSETTE RECORDER being used in FAST PICTURE SEARCH mode.

noise behind the signal see BIAS NOISE.

noise, burst see BURST NOISE.

noise-cancelling microphone a MICROPHONE used very close to the mouth, and fitted with filtering to control the excessive bass that this picks up, used to provide a speech commentary in very acoustically noisy situations.

noise, digital generator see DIGITAL NOISE GENERATOR.

noise factor the ratio of SIGNAL power to NOISE POWER. In TELEMETRY, this factor is measured for a receiver that is tuned to a desired signal, firstly with no MODULATION, so that the noise output of the receiver can be measured, then with full modulation so that the power of signal plus noise can be measured.

noise figure the NOISE FACTOR expressed in DECIBELS.

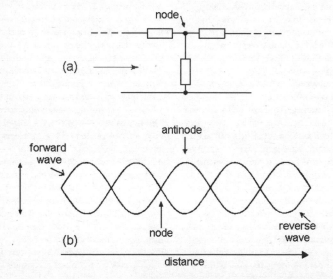

Fig. 80. **node**

noise, flicker see FLICKER NOISE.

noise gate a simple but imperfect analogue NOISE-REDUCING SYSTEM which gates the signal when a preset AMPLITUDE is exceeded, omitting all (mainly noise) signals below that amplitude.

noise generator the basic signal source of WHITE NOISE for a SYNTHESIZER, originally a DIODE.

noise immunity the ability of a DIGITAL radio signal to be unaffected by noise until the noise level exceeds a critical level.

noise, Johnson see THERMAL NOISE.

noise killer a circuit used in car radios that detects and mutes noise spikes.

noise limiter a circuit used in a radio receiver to clip IMPULSE NOISE from a carrier and thus reduce the received noise level. See also AUTOMATIC NOISE LIMITER; CLIPPER; MEDIAN FILTER.

noise margin for a digital LOGIC circuit, the amplitude of interfering pulse voltage that will make the device output change state.

noise, pink see PINK NOISE.

noise power ratio a measurement applicable to FREQUENCY DIVISION MULTIPLEX systems. With an input of random noise simulating a wideband signal, the noise output is measured. By using filtering, a quiet channel is simulated and the noise level again measured. The DECIBEL ratio of these values gives the noise power ratio.

noise, quantization see QUANTIZATION NOISE.

noise reduction circuitry circuits incorporated into tape RECORDING and replay so as to minimize noise, usually by a COMPANDER system.

noise, resistor the thermal noise generated when a current flows through a resistor, depending on absolute temperature and often quoted in terms of μV of noise per volt of DC across the resistor.

noise-shaper or **sigma-delta modulator** a circuit that carries out the action of BIT REDUCTION on oversampled DIGITAL DATA by feeding back the sum of filtered and unfiltered data to the input. The noise portion can then be allocated to unused bandwidth and removed.

noise, shot see SHOT NOISE.

noise temperature a method of NOISE measurement based on the idea that a resistor will emit an amount of noise that depends on ABSOLUTE TEMPERATURE, so that any noise source can be regarded as a resistor at some temperature, the noise temperature.

noise, white see WHITE NOISE.

noisy colour a PAL receiver problem indicating weak colour signals.

noisy picture or **snow** a white dotted appearance on a TV picture due to low signal strength, often caused by a poor AERIAL connection.

no-load condition the operation of an AMPLIFIER, OSCILLATOR or any other device without the LOAD that will normally be attached to it, i.e. no power is taken from the circuit. An amplifier should be stable and should not suffer damage under such conditions, and an oscillator should show no frequency DRIFT (sense 2).

nominal current rating, fuse the current rating for a FUSE that determines how long it will take to blow on an overload. See F; FF; M; T; TT.

nomogram a form of chart that allows the values of a variable to be estimated without resorting to a mathematical formula. One form taken by a nomogram is of a set of columns of values. By joining two columns with a straight line, values can be read from other columns that are intersected by the straight line. This can often be as precise as is needed, and allows very rapid estimates of quantities that would normally be time-consuming to calculate. See also FORM FACTOR (sense 2). See Fig. 81.

non-coherent demodulation or **envelope demodulation** the common form of demodulation that uses a rectifier to isolate the ENVELOPE shape of a CARRIER, (sense 1) followed by filtering. See also SYNCHRONOUS (or *coherent*) demodulation.

non-complementary system any form of noise reduction system that operates on one part of the tape process, usually on replay.

non-crystalline see AMORPHOUS.

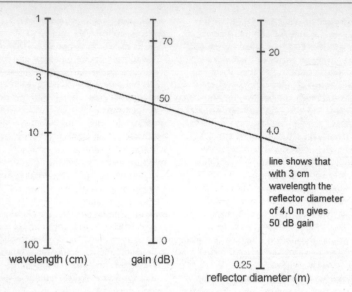

Fig. 81. **nomogram**

nondestructive test any form of testing
that does not damage the test specimen.
X-RAY examination is one form of
nondestructive test, as is ULTRASONIC
scanning.

non-deterministic network a NETWORK
(sense 2) whose action makes it
impossible to guarantee access within a
specified period.

non-inductive (of a wire winding) wound
so that its INDUCTANCE is a minimum.
Often applied to WIRE-WOUND resistors
in which the required length of resistance
wire is wound half in one direction and
half in the opposite direction. The effect
of this is to cancel most of the SELF-
INDUCTANCE of the winding. For most
purposes, the use of a metal FILM RESISTOR
is a more satisfactory solution if
inductance must be very low, but where
high DISSIPATION or great precision is
required, there may be no option but to
use wire-wound construction.

non-interlaced monitor a MONITOR that
does not use INTERLACE actions, so that
each LINE (sense 2) is scanned (see SCAN)
in turn, and one set of consecutive line

scans makes up a complete FRAME (sense 1).
Absence of interlacing is a feature of a
MULTISYNC MONITOR.

non-inverting amplifier an AMPLIFIER
whose output is in PHASE with its input.

non-inverting input the input to a
DIFFERENTIAL AMPLIFIER, particularly an
OPERATIONAL AMPLIFIER, at which the PHASE
of signal is the same as that at the output.
Contrast INVERTING INPUT.

nonlinear possessing a characteristic
shape that is not a straight line. The term
is usually applied to an AMPLIFIER or other
analogue signal device in which a plot
of signal out against signal in is not a
straight line. Passive networks that do not
contain metal-cored inductors are usually
linear. Nonlinearity in an amplifier is a
cause of HARMONIC DISTORTION and
INTERMODULATION. See also NEGATIVE
FEEDBACK. Contrast LINEAR.

nonlinear analogue circuit circuits such
as RECTIFIERS that are classed as analogue
but which are NONLINEAR.

nonlinear distortion a type of distortion,
such as HARMONIC DISTORTION and
INTERMODULATION that is caused by

NONLINEAR behaviour. The nonlinearity may be in an ACTIVE COMPONENT such as a transistor or IC, or in a passive device with HYSTERESIS, such as an iron-cored inductor.

nonlinear editing the editing of digital video or sound held on a hard drive or in the memory of a computer. The complete recording is then transferred to tape or DVD when the editing is finished. Compare LINEAR EDITING.

nonlinear mapping a MODEM technique that alters the distribution of data for a MULTI-LEVEL QAM coding to reduce the effect of nonlinear distortion.

nonlinear mixing the use of a device with non-linear characteristics fed with two signals so that INTERMODULATION takes place and a desired product can be extracted by filtering. See also SUPERHETERODYNE RECEIVER. Compare LINEAR MIXING. See also MIXER; MULTIPLICATIVE MIXER.

nonlinear resistor (NLR) a form of resistor whose resistance value decreases as the current through it increases. See also NON-OHMIC.

nonlinear scale a meter scale in which equal steps of the measured quantity are not represented by equal distances.

nonlinearity the result in signal terms of the NONLINEAR shape of a CHARACTERISTIC of an active or passive device.

nonlinearity errors, D-A errors in the ANALOGUE wave from a DIGITAL TO ANALOGUE CONVERTER due to errors in the ratio of currents or voltages in the converter.

nonlinearity, tape the NONLINEAR relationship between signal current and MAGNETIC FLUX DENSITY of recorded tape, corrected to some extent by using TAPE BIAS.

non-lossy (of a signal BIT REDUCTION system) having a totally reversible action so that repeated compression and expansion actions will not result in any loss of data.

non-lossy compression any form of BIT REDUCTION of a DIGITAL SIGNAL that is completely reversible, so that repeated compression and decompression will not

change the content of the signal. See also HUFFMAN; LZW.

non-maskable interrupt an INTERRUPT signal to a MICROPROCESSOR that will interrupt normal processing and which cannot be disabled by software.

non-modem connection a serial connection between computers that does not use a modem, see also NUL MODEM.

non-ohmic (of a device) with a NONLINEAR relationship between current and applied voltage.

non-persistent (of a network) not attempting to re-transmit a signal following a data COLLISION.

non-polar dielectric (of a CAPACITOR) using a solid dielectric, not an ELECTROLYTIC type.

nonreactive (of a component) having only RESISTANCE. The term is applied to a resistor or a TRANSMISSION LINE in which the phase of voltage is always the same as the phase of current under normal working conditions. See also IMPEDANCE; REACTANCE; RESISTANCE.

non-recursive filter a DIGITAL FILTER composed of DELAY units with signals fed forward to a summing stage from the start of each delay section, with no FEEDBACK elements (which would add RECURSION). These are used for LOW-PASS FILTERing, INTERPOLATION and EQUALIZATION.

non-resonant (of a component or circuit) having a frequency characteristic with no abrupt changes. A non-resonant component or circuit (see APERIODIC CIRCUIT) can be used at any frequency with no risk of sharp changes of phase or gain if the frequency is changed. See RESONANT FREQUENCY.

non-return-to-zero format (NRZ) a form of DIGITAL signal coding in which logic 1 is represented by a positive PULSE, and logic 0 by no pulse. The disadvantage of this system is that the signals have a DC COMPONENT, making them unsuitable for some RECORDING methods.

non-return-to-zero inverted (NRZI) or **invert on coding** a form of coding for digital signals in which the logic 0 bit is represented by a pulse transition, and a logic 1 by no transition. See also NON-RETURN-TO-ZERO FORMAT.

non-saturation a value for MAGNETIZATION of a material that is less than the saturated value.

non-sinusoidal (of a waveform) not being a sine wave, but (usually) a pulse or square wave.

nonvolatile (of memory storage) not depending on a power supply for the storage of data, i.e. any form of memory that uses MAGNETIC or ELECTROSTATIC storage that will be retained when power is no longer applied. Contrast VOLATILE. See also EAROM; EPROM.

nonvolatile memory any form of computer MEMORY that retains its information when power to the memory is switched off.

nonvolatile random access memory (NVRAM) a form of STATIC RAM that has a battery permanently connected to maintain data, or a type of EEPROM that can retain data without applied power.

non-weighted binary code any binary code, such as GRAY CODE or EXCESS-3 CODE, that does not arrange each bit in order of powers of two.

NOR a LOGIC action whose result is a LOGIC ONE output only when all of its inputs are at logic 0. See also AND; NAND; OR; NOT; XOR.

NOR gate a logic gate circuit that implements the NOR action, so that its output is at LOGIC ONE only when all of its inputs are at logic zero. For all other combinations of inputs, the output is logic 0. The gate can be imagined as a combination of OR GATE and INVERTER (sense 1), but is always manufactured as a gate in its own right. Like the NAND GATE, NOR gates can be used in combination to provide the action of any other type of gate.

normal blo fuse see F FUSE.

normal distribution see GAUSSIAN DISTRIBUTION.

normalized figure a figure that has been adjusted to fit a standard pattern. For example, RESONANCE curves are normalized around unity gain and RESONANT FREQUENCY. This means that the response is plotted with the peak gain shown as 1, and with the frequencies shown relative to the resonance frequency, rather than using actual measured values of gain and frequency for any one particular circuit. Normalization is encountered to a considerable extent in FILTER design, and in PROPAGATION calculations. See Fig. 82.

normally closed or **normally on** (of a switch contact) being closed until the switch is operated.

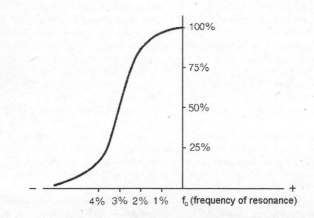

Fig. 82. **normalized figure**

normally open or **normally off** (of a SWITCH contact) being open until the switch is operated.

north bridge the chip used on a PC computer motherboard to derive PCI BUS and ACCELERATED GRAPHICS PORT bus signals from the processor bus signals. So called because on the system BLOCK DIAGRAM, this chip appears on the 'North side'. See also SOUTH BRIDGE.

north pole or **north-seeking pole** the end of a magnet that will point to the Earth's North pole if freely suspended.

Norton model the equivalent circuit using a source of TRANSCONDUCTANCE, used for analyzing a TRANSISTOR action.

Norton op-amp or **current-differencing amplifier** a form of operational amplifier whose output voltage is proportional to the difference between the currents at the two inputs.

Norton's theorem the current equivalent of THEVENIN'S THEOREM for finding an EQUIVALENT CIRCUIT. This states that any two-terminal LINEAR NETWORK to which a signal is applied can be simulated by a current GENERATOR (sense 2) in parallel with a resistor.

NOS network operating system.

NOT or **complement** a logic action that inverts a binary digit, so that NOT 0 = 1 and NOT 1 = 0.

NOT gate see INVERTER (sense 1).

notch filter or **wave trap** a filter with a sharp dip (*notch*) in its response around one frequency.

n-p-n transistor a BIPOLAR JUNCTION TRANSISTOR with a BASE of p-type material, and EMITTER (sense 1) and COLLECTOR of n-type. The n-p-n structure is the predominant one for silicon transistors.

NRZ see NON-RETURN-TO-ZERO FORMAT.

NRZI see NON-RETURN-TO-ZERO INVERTED.

NTC see NEGATIVE TEMPERATURE COEFFICIENT.

NTC thermistor a NON-OHMIC resistor with a large NEGATIVE TEMPERATURE COEFFICIENT value.

NTSC see NATIONAL TELEVISION STANDARDS COMMITTEE.

NTSC video replay a facility offered on some PAL VIDEO CASSETTE RECORDERS to process NTSC cassettes, providing the monitor can be made to run at a 60 Hz frame speed.

n-type (of a semiconductor material) being doped (see DOPING) with an electron-rich impurity. This causes the material to conduct predominantly by the movement of negative electrons. See also P-TYPE; SEMICONDUCTOR; TRANSISTOR.

nuclear electromagnetic pulse (EMP) see ELECTROMAGNETIC PULSE.

nuclear magnetic resonance an oscillation within the atoms of a material caused by application of strong fields, both electric and magnetic. The RESONANCE FREQUENCY can be detected and plotted against position to form an image.

nucleus the central part of an atom. The nucleus is positively charged, and contains most of the mass of the atom.

null a point or area in the signal around a TRANSMITTING AERIAL where the signal strength is zero or close to zero.

null-detector a DEVICE that detects when a signal has zero amplitude, often used in conjunction with the NULL METHOD of measurement to indicate balance. See also BRIDGE.

null method a measuring method in which adjustments are made in order to produce a NULL-DETECTOR reading. BRIDGES are the best-known null methods, because when a bridge circuit reaches its balanced condition, the signal or DC voltage across the detector is zero. This makes it unnecessary to use a detector that is calibrated in any way, and only high sensitivity is required. The size of the quantity that is being measured is calculated from the values of the other components in the bridge circuit and so is unaffected by any calibration error of the meter instrument.

null modem a connection from the SERIAL PORT of one computer to another without the use of a MODEM. The cable used for this purpose must have connections that are reversed at one plug so that the sending pin of one port is connected to the receiving pin of the other.

null steerable aerial (or antenna) an aerial array that is almost OMNIDIRECTIONAL but with a NULL whose direction can be altered electrically.

number base the digit in any numbering system that marks the point where two digits are required to express a number. For a number base of two, the permitted digits are 0 and 1, for a number base of 10 the permitted digits are 0 to 9. The hexadecimal (hex) scale used for binary numbers in groups of four needs fifteen digits represented by 0 to 9 and letters A to F.

numberpad see NUMERIC KEYPAD.

numerator the portion of a fraction that is above the bar. Contrast DENOMINATOR.

numeric keypad or numberpad a separate set of KEYS (sense 2) or buttons for entering numbers, usually placed on the right-hand side of a computer keyboard and therefore less useful to left-handed operators.

numerical control the control of any SYSTEM by digital signals, usually denoting the control of machinery by using digital signals from paper or magnetic tape.

NVRAM see NONVOLATILE RANDOM ACCESS MEMORY.

nybble see NIBBLE.

Nyquist bandwidth the figure of bandwidth for a DIGITAL signal, equal to half of the BIT RATE.

Nyquist criterion a method of determining if an amplifier will be unconditionally stable. This depends on whether the plot of a NYQUIST DIAGRAM encloses the point −1,0 on the conventional normalized (see NORMALIZED FIGURE) form of the diagram.

Nyquist diagram or vector response diagram a plot of a NORMALIZED FIGURE of GAIN against PHASE SHIFT for an AMPLIFIER. This shows the relationship between gain and FEEDBACK in an amplifier and is used as a measure of stability. See also NYQUIST CRITERION. See Fig. 83.

Nyquist filter see ANTI-ALIASING FILTER.

Nyquist interval the quantity obtained by calculating the reciprocal of the NYQUIST RATE.

Nyquist rate the maximum rate at which data can be sent over a channel with given BANDWIDTH.

Nyquist theorem the fundamental theorem for digital SAMPLING that shows that the minimum sampling rate must be twice the highest frequency in the analogue signal.

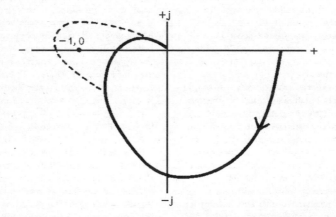

Fig. 83. **Nyquist diagram**

OC or **o/c**   see OPEN CIRCUIT.

o/c diode   a diode that has failed with an OPEN CIRCUIT.

OCR   see OPTICAL CHARACTER READER.

octal   (of a number) in BASE 8, used at one time in programming. In octal, digits 0 to 7 are used, and decimal 8 is represented by 10_8, 9 by 11_8 and so on to 16 which is 20_8.

octave   a doubling or halving of FREQUENCY. A change in response (such as of a FILTER or an AMPLIFIER) is often quoted as a number of decibels of attenuation or amplification per octave.

octet   see BYTE.

odd/even shuffle   a rearrangement of digital samples to avoid the worst effects of large errors. When the samples are put into correct order, INTERPOLATION will fill in for incorrect values.

odd function   a waveform whose FOURIER ANALYSIS shows that it is made up from SINE WAVE terms only. Compare EVEN FUNCTION.

odd parity   a PARITY scheme in which the number of 1 bits in a byte must be odd, otherwise an error is signalled.

OEM   original equipment manufacturer.

OFDM   see ORTHOGONAL FREQUENCY DIVISION MULTIPLEX.

off-axis response   the sensitivity of a MICROPHONE to sounds that come from a position that is not on the axis of a LOBE.

off-line   (of a computer system or communications unit) not connected to other parts of a NETWORK (sense 2). An off-line DEVICE may be working, with power applied, but is not in communication with other devices. Contrast ON-LINE.

off-line editing   video editing of DIGITAL TELEVISION, carried out using a computer. See also NONLINEAR EDITING.

off-line UPS or **voting UPS**   a form of UNINTERRUPTIBLE POWER SUPPLY that has to be switched on manually, not automatically taking over when power is lost.

off-load   (of a circuit) having its power output not connected to its load.

offset   a deviation from correct or normal VOLTAGE or CURRENT. The offset of an OPERATIONAL AMPLIFIER (using balanced power supplies) is the BIAS that is needed on one input to make the output reach earth voltage when the other input is at earth voltage.

offset angle   the angle between the TONE ARM of a VINYL DISC player and the axis of the CARTRIDGE (sense 2).

offset binary   an ANALOGUE TO DIGITAL CONVERTER system for waveforms with no DC content that simulates a DC COMPONENT by adding a constant number to the digital result of each sample.

offset dish or **offset feed aerial (or antenna)**   a MICROWAVE DISH, used particularly for DIGITAL TELEVISION, whose shape is that of a small section of a PARABOLIC REFLECTOR, enabling the dish surface to be almost vertical (avoiding rain gathering) and the head unit to be out of the arriving signal path.

offset, gate   an undesirable steady voltage difference between the output of an analogue GATE (sense 2) and its input.

offset null   an input to an OPERATIONAL AMPLIFIER whose voltage can be adjusted to reduce the DC OFFSET between signal inputs to zero.

offset superhet   a form of SUPERHETERODYNE RECEIVER for a PAGER in which the LOCAL OSCILLATOR is CRYSTAL controlled at a frequency that differs from the CARRIER (sense 1) by only half of the BANDWIDTH, resulting in a very low INTERMEDIATE FREQUENCY and no IMAGE FREQUENCY problems.

offset temperature drift   change of OFFSET VOLTAGE in an OPERATIONAL AMPLIFIER due to temperature changes.

ohm the SI unit of electrical RESISTANCE. The resistance in ohms between two points is defined as the DC voltage divided by the amount of steady current flowing between the points. Symbol: Ω. See also CONDUCTANCE; IMPEDANCE; REACTANCE.

ohmic (of a material) obeying OHM'S LAW, having a constant value of RESISTANCE at a steady temperature. If the value of resistance varies with applied voltage or current, then the resistance is *non-ohmic*. See also THERMISTOR.

ohmic contact an electrical contact with a steady value of CONTACT RESISTANCE.

ohmic loss a power loss caused by DISSIPATION in a resistor as distinct from radiation loss or HYSTERESIS loss, for example.

ohmic material any material that conducts and has a LINEAR voltage/current CHARACTERISTIC.

ohmmeter an instrument for measuring RESISTANCE. Simple ohmmeters use a CELL of constant voltage to pass a CURRENT through the unknown resistor, and measure this current. The disadvantage is a nonlinear reading scale. More elaborate ohmmeters use measuring BRIDGE circuits. See also MEGGER.

ohm-metre the unit of RESISTIVITY. Symbol: ρ. Unit: ohm-metre. The resistivity of a material is defined, at a steady temperature, by the equation:

$$R = \frac{\rho s}{A}$$

where R is resistance in ohms, s is length in metres, and A is the (uniform) area of cross section in square metres.

Ohm's law the principle that the RESISTANCE of a metallic conductor is constant at a constant temperature. For metallic and other ohmic conductors we can use the relationship V = R × I between (DC) current and voltage because the quantity R (resistance) is a constant. NON-OHMIC conductors do not have any constant resistance value, and the V = RI relationship can be used only if the value of R under the conditions is known.

ohms-per-volt a figure used to compare the sensitivity of analogue DC VOLTMETER movements that shows the series resistance of the voltmeter for any voltage range. For example if a meter is quoted as having 30K per volt, then on its 10V range, the resistance of the meter is 30 × 10 = 300k-ohms.

oil break switch a form of switch whose contacts are immersed in oil. This suppresses ARCOVER when the contacts separate.

oil-flame sensor a PHOTOCONDUCTIVE CELL that is most sensitive to red-orange light, used to detect when an oil burner has ignited correctly.

omega wrap the wrapping pattern of video tape around more than half of the circumference of the DRUM (sense 1) of a VIDEO CASSETTE RECORDER. Compare M-WRAP; U-WRAP.

omnidirectional capable of operating in any direction equally.

omnidirectional aerial an aerial whose RADIATION PATTERN is the same in all (horizontal) directions.

omnidirectional microphone a microphone whose sensitivity to sound is equal in all directions at a constant distance, giving a circular response pattern. See also BI-DIRECTIONAL; CARDIOID.

omni mode a MIDI mode in which transmitters use channel 1 and receivers respond to signals on all sixteen channels. This allows two synthesizers to be operated from one keyboard.

on-axis response the sensitivity of a MICROPHONE to sounds arriving along the axis of the main LOBE.

once-only assembly a mechanism that cannot be repaired, only replaced.

one-bit system see BITSTREAM.

one-key system or **one-time pad** an ENCRYPTION system that used only one KEY. This is secure only if the key can be transmitted securely between sender and recipient.

one-mode symptom a fault symptom that occurs only in one mode of operation.

one-shot see MONOSTABLE.

one time pad see ONE-KEY SYSTEM.

one time programmable (OTP) a READ-ONLY MEMORY that is programmed permanently at the time of manufacture.

one way function a mathematical function used for ENCRYPTING data. The function is reversible only if all of the KEYS are known, otherwise it is irreversible and cannot be decrypted.

on-line (of a computer system or communications unit) switched on and connected to other parts of a NETWORK (sense 2). Contrast OFF-LINE.

online UPS the more common form of UNINTERRUPTABLE POWER SUPPLY that switches into action automatically when power fails.

on/off control see BANG-BANG CONTROL.

on-off keying (OOK) a very primitive method of transmitting a digital signal by switching a CARRIER (sense 1) on for a '1' bit and off for a '0' bit.

on/off switch a switch that has two positions only, making (on) or breaking (off) a circuit.

on-screen display see OSD.

on-the-fly (of an action) carried out in REAL TIME rather than from stored data, such as conversion of analogue TV signals to digital.

OOK see ON-OFF KEYING.

opamp see OPERATIONAL AMPLIFIER.

open architecture see MOTHERBOARD.

open box testing see WHITE BOX TESTING.

open bus system a BUS in a computer that is connected to sockets into which EXPANSION CARDS can be plugged. See also ACCELERATED GRAPHICS PORT; ISA; LOCAL BUS; PERIPHERAL COMPONENTS INTERCONNECT BUS.

open circuit or **OC** or **o/c** a disconnection in an electrical CIRCUIT through which no CURRENT flows.

open-circuit impedance a measurement of IMPEDANCE of a NETWORK (sense 1). The open-circuit impedance at the input of the network is the impedance that it has with the output open circuited. The open circuit impedance of the output is the impedance value that it has when the input is open circuited.

open-circuit junction a BIPOLAR JUNCTION TRANSISTOR fault in which the internal circuit between BASE and EMITTER (sense 1) or base and COLLECTOR has failed.

open-circuit voltage the output signal voltage of an OPEN CIRCUIT or device when no LOAD is connected.

open-circuit voltage sensitivity a factor that indicates the efficiency of a diode for converting MICROWAVE input to signal output.

open-collector device or **open-ended device** or **open-collector output** a digital device in which the active PULL-UP TRANSISTOR of the output stage is omitted. If a number of device outputs have to be connected together, active outputs are undesirable because this may lead to an active low voltage on one device being connected to an active high voltage on another, with disastrous consequences. To avoid this problem, open-collector devices are used. The output can then only be made low (FALSE), or disconnected, and it is the responsibility of the designer to provide a PULL-UP RESISTOR so that in its disconnected state the output goes high. The pull-up resistor limits current and prevents any damage when conflicting output are connected. Open-collector devices can degrade the speed and noise immunity of a logic signal, and are best avoided by the use of a THREE-STATE LOGIC device.

open drain output an output from a FET IC that has no load or power connection, see also OPEN-COLLECTOR DEVICE.

open headphone or **velocity headphone** or **free-air headphone** a type of headphone that rests on ACOUSTICALLY TRANSPARENT foam, covering the ear lightly. The sound is described as light and airy, but is liable to intrusion of surrounding noise. Contrast CLOSED HEADPHONE.

open loop control a control whose setting cannot be altered by the output of the system, because there is no FEEDBACK. A simple example is a radiator with no thermostat, whose setting must be adjusted manually and cannot adapt itself to requirements.

open loop gain the gain of a FEEDBACK system when the FEEDBACK LOOP has been disconnected.

open loop mode the operation of an amplifier with no FEEDBACK, particularly of a feedback amplifier whose FEEDBACK LOOP is broken.

open systems interconnect (OSI) a set of standardized protocols for exchanging information between terminals, computers, and other devices.

open wire an un-insulated wire, as on an overhead line.

operating point a graph point that represents operating conditions. On a graph of output voltage plotted against input voltage for a device (a TRANSFER CHARACTERISTIC), for example, the operating point is the point on the graph that represents the static DC bias condition with no signal applied. See Fig. 84.

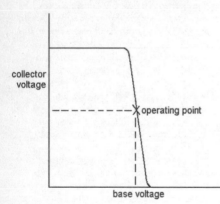

Fig. 84. **operating point**

operating system the software required to make use of a computer and control the action of other programs (*applications*).

operational amplifier or **opamp** a very high-gain linear DC-coupled DIFFERENTIAL AMPLIFIER with a single-ended output. The gain of an opamp will typically be between 10^5 and 10^6. An opamp will have a high INPUT IMPEDANCE of 1MΩ or more, and a low OUTPUT IMPEDANCE of between 50Ω and 5kΩ. Most opamps use a split power supply, typically ±15V. The symbol, Fig. 85(a), shows that the two inputs are marked, one with a + sign and the other

with a − sign. The output becomes positive when the + input is more positive than the − input, and vice versa.

An ideal opamp will have an output which is able to change instantaneously in response to the input. Practical opamps cannot do this; the maximum rate at which the output can change is called the SLEW RATE.

Almost all opamp circuits can be analyzed using two simple rules:
I. The voltage between the + and − inputs is almost zero.
II. The input draw no current.
Consider the application of these rules to the circuit in Fig.85(b):
(a) The + input is grounded, so that Rule I states that the − input must also be at earth potential.
(b) The whole of V_{in} appears across R_1, and the whole of V_{out} appears across R_2. Since Rule II states that the input pass no current, the current through R_1 must have an equal magnitude, but an opposite sign, to that through R_2. In other words, $V_{in}/R_1 = -V_{out}/R_2$. The gain of this circuit, V_{out}/V_{in} is therefore equal to $-R_2/R_1$.

This illustrates a common feature of opamp circuits. Because the intrinsic gain of the device and its input impedances are so high, Rules I and II can be applied, and the gain of an opamp circuit is determined solely by the input and FEEDBACK components.

opposition a SIGNAL which is a mirror-image of another signal. Two signals of identical frequency and waveshape are in opposition if their amplitudes at any instant are equal and opposite. The word ANTIPHASE is sometimes used, but for asymmetrical waves, a 180° phase shift does not produce an opposition (or inverted) wave.

optic, fibre see FIBRE OPTICS.

optical assembly see OPTICAL SYSTEM.

optical axis the straight line connecting the centres of lenses in an optical system.

optical beam proximity detector a security system that detects an intruder by interrupting a light beam.

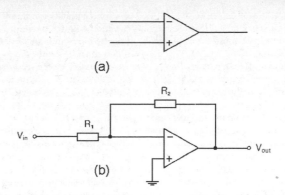

(a)

(b)

Fig. 85. operational amplifier

optical cavity a space in which a light beam can be reflected to and fro, the optical equivalent of a MICROWAVE cavity which is resonant to one particular frequency. See also GAS LASER.

optical character reader (OCR) a device that can SCAN printed characters and give a digital output to a computer. The scanning may be manual or automatic, and the output is usually in ASCII code form.

optical connector see SPDIF.

optical data link a connection between digital machines (often computers) using a light beam either in air or carried by a FIBRE OPTIC CABLE.

optical delay line a delay line for optical signals over a fibre guide, fabricated using silica on silicon. Delay values are small, typically 100 ps for a delay formed on a 2 cm × 2 cm area.

optical digitizer see OPTICAL ENCODER.

optical disc any form of storage system that is read using a LASER beam. This includes the COMPACT DISC and DIGITAL VERSATILE DISC.

optical encoder or **optical digitizer** any device that will convert ANALOGUE quantities into digital form, used particularly of transducers that convert linear or angular displacement into digital terms. See also ENCODER; LINEAR DIGITAL ENCODER; ROTARY ENCODER.

optical fibre a compound thread of two or more types of glass, used in FIBRE OPTICS.

optical filter a transparent material that passes only a limited part of the light spectrum.

optical grating a set of engraved fine lines, very closely spaced, on a transparent material so that, when one grating is moved relative to the other, light passing through both is periodically varied in intensity because of WAVE INTERFERENCE, allowing very precise measurement of displacement to be made.

optical image an image in light, using light and shade, or colour of various degrees of SATURATION (sense 2). A TV CAMERA TUBE or CHARGE COUPLED DEVICE would convert an optical image like this into a CHARGE image, and so into an electron beam image (camera tube) or a digital image (CCD).

optical inputs FIBRE-OPTIC connections that can be used as inputs to a digital recorder if optical signals are available.

optical mark reader a miniature, often pen-size, SCANNER (sense 2) that is used to read reply marks such as ticks or crosses on forms such as lottery ticket forms.

optical medium a storage medium such as a CD or DVD that uses OPTICAL RECORDING and replay.

optical mouse a computer MOUSE that uses visible light or infra-red signals to detect changes in its position. This does not mean that the link between the computer and the mouse is optical, though mice can be obtained that use radio (see BLUETOOTH) or infra-red signals rather than a cable.

optical pickup unit (OPU) the portion of a compact disc or digital versatile disc player or recorder that is concerned with the focusing and positioning of the laser beam and the conversion of reflected light into tracking information and digital output.

optical recording any system of recording DIGITAL DATA by optical methods, mainly applied to devices such as the COMPACT DISC and the DIGITAL VERSATILE DISC.

optical rotary encoder see OPTICAL ENCODER.

optical smoke detector an electronic smoke detector that operates by the reduction of light falling on a PHOTOCELL in the presence of smoke.

optical system or **optical assembly** the portion of a COMPACT DISC or DIGITAL VERSATILE DISC system that focuses the LASER beam on the disc surface and detects the reflected rays.

optical transmission any system of data communication using LASERS and OPTICAL FIBRES.

optical zoom the use on a camera of a lens whose FOCAL LENGTH is variable so that it can zoom from wide-angle (close-up) to telephoto (distant) with no loss of resolution. Contrast DIGITAL ZOOM.

optimum bias or **reference bias** the value of TAPE BIAS that provides the nearest to a flat frequency response over the audio range.

optimum bunching the bunching of electrons in a beam so that each bunch is separated by free space. See also BUNCHER; KLYSTRON.

optimum working frequency (OWF) the most suitable frequency for HF communications, calculated usually as 85% of the MAXIMUM USABLE FREQUENCY.

optocoupler or **optoisolator** a device consisting of a SEMICONDUCTOR PHOTODIODE in close contact with a LIGHT EMITTING DIODE. Signals into the LED are optically transferred to the photodiode, but there

is a considerable degree of isolation, depending on the packaging used, so that the input and output can be at very different DC potentials.

opto-electronics the study and use of optical devices in electronic circuits. Opto-electronic devices such as PHOTODIODES, PHOTOTRANSISTORS and LIGHT EMITTING DIODES can be used to build hybrid electronic-optical circuits in which an electrical signal is converted to light pulses, passed along an optical fibre and reconnected to electrical impulses at the other end. Some forms of signal processing can be carried out on a signal while it is in optical form; for example, filtering, mixing and switching. Developments in extremely high-speed switching are leading to the construction of optical computers and research is continuing in this area.

opto-isolator a circuit used in a MIDI system to allow connection between systems operating with different DC levels. See also OPTOCOUPLER.

OPU see OPTICAL PICKUP UNIT.

OR a logic action whose result is a LOGIC ONE output when any one, several or all of its inputs is at logic 1. See Fig. 86.

Oracle™ a TELETEXT system operated by the Independent Broadcasting Authority (UK), and identical technically to the BBC CEEFAX service.

order of filter a number for an ANALOGUE FILTER that is derived from the POLYNOMIAL expression for the filter, equal to the order of the polynomial.

or function or **logical sum** the OR logical operation as represented in a BOOLEAN EXPRESSION by the use of the + sign. See also AND FUNCTION.

organic semiconductor film a semiconductor material constructed from organic carbon compounds, used as a method of measuring contamination which alters the electrical properties.

OR gate a LOGIC gate that implements the or logic action. The action of the OR gate is inclusive, meaning that the output will be logic 1 no matter whether there is one logic 1 input or more than one. For some

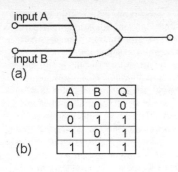

(a)

A	B	Q
0	0	0
0	1	1
1	0	1
1	1	1

(b)

Fig. 86. **OR gate**

applications it is necessary to exclude the case of more than one input being at logic 1, in which case the EXCLUSIVE-OR gate is needed. The NOR GATE (NOT OR) is the preferred version for manufacturing. See Fig. 86.

origin of graph or **0,0** the point on a graph where the axes meet representing a zero amount on each scale.

orthicon an obsolete type of TV CAMERA TUBE, superseded first by the IMAGE ORTHICON, then by the VIDICON before the wholesale adoption of solid-state imaging devices.

orthodynamic principle the forming of a coil on the surface of a DIAPHRAGM to make a headphone or loudspeaker, with the coil in a magnetic field.

orthogonal at right angles or at 90° phase.

orthogonal codes codes which when multiplied and summed over a time interval give a net result of zero.

orthogonal frequency division multiplex (OFDM) a method of DIGITAL MODULATION that generates a large number of closely-spaced CARRIER (sense 1) frequencies each digitally modulated with a portion of the signal and then filtered to produce a SPECTRAL RESPONSE that is almost flat. See also CODED ORTHOGONAL FREQUENCY DIVISION MULTIPLEX (COFDM).

oscillate to change position, voltage or other state alternately in each of two opposite directions at a regular speed. As applied to electronics, to produce a voltage that is a WAVEFORM.

oscillating current a CURRENT that varies in a periodic manner with time, a wave of current.

oscillating voltage a VOLTAGE that varies in a periodic manner with time, a wave of voltage.

oscillation the production of a periodic VOLTAGE or CURRENT, providing a waveform.

oscillation, flip-flop see FLIP-FLOP; see also APERIODIC OSCILLATOR.

oscillator a CIRCUIT that produces an AC signal output from a DC supply. Any circuit that has a negative value of AC resistance over a range of VOLTAGES can be considered to be an oscillator. Connecting a RESONANT CIRCUIT to this NEGATIVE RESISTANCE will result in a tuned oscillator whose output is close to a sine wave in shape. If the oscillating conditions only just produce negative resistance over a short range, the waveshape will be a reasonably pure sine wave. If the negative resistance is large, or if no tuned circuit is connected (see APERIODIC CIRCUIT), the output will be of square shape, as the oscillator output swings between BOTTOMING and CUT-OFF. A few devices, such as TUNNEL DIODES, have a negative resistance portion of their characteristic.

The other approach to oscillators is to produce a more controllable negative resistance characteristic by using an amplifier with POSITIVE FEEDBACK, so that the output signal from the amplifier provides enough input signal to sustain oscillation. This approach is the basis of common oscillator circuits such as the COLPITTS OSCILLATOR; FRANKLIN OSCILLATOR and HARTLEY OSCILLATOR. See also BUTLER OVERTONE OSCILLATOR; CLAPP OSCILLATOR; PHASE SHIFT OSCILLATOR.

oscillator, PSU see SWITCH MODE POWER SUPPLY.

oscillator tracking the correspondence of frequency between input tuning and local oscillator in a SUPERHETERODYNE RECEIVER.

oscillator tuned collector see TUNED-COLLECTOR OSCILLATOR.

oscillator, phase shift see PHASE SHIFT OSCILLATOR.

oscillator, quartz crystal see CRYSTAL OSCILLATOR.

oscillator, relaxation see RELAXATION OSCILLATOR.

oscillator, superhet see LOCAL OSCILLATOR.

oscillator, tape erase/bias see TAPE BIAS; TAPE ERASE.

oscillator, triangle wave see TRIANGLE WAVE OSCILLATOR.

oscillator, twin-T see TWIN-T OSCILLATOR.

oscillator, voltage controlled see VOLTAGE CONTROLLED OSCILLATOR

oscillator, Wien bridge see WIEN BRIDGE OSCILLATOR.

oscillator, Schmitt trigger see SCHMITT TRIGGER OSCILLATOR.

oscillator, unijunction see UNIJUNCTION OSCILLATOR.

oscilloscope see CATHODE-RAY OSCILLOSCOPE.

oscilloscope, digital storage see DIGITAL STORAGE OSCILLOSCOPE (DSO).

oscilloscope probe see PROBE (sense 1).

OSD on-screen display: the appearance on the screen of a TV receiver of information relating to a VIDEO CASSETTE RECORDER, DVD RECORDER, SET-TOP BOX, or other setting-up information.

OSI see OPEN SYSTEMS INTERCONNECT.

OTHR see OVER THE HORIZON RADAR.

OTP see ONE-TIME PROGRAMMABLE.

outer coding or **outer code** the REED-SOLOMON CODING of a DIGITAL DATA stream prior to other processes such as INTERLEAVING and INNER CODING.

outgassing the removal of absorbed gas from the metal, ceramic and glass of a THERMIONIC VALVE. This is done by eddy current heating while the valve is being evacuated. At later stages, outgassing can be assisted by running the valve filament and possibly passing ANODE current. Transmitting valves use no GETTER to absorb traces of gas, so it is particularly important to perform the outgassing very thoroughly while the valve is still connected to the vacuum pumps.

out-of-phase signal a signal whose phase is not in PHASE with respect to another signal. Out of phase is sometimes used to imply that the signal is INVERTED, but the two shapes are not identical for signals other than sine waves.

out of service testing the testing of equipment using artificially injected signals as distinct from making measurements on equipment that is still in use.

output the final signal-delivering STAGE of an electronic circuit. Contrast INPUT (sense 2).

output characteristic a graph plotting output current against output voltage for a circuit or device.

output current the current delivered by a device or absorbed by a device at its output.

output fuse a FUSE placed between an audio OUTPUT STAGE and a LOUDSPEAKER to protect the loudspeaker against excessive current. The fuse must be securely mounted to avoid variations in resistance.

output gap the part of a MICROWAVE device from which the microwave signal is taken.

output impedance the ratio of signal voltage to current, usually expressed as a COMPLEX NUMBER from which amplitude and phase can be obtained, at the OUTPUT of a DEVICE or CIRCUIT.

output level the AMPLITUDE of signal from a device (such as a tapehead or disc CARTRIDGE, sense 2) under standard conditions.

output meter a METER that can be connected to the OUTPUT of a CIRCUIT to measure the power at the output.

output offset voltage the value of output voltage of an OPERATIONAL AMPLIFIER when both input terminals are earthed.

output power the amount of power that a circuit can deliver to a load, usually quoted in watts, either for DC or for a sine wave. See also MUSIC POWER.

output regulation see REGULATION.

output resistance the ratio of signal voltage to signal current at the output of a device or circuit.

output stage or **output** the final signal-delivering stage of an electronic circuit.

output transformer a TRANSFORMER that is used at the OUTPUT of a CIRCUIT for COUPLING and IMPEDANCE MATCHING.

Output transformers were at one time used in domestic audio amplifiers, but are seldom seen nowadays because of the developments in power transistors. The form of output transformer used in AMPLITUDE MODULATION is known as a *modulation transformer*.

overall efficiency   the ratio of power supplied by a DEVICE to the power required to operate it.

overall noise factor   a figure for NOISE FACTOR for a multistage unit that takes into account the noise performance and gain of each stage.

overbunching   the separation of bunched electrons after optimum bunching has been achieved. See BUNCHER; KLYSTRON.

overclocking   running a MICROPROCESSOR at a speed above that for which it was intended. This is often used as a way of obtaining faster computing speeds, but at the cost of overheating and so shortening the life of the processor, perhaps drastically.

overcoupling   an excessive coupling (see CRITICAL COUPLING) between RESONANT CIRCUITs that will cause the amplitude-frequency graph to show a dip at the frequency of resonance. See also UNDERCOUPLING.

overcurrent protection   a circuit that will detect excessive current flowing in a circuit and either limit the current or switch off power (see OVERCURRENT TRIP).

overcurrent trip   a safety device that opens a CIRCUIT when excessive CURRENT flows.

overdamped   an amount of damping that prevents OSCILLATIONs completely and causes a voltage or movement to die away too slowly. See DAMPED; UNDERDAMPED.

overdriven   (of an amplifying STAGE) having too large an input signal. This causes DISTORTION of the output, and sometimes causes a DEAD TIME in which no output signal is produced.

overdubbing   a separate RECORDING of a piece of music from one instrument on a multi-track tape that can be used to replace another track made at an earlier time.

overflow, arithmetic   a word-length problem that arises when the result of an arithmetical operation requires more BITS than are allocated to a WORD.

over-horizon propagation   the broadcasting of a radio signal over the visible horizon. PROPAGATION over the near horizon can be due to signal refraction in the lower atmosphere but for greater distances, the propagation is carried out by reflections from the IONOSPHERE. Modern satellites allow a different form of over-horizon propagation by the re-broadcasting of transmissions that are beamed to the satellite.

overlapping gate   a form of construction for CHARGE-COUPLED DEVICES.

overlapping sidebands   a problem caused by excessively close spacing of CARRIERS (sense 1), causing interference to received signals.

overlay   see KEYING (sense 1).

overload   to take more than the RATED POWER from a DEVICE or CIRCUIT, either by using too small a load or by using too large an input. Overloading may cause a deterioration in the OUTPUT (such as an unacceptable waveform shape), or possibly damage to the device or circuit.

overload characteristic   the way in which OVERLOAD PROTECTION operates, often by reducing the voltage, see RE-ENTRANT OVERLOAD CHARACTERISTIC.

overload level   the amount of output power at which OVERLOAD sets in.

overload protection   any circuit or device, electromechanical or electronic, that will prevent too much power being taken from a circuit.

overmodulation   excessive AMPLITUDE MODULATION of a CARRIER (sense 1) so that the carrier amplitude is reduced to zero at each modulation trough. See Fig. 87.

overrun   loss of data in a computer input due to the data arriving at a PORT (sense 1) faster than it can be processed.

oversampling   an increase in BIT RATE of sampled data by adding interpolated (see INTERPOLATION) numbers.

overscan   the application of excessive scan amplitude to a TV CAMERA TUBE. This is

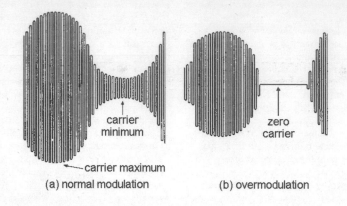

carrier
minimum

zero
carrier

carrier maximum

(a) normal modulation   (b) overmodulation

Fig. 87. **overmodulation**

done to ensure that the whole of the active surface is used at times when the camera is working with a test signal. Using overscan avoids any danger of marking the normal picture area with a burned-in image.

overshoot an excessive transient portion of PULSE amplitude. At the leading edge of a pulse, the voltage may momentarily rise above the normal amplitude level of the top of the pulse. This transient is the 'overshoot'. Compare UNDERSHOOT. See Fig. 38.

over the horizon RADAR (OTHR) RADAR that uses low frequencies, typically in the range 5 to 28 MHz, to obtain very long range reflections.

overtone see HARMONIC.

over-voltage cutoff a device, mechanical or electronic, that will cut off power supplies if the supply voltage rises to a level that is too high.

over-voltage diode a diode that forms part of an OVER-VOLTAGE PROTECTION circuit, conducting and triggering a protection circuit when the applied voltage is too high.

over-voltage protection the provision for preventing a rise in supply voltage from damaging an electronic circuit by cutting off or limiting the voltage.

overwind an additional winding on a transformer core as, for example, the

EHT winding on a television LINE OUTPUT TRANSFORMER.

overwrite to replace the contents of a memory, or data stored magnetically or on a CD REWRITER or DVD RECORDER, by other data.

oxidation a chemical process in which an element or compound is combined with oxygen (the gas that forms approximately 20% of air) to form a compound or compounds called 'oxides'. The oxides of metals are generally insulators, and the controlled oxidation of silicon to produce non-conducting silicon oxide is an essential part of the production of semiconductors of many types, particularly MOSFETS (see FIELD-EFFECT TRANSISTOR) and INTEGRATED CIRCUITS. Burning a fuel is a more familiar form of oxidation, but the term is also used more widely in chemistry to denote any process in which electrons are removed from an atom to form an ion, whether this process involves oxygen or not.

oxide masking the use of a layer of SILICON (IV) oxide to protect the underlying silicon. The oxide layer can be selectively etched with acid to allow the silicon to be treated further.

ozone smell a characteristic smell that indicates a CORONA DISCHARGE from high voltage points in a circuit.

PA 1. see POWER AMPLIFIER. 2. see PUBLIC ADDRESS.

package any form of enclosure for a component, particularly a SEMICONDUCTOR device.

packet see DATA PACKET.

packet assembler/disassembler (PAD) a circuit used as an intermediate between an ISDN line and a packet switched network for organizing data into packets (see DATA PACKET) and reassembling packets into a continuous data stream.

packet identification or **PID** a 13-bit portion of the MPEG signal that carries the identification for a DATA PACKET, placing it correctly in its data stream.

packet multiplexer a DIGITAL MULTIPLEXER that combines video, audio, data and service information into a digital stream with an output to a TRANSPORT STREAM.

packet or **data packet** a set of BYTES of DATA along with start and stop bytes and an identification code. A data transmission that is broken into packets can be reassembled even if the packets have been sent at intervals rather than in a continuous stream.

packet, digital TV a 204-byte unit consisting of DIGITAL DATA and error-correcting signals, with an identifying code so that it can be correctly reassembled when it arrives at a receiver.

packet radio a communication system that uses amateur radio transmitters operating along with computers to relay data.

packet switch node a computer used purely for relaying DATA PACKETS as part of a NETWORK (sense 2).

packet switched network a network in which DATA PACKETS, each containing information on route and destination, can be sent to receiving terminals.

packet switching the insertion of DATA PACKETS into a network.

packet synchronization the first byte in the header for an MPEG PACKET, conventionally allocated with a fixed value.

packet writing see INCREMENTAL WRITING.

packing density 1. the number of ACTIVE COMPONENTS per unit area in an INTEGRATED CIRCUIT. 2. the number of DATA BITS that can be recorded in a given space on a medium. 3. the number of molecules or atoms per unit volume in a crystalline material.

pad 1. a connection to a PRINTED CIRCUIT or an INTEGRATED CIRCUIT. 2. an ATTENUATOR circuit with a fixed division ratio.

padder a PRESET capacitor connected in series with an inductor, used to correct TRACKING (sense 2) for the OSCILLATOR of a SUPERHETERODYNE receiver. See also TRIMMER.

padding bit a bit added to a signal as part of a BIT STUFFING process.

paddle or **games paddle** a form of JOYSTICK, a controller that is held in the hand and used to control the position of an object, such as a CURSOR, on a computer MONITOR. Used mainly in games at one time, but now superseded by the JOYSTICK. See also MOUSE; TRACKERBALL.

page a unit of MEMORY for computer use.

Pagefax the system of transmitting complete pages of a newspaper for remote printing.

pair a TRANSMISSION LINE with two conductors. The conductors may be parallel (twin-line), twisted, or in coaxial form. See SHIELDED TWISTED PAIR; TWISTED PAIR.

paired cable a CABLE made from sets of twin conductors.

paired disparity code a type of BINARY CODE in which each input BIT of the original can be replaced by one of two signal levels of opposite polarity.

pairing an analogue TV display fault that accentuates the appearance of scanning lines on the screen (see SCAN). Pairing occurs as the result of a synchronizing fault that prevents correct INTERLACE action. As a result, the even-numbered lines are in the same screen positions (or very close to) the odd-numbered lines. This makes the screen appear to have much lower vertical resolution.

pair selected ternary a digital coding system that divides the stream of data into pairs of bits and then re-codes each pair with two TERNARY (three-state) digits.

Paknet™ an alarm signalling network for security in domestic, industrial, or public service premises.

PAL Phase Alternate Line: the standard European analogue COLOUR TELEVISION coding system. Like the SECAM system, PAL was devised to correct faults that were evident in the much earlier (1952) NTSC system. Of these faults, the most troublesome was the effect of phase variations in the colour signals, which caused frequent and random colour variations in the received picture. This led to the joke that NTSC was an abbreviation for 'never twice the same colour'.

In the PAL system, devised by Telefunken in Germany, the luminance (Y) signal is transmitted normally, and the colour information is coded into two signals, the U and V signals. The U signal (whose AMPLITUDE is proportional to B–Y), is transmitted by modulating a SUBCARRIER in phase, and the V signal (proportional to R–Y) is modulated on to the subcarrier at 90° phase. The V signal is inverted on alternate lines, hence the name of the system. The phase of the synchronizing burst signal is also alternated to +45° and –45° relative to a reference OSCILLATOR. At the TELEVISION RECEIVER, the alternation of the burst phase is used to identify (by generating an IDENT SIGNAL) the phase of the V signal, and to invert it when necessary. Because of the inversion, phase changes in transmission can be cancelled. The cancellation is done by delaying the colour signals for one line duration, and adding them to the colour signals for the next line. The colour signals are thus always

averaged over two lines, in one of which the V signals will have been inverted during transmission. The main disadvantage of both PAL and SECAM systems is that the vertical RESOLUTION is halved as compared to the NTSC system because of the averaging of the contents of adjacent lines. See also DIGITAL TELEVISION.

PAL matrix the adding and subtracting circuit which derives the separate R, G and B signals for a PAL colour receiver from the LUMINANCE signal and the two COLOUR DIFFERENCE SIGNALS.

PAL switch the circuit that switches the phase of the V CHROMINANCE SIGNAL in the PAL receiver before applying it to the V chrominance detector. This prevents the alternate line inversion from affecting the phase of the R–Y output.

PAM see PULSE AMPLITUDE MODULATION.

pan-and-scan an action used to convert 16:9 TV images to 4:3 ASPECT RATIO.

panchromatic display a grey scale display in which colours are correctly rendered as shades of grey with the luminance that the eye would see for the corresponding colour.

panel lamp a lamp fitted on a panel and used as a warning light or to indicate power on.

panel meters meters that are displayed permanently on a panel rather than temporarily connected as for servicing.

panoramic display a form of SPECTRUM ANALYZER for radio systems that displays the frequencies within the IF band of the receiver.

panoramic potentiometer a device used for STEREO signals, consisting of a pair of variable ATTENUATORs, one working clockwise the other anticlockwise to shift the position of a MONOPHONIC source to any point between loudspeakers.

panoramic receiver a radio RECEIVER that automatically tunes to a number of selected frequencies (see FREQUENCY) in sequence. Panoramic receivers are used to monitor international distress frequencies, or to monitor signals from a number of users of different frequencies.

panpot   see PANORAMIC POTENTIOMETER.

paper capacitor   a CAPACITOR whose DIELECTRIC is paper, usually impregnated with insulating oil. The metal conductors can be aluminium foil ribbons, or aluminium metallized coatings (see METALLIZED PAPER CAPACITOR). The sandwich of conductors and paper is rolled into the form of a cylinder with another layer of paper. Values of capacitance in the region of 1nF to 0.5μF can be achieved in a reasonable size, and the voltage rating can be high, typically 100V to 1kV.

paper-out switch   a switch fitted inside a printer that makes contact when no paper is present, sending a signal back to the computer to suspend printing.

paper tape   an obsolete method of permanent storage for computer data. The data is recorded by punching holes across the width of the tape, using up to eight preset positions. Each line of holes represents one character of a data file. The system is very slow, and has been superseded for all but vitally important archives by magnetic recording or OPTICAL DISC STORAGE. See also MAGNETIC RECORDING; MAGNETIC TAPE.

parabolic dish   a reflector for MICROWAVES consisting of a paraboloid shape that will reflect rays of a parallel beam to a focus point along the axis (the BORESIGHT).

parabolic reflector or **microwave dish**   a concave mirror of parabolic cross section that is used as a receiving or transmitting AERIAL for radio waves in the form of a parallel beam. For transmission, the signal source, often the HORN end of a WAVEGUIDE, is located at the FOCUS of the REFLECTOR, so that waves from the horn are reflected into a beam whose area of cross section is the same as that of the reflector. For reception, a beam of waves hitting the reflector is focused on to a small area at which the first receiver stage may be placed. Small parabolic reflectors are used domestically to pick up direct satellite broadcasts.

parabolic reflector microphone   a microphone situated at the focal point of a reflector providing a considerable gain of signals arriving on the axis, but scattering waves that arrive off axis.

parabolic waveform   a waveform added to the field timebase of a TV receiver in order to correct for PINCUSHION DISTORTION.

parallax error   error in reading the position of, typically, a needle over a scale because the position of the eye affects the apparent position of the needle. Parallax error does not occur when DIGITAL DISPLAYS are used.

parallel   1. (of a circuit or component) being connected so that it will share CURRENT with another circuit or component, having the same POTENTIAL DIFFERENCE. See PARALLEL CONNECTION. 2. (of lines or planes) evenly spaced so that the angle between them is zero, and they do not meet. 3. (of microprocessor chips) sharing tasks on data in a parallel processor computer.

parallel adder   a LOGIC GATE circuit that will add corresponding BITS of two WORDS, with terminals for a carry in and a carry out.

parallel capacitors   CAPACITORS connected in PARALLEL (sense 1) so that the combined capacitance C_T is given by: $C_T = C_1 + C_2 + C_3 + \ldots$ where C_1, C_2, C_3, etc. are the individual capacitor values.

parallel cells   CELLS connected in PARALLEL (sense 1) so that the voltage is that of a single cell, but with a current capability equal to the current that one cell can supply multiplied by the number of cells. This type of connection is discouraged because a fault in one cell can lead to rapid discharge of the others as they supply current to the faulty cell.

parallel changeover   a form of multi-connection switch that will change over a set of contacts.

parallel connection   a form of connection that makes it possible to share current across a common potential difference. PARALLEL RESISTORS form a total resistance that is smaller than any of the single values. PARALLEL CAPACITORS form a capacitance that is the sum of individual capacitance values. PARALLEL CELLS (each with the same voltage output) form a battery with higher current rating, but the same voltage output as a single cell. Contrast SERIES CONNECTION. See also PARALLEL TRANSMISSION.

parallel data transfer see PARALLEL TRANSMISSION.

paralleled input transistors the method of reducing INPUT RESISTANCE for an audio pre-amplifier by using transistors connected in parallel.

parallel feedback FEEDBACK that is applied in *shunt* or PARALLEL (sense 1) with the input signal to an amplifier.

parallel i/o a computer PORT (sense 1) that permits PARALLEL TRANSMISSION for both input and output.

parallel-in parallel-out (PIPO) a REGISTER constructed from a connected chain of FLIP-FLOP units. Each unit has a separate input and separate output. The units can load inputs and deliver outputs together, but there is no shifting of bits from one unit to another unless by external connections. Compare FIRST IN / FIRST OUT BUFFER; FIRST IN / LAST OUT BUFFER; PARALLEL-IN SERIAL-OUT; SERIAL-IN PARALLEL-OUT; SERIAL-IN SERIAL-OUT.

parallel input the provision, usually in a REGISTER, to place data into each FLIP-FLOP of a set simultaneously.

parallel-in serial-out (PISO) a register constructed from a connected chain of FLIP-FLOPS used for converting data from parallel to serial form. A PISO register can accept an input at each unit, but outputs

are obtained from one end only by clocking (see clock) the register. Compare FIRST IN / FIRST OUT BUFFER; FIRST IN / LAST OUT BUFFER; PARALLEL-IN PARALLEL-OUT; SERIAL-IN PARALLEL-OUT; SERIAL-IN SERIAL-OUT. See Fig. 88.

parallel-loading the loading (see LOAD) of a RESONANT CIRCUIT by connecting a resistor in PARALLEL (sense 1). The lower this value of resistance, the greater the loading or damping (see DAMPED).

parallel loading counter a COUNTER circuit consisting of FLIP-FLOPS (usually in a REGISTER) in which a number can be loaded in before counting starts by using the PARALLEL INPUTS.

parallel-plate capacitor a CAPACITOR consisting of two or more PARALLEL (sense 2) conducting plates that are separated by an INSULATOR called the DIELECTRIC. For such a structure, capacitance can be calculated from the dimensions of one plate and the thickness and RELATIVE PERMITTIVITY value of the dielectric. Most practical forms of capacitor are variations on this basic design.

parallel port a computer PORT (sense 1), used mainly for a printer, with typically 22 lines for communication using 8-bit PARALLEL TRANSMISSION in each direction along with control signals.

parallel-port device any device, such as a HARD DRIVE, a SCANNER (sense 2) or a TAPE STREAMER, that is connected through the parallel (printer) port rather than as a card inserted into the computer. This makes it

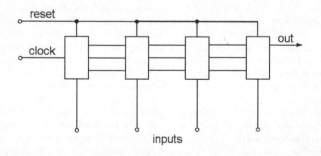

Fig. 88. **parallel-in serial-out**

easier to remove peripherals for reasons of security or moving from one machine to another. On modern computers, the use of connections such as USB or FIREWIRE is more common now.

parallel printer a PRINTER that makes use of parallel signals on eight data lines. The CENTRONICS standard of PARALLEL CONNECTION requires the use of eleven active lines, though a number of additional 'ground' lines are often added to the connector.

parallel processing a method of increasing processing speed. The traditional design of computer uses SERIAL PROCESSING, which means that instructions are carried out one after another. Parallel processing is a system, currently used mainly in mainframe machines, in which several instructions can be carried out simultaneously.

parallel resistors resistors connected in parallel so that the total resistance R_T is found from

$$R_T = \frac{1}{R_1} + \frac{1}{R_2} + \frac{1}{R_3} + \dots$$

where R_1, R_2, R_3, etc. are the individual resistance values.

parallel resonant circuit or **parallel tuned circuit** a RESONANT CIRCUIT that uses an inductor connected in PARALLEL (sense 1) with a capacitor.

parallel-T filter the combination of HIGH-PASS FILTER and LOW-PASS FILTER sections, usually constructed from resistors and capacitors, that provides a BAND-PASS FILTER action.

parallel-T network see TWIN-T NETWORK (sense 1).

parallel-T oscillator an oscillator circuit that uses a PARALLEL T FILTER in a NEGATIVE FEEDBACK loop to provide a 180° phase shift at a frequency determined by the values of the filter components.

parallel transmission or **parallel data transfer** a connection between a COMPUTER and a PERIPHERAL that consists of a number of lines, one for each digital bit in the data unit plus a set of control lines. Parallel transmission is fast and is used for connecting the computer to disk systems. It has also been widely used for connection to printers, using the Centronics standard. Fast SERIAL TRANSMISSION systems are now replacing parallel transmission for computer use.

parallel tuned circuit see PARALLEL RESONANT CIRCUIT.

parameter a quantity whose value is fixed only for one particular example. The parameters of a TRANSISTOR, for example, include quantities such as the forward current transfer ratio (current out/current in). This parameter may be constant for one particular transistor and set of conditions, but will have a different value under different test conditions, or in the next transistor that is tested.

parametric amplifier a form of AMPLIFIER that is used mainly for MICROWAVES. The parametric amplifier uses a device, such as a VARACTOR, for which a PARAMETER (capacitance in this example) is electrically variable. By using a signal to vary the parameter at a suitable frequency, a combination of amplification and frequency mixing can be achieved. The action of varying the parameter is called *pumping*.

parametric control a form of TONE CONTROL that allows a cut or lift in response as well as adjustment of the FREQUENCY at which this cut or lift occurs.

parametric equalizer a device used in PUBLIC ADDRESS systems that provides FILTER action with both the FREQUENCY and BANDWIDTH adjustable.

paraphase amplifier an amplifier that converts SINGLE-ENDED (unbalanced) signals into balanced form (see BALANCED AMPLIFIER) so that the sum of output signal amplitudes is always zero. The simplest form of paraphase amplifier is the transistor with equal loads in the emitter and the collector circuits. See Fig. 89.

parasitic element or **passive aerial** or **parasitic radiator** an aerial (antenna) element that does not receive or transmit signals and is used only to make an active aerial directional. See also DIRECTOR; REFLECTOR.

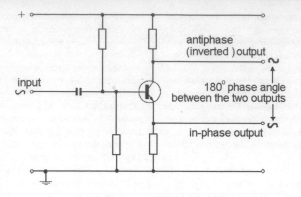

Fig. 89. **paraphase amplifier**

parasitic oscillation the unwanted oscillation caused by POSITIVE FEEDBACK in an AMPLIFIER. The feedback is usually through STRAY CAPACITANCE or INDUCTANCE, and so is at a very high frequency. In some cases, such as audio amplifiers, the existence of parasitic oscillations may not be suspected because they are usually above the audio range. See also MOTORBOATING.

parasitic radiator see PARASITIC AERIAL.

parasitic stopper a RESISTOR used to suppress PARASITIC OSCILLATION. When parasitic oscillation cannot be stopped by using screening, changes in layout, or other methods of avoiding STRAY CAPACITANCE and INDUCTANCE effects, parasitic stoppers may be used. These are resistors connected into the path of the oscillation to cause damping (see DAMPED). Stoppers are usually resistors of 100R to 1K value wired as close to the ELECTRODES of an ACTIVE COMPONENT as possible.

parity or **digit counting** a method of checking for errors in a DIGITAL message by counting the number of logic 1 bits. See also EVEN PARITY; ODD PARITY; PARITY BIT.

parity bit a BIT added to a BYTE before a digital transmission so as to make the total number of logic 1 bits even (for EVEN PARITY) or odd (for ODD PARITY). If the count of logic 1 bits at the receiver for a byte is incorrect, there has been an error, and a re-send is requested.

parity check code a set of bits used for error checking in a CYCLIC REDUNDANCY CHECK system. See also SYNDROME.

parity check polynomial an algebraic expression using several terms that describes how additional parity codes are used on a set of digits, such as a digital video frame.

parked head a READ/WRITE HEAD of a HARD DRIVE that is positioned on an unused track while inactive, minimizing damage if the drive is knocked.

partial gain the gain of a REFLECTOR AERIAL (antenna), intended to be used with two polarized carriers at 90° to each other, for one plane of polarization, see POLARIZATION, AERIAL.

partial response coding a coding system for BINARY (sense 1) data in which a LOW-PASS FILTER is used to remove high-frequency components, producing a MULTI-LEVEL SIGNAL with a narrower BANDWIDTH.

partition a section of a HARD DRIVE that is used by a computer as if it were a separate hard drive.

partition noise a form of NOISE in multi-electrode devices where an electron stream is divided. When THERMIONIC VALVES with several electrodes, such as pentodes, were used in receivers partition noise arose because of random fluctuations in the electron currents to the various electrodes. Partition noise is also a feature of BIPOLAR JUNCTION TRANSISTORS, hence the use of FIELD EFFECT TRANSISTORS for high frequencies.

PASC   see MPEG LAYER I AUDIO.

pascal   the unit of pressure equal to one newton per square metre.

pass band   the range of frequencies that a FILTER will pass from input to output with minimum attenuation. The range is usually defined in terms of the frequencies that are 3dB down as compared to the central frequency of the band. Contrast REJECTION BAND.

passivation   the protection of a SEMICONDUCTOR surface from unwanted contamination.

passive   requiring no power supply; using only PASSIVE COMPONENTS.

passive aerial   see PARASITIC AERIAL.

passive circuit   a circuit containing only PASSIVE COMPONENTS and requiring no power supply.

passive component   a COMPONENT that cannot cause a POWER gain. Components such as resistors, capacitors, and linear inductors (including transformers) are all passive. Nonlinear action along with a power supply, such as in a MAGNETIC AMPLIFIER, can cause a component to be classed as an ACTIVE COMPONENT.

passive crossover   a circuit that splits AUDIO signals into bass and treble to feed to separate loudspeakers, consisting only of PASSIVE COMPONENTS. Contrast ACTIVE CROSSOVER.

passive diaphragm or **passive radiator** a loudspeaker CONE and suspension connected into the same cabinet as a fully working loudspeaker and used as a form of loading system to improve response.

passive equalization   an audio EQUALIZATION circuit that uses only PASSIVE COMPONENTS, capacitors and resistors.

passive filter   a filter circuit that uses only passive components, as distinct from an ACTIVE FILTER.

passive infra-red (PIR)   a form of security detection operated by the heat from human or animal bodies. See also ACTIVE INFRA-RED DETECTOR.

passive-matrix screen   a form of LCD display that is controlled by using a

TRANSISTOR to drive each row and column (as distinct from each cell). This is cheaper and easier to manufacture than the ACTIVE-MATRIX LCD screen type, but the performance is inferior. See also TFT.

passive radar   a form of RADAR that does not transmit but uses MICROWAVE or INFRA-RED radiation emitted from a target to provide location information.

passive radiator   see PASSIVE DIAPHRAGM.

passive reflector   a reflecting surface for radio waves, the equivalent of a plane mirror for light, used to direct waves into a location that would otherwise by in shadow.

passive repeater   a form of relay for radio waves using two reflectors coupled by a length of WAVEGUIDE so the signals received by one can be retransmitted in another direction.

passive servicing   servicing using instruments such as METERS and CATHODE-RAY OSCILLOSCOPES only, with no attempt to inject signals.

passive substrate   a layer of INSULATION, often an intrinsic semiconductor or an insulating mineral crystal like sapphire, on which a SEMICONDUCTOR or other component can be formed or attached.

passive system   a detection system that emits no radiation, making it difficult to detect.

passive tone control   a tone control that makes use only of PASSIVE COMPONENTS. Contrast ACTIVE TONE CONTROL.

pass switch or **inhibit switch**   a switch, usable only by authorized personnel, that inhibits an alarm system.

PAT   see PROGRAM ASSOCIATION TABLE.

patchboard or **plugboard**   a board that contains sockets that are connected to CIRCUITs or devices. Experimental interconnections of circuits can then be arranged by connecting sockets with patch cords. See also BREADBOARD.

patch cord   **1.** a CABLE with a plug at each end, used for making connections on a PATCHBOARD. **2.** an extension cable, especially one that allows a board taken from a circuit to be run externally for fault-finding purposes.

patching I. the making of connections temporarily on a PATCHBOARD or BREADBOARD. This is done to test a circuit idea, or to make measurements without the need to have to construct a circuit or PRINTED CIRCUIT BOARD. Patching is feasible only for comparatively low-frequency circuits because of the large STRAY CAPACITANCES and INDUCTANCES of a patchboard system. **2.** in the US, making a connection between a radio link and a telephone system.

pattern generator a circuit or computer program that can generate signals that produce SCREEN patterns, used normally for checking the performance of a MONITOR or TV receiver.

pattern recognition the use of logic circuits to recognize patterns in binary data, whether these correspond to images or other forms of information.

patterning the appearance on TV screen of random patterns not related to the picture and usually caused by CO-CHANNEL INTERFERENCE.

P-bit one bit of the CONTROL WORD of a CD, used to indicate the start of music.

PC see PC COMPUTER.

PC card see CARD.

PC computer or **PC** see PERSONAL COMPUTER.

PCA see PROGRAM CALIBRATION AREA.

PCB see PRINTED CIRCUIT BOARD.

PCB diagram a diagram showing the connections on a PRINTED CIRCUIT BOARD, used for servicing purposes.

p-channel a conducting channel in a FIELD-EFFECT TRANSISTOR that uses P-TYPE doping. See also N-CHANNEL.

p-channel MOSFET a MOSFET IC that uses P-CHANNEL structures only.

PCI bus see PERIPHERAL COMPONENTS INTERCONNECT BUS.

PCM see PULSE CODE MODULATION.

PCM adapter a circuit added to a VIDEO CASSETTE RECORDER to allow it to be used for digital sound. A few early VCRs incorporated this adapter and were highly prized by audio enthusiasts.

PCMCIA see PERSONAL COMPUTER MEMORY CARD INTERNATIONAL ASSOCIATION.

PCS personal communications system.

PC-video converter the circuit whose inputs are the R, G and B set of signals for a computer monitor and whose output is a TV signal.

PD see POTENTIAL DIFFERENCE.

PD array the set of six photodiodes that are used to detect the reflected laser beam from a COMPACT DISC surface, and so control focus and position of the beam.

PDA see POST-DEFLECTION ACCELERATION.

PDC see PROGRAMME DELIVERY CONTROL.

PDM see PULSE-DURATION MODULATION.

PDN public data network.

PDP see PLASMA DISPLAY.

peak a maximum level, usually of amplitude of voltage or current.

peak amplitude the maximum level of AMPLITUDE of a WAVE.

peak clipping see CLIPPER.

peak detector a DEMODULATOR circuit that charges a capacitor to the peak value of each input CARRIER (sense 1) wave and whose TIME CONSTANTs permit this voltage to change up and down as the carrier wave amplitude changes. See also AVERAGE DETECTOR.

peak factor the ratio of PEAK AMPLITUDE to ROOT MEAN SQUARE (sense 2) value.

peak forward voltage the maximum permitted voltage across a RECTIFIER when current flows in the forward direction. The rectifier may be a DIODE, or a JUNCTION (sense 2) in a BIPOLAR JUNCTION TRANSISTOR.

peak inrush current the maximum amount of current that can flow into the RESERVOIR CAPACITOR of a power supply at the instant of switch on.

peak inverse voltage or **peak reverse voltage** the maximum permitted voltage across a RECTIFIER when BIAS is reversed, with no current flowing. This is a very important quantity for a DIODE or a semiconductor JUNCTION (sense 2), because if the peak inverse voltage is exceeded, the diode or junction may break down. Unless the amount of current can be limited, the diode or junction will then be destroyed.

peak limiter see CLIPPER.

peak load a load that causes maximum possible power to be dissipated from a circuit.

peak point the start of a NEGATIVE RESISTANCE region in the CHARACTERISTIC of a UNIJUNCTION or TUNNEL DIODE.

peak recorded velocity the maximum velocity of a stylus in the vinyl disc RECORDING, which can be as high as 60 cm per second.

peak reverse voltage see PEAK INVERSE VOLTAGE.

peak-riding clipper a form of self-adjusting CLIPPER. A peak-riding clipper charges a CAPACITOR to the value of the peak voltage of the signal, and uses this voltage as a clipping voltage. In this way, brief interference pulses can be clipped, but if the TIME CONSTANT is well chosen fluctuations in the PEAK AMPLITUDE of the wanted signal will not cause clipping of the signal.

peak sensitivity wavelength the WAVELENGTH of light for which a photocell has its maximum sensitivity.

peak-shift distortion see INTER-SYMBOL INTERFERENCE.

peak-to-peak amplitude a wave AMPLITUDE, particularly for an ASYMMETRICAL waveform, that is measured from the positive peak value to the negative peak value. See Fig. 90.

peak value an AMPLITUDE measured to one peak of a waveform from the zero voltage or from a steady BIAS level.

peak voltage clamp a circuit whose output is the PEAK LEVEL of the wave input. The simplest peak voltage clamp consists of a diode and the capacitor only.

peak white the level of AMPLITUDE of a TV signal that corresponds to peak brightness of white light on the screen.

pedestal a SQUARE WAVEFORM on top of which another pulse can be placed. The pedestal provides the starting voltage for the main pulse. See also SANDCASTLE PULSE. See Fig. 91.

peer-to-peer network or **p2p network** a form of NETWORK (sense 2) that does not use a SERVER. All computers on the network are equal partners, and each user can decide what files will be available on the network.

PEG see PRIMARY EARTH GROUND.

pel see PIXEL.

Peltier junction a metal JUNCTION (sense 3), part of a pair, whose temperature will rise or fall when current is passed through both. The usual requirement is for one Peltier junction to provide cooling.

pendulum switch a switch operated by a pendulum so that it responds to movement, used as part of a car security alarm system.

pentavalent element an element whose outer shell contains five electrons, used for DOPING a semiconductor to N-type.

Pentium™ a name for a large family of microprocessors produced over many years by Intel. The naming, rather than numbering, of microprocessor types was initiated because numbers could not be used as a trademark.

pentode a THERMIONIC VALVE with three GRIDS, a CONTROL GRID, *screen grid*, and *suppressor grid*. Such a valve has a characteristic in which the ANODE current is controlled almost entirely by the grid voltage, with anode voltage having only a negligible effect.

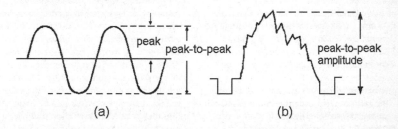

Fig. 90. **peak-to-peak amplitude**

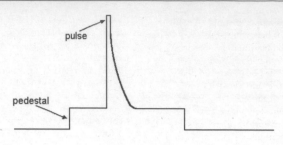

Fig. 91. **pedestal**

percentage modulation a measurement of linear AMPLITUDE MODULATION. The 'percentage modulation' is the amplitude of modulating signal divided by the amplitude of CARRIER (sense 1) signal, expressed as a percentage.

percentage regulation see REGULATION.

percentage ripple see RIPPLE.

percentage tolerance the permitted range of value of a component expressed as a percentage of the nominal value.

perceptual coding a method of compressing (see COMPRESSED AUDIO) DIGITAL AUDIO data based on RECORDING only what the ear can hear, as distinct from the sound that is available.

perceptual sub-band encoding the use of PERCEPTUAL CODING on each of a set of frequency bands, the *sub-bands*, that make up a complete audio signal.

perfect code for a code using words of length n and c PARITY bits, the code is defined as perfect if $2^c = (n + 1)$.

perfect crystal a CRYSTAL in which each atom is precisely in position, with no impurity atoms to alter its geometrical and chemical perfection.

perfect transformer a TRANSFORMER with no STRAY CAPACITANCE nor stray inductance, no EDDY CURRENTS, and no MAGNETIC HYSTERESIS in its core and hence 100% COUPLING of signal from primary to secondary.

performance figure for a RADAR system the ratio of peak transmission power to MINIMUM DISCERNIBLE SIGNAL at the receiver.

perigee the point in a satellite's orbit which is closest to the Earth's surface.

period or **periodic time** the duration of one CYCLE of a WAVEFORM, equal to the inverse of FREQUENCY.

periodic (of a WAVEFORM, OSCILLATION, coincidence or effect) occurring at regular intervals.

peripheral any device external to the main system, i.e. devices that can be connected to a COMPUTER, are controlled by the computer, but are not necessarily part of the computer. Examples include scanners and printers.

peripheral component interconnect bus the bus that has replaced older BUS types such as ISA or VLB for connections between the MICROPROCESSOR and the EXPANSION CARDS in PC computers. The PCI bus runs faster (up to 33 MHz) and is 32-bits wide.

peripheral interface adapter (PIA) an interfacing unit that will allow computer signals to be passed out from and into parallel ports, along with control and HANDSHAKE signals.

peritel connector or **SCART connector** or **Euro AV connector** a standardized 21-pin connector using flat pins, and with a shell that is shaped so as to allow connection to a socket only one way round. The connections provide for R, G, B lines each with a screen connection, along with two audio channels, composite video, and control lines so that, for example, an external device such as a SET-TOP BOX or a video recorder can switch a TV receiver to inputs from the SCART connection.

permalloy a nickel-iron alloy that has high PERMEABILITY and unusually low MAGNETIC HYSTERESIS loss.

permanent magnet a MAGNET made of material that has retained magnetism. The essential feature of a material for permanent magnets is high RETENTIVITY. The magnet can be demagnetized by heating above the CURIE POINT or by applying a strong enough alternating field which is then slowly reduced to zero. Permanent magnets are self-demagnetizing to some extent unless the flux path is kept closed by the use of a KEEPER.

permanent magnet erase a system once used on low-cost TAPE RECORDERS to erase the tape by passing it between the poles of a permanent magnet. This has the effect of considerably increasing the NOISE level of the tape and is no longer used except on a few tape dictating machines.

permanent magnet motor a type of DC electric motor that uses a PERMANENT MAGNET as FIELD MAGNET.

permeability the ratio of FLUX DENSITY (**B**) in a material to the MAGNETIC FIELD strength (**H**) that causes it. Symbol: μ (Greek mu); unit: henry per metre. All materials have a value of permeability, but for most materials this value will be close to the value of the permeability of free space, about 1.25×10^{-6} henry/metre. For FERROMAGNETIC materials, the values of permeability can be much higher, but are variable. Since the value of permeability of a ferromagnetic material is proportional to the slope of the MAGNETIC HYSTERESIS curve at any point, the value can vary from about the free-space value (at MAGNETIC SATURATION) to a very large value (many tens of thousands greater than the free space value) in the middle of the hysteresis curve. The permeability of a ferromagnetic material is usually quoted as the RELATIVE PERMEABILITY, and the conditions under which it is measured must be stated.

permeability of free space the magnetic constant for a vacuum. The symbol is μ_0 (pronounced mew-nought) and the value in modern units is approximately 1.25×10^{-6} henry/metre. The speed of light or any other electromagnetic wave in space is given by:

$$c = \frac{1}{\sqrt{(\varepsilon_0 \mu_0)}}$$

where c is the wave velocity and ε_0 (pronounced epsilon-nought) is the PERMITTIVITY OF FREE SPACE. See also PERMEABILITY; PERMITTIVITY.

permeability tuning tuning of a RESONANT CIRCUIT by varying the position of a core of an INDUCTOR rather than by variation of capacitance.

permeability tuning or **slug tuning** the tuning of a RESONANT CIRCUIT by varying the position of a core in a coil.

permeance the magnetic quantity equal to 1/reluctance. Unit: Weber/ampere-turn.

Permendur™ a cobalt-iron magnetic alloy that is notable for its very high FLUX DENSITY at the point of MAGNETIC SATURATION.

Perminvar™ a nickel-cobalt-iron alloy whose notable characteristic is a very constant value of RELATIVE PERMEABILITY over a wide range of applied MAGNETIC FIELD strength values.

permissible interference a level of INTERFERENCE that does not cause serious degradation of performance of a system.

permittivity a characteristic of an INSULATOR, defined as the ratio of displacement (**D**) to electric field strength (**E**) in a material. Symbol: ε (Greek epsilon); unit: farad per metre. Electric displacement is a quantity that describes the behaviour of charge in a DIELECTRIC subjected to an electric field. More practically, the permittivity value appears in the expression for the capacitance of a parallel-plate capacitor:

$$C = \frac{\varepsilon A}{d}$$

in which C is capacitance in farads, A is plate area in square metres, d is plate spacing in metres, and ε is the permittivity of the dielectric. If the dielectric is air or vacuum, then the value of permittivity is the PERMITTIVITY OF FREE SPACE, ε_0.

permittivity of free space the value of permittivity for a vacuum. Symbol: ε_0. The permittivity and the PERMEABILITY of a medium determine the speed of electromagnetic waves in that medium. See PERMEABILITY OF FREE SPACE.

permutation decoding a procedure for correcting errors in a word for which several PARITY errors have been discovered. This operates by shifting the bits in the received word and re-computing parity until agreement is found.

persistence the phenomenon of light being emitted from a PHOSPHOR screen after being struck by electrons or other radiation. See AFTERGLOW; LONG-PERSISTENCE SCREEN.

persistent memory see NONVOLATILE MEMORY.

Personal Computer (PC) the type of computer design using the design principles embodied in the IBM Personal Computer in 1982, and developed into the principles now used by a vast number of manufacturers. See EISA; ISA.

Personal Computer Memory Card International Association (PCMCIA) a standardizing agency whose initials are used for any memory storage card (or PC card) initially designed for plugging into laptop computers, and now also used on some DIGITAL CAMERAS. Other plug-in devices such as MODEMS and HARD DRIVES can be manufactured to make use of the same connecting system.

perveance a characteristic of a vacuum THERMIONIC VALVE. Perveance measures the DC conductivity of the valve per unit area of cross section at the ANODE.

PES see PROGRAMME ELEMENTARY STREAM.

peta a prefix denoting (for computing purposes) the number 2^{50}, so that one petabyte is equal to 1024 terabytes (see TERA). The prefix is also used outside computing applications for 10^{15} which is a lower number.

pet alley a VOLUMETRIC DETECTION zone in a security system that is close to ground level to allow small animals to move without triggering an alarm.

petabyte 2^{50} bytes.

PFM see PULSE-FREQUENCY MODULATION.

P-frame a form of predicted frame (sense 1) in an MPEG-2 set, accounting for three of the frames in a set of twelve. The information in a P-frame is predicted from the preceding adjacent I-FRAME or B-FRAME. See also GROUP OF PICTURES.

pH a logarithmic scale for measuring acidity, in terms of the logarithm of the concentration of hydrogen ions in a solution. Neutral conditions are indicated by a pH of 7, acidity by lower numbers and alkalinity by higher numbers (up to 15).

phase a time difference between two identical WAVEFORMS of the same FREQUENCY. Phase difference is expressed either as a fraction of a cycle or, more usually, as a phase angle found by expressing the phase as a fraction of the cycle time and multiplying this figure by 360. If the phase angle is to be expressed in radians, the time fraction must be multiplied by 2π. When the term is used to denote a single wave, the phase angle between current and voltage is meant.

phase accumulator a form of COUNTER used in a digital FREQUENCY SYNTHESIZER to establish phase.

phase alternate line see PAL.

phase and amplitude modulation the equivalent of amplitude modulating (see AMPLITUDE MODULATION a CARRIER (sense 1) with one signal at 0° phase and with another signal at 90° phase. See also QUADRATURE DEMODULATOR.

phase coincidence detector or **PCD** a form of DEMODULATOR for frequency modulated (see FREQUENCY MODULATION) signals that operates on a GATING system, not necessarily requiring any tuned circuit.

phase comparator the circuit that compares the PHASE of a signal input with the phase of a LOCAL OSCILLATOR and provides an output that is proportional to the phase difference between them.

phase constant the PHASE SHIFT per unit length of a TRANSMISSION LINE.

phase control a method of using a THYRISTOR to control power in an AC circuit. In a phase-control system, the point of switching on the thyristor in each cycle can be varied with respect to the phase of the voltage.

phase correction circuit   a circuit that restores the original PHASE (of voltage relative to current) of a signal to compensate for the effect of another network.

phased array aerial (or **antenna)** or **scanning array**   an AERIAL array in which the PHASE between elements can be changed so as to alter the direction of maximum sensitivity of the aerial without mechanical adjustment.

phase delay   the amount of PHASE SHIFT per unit frequency of a wave.

phase deviation   the difference in PHASE ANGLE of a phase-modulated wave compared to a standard (reference) phase. See PHASE MODULATION.

phase difference   the difference in PHASE between two waves expressed in terms other than PHASE ANGLE, e.g. time difference or fraction of a cycle.

phase discriminator or **phase-sensitive detector** or **phase detector** or **phase-sensitive demodulator**   a form of demodulator for phase-modulated signals (see PHASE MODULATION). The phase discriminator produces an output voltage that is proportional to the phase difference between the input signal and a reference signal.

phase displacement aerial (or **antenna)**   any type of aerial that uses a single driven element along with a group of reflectors, such as the YAGI.

phase distortion   the unwanted PHASE DIFFERENCE between current and voltage of a waveform. Phase distortion is caused by the presence of reactive components in the current path.

phase function   for an AERIAL (antenna), a mathematical function that relates the PHASE of the ELECTROMAGNETIC FIELD to that of a theoretically perfect spherical field form.

phase inverter   **1.** a signal waveform inverter, such as an INVERTING AMPLIFIER. **2.** a circuit that changes the phase of a signal by 180°. In common usage, the term usually denotes sense 1, but sense 2 is the more correct definition.

phase-inverted signals   a pair of signals of which one is the inverse of the other,

typically used as the input to a BALANCED AMPLIFIER.

phase-linear   (of a system) having a response in which PHASE plotted against FREQUENCY forms a straight line graph.

phase-locked loop   a CIRCUIT in which the PHASE of a LOCAL OSCILLATOR is locked to the phase of an incoming signal (see LOCK-IN). This implies that the frequencies of the two signals are also equal. The locking action is carried out by using a PHASE DISCRIMINATOR to generate a signal proportional to the phase difference between the signals, and then using this signal to correct the oscillator frequency until phase equality is reached.

phase modulation (PM)   the MODULATION of the PHASE of a CARRIER (sense 1) by a SIGNAL. The phase change of the carrier is made proportional to the amplitude of the modulating signal. The carrier amplitude remains constant, and the frequency of the variation is the same as the frequency of the modulating signal. The effect of phase modulation is indistinguishable from that of FREQUENCY MODULATION.

phase noise   the effect of a noisy OSCILLATOR signal on a MIXER stage producing noisy SIDEBANDS in the sum or difference signal.

phaser   a circuit used in an electronic SYNTHESIZER to add a delayed phase shifted signal to the original signal to produce a frequency sweeping effect.

phase response   for a circuit, the PHASE ANGLE of output relative to input.

phase reversal keying (PRK)   see PHASE SHIFT KEYING.

phase-sensitive demodulator   see PHASE DISCRIMINATOR.

phase-sensitive detector   see PHASE DISCRIMINATOR.

phase shift   a change in the relative PHASEs of two quantities; the term usually denotes a change in the phase of voltage relative to current in a single wave.

phase shift, capacitive   a phase shift of 90° with current leading voltage, as would be caused by a capacitor in a circuit.

phase shift, inductive   a phase shift of 90° with voltage leading current, as would be caused by an inductor in a circuit.

phase shift keying (PSK) or **phase reversal keying** or **phase shift modulation** a DIGITAL transmission system in which the data signal switches the CARRIER (sense 1) PHASE, typically no shift for logic 0 and 180° phase shift for logic 1.

phase shift keying demodulator or **PSK demodulator** a synchronous demodulator used to recover the data stream, followed by a low-pass filter to eliminate harmonics.

phase shift ladder oscillator see PHASE SHIFT OSCILLATOR.

phase shift modulation see PHASE SHIFT KEYING.

phase shift oscillator or **ladder oscillator** or **divider chain oscillator** or **R-C oscillator** a form of OSCILLATOR that uses an INVERTING AMPLIFIER. The phase of the output signal is shifted by 180°, normally using a CR network, and connected to the input. For a sine wave, the phase shift has the same effect as an inversion, so that the FEEDBACK is positive for the frequency at which the phase shift is 180°. The output of the phase-shift oscillator is a sine wave only if the gain is maintained at the minimum level needed for oscillation. See Fig. 92.

phase splitter a CIRCUIT that produces a WAVE and its inverse, used mainly as a DRIVER for a BALANCED AMPLIFIER.

phase velocity the apparent speed of a WAVE peak in a group of waves in a DISPERSIVE medium. If the GROUP VELOCITY is less than the wave speed, the phase velocity is greater than the wave speed.

phasing 1. the adjusting of two signals so as to be in PHASE. 2. the correct time adjustment of a synchronizing signal.

phasing burst a few cycles of a CARRIER (sense 1) signal in correct PHASE intended for synchronizing a local OSCILLATOR, such as for a FACSIMILE detector circuit.

phasing harness a connector that can be used to link aerials, ensuring that each is in PHASE.

phasing method a method of producing a single sideband suppressed CARRIER (sense 1) signal using two balanced mixers, one driven by the carrier and the modulating signal and the other driven by the same signals phase shifted by 90°. See also FILTER METHOD; WEAVER METHOD.

phasor diagram a diagram showing phase angle as 0° for a resistive component and phase angles of +90° and −90° for inductive and for capacitive components respectively. Formerly called *vector diagram*.

phono equalization see EQUALIZATION.

phono input input using a phono socket, preferably gold plated, for low resistance input connections with a higher resistance to contamination and tarnishing.

phono plug a popular type of plug (and socket) for audio use, particularly in the US. The plug is of the coaxial design, with a 3mm diameter pin and 9mm diameter shield.

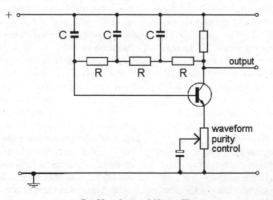

Fig. 92. **phase shift oscillator**

phonograph   the original name for what we now call a gramophone.

phonon   a mechanical wave QUANTUM used in connection with heat transfer and the propagation of ultrasonic waves.

phon unit   a subjective unit of LOUDNESS LEVEL compared to the perceived loudness of a standard note of 1000 Hz.

phosphor or **fluorescent coating**   a material used for coating CATHODE-RAY TUBE screens. Phosphors are metal compounds, usually sulphides or silicates of heavy metals, that have been *activated* by DOPING with other metals, notably silver. The effect is that incoming radiation, either as ultra-violet or electron beams, will cause light to be emitted by the phosphor. The emitted light is always at a lower energy level than that of the incoming radiation.

Phosphors can be manufactured for any colour of visible light (and for infra-red and ultra-violet) by suitable choice of materials. The white phosphor for monochrome television use is a mixture of phosphors, with a predominantly blue cast. Phosphors for colour TV use must be reasonably well matched, so that the ratio of beam currents for equal brightness is not too great. The red phosphor was in the past the least efficient, but steady advances in phosphor chemistry have reduced the difference.

phosphor dots   the method originally used for a colour CATHODE-RAY TUBE, in which each PIXEL consisted of a triangle of 3 phosphor dots, one green, one blue, and one red. See also PHOSPHOR STRIPES.

phosphor fatigue   the reduction in brightness caused by extended use of a MONITOR with an unchanging image. This can cause a static pattern to appear if the monitor shows the same picture for a prolonged period (several weeks).

phosphor stripes   the method of displaying colour in a COLOUR CRT. The screen face is coated with sets of phosphor stripes, one of which will glow red, one blue, and one green. The APERTURE GRILLE inside the tube ensures that only one beam will reach one colour stripe in a set of three.

photocathode   a thin layer of material that emits ELECTRONs in a vacuum when struck by light. Photocathodes are based on elements such as antimony, caesium, rubidium, potassium, and sodium. These are easily prepared as thin films by evaporation, but can exist only in a vacuum or a non-reactive gas atmosphere. For use in PHOTOCELLS and PHOTOMULTIPLIERS, the photocathodes are made after the tube has been evacuated.

photocell or **photoelectric cell** or **electric eye**   a DEVICE that will provide an electrical OUTPUT for a light INPUT (sense 1). See also PHOTOCONDUCTIVE CELL; PHOTOELECTRIC EFFECT.

photocell daylight sensor   see DAYLIGHT SENSOR.

photocell switch   a switch for security lights operated electronically from a PHOTOCELL so that the lights are switched on during the hours of darkness.

photoconductive cell or **photoresistive cell**   a form of PHOTOCELL that uses a material whose electrical conductivity is affected by light. Many SEMICONDUCTORs are photoconductive, but the materials that are used most frequently in photoconductive cells are cadmium sulphide and silicon (for small detectors) and antimony trisulphide or lead (IV) oxide for the (obsolescent) TV camera tubes (vidicons).

photoconductivity   a variation of CONDUCTIVITY caused by light in which the conductivity of the material increases (resistance decreases) when it is illuminated.

photoconductor or **photoresistor**   a material whose electrical CONDUCTIVITY is affected (usually reduced) by incident light.

photoconverter   a form of ANALOG TO DIGITAL converter that uses photocells, one for each BIT of a binary number, and beams of light whose position varies according to an input. The input can be from a rotating shaft or a sliding object, and the beams of light are obtained by shining a light through masks carried on the moving objects. See also ENCODER; LINEAR DIGITAL ENCODER; OPTICAL ENCODER; ROTARY ENCODER.

photocurrent an electric CURRENT produced in a PHOTOCELL by the action of light.

photodetector any electronic DEVICE that gives an electric output when struck by light.

photodiode a SEMICONDUCTOR diode that is light sensitive. The diode is operated with REVERSE BIAS, and is contained in a transparent material. When illuminated by light, a reverse current flows. The current is very small because the number of carriers is small, but the speed of response of most photodiodes is rapid.

photoelectric effect the EMISSION of electrons from materials exposed to energetic radiation such as light. The velocity of the emitted electrons depends on light frequency, and their quantity on light intensity. For each particular emitting material, there will be a LIGHT THRESHOLD FREQUENCY below which no emission can be obtained no matter how intense the radiation.

photoelectric transducer a TRANSDUCER that operates with a light input and an electrical output.

photoemission the EMISSION of electrons due to the impact of electromagnetic radiation. See PHOTOELECTRIC EFFECT.

photoemissive cell a form of photocell that makes use of PHOTOEMISSION.

photo-etching see PHOTOLITHOGRAPHY.

photolithography or **photo-etching** a method of making PRINTED CIRCUITS and INTEGRATED CIRCUITS. A material is coated with PHOTORESIST, a light-sensitive form of lacquer. The material is now treated like a photographic plate, and exposed to an image, often using ultra-violet rather than visible light. The effect of the exposure is to harden the lacquer selectively, so that washing the material will remove only the unexposed lacquer. This results in a lacquer image that is resistant to mild acids. The material that is not lacquer-coated can then be etched with acid, or otherwise chemically treated. Finally, the lacquer can be removed with solvents or by heating.

The technique is stretched to its limits in the manufacture of ICs, mainly because the distance between conducting lines in modern ICs is a comparatively small number of wavelengths of light.

photometer a light meter used for illumination measurements.

photomultiplier a combination of a PHOTOCATHODE and a set of secondary multipliers, or DYNODE CHAIN. The current output of a photomultiplier is very much greater than that of a photocathode. However, the signal from a photomultiplier can be subject to NOISE because the DARK CURRENT is multiplied as well as the wanted photocurrent.

photon a discrete amount of radiated energy that behaves like a particle. The energy of a photon of a given radiation is found by multiplying the frequency of radiation by Planck's constant, h.

photoresist the photosensitive lacquer that is used in PHOTOLITHOGRAPHY. The original photoresist was the gelatine-chromium (IV) oxide mixture that once formed the basis of the gum-bichromate photographic system. Modern methods use a form of lacquer.

photoresistive cell see PHOTOCONDUCTIVE CELL.

photoresistor see PHOTOCONDUCTOR.

photosensitivity the sensitivity of a material to light. For electronics use, photosensitivity is taken to apply to materials that give an electrical response to light.

photosensor any form of detector of light.

phototransistor a BIPOLAR JUNCTION TRANSISTOR with a transparent covering to the BASE region which allows light to reach it. The phototransistor is operated with no connection to the base. Base current is created by the PHOTOEMISSION effect of light striking the base region. The base current is then amplified by the normal transistor effect. The sensitivity is much higher than that of a photodiode, but the response time is longer.

phototube an evacuated tube that makes use of a PHOTOCATHODE to emit electrons.

The electrons may be collected by an ANODE at a positive voltage, or multiplied by a DYNODE CHAIN, as in a PHOTOMULTIPLIER.

photovoltaic cell a DEVICE that generates a VOLTAGE when exposed to light. The first photovoltaic cells used the element selenium, but these have been replaced by junctions formed between metals and a SEMICONDUCTOR (usually silicon).

photovoltaic effect the generation of a VOLTAGE at a junction of two materials when struck by light.

pi-attenuator an ATTENUATOR section with one series element and two parallel elements, whose shape resembles the Greek letter π.

PIC see PROPORTIONAL-INTEGRAL CONTROL.

pickup a TRANSDUCER for vinyl gramophone discs. The pickup converts the vibration of a stylus that tracks the groove of a RECORDING into electrical output. The pickup is usually in the form of a plug-in CARTRIDGE (sense 2) that can be attached to a TONE-ARM that holds the cartridge and guides it across the record surface.

The methods of converting vibration into electrical signals range from the PIEZOELECTRIC CRYSTAL pickup, for high output and relatively low quality, to the MOVING-COIL PICKUP for the lowest output and the highest quality. These systems are rapidly becoming obsolete due to the adoption of digital COMPACT DISC systems.

pico- prefix denoting 10^{-12}. Symbol: p.

picocell a very small area of coverage for CELLULAR PHONES.

picosecond a unit of time equal to 10^{-12} seconds.

picture controls the TV or monitor controls for such items as brightness, contrast, horizontal and vertical position, width, height and hold.

picture element or **pixel** the smallest part of a TELEVISION or monitor picture display that can be separately controlled. For TV reception purposes, this size is governed by the scanning frequencies, and (for colour) by the colour system and aperture grid dimensions. For LCD and PLASMA SCREENS, the pixel is the unit size of cell used in the construction of the display.

picture frequency the rate of transmission of a complete picture in television. See FRAME (sense 1); RASTER.

picture jitter a horizontal or vertical oscillation of a TV picture, usually caused by poor SYNCHRONIZATION.

picture noise the effect on a picture of a noisy signal. NOISE in a TV signal causes a speckled appearance on the picture. On a colour signal, noise is most noticeable on areas of saturated red.

picture signal the video COMPOSITE SIGNAL that carries all the television picture information.

picture tube a television CATHODE-RAY TUBE. The tube uses a large, usually rectangular, tube face, and is very short. The deflection is obtained using coils around the neck of the tube, often shaped so as to obtain the very large deflection angle that is required. The tube is operated at a comparatively high accelerating voltage of about 14kV for monochrome, 24kV for colour signals. The picture intensity variations are obtained by using the incoming video signals to control the electron beam current. A single electron gun is used for a monochrome tube, three guns for colour tubes. See also LCD MONITOR; PLASMA SCREEN.

PID see PACKET IDENTIFICATION.

Pierce oscillator a form of CRYSTAL OSCILLATOR circuit that requires no separate tuned circuit, using the crystal with a series capacitor in a negative FEEDBACK circuit.

piezoelectric crystal a CRYSTAL, such as quartz or barium titanate, that produces a voltage when stressed, and changes dimensions when a voltage is applied. The crystals are cut so that the effect is most marked between two parallel faces, and these faces are metallized (see METALLIZING), usually with silver. The crystals can then be used as electromechanical TRANSDUCERS.

piezoelectric cutter a sound-recording cutter for VINYL DISCS. The audio signals are applied to a PIEZOELECTRIC CRYSTAL that carries a cutting stylus. The cutter is forced to cut a spiral groove in a disc by being attached to a form of screw-cutting lathe. As the audio signal causes vibration of the stylus, the cut groove is modulated. Two cutters set at 90° are needed for stereo recording.

piezoelectric loudspeaker   a type of treble loudspeaker or TWEETER. The piezoelectric tweeter uses a PIEZOELECTRIC CRYSTAL that is attached to a small diaphragm. When an audio signal is applied to the faces of the crystal, the DIAPHRAGM is vibrated.

piezoelectric manometer   a pressure measuring instrument that operates by using pressure directly on a PIEZOELECTRIC CRYSTAL, or indirectly by way of a DIAPHRAGM.

piezoelectric microphone   a microphone making use of a PIEZOELECTRIC CRYSTAL, either directly or by way of a DIAPHRAGM. Sensitivity is high, but quality is generally low.

piezoelectric pickup   a PICKUP for VINYL DISC gramophone records that uses a piezoelectric material. The early crystal pickups used materials such as Rochelle salt that were unstable, and often failed in hot moist weather. Later types used 'ceramic' cartridges, with materials such as barium titanate. These produced fairly high outputs (tens of millivolts), but never with the linearity that could be obtained using pickups of the magnetic type, such as MOVING-COIL PICKUPS or MOVING-IRON PICKUPS.

piezoelectric sensor   any sensor using a PIEZOELECTRIC CRYSTAL to convert motion or vibration into an electrical output.

piezoelectric strain gauge   a method of obtaining an electric signal proportional to strain in a material. The piezoelectric strain gauge uses a PIEZOELECTRIC CRYSTAL material attached using epoxy resin to a structural material (such as metal, stone or brick). Changes in the stress of the material that cause strain are then read off as voltage signals from the piezoelectric material.

piezoelectric transducer   a converter of energy from electrical form into mechanical vibration, usually at ultrasonic frequencies.

pigtail   a flexible stranded wire connector, once used on variable resistors to connect the moving contact to a terminal.

pilot carrier   a low level CARRIER (sense 1) signal transmitted along with a SINGLE SIDEBAND SUPPRESSED CARRIER signal to make demodulation simpler by synchronizing a local OSCILLATOR.

pilot tone   the term used for a 19 kHz signal transmitted along with a STEREO FM audio signal, and used to regenerate the CARRIER (sense 1) in the correct PHASE for demodulating the L – R signals.

pinch-off   the reduction of CURRENT to zero in a channel of a FIELD-EFFECT TRANSISTOR. Pinch-off occurs when the channel contains no free conductors because of the bias at the GATE (sense 1).

pinch roller   see PINCHWHEEL.

pinchwheel or **pinch roller**   the wheel, made of synthetic rubber, that on a tape system holds the tape firmly against the CAPSTAN spindle so that the tape can be moved at a constant speed. Any dirt on this wheel will cause speed error problems such as FLUTTER and WOW.

pin-compatible   (of a chip) capable of being plugged into a socket intended for another make of chip.

pincushion distortion   the distortion of a TV picture from a rectangular shape to a shape in which the sides are curved inwards. Contrast BARREL DISTORTION.

p-i-n diode   a DIODE with a thin layer of INTRINSIC (sense 2) high resistance semiconductor between the P-TYPE and the N-TYPE layers. Used as a microwave source, the IMPATT diode, and as a PHOTODIODE (the DEPLETION LAYER DIODE).

pin grid array (PGA)   an IC pin format that uses a square or rectangular MATRIX of pins with 0.1-inch separation. Some pins are omitted to ensure that the IC is inserted correctly.

pink noise   noise whose power density distribution falls with increasing frequency at the rate of 3dB per octave. See also BAND-LIMITED NOISE; GAUSSIAN NOISE; RAYLEIGH DISTRIBUTED NOISE; RED NOISE; WHITE NOISE.

pin 1 indicator a method of indicating which strand of a flat cable is connected to pin 1 of a plug or socket, usually by colouring or striping that strand.

pinout a chart that shows the pin connections for an INTEGRATED CIRCUIT.

PIO or **parallel input/output** a PORT (sense 1) chip that controls PARALLEL DATA TRANSFER into and out of a computer.

pipelining the use within a MICROPROCESSOR of several BUFFERS (sense 2) each corresponding to a stage in the performance of a task, and working in parallel so as to provide faster processing.

PIPO see PARALLEL-IN PARALLEL-OUT.

PIR see PASSIVE INFRA-RED.

Pirani gauge a form of gauge for measuring low gas pressures (vacuum gauge) that operates by measuring the heat conduction through gas, and is suitable mainly for the lower levels of vacuum. See also IONIZATION GAUGE.

pi section a FILTER SECTION using one reactive element in series and two in parallel, named after its shape. See also T SECTION.

PISO see PARALLEL-IN SERIAL-OUT.

pitch the effect as perceived by the ear of the FREQUENCY of sound waves.

pixel see PICTURE ELEMENT.

pixel dropout failure of one or more PIXELS in an LCD screen to operate. This is incurable and, if serious, can be dealt with only by complete replacement.

pixelation a mosaic type of appearance of a picture due to the use of large PIXEL sizes.

PLA programmable logic array see PROGRAMMABLE LOGIC DEVICE.

plain text see CLEAR TEXT.

planar array a form of MICROWAVE AERIAL (antenna) constructed using an insulating substrate with an etched pattern of MICROSTRIP on one side and the other side totally metallized to act as a GROUND PLANE.

planar process a process for forming SEMICONDUCTOR junctions that uses a layer of silicon oxide on the surface of pure silicon to ensure that DIFFUSION processes affect only semiconductor surfaces that

have been exposed by etching away the oxide layer.

plane-polarization a type of polarization (see POLARIZED, sense 1) in which waves of light or other electromagnetic radiation have an electric component that is always in a fixed direction, the plane of polarization.

plano-convex waveguide laser see CHANNELLED SUBSTRATE LASER.

plan position indicator (PPI) a form of RADAR display in which the position of the receiver is indicated by the centre of the display tube. Distances from the radar receiver are proportional to distances from the centre of the tube face, and directions are read from a scale of compass positions around the tube face.

Planté battery a form of LEAD ACID CELL with a long life and very low maintenance requirements, used for backup on security systems.

plasma a totally IONIZED gas that is a good conductor, and which will emit light (due to RECOMBINATION of ions) while the ionization persists.

plasma display a form of ALPHANUMERIC display that uses the glowing gas of a PLASMA.

plasma oscillations the OSCILLATIONS of the current CARRIERS (sense 2), which are ions, in a PLASMA. These cause severe radio-frequency interference.

plasma screen or **plasma display screen** or **gas plasma display** a form of display first used for laptop computers that allows a flat display SCREEN to be constructed. The light is emitted by cells, one per PIXEL, of glowing gas that is ionized by the electrical voltage between metal electrodes. Plasma displays are now extensively used for large-screen TV receivers. See also ACTIVE MATRIX DISPLAY; LCD.

Plassche converter a DIGITAL TO ANALOGUE CONVERTER system using current addition rather than voltage addition and with a switching action to avoid the necessity for precise matching of resistor values.

plastic-film capacitor a capacitor of the rolled type that uses plastic film in place of paper (see PAPER CAPACITOR). The main types are polyester (Mylar™) and polystyrene.

plastic leaded chip carrier   a form of SOCKET for an IC.

plastic pin grid array   see PIN GRID ARRAY.

plate   see ANODE.

plateau   a part of a graph that remains horizontal over a considerable range of values.

plated-magnetic wire   a wire of nonmagnetic material, such as copper, which is covered with a magnetic coating deposited by ELECTROPLATING.

plated-through connection or **via**   a connection from one side to the other in a double-sided PRINTED CIRCUIT BOARD. The board is drilled, and metal deposited in the sides of the hole to link the copper strips on each side.

platinum resistance thermometer   a thermometer based on the change of resistance of platinum wire as temperature changes. This type of thermometer can be used for a large temperature range of –270°C to +660°C, and is used as a standard for calibrating other forms of thermometer.

platter   one MAGNETIC DISC in a HARD DRIVE that will typically use up to sixteen such discs.

playing weight or **stylus pressure** or **downforce** or **tracking weight**   the vertical force acting on the stylus of a VINYL DISC to keep it in close contact with the disc groove.

PLC   see PROGRAMMABLE LOGIC CONTROLLER.

PLCC   see PLASTIC LEADED CHIP CARRIER.

PLD   see PROGRAMMABLE LOGIC DEVICE.

plenum cable   a cable, usually for a NETWORK (sense 2), that will not emit hazardous fumes at high temperature, so that it can be installed in the space (the *plenum*) between a ceiling and the floor above.

plesiochronous transmission   a form of multiplexed signal where the CLOCKs for some of the multiplex are at slightly different rates, requiring the addition of PADDING BITs to the multiplex.

PLL   see PHASE-LOCKED LOOP.

plug   a MALE CONNECTOR for connecting signals or power. Compare SOCKET.

plug and play (PnP) or **hot swapping** a system that allows cards to be added or removed from a computer without the need to switch off and REBOOT.

plugboard   see PATCHBOARD.

plug-compatible   (of a socket-fitting device) capable of being plugged in to replace another make of such device and which will then work in the same way.

plug-in   (of part of a circuit) being connected or disconnected by a PLUG and SOCKET.

plug-in card   see CARD.

plumbicon   a form of VIDICON that uses a lead (IV) oxide photoconductor.

plumbing   a slang term for MICROWAVE signal connections through WAVEGUIDES.

PM   see PHASE MODULATION.

PMA   see PROGRAM MEMORY AREA.

PME   see PROTECTIVE MULTIPLE EARTHING.

PMOS   see P-CHANNEL MOSFET.

PMP   see POST METAL PROGRAMMING.

PMR   private mobile radio.

p-n junction   an area of contact between a P-TYPE and an N-TYPE semiconductor within a CRYSTAL. The junction cannot be created simply by bringing two materials together, because there must be no discontinuity in the crystal structure at the junction. At any such junction, a rectifying effect is obtained. Current will flow easily in the forward direction of the junction, with the p-type material at a higher positive voltage than the n-type material. No current flows until a THRESHOLD VOLTAGE is reached, after which the current-voltage graph is exponential (see EXPONENTIAL CURVE). In the reverse direction, current is negligible until the voltage reaches a level at which the junction breaks down.

p-n-p transistor   a BIPOLAR JUNCTION TRANSISTOR that is formed using P-TYPE material for the EMITTER (sense 1) and COLLECTOR regions, and N-TYPE for the BASE. In use, both the collector and the base must have negative bias with respect to the emitter. See also N-P-N TRANSISTOR; TRANSISTOR.

Poincaré sphere a form of graph depicting three dimensions used to illustrate the propagation of an ELECTRIC FIELD through space and to indicate forms of polarization (see POLARIZED, sense 1).

point contact an early form of semiconductor DIODE construction. A point contact diode uses a metal wire with a sharp point that makes contact with a semiconductor. The diode was used mainly for demodulation of high-frequency low voltage signals.

pointing accuracy the degree of precision with which a directional AERIAL is aimed.

poison an impurity in a material that prevents normal action. Contrast DOPING, a deliberate addition of impurity.

polar coordinates the use of a distance from a point and angle from a fixed direction to indicate position. See also CARTESIAN COORDINATES.

polar diagram plot a graphical diagram showing AERIAL (antenna) gain for various angles relative to the main axis of an aerial system.

polarity 1. a variety of charge; positive or negative. 2. a magnetic direction; north or south. 3. the joining of components such as a PLUG and SOCKET so that the correct connections are always made (see also KEYWAY). 4. the connection of a circuit so that one power connection is made to the positive supply and the other connection to the negative.

polarity, electrolytic the connection of an ELECTROLYTIC CAPACITOR so that the positive terminal is always connected to a positive voltage.

polarity, mains the connection of a mains lead to LIVE or NEUTRAL (sense 3).

polarization, aerial the direction of ELECTRIC FIELD strength produced by TRANSMITTING AERIAL or used by a RECEIVING AERIAL.

polarization, cell the effect of gas gathering on one electrode of a cell and acting as an insulator so that the current delivered from the cell drops to almost zero. See also DEPOLARIZER.

polarized (of an electromagnetic wave, an electronic component or a connector)

1. having the electric wave portion of an electromagnetic wave with a defined amplitude in a defined direction which is taken as the plane of polarization. In a very few cases (see TM WAVE) the direction of the magnetic portion is considered. 2. having a fixed charge, such as possessed by an ELECTRET, or requiring a potential of stated polarity on each of two connectors, like an ELECTROLYTIC CAPACITOR. 3. making the shape of a plug and socket combination so that the plug can be inserted only in the correct way, such as the 13A mains plug and socket used in the UK.

polarized plug a PLUG whose pins are arranged, or which is fitted with a keyway slot, so that it can be inserted in only one way into a matching SOCKET.

polarizing filter a light filter that will plane-polarize (see PLANE-POLARIZATION) the light that passes through it.

polarizing material a material that will POLARIZE electromagnetic waves, particularly LIGHT waves.

polarizing voltage the steady voltage that must be applied to ensure that the component, such as an ELECTROLYTIC CAPACITOR, operates correctly.

polarizing voltage, microphone the steady voltage required to charge the plates of a CAPACITOR MICROPHONE so that an electrical output can be obtained from it.

polar mount an AERIAL (antenna) mounting system that permits the aerial to be rotated and precisely pointed in a required direction.

polar orbit a SATELLITE orbit that covers both North and South poles.

polar pattern a POLAR DIAGRAM PLOT of response, particularly for a TRANSMITTING AERIAL.

polar signal a form of BINARY (sense 1) coded signal that uses pulses of one polarity only.

pole 1. a point on a POLE-ZERO DIAGRAM. 2. a centre of CHARGE or MAGNETISM. 3. a terminal, especially a CELL or battery terminal.

pole-pieces, tape head points on the TAPE HEAD from which the MAGNETIC FLUX appears to start and end.

pole, switch the moving contact of a
SWITCH. See also THROW.

pole-zero diagram a graph showing
the voltage responses (*poles*) and current
responses (*zeros*) of a circuit. The impedance
function for the circuit is derived as an
equation of the form:

$$Z(S) = SL + R + \frac{1}{SC}$$

and where this function is a maximum
represents a pole, a condition of natural
voltage response. Where the function
has zero value (a zero), this describes
the conditions for the natural current
response. Fig. 93 shows a typical pole-
zero diagram for a function with one zero
and two poles. The presence of a pole or
zero at the origin indicates integration or
differentiation, and the absence of any
poles on the right-hand side indicates that
stability is assured. For a comprehensive
explanation of pole-zero analysis, see any
textbook on electronic circuit analysis.

polling a method of reading an input,
such as the use of a keyboard, to a
computer by continually checking for a
signal becoming available. This is a time
inefficient method, and the method of
INTERRUPTS is more common.

pollywog a lump of magnetic material on
an otherwise smooth tape that will cause
poor RECORDING.

poly mode a MIDI mode in which an
instrument will respond to only one
MIDI channel selected by the user, so that
up to 16 different instruments can play
different parts.

polybinary coding the coding process
that converts a two-level BINARY (sense 1)
signal into a multi-level code with even
number levels representing one binary
value and odd number levels the other
binary value.

polybipolar coding a variation of
POLYBINARY CODING in which an odd number
of levels is produced, balanced around
zero so that there is no DC component.

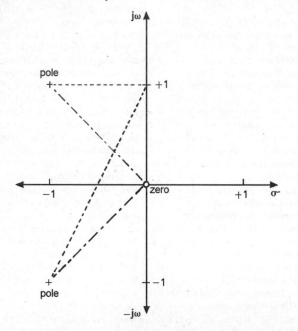

Fig. 93. **pole-zero diagram**

polycarbonate capacitor a form of rolled CAPACITOR using polycarbonate film as DIELECTRIC, and with very high level of specification. See also PAPER CAPACITOR; PLASTIC-FILM CAPACITOR; TUBULAR CAPACITOR.

polycrystalline silicon see POLYSILICON.

polyester-film capacitor a rolled CAPACITOR that uses polyester in place of paper. See PAPER CAPACITOR.

polynomial an algebraic expression of several terms, each of a different power of the variable, such as $X^5 + X^3 + X^2 + X^0$. A BINARY (sense 1) word can be expressed as a polynomial of powers of two, so that 1010 can be indicated as $X^3 + X^1$, using a power of X only where a logic 1 occurs.

polynomial code see CYCLIC CODE.

polyphase supply an electrical supply that uses more than two PHASES. The usual form is three-phase, in which the currents in the three lines are 120° out of phase with each other.

polyphase transformer a transformer with several windings that can be connected to a POLYPHASE SUPPLY.

polyphonic (of a synthesizer) able to produce more than one note simultaneously.

polypropylene capacitor a rolled type of CAPACITOR that uses polypropylene film in place of paper. See also PAPER CAPACITOR.

polysilicon heavily doped (see DOPING) silicon that is highly conductive, used for the electrodes of FETs.

polystyrene capacitor a rolled type of CAPACITOR that uses polystyrene film in place of paper. See also PAPER CAPACITOR.

polytetrafluoroethylene (PTFE) or **Teflon**™ a plastic material with very high resistivity, low dielectric loss, and which is almost unaffected by moisture. PTFE is extensively used in high-voltage insulation and in cable connectors.

POP post office protocol.

popcorn noise or **pops** a form of NOISE in transistor amplifiers occurring in bursts at frequencies below 100 Hz, due to transistor defects.

pops see POPCORN NOISE.

port 1. an INPUT/OUTPUT circuit, particularly for a computer system. A port must include storage, because there can be no certainty that the input or output will take place at a time when it can be used. In addition, a port includes a method of interrupting (see INTERRUPT) the action of the MICROPROCESSOR so as to trigger the reading of an input. 2. a terminal on a device.

portal any website that allows connection to the World Wide Web and all its facilities.

port chip an IC that carries out the storage and data transfer actions of a PORT (sense 1).

port concentrator a form of MULTIPLEXER (sense 3) that allows several PORTs to communicate over one transmission channel.

port, loudspeaker a hole or tunnel in a loudspeaker cabinet that will behave as a second DIAPHRAGM because of the mass of the air oscillating in the opening, acting to improve the bass response of the system.

POS point of sale.

position modulation see PULSE POSITION MODULATION.

position sensor a device, sometimes based on the HALL EFFECT, that can sense the position of a mechanical device. Other examples include optical-shift position sensors and ultrasonic proximity detectors.

positive (of a material) having a deficiency of ELECTRONs. The term is applied to any material in which the number of electrons is less than the number of PROTONs. Contrast NEGATIVE.

positive bias the application of a steady positive potential to a circuit or terminal of an active component such as the GATE (sense 1) of a FIELD-EFFECT TRANSISTOR. Contrast NEGATIVE BIAS.

positive charge the CHARGE type of a PROTON. Contrast NEGATIVE CHARGE.

positive earth or **positive ground** any system that has the positive side of its power supply earthed. At one time this was common practice in cars.

positive feedback or **regeneration** or **regenerative feedback**   the process of sending back a portion of the output to the input of an amplifier in such a way as to reinforce the input signal (see FEEDBACK). Positive feedback increases GAIN, narrows BANDWIDTH, increases DISTORTION, and can cause OSCILLATION. Contrast NEGATIVE FEEDBACK.

positive ion   an atom that has lost one or (sometimes) more ELECTRONs and is therefore positively charged. Because of the charge, the positive ion will experience a force in an electric field opposite in direction to that experienced by an electron. Contrast NEGATIVE ION.

positive logic   the digital logic system in normal use in which a positive voltage represents level 1, and zero or negative voltage represents level 0. Contrast NEGATIVE LOGIC.

positive peak detector   a circuit, typically using an OPERATIONAL AMPLIFIER and a DIODE that charges a CAPACITOR to the PEAK value of the input wave.

positive temperature coefficient (PTC)   a figure that expresses by how much a quantity increases in value as its temperature increases. Contrast NEGATIVE TEMPERATURE COEFFICIENT.

POST   see POWER ON SELF TEST.

post-deflection acceleration (PDA)   the acceleration of an electron beam in a CATHODE-RAY TUBE after the deflection of the beam. The method applies to electrostatically deflected tubes as used for oscilloscopes and other instruments. For high deflection sensitivity, the electron velocity must be low, for high brightness the velocity must be high. In a PDA tube, the accelerating voltage between the cathode and the deflection plates is low. Following the deflection plates, the beam is accelerated to a high velocity so as to produce a bright trace.

The separation of the low-velocity and high-velocity regions can be very complete, as in the MESH PDA TUBE system. An alternative is the SPIRAL PDA tube, in which an ANODE at the deflection plates is connected to the FINAL ANODE by a thin spiral of high-resistance graphite. This allows a graduated accelerating field to be created between the end of the deflection region and the screen.

post metal programming (PMP)   a method of programming a ROM using a high energy ion beam after the final METALLIZING stage has been carried out.

pot   see POTENTIOMETER (sense 1).

potential   see ELECTRIC POTENTIAL.

potential barrier   the difference in VOLTAGE between two points that forms an obstacle to the movement of a charged particle. A negative ELECTRODE, for example, forms a potential barrier to an ELECTRON.

potential difference (PD)   the difference in ELECTRIC POTENTIAL between two points. Symbol: U or V or ΔV; unit: volt. Potential difference is defined as the amount of work done per unit charge when a charge is moved from one point to the other, along any path.

potential divider   a series circuit of RESISTORS. A voltage is applied over the whole set, and fractions of the voltage can be obtained at each point where two resistors are connected. The division formula for the common case of two resistors is expressed as:

$$V_{out} = V_{in} \ \frac{R_2}{R_1 + R_2},$$

referring to Fig. 94. For alternating signals, capacitors or inductors can also be used to form potential dividers. See also COLPITTS OSCILLATOR; COMPENSATED ATTENUATOR.

potential energy   energy that is stored waiting to be released, such as the energy of a raised weight, a coiled spring, or a cell that is not delivering current.

potential gradient or **electric field strength**   the POTENTIAL DIFFERENCE between two points divided by the straight-line distance between the points. Units: volts per metre. See also ELECTRIC FIELD.

potentiometer or **pot**   1. a variable resistor having a moving contact that can be placed at any point between the terminals of a resistive coil or track.

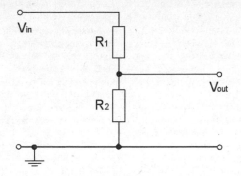

Fig. 94. **potential divider**

2. an instrument for measuring
ELECTRIC POTENTIAL using a tapped
voltage divider.

potentiometer law or **taper (US)**   the
relationship between the DIVISION RATIO
of a POTENTIOMETER (sense 1) and the angle
through which the shaft is turned,
generally either linear or logarithmic.

POTS   plain old telephone service.

powdered-iron core   see DUST CORE.

power   the rate of the production or
dissipation of energy. Symbol: P; unit:
watt. In DC circuits, power is calculated
from the product of POTENTIAL DIFFERENCE
and CURRENT, V × I. For AC, the
quantities must be measured in ROOT
MEAN SQUARE (sense 2) terms and be in
PHASE.

power amplifier (PA)   **1.** a stage that
provides output POWER to a LOAD. **2.** the
final RF AMPLIFIER that provides power to
the AERIAL from a transmitter. **3.** the audio
power amplifier stage that delivers the
signal to the loudspeaker(s).

power bandwidth   the range of
frequencies for an AMPLIFIER for which
the power output is half of the maximum
available power. This corresponds to the
3dB level.

power cleaner   see POWER LINE FILTER.

power component   the IN-PHASE
COMPONENT (sense 1) of current or voltage.

power derating   a reduction in the
maximum power rating for a circuit due
to a higher AMBIENT TEMPERATURE.

power dissipation   the amount of power
spent as heat, which can be as high as
100 watts for a MICROPROCESSOR.

power-down   to switch off.

power efficiency   the ratio of output
power to input power, particularly for
a TRANSDUCER.

power factor   the fraction by which
the product V × I for AC signals must
be multiplied to obtain true POWER.
The power factor is equal to the cosine
of the phase angle between voltage and
current.

power factor correction   a circuit,
usually capacitive, used to correct the
overall POWER FACTOR for an electrical
supply.

power flux density (PFD)   a measure
of the received field strength from a
SATELLITE transmission in terms of the
watts (or microwatts) per square metre
of power received on Earth. See also
FOOTPRINT.

power gain   the ratio of POWER output
to power input for any device or circuit.

power line filter or **power cleaner**   an
electronic circuit that will smooth out
voltage fluctuations in a supply line. This
is desirable if the fluctuations are serious

and are affecting computers, but the electricity supplier should be consulted first, as they have a statutory duty to supply a steady value of AC voltage.

power line surge a large change in mains voltage, caused either by lightning or by line faults, and potentially damaging for electronic equipment.

power MOSFET a form of MOSFET designed to pass large currents and with performance superior to that of BIPOLAR JUNCTION TRANSISTORS in respect of maximum operating frequency and linearity. See also D-MOS; U-MOS; V-MOS.

power on reset the action of clearing all of the memory locations in a MICROPROCESSOR whenever power is applied – the alternative is to allow each memory location to take a value of 0 or 1 at random, resulting in the memory containing garbage.

power on self test or **POST** the action of modern computers that checks memory and chip actions before loading the operating system ready to run a program.

power output stage the final stage of an AUDIO AMPLIFIER which provides little or no VOLTAGE GAIN but a large amount of CURRENT GAIN in order to drive a low impedance loudspeaker.

power pack the circuit that converts AC supply voltage into DC (usually at a different voltage) for an electronic device. The conventional power pack will consist of a mains transformer, RECTIFIERS, and smoothing, possibly with VOLTAGE REGULATOR stages. See also RESERVOIR CAPACITOR.

power rating, resistor the maximum dissipation of power permitted for a resistor, usually reduced when the AMBIENT TEMPERATURE is high.

power save mode an energy-saving system for a computer that reduces power consumption by switching off devices such as the DISPLAY, HARD DRIVE or other units when the computer is not active.

power spectral density (PSD) a method of displaying the effect of NOISE as a two-dimensional graph of the MEAN SQUARE noise voltage per hertz plotted against frequency.

power supply or **power supply unit** or **PSU** the source of POWER for an electronic circuit that can be mains, battery, solar cell, or other method.

power supply rating the figures for maximum power, voltage and current for a POWER SUPPLY unit.

power supply rejection ratio or **PSRR** for an OPERATIONAL AMPLIFIER, the dependence of INPUT OFFSET voltage on supply voltage level, usually of the order of $10 \ \mu V / V$.

power supply reversal a problem of battery operated equipment if the battery can be installed incorrectly, usually dealt with by a set of diodes that will not pass current if the battery polarity is incorrect.

power surge see VOLTAGE SURGE.

power transformer a TRANSFORMER whose PRIMARY WINDING is wound for connection to AC mains, and whose SECONDARY WINDINGS are used to supply power to a circuit.

power transistor a TRANSISTOR that is designed to handle large currents and dissipate heat efficiently. A power transistor will be designed with a large area of COLLECTOR or DRAIN with a good thermal contact to a metal casing. This allows the transistor to dissipate a large steady power providing that the case can be cooled by conduction or convection. See HEAT SINK.

Poynting vector a measure of power flow through space in a plane normal to the wave motion, given by the product of the values for ELECTRIC FIELD strength (E) and MAGNETIC FIELD strength (H) and the sine of the angle between them.

PPGA plastic PIN GRID ARRAY.

PPI see PLAN POSITION INDICATOR.

PPM see PULSE-POSITION MODULATION.

PPM meter a meter to indicate the AMPLITUDE of PEAKS in an analogue audio signal.

PPP point to point (internet) protocol.

PPS see PRECISE POSITIONING SERVICE.

PQFP plastic quad flat pack: an IC package.

PRBS   see PSEUDO RANDOM BINARY SEQUENCE.

preamp   see PREAMPLIFIER.

preamplifier or **preamp**   a STAGE or set of stages of low-noise voltage amplification, used in audio amplifiers in particular. In audio amplifiers, the preamp handles all the selection and mixing of inputs at various voltage levels. The system is arranged so that the output will be of about the same amplitude for any selected input. The output of the preamplifier is normally connected to the input of a POWER AMPLIFIER (sense 3) stage.

precipitation static   static noise caused by the ELECTROSTATIC charging on a structure due to the impact of rain, snow, ice or sleet.

precise positioning service or **PPS** a more precise version of GLOBAL POSITIONING SYSTEM available for military use.

precision approach radar   a RADAR system used for very accurate location at small distances, particularly for the guidance of ships or their craft in fog.

precision rectifier   a rectifier circuit that can rectify signals of less than 600 millivolts (the limit for a silicon diode), using an operational amplifier and a diode in conjunction to provide rectification for levels as low as 50 mV.

precision resistor chain or **switched potentiometer**   a set of resistors of very high precision connected in series to produce a switched ATTENUATOR, replacing the use of a continuously-variable POTENTIOMETER (sense 1). See Fig. 7.

pre-coated board   a form of blank PRINTED CIRCUIT BOARD which has already been coated with photoresist, ready for exposure to light.

pre-compensation   a method of combating high frequency loss by boosting the amplitude of high frequencies during recording.

predictive coding   a system in which a signal sample is used to predict the value of the next sample so that the (usually

small) difference between the prediction and the actual value can be coded and transmitted.

predictive frame or **P frame**   a DIGITAL TELEVISION frame that has been produced by prediction either from a previous frame or from a following frame.

predistortion   a method of reducing distortion for a system whose distortion pattern is precisely known, by distorting the input signal in the opposite sense.

pre-echo   a problem of tape recorders in which a strong signal can be heard faintly before its portion of tape arrives at the tape head. This is due to PRINT-THROUGH, caused by the strong signal magnetizing the piece of tape that it bears against on the tape reel.

pre-emphasis   a selective boosting of high audio frequencies. Pre-emphasis is used before transmitting FM signals, and before RECORDING on tape or on disc. In all these systems, the noise tends to be concentrated mainly in the treble, rather than spread evenly over the whole frequency range. By pre-emphasizing the signal, the receiver or playback stages can cut treble (DE-EMPHASIS), and the noise along with it. This restores the treble to its correct level, and reduces noise.

preferred values   a set of standardized figures between 1 and 10. These are based on a logarithmic scale, and are used to select values for resistors and capacitors. The principle is that if a set of values in a tolerance range of, say, 20% is selected, then no value of resistance or capacitance can possibly be rejected. A nominal 2K2 resistor, for example, in the 20% tolerance range, could have a value of up to 2K64, or down to 1K76. The next value of 3K3 could be as low as 2K64, and the previous value of 1K5 could be as high as 1K8. A range of resistors or capacitors can therefore be manufactured, and values selected for 5% accuracy. The remaining components can then be selected to provide a set of 10% components, and the remainder can be sold as 20% tolerance. See Table 4.

E6 series	E12 series	E24 series
20%	10%	5%
1.0	1.0	1.0
		1.1
	1.2	1.2
		1.3
1.5	1.5	1.5
		1.6
	1.8	1.8
		2.0
2.2	2.2	2.2
		2.4
	2.7	2.7
		3.0
3.3	3.3	3.3
		3.6
	3.9	3.9
		4.3
4.7	4.7	4.7
		5.1
	5.6	5.6
		6.2
6.8	6.8	6.8
		7.5
	8.2	8.2
		9.1

Table 4. **Preferred values for the E6, E12 and E24 resistor families**

pre-pulse trigger a TRIGGER PULSE for a CATHODE-RAY OSCILLOSCOPE. In a system, such as a RADAR transmitter, in which a master pulse is generated and used to trigger all the subsequent effects, it is useful to provide a pulse that immediately precedes the main pulse. This makes it possible to trigger an oscilloscope timebase just before the main pulse arrives, so that the shape of the whole of the main pulse can be displayed. If the main pulse is used for triggering, its LEADING EDGE cannot be seen on the oscilloscope display.

prescaler a FREQUENCY DIVIDER circuit used to provide a constant division ratio, typically for a FREQUENCY SYNTHESIS circuit.

preset or **set** an input to a FLIP-FLOP that will set the output state of the flip-flop to logic 1. Compare RESET.

pressure the force per unit area on a material. Symbol: P; unit pascal (Pa); equal to newtons per square metre. The average pressure of the atmosphere at the earth's surface is 10^5 Pa.

pressure operated microphone a MICROPHONE whose DIAPHRAGM is sealed on one-side so that it is operated by the pressure of the air on the open side rather than by the velocity of the air past the diaphragm. See also VELOCITY OPERATED MICROPHONE.

pressure pad a form of contact switch. A pressure pad will allow electrical contacts to close when pressure is applied to the unit. Pressure pads are used in burglar alarm systems and as limit switches on mechanical devices.

pressure pad, tape see TAPE PRESSURE PAD.

pressure unit the TRANSDUCER element or MOTOR UNIT for a LOUDSPEAKER.

pressure, unit see PASCAL.

Prestel™ an obsolete information service for computers that made use of the telephone network, now replaced by the use of the INTERNET.

pre-triggering the use of a TRIGGER pulse occurring before a main SYNCHRONIZING PULSE so that a CATHODE-RAY OSCILLOSCOPE can display the whole of the main pulse.

preventative maintenance maintenance carried out at intervals on portions of a working circuit that are known to be liable to faults.

previous word hold the action of the CD player in retaining a data WORD in memory until it can be compared with others to provide ERROR CORRECTION by INTERPOLATION if required.

PRF see PULSE REPETITION FREQUENCY.

PRI primary rate interface: an ISDN connection usually between a private branch exchange and a main telephone exchange.

primary cache the CACHE memory for a computer that is part of the MICROPROCESSOR itself and is usually manufactured in the form of STATIC RAM on the same chip.

primary cell a cell whose EMF is derived from a chemical reaction that is irreversible, so that the cell cannot be recharged. See also SECONDARY CELL.

primary circuit, relay   the circuit that includes the coil of the RELAY, as distinct from the switching contacts. See also SECONDARY CIRCUIT, RELAY.

primary code   the code used for a CLEAR TEXT message, as distinct from a SECONDARY CODE used for RECORDING or transmitting purposes.

primary colours, light   the colours red, blue and green which will combine to form white light. Note that primary *paint* colours are exactly the opposite of light colours.

primary earth ground or **protective earth** the EARTH connection to electrical equipment designed to provide protection against electrical shock. See also SECONDARY EARTH GROUND.

primary electron   an ELECTRON obtained from a cathode of any type. Compare SECONDARY ELECTRON.

primary IDE   the connector on a MOTHERBOARD for the first INTEGRATED DEVICE ELECTRONICS channel, usually serving the HARD DRIVE(s) of a PC computer.

primary line constants   the quantities of loop inductance, shunt capacitance, and shunt conductance (or leakage resistance), all per unit length. for a TRANSMISSION LINE.

primary radar   the conventional form of RADAR system in which the RETURN SIGNAL is due to the reflection of a small part of the transmitted signal from the target.

primary radiator   the main element in an AERIAL. For a TRANSMITTER, the primary radiator is the electrically connected AERIAL ELEMENT. For a RECEIVING AERIAL, the primary radiator is the element that is connected to the RECEIVER.

primary service area   the area of good reception around a TRANSMITTER. The primary service area is served by the GROUND WAVE (sense 1), and interference from reflected waves is small. This ensures a good standard of reception, day or night.

primary standard   a national or international standard of measurement, such as the National Physical Laboratory (UK) current balance for the ampere.

Secondary standards are calibrated from instruments of this type for everyday use, as primary standards may take a long time to set up and use.

primary voltage   the AC or signal VOLTAGE across the primary winding of a TRANSFORMER.

primary winding or **primary**   the WINDING to which the input signal for a TRANSFORMER is connected. In the conventional cored transformer, the primary winding is wound immediately next to the core. For modern TOROIDAL transformers, primary and SECONDARY WINDINGs are often interchangeable. See also TERTIARY WINDING.

principle of superposition   see SUPERPOSITION.

printed circuit   a CIRCUIT in which the interconnections between components consist of copper strips on an insulated board. The components are introduced by drilling holes for terminating leads, threading the leads through and soldering them to the copper strips. The pattern of connections on the board is printed on by PHOTOLITHOGRAPHY, and the unwanted metal is etched away in ferric chloride or ammonium persulphate. Double-sided boards have a pattern printed on each side, with PLATED-THROUGH connections between each side. Connections to the board are made using EDGE CONNECTORS, or by soldering sockets to the board. The advantages of printed circuits include uniformity, since the boards can be mass-produced, and the ease of automated assembly.

printed circuit board (PCB)   a board prepared by PHOTOLITHOGRAPHY ready for the insertion of components. The board material is usually SRPB (silicon-resin bonded paper) or fibreglass, and the copper sheet is bonded to the board as part of the manufacturing process for the board. The bonding must be sufficiently heat-resistant to allow DIP-SOLDERING of the whole board when the components have been threaded into place.

printer port   the PARALLEL PORT used to connect a printer to a computer.

printhead the set of nozzles and their actuators on an INKJET PRINTER, or the needles and solenoid system of a dot-matrix IMPACT PRINTER.

print-through a transfer of MAGNETISM from one layer of MAGNETIC TAPE to another. Print-through causes the effect of *pre-* or *post-echo*. This means that a loud sound can cause a faint copy to be heard just before and just after the correct position on the tape. Print-through is minimized if tape is frequently wound from reel to reel.

prism a polished glass solid with triangular cross section, used to deviate a beam of light and also to separate white light into its constituent colours.

private key the secret KEY (sense 1) in a two-key system, used to decipher a message sent using a PUBLIC KEY.

PRK phase reversal keying: see PHASE SHIFT KEYING.

probe 1. a lead for injecting or extracting signals, e.g. the sharp-pointed or clip-ended lead of a test instrument such as a voltmeter, signal generator or (particularly) an oscilloscope. 2. a conductor that is inserted permanently into a RESONANT CAVITY (of a microwave device) to inject or extract signals.

probe, low-capacitance a connector for, typically, a CATHODE-RAY OSCILLOSCOPE that provides a low value of parallel input capacitance.

processor see MICROPROCESSOR.

processor fan the cooling fan for a MICROPROCESSOR in a computer, attached either to a HEAT SINK on the processor or on a radiator when a heatpipe cooling system is used.

product detector or **product demodulator** a system in which two signals are multiplied together in a NONLINEAR device to form sum and difference signals, of which the difference signal is normally used as an INTERMEDIATE FREQUENCY.

product of sums see MAXTERM.

PRO-ELECTRON code a system of coding TRANSISTORS and other SEMICONDUCTOR devices. The PRO-ELECTRON code uses letters and numbers. The first letter is a material code, with A=germanium, B=silicon. The second letter denotes the device type, such as C for audio voltage amplifier, F for RF amplifier. A last letter of X, Y or Z is used to denote an industrial device. The number that follows is the makers' development number. The advantage of the PRO-ELECTRON code is that the type of device can be deduced from the code, unlike the US system of consecutive serial numbers.

program a set of instructions for a computer or a MICROPROCESSOR.

program association table or **PAT** a data table that is transmitted in an MPEG DATA PACKET for DIGITAL TELEVISION to a TV decoder and used to determine which television programmes appear in the MULTIPLEX and their position.

program calibration area or **PCA** the portion of a CD-R or CD-RW disc that is used for making a trial RECORDING to calibrate the LASER intensity needed for the disc that is being used. This allows for differences in disc materials, particularly between CD-R and CD-RW discs.

program counter the register within a MICROPROCESSOR that increments after each instruction to call up the next instruction in turn.

programmable (of a device) capable of being controlled by a stored set of instructions, usually in number form.

programmable attenuator see MULTIPLYING DIGITAL TO ANALOGUE CONVERTER.

programmable divider a circuit whose input is a waveform with stable frequency and whose output is another frequency related by an integer number to that of the input.

programmable frequency synthesizer a circuit that will perform a division action on a frequency input, usually from a CRYSTAL OSCILLATOR, to provide a precise desired frequency.

programmable logic array (PLA) see PROGRAMMABLE LOGIC DEVICE.

programmable logic controller or **PLC** a system making use of a MICROPROCESSOR or MICROCONTROLLER, used for machine control and replacing devices such as relays, cams or microswitches.

programmable logic device or **PLD** a form of IC based on a PROGRAMMABLE READ-ONLY MEMORY that can be used as a complete LOGIC CIRCUIT whose connections can be set by programming.

programmable output polarity the facility to use a logical inversion at the output of a gate in a PROGRAMMABLE LOGIC DEVICE.

programmable read-only memory see PROM.

programmable UJT a form of UNIJUNCTION whose INTRINSIC STANDOFF RATIO can be varied by altering the voltage on an electrode.

programme delivery control (PDC) or **video programming system (VPS)** a system for ensuring that a transmitted TV programme that has been delayed will nevertheless be recorded correctly by a VIDEO CASSETTE RECORDER that has been set for the published times. This is done by transmitting codes that the VCR can use, and is not available on all channels. It is not widely used on DVD or hard drive recorders.

programme elementary stream (PES) a set of DATA PACKETs, typically for 2–6 broadcast programs, assembled into a single data stream for transmission. See also PACKET MULTIPLEXER; TRANSPORT STREAM.

programme modulated noise or **breathing** a form of noise due to incorrect action of a noise reduction system on a TAPE RECORDER.

program memory area the portion of a CD-R or CD-RW disc that contains the table of track numbers along with start and stop positions for each track.

programming inputs the J and K terminals of a J-K FLIP-FLOP, used to determine how the flip-flop will operate on the next CLOCK PULSE.

progressive scan or **sequential scan** a NONINTERLACED scan, such as is used for computer MONITORs.

projection display a form of TV or computer display that is projected onto any flat white surface using a bright CATHODE-RAY TUBE or a brightly backlit LCD as the light signal source screen along with a projection optical system.

projector, LCD see LCD PROJECTOR.

prolate filter a form of LOW-PASS FILTER designed around the ELLIPTIC FUNCTION and with a good response to a STEP FUNCTION input.

Pro-Logic™ a Dolby circuit that extracts information from a STEREO audio signal to provide SURROUND SOUND outputs of left, right, centre and surround.

PROM programmable read-only memory: a form of permanent NONVOLATILE memory for a computer. The data stored on the chip can be read by the computer, but no new data can be written while the chip is in the computer. The chip can be removed from the computer, erased and reprogrammed if changes are needed. See also EAROM; EPROM; ROM.

PROM washing the erasure of a PROGRAMMABLE READ-ONLY MEMORY so that it can be reprogrammed with data.

proof voltage or **flash test voltage** a voltage applied for a short time between the PRIMARY and the SECONDARY windings of a TRANSFORMER to ensure that there is not likely to be any break down of insulation while in service. The proof voltage is usually 2 kV or more.

propagation the spreading of a radio wave from its source to all the points at which it can be received.

propagation coefficient a quantity that measures the attenuation and phase change, per metre, caused by a TRANSMISSION LINE.

propagation constant the COMPLEX NUMBER that represents ATTENUATION and PHASE SHIFT of a FILTER.

propagation delay the time delay between sending a signal into a TRANSMISSION LINE and its reception at the other end. Also used of a broadcast signal to mean the delay caused by the time taken for the wave to move from transmitter to receiver.

propagation loss the energy loss from a SIGNAL beam in the course of PROPAGATION by radio, cable or optical fibre.

propagation prediction a prediction of ionospheric weather conditions. Prediction of changes in the ionospheric layers is possible with reference to the condition of the sun, and past experience of changes. In this way, predictions of propagation conditions for various wavebands can be made in advance, so that important communications can be routed through channels that will be least affected by the expected changes.

propagation time the time for a GATE (sense 2) circuit to produce an output following an input. See also RACE HAZARD.

proportional control a control system that makes use of NEGATIVE FEEDBACK. The output of the system is measured, and the result of the measurement is used to correct the controlling signal.

proportional counter a form of radiation detector. The detector is biased so that the amount of current that is produced is proportional to the energy of the IONIZING RADIATION.

proportional-integral control a form of FEEDBACK control in which one signal proportional to the error amount is superimposed on a ramp obtained by integrating the output.

protecting diodes or **protective diodes** or **protection diodes** DIODES formed as part of a FIELD EFFECT TRANSISTOR that are used to prevent the ELECTROSTATIC DAMAGE by limiting the voltage between the points to which they are connected.

protection diodes see PROTECTING DIODES.

protection margin see PROTECTION RATIO.

protection ratio the ratio of wanted CARRIER (sense 1) power to interference power for a radio link. For practical reasons, this level is usually exceeded by an amount known as the *protection margin*.

protective earth see PRIMARY EARTH GROUND.

protective gap a spark gap that is used to protect high-voltage equipment. Any sudden voltage surge will cause a spark at the protective gap rather than causing BREAKDOWN of insulation or other irreversible damage to electronic circuits.

protective multiple earthing or **PME** the connection of all metal pipes and any isolated metalwork in a building to a safe earth.

protective relay a relay that will disconnect a circuit if a fault occurs. See also CONTACT BREAKER; OVERCURRENT TRIP.

protoboard see BREADBOARD.

protocol a set of rules that are drawn up to ensure that data can be passed without error between two or more parts of a system.

protocol converter a device or circuit that will convert the PROTOCOL of one system into the protocols of another to allow data to pass between the two.

protocol, serial the rules governing serial transmission of data, ensuring that sender and receiver are working in the same way.

proton a stable, positively charged elementary particle found in the nucleus of an atom. The number of protons in an atom is equal to the number of electrons (equivalent to the *atomic number* of the element). The nucleus of the atom also contains NEUTRAL (sense 4) particles called NEUTRONS. The charge of the proton is 1.6022×10^{-19} coulomb; this charge is of equal magnitude but opposite polarity to that of an ELECTRON. The rest mass of a proton is 1.67252×10^{-27} kilogram, 1,836 times that of an electron.

proximity coupler a device that provides a form of TRANSFORMER action or microwaves with 90° phase difference, implemented by using close sections of quarter-wavelength strip. See also LANGE COUPLER.

proximity detection sensing the nearness of an object, usually a conductor or a warm body.

proximity effect **1.** a form of INTERFERENCE between signal conductors. High-frequency signals are carried by currents that flow on the outsides of conductors. If two such conductors are close to each other, the repulsion of the electrons can cause the effective area of the conductors to be restricted, making the apparent resistance higher. **2.** an apparent boost in low-frequency that occurs when a microphone is placed too close to a sound source.

proximity switch   a form of electronics switch used in security systems to detect that an intruder is close to the detection point.

proxy gateway   see FIREWALL.

PRSG   pseudo-random sequence generator: see PSEUDO-RANDOM BINARY SEQUENCE GENERATOR.

ps/2 connector   a miniature 6-pin connector with a KEYWAY to polarize (see POLARIZED, sense 3) it, used extensively for connecting keyboards and mice to computers.

PSAE   see PERCEPTUAL SUB-BAND AUDIO ENCODER.

PSD   see POWER SPECTRAL DENSITY.

pseudo-chrome   a form of a coating for tape that produces characteristics similar to those obtained from chromic oxide.

pseudo-complementary circuit   a type of audio output circuit that uses a pair of low-power COMPLEMENTARY TRANSISTORS to drive a pair of emitter-follower high-power output transistors. See also LIN CIRCUIT.

pseudo noise   see PSEUDO-RANDOM BINARY SEQUENCE.

pseudo-random   (of a string of digits) appearing to be randomly picked but eventually repeating a sequence.

pseudo-random binary sequence or **PRBS**   a sequence of BINARY DIGITs that appear at random but is produced by an algebraic process starting with a key word. Though the sequence appears random, it will repeat when the same key word is used again.

pseudo-random digit generator or **PRDG**   see PSEUDO-RANDOM BINARY SEQUENCE.

pseudo-random binary sequence generator (PRBSG)   a circuit that generates a stream of the digital bits in a sequence that is almost, but not exactly, random.

pseudo-ternary code   a type of code that uses three signal levels for BINARY (sense 1) information, with the same BANDWIDTH and rate as the original code, unlike a true TERNARY CODE.

PSK   see PHASE SHIFT KEYING.

psophometer   an instrument that can be connected to a communications network to produce a figure for NOISE, weighted to indicate nuisance value.

PSPICE   a set of computer programs for drawing circuit diagrams and analyzing the action of circuits.

PSU   see POWER SUPPLY.

psychoacoustic masking system   see MASKING.

PTC   see POSITIVE TEMPERATURE COEFFICIENT.

PTC resistor   a RESISTOR whose value increases with the increase of temperature. See also NTC RESISTOR.

PTC thermistor   a THERMISTOR with a POSITIVE TEMPERATURE COEFFICIENT.

PTFE   see POLYTETRAFLUOROETHYLENE.

PTM   see PULSE-TIME MODULATION.

p-type   (of a semiconductor material) being doped with ACCEPTOR material. P-type material conducts by HOLE mobility, rather than by ELECTRON mobility.

p-type metal-oxide semiconductor (PMOS)   a variety of FIELD EFFECT TRANSISTOR construction used for ICs, using only p-channel devices. See also CMOS; NMOS.

public address (PA)   a sound-reinforcing system for large numbers of listeners that uses microphones, amplifiers and loudspeakers. Problems of PA systems include avoiding echoes and acoustic FEEDBACK, intelligibility and background noise.

public key   one key of TWO-KEY SYSTEM code which is made public and is used along with a second (secret) key for ENCRYPTION and DECRYPTION.

puff   a slang term for PICOFARAD.

pull-in power   the power that has to be dissipated in the coil of a RELAY to make the contacts changeover. See also HOLDING POWER.

pull-in range, PLL   the range of input frequencies for which the OSCILLATOR of the PHASE LOCKED LOOP will lock into synchronization.

pulling   the disturbance of OSCILLATOR frequency by another signal at a nearby frequency. Unless an oscillator is very stable, it can be made to synchronize with a strong signal at a close frequency. Pulling is minimized by isolating an oscillator as much as possible from other circuits. This can be done, for example, by using a separate stabilized supply, encasing the oscillator section and connecting its output through a BUFFER (sense 1) stage.

pull-up resistor a RESISTOR that is intended to BIAS an ELECTRODE to the potential of supply positive. Several types of logic ICs need pull-up resistors if their outputs are not connected directly to another input or if a number of outputs are connected.

pull-up transistor a transistor used usually as part of an integrated circuit to ensure that a LOGIC circuit can deliver a high OUTPUT (logic 1) that is as close as possible to the supply voltage level. By using a transistor for this purpose, the voltage drop is almost independent of current, unlike the voltage drop across a PULL-UP RESISTOR.

Pulsam system a form of SINGLE-SIDEBAND transmission that separates the signal into an amplitude component and a phase component, amplifies both, and reconstructs the original signal at a much higher power level.

pulsating oscillating in size, brightness or other quantity.

pulse a single cycle of abrupt VOLTAGE or CURRENT change. The usual pulse form consists of a sharp rise of voltage, followed by a drop to the original level, the BASE LEVEL. In most systems, pulses are used in a pulse train, meaning that the pulses repeat at regular intervals. The intended shape of a pulse is usually rectangular, but due to effects of STRAY CAPACITANCES and inductances, this shape is modified to give the effects of DROOP, OVERSHOOT and RINGING (sense 2).

A perfect rectangular pulse would require no time to change its voltage value, but in practice the requirement to charge and discharge stray capacitance means that a definite RISE TIME and FALL TIME can be measured. These times are usually measured between the 10% and 90% amplitude points. The width of the pulse is the time for which its amplitude exceeds the 90% level.

A pulse may be of current rather than of voltage. Pulse shapes other than rectangular are also used, such as triangular and cosine-squared pulses. (See also Fig. 38.)

pulse amplifier an amplifier that will increase the AMPLITUDE of a pulse without deterioration in the sharpness of the LEADING EDGE of the pulse.

pulse-amplitude modulation (PAM) a form of MODULATION based on PULSES of MICROWAVE frequency. The signal that is to be transmitted is used to modulate the amplitude of pulses in a pulse train. DEMODULATION is very simple (a LOW-PASS FILTER can be used), but the transmission is very susceptible to interference.

pulse and bar a form of test signal for television consisting of a TRIANGULAR PULSE and a SQUARE WAVE, used for checking the response of the LUMINANCE channel.

pulse-code modulation (PCM) a form of MODULATION based on the transmission of digital signals. The amplitude of an analogue signal is sampled at intervals by an ANALOGUE TO DIGITAL CONVERTER. The output of the converter is used to generate the pulses, so that a set of pulses, representing a number in binary code, is sent for each point on the waveform of the signal. At the receiver, these signals are decoded, and the signal recovered from a DIGITAL TO ANALOGUE CONVERTER. PCM is the almost universal method of pulse modulation now used.

pulse count triggering form of alarm system that reduces the incidence of false alarms by operating only if triggered twice within a short time.

pulse counter a circuit whose input is a stream of pulses and whose output is a binary number that is equal to the number of input pulses. The counter circuit requires gating so that the time for which the count is taken can be controlled.

pulse counting demodulator a very precise form of DEMODULATOR for a

frequency modulated signal (see
FREQUENCY MODULATION) consisting of a
ZERO-CROSSING DETECTOR followed by a
PULSE COUNTER. The output can represent
the modulated signal and is usually
followed by a LOW-PASS FILTER.

pulse density modulation   a form of
BITSTREAM that uses differing numbers
of pulses rather than differing widths
of pulses.

pulsed frequency modulation or **chirp**
a SPREAD SPECTRUM time-hopping system
in which the CARRIER (sense 1) frequency
is swept over a wide range.

pulse dialling or **loop disconnect**   the
older form of telephone dialling system
in which connections are made and
broken so as to operate rotary solenoids
at the exchange. Compare MULTI-FREQUENCY
DIALLING.

pulse discriminator   a CIRCUIT that selects
PULSES of a particular specification on the
basis of their AMPLITUDE, width (see PULSE
WIDTH) or repetition frequency (see PULSE
REPETITION FREQUENCY).

pulse dispersion   the spreading in width
(time) of a pulse, caused by passing
through any practical transmission system.

pulsed klystron   the use of a KLYSTRON for
television transmission with the ANODE
pulsed to reduce average BEAM CURRENT
without serious loss of output power.
The beam current is maximum only
during the period of SYNCHRONIZING PULSE.
This increases the klystron power
efficiency by up to 75%.

pulsed laser   a form of laser, typified
by GAS LASERS, which is activated by a
flashlamp source, as distinct from the
SEMICONDUCTOR LASER that produces
CONTINUOUS WAVE output.

pulse-duration modulation (PDM) or
pulse-width modulation (PWM)   a form
of MODULATION using a SIGNAL to modulate
the width of PULSES. The POWER AMPLIFIER
(sense 2) is switched according to the level
of the modulating signal, passing current
only when the output resistance is low
The width or duration of each pulse is
proportional to the amplitude of the
modulating signal at that instant. The

system operates with a very high depth
of modulation so that overall power
efficiencies of about 70% can be achieved.
Demodulation can be carried out by a
simple INTEGRATOR.

pulse duty cycle   the on to off ratio for
a pulse, also equal to pulse width/pulse
period.

pulse fall time   the time for the voltage
of a PULSE to fall from 90% of peak level
to 10% of peak level.

pulse-forming line   a line or cable with
a reflecting TERMINATION, either a short-
circuit or an open-circuit. The length of
this line will determine the time needed
for a PULSE to be propagated down the
line and then reflected back, and this
time delay can be used to control the
pulse width in a pulse generator circuit.
An artificial LUMPED PARAMETER line is
often used.

pulse-frequency modulation (PFM)
a form of MODULATION in which the
repetition frequency of PULSES is
proportional to the amplitude of the
modulating signal at any instant.

pulse generator   a CIRCUIT that generates
PULSES, usually for testing pulse circuits.
For comparatively long pulses,
MULTIVIBRATORS can be used, but for
pulses in microwave systems, pulse
generators based on PULSE-FORMING LINES
are more useful.

pulse-height analyzer   a measuring
instrument for received PULSES. The
analyzer shows how many received
pulses fall into each group of amplitude
size.

pulse interval modulation   see PULSE
POSITION MODULATION.

pulse modulated Doppler radar   a form
of DOPPLER RADAR which eliminates the
reflections from fixed objects.

pulse modulation   a form of MODULATION
using a train of pulses to carry
information. At MICROWAVE frequencies,
conventional modulation of oscillators is
almost impossible, and most oscillators
are operated by pulsing. Only a form of
modulating the pulses, then, can allow
these frequencies to be used for

communications. To take advantage of the large bandwidths that are available at microwave frequencies, MULTIPLEXER (sense 1) systems that allow more than one signal to modulate a pulse train are particularly useful. All pulse modulation systems operate on the basis that the pulse repetition rate will be very much greater than the frequency of the signal that is being modulated, so that the pulses carry a sample of the signal.

pulse oscillator an OSCILLATOR whose output is a stream of PULSES rather than a SINE WAVE or other smooth wave form.

pulse-position modulation a form of PULSE MODULATION using displacement of a pulse from its standard time position. This requires a CLOCK signal to be available both at the transmitter and at the receiver, so that the deviation of the pulse from its correct timing can be detected.

pulse regeneration the restoration of a PULSE to its original specification. All circuits and transmission systems will distort the shape and timing of a pulse. A regeneration system restores the original shape and timing. The regeneration system often consists of a PULSE GENERATOR that is triggered by the imperfect pulse. All digital devices incorporate pulse regeneration so that a degraded input pulse results in a 'perfect' output pulse.

pulse repetition frequency (PRF) the rate at which PULSES are transmitted in terms of pulses per second. The normal KILO- and MEGA- prefixes will be used with the unit of pps (pulses per second), so a rate of 5kpps means five thousand pulses per second.

pulse repetition time the average time between pulses in a pulse waveform, equal to 1/frequency.

pulse rise time the time for the voltage of a pulse to rise from 10% of peak to 90% of peak voltage.

pulse shaper a CIRCUIT that alters PULSE shape. The INTEGRATOR and DIFFERENTIATOR circuits are pulse shapers, and a PULSE REGENERATION circuit will consist of, or contain, a pulse shaper.

pulse spacing the time between pulses in a PULSE train.

pulse spreading see DISPERSION.

pulse step modulation or **PSM** a high efficiency form of SINGLE-SIDEBAND transmission system that separates AMPLITUDE and PHASE components and uses the amplitude component to switch a high-power amplifier whose output is combined with the phase component for transmission.

pulse-suppresser a simple circuit that will remove short pulses that may have been caused by a RACE HAZARD.

pulse-time modulation (PTM) a general title for any MODULATION system that affects timing rather than amplitude of pulses. See PULSE-DURATION MODULATION; PULSE-FREQUENCY MODULATION; PULSE-POSITION MODULATION.

pulse transformer a transformer, usually small in size, designed to pass a pulse waveform from one circuit to another.

pulse width the time between the LEADING EDGE and the TRAILING EDGE of a pulse, measured at 50% of pulse height.

pulse-width modulation see PULSE-DURATION MODULATION.

pulser, logic see LOGIC PULSER.

pump signal the power input signal for a PARAMETRIC AMPLIFIER.

pumped laser see GAS LASER.

pumping **1.** the periodic alteration of a PARAMETER in a PARAMETRIC AMPLIFIER. **2.** the irregular rise and fall in noise level of the sound from a tape that has been recorded with an unsatisfactory NOISE-REDUCTION system.

punch-through a BREAKDOWN of a region in a TRANSISTOR. Punch-through in a BIPOLAR JUNCTION TRANSISTOR means that the base region is destroyed by excessive collector-base voltage, so that the base no longer controls the collector-emitter current. A similar effect occurs in FIELD-EFFECT TRANSISTORS in which current punches through the SUBSTRATE layer, bypassing the GATE (sense 1).

puncture voltage the value of voltage that breaks down an insulator, particularly the DIELECTRIC of a CAPACITOR.

punctured code   a form of CONVOLUTION
CODE that selectively removes bits from
the encoder output, so making the
average code rate higher. The switching
action for removing the bits is controlled
by a database called the *puncture matrix*.

puncturing ratio   the fraction of the data
stream that is omitted in CONVOLUTIONAL
CODING to avoid the excess BANDWIDTH
that would be involved if both data
streams were transmitted unaltered.

purity   the purity of colour in a COLOUR
TELEVISION tube. Purity means that when
a single colour is displayed, it should
appear as the same colour with the same
amount of SATURATION (sense 2) over
the whole of the screen. The main cause
of impure displays is accidental
MAGNETIZATION of metal components
in or around the tube.

purity error   any cause of impure colour.
See PURITY.

purple plague   a fault of very early
TRANSISTORS. This was caused by the use
of gold and aluminium together, so
forming an alloy that diffused into the
SEMICONDUCTOR.

push-button switch   a switch whose on
and off actions are both performed by
pushing a button.

push-pull   an old term for a stage using
two transistors conducting alternately.
The original push-pull audio output
stages used thermionic valves, one
connected to each end of a transformer
primary winding whose centre-tap was

connected to HT, so that the valves
conducted alternately when driven by
antiphase (balanced) signals. Transistor
versions of this circuit used transformers
initially, but the single-ended version
(see SINGLE-ENDED PUSH-PULL) of the circuit
superseded the use of transformers.
See also BALANCED AMPLIFIER; LIN CIRCUIT.

push-pull oscillator   a symmetrical form
of OSCILLATOR that provides high output
levels and low distortion, used for tape
bias and erase circuits.

push-pull solenoid   a SOLENOID that can
exert a force in either direction.

PUT   see PROGRAMMABLE UNIJUNCTION
TRANSISTOR.

PVC   polyvinyl chloride, a plastic polymer
widely used as a general-purpose
insulator.

PWM   see PULSE WIDTH MODULATION.

pyramidal horn or **tapered horn**   a form
of FEED HORN that is tapered, in both
planes for a true pyramidal form, with
the interior sometimes corrugated.

pyroelectric   (of a material) generating
a voltage from a temperature gradient.
Pyroelectric materials are used in fire
alarms and other applications. Some types
of plastics films are strongly pyroelectric,
and also several types of crystals.

pyroelectric microphone   a microphone
making use of a PYROELECTRIC film as a
TRANSDUCER from vibration into electrical
signals.

PZM microphone   see BOUNDARY
MICROPHONE.

qam see QUADRATURE AMPLITUDE MODULATION.

Q band a MICROWAVE band in the wavelength range of approximately 6.5mm to 8.3mm, corresponding to the frequency range of 36 to 46 GHz.

Q-bit one bit of a control word stored on a CD to specify information on playing time, number of tracks, etc.

Q carrier the quadrature CARRIER (sense 1) PHASE of a QPSK transmission.

QCIF see QUARTER COMMON IMAGE FORMAT.

Q code a code used by radio amateurs, particularly on the MORSE CODE bands. The code uses a letter Q followed by other letters to indicate standard questions and answers.

Q component see QUADRATURE COMPONENT.

QDU see QUANTIZATION DISTORTION UNITS.

Q factor the magnification factor or quality factor for a RESONANT CIRCUIT used for describing the behaviour of a circuit near RESONANCE. The sharpness of response or selectivity of a circuit to inputs of different frequencies depends on the Q value. Q factor for a parallel LC circuit can be defined as the value of the resistive parallel paths divided by the impedance of the inductive parallel path at the frequency in question. Q factor can be estimated graphically, from a plot of the ratio of output voltage to input voltage, or output current to input current, against frequency. At the RESONANT FREQUENCY, the Q factor is equal to the resonant frequency divided by the width of the resonant peak between the –3dB points.

QFP see QUAD FLAT PACK.

QIC see QUARTER-INCH CARTRIDGE.

Q meter an instrument for measuring tuned circuit Q FACTOR values.

QPSK see QUADRATURE PHASE-SHIFT KEYING.

QPSK decoder the IC used to decode NICAM sound data and convert it to left and right channel analogue signals.

Q signal the NTSC signal that contains colour information for blue shades, and which requires only low definition.

quad aerial (or **antenna)** an AERIAL consisting of two square loops of conductor with quarter-wavelength sides, one with a FEED POINT acting as a radiator or receiver, the other used as a REFLECTOR.

quad detector system a security system using a set of four detectors that will trigger an alarm only if two or more detectors send a signal. This greatly reduces the incidence of false alarms.

quad flat pack a form of packaging for ICs that uses a row of pins along each side of a flat square package.

quad psk see QUADRATURE PHASE-SHIFT KEYING.

quadrature the state of a VOLTAGE or CURRENT having a PHASE difference of 90° to some reference phase. If, for example, the current wave has a phase angle of 90° with respect to the voltage wave then the two are in quadrature.

quadrature amplitude modulation (QAM) or **quadrature modulation** the use of a CARRIER (sense 1) split into two PHASES at 90°, each separately AMPLITUDE MODULATED, that are then combined so that one carrier is carrying two signals. This can also be seen as a carrier that is amplitude modulated with one signal and phase modulated with the other signal.

quadrature component the component of a QUADRATURE AMPLITUDE MODULATION carrier that is at 90° to the main CARRIER (sense 1) phase.

quadrature demodulator or **quadrature detector** a PHASE-SENSITIVE DEMODULATOR that can extract two channels of signal from a CARRIER (sense 1) that has been modulated both in phase and in AMPLITUDE.

quadrature mirror filter   a form of digital filter used to partition a wideband signal into sub-bands.

quadrature phase-shift keying or **quad PSK** or **QPSK**   a DIGITAL MODULATION system that uses a two-phase CARRIER (sense 1), with each PHASE modulated with either logic 1 or logic 0, so that one cycle of carrier can convey two bits as 00, 01, 10 or 11.

quadrifilar aerial (or **antenna)**   a form of HELICAL AERIAL using four metal tapes wound in a helix on a dielectric cylinder.

quadripole   a network, particularly a balanced FILTER network, having four separate signal terminals, two INPUTS (sense 2) in different phases and two OUTPUTS also in different phases.

quadrupler   a VOLTAGE MULTIPLIER circuit whose OFF-LOAD DC output voltage is approximately four times the PEAK AC input.

quad splitter   a four-way MULTIPLEXER (sense 1) for signals, particularly for security cameras.

qualifier   a trigger for a LOGIC ANALYZER, which can be a CLOCK pulse (*clock qualifier*) or other form of trigger depending on what waveforms are being analyzed.

quantization or **quantizing**   the SAMPLING of a signal to produce a number of values per second, an essential part of ANALOGUE TO DIGITAL CONVERTER operation.

quantization distortion units (QDU) a (poorly-defined) measure of SAMPLING ERROR when an ANALOGUE signal is converted to DIGITAL format. A SIGNAL TO NOISE RATIO of 30 dB of analogue signal corresponds roughly to 14 QDUs.

quantization noise   for a QUANTIZED signal, the signal that is the difference between the QUANTUM level and the actual amplitude of the sampled analogue signal at any point. This is proportionally worse for low-amplitude signals, see DITHER.

quantized   (of an analogue quantity) converted to a digital signal with a specified number of levels.

quantized feedback   a system for removing an AC component from a DIGITAL signal, using NEGATIVE FEEDBACK from a PULSE REGENERATION circuit.

quantizing   see QUANTIZATION.

quantum   a discrete minimum amount of energy. A photon is the quantum of electromagnetic energy and momentum absorbed or emitted in a single process by a charged particle. For a wave of frequency f, the energy quantum size is $E=\hbar f$ where $\hbar$ is Planck's constant. To liberate an electron from a photoemitter, the energy of the light quantum must be equal to or greater than the amount of energy that binds the electron to the atom.

quantum, digital   the size of step change of voltage in the permitted levels of a DIGITAL signal.

quantum efficiency   for a PHOTOELECTRIC device, the ratio of the usable electrons emitted to the incident PHOTON number in a given time.

quantum yield   a measure of the efficiency of a PHOTOCATHODE or other electron photoemitter, equal to the average number of electrons produced for each photon of suitable energy.

quarter common image format (QCIF) a digital VIDEOTELEPHONY format that reduces BANDWIDTH by using LUMINANCE sampling at 176 samples per line and 144 lines per frame, one quarter of normal resolution.

quarter-inch cartridge (QIC)   a standard form of digital TAPE cartridge used in TAPE STREAMER systems.

quarter-track   (of tape intended for STEREO recording) using two tracks on each side of the centreline of the tape.

quarter wavelength aerial or **quarter wave antenna**   an aerial wire cut to the length of one quarter of a WAVELENGTH (of the wave along a wire) that it is intended to receive.

quarter-wave match   a LINE (sense 1) that is a quarter of a WAVELENGTH long, used for matching two other lines.

quarter wave stub   see STUB AERIAL.

quarter wave transformer   see IMPEDANCE TRANSFORMER.

quartz crystal   the silicon-oxide crystal, found naturally, that is used as an electromechanical resonator. The crystal is cut to shape, and opposite sides are metallized (see METALLIZING). The crystal will then act as a TRANSDUCER of radio frequencies to mechanical vibrations and vice versa, and exhibits the behaviour of a RESONANT CIRCUIT with very high Q FACTOR. Such crystals are used to control the frequency of transmitters, to generate precise frequencies for timing (as in a quartz watch) or for SYNCHRONOUS DEMODULATION, and in FILTERS with a narrow PASS BAND or stop band.

quasi-complementary circuit or **quasi-complementary push-pull**   see LIN CIRCUIT.

quasi-impulsive noise   WHITE NOISE that has an added IMPULSE NOISE component.

quaternary signal   a signal that has four distinct states.

quench   to de-ionize an ionized gas (see IONIZATION). The term is applied to mean that ions in a gas-filled tube such as a GEIGER-MÜLLER TUBE, have been made to recombine so that the gas is no longer conductive.

queueing delay   the time between a DATA PACKET being ready for delivery and its launch on a network.

quick-acting fuse   see FF FUSE.

quick-start fluorescent   a fluorescent tube with electronic control circuitry, enabling quick starting with none of the flickering associated with switch starting.

quiescent   the state of a circuit with no signal inputs, only the normal DC bias voltages.

quiescent current   the steady current (BIAS current) that flows when no signal is applied to a circuit.

quiescent point or **Q point**   the point on the DC LOAD LINE of an amplifier that represents the QUIESCENT value of output voltage and current for the circuit.

quiet zone   the blank area at each end of a BAR CODE set.

quieting level   the reduction in noise from an FM receiver when a usable signal is found.

quincunx areas   the four corners and centre of a square, referring to a form of diagram for the SPECTRUM of a sampled (see SAMPLING) signal.

Quine-McKluskey minimization   a method of MINIMIZING a LOGIC GATE circuit, using BOOLEAN ALGEBRA and which can be implemented by a computer.

race around   see RACE HAZARD.

race hazard or **race around**   a problem in unsynchronized LOGIC GATE circuits. PULSES that form the inputs to a gate may be subjected to delays that are not the same for two different pulse paths. Because of this 'race', the two inputs to a gate may not arrive together, so that the gate action is never achieved. Race hazards are avoided by SYNCHRONOUS operation.

RACON or **radar beacon**   a transmitter and receiver that sends out coded information when it receives a radar signal. The bearings of the radar transmitter can be calculated from the coded information sent out.

radar   a method of finding the distance and bearings of a target, such as a ship, aircraft, missile or possibly a non-moving object. The term is derived from 'radio detection and ranging', and the method measures the time between transmitting a wave pulse and receiving the reflected echo.

   The simplest form of pulse radar generates a master pulse that is used to modulate a MAGNETRON, producing a short burst of waves. The pulse is also used to start a CATHODE-RAY TUBE timebase. The MICROWAVES are transmitted from an AERIAL, using a parabolic reflector type to form a beam. When the waves strike a target, particularly a metallic target, a small proportion will be reflected. The returning wave is picked up in the same aerial, amplified, demodulated (see DEMODULATION) to form a voltage pulse and displayed on the CRT screen. Because of the use of a timebase triggered by the initial pulse, the distance from the start of the sweep on the CRT screen represents the distance of the target.

   A more common modern system is to use a PLAN POSITION INDICATOR display, so that both distance and bearings can be displayed. Lower-power radar systems use continuous wave or FM systems, and the speed of moving objects can be measured using DOPPLER radar. See also PASSIVE RADAR.

radar beacon system or **RBS**   see IFF.

radar indicator   a CATHODE-RAY TUBE display for a RADAR system.

radar intruder alarm   an alarm based on the principle of radiating high frequency radio waves that are reflected from an obstacle such as an intruder and detected.

RADAS   see RANDOM ACCESS DISCRETE ADDRESS SYSTEM.

radial-beam tube   a vacuum electron tube intended for specialized purposes in nuclear instrumentation.

radial magnetic field   a MAGNETIC FIELD whose lines of FLUX (sense 1) are directed along the radii of a circle towards or away from a central point. This is the type of field used for a MOVING-COIL LOUDSPEAKER.

radial scan radar   see PLAN POSITION INDICATOR.

radian unit   the natural unit of angle equal to the angle subtended by the distance along the rim of a circle equal to the radius of the circle. This definition leads to the relation between radian as π radians $= 180°$.

radiant energy   energy radiated, usually through space, by means of ELECTROMAGNETIC waves.

radiated power see EFFECTIVE RADIATED POWER.

radiation   the transmission of ENERGY through a medium or through space by means of waves.

radiation angle   for an AERIAL, the angle between the ground and the axis of a LOBE.

radiation efficiency   a measure of efficiency for an AERIAL that is transmitting. The radiation efficiency η is given by

$$\eta = \frac{\text{power radiated from aerial}}{\text{electrical power into aerial}} \cdot$$

See also APERTURE EFFICIENCY.

radiation function a mathematical equation for radiation distant from an AERIAL in terms of three-dimensional coordinates.

radiation hardened (of systems and components) able to withstand the effects of nuclear ELECTROMAGNETIC PULSE.

radiation impedance the additional impedance of a vibrating DIAPHRAGM when it is in contact with air. This results in the change of the impedance of the electrical unit, such as a MOVING COIL, that drives the diaphragm.

radiation intensity the power radiated per unit solid angle at a distance from the AERIAL.

radiation pattern a diagram that represents the effectiveness of an AERIAL. For a TRANSMITTING AERIAL, it shows lines of constant field strength. For a receiver aerial, it shows lines of equal sensitivity. The usual pattern for a simple DIRECTIONAL AERIAL is a figure-of-eight, with unequal sized LOBES. The wanted direction is the direction of the major lobe, and the rear lobe is often undesirable and represents wasted power in a transmitter.

radiation resistance see AERIAL RESISTANCE.

radiation, transformer the field, mainly MAGNETIC, around a TRANSFORMER that can cause signals to be picked up in wiring and in INDUCTIVE components.

radio 1. the technology of communicating with electronically produced ELECTROMAGNETIC WAVES. 2. any device that transmits or receives sound signals with these waves, and for a FREQUENCY in this range.

radioactive emitting particles such as ELECTRONS, NEUTRONS and ALPHA PARTICLES and also high frequency radiation such as GAMMA RAYS.

radioactive background the normal rate of arrival of particles due to radioactive processes such as the RADIOACTIVITY of the core of the Earth, and to radioactive particles arriving from outer space. Any

measurements of a radioactive material must take into account the amount of background radiation that would be present in the absence of a radioactive material.

radioactive count rate the rate at which IONIZING PARTICLES are emitted from a radioactive material, and detected by a device such as the GEIGER-MÜLLER COUNTER.

radio astronomy the locating and analyzing of the radio signals that come from stars or other distant bodies. This has become an important branch of astronomy, because many of the sources of radio waves do not correspond to visible objects.

radio beacon see BEACON.

radio broadcast a public transmission of sound, vision or data (see TELETEXT) signals, available to all.

radiocommunication signalling from one point to another by use of RADIO (sense 1) waves.

radio compass a form of radio direction finder that makes use of a DIRECTIONAL AERIAL to locate the direction of a radio BEACON or other transmitter in a known location.

radio data system or **RDS** an additional DIGITAL DATA system carried on a radio signal to provide additional information. The RDS system also allows switching to an alternative frequency of the same station when the received signal strength drops below an acceptable level.

radio frequency (RF) a frequency in the accepted practical radio range. This covers about 100kHz to about 300GHz. At the lower end of the range, radiation is very difficult unless extremely long AERIALs can be used. At the upper end of the range, purely electronic methods for generating signals can no longer be used.

radio-frequency amplifier an amplifier for RADIO (sense 1) frequencies, often a TUNED AMPLIFIER.

radio-frequency generator an OSCILLATOR operating at RADIO (sense 1) frequencies.

radio-frequency heating the heating of objects by radio-frequency currents. The two main methods are induction heating (see EDDY CURRENT HEATERS) for metals and DIELECTRIC HEATING for insulators.

radio-frequency interference or **RFI** unwanted radio signals from transmitters, electrical devices, or power lines that can interfere with wanted signals.

radio-frequency probe or **RF probe** a probe containing a rectifier, used along with a meter to measure the amplitude of radio-frequency signals.

radio gastronomy a slang term for preparation of food using a MICROWAVE COOKER.

radio horizon the maximum distance of propagation for a GROUND WAVE (sense 1) signal.

radio intruder alarm an alarm, usually operating with PASSIVE INFRA-RED detection, whose signals are passed by short range radio signals to a central alarm unit.

radio microphone or **wireless microphone** a microphone with built in FM transmitter circuitry powered by a battery. This allows the microphone user to move anywhere within the range of receivers without the need for trailing wires. Either VHF or UHF frequency bands can be used.

radio noise the unwanted NOISE signals that affect radio broadcasts. Noise can be natural or man-made. Natural noise consists of radiation from the movement of ions in the ionosphere and upper atmosphere along with signals directly from the sun and from other radio sources in space. Man-made noise includes interference from other transmitters, car ignition systems, fluorescent lights, electrical equipment and other sources of radiation at radio frequencies. See also NOISE.

radio paging a one way radio communication system that uses a central TRANSMITTER to send text messages to a personal miniature RECEIVER (pager). The pager will beep or vibrate when a message arrives. The use of radio pagers in the UK has been largely supplanted by text messaging on mobile phones.

radio pill a pill-shaped capsule that contains a miniature radio TRANSMITTER. Most radio pills also contain TRANSDUCERS to measure such quantities as acidity, pressure, etc. in the digestive tract of the body. These measurements are modulated onto the CARRIER (sense 1) signal, so that a RECEIVER can plot conditions as the pill moves.

radio receiver a receiver for radio signals that carry sound MODULATION. The sound signals for entertainment radio will be either amplitude or frequency modulated onto the CARRIER (sense 1). Military and other communications equipment will often use SINGLE-SIDEBAND techniques. FREQUENCY MODULATION is used only for the transmissions on VHF bands, because of the large bandwidth that is needed. The almost universal receiver is the SUPERHETERODYNE, in which the received signal from the AERIAL is tuned, and may be amplified in one stage, but then converted to an INTERMEDIATE FREQUENCY for subsequent amplification. The demodulated (see DEMODULATION) IF signal is passed to the audio frequency stages, including any volume and tone controls, and so to the loudspeaker. At the demodulator, DC signals for gain and frequency control will be extracted. Special SYNCHRONOUS DEMODULATION techniques will need to be used if the transmission is of the single sideband type.

FM receivers often make provision for STEREOPHONIC signal reception. Radio receivers can also be bought as TUNERS, containing only the RF, IF and first audio stages. These offer a higher quality of reception (of FM/stereo) and are intended for use with high-quality (Hi-Fi) amplifier and loudspeaker systems. High quality reception of medium wave broadcasts is impossible because of the large number of (legal) transmitters that operate at closely spaced frequencies, plus various pirate transmitters that in some districts make the use of medium wave reception very difficult.

radiosonde an airborne measuring device employing data transmission by radio from the upper atmosphere. Radiosondes are used by meteorologists, and employ balloons to carry small transmitters and TRANSDUCERS to the required height. The transmitters send data on atmospheric conditions, and are ultimately lost.

radio spectrum the range of ELECTROMAGNETIC frequencies that can be used for radio communication.

radio tag a device that can range from credit card size to a very small dot size that can be attached to an item, allowing it to be tracked from its signals. The unit can be battery powered or can use the power of interrogating signals.

radiotelescope an instrument for receiving radio signals from space. The main AERIAL types are the parabolic dishes or arrays, and the rest of the receiving equipment follows conventional radio receiver designs.

radio wave see CARRIER (sense 1).

radio window the range of frequencies that are not reflected by the IONOSPHERE and can therefore be used in RADIO ASTRONOMY. The range is roughly from 15MHz (20m wavelength) to about 50GHz (6mm wavelength).

RAID see RANDOM ARRAY OF INDEPENDENT DISKS.

rail a conductor, usually providing a DC supply.

raised cosine shape a form of PULSE shape particularly favoured for DIGITAL communications because half of the energy of the pulse is contained within a BANDWIDTH of half of the BIT RATE.

RAKE receiver a type of receiver system for digital code using CODE DIVISION MULTIPLE ACCESS. The RAKE receiver uses multiple demodulators on differently phased signals and combines the outputs to provide the code pattern.

RAM see RANDOM ACCESS MEMORY.

Raman amplifier a form of PARAMETRIC AMPLIFIER for light signals implemented in fibre optics in order to achieve amplification.

Raman effect the appearance of additional lines in the SPECTRUM of light that has been scattered (*Raman scattering*) by a medium such as glass.

RAMDAC see RANDOM ACCESS MEMORY DIGITAL TO ANALOGUE CONVERTER.

RAM disk a computer HARD DRIVE used as if it were MEMORY.

ramp a steadily rising (ramp up) or falling (ramp down) voltage, such as the linear SWEEP portion of a timebase.

RAM refresh see REFRESH (sense 1).

RAN radio access network.

random access the ability to gain access to DATA without requiring to read other data first.

random access discrete address system or **RADAS** an early form of SPREAD SPECTRUM TECHNIQUE in which every receiver in the system used a unique binary address, and the sender used a table that contained the codes for each receiver.

random-access memory (RAM) a form of electronic MEMORY that allows data to be read from or written to any location independently of others. A *serial access memory* allows access to a unit of data only by shifting other units out. Random access permits only the wanted unit to be affected. This is done by allocating a number, the ADDRESS number, to each unit of data. A set of address connections to the memory can be used to convey an address number, so that when an address number is placed in binary form on the lines, the correct data unit is made available. Another connection is used to select between reading or writing. Compare READ-ONLY MEMORY.

random access memory digital to analogue converter (RAMDAC) a specialized IC used in VIDEO GRAPHICS CARDS. The memory can be accessed simultaneously for both input and output, and the digital signals into the converter are used to provide analogue R, G and B signals for a CATHODE-RAY TUBE or an LCD screen.

random array of independent (or inexpensive) disks or **RAID** a method of increasing the reliability of HARD DRIVE storage for a NETWORK (sense 2). Several hard drives are connected so that the data they hold is duplicated, so that the total failure of one drive will not bring down the whole system.

random errors, CD   small errors that may be scattered over the area of the disc, often due to imperfect moulding and relatively easy to correct. See also BURST ERRORS.

random noise   a waveform with no single frequency and whose amplitude at any time is unpredictable. See also WHITE NOISE; PINK NOISE; RED NOISE.

random sound field   the sound field in a closed and highly reflective room where the wavelength of the sound is considerably less than any dimension of the room.

range   the distance between TRANSMITTER and RECEIVER. The term is often used to denote the maximum range, the greatest distance at which reliable communication can be established.

ranges, meter   see METER RANGES.

range switch   a switch used on a measuring instrument to determine which range of measured values will be sufficient to cause a FULL-SCALE reading.

range tracking   a form of RADAR system that allows a moving target to be followed, but reduces other echoes. The echo from the target is used to generate a gating signal for the target echo.

RAPD   see REACH-THROUGH AVALANCHE PHOTODIODE.

rare earths   oxides of metals that are rare and little used except in electronics.

raster   a scanning pattern on a TV screen. Conventional analogue TV uses a SCAN pattern of horizontal lines that slope slightly. Each screen line starts on the left-hand side of the screen and sweeps across to the right, moving downwards slightly as it does so. The line pattern is produced by using a horizontal TIMEBASE waveform, and the vertical movement from a vertical (FIELD, sense 2) timebase. These timebase signals are applied to different sets of DEFLECTION COILS arranged around the neck of the tube. In this way, a pattern of parallel lines is traced out on the screen.

In a complete picture, two sets of lines are used, interlaced. This means that the first set of lines, the even-numbered lines, will be spaced so as to occupy the vertical dimension of the screen. The second set, the odd-numbered lines, will then occupy the spaces between the first lines. The reason for this pattern is to satisfy the contradictory requirements of good vertical resolution, lack of flicker and small bandwidth. By using two interlaced patterns of 310 lines each (UK system), each of 1/50 second duration, the screen flicker is at 50 Hz, but the resolution is of a 620 line picture (for monochrome), and the bandwidth is that of a 25Hz repetition rate. The electron beam is suppressed (see BLANKING) during the flyback time to prevent random noise from appearing on the raster. See also DIGITAL TELEVISION.

raster burn   a permanent pattern on a screen caused by long exposure of the PHOSPHOR to a still bright picture.

rat race   see HYBRID JUNCTION.

rate adaptation   see BIT STUFFING.

rate adapter   an interface that will convert an ASYNCHRONOUS data stream into a 64 Kbps stream by adding extra bits to pad out the bit rate.

rate of attenuation   the number of DECIBELS of ATTENUATION per OCTAVE of frequency change for a filtering action. Sometimes quoted as dB per decade of frequency change.

rate of flare, horn   the change of area of cross section per unit distance from the source for a horn, either a LOUDSPEAKER horn or a MICROWAVE horn.

rate of rise heat detector   a form of fire alarm used where a smoke detector is not acceptable. The alarm is triggered when the rate of rise of temperature becomes excessive or when the temperature reaches a dangerous level, typically 60°C.

rate, sampling   see SAMPLING RATE.

rating   a specification of maximum operating conditions. The ratings (of voltage, current, frequency, temperature, etc.) for a component or assembly are determined by the manufacturer.

ratio adjustor   see TAPCHANGER.

ratio arms the two resistors or impedances in a BRIDGE CIRCUIT that provide a fixed (switchable) ratio of values, such as 10:1, 100:1, etc.

ratio detector or **ratio demodulator** a form of FM DEMODULATOR. The ratio detector is useful only if there is no trace of amplitude modulation in the signal, and has to be preceded by a LIMITER stage to ensure this. See also FREQUENCY DISCRIMINATOR.

ratiometric A/D converter see DUAL-SLOPE ANALOGUE TO DIGITAL CONVERTER.

Rayleigh distributed noise the distribution of noise when GAUSSIAN NOISE is reduced in BANDWIDTH, making the distribution one-sided.

Rayleigh region the region of electromagnetic field very close to a transmitting AERIAL.

Rayleigh scattering losses in OPTICAL FIBRES caused by random variation of refractive index over distances that are small compared with a light wavelength. Contrast MIE SCATTERING.

R-C or **RC** see RESISTOR-CAPACITOR.

R-C coupling the connection from one STAGE to another using a resistor as a load in one stage and a capacitor to pass signal to the following stage. This is an untuned or APERIODIC COUPLING.

R-C (or RC) network see C-R NETWORK.

R-C oscillator see PHASE-SHIFT OSCILLATOR.

R-C substitution box a device used for servicing low-frequency circuits, consisting of a set of resistors and capacitors that can be connected to terminals by way of switches.

RC time constant the time in seconds obtained by multiplying capacitance in farads by resistance in ohms. More practical units are microseconds, nanofarads and kilohms. When a capacitor C is charged through a resistor R, 66% of the charging is complete in a time equal to one time constant, and the capacitor can be considered as completely charged in a time equal to four time constants.

RCA Radio Corporation of America, originator of the NTSC colour TV system.

RCA connector see PHONO CONNECTOR.

RCD see RESIDUAL CURRENT DEVICE.

RDAT see ROTARY-HEAD DIGITAL AUDIO TAPE.

RDRAM a fast operating MEMORY system for computers designed for transfer rates of around 500 MB/s using DIRECT MEMORY ACCESS.

RDS see RADIO DATA SYSTEM.

reach-through avalanche photo diode or **RAPD** a form of PHOTO diode with a very lightly doped layer between ANODE and CATHODE (sense 2) to reduce field strength at AVALANCHE BREAKDOWN. The sensitivity is less than that of a simple AVALANCHE PHOTODIODE but the noise level is lower.

reactance the ratio of SIGNAL voltage to signal current in an ideal CAPACITANCE or INDUCTANCE. Ideal in this case means with no measurable series resistance and infinite parallel resistance. The value of reactance depends on the signal frequency as well as on the value of capacitance or inductance. A pure reactance also causes a 90° phase shift between voltage and current. For a capacitor, the phase of current leads phase of voltage, and for an inductor, the phase of current lags the phase of voltage. See also IMPEDANCE; RESISTANCE. See Fig. 95.

reactance amplifier an amplifier circuit that simulates a REACTANCE by using FEEDBACK so that the current output is 90° out of PHASE with its voltage output. Unlike a true reactance, the characteristics of a reactance amplifier can be altered by changing bias.

reactance, capacitor see CAPACITIVE REACTANCE.

reactance chart a form of NOMOGRAM that is used to show values of REACTANCE for different values of capacitance, inductance and frequency.

reactance, inductor see INDUCTIVE REACTANCE.

reactance transformer an obsolescent form of power-control circuit that uses a third winding on a transformer fed with DC to alter the saturation of the core and so control the efficiency of the transformer.

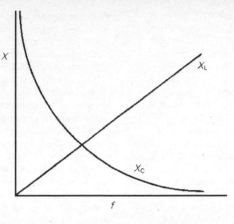

Fig. 95. **reactance**

reactivation the reviving of electron
EMISSION from a cathode or filament of a
THERMIONIC VALVE or CATHODE-RAY TUBE.
This usually involves running at higher
than normal temperature for some time,
often with GRID CURRENT being passed.

reactive circuit a circuit containing
REACTIVE COMPONENTS such as capacitors
and inductors.

reactive component any component that
causes a change of PHASE between current
and voltage.

reactive current or **idle current** the
component of current whose PHASE ANGLE
is at 90° to the phase of voltage.

reactive ion etching a method of creating
very narrow slots of less than one μm in a
semiconductor, using a stream of ionized
reactive gas molecules at high speed.

reactive load any LOAD that contains
REACTANCE and therefore causes a phase
angle between the current and the voltage
of a signal wave applied to it.

reactive power or **imaginary power** or
wattless power the figure that is the
product of volts and current for a perfect
REACTOR, or the V × I component at 90°
PHASE, not corresponding to any real
DISSIPATION of power because of the phase
difference.

reactive reflector a form of AERIAL
reflector constructed from WAVEGUIDE

sections each containing a phase shifter so
that the aerial DIRECTIVITY can be altered.

reactive voltage the component of
voltage whose PHASE ANGLE is at 90° to the
phase of current.

reactive volt-amperes the product of
voltage and current when a phase angle
exists. The true dissipated power is less
than this value, and is found by
multiplying the reactive volt-amperes
figure by the POWER FACTOR (the cosine
of the phase angle).

reactor a COMPONENT that is REACTIVE,
such as a capacitor or inductor.

read to copy stored information,
particularly in a computing storage system.
A non-destructive read process will allow
the copy to be made in the form of voltage
pulses on a line without any change in
the stored information. Contrast WRITE.
A DESTRUCTIVE READ process destroys the
stored information in the course of copying
it. For example, the stored charge image
in a TV camera tube is read by measuring
the electron current needed to discharge it.

READ diode see IMPATT DIODE.

reading memory the action of copying
DATA from a memory location to another
location, such as a REGISTER. If the type of
memory dictates a DESTRUCTIVE READ, then
the data must then be replaced in the
memory unless it can be discarded.

read-only memory (ROM) a form of memory for MICROPROCESSOR or computer use. The usual form of ROM permits random access to any unit, but allows reading only. This form of memory is NONVOLATILE, and is used for all programs that must be present from the instant of switching on. Contrast RANDOM-ACCESS MEMORY. See also PROM.

read-out pulse a PULSE applied to a MAGNETIC CORE (sense 2) memory system that allows a selected part of the memory to be read.

read-write head the TRANSDUCER of a tape or magnetic disk RECORDING system in which separate read and write heads are not used. See MAGNETIC RECORDING.

read-write line the signal line connecting to a MICROPROCESSOR input whose voltage level determines whether a READ or a WRITE operation is taking place.

read-write memory memory that can be read or written according to the voltage applied to the form of the memory chip.

real axis the x-axis of a graph used to represent the real part of a COMPLEX NUMBER; with the IMAGINARY PART represented on the y-axis.

real estate a slang term for the amount of space used on a chip.

real time (of an action) happening at the present time as distinct from an action on stored data that had been gathered earlier.

rear gap a gap at the rear of a tape head, which minimizes the problem of change of permeability of the core material with frequency, and makes RECORDING less dependent on tape to head contact.

rear projection a method of obtaining large screen television pictures by using a projector at the rear of a translucent screen. Compare FRONT PROJECTION. See also BEAMER; DIGITAL LIGHT PROCESSOR; PLASMA SCREEN.

reboot switch a switch on a computer that will force the machine to re-start, losing any unsaved data.

receiver a device that processes radio signals from an AERIAL into their final form (audio, video, digital code, etc.). Compare TRANSMITTER.

receive register a SERIAL REGISTER used to receive data on a network. See also TRANSMIT REGISTER.

receiving aerial an aerial design along the same principles as those for a TRANSMITTING AERIAL, but with no requirement for large currents to flow.

reception the interaction between an electromagnetic wave and any form of AERIAL that results in a signal being received. Compare TRANSMISSION.

rechargeable cell a CELL using a chemical reaction that is easily reversible by applying a voltage that is higher than the normal cell EMF to the terminals.

recharging see CHARGING.

reciprocal mixing see PHASE NOISE.

reciprocal theorem a theorem relating to NETWORKS (sense 1). Imagine two points, A and B in a linear network. If a signal voltage V at point A causes a signal current I at point B, then a voltage V at point B will generate a current I at point A.

recombination the removal of CHARGE carriers from a semiconductor or an ionized gas. Recombination can occur when an ELECTRON and a HOLE meet and release energy, so that the electron is no longer mobile, and the hole no longer exists. Both electrons and holes may also be trapped by impurity atoms.

recombination noise NOISE in BIPOLAR JUNCTION TRANSISTORS caused by the random RECOMBINATION of HOLES and ELECTRONS, more noticeable at higher frequencies.

record 1. a permanent store of data. 2. a gramophone record, see RECORDING OF SOUND.

record amplifier the amplifier circuit used in a TAPE RECORDER for the inputs from the microphone or other sources. Low-pass filtering is usually included to reject the PILOT TONE of a stereo broadcast and at the output the bias oscillator frequency must also be rejected. The record amplifier also contains part of the NOISE REDUCTION CIRCUITRY system along with the circuitry to indicate and control RECORDING LEVEL.

record head gap the space between the FERROMAGNETIC poles of a TAPE HEAD used for RECORDING and normally packed with hard non-magnetic material. Typical gap size for a record head is 6 to 10 MICRONS. See also REPLAY HEAD GAP.

recordable CD see CD-R; CD-RW.

recordable DVD a form of DIGITAL VERSATILE DISC that can be recorded on domestic equipment. The recording may be read-only (R), in which case the recording can be deleted but not edited nor added to, or it can be read-write (RW), in which case the DVD can be used in a similar way to video-cassette tape and recorded and rerecorded as often as required. Unfortunately, three competing systems exist, see DVD COMPATIBILITY.

recorded wavelength the distance along a portion of tape required to record one cycle of signal. If this distance is equal to the REPLAY HEAD GAP, the output will be zero.

recorder a piece of RECORDING equipment, for example, a tape (or cassette) or RANDOM-ACCESS MEMORY recorder, or (in data recording) a multichannel TAPE RECORDER.

recorder, strip-chart see STRIP-CHART RECORDER.

recording the storing of data in permanent form.

recording head the head of a TAPE RECORDER or of a HARD DRIVE that is used for recording signals on a magnetic medium. For many lower priced tape recorders the same head is used both for recording and for reading (replay). Hard drives also use the same head for both reading and writing data. See also ERASE HEAD.

recording level the peak or average value of signal delivered to tape RECORDING heads. If the recording level is too low, the output will have a poor SIGNAL-TO-NOISE RATIO. If the recording level is too high, the output will be distorted.

recording level indicator a device that provides a visible measure of RECORDING LEVEL. For professional tape recordings, a meter system is normally used, but for all other purposes a set of the LEDs indicates the level.

recording of sound the use of a system of TRANSDUCERs to convert sound into signals that can be recorded. The main systems are mechanical analogue, mechanical digital, magnetic, and optical. The mechanical analogue system uses the vibration of a stylus to modulate the shape of a groove that is cut into a gramophone DISC. The mechanical digital system uses an ANALOGUE TO DIGITAL CONVERTER, and records the digital signals by melting pits into the surface of a plastic disc with a laser beam. The storage density is very high, and the system permits the highest standard of domestic SOUND REPRODUCTION that has been achieved to date, the COMPACT DISC system. The magnetic systems use either analogue or digital recording on magnetic tape, see TAPE RECORDER. The optical system is used only for film soundtracks, in which the width or density of a strip of film is modulated by the audio signals. Optical systems suffer from poor signal to noise ratios, and noise-reducing techniques such as the DOLBY SYSTEM are very useful. Tape systems that use slow-moving, narrow tapes also suffer from noise problems, and the same solutions are used. See also DBX.

recording of video the use of a system for recording and replaying video signals, usually on tape (see VIDEO CASSETTE RECORDER). The analogue recording of video signals on tape requires processing of the signals to reduce their BANDWIDTH. The video recording heads are moved to sweep along and across the tape, so that the speed of the tape can be comparatively low while permitting the speed of the head relative to the tape to be high. The tape is considerably wider than conventional audio recording tape.

The sound track is separately recorded, usually on a strip that runs longitudinally, though on most modern machines much higher-quality sound reproduction is obtained by using an additional track swept with the video head. See Fig. 96.

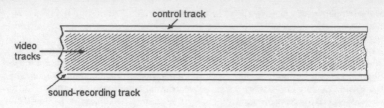

control track

video tracks

sound-recording track

Fig. 96. **recording of video**

Video recording of a much higher standard is also possible on discs, using the same laser read and write techniques as are used for DVD.

recovery time, compressor or **release time, compressor** the time required for the compressor action of a tape COMPANDER system to restore its gain to normal value after the signal falls below the threshold value at which compression starts to be applied.

rectangular coordinates see CARTESIAN COORDINATES.

rectangular wave a wave whose plot of voltage against time is of rectangular shape.

rectangular window a form of digital WINDOW FUNCTION used to reduce OVERSHOOTs or OSCILLATIONs due to a sharp cut-off digital filter.

rectification the conversion of a WAVEFORM into a voltage or current in one direction (unidirectional) only, the first step to converting AC to DC.

rectifier a COMPONENT, such as any type of DIODE, that passes current easily in one direction only. A rectifier, used in a half-wave or full-wave circuit will convert AC into UNIDIRECTIONAL CURRENT. This can be used to charge a RESERVOIR CAPACITOR in order to obtain smooth DC.

rectifier bridge see BRIDGE RECTIFIER.

rectifier diode a DIODE designed for use as a RECTIFIER for a POWER SUPPLY unit as distinct from use with signal waveforms. See also DEMODULATION.

rectifier instrument a measuring instrument that can be used with AC because it contains a RECTIFIER. The rectifier bridge circuit is normally used.

rectifier, precision see PRECISION RECTIFIER.

rectifier voltmeter a VOLTMETER that can measure sine wave AC values (see ROOT MEAN SQUARE, sense 2) because it incorporates a rectifier. The rectifier may be switchable, so that the voltmeter can be used for either DC or AC.

rectifying contact a CONTACT between two materials that has a rectifying action. The difference between the forward and the reverse resistance values may be small, but the presence of the rectifying contact can cause nonlinear effects in a signal.

recurrent code see CONVOLUTION CODE.

recursion the use mathematically of a single formula action repeated on a number. If a number is calculated from a procedure, and the result is then modified using the same procedure, and this is repeated until some limit is reached, the actions are said to be recursive. One well-known 'definition' is:

recursion see RECURSION.

recursive filter a form of INFINITE IMPULSE FILTER in which data is passed through more than once.

red-green-blue or **RGB** one of the methods of specifying a colour in terms of the relative amounts of three primary colours of light. A suitable mix of all three provides white light. A MONITOR that requires separate R, G and B signals is called an *RGB monitor* and cannot be used with a COMPOSITE VIDEO signal (such as from a video recorder) unless a separate composite input socket is present. The RGB system is used to obtain the highest possible RESOLUTION from a monitor. See also CMY; HUE; SATURATION (sense 2); BRIGHTNESS.

red gun one gun of a COLOUR CRT. The red gun is the gun whose electrons will pass through the APERTURE GRILLE to strike only the parts of PHOSPHOR that glow red.

red noise noise whose power density distribution falls with increasing frequency at the rate of 6dB per octave.

reduced bandwidth QPSK or **RBQPSK** a QUADRATURE PHASE SHIFT KEYING signal that has been narrowly filtered to reduce BANDWIDTH.

reduced carrier transmission or **reconditioned carrier reception** or **pilot carrier system** or **pilot tone system** a system used in single or double sided band suppressed carrier transmissions in which a lower level of CARRIER (sense 1), see PILOT TONE, is transmitted. This is used at the receiver to regenerate and synchronize a locally generated carrier.

reduced instruction set computer or **RISC** a computer designed around a MICROPROCESSOR CHIP with a very limited range of instruction codes. The set contains only the most-used instructions, that are arranged to be performed very rapidly, and more complex actions are obtained by using software at the cost of comparatively slower execution. The advantage as compared to the more usual complex instruction set computer (CISC) is speed, but if programming requires a large number of complex actions, the speed advantage of the RISC can be eroded.

reduction, noise see NOISE REDUCTION CIRCUITRY.

redundancy a deliberate or natural duplication. Redundancy in a circuit means that additional components are provided that will take over from other components in the event of failure. This idea can extend to complete systems, such as on-board computers for space or aircraft systems. Redundancy in a signal means information that is not needed. In an analogue TV signal, for example, over 90% of the data that is transmitted on one frame is also transmitted on the next frame, unless there is a change of scene. Some types of narrow bandwidth analogue systems operate by removing

redundancy from signals, and DIGITAL TELEVISION systems also reduce bandwidth in this way.

redundant bits BITS added to a DIGITAL signal to enable errors to be corrected.

reed relay or **reed switch** a form of RELAY for light-current applications, consisting of two thin magnetized strips in a glass tube, usually evacuated. When a magnetic field is applied, either by an energized coil or by a PERMANENT MAGNET, the strips are attracted and snap together, operating switch contacts at the ends of the strips. Reed relays can be obtained as NORMALLY CLOSED, NORMALLY OPEN or CHANGEOVER designs.

Reed-Solomon code a form of CYCLIC CODE that will correct any combination of n or fewer errors using no more than $2n$ PARITY bits. A GENERATOR POLYNOMIAL is used for encoding and on decoding a SYNDROME will be produced to identify the error pattern.

reed switch see REED RELAY.

re-entrant horn a form of compact horn loudspeaker that uses a folded and reflected sound path. The sensitivity is high but the bandwidth is limited and this type of loudspeaker is usually used for paging or PUBLIC ADDRESS only.

re-entrant overload characteristic a characteristic of a REGULATED POWER SUPPLY that will force the supply voltage to collapse to a low level in the event of a short-circuit occurring.

reference bias a figure of bias for a TAPE RECORDER that provides a reasonably flat frequency response with low distortion. One method of obtaining this is to find the bias that provides the lowest value of third harmonic distortion at 1 kHz.

reference diode a form of ZENER DIODE used to provide a REFERENCE VOLTAGE.

reference generator an OSCILLATOR, usually CRYSTAL controlled, used to generate a reference signal to act as a PHASE comparison in a PHASE-SENSITIVE DETECTOR.

reference pilot a single frequency that is included in a MULTIPLEX and monitored so that any change will indicate errors.

reference signal a signal of constant frequency and PHASE used as a comparison for phase demodulation.

reference voltage a steady and precise voltage, usually from a ZENER DIODE, that is used by a REGULATOR circuit as a comparison.

reflected current the signal current reflected from a faulty termination of a TRANSMISSION LINE.

reflected impedance an impedance whose effect can be measured in a circuit, but which is connected to that circuit by means of a transformer, line or other coupling. The reflected impedance of the secondary of a transformer is the amount of impedance measured at the PRIMARY that is due to the presence of the secondary load.

reflected power the power that is not absorbed by a LOAD, and is returned to the generator. This applies typically to a TRANSMISSION LINE system that is not correctly matched. In a MICROWAVE system, such reflected power can cause overheating and failure of the microwave generator.

reflected wave 1. a wave reflected in a TRAVELLING WAVE TUBE. 2. see SKY-WAVE.

reflection a reversal of direction of travel and PHASE of a wave, usually by striking a metal or other conducting surface, or from a discontinuity in a transmission line or other medium.

reflection coefficient the ratio of reflected current to forward current in a line. The currents will not, in general, have the same PHASE.

reflection error the errors in RADAR or RADIO COMPASS systems caused by false REFLECTIONS of signals.

reflection factor a measurement of MATCHING in a TRANSMISSION LINE. The reflection factor is the ratio of the current sent to a reflecting load to the current that would be sent to a perfectly MATCHED LOAD. The factor is often converted into decibels.

reflective array aerial see REACTIVE REFLECTOR.

reflective display or **RD** a form of colour LCD unit that is illuminated by white light and reflects a colour from each liquid crystal PIXEL. See also TRANSFLECTIVE DISPLAY; TRANSMISSIVE DISPLAY.

reflector an element of a DIRECTIONAL AERIAL. The reflector is placed behind the active portion of the aerial, which is usually a DIPOLE AERIAL. Its action is to reflect signal back to the dipole and so greatly reduce the size of the rear LOBE. The reflector can be another rod or be a metal sheet or wire mesh. The length of the reflector is always greater than that of the dipole, usually by a factor of about 10%, and the spacing between the reflector and the active element is of the order of a quarter of a wavelength.

reflector aerial (or **antenna)** an aerial for frequencies of 1 GHz upwards that uses a reflector whose size is large compared with the WAVELENGTH. The reflector is usually a paraboloid so that the energy reaching any part of the surface will all be reflected to a single focal point at which a waveguide or dipole can be placed.

reflector, aerial an AERIAL ELEMENT placed so as to reflect oncoming waves to a pickup unit such as a DIPOLE AERIAL. See also DIRECTOR; YAGI.

reflector surface errors errors in reception caused by the surface of a parabolic reflector not being a perfect paraboloid, in particular with surface blemishes.

reflex cabinet a form of loudspeaker ENCLOSURE that consists of a closed box with a hole or tunnel in one wall. The area of this *port* is equal to or smaller than the area of the MOTOR UNIT.

reflex circuit an obsolete circuit that was used as an amplifier for two sets of signals at different frequencies; a way of economizing on valves in early radio receivers.

reflex klystron a form of KLYSTRON in which the beam is reflected back after bunching. The effect is to make the device into a MICROWAVE oscillator, whose frequency is determined by the CAVITY RESONATOR dimensions and the voltage applied to the reflecting electrode. Reflex klystrons were once the only available devices for use as local oscillators in microwave receivers, but have now been almost completely superseded for low power applications by GUNN DEVICES.

reflow soldering a SOLDERING method used for SURFACE MOUNT DEVICES (SMD), in which a solder cream or paste is applied to the pads on a PRINTED CIRCUIT BOARD, and the SMD located on the pads. The board is then passed through a furnace to reflow the solder. A variation of this is vapour phase reflow soldering, in which the heating is carried out (more controllably) by condensing the vapour of a boiling hydrocarbon liquid on to the printed circuit board. See also WAVE SOLDERING.

reform electrolytic to apply steady POTENTIAL DIFFERENCE across an ELECTROLYTIC CAPACITOR until the LEAKAGE CURRENT reaches a minimum. Reforming is sometimes needed after an electrolytic capacitor has been stored unused for a long period, or after exposure to cold conditions. The reforming voltage re-establishes the film of aluminium oxide that acts as the insulator.

reforming nicad the application of brief large voltage pulses to a NICKEL-CADMIUM CELL to make it usable after an excessive discharge has caused it to fail to charge normally.

refraction the change of direction of a beam of ELECTROMAGNETIC WAVES when they pass from one material into another with different REFRACTIVE INDEX.

refraction, ionosphere the change of direction of radio waves as they pass from one layer of the IONOSPHERE to another. The amount of refraction may be enough to reflect the waves of some frequencies back to earth.

refractive index a measure of the angle through which a light beam will be bent when it passes into or out of a transparent substance.

refresh 1. (or RAM refresh) a signal or set of signals applied to a DYNAMIC RAM in order to maintain the level 1 voltage in each CELL. The MOS capacitors store data in the form of charges and because unavoidable leakage discharges these capacitors, the memory must be refreshed

by recharging at intervals of, typically, one millisecond. **2.** to regenerate the condition of a signal. A refresh operation has to be used in storage devices that use destructive readout.

refresh CRT to maintain a display of data on the SCREEN of a CATHODE-RAY TUBE. A CRT display exhibits a picture that is built up from a line pattern by brightening the beam at selected places. This picture is transient, because the glowing material (the phosphor) on the tube face glows only for a very short time after the electron beam has struck it. The process must be repeated at a rate of 25 times per second if the picture is to be shown continuously. This action is termed *refreshing*, and is carried out either by using a TV type of signal, or by the use of a video processor circuit.

refresh rate the number of REFRESH (sense 1) actions per second required to sustain the memory or display action.

regeneration see POSITIVE FEEDBACK.

regenerative detector a detector (demodulator) circuit using an amplifier stage in which POSITIVE FEEDBACK is used to keep the stage almost at the point of oscillation.

regenerative feedback see POSITIVE FEEDBACK.

regenerative receiver an early type of RECEIVER that achieved very high GAIN and SELECTIVITY by using RF positive FEEDBACK. See also SUPER-REGENERATION.

regional coding or **regionalization** coding placed on to a DVD disc to ensure that it can be played only in one part of the world. The system is designed to allow a film to be released in one region before it is available in others, but most DVD players can be set to ignore these regional codes and play any disc.

regionalization see REGIONAL CODING.

register an assembly of connected FLIP-FLOPS in which loading, storage and serial shifting (see SERIAL MEMORY) can be performed. Registers are used in microprocessors and in the CPU sections of computers. The use of registers is to store data temporarily, in particular the results of arithmetic and logic actions on data.

register insertion a NETWORK (sense 2) technique in which a NODE (sense 1), waiting to transmit, loads its data into a SHIFT REGISTER which is then switched in series with the network when a gap is detected. See also RECEIVE REGISTER; TRANSMIT REGISTER.

register with feedback a circuit used in a SIGNATURE ANALYZER that produces a unique pattern of BITs for any given input.

registration, image the precise ALIGNMENT of red, green, and blue images on the screen of a colour CATHODE-RAY TUBE so that there is no blurring of the image.

regulated power supply or **stabilized power supply** a power supply whose DC output remains constant despite variations in the AC mains voltage or in the current taken from the supply by a varying LOAD.

regulated voltage or **stabilized voltage** a voltage that remains steady, unaffected by changes in LOAD current or mains supply voltage.

regulating pilots a number of SINE WAVE signals at different frequencies spread throughout a multiplex and monitored so that their levels can be used to control the system gain-frequency characteristics. See also REFERENCE PILOT.

regulation or **stabilization** a circuit technique for making a quantity resist changes in inputs or loads. VOLTAGE REGULATORs are circuits whose output voltage remains stable despite changes in load current or supply voltage. Current regulators are circuits that supply a constant current despite changes in load resistance or supply voltage. Regulation of the gain of an amplifier against changes in component values can be achieved by using NEGATIVE FEEDBACK. A circuit can also be said to be regulated if phase correction is used to prevent unwanted oscillations or RINGING (sense 2).

regulation, cell the amount by which the voltage across a CELL drops when current is taken. This can be expressed in the form of OUTPUT RESISTANCE.

regulation, electromechanical an old system for regulating the output of a dynamo by switching windings in and out of use as output voltage varies.

regulation factor or **regulation** or **output resistance** the ratio of voltage drop to regulated voltage level at full load current, expressed as a percentage, for a POWER SUPPLY UNIT.

regulation, transformer the fractional drop in voltage at the secondary of a transformer, expressed as:

$$\frac{\text{open circuit voltage} - \text{full-load voltage}}{\text{open circuit voltage}}.$$

regulator or **stabilizer** a CIRCUIT that can maintain the value of either VOLTAGE or CURRENT constant over a wide range of conditions of changing LOAD value or mains voltage variation.

regulator interference interference on a car radio caused by the regulator for the battery recharging circuit.

reignition voltage the VOLTAGE that is needed to start CURRENT flowing again in a gas-filled device. If there is some trace of IONIZATION from previous current, the reignition voltage will be lower than the usual cold striking voltage.

rejection band see STOP BAND.

rejection filter a STEEP-CUT FILTER designed to reject one particular frequency or narrow band of frequencies, such as the TAPE BIAS reject filter fitted to a RECORD AMPLIFIER.

rejection ratio a measure of interference for a system which should be as low as possible. The rejection ratio, in decibels, is given by:

$$20\log \frac{\text{demodulated interference signal}}{\text{demodulated wanted signal}}.$$

rejector a filter CIRCUIT with very high IMPEDANCE at one frequency. The term usually denotes a PARALLEL RESONANT CIRCUIT used as a BAND-STOP FILTER.

relative frequency shift keying or **RFSK** a digital keying method in which a data signal using FSK modulation is used in turn to modulate a CARRIER (sense 1) so that two pairs of sideband frequencies are generated, one representing logic 0 and the other logic 1. This produces a better signal-to-noise ratio and a lower error rate.

relative humidity the amount of water vapour in a space, expressed as a fraction of the amount that could be held in air that was completely saturated with water.

relative permeability the ratio of the PERMEABILITY of a material relative to the PERMEABILITY OF FREE SPACE. Symbol: μ.

relative permittivity the ratio of the PERMITTIVITY of a material relative to the PERMITTIVITY OF FREE SPACE. Symbol: ε.

relaxation oscillator or **aperiodic oscillator** a form of untuned oscillator in which the ACTIVE COMPONENTS pass current only for brief intervals. MULTIVIBRATORS, UNIJUNCTION oscillators and BLOCKING OSCILLATORS are all relaxation oscillators. The output waveform of such an oscillator is aperiodic, and consists of steep-sided waveforms with comparatively long periods of steady voltage, either at zero or supply voltage.

relaxation time the recovery time for a CAPACITOR following a sudden change of charge.

relay an electromechanical SWITCH. A current flowing through a coil causes a magnetic field that attracts an armature. The armature moves, opening or closing switch contacts that are mechanically connected to it. Many uses of relays have now been taken over by purely electronic components, such as THYRISTORS and TRIACS. In some cases, however, wiring regulations insist on the use of mechanical relays.

relay contacts the switching contacts of a RELAY, nominally plated with silver, gold, or other metals.

relay driver a CIRCUIT that provides the current to the coil of a RELAY. When a TRANSISTOR is used as a relay driver, a DIODE must be connected so as to absorb the pulse of BACK-EMF that will be generated when current is switched off.

relay transmitter a low power transmitter, usually for UHF, designed to pick up signals from the main station and retransmit them into areas that cannot be reached from the main station.

release the last section of the waveform for a musical note in which the amplitude returns to zero. See also ATTACK; DECAY; SUSTAIN.

release time, compressor see RECOVERY TIME, COMPRESSOR.

reliability a measure of confidence in the ability of a DEVICE to keep working. Unlike mechanical devices, the reliability of electronic equipment is too high to measure in terms of probability. A more useful measure is the inverse, FAILURE RATE.

reluctance a magnetic circuit quantity that is analogous to resistance in the magnetic circuit equation mmf = flux × reluctance. See also FLUX (sense 1); MAGNETOMOTIVE FORCE.

remanence or **residual magnetism** or **remanent magnetism** or **remanent flux** the retained MAGNETISM of a magnetic material. The remanence is the FLUX DENSITY remaining in material that has been magnetized to MAGNETIC SATURATION, after which the magnetizing field has been removed. See also MAGNETIC HYSTERESIS.

remanence relay a form of relay that uses a small PERMANENT MAGNET as part of the CORE so that once the relay has been operated it will remain switched over without further application of power, and is released by applying a REVERSE POLARITY pulse.

remote control the control over a DEVICE at a distance, either by wire signals, by radio, or by INFRA-RED BEAMS.

remote control extender or **remote eye** a small unit, resembling a computer mouse, that carries a PHOTOCELL and an LED. This unit is connected by cable or radio link to the device that is remotely controlled, typically a satellite or Freeview digital box, so that the main box can be hidden away, or even in another room, while only the extender needs to be visible.

remote eye see REMOTE CONTROL EXTENDER.

removable hard drive a HARD DRIVE for a computer that is mounted so that it can be removed or replaced without removing the cover of the machine. The drive is usually attached to a holder (caddy) that will ensure good contacts being made when placed into a receptacle.

REN see RING EQUIVALENCE NUMBER.

rendering the process of editing DIGITAL VIDEO, separating AUDIO and VIDEO tracks and making alterations followed by reassembly into a COMPRESSED VIDEO format.

repeater a form of signal BOOSTER (sense 1). A repeater in a telephone line amplifies the audio signals to compensate for attenuation in the lines. Repeaters can be made that are bi-directional, operating in either direction, or which restore the original waveform of signals such as pulses.

repeller an electron used in a REFLEX KLYSTRON whose negative potential reflects the electron beam back along the drift tube and through the cavity (see CAVITY RESONATOR), causing BUNCHING at each pass.

replay amplifier the amplifier whose input is the feeble signal from a tape head and whose output is to loudspeakers, incorporating equalizing stages and designed for good signal-to-noise performance.

replay equalization the process of compensation for the frequency response of a tape system. The equalization in the REPLAY AMPLIFIER usually requires a boost for bass frequencies and another boost for the higher treble frequencies above around 2 kHz.

replay head the head of a TAPE RECORDER used only for reading. Lower priced tape recorders use the same head for both reading and writing actions. See also ERASE HEAD; RECORDING HEAD.

replay head gap the space between the FERROMAGNETIC poles of a TAPE HEAD used for replay and normally packed with hard non-magnetic material. Typical gap size for a record head is 1 MICRON or less.

resampling 1. the process of converting analogue TV image information from one format (standard) to another. 2. In digital imaging, the process of altering an image by operating on samples of PIXELS.

reservoir capacitor an essential part of AC to DC conversion. The reservoir capacitor is charged by a conducting RECTIFIER to the PEAK VOLTAGE of the waveform. When the input voltage to the rectifier drops, the reservoir capacitor supplies current to the LOAD until the rectifier can conduct again.

reset or **clear** to restore anything to its original setting or settings. As applied to a REGISTER means that each output will be put at logic 0.

reset button a button that, when pressed, will restart a system, particularly a computer, with the settings that are used at initial switch on.

reset input the input to a MICROPROCESSOR that will restore all default settings.

reset mode an operating mode of a J-K FLIP-FLOP with J = 0, K = 1 so that the output is reset to 0 at the edge of the CLOCK pulse. See also HOLD MODE; SET MODE; TOGGLE MODE.

residual charge see SOAKAGE.

residual current a current that continues to flow in a semiconductor device for a short time (measured in nanoseconds) after applied voltage has been reduced to zero. The effect is caused by the momentum of the CHARGE CARRIERS.

residual current device or **RCD** a form of sensitive RELAY used in a mains distribution box that can break off supply if there is a leakage of current to earth.

residual error rate the ratio of the number of uncorrected errors to the total number of BITS in a message.

residual magnetism see REMANENCE.

resistance the ratio of DC voltage to DC current for a conductor. Symbol: R; unit: ohm (Ω). The inverse of resistance is CONDUCTANCE. See also OHM'S LAW.

resistance-capacitance coupling or **resistor-capacitor coupling** or **RC coupling** a method of transferring signal from one amplifier STAGE to another. A resistor is used as a load in the output stage of one device, and a capacitor is used to transfer AC signal without affecting the DC level of the next stage.

resistance (Joule) loss loss of power in a circuit due to the conversion of energy into heat following JOULE'S LAW.

resistance pressure gauge a form of TRANSDUCER that measures pressure by its effect on a resistor.

resistance ranges the measuring ranges for RESISTANCE that are available on a MULTIMETER.

resistance strain gauge or **resistive strain gauge** a STRAIN GAUGE that uses a wire element. The wire is attached to a material and changes in stress cause variations of wire length and of area of cross section that alter its resistance. Semiconductor strain gauges are easier to use because of their much greater sensitivity.

resistance thermometer an instrument for measuring temperature electrically. The resistance of any metallic conductor changes with temperature, becoming greater as temperature rises. Resistance thermometers use wire coils (nickel alloy or platinum) as sensors, and the resistance is measured in a BRIDGE circuit, using COMPENSATING LEADS.

resistance, tuned circuit see DYNAMIC RESISTANCE (sense 1).

resistance values see PREFERRED VALUES.

resistance wire a wire that is made from high-RESISTIVITY material. Typical materials are nickel-chromium alloys such as Nichrome or Constantan.

resistive component the part of an IMPEDANCE for which voltage is in PHASE with current.

resistive loading the use of a resistor as a LOAD across, for example, a resonant circuit to introduce damping, or across the loudspeaker terminals of an amplifier to provide a constant load for test purposes.

resistive loss, transformer the losses due to heating in the windings of a transformer because of the resistance of the windings.

resistive power or **true power** the power dissipated in a RESISTOR when either AC or DC flows, or the power dissipated in the resistive component of an IMPEDANCE when AC flows.

resistive strain gauge a form of SENSOR for strain in a material based on the change of resistance of a conductor as it is stretched.

resistive temperature detector a form of SENSOR for temperature making use of the change of resistance that occurs for a conductor or a SEMICONDUCTOR when temperature changes.

resistivity a quantity that measures the resistance characteristic of a material. The figure of resistivity for a material is independent of shape or size and can be used to calculate the resistance of any specimen of that material. Symbol: ρ (Greek rho); units: ohm-metre. For a sample with area of cross section A and length d, and with resistance R, the resistivity is given by RA/d. Compare CONDUCTIVITY.

resistor a COMPONENT that is used for its resistance value. In the past, most resistors were manufactured from carbon composition, a baked mixture of graphite and clay. These have been almost completely superseded by carbon or metal FILM RESISTORS. WIRE-WOUND RESISTORs are used for comparatively low values of resistance where precise value is important, or for high dissipation. They are unsuitable for RF use because of their reactance. See also VARIABLE RESISTOR.

resistor-capacitor or **R-C** or **RC** a coupling method for an amplifier, or a tuning system for a low-frequency oscillator, that makes use of resistors and capacitors.

resistor colour code the set of colours for digits 0 to 9, along with colours for TOLERANCE values, used to mark values on resistors and capacitors.

resistors, parallel see PARALLEL RESISTORS.

resistors, series see SERIES RESISTORS.

resistor tolerance series see PREFERRED VALUES.

resistor-transistor logic (RTL) an obsolete system of logic circuitry for INTEGRATED CIRCUIT construction. These circuits used integrated resistors and transistors to form logic GATES (sense 2).

resolution or **definition** the ability of a display system to show fine detail, particularly CATHODE-RAY TUBE and LCD displays.

resolution of potentiometer a measure of the ability of a variable POTENTIOMETER (sense 1) to produce a small voltage change by a small adjustment. When wire-wound potentiometers are used, the smallest percentage change in resistance is given by the change from one turn of the winding to the next. For continuous metal-film potentiometers, this restriction does not apply, and greater resolution can be obtained.

resonance the maintenance of OSCILLATION with minimum driving signal. A resonant circuit will show little response to signals until a signal at the natural RESONANT FREQUENCY is used. At the resonant frequency, maximum current flows in the resonant circuit components for minimum input signal. There is usually current or voltage magnification, so that the circuit acts as a form of selective amplifier for one frequency.

resonance bridge a form of BRIDGE circuit in which one arm consists of a series RESONANT CIRCUIT. The bridge can be balanced only at the RESONANT FREQUENCY of the tuned circuit. From the balance conditions, the resistance of the tuned circuit can be found.

resonance, quartz crystal see QUARTZ CRYSTAL.

resonance-tunnelling hot-electron transistor or **RHET** a form of BIPOLAR JUNCTION TRANSISTOR that uses QUANTUM TUNNELLING across the base region to control current flow. Such transistors are capable of operating at frequencies of 120 GHz or more, with very high gain.

resonant cavity a closed space surrounded by metal that acts as a RESONANT CIRCUIT for MICROWAVES.

resonant circuit or **tuned circuit** a circuit that will resonate at some frequency. 'Lumped' resonant circuits use a capacitor and an inductor, but resonance can also

occur in a QUARTZ CRYSTAL, in a TRANSMISSION LINE, and in a CAVITY RESONATOR.

resonant frequency or **natural frequency** the frequency of natural RESONANCE of a circuit or any other system that can oscillate. Any system that is set into oscillation by a brief stimulus will from then on oscillate at its natural frequency of resonance. An OSCILLATOR is most stable when the stimulus is so small that the frequency of oscillation is the natural frequency for the network.

A CAPACITOR presents a high IMPEDANCE to low-frequency alternating current, but has a low impedance at high frequency. The opposite is true of an INDUCTOR, which has a high impedance for high frequencies and a low impedance for low frequencies. In addition, the direction of PHASE shift for a circuit containing an inductor is opposite to that for a capacitor.

In a series circuit containing inductance, capacitance and resistance (as illustrated in Fig. 97) the impedance LOAD of the signal generator will be large at high frequencies (because of the inductor) and also at low frequencies (because of the capacitor). At some intermediate frequency there will be a minimum impedance, and this is called the 'resonant frequency' or 'natural frequency'. In the circuit of Fig. 97, which is called a *series resonant circuit*, resonance will occur when the ANGULAR FREQUENCY of the signal generator is:

$$\omega = \frac{1}{\sqrt{LC}}.$$

Resonance occurs at the frequency at which the inductive and capacitive REACTANCES are exactly equal and opposite, so that they cancel. Under these conditions the impedance is real and has the value R as if the circuit contained only resistance.

A circuit excited into oscillation by an IMPULSE (sense 1) will resonate until all the energy contained in the capacitive and inductive components has been lost through damping, in the resistor in this example. Resonant circuits are used to

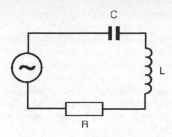

Fig. 97. **resonant frequency**

'select' signals that are at or near their
resonant frequency, and also to determine
the frequency of an OSCILLATOR. See also
RINGING (sense 1).

resonant line   a TRANSMISSION LINE whose
inductance and capacitance resonate at
the operating frequency.

resonant mode converter   a type of
circuit used for a SWITCH MODE POWER
SUPPLY in which the switching pulse width
is held constant, allowing switching
speeds as high as 1 MHz to be used.

response curve   a graph of output
amplitude plotted against frequency for any
circuit, particularly for a filter or amplifier.

response time   the time needed for a
system to respond to a signal.

responsivity   a measure of efficiency for
an energy conversion, equal to (output
signal)/(input signal), and usually
expressed as a percentage. See also
TRANSDUCER.

restore   to return to original conditions.

retentivity   the quantity that measures
the amount of retained MAGNETISM of a
magnetic material after an applied field
has been removed. The units are as for
flux density, webers per square metre.
See also COERCIVITY; MAGNETIC HYSTERESIS.

retrace   see FLYBACK.

retroflective photodetector   a
PHOTOELECTRIC sensing system that uses
a light source and a detector in the same
place, with the light reflected from a
mirror back to the detector.

retroflective scan   a method of
recognizing an object with diffuse
contours using a scanned light beam and

analyzing the reflected signal. See also
IMAGE ANALYSIS.

return loss   for a TRANSMISSION LINE, the
ratio of reflected power to incident power
at the load.

return signal   the weak MICROWAVE signal
returning to a RADAR aerial from a
target.

return-to-zero format or **RZ**   a method
of coding BINARY (sense 1) signals using
narrow PULSES, with logic 1 represented by
a positive pulse and logic 0 by a negative
pulse, so that the signal level returns to
zero between pulses. The format is
seldom used because it is wasteful of
energy and BANDWIDTH.

reverberation time   the time for which
a sound will echo in a space until it
becomes inaudible.

reverberation unit or **reverb**   a form of
ULTRASONIC DELAY LINE or digital delay
used to provide artificial echo in a sound
recording.

reverse AGC   a form of AUTOMATIC GAIN
CONTROL that uses NEGATIVE BIAS. Reverse
AGC is used when the gain of the
amplifier stages is reduced by reducing
their operating current. Compare
FORWARD AGC.

reverse bias   a BIAS that opposes the flow
of current in a device. Compare FORWARD
BIAS.

reverse breakdown voltage   the REVERSE
BIAS voltage applied to a DIODE or
JUNCTION (sense 2) that will cause large
amounts of current to flow as distinct
from the very small reverse current that
flows when smaller levels of reverse
voltage are applied. See also AVALANCHE
BREAKDOWN; ZENER DIODE.

reverse current   current flowing in the
REVERSE DIRECTION, such as from CATHODE
(sense 2) to ANODE (sense 2) of a DIODE.

reverse direction   the direction of high
resistance to current flow through a
device that is not OHMIC.

reverse-EMF   the EMF that is generated
when current through an inductor is
suddenly changed. By LENZ'S LAW the
direction of this EMF will always oppose
the change of current that caused it.

reverse polarity the connection of a device the wrong way round, such as to a power supply with positive and negative connections reversed.

reverse polarity protection the use of circuits, usually containing DIODES, to avoid connecting a sensitive unit to the incorrect voltage polarity.

reverse saturation current the small current that flows through a DIODE that is reverse biased (see REVERSE BIAS). This reverse current varies with temperature and is affected by light striking the SEMICONDUCTOR, see PHOTODIODE.

reverse video see INVERSE VIDEO.

reverse voltage a voltage applied to a DIODE with the CATHODE (sense 2) positive and ANODE (sense 2) negative.

reversible aerial or **reversible antenna** a form of DIRECTIONAL AERIAL whose main lobe can be switched through 180° by changing the feed.

rewritable CD see CD-R; CD-RW.

RF see RADIO FREQUENCY.

RF amplifier an amplifier stage, usually tuned, that precedes the MIXER STAGE of a SUPERHETERODYNE RECEIVER.

RF bands a form of classification of high radio frequency bands by letter, ranging from A (100 to 300 MHz) to M (60 to 100 GHz).

RFC radio frequency choke: see INDUCTOR.

RF cable a cable designed specifically for RF transmission, and graded into groups by the figure of ATTENUATION (for a 10 metre length) at various frequencies.

RF condenser microphone see CAPACITOR MICROPHONE.

RF connector any form of plug and socket connection designed specifically for use with radio frequencies to terminate an RF CABLE.

RF distribution the use of RADIO FREQUENCY signals to distribute television or radio signals among a large number of receivers.

RF heating eddy current heating (see EDDY CURRENT HEATER) or DIELECTRIC HEATING using radio frequencies.

RFID radio frequency identification.

RF interference (RFI) interfering signals at RADIO FREQUENCY, either natural or generated from other electrical equipment.

RF transformer a transformer designed specifically for RADIO FREQUENCY signals and normally using either an AIR CORE or a form of DUST CORE.

RF transistor a TRANSISTOR specifically designed to be used for high frequency signals.

RFSK see RELATIVE FREQUENCY SHIFT KEYING.

RGB see RED-GREEN-BLUE.

RGB connection a connection for VIDEO SIGNALs that carries the red, green and blue signals separately, providing considerably better quality in the resulting picture than a COMPOSITE SIGNAL.

RGB guns the three separately controlled ELECTRON GUNS of a colour CATHODE-RAY TUBE.

RGB matrix the arrangement of individual colour LCD cells on a display screen, usually following an offset pattern so that each line of cells is displaced by half of a cell width.

RGB projection a TV PROJECTION system that uses three sources, red, green, and blue, rather than attempting to project a single picture.

rheostat an old form of VARIABLE RESISTOR, usually wire-wound.

RHET see RESONANCE-TUNNELING HOT-ELECTRON TRANSISTOR.

rho Greek letter ρ used as a symbol for RESISTIVITY.

rhombic aerial (or antenna) a four-sided wire structure that acts as a DIRECTIONAL AERIAL.

RIAA curve the characteristic devised for cutting VINYL RECORDs which reduces bass frequencies to avoid large excursions of the cutting stylus and boost treble frequencies to raise the signal-to-noise ratio at these frequencies. This characteristic is reversed in an equalizing stage on replay.

ribbon cable a cable, used extensively in computer construction. with a large number of connecting wires that are laid flat rather than being compacted into a circular form. The flat form reduces interference between signals, but the use of ribbon cable is declining because of the adoption of SERIAL data cables.

ribbon loudspeaker a form of loudspeaker MOTOR UNIT using a very powerful magnet with a metal ribbon between its poles. Passing signal current along the ribbon will cause it to vibrate at the frequency of the signal.

ribbon microphone or **induction microphone** a form of dynamic-induction microphone. A thin metal ribbon is stretched between the poles of a high-flux magnet. Vibration of the ribbon by sound waves causes an induced signal voltage that can be amplified. The microphone uses no separate DIAPHRAGM, so greatly reducing unwanted resonances, and is particularly suitable for high-quality work. The output is very small, but because of the low impedance it is not difficult to avoid interference pickup. See also VELOCITY OPERATED MICROPHONE.

RIE see REACTIVE ION ETCHING.

right-hand rule see FLEMING'S RULES.

ring counter a form of digital counter that uses FLIP-FLOPS connected in a circular arrangement, so that output of the last flip-flop is connected to the input of the first flip-flop.

ring equivalence number or **REN** the number of telephones or their equivalent that can be loaded on to a single subscriber line. The usual maximum is REN 4, beyond which the line cannot support the ringing current.

ring indicator a signal that shows that an incoming call to a MODEM is being received.

ringing **1.** the oscillation of a RESONANT CIRCUIT caused by a pulse signal (see SHOCK EXCITATION). **2.** unwanted oscillations appearing in a pulse.

ringing choke converter see FLYBACK CONVERTER.

ring magnet a magnet in annular shape designed typically to fit around the neck of a CATHODE-RAY TUBE.

ring network a form of NETWORK (sense 2) in which each terminal is connected

to two others in a ring. See also STAR NETWORK.

ripple **1.** the proportion of AC remaining in a steady voltage from a power supply. The ripple is due to the fluctuations of voltage across the RESERVOIR CAPACITOR as it is charged and discharged. For a full-wave rectifier system, the ripple frequency is twice supply frequency, but for a half-wave circuit, the ripple will be at supply frequency. The ripple waveform is generally a sawtooth rather than a sine wave. **2.** a fault in amplification of a square wave that results in a damped high-frequency oscillation, (see Fig. 38).

ripple counter or **asynchronous counter** a form of digital counter that consists of a chain of FLIP-FLOPS. The input pulses are used to switch the first flip-flop, and the output of this flip-flop is used to toggle the next in the chain. The number of pulses is shown in terms of the digital number stored by the outputs of each flip-flop. As each flip-flop input is the output of the previous stage, incrementing the count by one will cause a successive series of changes to 'ripple through' the device, so that the flip-flops do not change simultaneously.

ripple factor the percentage of RIPPLE (sense 1) in a DC supply. This is expressed as the percentage of ROOT MEAN SQUARE (sense 2) ripple, assuming that the ripple is a SINE WAVE – which is seldom true.

ripple filter an integrating or smoothing circuit that removes RIPPLE (sense 1). The circuit is a simple form of LOW-PASS FILTER, using series inductance or resistance and parallel capacitance.

ripple frequency the frequency of RIPPLE (sense 1), in terms of supply frequency. If a bridge rectifier is used, ripple occurs at twice the supply frequency; if a half-wave rectifier is used the ripple is at supply frequency.

ripple, picture a TV picture fault that causes severe distortion of the picture at a frequency of double the mains frequency, caused usually by failure of the SMOOTHING (sense 1) circuits in the POWER SUPPLY unit.

ripple rating the maximum current at RIPPLE FREQUENCY that can be applied to an ELECTROLYTIC CAPACITOR.

ripple rejection the action of a REGULATED POWER SUPPLY in reducing any RIPPLE (sense 1) from a RECTIFIER and RESERVOIR CAPACITOR unit.

ripple voltage the amount of RIPPLE (sense 1), usually measured in terms of an RMS sine wave, that exists on a nominally smooth DC supply.

rippling through the process of passing a BIT from one stage of a LOGIC CIRCUIT to another, such as passing a carry bit in an ADDER CIRCUIT or passing a counter bit from one counter stage to another in a RIPPLE COUNTER.

RISC see REDUCED INSTRUCTION SET COMPUTER.

rise time the time of a pulse LEADING EDGE. This is usually taken as the time for the voltage to change from 10% to 90% of the pulse peak voltage. (See Fig. 38.)

Rivest-Shamir-Adleman algorithm or **RSA algorithm** a DATA ENCRYPTION method that relies on two large prime numbers chosen at random and used to calculate their product. From knowledge of the prime numbers an ENCRYPTION KEY and DECRYPTION KEY can be calculated, and the modulus of the product can be used as a PUBLIC KEY.

RL differentiator a DIFFERENTIATING CIRCUIT formed from a series inductor followed by a parallel resistor.

RLE see RUN-LENGTH ENCODING.

RL filter a FILTER, HIGH-PASS or LOW-PASS, formed from a resistor and an inductor.

RL integrator an INTEGRATING CIRCUIT formed from a series inductor and a parallel resistor.

RLL see RUN LENGTH LIMITED.

RMS see ROOT MEAN SQUARE.

RMS detector a circuit whose input is a signal of any waveform, and whose output is a DC level equal to the exact ROOT MEAN SQUARE (sense 2) value of the signal at that instant.

robot or **automaton** any machine that has been programmed to carry out a set of repetitive mechanical actions with minimum human intervention.

robotics the study of machines with some form of intelligence.

Rochelle salt a PIEZOELECTRIC CRYSTAL material that is seldom used now because of its deterioration in the presence of water vapour.

rolled capacitor a CAPACITOR formed from a thin ribbon of a DIELECTRIC, METALLIZED on each side and rolled into a cylinder with connections to each metallized surface. See also PAPER CAPACITOR.

rolling picture a TV picture fault in which the whole picture appears to be rolling vertically, caused by poor FRAME SYNCHRONIZATION.

roll-off or **roll-off rate** the rate in terms of dB per octave, at which the GAIN of an amplifier is reduced when the applied frequency is outside the normal BANDWIDTH.

ROM see READ-ONLY MEMORY.

ROM signature a number obtained by adding all the BYTES in a ROM, discarding CARRY bits. Any change in this number indicates a fault in the ROM.

room modes see EIGENTONES.

root-mean-square (RMS) **1.** the square root of the average of the squares of a set of numbers. **2.** the root of the average value of the square of wave amplitudes over a complete cycle. This quantity is used to find the DC equivalent of an AC voltage or current. The principle is that power can be correctly calculated for AC circuit using RMS values (providing that phase shifts are correctly taken into account). For a sine wave shape, the RMS value is equal to peak value divided by $\sqrt{2}$. A different factor must be used for other waveforms. See also TRUE RMS.

rosin or **colophony** an old form of FLUX (sense 2) for SOLDERING, now out of favour because of the fume hazard.

rosin-cored solder SOLDER made in the form of hollow wire that is filled with rosin or other FLUX (sense 2).

Rosing, Boris (1869–1933) the inventor of a scheme (in 1904) for using a cathode-ray tube as part of a television receiver system, with a mechanical system used as a transmitter.

rotary encoder an ANALOGUE TO DIGITAL CONVERTER for a rotating shaft which often uses an optical source and sensor arrangement and a slotted disc. See also LINEAR DIGITAL ENCODER; OPTICAL ENCODER; PHOTOCONVERTER.

rotary head digital audio tape or **RDAT** the digital audio tape system that uses the same type of rotary head design as a VIDEO CASSETTE RECORDER. The technology allows very high density RECORDING with exceptional quality, and though it has been taken up by professional recording engineers, totally replacing older forms of tape recording, it has made no impression on domestic recording because of the restrictions imposed by the records industry to prevent copying. As a format for domestic recording, it has now been superseded by hard drive systems and recordable CDs and DVDs.

rotary solenoid a form of SOLENOID that produces torque rather than force and rotates a shaft when energized. The shaft turns back to its starting position by means of a spring when the solenoid is de-energized.

rotary switch a switch that is operated by turning a shaft, rather than by depressing a lever. Rotary switches are often MULTI-POLE, MULTI-WAY designs.

rotary transformer 1. or **rotating transformer** a transformer, one of whose windings can rotate with respect to the other without compromising the transfer of signals between the windings. A transformer of this type is an essential part of the signal system to and from the heads of a VIDEO CASSETTE RECORDER. 2. A very old method of power conversion in which the input power, AC or DC, operates a motor that turns the shaft of a dynamo or alternator for a DC or AC output at a different voltage level.

rotating-anode tube a form of X-RAY TUBE in which the ANODE can be rotated to avoid overheating.

rotation or **endaround shift** a serial memory or REGISTER action in which the most significant bit from the end of a memory or register is loaded in at the least significant end, the remaining bits being shifted one place to make room.

rotation detector a circuit, using TACHOMETER pulses, that detects the rotation of the head DRUM (sense 1) of a VIDEO CASSETTE RECORDER.

rotational speed speed of turning expressed usually as radians per second or complete turns per second.

rotator a portion of a WAVEGUIDE that changes the plane of POLARIZATION (see POLARIZED, sense 1) of the waves.

Rotomode coupler a MICROWAVE directional coupler used as a BAND-PASS FILTER or as a method of combining two signals for transmission over one line.

rotor the rotating part of a motor or generator. Contrast STATOR.

round the world echo an echo effect on low-frequency signals that can propagate around the world to arrive at the RECEIVING AERIAL some time following the DIRECT SIGNAL. See also BACKWARD ECHO; FORWARD ECHO.

Round-Travis detector a form of DEMODULATOR for FM that uses a pair of tuned circuits with diode rectifiers, one tuned above the incoming signal frequency and the other tuned below the signal frequency.

router a connecting device for NETWORKS (sense 2) that passes signals between networks only when the networks use identical PROTOCOLS.

routing the action of passing data packets from one network to another. See also BRIDGING; BROUTER.

row and column address a position in a keyboard MATRIX or a memory, formed by using a numbered row and a numbered column.

R-S flip-flop or **S-R flip-flop** the simplest type of flip-flop constructed from NOT gates and not available in IC form. An output is obtained if one input at the two terminals, R and S, is at LOGIC ONE. The output is then stored for as long as both inputs are held at LOGIC ZERO. The R-S flip-flop was superseded by the J-K FLIP-FLOP except for the purposes of SWITCH DEBOUNCING. See Fig. 98.

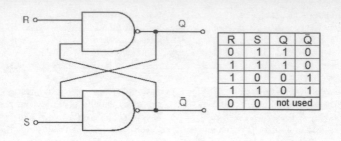

R	S	Q	Q̄
0	1	1	0
1	1	1	0
1	0	0	1
1	1	0	1
0	0	not used	

Fig. 98. **R-S flip-flop**

RSA   see RIVEST-SHAMIR-ADLEMAN ALGORITHM.

RS-423   a modern version of serial protocol similar to RS-232 but using fewer lines and with signal voltages of +5 V and 0 V to match the levels used on a computer MOTHERBOARD. A 9 pin D-TYPE CONNECTOR is used.

RS232   an internationally agreed standard for serial data transmission. It specifies high and low voltage levels, timing and control of signals.

RTD   resistance temperature detector: see RESISTANCE THERMOMETER.

R-2R ladder   a form of DIGITAL TO ANALOGUE converter that uses only two resistor values in a 2:1 ratio, for which accuracy is easy to obtain.

rubber Zener or **V$_{be}$ multiplier**   a circuit consisting of a BIPOLAR JUNCTION TRANSISTOR biased by a potentiometer (sense 1) and used to set the bias for a class B output stage. See Fig. 99.

rumble   a low-frequency NOISE. The term usually denotes the low-frequency audio signals that are caused by mechanical vibrations of the motor or bearings of a gramophone vinyl disc player.

runaway   loss of control, e.g. THERMAL RUNAWAY, the loss of control of temperature. If the temperature of a transistor increases to such an extent that the base current is no longer able to control collector current, the current and temperature will increase until the junctions are destroyed. Thermal runaway is very rare with modern silicon transistors correctly used.

run-length encoding (RLE)   a simple method of NON-LOSSY COMPRESSION for data

that contains repeated items, such as PIXELS of an image. Instead of using the data for each repeated pixel, the data for one pixel is used along with the number of consecutive pixels using the same data.

run length limited (RLL)   a form of DISK DRIVE recording system used for a HARD DRIVE that permits tighter packing of data than the MODIFIED FREQUENCY MODULATION system.

run-length limits   the maximum and minimum limits on transitions of voltage in digital codes. Recording processes cannot cope with a long stream of bits of the same polarity, nor can they cope with rapid transitions such as would be caused by a stream in which the polarity alternated on each pulse.

runt   an error signal caused by processing a GLITCH that was part of a serial BITSTREAM.

RZ   see RETURN-TO-ZERO FORMAT.

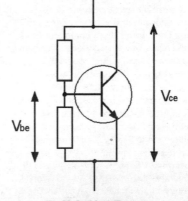

Fig. 99. **rubber Zener**

SAB see SELF-ACTIVATING BELL.

Sabine formula a method of finding the REVERBERATION TIME for a recording studio of given dimensions.

saddle-shaped field the shape of the ELECTROSTATIC FIELD required of an ELECTRON LENS to focus a beam of electrons. The field can be obtained from a set of three electrodes, with the central electrode at a lower potential than the other two.

safe operating area (SOA) or **safe working area (SWA)** the conditions of voltage and current that can be used for a transistor without danger of over-dissipation.

safe working area or **SWA** see SAFE OPERATING AREA.

safety-critical component a component that is marked out by a special symbol on a CIRCUIT DIAGRAM as being critical to safety, and which must be replaced by an identical component, not by a substitute.

safety-critical system any system whose failure can have catastrophic results.

safety switches switches that are built in to cabinets for electronic equipment to switch off the mains supply when covers are removed.

safety tab the plastic tab on a video cassette (see VIDEO CASSETTE RECORDER) that can be removed to prevent the tape being used for recording. If the tape needs to be recorded over, the space can be covered by sticky tape.

safety-valve, cell a thin section of container wall, used particularly in a lithium cell, to allow gas to blow out in the event of excess pressure.

sag see DROOP.

Sallen & Key filter a filter circuit that uses in-phase FEEDBACK from a compound EMITTER FOLLOWER (see DARLINGTON PAIR) to a C-R NETWORK to produce a LOW-PASS FILTER or HIGH-PASS FILTER with a SLOPE of typically 12 dB per octave.

sample and hold a circuit that produces a stored output that is the VOLTAGE of a WAVEFORM at a particular instant when it has been sampled.

sampler a form of digital RECORDING device using an ANALOGUE TO DIGITAL CONVERTER, a RANDOM ACCESS MEMORY, and a DIGITAL TO ANALOGUE CONVERTER. This allows short messages to be recorded and replayed at will as for a telephone answering machine.

sampling the making of measurements at intervals. Sampling is an essential part of ANALOGUE TO DIGITAL CONVERTER operation, and the conversion will be useful only if the sampling rate is high enough. A minimum sampling rate of twice the sample frequency is often quoted, but in practice this would seldom be totally satisfactory.

sampling clock the clock signal generated by a digital recorder (see DIGITAL RECORDING) using a CRYSTAL OSCILLATOR to control the rate of sampling.

sampling rate the rate at which an ANALOGUE SIGNAL is sampled in order to convert it to a DIGITAL signal. See also SHANNON'S LAW.

sampling rate, DSO the rate at which a DIGITAL STORAGE OSCILLOSCOPE must sample an input signal, equal to at least twice the signal frequency.

sandcastle pulse a combination of COLOUR BURST gating pulse, line-blanking pulse and field-blanking pulse generated in an APPLICATION SPECIFIC INTEGRATED CIRCUIT for a TELEVISION RECEIVER so as to avoid the need for multiple pulse outputs. The combined pulse (named because of its shape) is separated into separate pulses by the luminance and chrominance ICs. See Fig. 100.

SAR see SYNTHETIC APERTURE RADAR.

SARAM see SEQUENTIAL ACCESS; RANDOM ACCESS MEMORY.

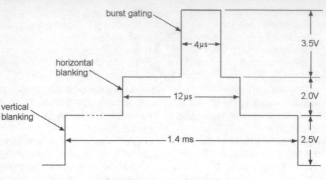

Fig. 100. **sandcastle pulse**

satellite a man-made object in orbit round the Earth, usually carrying electronic equipment for communications, scientific or military purposes. See also APOGEE; GEOSTATIONARY ORBIT; PERIGEE.

satellite communications the use of a satellite as a relay station, accepting signals from earth and re-transmitting them to other points on Earth.

satellite dish a receiver for MICROWAVE signals from a SATELLITE using a parabolic dish to focus a wide beam on to a small area and so pick up a signal of reasonable amplitude.

satellite TV the direct broadcasting of television programmes, now usually in digital format, from a satellite above the Earth.

saturable reactor or **transductor** an INDUCTOR whose inductance value can be considerably changed by passing DC through another coil wound on the same core. See also MAGNETIC AMPLIFIER.

saturable transformer a transformer whose output can be controlled by passing DC through a winding, used to provide a regulated AC supply. See also REACTANCE TRANSFORMER; SIGNAL WINDING; TERTIARY WINDING.

saturated mode the constant-current operation of a FIELD-EFFECT TRANSISTOR. A FET is being operated in saturated mode when the DRAIN voltage is kept at a level at which only the GATE (sense 1) voltage affects the drain current.

saturated region the portion of the characteristics of a BIPOLAR JUNCTION TRANSISTOR or FET in which the COLLECTOR or DRAIN voltage is so low that change of BASE current or GATE (sense 1) voltage has no effect on the collector or drain current.

saturation 1. a limiting state. A magnetic material is saturated when the MAGNETIC FLUX DENSITY of a material is almost unaffected by changes in the MAGNETIZING FIELD. 2. a measure of intensity of colour of light in terms of comparison to white light. A completely saturated colour has no white light content; it is 100% saturated. Addition of white to this light will reduce the saturation, and at 0% saturation the light is perfectly white.

saturation, core the state of a magnetic core in which the MAGNETIZING FORCE has reached the magnitude that completely magnetizes the material, so that FLUX DENSITY does not increase appreciably with increase of magnetizing force.

saturation current a state of maximum current, unaffected by a rise of voltage. See SATURATED MODE.

saturation humidity the water content of air that cannot hold any more water vapour without precipitation. See also RELATIVE HUMIDITY.

saturation output level or **SOL** the maximum tape replay level from a tape that is magnetically saturated on signal peaks, measured at a high frequency, usually 10 kHz. See also MAXIMUM OUTPUT LEVEL.

saturation recording recording on a MAGNETIC material by using signals that magnetize the material to MAGNETIC SATURATION in either POLARITY (sense 2), using one polarity for logic 0 and the other for logic 1.

saturation resistance the resistance between COLLECTOR and EMITTER (sense 1) of a saturated BIPOLAR JUNCTION TRANSISTOR. SATURATION (sense 1) occurs because the resistance falls to such a low value that the current is determined by the load resistor rather than by the base current.

saturation signal a SIGNAL that overloads a RADAR receiver.

saturation voltage the voltage between COLLECTOR and EMITTER (sense 1) of a saturated BIPOLAR JUNCTION TRANSISTOR. For a silicon transistor, this is typically less than 200mV.

SAW see SURFACE ACOUSTIC WAVE.

sawtooth current a current whose waveform, plotted by a CATHODE-RAY OSCILLOSCOPE appears as a sawtooth shape.

sawtooth distortion or **jaggies** the appearance of a diagonal line on a SCREEN with low RESOLUTION.

sawtooth oscillator an OSCILLATOR whose output is a voltage or current sawtooth wave. The sawtooth oscillator is a form of RELAXATION OSCILLATOR.

sawtooth waveform or **sweep waveform** the output WAVEFORM from a SAWTOOTH OSCILLATOR. An ideal sawtooth waveform consists of the linear SWEEP section, a brief FLYBACK, and a waiting period between the end of the flyback and the start of the next sweep.

S band a MICROWAVE band, with wavelength range from 5.77cm to 19.3cm, corresponding to the frequency range of 1.55GHz to 5.2GHz.

SBC single board computer.

Sbus a bus system developed by Sun Microsystems providing a 32- or 64-bit data bus with a maximum transfer rate of 80 MB/s.

Scalable Processor Architecture or **SPARC** a technology developed by Sun

Microsystems Inc. using a REDUCED INSTRUCTION SET COMPUTER chip for either large or small computers.

scalar (of a physical quantity) that has size but no directional dimension. Contrast VECTOR.

scalar feedhorn a form of MICROWAVE aerial for reception, using several concentric rings that behave as slots around a waveguide. The advantages are that wave polarization is unimportant, and the VOLTAGE STANDING WAVE RATIO is low with good side-lobe discrimination.

scalar network analyzer a measuring instrument consisting of a CATHODE-RAY OSCILLOSCOPE controlled by a MICROPROCESSOR with DIGITAL processing of the signal to be used for measurements such as INSERTION GAIN or loss, RETURN LOSS, VOLTAGE STANDING WAVE RATIO, GAIN COMPRESSION, etc.

scale modelling simulation of the behaviour of a large AERIAL using a model with scaling factors to indicate the results that will be achieved with the full size aerial.

scale of 8 see OCTAL.

scale of integration a description of the number of devices that can be obtained on a single semiconductor CHIP (sense 1). The integration scales range from SSI (small scale), through MSI, LSI to VLSI (very large scale integration).

scale of two see BINARY SCALE.

scaler a form of PULSE count divider. A scaler gives a pulse output after a fixed number of input pulses have been received. Most scaler units are decade (ten pulses in for one out) or binary (two, four, eight or sixteen pulses in for one out).

scaling factor the method used in a NICAM receiver to expand the 10-bit DATA words into 14-bit samples to convert back to ANALOGUE form.

scan the movement of an ELECTRON BEAM across a target or screen (scanning). Television requires both a horizontal and a simultaneous vertical scan. See also RASTER.

scan coils the set of coils fitting over the neck of the magnetically deflected CATHODE-RAY TUBE so that the beam can be deflected in any direction. See also SCANNING YOKE.

scanner 1. a detector system for medical use. One form of scanner is a detector of radio tracers in the body, allowing a map to be made of suspect tissue. Other forms scan using ultrasonics or magnetic resonance. 2. a device controlled by a computer that can make a digitized copy of an image or of text. 3. a slang term for a TV outside-broadcast van.

scanning see SCAN.

scanning array see PHASED ARRAY AERIAL.

scanning receiver a receiver using FREQUENCY SYNTHESIS for the LOCAL OSCILLATOR so that it can scan a particular WAVEBAND automatically and stop when it finds a signal that has a desired set of characteristics.

scanning yoke or **yoke** an arrangement of DEFLECTION COILS for a TV or radar CATHODE-RAY TUBE.

SCART connector see PERITEL.

scattering the loss of light energy in FIBRE OPTICS systems due to imperfections and impurities in the glass. See also BRILLOUIN SCATTERING; MIE SCATTERING; RAMAN SCATTERING; RAYLEIGH SCATTERING.

scattering factor the ratio of scattered (lost) power to incoming power for a RECEIVING AERIAL.

scattering loss the loss of energy from an electron or light or radio BEAM by irregular reflections. Loss by scattering is particularly noticeable when the wavelength of the radiated energy is close to the dimensions of scattering particles, e.g. the effect of fog on light. The use of metal strips (called chaff or window) to confuse radar is an early example of deliberate scattering of electromagnetic waves. An electron beam is scattered when it passes through dense matter.

schematic see CIRCUIT DIAGRAM.

Schering bridge a form of measuring BRIDGE for measuring CAPACITANCE and leakage resistance.

Schmitt optical system a curved mirror that is used on PROJECTION TELEVISION systems to form beams that focus on to a screen.

Schmitt trigger a form of level-triggered BISTABLE CIRCUIT with SQUARE-LOOP HYSTERESIS. The output of a Schmitt trigger remains low until the input voltage reaches a critical level. The output then rapidly switches high. The input voltage must then be lowered to a different and lower critical level in order to switch the output voltage low again. The Schmitt trigger is a particularly useful circuit for PULSE REGENERATION. See Fig. 101.

Schmitt trigger oscillator a simple form of SQUARE WAVE oscillator using a Schmitt trigger IC LOGIC GATE with FEEDBACK through an R-C NETWORK to an input.

Schottky diode or **hot-carrier diode** a DIODE that uses a metal-semiconductor JUNCTION (sense 2), usually aluminium-silicon. The diode has a very low forward voltage for conduction, fast switching speed, and fast cutoff on reverse bias. Schottky diodes are incorporated into a range of digital logic ICs (the TTL LS series) in order to achieve faster switching with lower values of current.

Schottky noise or **shot noise** a form of NOISE caused by the random emission of electrons, particularly in vacuum devices.

scientific calculator a pocket calculator that, in addition to the usual arithmetic functions, will carry out actions such as square roots, powers, sines and cosines and expressions using brackets, all with numbers in STANDARD FORM if necessary.

scientific notation see STANDARD FORM.

scintillation 1. the flash of light in some types of CRYSTAL when struck by an ionizing particle. 2. the random variation of amplitude of a radio signal that has been transmitted over a long distance.

scintillation counter a detector and counter of IONIZING RADIATION. The active elements consist of a scintillating crystal and a PHOTOMULTIPLIER. The flash of light from the crystal for each particle is detected by the photomultiplier, and the output pulse from the photomultiplier is amplified and used to operate a SCALER or COUNTER. The colour of light from the scintillation counter depends on the energy of the particle that produced it,

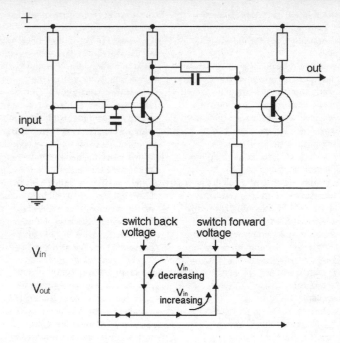

Fig. 101. **Schmitt trigger**

and the pulse amplitude from the photomultiplier is also affected by the energy of the radiation. This makes it possible to analyze the output of a scintillation counter in more detail than is possible if a GEIGER MÜLLER detector is used.

SCMS see SERIAL COPY MANAGEMENT SYSTEM.

S connector a connector designed for S-VIDEO signals.

SCPC see SINGLE CHANNEL PER CARRIER.

SCPI see STANDARD COMMANDS FOR PROGRAMMABLE INSTRUMENTS.

SCR see THYRISTOR.

scrambler a DEVICE for making telephone, TV, or satellite communications secure. The signal is treated, for example by inverting the frequency bands, so that it makes no sense to any listener who cannot make use of an unscrambler for decoding.

scratched CD a problem that can cause a CD PLAYER to skip TRACKS. The scratch is much more serious if it lies along the track as distinct from across the track, hence the advice to clean CDs by wiping from centre to edge.

scratch filter or **whistle filter** a LOW-PASS FILTER used particularly for replaying older vinyl or shellac recordings to reduce the noise from surface scratching, or excessive treble.

screen the endplate of a CATHODE-RAY TUBE, or its metal shield against electric or magnetic fields. See FARADAY CAGE; MAGNETIC SCREENING.

screen burn see ION BURN.

screened cable a cable whose insulation is covered with a layer of copper braid or aluminium foil wrapper to provide an electrostatic shield. Such cables should not be kinked or bent to a small radius.

screened pair two insulated signal-carrying wires surrounded by a conducting braiding. A screened pair is very commonly used for stereo audio signals, with one wire for each channel and the braiding used for the earth connection.

screen grid an additional grid electrode run at high voltage and placed between the CONTROL GRID and ANODE of a THERMIONIC VALVE to reduce the FEEDBACK effect of capacitance between anode and control grid. See also PENTODE.

screen, high-mu a magnetic shield, usually for a TRANSFORMER, with high magnetic PERMEABILITY.

screening the encasing of a CIRCUIT with metal to reduce the effect of MAGNETIC or ELECTRIC FIELDS. The screening is usually against external fields, but can be used to prevent internal fields from escaping. For electrostatic screening, the metal should be a good conductor, and earthed. For magnetic screening, the metal must be of very high PERMEABILITY, and in the form of a complete loop.

SCS see SILICON CONTROLLED SWITCH.

SCSI see SMALL COMPUTER SYSTEMS INTERFACE.

SDAT a form of DIGITAL TAPE RECORDER using stationary heads, now obsolete. See RDAT.

SDH see SYNCHRONOUS DIGITAL HIERARCHY.

SDLC see SYNCHRONOUS DATA LINK CONTROL.

SDRAM see SYNCHRONOUS DYNAMIC RANDOM ACCESS MEMORY.

sealed cell a CELL that is sealed so that neither liquid nor gas can escape. Some such cells include a vent that can burst to release gas in an emergency.

search coil a small COIL that was used along with a BALLISTIC GALVANOMETER as a former method of measuring MAGNETIC FLUX. This method of measuring flux has been superseded by the use of HALL EFFECT devices.

search tuning see AUTOMATIC TUNING.

SECAM see SYSTEME ELECTRONIQUE COULEUR AVEC MEMOIRE.

secondary aerial (or antenna) properties a set of PARAMETERS for aerial behaviour, including EQUIVALENT NOISE TEMPERATURE, POINTING ACCURACY, SECONDARY RADIATION, BLOCKING LOSSES, SIDELOBE RESPONSE and VOLTAGE STANDING WAVE RATIO.

secondary cache CACHE memory placed on the MOTHERBOARD of a computer and used in conjunction with the PRIMARY CACHE that is located on the microprocessor itself.

secondary cell a CELL whose chemical action is easily reversible. The cell will provide electrical energy until the chemical reaction is almost complete, at which point the action can be reversed by connecting the cell to a source of potential difference that is higher than the normal EMF of the cell. This recharging action can be continued until the chemicals in the cell have been completely restored to their original state, allowing the cell to be used again. See also LEAD-ACID CELL; NICKEL-CADMIUM CELL.

secondary circuit, relay the circuit that includes the switching CONTACTS of a RELAY. Contrast PRIMARY CIRCUIT, RELAY.

secondary code see SECONDARY ENCODING.

secondary colours the colours cyan, yellow and magenta, produced by subtracting the primary colours of red, blue and green respectively from white light.

secondary earth ground or **signal earth** an earthing point for signal circuits. Compare PRIMARY EARTH GROUND.

secondary electron an ELECTRON that has been emitted from a material in a SECONDARY EMISSION process. Compare PRIMARY ELECTRON.

secondary emission the EMISSION of electrons from a material in a vacuum because of electron bombardment (of PRIMARY ELECTRONS). The effect occurs only for a limited range of accelerating voltage of the primary electron beam, between the crossover voltages. Below the first crossover voltage (30 to 100V usually) primary electrons land or are reflected. Above the second crossover voltage (in the region of 2500 to 4000 volts), primary electrons penetrate the material and are retained. In the secondary emitting region more electrons are emitted, with low velocities, than land. If the material is an insulator, it will become positively charged as a result of the secondary emission.

secondary encoding   methods of transforming a DIGITAL stream of bits into signals that can be transmitted or recorded. This usually requires any digital signal to avoid rapid changes of state or long strings of one single digit. See also HIGH-DENSITY BIPOLAR CODE; ZERO SUPPRESSION (sense 2).

secondary IDE   a second IDE connector on a computer MOTHERBOARD intended for items such as CD and DVD drives rather than for HARD DRIVES.

secondary radar   a radar system in which reflections are not used, see IFF; INTERROGATING SIGNAL; TRANSPONDER.

secondary radiation   the retransmission of interference from a system because of poor EARTHING.

secondary standard   a standard of measurement that can be used for calibrating instruments. A secondary standard, sometimes confusingly known as a substandard, is calibrated from a PRIMARY STANDARD that is usually a cumbersome and impractical device. The secondary standard then becomes the practical implementation of the standard.

secondary supplies   backup systems to provide for mains failure, particularly for electronic security systems.

secondary surveillance RADAR or **SSR** any system such as IFF that involves exchange of signals between RADAR systems.

secondary voltage   the AC voltage across the SECONDARY WINDING of a TRANSFORMER.

secondary winding   the TRANSFORMER WINDING across which an output of AC is taken. In the older core type of transformer, the secondary winding was the outside winding, wound over the primary winding. In modern toroidal and shell-construction transformers, the primary and secondary windings are interchangeable, and the difference is only in function. See also TERTIARY WINDING.

sector   a portion of one track of a magnetic disk, storing 512 BYTES.

sectoral feedhorn   a form of HORN aerial that is favoured or flared in one dimension only so that it has one pair of parallel sides. See also E-PLANE HORN.

security coding   a method of protecting portable equipment, and also in-car electronic systems, from theft by ensuring that the unit cannot be used, if it has been disconnected from its power supply, until a code is entered.

security fuse   an additional fuse link within a PROGRAMMABLE LOGIC DEVICE that may be blown to disable the verification logic, making it difficult to copy the stored data.

SED   see SINGLE ERROR DETECTION.

Seebeck effect   the THERMOCOUPLE action that occurs when two wires of dissimilar metals are joined to form a loop. When the JUNCTIONS (sense 3) are held at different temperatures an EMF (the *Seebeck potential*) will be produced, proportional to the temperature difference, and current will flow.

seek time   a PARAMETER of a HARD DRIVE, the time taken to place a HEAD on the selected track.

see-saw circuit or **paraphase amplifier** an INVERTER (sense 1) circuit with unity gain. The see-saw circuit uses 100% negative FEEDBACK in an inverting amplifier, and its main application is for inverting a signal to apply to a BALANCED AMPLIFIER. See Fig. 102.

SEG   see SECONDARY EARTH GROUND.

segmented encoding law   the use of a set of LINEAR FUNCTIONS to make an approximation of the smooth curve required for companding (see COMPANDER) data.

selective fading   a form of FADING in which some frequencies of a signal are affected more than others, causing severe distortion that cannot be remedied by devices such as AUTOMATIC GAIN CONTROL.

selective interference   a form of interference, such as deliberate JAMMING, that affects one or a few particular frequencies.

selectivity   the ability to select a particular FREQUENCY. The simplest measurement of selectivity is the BANDWIDTH of the circuit or complete device. See also Q FACTOR.

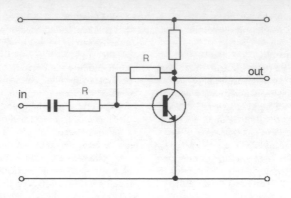

Fig. 102. **see-saw circuit**

selenium   an element related to sulphur that was one of the first known SEMICONDUCTORS. It exhibits PHOTOCONDUCTIVITY, and when in contact with a metal acts as a PHOTOVOLTAIC CELL.

selenium rectifier   a RECTIFIER diode that uses selenium-iron junctions. Selenium rectifiers were once extensively used for power supplies. They have now been replaced with the smaller and more efficient SILICON DIODES. An incidental advantage of this is the elimination of the hazard of the poisonous fumes from burning selenium that used to be a predominant smell in electronics workshops.

self-activating bell or **SAB**   a form of alarm bell that contains its own power supply so that removal of the mains supply will not affect the alarm function.

self-adjusting bias   any bias system that uses DC FEEDBACK to keep the bias constant despite changes in characteristics of transistors due to change of temperature.

self biasing   the circuit using a resistor in the source circuit of an FET so that the bias for the gate is equal to the voltage drop across the source resistor.

self-capacitance   the STRAY CAPACITANCE between adjacent turns of wire in a coil. This causes a coil to have a self-resonant frequency, and an equivalent single value of capacitance can be calculated from the inductance value and the resonant frequency.

self-clocking code   a form of modulated binary code that contains a guaranteed minimum number of transitions per second at a multiple of a basic clock rate.

self-demagnetization   the effect of reduction of magnetization in any portion of a recorded tape where the distance between adjacent North and South poles is very small.

self-discharge   the gradual reduction of EMF and stored charge of a CELL that is not passing current.

self-excited   (of an oscillator or generator) being self-starting. Some very stable oscillators are not self-starting, and need an applied signal to start oscillation.

self-heating, thermistor   the rise in temperature of a THERMISTOR due to current flowing through it, so that any thermistor used for measurement purposes must be placed in a circuit that passes a very low value of current.

self-inductance   the quantity that relates the magnetic flux of an inductor to the current flowing in the windings. Symbol: L; unit: henry. For a given size, shape and number of turns of an inductor and in the absence of FERROMAGNETIC material, the self-inductance is constant. Compare MUTUAL INDUCTANCE.

self-latching   the action of a THYRISTOR or TRIAC in which the device remains conducting until it can be switched off.

self-noise 1. NOISE generated by any conducting material depending on its RESISTANCE value and its ABSOLUTE TEMPERATURE. **2.** for a SPREAD SPECTRUM system, the affects resembling noise that are generated by other transmissions within the spectrum.

self-parking heads a system used in all modern HARD DRIVES in which the heads park over an unused track automatically when power is switched off. See also STEPPER MOTOR; VOICE-COIL DRIVE.

self-resonance resonance of STRAY CAPACITANCE and STRAY INDUCTANCE in a circuit.

self-sealing capacitor a CAPACITOR that resists damage by excessive voltage. If the DIELECTRIC is punctured, the local heating oxidizes the metal electrode around the puncture, restoring the insulation.

self-seek the tuner action that will scan over the frequency bands for television signals and store the settings for the strongest local signals ready for use. The order of these programmes can be altered later if required.

self-shrouding plug a plug whose pins are protected by a metal collar or shroud, so avoiding short circuits when plugs are close to each other or to other metalwork.

selsyn see SYNCHRO.

SEM scanning electron microscope: see ELECTRON MICROSCOPE.

semiconductor a material whose CONDUCTIVITY can be controlled by the presence of IMPURITIES. The conductivity of a doped semiconductor (see DOPING) may be one or more orders of magnitude lower than that of a good conductor. Semiconductors can be elements, such as selenium, germanium, silicon, or compounds such as gallium arsenide, antimony trisulphide, or cadmium sulphide. In the pure state, semiconductors are reasonably good insulators, but they have a NEGATIVE TEMPERATURE COEFFICIENT of resistivity, unlike metals.

Traces of impurity have a very considerable effect on resistivity, lowering the value to levels that are close to the resistivity values of some metals. In addition, the type of MAJORITY CARRIER, electron or hole, can be determined by the type of material that is used as an impurity, or doping material. See ACCEPTOR; DIFFUSION; DONOR; INTRINSIC (sense 2); JUNCTION (sense 2).

semiconductor diode a DIODE that makes use of a SEMICONDUCTOR material. JUNCTION (sense 2) DIODEs make use of the contact between n-type and p-type semiconductors, POINT CONTACT diodes use a metal point contact to a semiconductor surface, and SCHOTTKY DIODES use a metal in contact with a larger area of semiconductor.

semiconductor image sensor see CHARGE-COUPLED DEVICE.

semiconductor laser a SEMICONDUCTOR device similar to an LED, but using an OPTICAL CAVITY to produce MONOCHROMATIC RADIATION of light in a continuous beam. Contrast GAS LASER.

semiconductor laser amplifier a SEMICONDUCTOR LASER used in a FIBRE OPTICS system to provide amplification as distinct from the regeneration of the original signal.

semiconductor package or **package** the container used for a SEMICONDUCTOR providing protection against contamination from the air and easy connection to a printed circuit board.

semiconductor strain gauge a form of STRAIN GAUGE using the change in resistance of a SEMICONDUCTOR which provides much higher outputs than a simple resistance strain gauge.

semiconductor temperature sensor any form of temperature sensor that makes use of the large changes in SEMICONDUCTOR characteristics that occur as temperature is changed.

semitransparent cathode a PHOTOCATHODE that is partly transparent to the light that causes EMISSION. Such a material can be used in the form of a thin film on a glass plate, with light striking the surface from the glass side, and electron emission from the other side. Such photocathodes were used in early types of TV CAMERA TUBES, and are still used in PHOTOMULTIPLIERS.

Sendust™ a hot pressed composite of powdered metallic alloys that have high permeability and hardness, used for tape heads.

sense wire the wire that threads a MAGNETIC CORE and detects a change of magnetization.

sensitivity the ratio of OUTPUT change to INPUT (sense 1) change for a measuring device. For a measuring instrument, sensitivity is quoted in terms of the amount of input for FULL-SCALE DEFLECTION, or the amount of input for unit deflection. For example, a milliammeter may be quoted as 1.0mA for FSD, and an oscilloscope Y-amplifier as 1V PEAK TO PEAK per cm. For a radio receiver, the sensitivity would be quoted as the minimum input signal in microvolts that is needed to ensure a useful SIGNAL-TO-NOISE RATIO.

sensitivity/selectivity characteristic or **signal + noise to noise ratio** for a radio receiver, the minimum input signal voltage to produce a given output level at the stated SIGNAL-TO-NOISE RATIO and specified degree of SELECTIVITY.

sensor a term for any type of measuring or detecting element. A sensor will detect changes in the quantity to which it is sensitive (light, temperature, strain, rotation, etc), and transmit this change as an electrical signal. The energy conversion efficiency of a sensor is unimportant. Compare TRANSDUCER.

separation control an AUDIO circuit using MATRIX addition or subtraction to increase or decrease the apparent channel separation of STEREO signals.

sequence generator a circuit based on a SHIFT REGISTER with FEEDBACK either from output to input or from other intermediate stages to the input. See also LINEAR FEEDBACK SHIFT REGISTER; RE-ENTRANT SHIFT REGISTER.

sequencer a device that can be used to provide a sequence of actions, usually operating from one or more programs of sequences.

sequential of or relating to anything following a sequence or series; one by one.

sequential access random access memory or **SARAM** a type of static ram that has two ports which can be accessed at the same time, one providing random input or output and the second fed serially from a clocked shift register.

sequential circuit a LOGIC circuit in which the output is determined by the sequence of inputs rather than the combination of inputs. See also COMBINATIONAL CIRCUIT.

Sequential Couleur à Memoire see SECAM.

sequential colour any type of COLOUR TELEVISION signal in which the colours are used in sequence rather than simultaneously, see SEQUENTIAL FIELD; SEQUENTIAL LINE.

sequential control the control of any device by a sequence of instructions. MICROPROCESSOR-controlled equipment uses sequential control, and the controlling sequence of instructions is known as the program.

sequential copying see SERIAL COPYING.

sequential field an early type of COLOUR TELEVISION system. In a sequential field system, a complete picture in each PRIMARY light colour was transmitted and shown in sequence. The rate of display had to be fast enough to appear as one picture to the eye. Field sequential methods, in which three complete fields are used per picture, are not compatible with MONOCHROME reception, but are still used for narrow-bandwidth colour TV. See also LINE-SEQUENTIAL TV.

sequential logic a LOGIC system in which the output depends on the sequence of inputs rather than the instantaneous combination of inputs. The FLIP-FLOP is a sequential device, because its output, unlike that of a GATE (sense 2), is usually determined by the sequence of past inputs rather than a present input. For example, an R-S FLIP-FLOP with both inputs at zero can have an output that is 1 or 0, depending on what the *previous* input was. Contrast this with a gate, in which the output is determined completely by the inputs that are present at the time.

sequential processing   see SERIAL PROCESSING.

sequential scan   see PROGRESSIVE SCAN.

sequential system, TV   a system for COLOUR TV in which a picture or portion of picture appears in one colour for a short time and then in the other two primary colours, one after another, also for a short time. See also FRAME SEQUENTIAL; LINE SEQUENTIAL.

serial   one after another, in succession.

serial access memory   memory that makes use of a form of SERIAL REGISTER so that any data read in has to be read out by emptying the register from one end and refilling it from the other.

serial adder   an ADDER circuit that operates on only two BITS at a time, with a bit carried in and a bit carried out.

serial astable   see SERIAL MULTIVIBRATOR.

serial ATA or **SATA**   a fast serial connection system used in a computer to connect the motherboard to drives.

serial code   any code in which bits are arranged in a serial stream as distinct from being transmitted in parallel.

serial communication   transfer of DIGITAL signals one BIT at a time, as for example using RS 232.

serial control port   a PORT (sense 2) found on some CAMCORDERS so as to allow editing control from an external console.

serial copying or **sequential copying**   the actions of making a copy of a recorded item, then making a copy of that copy, and so on. For ANALOGUE recordings this results in unusable sound after a few generations of copies, but DIGITAL recordings can be serial copied indefinitely unless some form of limiting system is used.

serial copying management system or **SCMS**   a system forced on manufacturers of digital tape cassette recorders to prevent more than a single generation copy being made. The delays in enforcing this retarded the sales of digital tape recorders which eventually became obsolescent when compact disc RECORDING became easily possible.

serial counter   see ASYNCHRONOUS COUNTER.

serial data recording   the recording of a single channel of serial data, as distinct from using parallel data recordings with multiple recording heads.

serial-in parallel-out register or **SIPO**   a type of REGISTER in which data is fed in serially, using one CLOCK pulse per BIT of data, and then read out on a set of PARALLEL TRANSMISSION lines, using one line output for each FLIP-FLOP in the register. See Fig. 103.

serial-in serial-out (SISO) register   a conventional serial REGISTER constructed from a set of FLIP-FLOPS with the output of a flip-flop forming the CLOCK for the next in line. The REGISTER can be loaded with a set of serial BITS, one at each clock pulse, and will make these bits available at a serial output, one after the other, after they have passed through the register. This is a form of DIGITAL DELAY. See Fig. 104.

serial input/output or **serial i/o** or **SIO**   the action of a SERIAL PORT that can transmit serial signals in either direction.

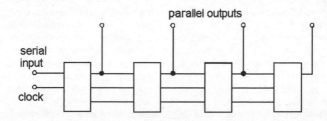

Fig. 103. **serial-in parallel-out register**

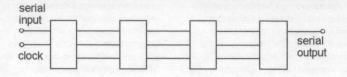

Fig. 104. **serial-in serial-out register**

serial interface an INTERFACE for transmitting and receiving SERIAL signals. Such an interface would normally be of the RS-232 type, but faster serial systems such as FIREWIRE and USB are now in use for short-distance serial links. The main merits of a serial interface are that it uses fewer connections.

serial i/o see SERIAL INPUT/OUTPUT.

serial line a wire or cable connecting SERIAL PORTS and carrying SERIAL FILE data.

serial memory a MEMORY that makes use of devices such as FLIP-FLOPS connected in series. A set of flip-flops in series (a SERIAL REGISTER) can be clocked by a common PULSE so that an input at one end can be shifted through the register by clocking. The data bit moves along by one flip-flop for each clock pulse. Data stored in such a register can be obtained only by clocking out all the previously stored data. Modern computers make more use of RANDOM ACCESS MEMORY systems.

serial mouse a type of computer MOUSE that can be plugged into a SERIAL PORT rather than into a dedicated port, contrast BUS MOUSE.

serial multivibrator or **serial astable** a circuit that uses a COMPLEMENTARY PAIR of transistors each connected COLLECTOR to BASE to form an oscillating circuit with a single TIME CONSTANT.

serial port the INTERFACE that allows the use of SERIAL signals as inputs or outputs.

serial protocols a set of rules for ensuring that DATA transmitted in SERIAL form can be correctly received. Protocols govern such items as standard BIT RATES, use of START BITS and STOP BITS, PARITY, signal format, etc.

serial register a register that has one input, reading one BIT at each CLOCK pulse

and shifting previously-read bits along to the next stage of the register at each clock pulse. The output can be from each stage in the register (*parallel*) or from a single output on the last stage (*serial*). See also PARALLEL-IN SERIAL-OUT; SERIAL-IN SERIAL-OUT.

serial to parallel converter a HARDWARE device that will convert a stream of signals from SERIAL form into PARALLEL TRANSMISSION form, useful for attaching a printer to equipment whose data output is in serial form.

serial transfer the movement of DIGITAL DATA in binary form along a single cable. Each bit is transferred as a logic 0 or 1 signal along the cable, and for a group of bits the transfer is controlled by a master clock rate. See also SERIAL TRANSMISSION.

serial transmission the transmission of DIGITAL DATA along a single serial link. The transmission can be SYNCHRONOUS or ASYNCHRONOUS, and both types rely on generating identical clock pulse rates. In the synchronous system, the sending terminal sends out a synchronizing character, a set of 1s and 0s. This is used by the receiver to achieve synchronization, and from that time on, the two are held in synchronization by transmitting either data or the synchronizing character. In the asynchronous system, data is sent at intervals, with nothing on the line when there is no data. Each group of data (usually each byte) carries its own synchronizing signals in the form of a start bit and two stop bits.

series the connection of COMPONENTS so that the same current flows through each in turn. Compare PARALLEL.

series capacitors capacitors connected in series so that the total capacitance is related to the individual capacitance values by the expression:

$$\frac{1}{C_T} = \frac{1}{C_1} + \frac{1}{C_2} + \ldots$$

where C_T is the total capacitance and C_1, C_2, ... are the individual capacitances.

series cells for CELLS connected in series, the total EMF is equal to the sum of the EMFs for each cell.

series circuit a circuit in which the components are connected in a chain, one to another, so that the same current passes through all the components.

series current feedback feedback that is proportional to the current at an output and applied in series to the input of an amplifier.

series feedback a form of FEEDBACK in which some of the output current waveform is fed back to the input.

series LCR see SERIES RESONANCE.

series loaded aerial (or **antenna)** an aerial whose length makes it non-resonant with series reactance added to improve current distribution and radiation efficiency.

series network a NETWORK (sense 1) in which components are connected in series with the signal.

series-parallel (of a CIRCUIT or NETWORK, sense 1) having some components in series with the signal and others in parallel.

series regulation a method of regulating current or voltage that uses a controller, such as a transistor, in series.

series resistors resistors connected in series so that the total resistance is given by: $R_T = R_1 + R_2 + \ldots$ where R_T is the total resistance and R_1, R_2 ... are the individual resistor values.

series resonance a RESONANT CIRCUIT in which the impedance becomes a minimum at resonance. The series connection of an inductor and a capacitor is the simplest series resonant circuit. At resonance, the impedance of this circuit is simply the resistance of the inductor, and voltage is in phase with current.

series stabilization see SERIES REGULATION.

series, triboelectric see TRIBOELECTRIC SERIES.

series voltage feedback FEEDBACK that is proportional to the voltage at an output and applied in series to the input of an amplifier.

server a fast-acting computer with a very large amount of HARD DRIVE capacity, used to contain websites that can be accessed from the Internet.

service area the area within which a TRANSMITTER can be usefully received. The area is shown as a set of field-strength contours on a map, and is often divided into primary and secondary regions. Outside the secondary region, reception is unsatisfactory because of severe FADING, or interference from other transmitters.

service-induced fault a fault in a circuit caused by servicing actions on the circuit, often because of overheating during soldering.

service mode an optional mode of operation of a system that provides diagnostic data for the benefit of a service engineer.

service sheet a CIRCUIT DIAGRAM and brief description of a piece of equipment along with values for components, intended for use by a service engineer to help locate faults.

servo any mechanical system that is electrically controlled, particularly a motor that is remotely controlled and will duplicate the movements of a master generator shaft.

servo IC the control chip for all the motor functions in a VIDEO CASSETTE RECORDER.

servomotor a small motor used in a FEEDBACK LOOP to position an object very precisely.

servo surface one surface on a set of HARD DRIVE PLATTERS reserved for speed and position control data.

session a RECORDING made on CD-R or CD-RW that can consist of between 1 and 99 tracks, preceded by a LEAD-IN (sense 1) and ending with a LEAD-OUT. See also MULTISESSION.

set or **preset** an input to a FLIP-FLOP that can be used to switch the output to its logical one state irrespective of the CLOCK state. See also RESET.

set channel display a pattern used to modulate the output CARRIER (sense 1) of a VIDEO CASSETTE RECORDER to make it easier to tune in the TV receiver to this frequency.

set mode the use of the J-K flip-flop with J = 1, K = 0. The output (Q) will then be set to 1 at the clock irrespective of its previous state.

set-reset latch see R-S FLIP-FLOP.

set-top box or **STB** a box of electronic circuits connected to a TV receiver, intended to decode digital signals from satellite, the AERIAL, or CABLE TELEVISION networks.

set zero, meter an adjustment to an ANALOGUE METER that allows the pointer to be set precisely to zero when there is no input.

seven-segment decoder a circuit that transforms binary inputs into a set of seven signals for operating a SEVEN-SEGMENT DISPLAY.

seven-segment display a method of displaying digits and some letters with seven bar shapes. The seven-segment display is extensively used for LIGHT EMITTING DIODE and LIQUID CRYSTAL DISPLAYS, particularly for calculators. The alternative is a DOT MATRIX type of display. See Fig. 105.

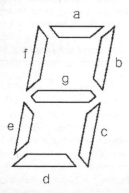

Fig. 105. **seven-segment display**

SFDR see SPURIOUS FREE DYNAMIC RANGE.

SFN see SINGLE FREQUENCY NETWORK.

shaded-pole motor a type of AC motor in which a phase shift is created in the field by a copper ring placed over part of the field core. The presence of this phase shift creates a rotating field, and the metal rotor will try to keep in step with the rotation at the frequency of the AC supply.

shading an unwanted AMPLITUDE change in a TV signal. This usually causes a uniformly-lit scene to appear to contain shadows when the image is viewed.

shadow the ATTENUATION of radio signals caused by obstructions between the TRANSMITTER and the RECEIVER. Hills, power-lines and large metal objects can all cause shadowing, and the effect can be particularly severe at the higher frequencies.

For TV signals, improvements can sometimes be achieved by using a DIRECTIONAL AERIAL pointed to a local reflection, but in very bad cases, it may be necessary to use a REPEATER of some sort. A passive repeater, consisting of a RECEIVING AERIAL on one side of a hill connected to a TRANSMITTING AERIAL on the other, is often very successful. Direct broadcasting from satellites (DBS) eliminates these problems of shadowing.

shadow losses or **shadowing losses** see BLOCKING LOSSES.

shadow mask the original type of TV receiver colour tube. The shadow mask was made from nickel-steel, with a low expansivity, and was perforated with holes in groups of three, using a triangular arrangement. This, combined with the deposition of phosphor dots on the screen in the same pattern, ensured that electrons from three separate electron guns arrived on the correct PHOSPHOR dots. The guns were also arranged in a triangular structure.

The weakness of the system lay in the number of controls and adjustments that were needed in order to preserve good CONVERGENCE, since each control had to deal with both vertical and horizontal effects. Very often, convergence had to be re-established if a receiver was moved. The later development of the APERTURE GRILLE greatly reduced convergence problems, because it allowed the three guns to be constructed in line, so making all corrections along one axis only.

shadowing losses see BLOCKING LOSSES.

Shannon, C.E. (1916–2001) the pioneer of digital signal communications whose work is the basis of most of the digital theory of today.

Shannon's law or **Shannon's sampling theorem** a theorem stating that an analogue signal must be sampled at a rate that is at least twice the frequency of the highest components contained within the signal if ALIASING errors are to be avoided.

shaped-beam tube a form of specialized display CATHODE-RAY TUBE for ALPHANUMERIC displays. The characters are formed by acting directly on the shape of the beam with electric or magnetic fields, rather than by the scanning of the beam.

shape factor a measure of the rate at which a FILTER reaches its STOP BAND, taken as the stop band BANDWIDTH divided by the PASS BAND bandwidth at a given level of ATTENUATION.

shaping circuit a circuit that alters the shape of an ANALOGUE WAVEFORM, such as a DIFFERENTIATING CIRCUIT or an INTEGRATING CIRCUIT.

shared wireless access protocol or **SWAP** a short-range communication system for the home intended to carry voice and data at the rate between 10 and 20 Mbps. The 2.4 GHz frequency band is used, with FREQUENCY HOPPING.

sharp-cut filter or **spot filter** a FILTER that rejects one particular frequency along with a small band of frequencies around it.

sharpness control a TV receiver circuit that performs a sharpening action on leading or trailing edges of pulses to improve the picture definition.

sheathed thermocouple a THERMOCOUPLE with an external protective layer to prevent corrosion. Suitable materials range from mild steel, through nickel alloys to ceramics.

shelf life the time for which any component can lie unused without significant deterioration.

shell or **band** a set of ELECTRONS in an ATOM that all have the same value of energy.

shell, connector a protective cover for a (plug or socket) connector, either plastic or metal, which also supports the cable.

SHF see SUPER HIGH FREQUENCY.

shield a metal screen used to protect a circuit from incoming interference (either electric or magnetic) or to prevent outgoing signals from interfering with other equipment such as radio and TV receivers.

shielded loop aerial (or **antenna)** a DIRECTION-FINDING AERIAL consisting of one or more terms of wire enclosed in a tubular metal sleeve. A gap in the sleeve avoids the effect of a short-circuited turn.

shielded twisted pair or **STP** the usual type of cable used for NETWORK (sense 2) connections, consisting of two insulated wires twisted together with an outer (earthed) metal shielding.

shielding protection of equipment against ELECTRIC and MAGNETIC fields by the use of earthed metal cases.

shift and add the binary actions that amount to the process of multiplication.

shifting the action of moving binary digits in a REGISTER. In a shift action, the bits are moved from one FLIP-FLOP to the next in line. The bit at one end of the register will be lost, and a new bit will be loaded in at the other end.

shift register a set of FLIP-FLOPs connected in series. The flip-flops are connected with the output of one taken as the input to the next. When a clock pulse is applied to all of the flip-flops together, the bit (0 or 1) in each flip-flop will be transferred to the next in line. The connections can be made either for left-shift or for right-shift, or by way of gates so that both left- or right-shift can be obtained by using a shift-direction signal. The shift register is the basis of SERIAL MEMORY.

shock excitation the production of OSCILLATIONS by a PULSE. This causes RINGING (sense 1).

Shockley diode a general name for a pnpn diode, such as a THYRISTOR or SILICON CONTROLLED SWITCH.

short see SHORT CIRCUIT.

short aerial (or **antenna)** an aerial that is physically shorter than a quarter wavelength. Such an aerial is used along with an inductive loading, either at the base of the MONOPOLE or centrally, or the aerial is made in the form of quarter wave wire wound in a helix over a short length.

short circuit or **short** a low-RESISTANCE connection, wanted or (more usually) unwanted. The effect of a short circuit is to equalize voltages at two points, and to allow current to flow. If the short circuit is a fault condition, it will usually cause problems such as loss of signal, loss of control, or damage to components. Deliberate short circuiting is used in signal switching, or for making high-voltage circuits safe to touch.

short-circuit current the current that can flow from a power supply in the event of a short circuit. In most circuits this will cause a fuse to blow, but many supplies incorporate protective circuits to limit such current to the safe amount.

short-circuit impedance a measurement on a NETWORK (sense 1). The short-circuit IMPEDANCE at the input of a network is the impedance at the input when the output is short-circuited to signals. The short-circuit impedance at the output is the output impedance when the input is short-circuited to signals.

short-haul network a NETWORK (sense 2) that operates over short distances, as between offices in the same building.

short message service or **SMS** the text service used on mobile phone networks.

short wave a radio signal in the frequency range of about 3 to 30MHz. This range contains many of the most-used amateur bands, as well as many international communications channels.

short-wave converter an add-on circuit to allow short-wave reception by a MEDIUM-WAVE receiver. The converter contains a LOCAL OSCILLATOR and MIXER that converts short-wave signals into

signals in the medium-wave band, so that the receiver is being used as the second part of a DOUBLE SUPERHET.

shotgun microphone or **line microphone** an acoustic line or pipe with a MICROPHONE element fitted at the rear end, used for its very directional character.

shot noise see SCHOTTKY NOISE.

shrouded pins pins that may be live on a plug and which are covered in such a way as to be inaccessible to the finger.

shuffling the rearrangement of DIGITAL DATA from widely separated areas of a digitally-coded picture.

shunt **1.** a COMPONENT connected in PARALLEL (sense 1) with a SIGNAL. A *meter shunt* is a low-value RESISTOR that is connected in parallel with an ANALOGUE METER movement in order to allow measurement of currents greater than the FSD current of the movement. **2.** to connect a COMPONENT in PARALLEL (sense 1) with another.

shunt current feedback FEEDBACK that is proportional to the current at an output and applied in parallel to the input of an amplifier.

shunt-derived filter a form of FILTER in which parallel (*shunt*) resonant circuits are used.

shunt network a NETWORK (sense 1) that is connected in PARALLEL (sense 1) with a signal.

shunt regulation or **shunt stabilization** the regulation, usually of voltage, by a device connected in parallel with the load. The simple use of a ZENER DIODE is an example of shunt voltage stabilization. The stable voltage is the voltage across the diode, with a series resistor used as a load. Variations in the supply voltage cause current variations that appear as voltage changes across the resistor, not across the Zener diode. Changes in the load current cause changes in the current through the Zener diode, with negligible effect on the voltage output. The regulation breaks down if the current through the Zener diode falls below the stabilizing limit, or if the supply voltage drops to about the level of the regulated voltage. See Fig. 106.

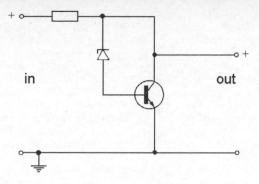

Fig. 106. **shunt regulation**

shunt resistance loss loss of energy in a circuit expressed by a value of resistance in PARALLEL (sense 1) that would account for such a loss.

shunt resistor a resistor connected in parallel with another component.

shunt stabilization see SHUNT REGULATION.

shunt voltage feedback FEEDBACK that is proportional to the voltage at an output and applied in parallel to the input of an amplifier.

shunt, universal see UNIVERSAL SHUNT.

shunt-wound motor a DC motor whose field magnet is an electromagnet, the *shunt*, fed from a separate supply. For a shunt-wound motor with a constant rotor current, the motor speed increases as the shunt current decreases and vice versa.

shuttle action a professional TAPE RECORDER action that moves the tape to and fro across the REPLAY HEAD to allow precise location of an editing point.

SI unit any of the units adopted for international use (Système Internationale) in science and engineering, based on the metre, kilogram, second and ampere.

SID see SUDDEN IONOSPHERIC DISTURBANCE.

sideband a range of frequencies caused by the MODULATION of a CARRIER (sense 1). Any form of modulation of a carrier will result in the appearance of sidebands. One set, the upper sideband, will be at higher than carrier frequency, with the other set, the lower sideband, at a (symmetrically) lower frequency. For

AMPLITUDE MODULATION, the sideband frequencies are directly related to the modulating frequency. Each upper sideband frequency is the sum of the carrier frequency and a modulating frequency, and each lower sideband signal is the difference between the carrier frequency and a modulating frequency. The useful part of the signal is carried in the sidebands, but these together constitute only up to 50% of the total signal energy. For FREQUENCY MODULATION, the inner sidebands have the same frequencies as for AM, but there are also outer sidebands unless the MODULATION INDEX is very small. See Fig. 107.

sideband distortion signal distortion at a TRANSMITTER caused by overloading of the POWER AMPLIFIER (sense 2).

sideband folding see KENDALL EFFECT.

side frequency one single frequency in a SIDEBAND.

side lobe a region of sensitivity or signal strength to the side of the wanted direction axis of an AERIAL (antenna). Most DIRECTIONAL AERIALS allow some side-lobe formation, but this is harmless unless it causes interference.

side-lobe response an undesirable feature of a receiving AERIAL that allows interfering signals to enter along the direction of a LOBE that is not the main receiving lobe.

sidereal time a timescale based on the Earth's period of rotation relative to distant stars, slightly less than solar time and important for satellite communications.

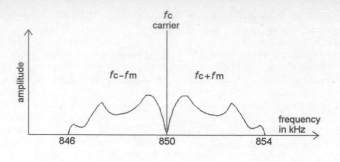

Fig. 107. **sideband**

siemens or (formerly) **mho** the unit of conductance, that is equal to the inverse ohm. Symbol: S.

SiGe alloy an alloy of SILICON and GERMANIUM used for SEMICONDUCTORS because of its ability to operate at higher frequencies with lower power consumption.

sigma-delta modulator see NOISE-SHAPER.

sign bit the MOST SIGNIFICANT BIT of a digital number, used to indicate sign as 1 for negative and 0 for positive.

signal a variation in VOLTAGE or CURRENT that is used for carrying information.

signal clipping see CLIPPING.

signal conditioning the processing of the WAVEFORM or pattern of a SIGNAL, usually to ensure compatibility with a DEVICE.

signal diode a diode with a small area of JUNCTION (sense 2), intended for use with small signals at high frequency, as in a demodulation circuit.

signal earth see SECONDARY EARTH GROUND.

signal electrode an ELECTRODE from which a signal output is taken. The term usually denotes the signal output electrodes of TV CAMERA TUBES, PHOTOMULTIPLIERS, and TRANSDUCERS.

signal fade margin the allowance of around 3 to 5 dB, due to atmospheric conditions, that needs to be made in estimates of signal strength from a satellite. For terrestrial broadcasting, a margin of more than 30 dB is more usual.

signal generator or **frequency generator** a laboratory or workshop diagnostic instrument which is a combination of controllable calibrated OSCILLATOR (see CALIBRATION) and ATTENUATOR. Signal generators are used to supply signals of known amplitude at a known frequency within audio or radio ranges for test purposes. See also PULSE GENERATOR.

signal intrusion the breakthrough of RIPPLE (sense 1) frequencies on a POWER SUPPLY into a signal circuit, causing HUM on an audio output.

signal level the AMPLITUDE of a SIGNAL. This is often quoted relative to some standard, such as the 1V peak-to-peak video signal. When the standard level is well known, the signal level is often quoted in (voltage) dB.

signalling rate the rate of change of any aspect of a SIGNAL, such as AMPLITUDE, FREQUENCY or PHASE SHIFT. See also SYMBOL RATE.

signal-matching transformer see MATCHING TRANSFORMER.

signal + noise to noise ratio see SENSITIVITY/SELECTIVITY CHARACTERISTIC.

signal polarity the polarity of a PULSE or other unidirectional signal, positive or negative.

signal rise time see RISE TIME.

signal strength meter a meter that measures the strength of signal at an AERIAL, used to align aerials or test for aerial damage.

signal-to-noise ratio (S/N or SNR) the ratio of levels of desired SIGNAL to unwanted NOISE, in decibels, a measure of signal quality for an ANALOGUE transmission. The usefulness of a received signal is determined by its S/N. An acceptable analogue video signal needs an S/N in the region of 45dB, a hi-fi audio signal requires at least 60dB. For a DIGITAL system, the BIT ERROR RATE (BER) is a more useful guide to signal integrity.

signal to quantization noise ratio or **SQNR** the ratio of RMS signal to RMS noise for a quantized signal, calculated from $(1.76 + 6n)$ where n is the number of bits per sample.

signal winding the WINDING of a MAGNETIC AMPLIFIER to which the low frequency AC signal is applied.

signature a set of BYTES used to check that a component such as a ROM or a complete microprocessor system is not corrupted or damaged.

signature analyzer equipment that can be connected to a digital circuit to produce a unique digital WORD from the equipment. If the signature of working equipment is known, then failure to reproduce this digital number indicates a fault.

signature-checker a circuit or, more likely, a software routine, for checking the SIGNATURE of a component or system.

signature profile a set of waveforms from test points in a system under test that can be compared with those derived from a good system using automatic test equipment.

significance the weighting of a digit in a number, indicated by its position in the number. See also LEAST SIGNIFICANT BIT; MOST SIGNIFICANT BIT.

SIL see SINGLE INLINE PACKAGE.

silect package a plastic encapsulation PACKAGE for small transistors.

silent zone see DEAD ZONE.

silicon a semiconducting ELEMENT, obtained from sand (silicon oxide).

silicon cell a PHOTOCELL that uses silicon as its sensitive material.

silicon chip see CHIP (sense 1).

silicon-controlled rectifier (SCR) see THYRISTOR.

silicon-controlled switch (SCS) a four-layer (pnpn) DIODE in which connections are made to the inner P-LAYERS and N-LAYERS. A positive voltage is applied to the ANODE (sense 2), the outer p-layer, and the CATHODE (sense 2), the outer n-layer, is at zero voltage. In this condition, a pulse to the first gate, the inner p-layer, will switch the device on. A positive pulse on the second gate, the inner n-layer, will switch current off. The SCS is used for low-power switching as compared to the THYRISTOR, which has a similar structure, and can be used only for comparatively low switching rates because of its comparatively long turn-on and turn-off times.

silicon diode a diode that uses a rectifying silicon JUNCTION (sense 2). The FORWARD DROP is rather high, of the order of 0.6V, but the resistance in the REVERSE DIRECTION is also very high.

silicon disk or **RAMdisk** MEMORY used by a computer as if it were a DISK.

silicone grease a synthetic grease that is an excellent electrical INSULATOR, but a reasonably good heat conductor. It is used as a way of improving the heat transfer from a TRANSISTOR or IC to a heatsink. The grease is similar in chemical structure to a natural grease but with silicon substituted for carbon, hence the name.

silicone resin bonded paper or **SRBP** a hard insulating material that can be produced in flat sheets; used for PRINTED CIRCUIT BOARDS.

silicone rubber a form of synthetic rubber in which carbon atoms have been replaced by silicon atoms, used for its high INSULATION quality and resistance to high temperatures.

silicon on insulator or **SOI** the method of construction of SEMICONDUCTORs, usually on sapphire insulation, that results in RADIATION HARD devices.

silicon-on-sapphire (SOS) a construction for METAL-OXIDE SEMICONDUCTOR ICs, used particularly for military and other applications where high reliability is required. Synthetic sapphire is used as a SUBSTRATE, and silicon is deposited on it by EPITAXY. The resulting chips have a very high performance, but the construction is difficult and costly. The rapidly reducing price of synthetic diamonds makes this material an attractive alternative to sapphire.

silicon power transistor   see POWER TRANSISTOR.

silicon rectifier   a SILICON DIODE of any type used as a RECTIFIER.

silicon transistor   a conventional BIPOLAR JUNCTION TRANSISTOR formed from silicon.

silver leaching   the dissolving of silver from silver plated contacts on a component by contact with hot solder. If repeated, this can lead to DRY JOINTs.

silver mica   the highest quality of mica used for mica CAPACITORS.

silver oxide cell   a PRIMARY CELL whose active components are silver oxide mixed with graphite as the ANODE (sense 3), a zinc CATHODE (sense 3), and an ELECTROLYTE of potassium hydroxide. The EMF of 1.5 V is maintained at a steady level for most of the long life of the cell.

silver solder   a solder alloy with 10% of silver which provides joints of lower resistance, though its melting point of 370°C is more than most electric soldering irons can provide.

SIM   see SUBSCRIBER IDENTITY MODULE.

SIMM   see SINGLE INLINE MEMORY MODULE.

simple cell   a PRIMARY CELL, no longer used in its original (wet) form, with a zinc CATHODE, copper ANODE, and sulphuric acid ELECTROLYTE.

simplex   a data channel that allows communication in one direction only. Compare DUPLEX; HALF-DUPLEX.

simulator   a SYSTEM, usually computer-based, that imitates the behaviour of another system. The simulator may imitate the action of a NETWORK (sense 1) to a PULSE, the response of an aircraft to a downwind, the reaction of an office organization to the death of a manager. The importance of simulation is that any system that is reasonably well understood can be simulated, and the simulation used to predict behaviour of the main system. For a partly-understood system, the simulation may be used to gain understanding by comparing the

predictions of the simulator with the actual outcome of an experiment.

simulator software   computer software that can simulate the action of a DIGITAL circuit and point to any difficulty such as GLITCHes.

simulcast   a broadcast carried out simultaneously in two different forms, such as a concert broadcast both on Radio 3 and on television.

SINAD ratio   a measurement to describe the total effects of both noise and distortion on a signal. The SINAD ratio =

$$\frac{\text{signal} + \text{noise} + \text{distortion}}{\text{noise} + \text{distortion}}.$$

sine/cosine potentiometer   a POTENTIOMETER (sense 1), seldom encountered in modern use, in which the DIVISION RATIO is proportional to the sine or cosine of the angle of rotation of the shaft.

sine squared pulse and bar   a form of INSERTION TEST SIGNAL placed in the VERTICAL BLANKING INTERVAL of a TV transmission to test the LUMINANCE channel.

sine wave   a WAVEFORM whose cycle shape is that of a graph of the sine of an angle plotted against the angle. A sine wave is the natural waveform of voltage generated by a coil of wire revolving in a uniform magnetic field.

singing   an OSCILLATION with an audible output.

single channel per carrier or **SCPC** using one channel of information for each CARRIER (sense 1) frequency, unlike a MULTIPLEX transmission.

single-ended or **unbalanced**   (of a circuit) having one signal terminal at earth at both input and output. The signal at the input or output consists of a voltage that will vary with respect to earth. See also BALANCED AMPLIFIER; DIFFERENTIAL AMPLIFIER.

single-ended push-pull   an output stage consisting of two transistors in series biased to a voltage half way between the supply voltage and ground. The output signal is produced by operating the transistors so that as the current through one increases, the current through the other decreases by an identical amount. See COMPLEMENTARY CIRCUIT; LIN CIRCUIT; PSEUDO-COMPLEMENTARY CIRCUIT.

single error detection (SED) the ability of an error detecting system, such as PARITY, to find a single bit error in a byte.

single frequency network (SFN) the use of the same channel countrywide for the same digital program multiplex, possible only because COFDM is immune to ghosting effects that make this impossible for analogue signals.

single inline memory module or **SIMM** a form of memory, now obsolescent, that contains a set of memory chips making up an extension to the memory of a computer, usually 8 megabytes, 16 megabytes, or more in each unit. See also DOUBLE INLINE MEMORY MODULE (DIMM).

single inline package a package, usually of resistors in thick-film form, containing a set of passive components connected to a single line of pins.

single-layer solenoid an inductor consisting of a single layer of winding in SOLENOID (sense 1) form.

single mode laser a LASER that produces a single SPECTRAL LINE, used for long haul wide band systems.

single-phase (of an AC system) having one supply conductor and a return.

single polarized aerial (or **antenna)** an aerial that is designed to receive or transmit one single POLARIZATION (see POLARIZED, sense 1) of wave only.

single-pole changeover or **SPCO** see SINGLE-POLE DOUBLE-THROW.

single-pole double-throw or **SPDT** or **single-pole changeover** or **SPCO** a SWITCH format in which one moving contact (pole) can be connected to either of two static contacts.

single-pole single-throw or **SPST** or **single-throw switch** a SWITCH format in which one moving contact can be in contact with a static contact (on) or not in contact (off).

single-pole switch a switch that changes the connection of one line only.

single-shot see MONOSTABLE.

single sideband or **SSB** (of a transmitter or receiver) transmitting or receiving radio signals with one SIDEBAND only. In a conventional amplitude-modulated signal, all of the information of the modulating signal is held in each one of the sidebands. This means that there is redundancy of signal that can be reduced by transmitting only one sideband. Since one sideband represents only one quarter of the total transmitter power of a double sideband system, this implies that the transmitted power can be reduced with no loss in reception range. By eliminating the CARRIER (sense 1) as well, all of the power of the transmitter can be devoted to the information-bearing sideband. The drawback is that much more elaborate transmitters and receivers are needed.

single-sideband suppressed carrier or **SSBSC** a very efficient AM transmission system that has filtered out the CARRIER (sense 1) and one SIDEBAND, leaving only a single sideband that carries the information. The carrier signal in correct phase must be reinserted to demodulate (see DEMODULATION) such a signal.

single slope A/D a simple form of ANALOGUE TO DIGITAL CONVERTER in which clock pulses are gated to an INTEGRATOR until the integrated output equals the input voltage. The clock pulse counter is then the digital number representing the analogue input at that instant.

single slope ADC or **voltage to frequency converter** a simple form of ANALOGUE TO DIGITAL CONVERTER in which a set of PULSES is integrated and counted. When integrated output reaches the same level as that of a sample signal, the count is used as a digital output and the process starts on the next sample. The system is slow, not particularly precise, and seldom used.

single station locator a tracking system using the HF bands and reflections from the F2 LAYER to find azimuth and range information for a distant transmitter.

single throw switch see DOUBLE-POLE SINGLE-THROW; SINGLE-POLE SINGLE-THROW.

sink 1. to accept CURRENT from a TERMINAL (sense 1) or a device that accepts such current. TRANSISTOR-TRANSISTOR LOGIC ICs require any driving device to be able to accept (sink) a current of up to 1.6mA to earth when a terminal is at logic 0. 2. see HEAT SINK.

sintered plate cell a cell using plates that are made of compressed powdered metal that presents a very large surface to the electrolyte. Compare MASS-PLATE CELL.

sinusoidal (of a WAVEFORM) having the shape of a SINE WAVE.

SIPO see SERIAL-IN PARALLEL-OUT REGISTER.

SISO see SERIAL-IN SERIAL-OUT REGISTER.

six band resistor coding a method of coding value, tolerance, and temperature coefficient rating of a resistor using six coloured bands.

600 ohm line a form of TWIN CABLE feeder with a characteristic impedance of 600 ohms.

skeleton slot a form of SLOT AERIAL in which the metal surrounding the slot has been reduced to a tube or wire frame.

skeleton trimmer a miniature POTENTIOMETER (sense 1) with no casing, used on a PRINTED CIRCUIT BOARD to make small adjustments.

skew the time difference between signals, particularly PULSE signals.

skew symmetric the shape of the filtered SPECTRUM for a VESTIGIAL SIDEBAND signal that will produce no low-frequency distortion on DEMODULATION. See Fig. 108.

skin effect the conduction of high-frequency currents on the outside surface of a CONDUCTOR. Conductors for high-

frequency currents can be made from thick wire or tube, and use silver plating to increase conductivity.

skip distance the distance between a TRANSMITTER and the region in which the first reflection from the IONOSPHERE is received. There will be a SILENT ZONE in the area that lies between the skip distance and the greatest distance covered by the ground wave.

skipping, CD movement of the reading beam of a CD player from one TRACK to another caused by vibration.

skip zone see DEAD ZONE.

skirted monopole a form of MONOPOLE AERIAL, one quarter wavelength long, projecting above a conical skirt of metal or mesh one-third of a wavelength long and enclosing the COAXIAL feeder to the monopole.

skying effect see SWEEPING EFFECT.

sky noise the combination of GALACTIC NOISE and ATMOSPHERIC NOISE, usually measured as an equivalent NOISE TEMPERATURE.

sky wave a RADIO (sense 1) wave reflected back to earth from a layer in the IONOSPHERE.

slab laser form of crystal laser using a pumping cavity and two resonator mirrors that can produce several kilowatts of output power.

slave circuit a LOGIC CIRCUIT that is completely driven by the output of another, and which reproduces this waveform. The slave portion of a MASTER-SLAVE FLIP-FLOP, for example, reproduces a voltage level from the master section, but is clocked at a different time.

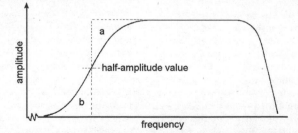

Fig. 108. **skew symmetric**

slave processor or **co-processor** a MICROPROCESSOR in a computer or controller circuit that is totally controlled by a main microprocessor. The usual type of slave processor is used for memory access, screen control, or mathematical operations.

SLDRAM see SYNCHRONOUS LINK DYNAMIC RANDOM ACCESS MEMORY.

sled servo see CARRIAGE SERVO.

sleep (of power-consuming devices) to run on low power until required.

sleeve dipole or **sleeved dipole** a type of DIPOLE AERIAL whose FEED section is enclosed in a short COAXIAL sleeve to improve the impedance matching and radiation efficiency.

slew rate the rate of change of SIGNAL voltage. This is a better guide to the FREQUENCY RESPONSE of transistors and amplifiers (particularly OPERATIONAL AMPLIFIERS) to large signals than the use of high-frequency cutoff figures that relate to small signals. Slew rate is often very important to FEEDBACK amplifiers because of the possibility of breakdown of feedback. If the slew rate is slower than the response of the FEEDBACK LOOP, for example, the amplifier will effectively be operating without feedback during the time of rapid voltage change at the input.

slew-rate distortion or **transient intermodulation distortion** the distortion in an amplifier stage when its input is a sharp change of voltage which is faster than the SLEW RATE of the stage.

slew-rate limiting the inability of a transistor amplifier to reproduce a sharp rate of rise of voltage. This can be overcome only by using a transistor with better characteristics.

slide potentiometer a form of linear POTENTIOMETER (sense 1) operated by altering the position of a sliding contact over a linear track.

slider servo see CARRIAGE SERVO.

slide switch a form of linear switch operated by a sliding knob or bar.

sliding stereo separation an FM TUNER circuit method of reducing the hissing NOISE on a STEREO signal when the incoming FM signal strength falls on the optimal value. The stereo separation is reduced as the signal strength reduces, eventually becoming a MONOPHONIC signal.

SLIP serial line interface protocol.

sliprings circular metal rings located on a shaft and connected to the windings of a ROTOR. Using a BRUSH connection to each slipring allows current to be passed to the rotor. A similar system is used to connect signals to and from the RECORDING HEADS of a VIDEO CASSETTE RECORDER.

slope the ratio of vertical increment to horizontal increment for a portion of a graph. In the general equation for a straight line: $y = mx + c$, the slope of the graph is the constant m. See also INTERCEPT. See Fig. 109.

slope control a form of AUDIO TONE CONTROL to alter the relative balance of low and high frequency components of the signal with reference to a mid point.

slope detector or **slope demodulator** a simple and inefficient method of demodulating an FM signal by tuning a resonant circuit to one sideband and using ENVELOPE DEMODULATION.

slope of attenuation the rate of attenuation for a filter in terms of decibels per octave.

slope resistance see INCREMENTAL RESISTANCE.

slot aerial an aerial that consists of a rectangular slot in a metal sheet or in a metal mesh. The long dimension of the slot is along the plane of the magnetic field, so that the transmitted wave is POLARIZED (sense 1) at 90° to the polarization of a conventional DIPOLE AERIAL. The balanced feed is to or from the midpoints of the edge of the slot, and the CHARACTERISTIC IMPEDANCE is of the order of 500 ohms. See also SKELETON SLOT.

slot line a form of MICROWAVE INTEGRATED STRUCTURE using a dielectric metallized on one side only, with an etched slot to guide the wave.

slotted waveguide a WAVEGUIDE into which slots are cut in places to allow a PROBE (sense 2) to be inserted.

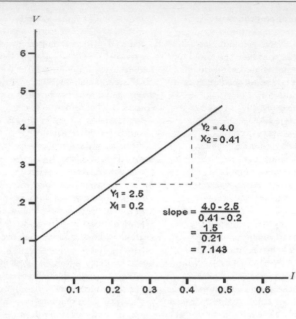

Fig. 109. slope

slow acting relay a relay which will not operate immediately on energizing the coil.

slow-blo fuse see T FUSE.

slow-break switch a SWITCH that uses no form of spring-assisted snap-over action. An example is the old-fashioned KNIFE SWITCH.

slow-scan television or **SSTV** a form of television signal that uses low SCAN rates allowing signals to be sent over telephone lines or recorded at low speeds.

slow-wave an electromagnetic wave that has been slowed to about the speed of ELECTRONs in a beam. The slowing can be achieved by propagating the wave in a spiral path, as in a TRAVELLING-WAVE TUBE.

slugged relay a form of RELAY in which a copper loop, the *slug*, has been placed over the magnetic circuit. This makes the action of the relay slower because of the effect of EDDY CURRENTs.

slug tuning see PERMEABILITY TUNING.

SMA connector a family of connectors for HF cables to the BS9210 specification that are screw-retained for more rigidity.

The voltage rating is up to 450V peak, and frequency limit is up to 18 GHz. See also BNC CONNECTOR; SMB CONNECTOR.

small computer systems interface or **SCSI** a system for connecting a computer to DISK DRIVES and other peripherals, not so common nowadays. The SCSI system allows for very fast data transfer between a variety of peripherals and the main computer. See also EXTENDED IDE; INTEGRATED DEVICE ELECTRONICS.

small outline or **SO** or **SOL** a form of SURFACE MOUNT PACKAGE for active components.

small outline transistor or **SOT** a form of SURFACE MOUNT PACKAGE for a TRANSISTOR.

small-scale integration or **SSI** the SCALE OF INTEGRATION in which the number of ACTIVE COMPONENTS on one chip is in the range 100 or less.

small-signal gain the GAIN figure of a system obtained from the ratio of output to input signal amplitudes for signals that are of small amplitude compared to the power supply voltage.

small-signal parameters the PARAMETERS such as input resistance, transfer current ratio, etc., that are measured for small signal (not DC) quantities. The term denotes particularly the parameters that are used to specify transistor action.

small-signal transistor a transistor designed to be used with low voltage supplies and signals of small amplitude and low power.

Smart Battery a battery system composed of charger, battery and control unit, that provides information on the state of charge and controls charging rate to cope with demands made on the battery.

smart card a card inserted into a satellite decoder to permit programmes to be received with payment charged to the card account.

smart modem a modem that includes facilities of LINE PROBING, FORWARD ERROR CONTROL, PRE-EMPHASIS, and NONLINEAR MAPPING.

smart system a computer-controlled system with the ability to learn from experience.

smart terminal see INTELLIGENT TERMINAL.

SMB connector sub-miniature bayonet connector: a bayonet fitting connector to BS 9210 of 6 mm diameter and rated for 500 V peak signal at frequencies up to 4 GHz. See also SMA CONNECTOR.

SMC see SURFACE MOUNT COMPONENT.

SMD surface mount device: see SURFACE MOUNT COMPONENT.

smeared picture a TV fault in which resolution is severely reduced, generally caused by poor frequency response.

Smith's chart a method of solving TRANSMISSION LINE problems by graphical methods.

smoke detector see SMOKE SENSOR.

smoke sensor or **smoke detector** a device using either a photoelectric sensor and light beam, or the ionization due to a radioactive source to provide an electrical output in the presence of smoke.

smoke test a simple test for HARDWARE, usually following a bodged repair, to check that nothing drastic has gone

wrong. If no smoke emerges after switching on, the equipment can be passed to the customer or for further testing.

smoothing 1. the removal of unwanted AC content from DC. **2.** the filtering of any signal by a LOW-PASS FILTER.

smoothing capacitor a capacitor used to remove RIPPLE (sense 1) from a DC power source.

SMPS see SWITCH-MODE POWER SUPPLY.

SMPTE see SOCIETY OF MOTION PICTURE AND TELEVISION ENGINEERS.

SMS 1. see SWITCH-MODE POWER SUPPLY. **2.** see SHORT MESSAGE SERVICE.

SMT see SURFACE MOUNT TECHNOLOGY.

S/N see SIGNAL-TO-NOISE RATIO.

snap-off diode see CHARGE STORAGE DIODE.

Snell's law the law of wave REFRACTION, linking angles of incidence and refraction to the refractive indices for two media. The law can be stated in equation form as: $n_1.\sin\theta_1 = n_2.\sin\theta_2$ where n_1, n_2 are the refractive indices of layer 1 and layer 2, and θ_1 and θ_2 are the angles in the respective media.

SNOS silicon nitride oxide semiconductor: a variant of MOS technology.

snow a slang term for the effect of NOISE on a TV or radar picture signal.

SNR see SIGNAL TO NOISE RATIO.

snubber circuit an inductor and capacitor wired into the ANODE circuit of a THYRISTOR to suppress RADIO-FREQUENCY INTERFERENCE.

SO small outline, a SURFACE MOUNT PACKAGE for TRANSISTORs.

SOA see SAFE OPERATING AREA.

soakage or **dielectric absorption** or **voltage remanence** the effect of retained charge on a CAPACITOR after a SHORT CIRCUIT. Some types of capacitors have virtually no soakage, older types will very often require to be discharged several times before the voltage across their terminals becomes negligible.

soak test a test of electronic equipment, particularly following servicing, in which the equipment is left running for a long period connected to diagnostic instruments.

SOC   see SYSTEM ON A CHIP.

Society of Motion Picture and Television Engineers or **SMPTE**   a standardizing body, founded in 1916 and based in New York, serving the motion picture and television industries.

socket   a form of FEMALE CONNECTOR. Compare PLUG.

soft   (of part of a digital system) able to be changed easily by issuing typed commands, like a program in memory. Compare HARD.

soft breakdown   a comparatively slow change of REVERSE CURRENT in a DIODE that is strongly doped. This is the true ZENER EFFECT, occurring at levels of 6V and lower, as distinct from the hard breakdown of a diode that has lower doping and breakdown levels of more than 6V, see AVALANCHE BREAKDOWN.

soft decision decoding   a method of using ERROR CORRECTION so that the decoding methods are adapted to changing channel conditions, such as SIGNAL-TO-NOISE RATIO.

soft error   a data error that can be corrected if the data is read again.

soft failure   the results of electrostatic discharge or electromagnetic interference that cause data errors but do not affect system hardware.

soft handover   a period in which a mobile phone is in contact with two BASE STATIONS during the transition from one to another.

soft magnetic material   a material with very high PERMEABILITY but very low RETENTIVITY. Such a material will become very strongly magnetized when in a magnetic field (from a coil or another magnet), but retains practically no magnetism when the field is removed. See MOVING-IRON METER.

soft setting   settings for equipment that can be made by using SOFTWARE rather than by altering connections on a board.

soft-start   (of a power supply) reaching its full voltage comparatively slowly.

software   the programs for a MICROPROCESSOR-controlled system. Compare hardware.

software multiplexing   the use of a computer to separate channels from a MULTIPLEX using software.

soft x-ray   an X-RAY beam that has been created using a comparatively low-energy ELECTRON beam. Soft x-rays have a lower frequency range than the more penetrating hard x-rays.

SOI   see SILICON ON INSULATOR.

SOL   see SMALL OUTLINE.

solar cell   a PHOTOVOLTAIC CELL that is used to obtain electrical power from light. Cells based on gallium arsenide have been used for satellites and spacecraft to provide power over long periods. The voltage output is low, a fraction of a volt per cell, and the efficiency is also poor, about 10%. For situations where no practical alternative exists, however, solar cells can provide useful power, and development is steadily raising efficiency levels.

solar constant   the average rate of radiated energy that reaches the Earth from the surface of the sun, about 1.35 kW per square metre.

solar cycle   the reasonably regular 11-year cycle of solar flares and eruptions, allowing future peaks to be predicted for several days ahead.

solar noise   the radio NOISE that is generated from the random movement of ions in the sun.

solar winds   streams of ionizing particles that flow from the sun during a solar flare, causing ELECTROMAGNETIC INTERFERENCE and effects such as the *Northern lights*.

solarization   the effect of removing two, three or even four of the lowest order BITS from each BYTE of a digital picture signal. This gives an effect similar to that of solarization (excessive exposure to sun) on a conventional photograph.

solder   an alloy with a low melting point. The traditional alloy is 60% tin and 40% lead, but health fears associated with the use of lead have encouraged the use of lead-free alloys containing silver, bismuth, or both.

solder braid   thick braided copper wire used to absorb solder from joints when the joint is heated with the braid in contact. See also DESOLDERING; SOLDER SUCKER.

solder bridge an undesirable short-circuit between two parts of a PRINTED CIRCUIT BOARD caused by a piece of solder.

solder flux material with a low melting point that coats metals, protecting against oxidation, while SOLDER is applied. The most common flux material, rosin (colophony), produces fumes that may cause industrial asthma.

soldering the joining of metals with SOLDER alloy. Soldering is the most common method of making mechanical and electrical connections to electronic components. For hand work and repair work, an electrically heated soldering 'iron' is used, along with a solder alloy that is in the form of hollow wire, with a core of FLUX (sense 2). Mass-produced printed circuit boards are soldered using a HOT DIP system. For very high-reliability systems, assemblies are made by robot systems, using spot-welding rather than soldering.

soldering change the change in value of components such as a RESISTOR or CAPACITOR due to the heating that takes place on SOLDERING.

soldering iron a soldering tool using a copper rod heated electrically, used to melt solder onto a metal surface.

solderless breadboard a form of BREADBOARD with a matrix of holes that are sockets for wire and are interconnected. A circuit can be made by plugging in the leads of components into the correct positions on the matrix.

solder pad metal coated areas on a PRINTED CIRCUIT BOARD intended for soldering SURFACE MOUNT components and providing reliable joints with good heat dissipating properties.

solder paint finely powered SOLDER in a suspension that can be painted onto joints so that the soldering operation can be carried out by using a furnace or by blowing hot gas over the joint.

solder pot an electrically heated pot containing molten SOLDER along with a device for removing the film of oxide from the surface. Small units can be dipped into the pot to solder joints that have been coated with FLUX (sense 2).

solder pump see SOLDER SUCKER.

solder sucker or **solder pump** a simple form of vacuum pump, used in conjunction with a soldering iron to remove molten solder from a joint.

solenoid 1. a tubular coil of wire whose length is large compared to the diameter. 2. an electromechanical actuator that consists of a coil with a moveable core. When current flows in the coil, the core is drawn into the coil, and this mechanical action is made use of.

solid conductor a single core wire, as opposed to stranded or hollow-cored wire.

solid-electrolyte capacitor see TANTALUM ELECTROLYTIC.

solid-state (of an electronic system) using non-moving solid materials such as SEMICONDUCTOR devices in place of THERMIONIC VALVES and mechanical components such as RELAYS.

solid-state camera a TELEVISION CAMERA that dispenses with the old-style vacuum tubes (VIDICONs) for image pickup. Modern still or movie digital cameras use CCDs as photosensors. This allows charge that has accumulated in a row of CCD cells to be read out in the time of a line flyback pulse by a number of clock pulses. Simple CCD cameras (see WEBCAM) have appeared for use with computers, and the combination of a CCD camera and DIGITAL TAPE RECORDER forms the basis of the digital CAMCORDER.

solid-state circuit any CIRCUIT that makes use of semiconductors as active components, with no mechanical moving parts or any vacuum devices other than a CATHODE-RAY TUBE.

solid-state memory a MEMORY system that uses semiconductors as distinct from magnetic tape or disk devices. See also DYNAMIC RAM; RAM; ROM; VIRTUAL MEMORY.

solid state microwave amplifier the use of many SEMICONDUCTOR devices connected in parallel for microwave amplification to overcome the low power of a single amplifying device.

solid-state physics the branch of physics that deals with structure and behaviour of solids, particularly of SEMICONDUCTORS.

solid-state relay a SEMICONDUCTOR device that switches large currents, such as a THYRISTOR or TRIAC.

soliton a light pulse with the duration of less than one picosecond that can propagate through 10,000 km of OPTICAL FIBRE without loss of shape, due to its very small DISPERSION.

SONAR see SOUND NAVIGATION AND RANGING.

sone a unit of LOUDNESS, defined as the loudness of a pure SINE WAVE of 40 dB sound pressure level at 1000 Hz.

SONET see SYNCHRONOUS DIGITAL HIERARCHY.

SONOS silicon oxide nitride oxide semiconductor: a variant of MOS.

soot-and-whitewash the appearance of a monochrome TV picture in which CONTRAST is excessive.

SOS silicon on sapphire: see SILICON ON INSULATOR.

SOT see SMALL OUTLINE TRANSISTOR.

sound any audible pressure waves in air. Sound waves can also be transmitted at higher speeds in liquids and in solids. The frequencies above the range of hearing are called ULTRASONIC, these below the range of hearing SUBSONIC or infrasonic.

sound activated lighting lighting that can be turned on by the effect of sound picked up by a microphone and used to activate an ELECTRONIC SWITCH.

sound board or **sound card** a PRINTED CIRCUIT BOARD added to a COMPUTER by way of an EXPANSION SLOT so as to add sound capabilities.

sound card see SOUND BOARD.

sound carrier the radio frequency CARRIER (sense 1) for the sound of a TV picture. In the UK PAL system, the sound is frequency modulated on to a separate carrier whose frequency is 6MHz higher than the vision carrier. See also INTERCARRIER SOUND.

sound channel the range of frequencies used in a TELEVISION RECEIVER to carry the sound signal.

sound chip an IC that executes software instructions to create sounds, used in a SOUND BOARD.

sound mixer a circuit containing amplifiers and adding stages that allow sound from various sources to be blended, faded and mixed for RECORDING onto a master tape or other storage device.

sound navigation and ranging (SONAR) a form of acoustic RADAR. Ultrasonic waves in water are used to locate objects in the water, using the reflection from a pulse output. The principles are used also in echo sounding.

sound on vision the appearance of fluctuating bars on a TV picture due to some of the sound signal entering the vision circuit.

sound pressure level or **SPL** a measure of intensity of sound based on the pressure exerted by the sound wave. The definition is

$$SPL = 20\log{}^P/_{P_{ref}} \text{ dB,}$$

where P_{ref} is approximately the threshold of hearing, taken as 2×10^{-5} N/m² (0.0002 microbar).

sound recording see RECORDING OF SOUND.

sound reproduction the recovery of AUDIO signals from a RECORDING and their conversion into sound. A sound reproduction system consists of a replay TRANSDUCER, amplifier and loudspeaker system.

A general description of a good hi-fi system shows what is required for each type of reproduction system separately. The replay transducer converts the form of recorded sound into audio signals. For the older form of recording, the mechanical vinyl disc, the transducer took the form of a PICKUP head. This uses a stylus fitting in the groove of the disc to vibrate, driven by the modulation of the groove. The disc has to be spun at a steady speed, generally $33\frac{1}{3}$ revolutions per minute, though 45 revolutions per minute was used for shorter recordings. For a stereo recording, this modulation will be picked up as vibration in two directions at 90° to each other. Transducers connected to the stylus will then convert these vibrations into electrical signals. The transducers can use PIEZO-LECTRIC CRYSTALS, or the MOVING IRON PICKUP, or MOVING COIL PICKUP principles.

The small signals from the pickup are voltage-amplified by a PREAMP, and any corrections, such as EQUALIZATION are performed.

If the source of signals is tape, then a tape transcriptor must be used to pull the tape at a constant (and correct) speed past the replay head. The fluctuations of magnetic field on the tape are converted into induced voltages in the head, and these signals are de-emphasized as required in the preamplifier. The signals from a cassette unit may require to be expanded (see COMPANDER) if they have been compressed during recording for noise-reduction purposes.

For COMPACT DISCS, the speed of the disc is controlled by a motor in such a way as to present a constant linear speed to the pickup unit. The start of the recording is in the inner track, and reading is carried out by a solid-state LASER and optical system. The reflection of light from a flat surface indicates that a 0 is present, its scattering by an etched pit indicates a logic 1. The digital bit signals are detected by a photocell, and these signals are amplified before being passed to the DIGITAL TO ANALOGUE CONVERTER and then to the preamp unit.

For radio signals, a TUNER is used. This will normally be an FM tuner, though several designs allow for medium wave reception also, and new designs feature a tuner for digitally coded (see COFDM) broadcasts. The signal from the AERIAL is tuned, converted to IF, amplified and demodulated (see DEMODULATION). The audio signal is de-emphasized (see DE-EMPHASIS), and then passed to the preamp.

At the preamp, a switch allows the user to select any of the sound sources for reproduction. Simple systems make use of mechanical switches directly, but good-quality systems use the switch to operate separate MOSFET switches, so that switch pulse noise and switch contact noise are eliminated. The signal is then voltage-amplified, and POTENTIOMETER (sense 1) controls for gain, bass and treble are included. The signal then passes to the main amplifier in which several stages of voltage amplification are followed by a power amplifier stage. This provides an output with enough power to drive a loudspeaker, usually of the magnetic type. See also RECORDING OF SOUND; SOUNDTRACK.

sound synthesis   the production of sound without the use of musical instruments, based on the use of OSCILLATORS or a combination of NOISE GENERATORS and FILTERS.

soundtrack   the edge of a cinema film that is used to carry the sound MODULATION. Traditionally, the sound is modulated in the form of variable width or variable density bands in which the density or width is proportional to amplitude. Because the film passes through the projection gate in pulses, being held for about   second, and then rapidly jerked on, the sound recording and reproduction must be done at a different part of the film that is moving steadily. This part of the film is ahead of the picture, following the loop that allows the film to regain steady motion after its intermittent movement through the projection gate. Because of this, any splicing because of film breakage can cause sound synchronization to be lost. The SIGNAL-TO-NOISE RATIO for film sound is very poor unless methods such as the DOLBY SYSTEM are used. The reproduction of film sound makes use of a light source and a PHOTOCELL. The photocell must be capable of reasonably fast response, so that sensitivity has to be sacrificed, and a high-gain amplifier needs to be used for the output signals. For modern films, the soundtrack is contained on a magnetic tape rather than as part of the film.

sound wave   a wave of alternate compression and rarefaction in a solid, liquid, or gas. This is a LONGITUDINAL WAVE meaning that the vibrations of the molecules that carry the energy are in the same direction as the movement of the wave.

source   **1.** an emitter of CHARGE CARRIERS in a FET. **2.** any device that produces signals. **3.** to provide CURRENT to drive a

LOAD, such as for a logic device, or a device that provides current. See also SINK (sense 1).

source follower a FIELD-EFFECT TRANSISTOR common-drain amplifier circuit. This is the FET equivalent of an EMITTER FOLLOWER, with high INPUT IMPEDANCE and low output impedance.

source impedance the (complex number) ratio of voltage change to current change for any source of signal, taking any phase changes into account. See IMPEDANCE.

south bridge a chip used on a computer MOTHERBOARD to derive various slower signals (such as USB, keyboard, mouse, serial port, etc.) from the PCI BUS signals. So called because on the system block diagram, this chip appears on the 'South side'. See also NORTH BRIDGE.

south pole the pole of a magnet that, when freely suspended, will point south. MAGNETIC FLUX lines are imagined to leave the NORTH POLE and circulate round a magnet into the south pole.

SP the normal (standard play) setting for a VIDEO CASSETTE RECORDER, allowing the nominal time (such as 180 minutes) for a cassette to be used. See also LP VIDEO.

space charge a cloud of ELECTRONS or other CHARGE CARRIERS, originally denoting the electrons around the hot CATHODE (sense 1) of a vacuum emitter. Space charges also exist in semiconductors around a JUNCTION (sense 2). The existence of space charge causes a form of bias to exist even when no external voltage is applied because the charge acts as a POTENTIAL BARRIER to the movement of electrons.

space charge density a measure of the SPACE CHARGE effect equal to the amount of charge per unit volume in a space charge region.

space charge limiting the limiting of CURRENT in a vacuum THERMIONIC VALVE because of the effect of a SPACE CHARGE. This type of limiting means that the electron current that can be drawn from the region around the CATHODE (sense 1) is not greatly affected by variations in the cathode temperature, provided that the cathode can maintain the space charge.

Most transmitting valves operate under space charge limited conditions rather than in the alternative temperature limiting conditions.

space-time-space switching a form of digital switching, with a memory used to manage time slot interchanges.

space wave a frequency above about 25 to 30 MHz which is not reflected by the ionosphere and therefore escapes into space. These frequencies are used mainly for shorter distance terrestrial communications links.

spacial codes code patterns that are in parallel format.

spacial sound a method of processing of a MONOPHONIC sound signal to make it appear like a stereo signal by altering the phase and amplitude of the left and right channels; used also to enhance a stereo signal.

SPARC see SCALABLE PROCESSOR ARCHITECTURE.

spark an electrical discharge caused by the BREAKDOWN of air INSULATION. Sparking can occur through the air much more easily if the air is ionized (see IONIZATION) by, for example, radioactive particles.

spark counter a detector for ALPHA PARTICLES. Alpha particles have very high ionizing (see IONIZATION) capability, but are stopped by thin layers of materials of ordinary density. A spark counter detects alpha particles in air by using a high voltage between a positive *anode* and a negative *cathode*. The presence of an alpha particle will ionize the air and cause a spark. If the anode is supplied through a large value load resistor, there will be a voltage pulse at the anode that can be amplified and used as the input to a counter.

spark gap an arrangement of ELECTRODES to encourage a spark to pass under fault conditions. The arrangement is used to protect devices like CATHODE-RAY TUBES from voltage surges that would otherwise cause internal sparking. See SURGE DIVERTER.

sparking see ARCING.

sparkly a bright spot on the screen of a TELEVISION RECEIVER, caused by a noise spike in the VIDEO signal. See also CLICK.

spark suppression circuit a CIRCUIT intended to reduce sparking at SWITCH or RELAY contacts. Typical circuits use capacitor-resistor networks that form a damped oscillating circuit, greatly reducing the rate of change of voltage as the contacts open. Spark suppression is particularly important if the contacts switch an INDUCTIVE LOAD, and suppression using DIODES is then more useful.

spark transmitter the primitive form of radio TRANSMITTER used at the start of the 20th century with a high frequency spark producing CARRIER (sense 1) waves that can be switched on and off to provide a Morse code signal.

SPCO see SINGLE-POLE CHANGEOVER.

SPDIF interface a two-channel serial DIGITAL interface for a computer, with 75 ohm termination intended for use with COAXIAL cable.

SPDT see SINGLE-POLE DOUBLE-THROW.

speaker see LOUDSPEAKER.

speaker, active see ACTIVE SPEAKER.

specific cymomotive force the CYMOMOTIVE FORCE produced in a given direction for 1 kW of AERIAL power.

spectral efficiency the data capacity of a channel in terms of BITS PER SECOND per Hz of bandwidth.

spectral line a line in a SPECTRUM of light, often a characteristic of the source of that light.

spectral response a graph of the output of a photosensitive device plotted against WAVELENGTH of light.

spectral shaping the alteration of the SPECTRUM of a serial waveform to make it more efficient and to prevent data from interfering with control signals. See also CHANNEL CODING.

spectral skewing unequal treatment of different AUDIO frequencies, and in an audio COMPANDER.

spectral transposition a scrambling (see SCRAMBLER) system for analogue voice communications in which the audio signal is broken into SUB-BANDs that are either inverted or changed to new frequencies and reassembled into a new analogue signal of the same frequency range. See also TEMPORAL TRANSPOSITION.

spectrum a range of frequencies or WAVELENGTHs. The ELECTROMAGNETIC SPECTRUM consists of all electromagnetic waves, from the very low frequencies up to the gamma-ray range and beyond. The term is often used to denote a band of frequencies, e.g. *microwave spectrum*.

spectrum analyzer an instrument whose output is a graph that shows a plot of amplitude or phase against frequency for a complete FREQUENCY BAND.

speech bandwidth the minimum BANDWIDTH that is needed for intelligible speech, about 300Hz to 2.7kHz.

speech coil the active part of a moving-coil LOUDSPEAKER. The speech coil is located by the SPIDER inside the gap of the magnetic circuit. A current flowing through the speech coil causes the coil, the core on which it is wound, and the cone attached to it, to move. This in turn moves the air around the loudspeaker so producing sound.

speech dialler or **communicator** a security system that uses a voice RECORDING stored in memory, played to a prearranged number in the event of the alarm being triggered.

speech digit signalling the use of one bit in a time slot, or a complete frame, to add channel signalling bits in a slot used mainly for encoding speech signals. See also BIT STEALING.

speech recognition a method of controlling a computer by spoken commands, or dictating text into a word processor program. The voice sounds are picked up by a microphone, and processed into pulses. The pulses are analyzed and converted into digital codes that are compared with stored, standard, codes. If an input causes a code to be generated that is sufficiently similar to a stored code, then the action of the stored code is executed. This action can be to carry out a command or to enter a word into a word processor. See also DIRECT VOICE INPUT.

speed loop the servo control loop in a VIDEO CASSETTE RECORDER that ensures that both the CAPSTAN and the DRUM (sense 1) are running at the correct speed.

speed of light the speed of light and all other electromagnetic waves in free space is taken as 3×10^8 metres per second. The speed of light in glass, or of electromagnetic waves through materials, is lower than the speed in free space.

speed of sound the speed of sound in air is usually taken as 300 metres per second, but is affected by changes in air pressure and humidity. The speed of sound in liquids and solids is considerably greater.

speed-up capacitor a capacitor added to the base circuit of a bipolar junction transistor SWITCHING CIRCUIT to provide positive feedback and so make the switching action faster.

spherical aberration a fault of simple glass lenses that are sections of a sphere, causing parallel rays at a distance from the centre of the lens to focus at different points along the axis. The result is that a point object is imaged as a disc rather than as a point.

spherical wave the shape of a wave of any type emitted from a point source.

SPI see SYNCHRONOUS PARALLEL INTERFACE.

SPICE a computer software model for analogue circuits that can be used to analyze behaviour and plot response.

spider a metal or plastic flat spring that locates a LOUDSPEAKER cone and SPEECH COIL in place. The term arises from the traditional shape of the spring.

spill over loss loss of transmitted signal from a REFLECTOR AERIAL because of energy radiated from the focal point that does not fall on the reflector.

spike a narrow pulse of voltage, usually unintended and unwanted interference.

spin speed the rate at which the PLATTERS of a HARD DRIVE spin. The faster the rate, the faster data can be written and read, and speeds of 10,000 RPM are now common.

spin-up time the time needed for a motor driving a COMPACT DISC to spin to the correct speed, usually from five to ten milliseconds.

spiral PDA a form of POST-DEFLECTION ACCELERATION that uses a spiral of high-resistivity film.

spiral scanning a form of CATHODE-RAY TUBE scanning. A spiral SCAN starts at the centre of the face of the tube, and traces out a spiral path until it reaches the edges.

splitter a filter network that provides a signal for several outputs without mutual interaction between the outputs.

sporadic-E an effect that causes unusual radio PROPAGATION conditions. At times, very highly ionized (see IONIZATION) layers form in the E LAYER, about 100km above the Earth's surface. This heavily-ionized layer reflects frequencies that normally pass through the IONOSPHERE, and therefore causes long-distance reception of signals, such as VHF TV signals whose range is normally 'line of sight'. This in turn causes severe INTERFERENCE between transmissions that are normally not within range of each other. Sporadic-E conditions are associated with intense sun-spot conditions, and are usually predictable. See also SUNSPOT CYCLE.

spot 1. the area on the screen of a CATHODE-RAY TUBE that is lit by the electron beam. 2. an imperfection on a screen that will not illuminate.

spot cutter a tool for cutting tracks on a PRINTED CIRCUIT BOARD or MATRIX STRIPBOARD.

spot filter see SHARP-CUT FILTER.

spot noise factor the NOISE FACTOR for a single frequency only.

spot speed the rate of scanning of a CATHODE-RAY TUBE in terms of spot (sense 1) diameters per second.

spread spectrum or **frequency agile** or **frequency hopping** (of a radio transmission system) designed for secure communications in which channels are changed according to a programming sequence that has to be used also at the receiver.

spreading resistance the internal RESISTANCE of collector or base connection of a transistor due to the semiconductor material between the junction and the contact.

spring line reverb a metal spring with a TRANSDUCER at either end, one converting electrical AUDIO signals into vibrations the other reconverting to electrical signals with a time delay depending on the length of the spring. This unit adds reverberation to a synthesized sound.

SPST see SINGLE-POLE SINGLE-THROW.

spurious free dynamic range or **SFDR** the amplitude range between a fundamental frequency and the first spurious noise component, measured in decibels.

spurious response an unwanted return signal, particularly in a RADAR system.

spurious outputs signals other than the desired signal, such as intermodulation products and harmonics.

sputtering a coating method that makes use of a low-pressure gas discharge in which the material to be coated is connected to a positive voltage to act as an ANODE and the coating material is negative, the CATHODE. Any material can be coated by sputtering, and almost any refractory coating material can be used, such as tungsten, platinum, diamond (carbon), silica, etc.

SQNR see SIGNAL TO QUANTIZATION NOISE.

square-law characteristic a graph of signal output plotted against input where the output is proportional to the square of input signal AMPLITUDE. A JUNCTION FET will produce such a characteristic, used for a MIXER.

square-law detector a form of amplitude DEMODULATOR. The output voltage of a square-law detector is proportional to the square of the input voltage. A small amount of modulation of a CARRIER (sense 1) can therefore produce a comparatively large output from the circuit, so that the detector is sensitive. MOS devices are particularly good square-law detectors.

square-loop hysteresis a characteristic shape of HYSTERESIS LOOP that is straight-sided. See also SCHMITT TRIGGER. (See Fig. 58.)

square wave a WAVEFORM with a square shape. The waveform has vertical sides, representing a rapid switch between low voltage and high voltage. The time spent at high voltage is equal to the time spent at low voltage, making the MARK-SPACE RATIO equal to unity. Waves with steep sides that do not have unity mark-space ratio should be described as *rectangular waves*, but are generally known as square waves unless the mark-space ratio is very low, when the waves are called PULSES.

square-wave defects imperfections that change the shape of a SQUARE WAVE, such as long RISE TIME or FALL TIME, OVERSHOOT, DROOP, and UNDERSHOOT.

square-wave response the OUTPUT of a CIRCUIT for a SQUARE-WAVE input. Poor high-frequency response (or low SLEW RATE) shows up as sloping sides in the output wave, and poor low frequency response as a sagging top (see DROOP). Any instability also shows itself as RINGING (sense 1) after a change of voltage.

squaring the effect of flattening the PEAKS of a WAVEFORM, due to a LIMITING action in an amplifier.

squegging (of an oscillator) biasing off at intervals. A squegging oscillator uses too much FEEDBACK, driving the circuit into NONLINEAR conditions and causing a capacitor in the circuit to charge, so biasing off the oscillator. The oscillation then resumes when the capacitor has discharged. The BLOCKING OSCILLATOR is a deliberately designed form of squegging oscillator.

squelch a circuit technique for reducing radio interstation NOISE. The voltage on the AUTOMATIC GAIN CONTROL line is used to suppress the audio stages unless a signal is tuned that is strong enough to operate the AGC line. This allows a radio to be tuned from one station to another without hearing the noise in between carriers. The squelch technique has obvious benefits in, for example, car radio reception.

SRAM see STATIC MEMORY.

SRBP see SILICONE RESIN BOLDED PAPER.

S-R flip-flop see R-S FLIP-FLOP.

SSB see SINGLE SIDEBAND.

SSBSC see SINGLE-SIDEBAND SUPPRESSED CARRIER.

SSI **1.** see SMALL-SCALE INTEGRATION.
2. see SYNCHRONOUS SERIAL INTERFACE.

SSIP small inline package: a form of SURFACE MOUNT PACKAGING for TRANSISTORS.

SSR see SECONDARY SURVEILLANCE RADAR.

SSTV see SLOW-SCAN TELEVISION.

stabilization see REGULATION.

stabilization, diode a measure of the regulation of a ZENER or AVALANCHE BREAKDOWN diode by its dynamic resistance =

$$\frac{\text{voltage change}}{\text{current change}}.$$

stabilized power supply see REGULATED POWER SUPPLY.

stabilized voltage see REGULATED VOLTAGE.

stabilizer see REGULATOR.

stabilizing amplitude controlling the AMPLITUDE of oscillation so that the output of an OSCILLATOR is a reasonably pure SINE WAVE.

stable circuit a circuit that will not break into OSCILLATION under any normal working conditions. If the circuit is truly stable, it will not show RINGING (sense 1) under SQUARE WAVE testing. See also ASTABLE; BISTABLE.

stage a clearly defined unit of a CIRCUIT in which signals are processed in several steps, such as the circuitry around one transistor or IC.

stage coupling or **interstage coupling** the circuitry that passes signal from one stage to another, often required to block DC.

stage efficiency the ratio of power output from a STAGE to the power that has to be supplied to it (DC supply as well as signal power), used mainly of TRANSMITTER stages.

stage gain the gain, usually VOLTAGE GAIN, of a STAGE. This is often expressed in dB, using 20logVout/Vin.

staggercasting a VIDEO ON DEMAND system where programmes are transmitted at staggered starting times on a set of channels.

stagger tuning a method of obtaining a large BANDWIDTH in a TUNED AMPLIFIER. Several tuned circuits in different STAGES of an amplifier are tuned to slightly

different frequencies, so that the overall tuning is wideband.

staircase voltage a voltage waveform that takes the form of a RAMP with a number of level sections so that the shape is that of a flight of stairs.

standard cell a cell whose EMF is constant under no-load conditions, so that it can be used as a voltage reference. The use of standard cells has greatly diminished owing to the availability of REFERENCE DIODES.

standard commands for programmable instruments or **SCPI** a PROTOCOL that allows instruments that are not compatible with the GPIB bus to use that bus.

standard form or **scientific notation** or **exponent-mantissa form** the expression of a number in the form of $A \times 10^n$ where A (the MANTISSA) is a number less than 10 and n (the EXPONENT) is an integer.

standard M gradient the variation of refractive index for radio waves with altitude above the Earth's surface.

standard product form a BOOLEAN EQUATION format in which each factor is combined by OR so that it appears as a PRODUCT OF SUMS.

standard radio atmosphere an atmosphere with the STANDARD M-GRADIENT.

standard radio horizon the RADIO HORIZON that would exist for transmission through a STANDARD RADIO ATMOSPHERE.

standard refraction the amount of REFRACTION in a STANDARD RADIO ATMOSPHERE.

standard sum form a BOOLEAN EQUATION format in which each factor is combined by AND so that it appears as a SUM OF PRODUCTS.

standard TTL the original form of TTL circuit that requires an input current of −1.6 milliamps for operation. This form of circuitry is obsolete and has been replaced by others including LOW-POWER SCHOTTKY and CMOS. There are many variations on these other forms of digital ICs.

standard voltage cell   a cell, such as the old-fashioned Weston standard cell, that can be used to calibrate the accuracy of a VOLTMETER.

standardization   the setting up of a basis of comparison of units of measurement. Standardization of an instrument, such as a voltmeter or oscilloscope, means that its readings are compared with those of a standard, usually a SECONDARY STANDARD. The instrument is then corrected or calibrated. The term is also used to denote the establishment of written standards for the manufacturing, testing and specification of components and devices.

standards conversion   the electronic conversion from one form of TV signal (NTSC, PAL, SECAM, and for different line and field rates) to another.

standby   a mode of operation for electronic equipment in which the minimum of consumption of power is achieved. Typically for a TV receiver this means supplying power only to the remote-control receiver, and the standby mode for a VIDEO CASSETTE RECORDER or DVD player will operate at much lower levels of power. For a computer, standby involves switching off the HARD DRIVES and the MONITOR, and using the mouse or any key will restore normal operation.

standing wave or **stationary wave**   a wave fixed in space, so that the amplitude of wave oscillation at a given point is fixed for as long as the wave pattern persists. A NODE (sense 2) of the standing wave pattern is a point of minimum amplitude, and an ANTINODE is a point of maximum amplitude. The pattern has the same

wavelength as the wave that generates it, so that wavelength can be measured from the pattern (see LECHER LINES). Compare TRAVELLING WAVE.

standing wave aerial (or antenna) or **resonant aerial**   a DIPOLE AERIAL of length that is an integral multiple of half a wavelength of the frequency used, and which therefore supports STANDING WAVES.

standing wave ratio (SWR)   a measurement of the efficiency of line transmission that applies also to WAVEGUIDES and AERIALS. The SWR is the ratio of the maximum amplitude at any point on the line to the minimum amplitude. The smaller the SWR (the minimum possible value is unity), the better the MATCHING of the line. See also SWR METER.

star connection   a connection to three-phase AC mains that requires four connectors, three live and one neutral. Compare delta connection, see also STAR-DELTA TRANSFORMATION.

star-delta transformation   a theorem for finding the equivalent component values for the arrangements of connections for a THREE-PHASE SUPPLY of AC given the star arrangement values. The principle states that the star network is equivalent to a delta network (Fig. 110) if the component values conform to the equations:

$$R_1 = r_1 + r_2 + \frac{r1r2}{r3} \; ; \; R_2 = r_3 + r_1 + \frac{r3r1}{r2} \; ;$$

$$R_3 = r_2 + r_3 + \frac{r2r3}{r1} \; .$$

There is a similar set of transformations for finding the star values from delta values.

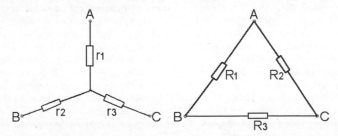

Fig. 110. **star-delta transformation**

star network a form of network controlled by a central HUB with terminals radiating from the hub, so that each terminal can communicate with another only by way of the hub.

start bit or **start flag** a BIT that marks the start of a set of DATA such as a DATA PACKET.

start flag see START BIT.

start pulse a PULSE used to start an action such as that of a COUNTER.

starter 1. an additional ELECTRODE in a GAS-FILLED TUBE that starts IONIZATION. 2. the DEVICE that generates a voltage impulse to start the discharge in a fluorescent tube.

starting current the current flowing during starting conditions. The term usually denotes the heater current of a MAGNETRON that can be reduced when oscillation starts.

Star-Track an automatic vehicle location and data collection system that uses the GLOBAL POSITION SYSTEM and mobile communications technology.

state the condition of output or signal level of a device, or level of any measurable quantity relating to the device. For many electronic devices, the state of the device will denote the voltage level at the output. Digital devices will allow two states only, 0 and 1.

state table a table used to describe the action of a FLIP-FLOP by listing the state of each output and input and the effect of each clock pulse.

state transition diagram a SEQUENTIAL LOGIC diagram that shows current states and inputs that cause a transition from one state to another. See also MEALY MACHINE; MOORE MACHINE.

static a form of radio or television interference. Static is produced by ELECTROSTATIC DISCHARGES, and is most prominent in thundery conditions.

static characteristic a graph-plot of one quantity against another with all other variables held at constant values, such as a plot of transistor output current against input voltage, with collector voltage held constant. In a *dynamic characteristic*, the effect of varying collector voltage would have to be considered, as this would then represent the changes in a working transistor.

static-charge damage see ELECTROSTATIC DAMAGE (ESD).

static convergence an adjustment for a colour cathode-ray tube that ensures purity of colour for a dot in the centre of the screen, with no scanning. Compare DYNAMIC CONVERGENCE.

static electricity a large ELECTRIC FIELD generated usually by rubbing materials together. See TRIBOELECTRICITY.

static error an error in reading an instrument as distinct from an error due to the instrument itself. See DYNAMIC ERROR.

static loop phase error an offset in the normal 90° phase shift of a PHASE LOCKED LOOP.

static memory any form of memory that will store information without the need to rewrite the data at intervals (see REFRESH, sense 1). Static memory may be VOLATILE, like STATIC RAM, or NONVOLATILE, like the obsolete MAGNETIC CORE (sense 2) storage. Neither type, however, needs any signals to maintain storage, unlike a DYNAMIC RAM memory.

static RAM (SRAM) a form of semiconductor MEMORY based on FLIP-FLOPs. Each flip-flop stores one bit of data, but only one part of each flip-flop is connected to each output. The same current will flow through each flip-flop whether a 1 or a 0 is stored, so that the power consumption and the device count for a static memory is greater than for a DYNAMIC RAM memory.

static reverse current the low reverse current through a ZENER DIODE when the reverse voltage is below the level at which Zener or AVALANCHE action starts.

static-sensitive components components that are readily damaged by fairly small ELECTROSTATIC VOLTAGES, typically MOSFETs, CMOS and gallium arsenide semiconductor devices. The risk of damage is very much lower once the components have been soldered into place. See also EARTHING STRAP.

stationary head recorder a form of
DIGITAL TAPE RECORDER in which the digital
signals are recorded on several parallel
channels each using a separate TAPE HEAD.
See also ROTARY HEAD RECORDER.

stationary wave see STANDING WAVE.

statistical multiplexer see CONCENTRATOR.

statistical multiplexing see DYNAMIC
BANDWIDTH ALLOCATION.

statistical sampling the random selection
of components or circuits from a
production line to test quality and
reliability.

stator the stationary part, usually a
magnet, of a motor, generator, or moving-
coil meter. Compare ROTOR.

stator time constant the time required
for the STATOR winding of a MOTOR or
other electromechanical device to reach
its final working temperature following
switch on.

STB see SET-TOP BOX.

steady-shot or **anti-shake system** or **image
stabilizer** see ELECTRONIC IMAGE
STABILIZER.

steady state the state of any system after
any transient OSCILLATIONS or other initial
disturbances have died away.

steep-cut filter a filter which has a steep
SLOPE OF ATTENUATION from its pass band
to its stop band.

steerable aerial (or **antenna)** an aerial
system whose main LOBE can be pointed

in different directions. This can be done
either by moving the whole aerial
structure (like a radar DISH) or by altering
the phases of signals to separate
components of the aerial array.

steering diode a DIODE that is used as part
of a FLIP-FLOP circuit to permit TOGGLING.
For a conventional flip-flop, two steering
diodes are needed. The diodes are biased
by the collector voltages of the transistors,
so that a voltage input pulse can pass
through only one diode. This will be the
diode that is connected to the input of
the shut-off transistor, so that the pulse
switches over the state of the flip-flop.
After the changeover, the bias on the
diodes will have changed also so that the
state will reverse again on the next pulse
input. See Fig. 111.

steering logic gating used to ensure that
the inputs to a FLIP-FLOP do not lead to a
FORBIDDEN STATE.

step-down transformer a TRANSFORMER
constructed and connected so that its
signal output is of lower voltage than its
input. This is because the SECONDARY
WINDING has fewer turns than its PRIMARY
WINDING. Compare STEP-UP TRANSFORMER.

step function a sharp change of voltage
from one level to another, equivalent to
half of a SQUARE WAVE.

step-index fibre an OPTICAL FIBRE
construction in which there is a sudden

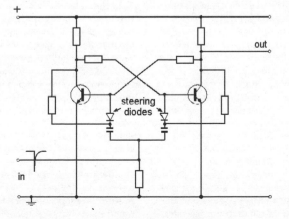

Fig. 111. **steering diode**

change of REFRACTIVE INDEX at the fibre wall between the core and the cladding. See also GRADED-INDEX FIBRE; MULTI-MODE GRADED INDEX FIBRE.

stepped lens see FRESNEL LENS.

stepped lens aerial (or **antenna)** a lens type of aerial whose surface consists of a set of concentric rings with each stepped by an integer multiple of a wavelength. See also ZONE PLATE.

stepped pulleys a set of pulleys with different diameters placed together so that a speed change can be effected by moving a belt from one pulley to another. The system was used on turntables for vinyl disc records.

stepper motor or **stepping motor** a motor operated by PULSE inputs whose shaft will move a few degrees round for each pulse.

stepping relay a type of RELAY once used in telephone exchanges of the Strowger pattern. The relay has a contact arm that can touch several contacts (usually ten) in sequence as the arm rotates.

step recovery diode see CHARGE-STORAGE DIODE.

step-down regulator a form of SWITCH-MODE POWER SUPPLY used to convert an input DC level to a lower level of DC output.

step-up regulator a form of SWITCH-MODE POWER SUPPLY used to convert an input DC level to a higher level of DC output.

step-up transformer a TRANSFORMER constructed and connected so that its signal output is of higher voltage than its input. This is because the SECONDARY WINDING has more turns than its PRIMARY WINDING. Compare STEP-DOWN TRANSFORMER.

step waveform a waveform consisting of a sudden change to a new voltage level.

Sterba array or **Sterba curtain** an AERIAL system consisting of two quarter-wave and one half-wave DIPOLE AERIALS.

stereo or **stereophonic** (of a sound reproducing system) using more than one independent channel to produce the effect of sound that appears to come from an extended source, rather than from a single small LOUDSPEAKER. Contrast MONOPHONIC.

stereo amplifier an audio AMPLIFIER that has two channels. The channels must be separate, allowing virtually no CROSSTALK. They must, however, use ganged volume, treble and bass controls (see GANGED CIRCUITS).

stereo broadcasts the broadcasting of STEREO sound either on FM radio or through television. FM stereo uses a subcarrier for the L – R signal. TV stereo sound uses the NICAM system.

stereo disc recording the simultaneous RECORDING of left and right stereo signals on a vinyl disk. For CD recording the signals are recorded alternately in short bursts.

stereo hiss the noise present on a STEREO radio broadcast when the SIGNAL STRENGTH is low.

stereo loudspeakers loudspeakers used in pairs, one for each channel of a STEREO received broadcast.

stereo receiver a radio receiver or TUNER that can make use of stereo transmissions. The FM signal is demodulated (see DEMODULATION) to recover the L + R signal, where L and R mean the left- and right-channel signals. At the same time, the sideband of the SUBCARRIER of the L – R signal is amplified, the subcarrier regenerated, and the L – R signal recovered by DEMODULATION. The L + R and L – R signals are then combined so as to separate the L and R signals.

stereo tape recorder a TAPE RECORDER that uses separate amplifying systems to record and replay stereo signals on two separate tracks of tape. A stereo record/replay head is needed, with two separate magnetic circuits, gaps and coils.

stereoscopic (of an imaging system) producing an optical image that appears to have three dimensions, as a LASER hologram.

still frame a VIDEO CASSETTE RECORDER effect that allows a single FRAME (sense 1) of a picture to be repeated. On a simple two-head DRUM (sense 1), this usually causes a band of noise across the still picture, but much more satisfactory still frame effects can be obtained using a four-head drum.

stock faults faults on electronic equipment that recur fairly frequently and whose repair procedure is well-established.

stop band or **rejection band** the range of frequencies that a FILTER is designed to reject. Compare PASS BAND.

stop bit a bit at the end of a set of data bits to indicate the end.

stopped down (of an optical lens) having an aperture considerably reduced, passing less light but providing much larger *depth of field* so that both near and far objects are equally well in focus.

stopper a RESISTOR used to suppress OSCILLATIONS. The stopper is connected close to a terminal of an ACTIVE COMPONENT. Its action is as a damper (see DAMPED) in an unintentionally oscillating circuit. See also BASE STOPPER.

stopping potential the reverse voltage that is needed to prevent an ELECTRON from landing on a surface. The stopping potential required on an ANODE measures the energy of the electrons liberated by light from a PHOTOCATHODE.

stop pulse a pulse applied to a circuit to stop an action, typically COUNTING.

storage oscilloscope an oscilloscope that can retain a trace of a transient input, such as a short pulse. This was originally done using a direct-view STORAGE TUBE, but is now performed by using digital storage, see DIGITAL STORAGE OSCILLOSCOPE.

storage time the time for which data can be stored before requiring to be refreshed. See DYNAMIC RAM; REFRESH (sense 1).

storage tube or **charge storage tube** a form of CATHODE-RAY TUBE that uses charge storage to retain its trace. Most types of TV CAMERA TUBES were storage tubes in this sense, but the term is usually reserved to denote direct-view display storage tubes. These tubes, developed in the 1950s, used metal mesh coated with an insulator, and 'written' with positive charges by an electron beam, using SECONDARY EMISSION to charge the insulator. The pattern of charge then affected the passage of an overall FLOOD GUN beam through the apertures in the mesh. This type of tube, the *direct-view*

storage tube (*DVST*) has now been superseded by the use of digital storage of waveforms for most purposes.

store and shift a description of the actions that are needed using REGISTERS and GATES (sense 2) to carry out multiplication and subtraction.

stored charge the charge that exists in a junction, particularly in the BASE region of transistor which cannot instantly be dissipated when the base bias is suddenly reversed. The result of stored charge is that the transistor will conduct momentarily in the reverse direction. The same effect will cause a conducting diode to continue conduction for a short time after the bias voltage has been reversed.

stored energy, capacitor the energy, in units of JOULES, that is stored by a charged capacitor. In terms of capacitance and voltage this is equal to $\frac{1}{2} CV^2$ where C is capacitance in farads and V is potential difference in volts.

stored energy, cell the energy content for a cell, calculated as the average terminal voltage, multiplied by rated current, multiplied by the time for which the cell can be used.

STP see SHIELDED TWISTED PAIR.

straight ring connection a set of FLIP-FLOPs, each with its Q output connected to the J input of the next and the Q-bar output connected to the K input of the next, with the last flip-flop connected back to the first. This circuit will act as a counter, but its output is not a BINARY CODE. See also JOHNSON COUNTER.

strain the fractional change in size of an object when a *stress* (force per unit area) is applied to it.

strain gauge a method of measuring mechanical strain by electrical methods. The most useful methods are the RESISTANCE STRAIN GAUGE and the SEMICONDUCTOR STRAIN GAUGE. See ELASTORESISTANCE.

stranded conductor a wire made out of a set of strands twisted together.

strapping a technique for stabilizing MAGNETRON operating frequency. Strapping means the connecting of alternate cavities (see CAVITY) so that they share signals in the correct phase.

stratosphere   the layer of the atmosphere between about 10 and 40 km above the surface.

stray capacitance   the CAPACITANCE that exists between parts of a circuit but is not deliberately designed into the circuit. This consists of the capacitance of connectors, wires, leads, and components themselves, both to earth and to other components. Stray capacitance is unwanted, but cannot be forgotten. It causes unwanted resonances, sometimes oscillations, and is responsible for the loss of gain at high frequencies in wide-band amplifiers.

stray inductance   inductance, such as that of component leads and wiring, that is not deliberately designed into a circuit and which can cause unwanted RESONANCES or OSCILLATIONS, particularly in circuits for high frequency units.

streaming   continuous delivery of DIGITAL DATA, such as sound or video sent over the INTERNET, or data being saved in a tape backup system.

striking potential   the POTENTIAL DIFFERENCE between two electrodes that is needed to start a gas discharge. See also STARTER (sense 1).

stripboard   see MATRIX STRIPBOARD.

strip-chart recorder   a form of data recorder that can draw charts for several channels of information and print time and date on a long strip of paper.

strip core   a magnetic core for an inductor that is made by winding a ribbon of SOFT MAGNETIC MATERIAL. Using a ribbon rather than a LAMINATED CORE allows the use of a material that is highly ANISOTROPIC magnetically.

stripe geometry laser   a form of HETEROJUNCTION laser in which the active area width is reduced by creating a higher resistance area on each side.

strip line   a form of TRANSMISSION LINE using a broad conductor on one side of an insulating strip and a narrow conductor on the opposite side.

stripline inductor   an INDUCTOR formed from a short straight piece of conductor

on a DIELECTRIC, which has sufficient inductance for UHF tuning.

strobe   **1.** a gating pulse for a signal. See STROBED DISPLAY. **2.** see MOIRÉ PATTERN.

strobed display   a display, usually of the SEVEN-SEGMENT type, that is displayed section by section. The display is operated by ENABLING (strobe) pulses that connect the ANODE voltage and so illuminate each section of the display in turn. The rate of pulsing is such that all of the units appear to be operating together. Strobing allows all the connections to the segments to be taken to seven inputs irrespective of the number of digits in the display. When a strobe pulse is applied, the data for the correct unit is applied to the inputs. For example, when the 'tens' unit is strobed, the data that is applied is for the tens figure. This data will also affect the bars of all the other units, but only the tens unit is visible because of the strobing.

strobe pulse   a PULSE that is used to select one of a number of units, or a connection to a MULTIPLEXER (sense 2).

stroke, solenoid   the distance over which a SOLENOID (sense 2) can operate at sufficient force to be useful.

STTL   see STANDARD TTL.

stub   a short length of TRANSMISSION LINE or WAVEGUIDE used for MATCHING other sections. The stub may be either short circuited or open circuited at its far end. It is connected to the main line at a point where matching is needed, such as where the line joins to a device. The stub is then adjusted by cutting or by using a tuning capacitor connected to the end so as to achieve the minimum STANDING WAVE RATIO.

stub aerial   a short form of AERIAL, usually consisting of a quarter wave wire wound in a short length helix, as used on MOBILE PHONES.

studio monitor   a loudspeaker and enclosure for use in a professional RECORDING studio, featuring higher maximum sound level and lower distortion levels than its domestic counterpart.

stud packaging   a form of PACKAGE, mostly for RECTIFIER DIODES, in a casing that has a metal stud, allowing it to be screwed tightly to a HEAT SINK.

stylus   a sharp tip, usually of diamond or sapphire, on a metal holder that is vibrated by the groove of a conventional vinyl record disc and transmits the vibration to a transducer, the pickup CARTRIDGE (sense 2).

stylus pressure   see PLAYING WEIGHT.

subassembly   a set of components bunched into an assembly to be inserted as one unit or replaced as one unit during servicing.

subatomic   (of particles) smaller than an atom, such as electrons, protons and neutrons.

sub-audible tones   see CONTINUOUS TONE CODED SQUELCH SYSTEM.

sub-band   a small portion of a complete frequency band, often used in SCRAMBLER systems. See also SPECTRAL TRANSPOSITION; TEMPORAL TRANSPOSITION.

subcarrier   a second CARRIER (sense 1) that is itself modulated onto a main carrier. See also COLOUR TELEVISION; PAL; STEREO RECEIVER.

subcode   part of the data in a digital video cassette RECORDING consisting of TIMECODE (sense 1) and cue flags for locating the shot and for marking still frames.

subcode detector   part of the DECODER system for a COMPACT DISC player, used to detect the 8-bit control WORD.

subharmonic   a frequency that is an integer fraction ($1/2$, $1/4$, etc.) of a FUNDAMENTAL FREQUENCY. Compare HARMONIC.

subharmonic mixing   a method of minimizing noise problems of FREQUENCY CHANGERS for MICROWAVE reception by running the LOCAL OSCILLATOR at a sub-multiple of the frequency and multiplying it up to the correct value.

subreflector   a second, smaller, reflector used along with parabolic reflector AERIAL so that the electronics unit does not have to be placed at the focal point. See also CASSEGRAIN REFLECTOR; GREGORIAN REFLECTOR.

subscriber identity module or **SIM** or **Simcard**   a small MEMORY in card form that can be loaded into a mobile phone to hold personal information that is set up on the phone. The card can also be transferred to a new phone.

subsidence inversion   a layer of warm air below a cold layer that causes increased co-channel interference problems for radio transmissions.

subsonic or **infrasonic**   (of frequencies) being below the range of audible sound frequencies, less than 20Hz.

substandard   an instrument that is a SECONDARY STANDARD.

substitution box   a box containing a variety of PASSIVE COMPONENTS connected to terminals to allow easy substitution in circuits operating at comparatively low frequencies.

substrate   the material of a chip on which (and of which) an INTEGRATED CIRCUIT is constructed, applied mainly to the main part of the semiconductor chip on which the IC components and connections are made. Also applied more generally to any supporting insulating material on which conductors are deposited.

subtitles   TELETEXT lines that have precedence over other items, used to add text data to a picture.

subtractive light mixing   a method of obtaining SECONDARY COLOURS by subtracting PRIMARY COLOURS from white light, used for colour photography on film. Contrast ADDITIVE LIGHT MIXING.

subtractor amplifier   see DIFFERENTIAL AMPLIFIER.

sub-woofer   a loudspeaker and enclosure specifically designed for boosting the level of AUDIO signals below 100 Hz.

successive approximation converter   a form of ANALOGUE TO DIGITAL CONVERTER in which the output from the converter is compared to the input, and the difference used in each step of comparison to set or reset one of a set of a FLIP-FLOPS. This allows a lower number of comparisons to be made for a given size of digital work.

sudden ionospheric disturbance or **SID**   a violent change in ionospheric conditions, usually caused by a sun flare.

sum of products   a BOOLEAN EXPRESSION that consists of products within

brackets that are then added, such as
(A·B) + (C·D).

summing amplifier   an OPERATIONAL
AMPLIFIER circuit with several inputs and
one output, so that the analogue output
is the sum of the signal amplitudes at
the inputs.

sun-and-planet model   a simple model
of an ATOM in which the NUCLEUS is
surrounded by spinning ELECTRONS.

sunspot cycle   the periodic changes of
conditions in the outer layers of the sun.
These cause considerable changes in the
IONIZATION of layers in the IONOSPHERE,
thus affecting radio reception.

super high frequency or **SHF**   the range
3 to 30GHz (wavelength 1 to 10cm) in
the MICROWAVE range.

supercomputer or **big iron**   a computer
intended for performing a very large
number of operations (see FLOP) per
second, so that it can be used for large
amounts of rapidly-changing data, such
as is required for weather forecasting.

superconducting magnet   an ELECTRO-
MAGNET run at such a low temperature
that the windings have zero resistance,
allowing very large currents to be used
to create very large MAGNETIC FIELDS.

superconductivity   a complete loss of
electrical RESISTANCE. This occurs in
many metals at very low temperatures
close to absolute zero. See also JOSEPHSON
EFFECT.

superframe   a set of 12 or 24 FRAMES
(sense 2) of DIGITAL information.

superheterodyne (superhet) receiver
the most important type of RADIO RECEIVER
circuit for virtually all usable frequencies.
A superhet receiver is based on the principle
of changing the frequency of received
signals to a fixed lower frequency, the
INTERMEDIATE FREQUENCY, at which most of
the amplification is carried out. This ensures
that any unintended FEEDBACK, such as is
inevitable in the early tuned stages of a
receiver, will not be at a frequency that
will cause oscillation. In addition, the
main amplification will be carried out at
a fixed frequency, allowing greater gain
and bandwidth than would be possible if
a variable frequency had to be amplified.

The intermediate frequency is obtained
by mixing the incoming frequency with
the signal from a LOCAL OSCILLATOR. The
oscillator tuned circuit is adjustable, and
the tuning of the oscillator is ganged
(see GANGED CIRCUITS) to the tuning of the
mixer input stage, and to any tuned pre-
mixer stage. In this way, the frequency
of the oscillator is kept in step with that
of the input signal so as always to produce
the correct intermediate frequency.
By convention, the oscillator frequency is
usually higher than that of the incoming
signal. The name is derived from the
original description of the action,
supersonic heterodyne. See Fig. 112.

Supermalloy™   a magnetic nickel-iron alloy.
Supermalloy contains 5% molybdenum
and has very high permeability and low
saturation field strength.

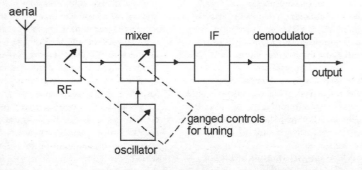

Fig. 112. **superheterodyne**

supermatched devices sets of transistors simultaneously formed on the same IC chip. These have virtually identical characteristics and are used to provide a low-impedance low-noise input stage for AUDIO signals.

Supermendur™ a magnetic cobalt-iron alloy. Supermendur contains Vanadium and has very high saturation field strength.

Super-Permalloy™ a nickel, iron, molybdenum alloy that has been heat-treated in hydrogen to improvement magnetic properties and wear resistance.

superposition theorem or **superposition principle** a useful electrical theorem for linear NETWORKS (sense 1) of PASSIVE COMPONENTS. In a linear network that contains several sources of voltage, the effect of each voltage at a selected point can be found separately, and these effects added to find the effect of all the voltages at that point. Suppose, for example, a network contains two signal voltages. To find the voltage across one resistor in the network, imagine one signal source replaced by its internal resistance. Calculate the voltage across the resistor that is due to the remaining signal. Now reverse the situation, replacing the first signal, but removing the second and substituting its internal resistance. Calculate the voltage across the resistor due to the second signal. Now add these voltages. The result is the voltage that would be caused by the two signal sources. The use of the superposition theorem is often simpler and quicker than methods based on KIRCHOFF'S LAWS.

super-regeneration a method of operating a RECEIVER circuit for exceptionally high SENSITIVITY. The circuit is regenerative, meaning that POSITIVE FEEDBACK is used. The amount of positive feedback is so high that the circuit oscillates, but the circuit is arranged as a SQUEGGING oscillator, with the squegging at an ultrasonic frequency and suppressed by the incoming signal. Super-regenerative receivers can achieve astonishingly high gain, allowing the use of two-transistor

receivers, for example, but with poor SELECTIVITY. In addition, the radiation that they set up by their oscillation interferes with other receivers around them, so super-regeneration is a technique that is used only in receivers for emergency use that must be of minimal size and power consumption. See REGENERATIVE RECEIVER.

super turnstile aerial (or **antenna)** an aerial consisting of four metal fins electrically coupled and mounted at 90° to each other on a vertical mast.

supertwist LCD a form of LCD construction that offers faster operation and greater contrast, now superseded by THIN-FILM TRANSISTOR (TFT) types.

supply voltage the operating voltage, usually DC, for a circuit.

support chip an IC that is designed to work along with a specific MICROPROCESSOR either to extend the action or to make an action more efficient. Support chips are used typically for supplying CLOCK pulses, for carrying out DMA, and for controlling BUS allocation. See also NORTH BRIDGE; SOUTH BRIDGE.

suppressed aerial (or **antenna)** see CONFORMAL AERIAL.

suppressed-carrier transmission a system of TRANSMISSION and reception of AMPLITUDE MODULATION. In the suppressed-carrier system, the CARRIER (sense 1) frequency is suppressed or filtered to very low amplitude at the transmitter. Since half of the power of a conventional AM transmitter is used to transmit the carrier, but all of the information lies in the SIDEBANDS, the suppression of the carrier greatly improves the efficiency of transmission. This can be increased still further if only one sideband is transmitted. The missing carrier must be regenerated at the receiver for purposes of DEMODULATION. This can be done either by CRYSTAL CONTROL of both transmitter and receiver, or by transmitting a small-amplitude carrier signal (see PILOT TONE) that can be filtered, amplified and used to synchronize a LOCAL OSCILLATOR in the receiver.

suppressed-zero indicator an indicator in which the scale does not start at zero. A simple example is a voltmeter for a car that has a range of about 10V to 14V only.

suppressor a DEVICE that reduces the radiation of INTERFERENCE, applied mainly to series resistors fitted in spark-ignition systems. These damp out the VHF oscillations in the system. Other suppressors make use of c-r networks, diodes, inductors and other components to slow down sudden voltage changes and damp out oscillations.

surface acoustic wave (SAW) an ULTRASONIC wave along the surface of a QUARTZ CRYSTAL or other material. Surface acoustic waves are generated by crystal TRANSDUCERS, and can be of very high frequencies. The wave can be very precisely filtered by mechanical treatment of the surface along which it travels. SAW filters are therefore extensively used wherever a purely electronic filter could not provide sufficiently sharp band edges and/or amount of attenuation.

surface-barrier device a transistor that makes use of SCHOTTKY DIODE junctions in place of the normal p-n type of JUNCTION (sense 2).

surface leakage a leakage current along the surface of a material rather than through it.

surface mounted component (SMC) or **surface mount device (SMD)** any component that has been manufactured in SURFACE MOUNT TECHNOLOGY packaging. It is often difficult, looking at the printed circuit board, to distinguish such components from blobs of solder.

surface mount technology or **SMT** a form of miniature packaging for components, active or passive, that dispenses with connecting wires and solders these components directly onto the printed circuit board (see SOLDER PAD). This reduces stray inductance and also allows better heat dissipation.

surface passivation the treatment of a SEMICONDUCTOR or other surface so that it cannot be affected by the environment.

surface recombination noise TRANSISTOR noise caused by the RECOMBINATION of ELECTRONS and HOLES in BASE region.

surface resistivity the RESISTANCE per unit square of a surface of uniform thickness. The resistance is measured between two opposite sides of a square of any size.

surface wave a CARRIER (sense 1) wave that follows the ground contours between TRANSMITTER and RECEIVER.

surface wave aerial (or antenna) any aerial, such as an END FIRE ARRAY, whose radiation is due to an electric magnetic wave travelling along the surface.

surge a large and abrupt change of VOLTAGE. Surges are produced by lightning striking power cables, cable faults, reflections on a transmission line, or switching transients.

surge arrester a DEVICE that opens a CIRCUIT when a SURGE occurs.

surge current a large current flowing in a circuit, usually at switch-on when CAPACITORS are being charged.

surge diverter a CIRCUIT that limits the effect of a SURGE by limiting the surge voltage. A SPARK GAP is a simple form of surge diverter.

surge impedance the IMPEDANCE of a TRANSMISSION LINE to a sudden step of voltage. The value is determined by the values of inductance and capacitance per metre of line.

surge limiter a resistor designed to limit the amount of charging current to the RESERVOIR CAPACITOR of a power supply at the instant of switching on.

surround sound a method of using two conventional stereo channels to carry additional information, allowing the use of multiple loudspeakers for replay. See also DISCRETE 5.1 AUDIO.

suspended strip line a form of MICROWAVE INTEGRATED STRUCTURE in which the ground plane of an INVERTED STRIP LINE totally encloses the substrate.

sustain the middle section of waveform for a musical note in which the amplitude remains almost constant. See also ATTACK; DECAY; RELEASE; SUSTAIN.

SVGA or **super video graphics array**
a standard system for computer MONITOR
displays with RESOLUTIONs ranging from
800 × 600 to 1280 × 1024 or higher.

S-VHS　a high-definition form of VHS
RECORDING for analogue television
pictures, used for some analogue
CAMCORDERs but now rendered
obsolescent by the development of digital
methods.

S-video　a form of video connection that
uses separate cables for LUMINANCE and
CHROMINANCE, providing better pictures
than a COMPOSITE VIDEO system, but
inferior to a full RGB CONNECTION.

SWA　safe working area: see SAFE
OPERATING AREA.

swamp resistor　a resistor placed in
series with a device whose resistance
is variable, so that the total resistance
is almost constant.

SWAP　see SHARED WIRELESS ACCESS
PROTOCOL.

sweep　a waveform that is a combination
of a RAMP and a FLYBACK.

sweep generator　see·TIMEBASE.

sweeping effect or **skying effect**　a sound
synthesis effect that uses a phase shift
and delay.

sweep voltage　the linear rate of change
of VOLTAGE from a TIMEBASE circuit that is
used to deflect an ELECTRON BEAM. For
magnetically deflected CATHODE-RAY TUBES,
sweep current is a more useful quantity.

sweep waveform　see SAWTOOTH WAVEFORM.

SWG　standard wire gauge: the old
system of measuring wire cross sections,
now replaced by metric measurement of
the diameter of each strand. A similar
system to SWG is still used in the US, the
Standard American Wire Gauge (AWG).

swimming display　a screen display in
which the items move up and down or
from side to side. This is usually due to
the presence of an alternating magnetic
field, often from another MONITOR.

swing　a range of values of VOLTAGE or
CURRENT that is used by a DEVICE. The
output swing of an amplifier stage might,
for example, be between 1V and 9V when
a 10V supply was used.

swinging burst　the subcarrier BURST used
for synchronizing colour for the PAL
system that alternates 90° in phase so as
to synchronize the phase changes of the
V-subcarrier.

swinging choke　an INDUCTOR whose
inductance is deliberately made
NONLINEAR. The inductance value of a
swinging choke decreases as the current
increases, so that the filtering effect of the
choke is less effective for high currents.

switch　a method of making, breaking,
or changing electrical connections.
Mechanical switches use moving contacts
to make connections, but switching can
also be carried out by semiconductor
devices such as DIODEs, FETs, SILICON
CONTROLLED SWITCHes, THYRISTORS,
TRANSISTORs, etc.

switch de-bouncer　a circuit connected
to a switch that will remove any excess
PULSEs arising from the switch contacts
bouncing as the switch is closed.

switched attenuator　see ATTENUATOR.

switched capacitor filter　a form of low-
frequency ACTIVE FILTER in integrated form
that operates by switching the signal to a
pair of capacitors, so that different filter
actions can be achieved by controlling
the switching action.

switched potentiometer　see PRECISION
RESISTOR CHAIN.

switched-star　a form of NETWORK (sense 2)
system for CABLE TELEVISION in which
available programmes are cabled to a central
point from which the subscriber can
request programmes to an individual line.

switching circuit　a circuit capable of
changing rapidly from one state of output
to another for a small change of input.

switching diode　a diode chosen for a very
low JUNCTION CAPACITANCE so that it can be
used as a switch for very high frequency
circuits.

switching transients　brief PULSEs on a
WAVEFORM, caused by the effect of
switches in the circuit through which
the waveform is passing.

switching transistor　a TRANSISTOR
designed to have a small value of STORED
CHARGE so that the collector current can

be switched rapidly by altering the base voltage.

switch logic the representation of the LOGIC actions of AND and OR by using SINGLE-POLE SINGLE-THROW SWITCHes.

switch-mode power supply (SMPS) or **switch-mode supply (SMS)** a form of REGULATED POWER SUPPLY that is much more efficient than older linear types. For a switch mode supply the mains voltage is rectified and this output is used to operate an OSCILLATOR working at high frequency. A small transformer changes the high frequency voltage to the level required, and this is rectified and smoothed with comparatively small values of capacitance. Regulation is achieved by feeding back one of DC outputs to control the oscillator.

switch-start fluorescent a fluorescent tube with a starting arrangement consisting of an INDUCTOR and a THERMAL SWITCH. When the switch contacts open, the BACK EMF across the inductor is more than the BREAKDOWN VOLTAGE for the vapour in the tube, so starting a discharge that will then continue at a lower voltage.

SWR see STANDING WAVE RATIO.

SWR meter a form of radio-frequency measuring bridge that can measure the amplitude of forward and reverse waves on a line. By doing so, it indicates the value of voltage STANDING WAVE RATIO.

symbol any bit, byte or word that carries a recognizable piece of information.

symbol rate see BIT RATE. Contrast BAUD RATE.

symmetrical binary code see FOLDED BINARY CODE.

symmetrical network a NETWORK (sense 1) in which input and output terminals can be interchanged without changing the electrical properties.

symmetrical waveform a waveform with the same shape and size above the time axis as below so that there is no DC component.

sync see SYNCHRONIZING PULSE.

sync generator the master OSCILLATOR, generating the frequency that will be divided down to supply both line and field signals for a television system.

sync separator a circuit used in an analogue TELEVISION RECEIVER to separate the two SYNCHRONIZING PULSES from the VIDEO SIGNAL and from each other. The sync separator firstly separates the synchronizing signals from the video waveform using a biased amplifier stage. A differentiator circuit is used to give a sharp spike for each sync pulse, so providing a horizontal (line) synchronizing pulse (see RASTER). The differentiator will also give an output for each of the field sync pulses, but this is unimportant. An integrating circuit

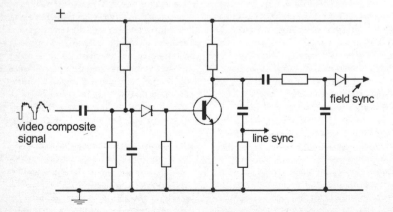

Fig. 113. **sync separator**

provides a negligible output for each line sync pulse, but the more closely-spaced field sync pulses cause a rise in voltage that can be used to synchronize the vertical (field) timebase generator. See Fig. 113.

synchro or **selsyn**   a method of synchronizing mechanical motion. The synchro transmitter and receiver units consist of a ROTOR on a shaft and a three-phase STATOR. The stator coils of transmitter and receiver are connected, and the same AC supply is used for both the rotors. When one rotor is turned, the induced currents in the stators will ensure that the other rotor maintains the same position as that of the transmitter.

synchrodyne   see HOMODYNE.

synchro edit   a system of connecting together a CAMCORDER and a VIDEO CASSETTE RECORDER so that editing actions can be carried out during the process of copying signals from one to the other.

synchronization   (of a circuit or device) being adjusted to run at the same timing as another circuit or device.

synchronizing pulse or **sync**   a PULSE that is used to start an action so that the action will be in time with the pulse. The source of a sync pulse is called a *clock generator*. Synchronizing pulses are essential in MICROPROCESSOR equipment, and are used extensively also in analogue TELEVISION circuitry. See also RASTER.

synchronous   (of a SIGNAL) being forced into step with another signal. When different circuits are fed with the same sync pulse, they will be acting in a synchronous way. The action of an analogue television SYNCHRONIZING PULSE is to make the TIMEBASE of a TV receiver operate in a synchronous way with respect to the transmitted signals. Synchronous action is also important in a computer system, in which virtually every waveform is synchronized to a main CLOCK PULSE. Contrast ASYNCHRONOUS, see also SYNCHRONOUS COUNTER.

synchronous AC motor   a form of the AC motor whose rotating speed is synchronized to the frequency of the mains input, so that speed can be 3000 rpm or a sub-multiple.

synchronous AM demodulation   see SYNCHRONOUS DEMODULATION.

synchronous communication   a system of transmitting SERIAL data in which a master CLOCK pulse determines the timing of each transmitted bit. SERIAL COMMUNICATIONS generally use ASYNCHRONOUS TRANSMISSION.

synchronous counter   a set of FLIP-FLOPS arranged so as to act as a counter of PULSES that are fed to each flip-flop in the counter. Unlike the ASYNCHRONOUS COUNTER in which each flip-flop is toggled (see TOGGLING) by the previous flip-flop, the synchronous counter applies the input pulses to the clock terminals of each flip-flop, so that the clocking rate is the same for each unit. The counter uses J-K FLIP-FLOPS, and the counting logic is determined by the way in which the J and K inputs are inter-connected using GATES (sense 2).

synchronous data link control or **SDLC**   an international PROTOCOL for data communications.

synchronous demodulation or **synchronous detection** or (*formerly*) **homodyne detection**   a form of DEMODULATION in which a modulated signal is mixed with a sine wave that is at CARRIER (sense 1) frequency. The modern synchronous detector is phase sensitive (see PHASE DISCRIMINATOR), so its output is affected by any difference between the phase of the incoming signal and the phase of the locally-generated carrier.

synchronous detection   see SYNCHRONOUS DEMODULATION.

synchronous digital hierarchy (SDH) or **synchronous optical network (SONET)**   a worldwide standard for interconnection of broadband ISDN services.

synchronous dynamic random access memory or **SDRAM**   a form of DYNAMIC RAM that can be run at the speed of the system clock, typically 100 or 133 MHz. Faster effective rates can be attained by developments of this system such as DDR-SDRAM.

synchronous gating a method of opening and closing circuit paths in response to a SYNCHRONIZING PULSE.

synchronous link dynamic random access memory (SLDRAM) a type of SDRAM that uses a multiplexed command bus so that fewer pins are needed on the package, along with the advantages of greater bandwidth and higher operating speed.

synchronous logic the use in a LOGIC CIRCUIT of FLIP-FLOPS that are clocked (see CLOCK). The clock signal is independent of the inputs to the flip-flops, and the advantage of the system is that it avoids RACE HAZARDS by ensuring that all logic stages operate at precisely controlled times.

synchronous motor a form of AC motor in which the rotating speed is determined entirely by the supply mains frequency. In general, the synchronous motor will either run at its synchronous speed or not at all. Some types, such as those once used in mains electric clocks, are not self-starting.

synchronous operation the connection of FLIP-FLOPS into a COUNTER circuit so that the same clock pulse is used on each flip-flop.

synchronous optical network or **SONET** see SYNCHRONOUS DIGITAL HIERARCHY.

synchronous parallel interface or **SPI** a standardized parallel interface for MPEG signals designed for short to medium distances. One sync signal is used to identify the beginning of each DATA PACKET and another line is used to flag empty bytes. The clock signal is equal to the useful bit rate, not exceeding 13.5 MHz, and the mechanical interface uses a D25 plug and socket.

synchronous serial interface or **SSI** a standardized serial interface for MPEG signals. There is no fixed rate because the data is directly converted to serial from its parallel form, and is BIPHASE encoded. The standard is not widely implemented.

synchronous switching decoder a method of extracting left and right stereo signals from the composite FM stereo input using switching operated at 38 kHz.

synchronous transmission any form of digital transmission that is synchronized to a clock pulse.

syndrome a number, produced from the PARITY checking action of Hamming code, whose value reveals the position of the error in the data.

synthesis the construction of a WAVEFORM or a desired response from standardized components. An example is *filter synthesis*, the technique of designing filters of desired characteristics from standard values of inductors, capacitors and resistors.

synthesizer a DEVICE that uses electronic CIRCUITS for generating sounds. Synthesizers are based on the generation of SQUARE WAVES in the audio range. These waves are rich in HARMONICS. FILTERS are used to modify the shape of the waves, and modulators, limiters, clippers and other devices are used to shape the sound wave and form an envelope of waves. This permits a synthesizer to imitate the sounds of instruments and, more important, to create new types of notes and effects. Many synthesizers can be interconnected to computers using the MIDI (musical instrument digital interface) system to permit a degree of control that is difficult to achieve manually.

synthesizer, direct digital see DIRECT DIGITAL SYNTHESIZER.

synthetic aperture RADAR or **SAR** a form of satellite-borne RADAR in which the radar pulses are emitted by the satellite which has moved several kilometres along its track by the time the returns from the Earth are received so providing the effect of an AERIAL several kilometres wide with high GAIN and very narrow BEAMWIDTH. This system is used with DIGITAL processing to produce highly accurate maps of the Earth's surface.

synthetic resin bonded paper (SRBP) a material made by soaking paper in a resin that hardens so that the result is a stiff sheet with excellent insulating properties used to make PRINTED CIRCUIT BOARDS.

system a set of interacting parts that make up a working entity. The term can denote a circuit, device, a construction such as a radio receiver or a radar station, or a large assembly such as a steelworks. Anything can be treated as a system if it has definable inputs, outputs and control actions.

system control   a MICROPROCESSOR based circuit used on electronic equipment to carry out control actions such as tuning, volume adjustment, starting and stopping tape mechanisms, often in conjunction with a remote control.

system deviation   the error signal that is fed back in a control system to correct the output.

systeme electronique couleur avec memoire or **SECAM**   the name of the French COLOUR TV transmission system that differs in several respects from the NTSC and PAL systems. In the SECAM system, the COLOUR DIFFERENCE SIGNALS, R-Y and B-Y, are sent alternately.

The signals are frequency modulated (see FREQUENCY MODULATION) onto the SUBCARRIER, and a delay line is used at the receiver to allow both sets of signals to be available. The use of sequential signals effectively halves the vertical resolution, as the summing of signals does in the PAL system, and the use of frequency modulation causes marginally more visible dot-patterning on monochrome receivers than the PAL system. Pre-emphasis is used to reduce the effect of the frequency variation of the subcarrier.

system noise performance   see FRIIS' EQUATION.

system on a chip or **SOC**   a SURFACE MOUNT PACKAGING for an IC containing several million transistors.

system parameters   measurements that can be made on a communications system to assess its quality.

table of contents or **TOC**   the information on number of tracks, track time and total playing time for a CD that has to be read by a CD player before playing a disc.

tachogenerator or **tacho**   a miniature electrical GENERATOR (sense 1) for rotational speed measurement. The tacho is designed to give a linear graph-shape of voltage output plotted against the speed of rotation of the shaft. This allows rotating components to be included in a FEEDBACK LOOP, with the tacho providing the feedback signal proportional to speed.

tachometer   any form of angular speed sensor. Electronic tachometers can use revolving magnets with static pickup coils, light beams that are interrupted by a revolving object, TACHOGENERATORS, etc.

tacho pulse   a pulse received from a tachogenerator to provide rotational speed information.

tag   an identifier, often one BIT or one BYTE used to identify the remainder of a byte or WORD.

tag byte   part of an item of DATA used as an identifier where data is not accessed by using ADDRESS numbers.

talker or **talker device**   a device connected to the GENERAL PURPOSE INTERFACE BUS that sends data to a LISTENER. See also CONTROLLER.

tamper loop   a security system wiring method that ensures that an alarm will sound if any unit is disconnected or has its cable cut.

tangential error   an incorrect setting of the angle of the optical pickup unit of a CD player relative to the disc.

tangential sensitivity   the NOISE FIGURE for a MICROWAVE detector DIODE working into a matched load. See also OPEN CIRCUIT VOLTAGE SENSITIVITY.

tank circuit   a tuned circuit that continues to resonate when signals from an ACTIVE COMPONENT are cut off. The term is normally applied to the tuned circuit of a transmitter OUTPUT STAGE operating in CLASS C.

tantalum electrolytic   an ELECTROLYTIC CAPACITOR using tantalum in place of aluminium electrodes. Such capacitors can operate with low or zero polarizing voltage (see POLARIZED, sense 2), and almost dry.

tantalytic   see TANTALUM ELECTROLYTIC.

tap   see TAPPING.

tap changer or **ratio adjuster**   a device for changing a TRANSFORMER ratio. The term is usually reserved to denote a switching type of changer that can be used while the transformer is energized. An alternative to tap changing is to use a fixed ratio transformer along with a variable transformer such as a VARIAC.

tape   see MAGNETIC TAPE; PAPER TAPE.

tape bias   a high-frequency signal applied along with the recording signal to the recording head of a TAPE RECORDER in order to overcome the NONLINEAR response of the magnetic material.

tape cartridge   an enclosed pair of reels wound with MAGNETIC TAPE in the style of a video cassette. The standard tape width of quarter-inch is often used for cartridges intended for computer data backup. See MAGNETIC TAPE DRIVE.

tape cassette   a small casing containing two reels of narrow (0.125 inch) MAGNETIC TAPE, along with guide bars and a PRESSURE PAD. When the cassette is inserted into a recorder, the read/write tape head is pressed against the tape and the mechanism is enabled. On recording, the erase head is also pressed against the tape at a point just before the tape reaches the read/write head.

tape counter   an indicator of tape use in a TAPE RECORDER. At its simplest this counts the number of revolutions of the CAPSTAN spindle.

tape drive   see STREAMER.

tape equalization   filtering of signals to or from tape heads to take account of the characteristics of the head and of the tape.

tape erase   the removal of a recording from a MAGNETIC TAPE by taking the magnetic material through its HYSTERESIS cycle at progressively lower amplitudes until the tape is almost completely demagnetized.

tape guide   a smooth bar, roller, or plastic cylinder that acts to guide TAPE past a TAPE HEAD. The tape guide normally uses shoulders to prevent the tape from moving sideways. Any side movement of the tape will cause incorrect placing of tracks, leading to CROSSTALK. A tape cassette or cartridge contains some plastic tape guides, but the tape head also has its own guides.

tape head   a HEAD intended for a tape or cassette recorder for reading, writing or erase.

tape hiss or **tape noise**   the NOISE that is heard when an audio magnetic tape is replayed. The noise is concentrated in the higher audio frequencies, so that it sounds like a hiss rather than a rumble or boom. The hiss can be minimized by using a wide section of tape for recording, and moving the tape rapidly past the head. Where these solutions are not available, noise-reduction systems that rely on companding (see COMPANDER) must be used. See also DBX; DOLBY SYSTEM; RECORDING OF SOUND.

tape noise   see TAPE HISS.

tape pressure pad   a soft felt pad used to hold tape against a recording head. On high-quality tape machines, the pressure pad is not used and tape tension is adjusted to ensure that the tape is in perfect contact with the head.

taper   see POTENTIOMETER LAW.

tape recorder   a device for recording signals on MAGNETIC TAPE. The simplest types record analogue sound by passing the signal through an electromagnet, the TAPE HEAD, so that the varying amplitude of the signal is recorded as varying magnetic field applied to the steadily moving magnetic tape. A high frequency TAPE BIAS signal is also applied to the tape head so that the portion of the HYSTERESIS

curve for the magnetic material that is used is approximately straight. On replay, the tape is moved steadily at the same speed, and the same head (see replay head) can be used, though high-quality recorders use a separate head. The varying magnetism of the tape generates varying amplitudes of signal, in the windings of the head, and this signal is amplified and constitutes the audio output. A third head, the ERASE HEAD is used when recording to demagnetize the tape before recording so as to remove any trace of a previous recording.

tape recording   see RECORDING OF SOUND.

tapered feedhorn   see PYRAMIDAL HORN.

taper, potentiometer   see POTENTIOMETER LAW.

tape streamer   a DIGITAL TAPE RECORDER used for backing up computer data. A streamer uses a CARTRIDGE TAPE and can store very large amounts of data, typically twenty GB or more.

tape threading   see THREADING.

tapped-coil oscillator   see HARTLEY OSCILLATOR.

tapping or **tap**   a connection to a component that is not to a terminal at either end. RESISTORS and INDUCTORS are the most common tapped components.

tapping element   see COUPLER / MULTIPLEXER.

target   an ELECTRODE at which an ELECTRON BEAM is aimed. The electrode is used in TV CAMERA TUBES and other charge STORAGE TUBES. The target of an X-RAY TUBE is also called *anticathode*.

target voltage   **1.** the voltage between the CATHODE (sense 1) of an electron gun and the TARGET of a TV camera tube. This voltage is normally low, in the order of 10 to 30V. **2.** the voltage between the filament and the target of an X-RAY TUBE. In this case, the voltage will be very high, of the order of 100kV.

TASI   see TIME ASSIGNMENT SPEECH INTERPOLATION.

Tchebychev, Tschebycheff or **Chebisheff response**   a form of FILTER characteristic that has a steep SLOPE between BANDS, but some undulating variation in the response level in the PASSBAND. See also BUTTERWORTH FILTER. See Fig. 114.

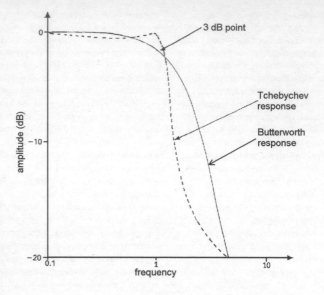

Fig. 114. **Tchebychev response**

T-coupler or **tapping element** an optical component that will combine the signals from two fibres, or split a single light source to a fibre into two outputs.

TD transmit data.

TDM see TIME DIVISION MULTIPLEXING.

TDMA see TIME DIVISION MULTIPLE ACCESS.

TE wave see TRANSVERSE ELECTRIC WAVE.

tearing the breakup of a TV image because of faulty synchronization of timebase waveforms (see RASTER). The most common form is line tearing, in which the picture seems to be torn horizontally. In colour receivers, faulty colour synchronization can cause colour tearing (see HANOVER BARS).

Teflon see PTFE.

telecommunications the transmission and reception of signals in electrical form by wire or by electromagnetic waves.

teleconferencing the use of networked (see NETWORK) computers along with video cameras (web cameras) to link people and places with both sound and vision interchange.

Telegraphone the name devised for the original form of metal wire recorder by Valdemar Poulsen, forerunner of all TAPE RECORDING systems.

telegraphy communication by signal codes along wires or by radio. For message telegraphy, MORSE CODE is still in use, but the increasing use of computers has led to the predominance of BINARY CODE systems.

teleinformatics the term covering all the non-voice telecommunications services such as FACSIMILE, TELEX, TELETEXT, etc.

telematics see TELEINFORMATICS.

telemetry the remote measurement of physical quantities by TRANSDUCERs and some form of radio transmitter. See also RADIO PILL; RADIOSONDE.

telephone a combination of MICROPHONE and EARPHONE connected through copper lines to an exchange so that connection can be made to any other telephone to allow speech communication.

telephone answering machine a machine that responds to an incoming call after a preset number of ring tones by sending out a message and then a tone and recording the answer. The machine indicates the number of calls that have been received, and in some cases also, the name of the caller.

telephone line a wire connection (see COPPER TAIL) between a telephone instrument and an exchange, or a FIBRE-OPTIC link between exchanges.

telephony any method of transmitting audio-frequency signals, either by wire or by radio.

teleprinter an electrically-operated typewriter that is controlled by digital signals. The term is now restricted to denote the obsolete type of electromechanical device that has been superseded by inkjet and laser printers.

telescopic aerial a form of rod aerial made from coaxial metal tubes that can be extended when required, or retracted for portability.

Teletex an enhanced form of TELEX that allows information exchange on a 24 hour basis, including transmission of still images.

teletext a television information service providing data consisting of digits, letters and some standardized graphics symbols. These are coded, using the digital ASCII code system, and transmitted along with the TV signal. The transmission of teletext takes place during the field-flyback period, and the signals are decoded, stored, assembled and displayed by a suitable receiver. In the UK, both BBC and ITA use identical systems, called CEEFAX and ORACLE respectively.

teletypewriter or **teletype** an obsolete form of electric typewriter that can send and receive coded signals. See also EMAIL; FACSIMILE; TELEX; TEXTING.

television (TV) a method of transmitting sound and animated vision signals. The TELEVISION CAMERA uses light-sensitive CAMERA TUBES or CCD devices, on the face of which the image is projected by lenses. The sensors are scanned, so that data on brightness (and colour) is extracted serially to form the VIDEO SIGNAL. In the older analogue system, BLANKING and SYNCHRONIZING PULSES are added, and the modulated colour SUBCARRIER signals, forming a COMPOSITE video signal. The sound signals from the microphones are separately amplified. The two sets of signals are modulated onto separate UHF carriers, with the SOUND CARRIER 6MHz (in the UK) above the vision carrier frequency, and frequency modulated. See also COLOUR TV; DIGITAL TELEVISION; TELEVISION RECEIVER.

television camera a camera whose input is an optical image and whose output is a VIDEO waveform. The camera consists of an optical system, CAMERA TUBES or CCD sensors, and PREAMPLIFIER stages. For a colour camera using VIDICONs, at least three pickup tubes will be used, and the optical system is very elaborate. It must consist of a main lens, often of the zoom variety, in which the image path is split into as many sections as there are camera tubes, so that each tube has an image focused on its face. By using dichroic prisms or mirrors, these images will be in the primary colours of blue, red and green – some designs use a black/white image also.

The electron beams of the vidicons are deflected by TIMEBASE signals, all of which are synchronized to a master generator in a camera control unit, often separate from the camera. BLANKING pulses are used to suppress the output from the vidicons during the FLYBACK time of the timebase. The separate video signals are each amplified in a preamplifier, and any frequency corrections and corrections for other distortions such as aperture distortion are made at this point.

Miniature cameras and camcorders inevitably use a CCD form of sensor which can be manufactured in colour-sensitive form as a filtered CCD. A filtered CCD has a colour filter applied to each sensor in a set of four, and each set constitutes a PIXEL. In a set, one cell will be filtered blue, one red and two green. This is done to match the higher sensitivity of the human eye to green light. The output signals from the CCD array constitute a video signal.

The convention is that the video waveforms are amplified to a PEAK-TO-PEAK AMPLITUDE of 1V. The video signals are then transmitted from a low output impedance current amplifier through a cable to the camera control unit. In this unit, further correction is carried out, sync signals are added, and the colour signals are processed. This consists of forming a LUMINANCE signal (black/white) from the colour signals if no separate luminance signal has been generated. The colour signals, in pairs, are then mixed to form the U and V signals of the PAL system, and these signals are modulated on to SUBCARRIERS, using in-phase and quadrature phase modulators. The COLOUR BURST of subcarrier frequency is added to the BACK PORCH of the line sync pulse, and the modulated subcarrier signals are added to the video signal, with the CARRIER (sense 1) itself suppressed.

television receiver a device containing circuitry for receiving TV signals and producing an image. The older analogue receiver follows the pattern of a SUPERHETERODYNE RECEIVER system, and a wideband IF signal is obtained, containing both video and sound signals. The vision demodulator produces the main LUMINANCE signal, and allows the colour signals (modulated on to a SUBCARRIER) and the INTERCARRIER SOUND signals to be separated off. The sound signal is separately amplified, demodulated (see DEMODULATION) and passed to the audio stages. The COLOUR BURST is used to synchronize a local colour oscillator, and the output of this is used in two synchronous detectors (see SYNCHRONOUS DEMODULATION) to obtain the two COLOUR DIFFERENCE SIGNALS. These signals are then mixed with the luminance signal in the correct proportions to recover the separate red, green and blue signals for the guns of the colour cathode-ray tube.

Picture synchronization is achieved by separating off the mixed sync pulses from the luminance signal in a sync separator that also separates the sync pulses from each other. These pulses are used to synchronize the TIMEBASE circuits that generate the linear sweep (ramp) currents for the deflection coils. The line sweep current must be switched off rapidly to achieve a fast flyback, and the voltage that is produced by this rapid change of current in the line output transformer is stepped up in a WINDING, rectified by a VOLTAGE MULTIPLIER, and used to provide the accelerating voltage (EHT) for the picture tube. See also DIGITAL TELEVISION.

telex a system of telegraphy for digitally coded signals. Telex users can type or receive messages on a TELEPRINTER, and adaptors can be used to allow computers to be linked to the network.

temperature comparative hotness of any object on a scale determined from a zero point and a 100° point. See also KELVIN.

temperature coefficient a measure of the effect of changing temperature on a physical quantity. The coefficient is defined as the fractional change of quantity per unit temperature change. The temperature coefficient may be positive (increasing quantity for increasing temperature) or negative (decreasing quantity for increasing temperature). The most important temperature coefficients are of RESISTIVITY (or resistance) and of CAPACITANCE. Most OHMIC CONDUCTORs have a positive temperature coefficient of resistivity or resistance, semiconductors generally have a negative coefficient. Either PTC or NTC capacitors can be obtained, and oscillator circuits often use a mixture of capacitor types in order to balance out the effect of temperature changes on the tuned circuit.

temperature-compensated diode a form of ZENER DIODE with very low TEMPERATURE COEFFICIENT of regulated voltage.

temperature compensation capacitor a low PERMITTIVITY capacitor with a NEGATIVE TEMPERATURE COEFFICIENT intended to be used along with a main capacitor with a POSITIVE TEMPERATURE COEFFICIENT so that the combination has the desired capacitance value with almost zero temperature coefficient.

temperature cycling   repeated rising and falling temperatures, often a way of revealing weakness in a circuit.

temperature gradient   a measure of distribution of TEMPERATURE through a THERMAL CONDUCTOR in terms of degrees Celsius per unit length of heat path.

temperature monitoring   the reading of temperatures within a computer or other equipment, usually to ensure automatic shutdown in the event of overheating.

temperature sensing   the detection of temperature using the devices as THERMOCOUPLES, RESISTANCE THERMOMETERS, PYROELECTRIC films, and THERMISTORS.

tempest   electromagnetic radiation from a computer system, that can be picked up and recorded illegally on another nearby system.

temporal aliasing   a visual effect seen only in interlaced (see INTERLACING) RASTERS which causes flickering or line crawling effects.

temporal code   see SERIAL CODE.

temporal masking   the effect in which a sound of high amplitude will mask sounds immediately preceding it or immediately following in time.

temporal transposition   a method of scrambling (see SCRAMBLER) voice signals in DIGITAL format by dividing the datastream into blocks which are time reversed and then added together and reconverted to analogue form.

TEM wave   see TRANSVERSE ELECTROMAGNETIC WAVE.

tension servo   a SERVOMOTOR used in a tape drive system to provide constant tension in the tape.

tera-   a prefix denoting 10^{12}, a million million. In computing, the nearest powers of two are used, in this example 2^{40}.

terabyte or **TB** or **Tbyte**   a unit of computer data storage equal to 2^{40} bytes.

terminal   **1.** a place to which leads can be attached into or out from a CIRCUIT. **2.** the remote keyboard and display unit of a computer system.

terminal block   a set of connectors for cables that allow the connections to be changed.

terminal device   see TERMINAL (sense 2).

terminal impedance or **terminating impedance**   the IMPEDANCE at the end of a TRANSMISSION LINE.

termination   a MATCHING load for a TRANSMISSION LINE that prevents reflections.

ternary code   any code that uses three levels to code DIGITAL DATA.

terrestrial digital broadcasting   the transmission of DIGITAL sound and television from existing land-based TRANSMITTING AERIALS, using the COFDM method of digital modulation. The digital radio uses the older band 3 frequencies, but digital television is multiplexed onto UHF channels.

tertiary winding   an additional WINDING on a TRANSFORMER. The tertiary winding may be used to supply a FEEDBACK signal, to provide a voltage level that differs from that on the secondary winding, to be used with DC flowing to control saturation of the core (see SATURABLE TRANSFORMER), or to ensure insulation. For example, a well-insulated tertiary winding is used on a transformer for an oscilloscope to supply the heater voltage for the CATHODE-RAY TUBE, because the cathode may be operating at a large negative voltage. A tertiary winding that is electrically connected to another winding is often called an OVERWIND. See also PRIMARY WINDING.

test mode   the use of AUTOMATIC TEST EQUIPMENT to compare each test value with standard parameters. See also LEARN MODE; SIGNATURE PROFILE.

test pattern   a definition and shading pattern used to check a TELEVISION system. The chart contains fine close-spaced lines and shaded blocks that should be distinguishable from each other, even by domestic TELEVISION RECEIVERS.

test point   a terminal to which a measuring instrument can be attached to check the operation of a circuit.

test program   built-in SOFTWARE that can be run as an aid to fault diagnosis for equipment controlled by a MICROPROCESSOR.

test tape a videotape produced by a manufacturer in order to set up the tape ALIGNMENT and drive of machines undergoing servicing.

tetravalent (of an element) having four electrons in its outermost shell, such as silicon or germanium.

tetrode see THERMIONIC VALVE.

tetrode thyristor a form of THYRISTOR with two gates that allows current to be switched on or off.

tetrode transistor a form of FET designed to operate at frequencies of 1 GHz upwards using a short CHANNEL (sense 2) with two GATE (sense 1) electrodes, each capable of controlling SOURCE to DRAIN current. The second gate may be used for gain control or to allow operation as a MIXER.

text generator a circuit that generates a TV image of text using data stored in memory.

texting the sending and receiving of short text messages (short message service or SMS) using MOBILE PHONES.

TFT thin-film transistor, a form of construction, particularly for LCD screen displays in which a transistor is formed on a thin substrate along with another device such as an LCD cell.

TFT screen a form of large screen LCD display in which each PIXEL is controlled by a THIN FILM TRANSISTOR.

T fuse or **time-lag fuse** or **slo-blo fuse** a fuse that will rupture in 100 milliseconds for a tenfold overload and in about 20 seconds for a twofold overload.

THD see TOTAL HARMONIC DISTORTION.

theremin a pioneering form of electronic musical instrument using an OSCILLATOR whose frequency depended on STRAY CAPACITANCE between a metal plate and the hands of the user.

thermal breakdown the complete loss of correct action of a component due to overheating. The overheating may in turn be caused by THERMAL RUNAWAY.

thermal conductivity a quantity that measures the ability of a material to conduct heat through its bulk. The thermal conductivity coefficient for a material is defined as the quantity of heat (expressed in watts) conducted per unit temperature difference multiplied by the length per unit area of cross section of the sample. The coefficient is independent of sample size and shape. See also THERMAL RESISTANCE.

thermal conductor a material that conducts heat relatively easily, such as a metal.

thermal EMF the EMF at a junction of two metals that varies with temperature.

thermal imaging the process of producing an image of an object from its heat radiation. Thermal imaging cameras use TV techniques with infra-red sensitive CAMERA TUBES. The system is used for military purposes and in crime prevention and detection. It is also applicable to medicine, because tumour cells are often at a slightly higher temperature than healthy tissue, and show up differently on the thermal display.

thermal instrument any type of measuring instrument that makes use of heating. See HOT-WIRE.

thermal limit circuit a circuit that will limit the current in a device or circuit when the temperature becomes too high.

thermal noise or **Johnson noise** the electrical NOISE signal caused by the thermal agitation of current CARRIERS (sense 1). In any conductor, the current carriers vibrate as well as moving along a current path. The vibration constitutes a noise signal, and its amplitude depends on the square root of (absolute) temperature. If very low noise is required an amplifier may have to be operated at a very low temperature.

thermal paper printing paper that discolours on heating. Thermal paper was at one time used by some types of printers because it allows silent printing.

thermal protection circuitry, often included within an IC, to protect against excess temperatures. see also FOLDBACK PROTECTION.

thermal relay a form of RELAY triggered by temperature, usually for protection against overheating.

thermal resistance a measure of the resistance to heat flow. The practical units used in electronics are of degrees Celsius per watt, and the measurement expresses the change of temperature caused by the dissipation of each watt of power. The thermal resistance of a collector JUNCTION (sense 2) to the case of a transistor is a very important PARAMETER of a power transistor, because it decides at what maximum power level the transistor can be used.

thermal runaway or **runaway** the loss of control of temperature. If the temperature of a transistor increases to such an extent that the base current is no longer able to control collector current, the current and temperature will increase until the junctions are destroyed. Thermal runaway is very rare with modern silicon transistors correctly used.

thermal shock a testing method in which test temperatures change rapidly in each direction.

thermal stability ability of a CIRCUIT to function correctly at a wide range of temperature levels.

thermal switch a form of switch that opens at high temperatures to provide protection from excessive power dissipation. A similar device can be used on a freezer to warn that temperatures are dangerously high.

thermal transducer any form of TRANSDUCER that converts heat energy to electrical energy or vice versa.

thermionic (of any device) using ELECTRONS emitted from a hot surface into a vacuum.

thermionic cathode a hot electron-emitting surface. This may be a tungsten or tungsten/thorium wire that is heated to temperatures of around 2,500K by passing direct current through it. A cathode of this type is called directly-heated, i.e. a FILAMENT.

Indirectly heated cathodes are used in CATHODE-RAY TUBES, CAMERA TUBES, thermionic MICROWAVE devices, and some small VACUUM VALVES. These use cathodes that are hollow nickel tubes coated with a mixture of oxides of barium, strontium and calcium. This material emits electrons copiously at comparatively low temperatures, around 1,000K. The cathode is heated by an insulated molybdenum spiral filament inside the nickel tube. The disadvantage of using such materials is that the cathode material is easily damaged, particularly by sparking or by the electrostatic removal of the coating in large fields, and it tends to liberate gas when used for high currents. For these reasons, transmitting valves use tungsten or thoriated tungsten filaments.

thermionic emission the release of ELECTRONS from hot filaments or cathodes into a vacuum.

thermionic valve (UK) or **vacuum tube (US)** an evacuated tube that contains a THERMIONIC CATHODE and other ELECTRODEs. The most common form of valve nowadays is the TRIODE or transmitter valve, which is the thermionic equivalent of a BIPOLAR JUNCTION TRANSISTOR. This uses a directly heated FILAMENT that is surrounded by a framework carrying a metal spiral, the control grid. In a triode, this in turn is surrounded by a metal cylinder, the ANODE (*plate* in the US). For high-power valves, the anode is the exterior casing of the valve and will be finned on the outside, or attached to a water jacket for cooling.

Small valves, now obsolete but still obtainable, contain the anode and other electrodes inside a glass tube, the *envelope*. The valve that uses one grid is a triode, adding another grid between the first grid (control grid) and the anode makes the valve a tetrode, and the type with a third grid is a pentode. The cathode is heated to provide electrons, and the anode is connected to a high voltage, typically 300 volts. The flow of electrons is controlled by the control grid voltage, and a sufficiently negative voltage on this electrode will cut off the electron stream. In transmitting use higher anode voltages are used and the grid voltage is often swung between negative and positive voltage values relative to the cathode, so that current will flow to the grid during the positive parts of the cycle.

thermistor a non-ohmic resistor (see OHMIC). Thermistors are made from semiconducting materials, and most types have very large NEGATIVE TEMPERATURE COEFFICIENTS. They are used for temperature measurement, temperature warning devices, and also for temperature compensation. Thermistors are also used in the FEEDBACK circuits of R-C OSCILLATORS to stabilize amplitude of oscillation by increasing NEGATIVE FEEDBACK when the amplitude of oscillation becomes too great.

thermoammeter a current METER that uses the heating effect of current. The thermoammeter uses either the HOT-WIRE METER principle, or a THERMOCOUPLE heated by current through a strip of resistive material. Thermoammeters are imprecise, but are often the only way of measuring a radio-frequency current. They can also be calibrated in terms of true RMS values.

thermocouple a JUNCTION (sense 3) between two different metals. Two thermocouples connected in series will generate a voltage if the junctions are at different temperatures. The voltages are of millivolt level, but comparatively large currents can be passed. Thermocouples are used extensively for measuring temperature because the sensor (junction) can be remote from the meter at which the reading is taken. See also THERMOELECTRIC EFFECTS.

thermoelectric effects a set of discoveries by Thomas Seebeck (1770–1831), Jean Peltier (1785–1845) and Lord Kelvin (1824–1907). The *Seebeck effect* is the action of the THERMOCOUPLE. The *Peltier effect* is the opposite – the heating of one junction and the cooling of the other when current is forced to flow through two junctions. Using metal/semiconductor junctions, large temperature changes can be obtained, so that refrigeration by Peltier junction is possible. The *Kelvin effect* is a voltage in a

single conductor caused by temperature differences that affect the electron ENERGY BANDS.

thermography a form of THERMAL IMAGING that produces a permanent pattern on paper or on film.

thermojunction a single junction of a THERMOCOUPLE. The favourite pairs of materials for junctions include copper and constantan, iron and constantan, platinum and rhodium.

thermometer an instrument for measuring TEMPERATURE.

thermometry the science and practice of temperature measurement.

thermopile a set of THERMOCOUPLES wired in series or in series-parallel to form a source of EMF comparable to that of a chemical battery.

thermosphere the part of the upper atmosphere in which temperature *increases* with increasing altitude.

thermostat a temperature-operated SWITCH. The usual thermostat principle uses a BIMETALLIC STRIP carrying a switch contact. This device, however, suffers from considerable HYSTERESIS that limits its usefulness as a method of maintaining a constant temperature. The simple thermostat is now being superseded by the use of THERMISTORS, often as part of a MICROPROCESSOR system.

thermostat hysteresis the HYSTERESIS of a BIMETALLIC THERMOSTAT, causing the contacts to open at higher than the set temperature and to close at a lower temperature than the set temperature. This causes temperature fluctuations in a room controlled by this type of thermostat.

Thevenin's theorem a useful method of analyzing linear resistance networks. Thevenin's theorem states that any two-terminal LINEAR NETWORK that contains sources of voltage (DC or signal) can be represented by a single voltage source and a series RESISTANCE. The use of Thevenin's theorem therefore allows an EQUIVALENT CIRCUIT to be drawn up for any linear network. See also NORTON'S THEOREM.

thick ethernet   a NETWORK (sense 2) connecting system that uses COAXIAL CABLE of 1 cm diameter. This cable permits efficient networking up to distances of about 1 kilometre.

thick-film circuit or **hybrid circuit**   a type of miniature PRINTED CIRCUIT BOARD, but with PASSIVE COMPONENTS formed in the connections. The circuit is formed by photolithographic techniques, and uses metal films for connections and for resistors, with capacitors formed from metal and oxide layers. INTEGRATED CIRCUITS can be bonded to the thick-film circuit by compression welding to bonding pads. Compare THIN-FILM CIRCUIT.

thin ethernet   a NETWORK (sense 2) connecting system that uses COAXIAL CABLE of 0.5 cm diameter. This cable permits efficient networking up to distances of about 300 metres.

thin-film circuit   a form of circuit that uses sputtered (see SPUTTERING) or vacuum-deposited films rather than thick films. Compare THICK-FILM CIRCUIT.

thin-film thermo-electric sensor   a set of SEMICONDUCTOR thin-film DIODES forming a junction that delivers a DC voltage output proportional to the RF power striking the sensor.

thin-film transistor   see TFT.

third-harmonic distortion   a form of nonlinear distortion of a sine wave that introduces the third harmonic of the sine wave. Third-harmonic distortion is particularly undesirable in audio equipment because the effect is to make sounds unpleasantly shrill.

third order intercept   the point on a graph of power output plotted against power input for an amplifier where the extrapolated linear line, whose slope is the gain, intersects with the line for the third order harmonic.

Thomson effect   the EMF, of the order of $87\mu V/°C$, that is set up when there is a temperature difference between the ends of a metal strip.

thoriated tungsten   a thorium-tungsten alloy material, used for directly-heated CATHODES (sense 1) in transmitting valves.

The presence of thorium allows electron EMISSION at considerably lower temperatures than tungsten alone. When a thoriated tungsten cathode starts to lose emission, it can often be regenerated by running the FILAMENT for a short time at a higher temperature than normal, so allowing more thorium to diffuse to the surface.

thrashing   excessive HARD DRIVE activity when a large number of short data items are being retrieved from different parts of the disk.

threading or **lacing**   the initial action of a VIDEO CASSETTE RECORDER pulling tape out of the cassette and winding it around the DRUM (sense 1) so as to replay or record the tape. Also applied to the manual threading of reel-to-reel tape in the older type of tape recorder.

three-beam projector   an image projector for large-screen displays that uses three scanning coloured beams to project images from a computer or a VIDEO CASSETTE RECORDER. The beams may be derived from quartz-halogen lamps or LASERS.

3dB frequency or **break frequency** or **transition frequency**   the frequency at which the GAIN of an amplifier, or the response of filter, is 3dB down (often written as −3dB) from the average MIDBAND GAIN. This can be at either the low end of the frequency response (*lower 3dB point*) or the high end (*upper 3dB point*). See Fig. 115.

three-head machine   an audio TAPE RECORDER with separate heads for the three functions of record, replay, and erase.

three key system   a variant of the PUBLIC KEY system that uses two secret codes, primary and secondary, and a third (public) key, providing a very high degree of security.

three-phase distribution   see THREE-PHASE SUPPLY.

three-phase rectifier   a set of rectifiers arranged to produce a rectified output from a three-phase input, usually with lower ripple (and at higher frequency) than is possible from a two-phase supply.

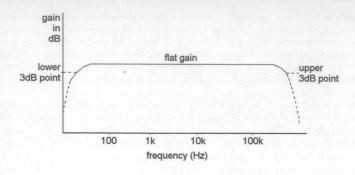

Fig. 115. **3dB frequency**

three-phase supply or **three-phase distribution** a supply of AC along three separate lines, with 120° between the voltage phases of any two lines.

three-pin plug a mains plug with three pins, one of which is an EARTH contact, using the other two for live and NEUTRAL (sense 3) (in the UK) or for live supplies balanced around earth (in other countries).

three-state logic or **tri-state logic** or **three-state control** a logic circuit arrangement for INTEGRATED CIRCUITS. In a three-state logic terminal, the voltage may be at logic 0, logic 1, or FLOATING. In the floating state, the voltage may be changed by external voltages without any damage to the internal circuits of the chip. The floating state is the third state of the title.

threshold the point at which a cause just produces an effect. The threshold frequency for the PHOTOELECTRIC EFFECT is the light frequency for which EMISSION can just be detected. The THRESHOLD VOLTAGE for a conducting device is the voltage at which the device just starts to pass current. The threshold signal for a receiver with SQUELCH is the signal that overcomes the squelch and thus enables the audio section of the receiver.

threshold decoding a digital DECODING system that uses a LOOK-UP TABLE in memory for all correctable error patterns and the corresponding SYNDROMES. Non-correctable errors are beyond the

threshold of the table, but some may still be detectable.

threshold extension a technique that allows the CARRIER TO NOISE RATIO of FM to be reduced to a very low level by lowering the detection bandwidth without reducing signal energy.

threshold frequency, light see LIGHT THRESHOLD FREQUENCY.

threshold of hearing the minimum audible intensity of sound for an average ear; the threshold is not a fixed amount but varies with frequency of sound and from one ear to another.

threshold voltage a voltage level below which an input has no effect on the system.

through-scan one form of use of an OPTICAL BEAM PROXIMITY DETECTOR in which the light source is aimed at the receiver and will respond if the beam is interrupted. See also RETROFLECTIVE SCAN; DIFFUSE SCAN PHOTO DETECTOR.

throw the number of different contact positions or ways that a SWITCH can make. See also POLE (sense 3).

thyratron a GAS-FILLED TUBE that acts as a form of RELAY, conducting when triggered by a pulse. Thyratrons have been largely replaced by their semiconductor equivalent, the THYRISTOR.

thyristor or **silicon-controlled rectifier (SCR)** a SEMICONDUCTOR pnpn rectifying device. The thyristor has three electrodes, ANODE (sense 2), CATHODE (sense 2) and

GATE (sense 1). A voltage that can be in either polarity is applied between the anode and the cathode. Current will flow between the anode and the cathode only when the anode is positive with respect to the cathode, and when the gate has been triggered. The TRIGGER pulse is applied to the gate at the time when the anode is positive. The effect of the trigger pulse is to make the device conduct heavily. Conduction then continues until the anode voltage drops to almost the cathode voltage level, or the current falls to a very low value. Thyristors have almost completely replaced THYRATRONS for most purposes.

thyristor regulator   a voltage controller circuit that acts to control the AC supply to a power supply so that it can control the output voltage. See also BURST FIRING; PHASE CONTROL.

tight coupled   (of a pair of coupled resonant circuits) whose coupling is tight, see TIGHT COUPLING. Contrast LOOSE COUPLED.

tight coupling   a form of TUNED TRANSFORMER coupling in which the COUPLING COEFFICIENT is large so that a large fraction of the input signal is transferred to the output. A tight coupling is efficient in terms of signal transfer and can provide optimum signal transfer conditions if the coupling is critical (see CRITICAL COUPLING). If the coupling exceeds the critical value then OVERCOUPLING will occur, causing the bandwidth to increase considerably and the shape of the transfer characteristic (the graph of output plotted against input) to develop a trough between two peaks. Compare LOOSE COUPLING.

tile   a set of PIXELS forming a small image that is repeated in a pattern.

tilt angle   see BORESIGHT ERROR.

tilting head drum   a mechanism devised by JVC of tilting the head DRUM (sense 1) of a VIDEO CASSETTE RECORDER in order to achieve good still-frame pictures.

tilt switch   a switch, usually containing mercury, that will make contacts when the body of the switch is tilted.

time assignment speech interpolation or **TASI**   a digital technique that assigns a transmission channel to the user only when needed, so increasing total traffic capacity of a network.

timebase   a CIRCUIT that produces a WAVEFORM for ELECTRON BEAM deflection. The most common type is the linear RAMP (or sweep) circuit that produces a SAWTOOTH WAVEFORM. Timebase generators use a combination of a SQUARE WAVE generator and an INTEGRATOR to produce the linear ramp (the sweep), and some type of switch circuit to produce a rapid FLYBACK. By separating the square wave generator portion from the integrator, it is possible to control the frequency and the slope of the timebase sweep separately. The square-wave generator may be a MONOSTABLE, in which case the timebase is a triggered one, producing a sweep voltage only when a TRIGGER PULSE arrives.

timebase corrector   a system used in a DIGITAL TAPE RECORDER to eliminate WOW and FLUTTER by reading the data from the tape into a MEMORY from which it is read as a constant rate.

timebase, Miller   see MILLER TIMEBASE.

timecode   1. a binary coded form of timing of the hours, minutes and FRAMES (sense 1) on a tape used by a CAMCORDER to assist postproduction editing. 2. a MIDI protocol that is used to keep two devices correctly synchronized.

time constant   a measure of the time required to change the VOLTAGE across a CAPACITOR or INDUCTOR. For a capacitor-resistor circuit, the time constant is given (in seconds) by $C \times R$, where C is in farads and R in ohms. For an inductor-resistor circuit, the time constant is L/R, with L in henries and R in ohms. The time that is obtained from these calculations is the time needed for the voltage across the capacitor or the current through an inductor to decrease to $1/e$ or 36.8% of the starting value. Time constant values are particularly useful in estimating the effect of a CR or LR network on a square wave.

time delay or **time lag** the time between a signal being applied to an INPUT (sense 2) and appearing at the output of a CIRCUIT.

time delay stereo an illusion of STEREO sound that occurs when there is a time difference of two milliseconds or more between sounds to left and right loudspeakers.

time-delay switch a SWITCH that operates after a specified time delay. In equipment that makes use of indirectly-heated CATHODES (sense 1), a time-delay switch is often used to ensure that no high voltage is applied until the cathode has warmed up.

time discriminator a demodulator for pulse-time modulated signals. The time discriminator generates a signal whose amplitude is proportional to the time between pulses. A simple form of time discriminator is a TIMEBASE that is triggered by one pulse and terminated by the next.

time division multiple access or **TDMA** a DIGITAL technique for MULTIPLEXING that uses DATA PACKETS. Contrast FREQUENCY DIVISION MULTIPLE ACCESS.

time division multiplex a method of using the entire bandwidth of a SATELLITE broadcast for signals, usually digitally coded, so that a portion of coded signal is transmitted for each channel in turn. At the receiver the coded DATA PACKETS are reassembled for the channel that is to be used.

time-division multiplexer a system by which a cable or radio channel may be shared by several signals. Each signal is sampled and the sample amplitudes are transmitted in sequence. At the receiver, the same rate of sampling has to be used to reconstitute the signals correctly. SYNCHRONIZING PULSES can be transmitted at intervals to keep the transmitter and the receiver in step.

time domain the use of time as the independent variable of a graph, plotted on the x-axis.

time-domain analysis analysis of the behaviour of a CIRCUIT from its graph of AMPLITUDE plotted against FREQUENCY.

time expansion the expansion of time compressed signals by writing the samples in bursts into memory at the incoming clock rate but reading out at the standard digital audio sampling rate. The average rates must be equal if the memory is not to be overloaded.

time hysteresis a method of TEMPERATURE SENSING used in systems controlled by a MICROPROCESSOR in which temperature is sensed at intervals and a change is registered only if the same direction of temperature change is registered twice consecutively. This avoids excessive switching of heating on and off due to minor fluctuations around the sensor.

time invariant (of a network or system) producing a particular response for an input at one time and an identical response for the same input at another time.

time lag see TIME DELAY.

time-lag fuse see M FUSE.

time multiplexing the use of a single CARRIER (sense 1) to carry several transmissions by allocating a channel to each carrier in turn for brief intervals. A carrier can also carry two simultaneous analogue transmissions if one is AM and the other FM.

timeout a cancellation action that will take place if the user waits too long to respond to a prompt.

time period the time of one OSCILLATION, mechanical or electrical.

timer circuit or **timer** a circuit using an accurate CLOCK combined with a PULSE COUNTER with provision for switching on or off, used for measuring time intervals.

time sharing the sharing of the use of a computer among several users. By interleaving the signals to and from the main computer, each user can be served with almost unnoticeable time delays. The system becomes unworkable if each user simultaneously needs the full speed of the computer.

time-slicing a method of allocating the use of a MICROPROCESSOR to several actions. This involves switching the microprocessor from one program to another at short intervals, particularly when the microprocessor would otherwise be idling.

time switch a form of clock, either electromechanical or DIGITAL quartz, that will switch circuits on or off.

time to trip the circuit-breaking time for a RELAY. This is the time between activating the coil (or deactivating it) and breaking the circuit that is operated by the relay.

timing diagram display or **timing domain analysis** a form of display on the LOGIC ANALYZER that shows the various logic levels for each line displayed in sequence against the time axis running from left to right.

timing domain analysis see TIMING DIAGRAM DISPLAY.

timing jitter see JITTER.

tin/lead solder the conventional SOLDER alloy with the melting point of 180°C.

tinning the application of a thin film of SOLDER to a metal surface.

TIP terminal interface processor.

tizziness a buzzing effect on high frequency sounds, often due to slew rate limiting in an audio amplifier.

T-junction see HYBRID JUNCTION.

TM wave see TRANSVERSE MAGNETIC WAVE.

T-MOS a form of power MOSFET configuration in which the gate is built up over the level of the SOURCE and DRAIN.

toggle mode a mode of using a FLIP-FLOP in which the output state changes for each clock pulse received.

toggle output the action of switching an output on or off, or from one signal to another.

toggle switch the conventional form of on/off SWITCH that is spring loaded to snap to either position.

toggling the switching of STATE, as of a FLIP-FLOP in which each pulse at the input causes the OUTPUT to change state. A toggling circuit is a divide-by-two COUNTER, because two complete pulses at the input produce one complete pulse at the output. A series of connected toggling circuits may be used to provide divide-by 4, 8, 16, and so on, counters.

token a special DATA PACKET of a specific bit pattern used as the signal in a token ring network.

token passing the interception of a TOKEN on a NETWORK (sense 2) by a NODE (sense 1). The node will replace the token with its own data for transmission and when the data reaches its destination it is removed and a FLAG BIT is added to the DATA PACKET to indicate the reception. The packet is then returned to the sender when the flag indicates receipt, and the token is restored.

token-ring network a NETWORK (sense 2) in which a set of BITS, the *token*, circulates. Any message following the token will be transmitted throughout the system.

tolerance the amount of variation about a nominal value. Most passive components in electronic circuits are specified to quite wide tolerances, up to 20%. The tolerance of value for electrolytic capacitors can be as high as 50% of nominal value, and semiconductors also have very large tolerance values.

The problem is dealt with in analogue circuits by using NEGATIVE FEEDBACK circuits in which only a few components in the FEEDBACK LOOP need be of close tolerance. In digital circuits, tolerances have very little effect on the action of a correctly designed circuit.

tolerance band a silver or gold band or spot used on a resistor or capacitor to denote tolerance percentage.

toluene a cleaning solvent used particularly for switches and for removing adhesives, which produces toxic fumes.

tone arm the arm that holds and guides the PICKUP of a gramophone for vinyl discs. The design of a tone arm is complicated by conflicting requirements, among them the need to hold the pickup head rigidly, yet allow free movement to follow the record track, with no vibrational resonance that will cause peaks in the response.

tone burst a FUNCTION GENERATOR output that consists of a SINE WAVE modulated with a parabolic envelope and generated in bursts. This is used to test full bandwidth audio systems or circuits where RESONANCES are suspected.

tone control a control over the FREQUENCY RESPONSE of an audio AMPLIFIER. Simple radio receivers sometimes incorporate a treble cut control, but good quality sound reproduction demands a more comprehensive system of tone controls. These should include the actions of boosting or cutting BASS response, with a choice of the CROSS-OVER (sense 2), and a similar variable boost or cut for TREBLE with a choice of crossover. See ACTIVE TONE CONTROL; BAXANDALL TONE CONTROL; CLAPHAM JUNCTION TONE CONTROL; PARAMETRIC CONTROL; PASSIVE TONE CONTROL; SLOPE CONTROL.

TO package a form of packaging for small transistors distinguished by serial numbers or names.

topology the geometric design of a NETWORK (sense 2) such as bus, ring, star, etc.

toroidal inductor or **toroidal core inductor** an INDUCTOR wound around a ring-shaped core. The toroidal shape of MAGNETIC CORE (sense 1) is particularly efficient because it is easy to ensure that all of its flux passes through the coils that are wound round it. Now that machines for winding toroidal coils are widely available, toroidal transformers are displacing the older LAMINATED CORE type.

toroidal transformer a transformer wound on a toroidal core, providing high efficiency and good coupling between primary and secondary.

total access time for a computer, the time between a request for data from the HARD DRIVE and delivery of the data.

total emission the total electron current from a CATHODE (sense 1) to all forms of GRID or ANODE in a THERMIONIC VALVE.

total harmonic distortion (THD) the sum of the ROOT MEAN SQUARE (sense 2) amplitudes of all HARMONICS that are generated by an amplifier whose input is a pure sine wave. The THD is usually expressed as a percentage, and quoted for full rated power, or shown as a graph plotted against power. For ordinary

purposes, a THD of up to 10% is tolerated. Hi-fi sound systems deal with THD amounts in the region of 0.1% or less.

total internal reflection reflection of light that is passing from a dense optical material (such as glass) to a less optically dense material (such as air). If the angle between the ray in the glass and the glass surface is too small, the beam will be reflected, not refracted. See also REFRACTION.

totem-pole circuit see LIN CIRCUIT.

touch control a form of SWITCH that is operated by touching. The switch contains contact areas, and touching with the finger makes a high resistance connection that triggers a TRANSISTOR circuit and operates a THYRISTOR. The touch portion of the circuit must be completely isolated from the thyristor circuit. Some touch switches ensure safe use by making use of the capacitance between an insulated contact and the body of the user.

touch pad an INPUT (sense 2) device that uses switch contacts placed under a plastic pad that may be inscribed with symbols.

touch screen or **active picture technology** a system of making computer inputs without using the KEYBOARD. When a finger interrupts a pair of infra-red beams that cross the SCREEN, the position of the finger can be digitized (see DIGITIZE) into X and Y COORDINATE numbers, and used to launch appropriate software.

touch tone a method of telephone dialling that uses combinations of tones to represent each digit. See also PULSE DIALLING.

TPDF see TRIANGULAR PROBABILITY DENSITY FUNCTION.

T pulse a form of INSERTION TEST SIGNAL for testing frequency response of the TV system.

TR switch see TRANSMIT/RECEIVE SWITCH.

TR/ATR or **TR switch** see TRANSMIT-RECEIVE SWITCH.

trace the shape drawn by the SPOT (sense 1) of light on the face of a CATHODE-RAY TUBE.

track   a conducting line on a PRINTED-CIRCUIT BOARD or a line of stored information on a TAPE or a DISC.

track at once   a mode of RECORDING a CD-R or CD-RW disc so that the SESSION is written as a set of TRACKs, each a complete entity. Contrast DISC AT ONCE.

trackball   a form of controller initially used for radar and now common on computer systems. The trackball is like an inverted mouse with a large ball moved with the palm of the hand to alter the screen cursor position.

track crossover   crossing of two circuit lines on a PRINTED CIRCUIT BOARD without making contact between them, carried out by using the opposite surface of the board to create a loop. See also VIA.

tracking   1. the maintenance of a fixed relationship between quantities. 2. in a SUPERHETERODYNE RECEIVER, the maintenance of correct tuning in the RF and oscillator circuits, so that the difference between their frequencies is constant, see also GANGED CIRCUITS. 3. the locking of a RADAR beam onto a target which will continue to follow that target to the extremes of its range until reset. 4. In a GRAMOPHONE transcriptor for vinyl discs, the arrangement of the TONE ARM so that the stylus is always correctly located in the groove of the disc. 5. the formation of conducting tracks that will cause sparking on an insulator.

tracking coils   the coils that are used to actuate the movement of the OPTICAL PICKUP UNIT of a CD player/recorder so that the beam is exactly over the correct track.

tracking control   an adjustment for a VIDEO CASSETTE RECORDER that ensures that the HEADs will be perfectly aligned with the magnetic tracks on the tape.

tracking error   failure to follow a track correctly, applying to a VIDEO CASSETTE RECORDER, CD or DVD player.

tracking filter   an ACTIVE FILTER with a narrow band whose CENTRE FREQUENCY can be made to track the DEVIATION (sense 2) of an FM CARRIER (sense 1).

tracking range   see HOLD RANGE.

tracking servo   the SERVO system in an OPTICAL PICKUP UNIT for a CD or DVD player that enables the LASER beam to follow a track precisely.

tracking weight   see PLAYING WEIGHT.

track skipping   a fault of CD and DVD players in which the LASER BEAM moves unintentionally from one TRACK to another, often caused by dirt on the surface of the disc.

track-to-track access time   the time, measured in MILLISECONDS, needed to move the READ/WRITE HEAD of a HARD DRIVE from one TRACK to the next. This is one measure of hard drive speed.

track-to-track seek time   the average time taken for a HARD DRIVE to move from one track to another specified track.

tractor feed   a method of feeding paper into a printer, using sprocket holes on each side of the paper engaged by sprocket wheels on the printer.

traffic   the volume of DATA flow along a network or connecting link.

trailing edge   the rear, falling-voltage, edge of a PULSE.

tram lines   a form of CATHODE-RAY OSCILLOSCOPE measurement used as an alternative to EYE HEIGHT DISPLAY measurements. The raw datastream is applied to the Y-input and the timebase set to a low speed so that logic 1 and 0 levels will produce bright parallel lines.

transceiver   a unit that can both transmit and receive data, such as a radio transmitter/receiver or a MODEM.

transcoder   a unit designed to convert signals from one COLOUR TELEVISION format to another, usually between NTSC and PAL.

transconductance   see MUTUAL CONDUCTANCE.

transconductance amplifier   see OPERATIONAL TRANSCONDUCTANCE AMPLIFIER.

transcriptor   an assembly comprising a gramophone turntable, TONE-ARM and pickup CARTRIDGE (sense 2) for replaying recordings on vinyl or shellac discs.

transducer   a CONVERTER of energy from one form to another. For electronics purposes, the transducers of interest are those that have either an electrical input, electrical output or both. The linearity of a transducer is unimportant, but conversion efficiency is important. Compare SENSOR.

transductor see SATURABLE REACTOR.

trans-equatorial skip an occasional long propagation distance between Northern and Southern hemispheres due to the merging of the F1 and F2 layers of the IONOSPHERE.

transfer characteristic a graph plot of OUTPUT against INPUT (sense 1) for a device or circuit. The characteristic may be of current (output current/input current), voltage, or a hybrid such as output voltage/input current.

transfer current the current to the STARTER (sense 1) of a gas-filled device.

transfer function a mathematical description of how a given signal input to a device or circuit produces a signal output.

transfer parameter a PARAMETER that is calculated from the slope of a TRANSFER CHARACTERISTIC.

transfer rate the rate at which data can be moved to and from a storage medium, or the rate at which data can be moved from a transmitter to a receiver.

transferred electron device or **TED** a Schottky Gunn effect device that provides very high-speed binary logic switching.

transfer standard a calibrated measuring instrument used to check the precision of others.

transflective display a form of LCD display which can be used either with backlighting in dark conditions or with frontal lighting in a well-lit room.

transform a change or set of changes made to an algebraic equation or a geometrical shape that maintains the essential features of the original but allows manipulation in a different way.

transformer a general term for a pair of mutual inductors (see INDUCTANCE). For high-frequency signals, a transformer can take the form of two coils placed close to each other. For lower frequencies, MAGNETIC CORES (sense 1) must be used to

concentrate the FLUX (sense 1) and ensure that all the flux from one winding cuts the turns of the other winding. The winding to which a signal is applied is the PRIMARY WINDING, the winding from which a signal is taken is the SECONDARY WINDING. For an IDEAL TRANSFORMER, the ratio of secondary voltage to primary voltage is the same as the ratio of secondary turns to primary turns.

transformer coupling the transfer of signal from one STAGE to another by means of a TRANSFORMER.

transformer equation or **transformer law** the equation for a PERFECT TRANSFORMER in which no power is lost, so that $V_p I_p = V_s I_s$ in which p = primary, s = secondary, V = voltage, I = current.

transformer induction the induction of an alternating EMF in one conductor due to change of current in another.

transformer law see TRANSFORMER EQUATION.

transient a brief PULSE of voltage or current.

transient defects or **transient distortion** an audio system problem where brief TRANSIENT signals or sudden changes in level are superimposed on the normal slow-changing signal levels.

transient event a very brief signal, such as a GLITCH pulse, that cannot be detected using a conventional CATHODE-RAY OSCILLOSCOPE. Transient testing requires the use of a digital storage oscilloscope.

transient intermodulation distortion see SLEW-RATE DISTORTION.

transistor a three-electrode SEMICONDUCTOR device. The main types of transistor are the BIPOLAR JUNCTION TRANSISTOR (BJT) and the FIELD-EFFECT TRANSISTOR (FET). In either type of device, a main current between two of the electrodes is controlled either by a much smaller current at the third electrode (bipolar junction transistor) or by a small voltage at the third electrode (FET). Both types make use of semiconductor material of both DOPING types, p-type and n-type, but they differ in the way in which the main current is conducted and controlled.

In the bipolar junction transistor, the main current between the emitter and collector terminals flows through two JUNCTIONS (sense 2) and is controlled by passing current into or out from the (base) region between the junctions. In the field-effect transistor, the main current flow between SOURCE and DRAIN terminals is along a path (channel) of one material type, which can be p-type or n-type.

The modern methods of fabrication of transistors are EPITAXY and ION IMPLANTATION, and although discrete devices are still manufactured in huge numbers, most transistors are now formed (using field effect technology) as parts of INTEGRATED CIRCUITS.

transistor coding any method of labelling transistors. The US JETEC scheme assigns a number to each type, but the European PRO-ELECTRON system allocates letters that indicate the type of device along with allocation numbers.

transistorized relay a RELAY whose coil current is controlled by a TRANSISTOR so that the relay can be operated by a very small current into the BASE of the transistor.

transistor package the casing used around a transistor to protect the active portion of the ship from light and contamination.

transistor parameters the measurements that allow the action of a transistor to be represented in an EQUIVALENT CIRCUIT. Many sets of parameters were devised during the development stages of transistor technology, and many are no longer used. The almost universal adoption of silicon as a transistor material has meant that many of the old transistor parameters can be ignored. A useful equivalent circuit of a silicon bipolar transistor is one in which the transistor is considered as a current generator producing 40mA per input volt for each milliamp of bias current. This leads to a figure of voltage gain of $40 \times$ (bias current in mA.) for transistors operated with small signals in the audio frequency region. More detailed analysis is needed if the transistors are being used in radio frequency or wideband circuits, and for SWITCHING CIRCUIT design, the large-signal equivalent circuit must be used.

transistor switching the use of BIPOLAR or FET transistors as switch devices for audio signals, allowing remote control and the elimination of noises due to differences in the DC levels.

transistor tester a device for measuring the PARAMETERS of a TRANSISTOR so that its fitness in a circuit may be assessed.

transistor-transistor logic (TTL) a system of constructing GATE (sense 2) and other LOGIC CIRCUITS in INTEGRATED CIRCUIT form with BIPOLAR JUNCTION TRANSISTOR techniques. The gates use integrated transistors whose bases are connected through a resistor to the supply positive terminal, Fig. 116. The input logic signals are to the EMITTERS (sense 1) of these transistors. A logic 1 input, therefore, requires no current to or from the source. A logic 0, however, requires the source voltage to drop to zero, and to accept current from the IC input (the driving circuit must be able to SINK (sense 1) current). TTL circuits are fairly fast-acting, but require a considerable amount of supply current. The later Schottky devices make use of SCHOTTKY DIODES in circuits that permit input to the base of a transistor. These devices require much lower driving currents, and are very fast in operation.

transistor zenering a limiting voltage between the BASE and EMITTER (sense 1) of a TRANSISTOR when the base is reverse-biased, due to AVALANCHE effect. This causes the frequency of a MULTIVIBRATOR to become dependent on supply voltage when the limiting action starts.

transit time the time that an ELECTRON or HOLE takes to travel from one ELECTRODE to another in an ACTIVE COMPONENT. The transit time for a device limits its ability to operate with high-frequency signals.

transition a sudden change from one STATE to another, such as voltage levels in a PULSE waveform or electron energy level inside an ATOM.

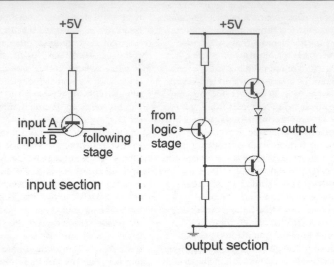

Fig. 116. **transistor-transistor logic**

transition frequency see 3DB FREQUENCY.

transliteration the conversion of characters from one alphabet set into another, a simple form of ENCRYPTION.

transmission the sending of SIGNALS from one place to another. Contrast RECEPTION.

transmission gate a form of SEMICONDUCTOR switch used to gate a signal on or off.

transmission line a CABLE or arrangement of cables for transmitting SIGNALS. The important features of a transmission line are that it should not radiate nor reflect signals. If the signal at the input of the line is to reach the end of the line substantially unaffected, then the line must be matched (see MATCHING) to the impedances of the load and the source so that the STANDING-WAVE RATIO is as low as possible. The use of a balanced or a shielded line reduces radiation, and correct matching reduces reflection to a minimum. The loss of power on the line can be minimized by good construction and suitable materials.

transmission lobe see LOBE.

transmission loss the ratio of power out to power in for a TRANSMISSION LINE or other system. The loss figure is often converted into DECIBELS.

transmission primary a primary colour for COLOUR TELEVISION use. The transmission primaries are red, blue and green. These are not the primary colours of paint, because the primary light signals add to give white light; the paint primaries add to give black paint.

transmission time the time for a DATA PACKET to reach its destination in a network, dependent on packet length and network BIT RATE.

transmissive display a form of LCD display that is used with a white backlight, ideal for use in low lighting conditions. See also REFLECTIVE DISPLAY; TRANSFLECTIVE DISPLAY.

transmit register a REGISTER used at a NETWORK NODE to store data waiting for a gap. See RECEIVE REGISTER; REGISTER INSERTION.

transmit/receive (TR) switch a gas-discharge device used in a RADAR system.

The gas ionizes (see IONIZATION) during the transmission period, placing a short circuit across the receiver waveguide. This prevents the receiver from being paralysed by the transmitted signal. Following transmission, the gas de-ionizes, and the receiver waveguide opens again. Compare ANTI-TRANSMIT / RECEIVE SWITCH.

transmitted-carrier transmission a conventional amplitude modulation system with full CARRIER (sense 1) amplitude present. See SUPPRESSED-CARRIER TRANSMISSION; VESTIGIAL SIDEBAND.

transmitter a device that sends out a CARRIER (sense 1) signal at RADIO FREQUENCY modulated by audio, video or other waveforms. Contrast RECEIVER.

transmitting aerial an aerial used only for transmitting purposes and designed to provide the maximum field strength in the required direction.

transmitting valve a very large THERMIONIC VALVE, usually very high dissipation, used as the final stage of a transmitter circuit to feed power to the aerial.

transparent latch see D-TYPE FLIP-FLOP.

transponder a device that receives a coded signal, the interrogating signal, from a distant TRANSMITTER, and responds with another coded signal for recognition purposes. The transponder is the basis of the IFF system, a form of SECONDARY RADAR.

transport demultiplexer a section of a DIGITAL TELEVISION receiver in which the various DATA PACKETS are assigned and assembled into continuous streams, one to each channel. The video and audio portions are also extracted and synchronized.

transport stream a set of DATA PACKETS from several DIGITAL TELEVISION program channels, usually four or five, assembled together to a continual series of 188-byte data packets, each with a 4-byte header and 184 bytes of audio, video or control data.

transposed line a LINE (sense 1) or cable in which the positions of the conductors are interchanged at intervals to reduce

any possibility of losses caused by any asymmetry of capacitance or inductance.

transputer™ a complete computer, including the MICROPROCESSOR and its MEMORY, fabricated on a single CHIP (sense 1).

transresistance amplifier an OPERATIONAL AMPLIFIER circuit with a virtual earth at the inverting input, used as a current to voltage converter and as an amplifier for transducers with a current output.

transversal filter or **transversal SAW** a form of SURFACE ACOUSTIC WAVE FILTER that uses an unconnected set of strips to act as a damper for unwanted waves.

transverse electric wave an electric wave in a WAVEGUIDE in which the electric field is POLARIZED (sense 1) at right angles to the direction of propagation, but with a magnetic field component whose polarization varies with the distance travelled along the waveguide. See MODE (sense 2).

transverse electromagnetic wave (TEM) a wave in which the electric and the magnetic fields are perpendicular to each other and also to the direction of PROPAGATION. This is the type of wave that is propagated through space and along TRANSMISSION LINES. It cannot be propagated along a WAVEGUIDE.

transverse junction stripe laser a laser formed on a semi-insulating substrate so as to minimize temperature dependent leakage current. The carriers are confined to a very small active region, giving relatively high output power for a low threshold current.

transverse magnetic wave (TM) a wave in a WAVEGUIDE in which the magnetic field is POLARIZED (sense 1) at right angles to the direction of propagation, but with an ELECTRIC FIELD component whose polarization varies with distance travelled along the waveguide.

transverse scan the form of scanning used initially for VIDEO RECORDING and subsequently for all data recording on tape. This uses a HEAD or heads mounted on a revolving DRUM (sense 1) which is inclined so that the magnetic tracks written on to the tape are at a small angle to the edge of the tape. This permits a high recording speed to be used at a low tape speed.

transverse wave any wave in which the OSCILLATION occurs at right angles to the direction of PROPAGATION. All electromagnetic waves are transverse, but ACOUSTIC WAVES are longitudinal, oscillating along the direction of propagation.

Transzorb™ a form of AVALANCHE BREAKDOWN diode developed for use as a TRANSIENT suppressor, with a turn-on time of less than 1 nanosecond.

trap a form of FILTER that reduces the amplitude of one particular frequency, usually by means of a resonant tuned circuit. A trap is used in a colour TV receiver, for example, to eliminate the 4.43MHz colour SUBCARRIER signal from the LUMINANCE signal before the luminance signal is applied to the CATHODE-RAY TUBE.

trapezium distortion a form of distortion of a TV image in which the normal rectangular shape is distorted into the shape of a trapezium.

TRAPPATT diode a DIODE using the trapped plasma avalanche triggered transit time effect. This is used as an amplifier or an oscillator below about 10 GHz.

trapped inverted microstrip a form of INVERTED STRIP LINE in which the GROUND PLANE is formed into a channel shape so that the conductor is screened on three sides. This is usable at frequencies of up to 100 GHz.

travelling wave an electromagnetic wave (see ELECTROMAGNETIC RADIATION) travelling in space or along a TRANSMISSION LINE with no reflections. At any point along the direction of travel, the wave amplitude will vary with time at the wave frequency. Compare STANDING WAVE.

travelling-wave aerial (or antenna) a long wire aerial varying from one to several wavelengths. The aerial is non-resonant and the end remote from the generator must be terminated in a matching resistance.

travelling-wave tube (TWT) a type of AMPLIFIER for MICROWAVES. The waves are forced to travel in a spiral path along a line inside a vacuum tube. A beam of electrons from a CATHODE (sense 1) is made to travel down the axis of the tube at the same speed, with the result that the ELECTRON BEAM is modulated by the waves. The electron beam, which is now bunched by the interaction, passes its power back to the wave at a later part of the spiral, so that the output power is much greater than the input power. In another variation of the principle, the direction of the electron beam is opposite to the direction of the wave, constituting a BACKWARD-WAVE TUBE. The travelling-wave tube has been an important method of low-noise amplification of microwave frequencies, but it has been eclipsed to some extent in this role by the MASER.

traverse servo or **traverse system** or **sled feed** the servo system that controls the movement of the OPTICAL PICKUP UNIT across an optical disc (CD or DVD) from one track to another.

treble the audio frequencies in the range 2kHz upward.

treble boost or **treble emphasis** an AUDIO control used to increase the amplitude of high frequencies relative to MID-BAND RESPONSE.

treble cut an AUDIO control used to decrease the amplitude of high frequencies relative to MID-BAND RESPONSE.

treble response a feature of an AMPLIFIER or SYSTEM that is measured by the amplitude of treble frequencies relative to lower frequencies. The standard frequency for response is often that of a 1kHz wave, and the relative values of amplitude are usually expressed in dB.

tree and branch the older form of CABLE DISTRIBUTION in which all available programmes are continuously sent over the network in separate channels with user selection at the receiving point. See also SWITCHED STAR.

trellis coding a form of FORWARD ERROR CONTROL used in a MODEM to improve BIT ERROR RATE.

TRF see TUNED RADIO FREQUENCY.

triac a form of two-way THYRISTOR. The triac uses an electrode (the gate) to trigger conduction between two other electrodes, usually labelled M1 and M2 since the terms anode and cathode are not appropriate. The conduction ceases when the current through the device falls to below the HOLDING CURRENT value or the voltage between M1 and M2 drops to below the holding value.

triad a group of three colour PHOSPHORS, one red, one green, one blue, constituting a single visible point on a COLOUR TV picture.

triangle wave oscillator an oscillator that delivers a continuous triangular wave, usually by combining a square wave generator with an integrator.

triangular probability density function or **TPDF** the shape of a DITHER signal added to reduce the overall noise in digital recording.

triangular pulse a pulse of triangular shape, used for testing purposes.

triangular wave a wave that consists of a LINEAR SWEEP of increasing voltage followed by a linear downward sweep, each taking the same time.

triangular window a form of WINDOW FUNCTION whose graphical plot has a triangular shape. See also BARTLETT WINDOW; HAMMING WINDOW; HANNING WINDOW; RECTANGULAR WINDOW.

triboelectricity ELECTROSTATIC charge produced by the rubbing of one material against another.

triboelectric series a list of materials ranging from positive to negative and indicating how much electric charge will be produced when two materials are rubbed together. The further apart materials are in the series, the greater the charge produced on rubbing them together.

trickle charge a supply of a small amount of current supplied to a SECONDARY CELL in order to charge the cell slowly or maintain it in a fully charged state.

trigger see TRIGGER PULSE.

triggering the use of a TRIGGER PULSE to start an action.

trigger level a critical level of VOLTAGE that must be exceeded by a TRIGGER PULSE in order to start an action.

trigger pulse or **trigger** a brief PULSE that will start an action. A trigger pulse will normally have a very sharp rise, but may not have a fixed duration, though its amplitude may be critical.

trigger qualifier use of a TRIGGER PULSE to start the operation of the LOGIC ANALYZER. See also CLOCK QUALIFIER.

trimmer a small-value preset VARIABLE CAPACITOR or VARIABLE RESISTOR used for the fine adjustment of a CIRCUIT. A trimmer is adjusted only during manufacture or calibration of a circuit. One example of a trimmer in use is in the oscillator TRACKING (sense 2) of a SUPERHETERODYNE RECEIVER. The trimmer capacitor is connected in parallel with the main tuning capacitor, and another form of trimmer, a PADDER, is sometimes connected in series. By adjusting both of these capacitors, the tracking of the oscillator frequency can be made almost perfect at the two extremes of the frequency range.

trimpot a miniature POTENTIOMETER (sense 1) used to make an adjustment for set-up purposes.

Trinitron™ the Sony APERTURE GRILLE colour TV tube.

triode see THERMIONIC VALVE.

trip a RELAY connected so as to open-circuit a supply in the event of a fault. See also OVERCURRENT TRIP.

triple beat a form of BEAT FREQUENCY interference caused by system NONLINEARITY when a communications system uses a FREQUENCY DIVISION MULTIPLEX band of carriers.

triple conversion the use of three frequency converting stages in a SUPERHETERODYNE design of receiver.

triple detection see DOUBLE SUPERHET.

tripler a form of AC VOLTAGE MULTIPLIER circuit whose output is three times the input voltage.

triplexer see COMBINER.

tri-state device™ a logic INTEGRATED CIRCUIT that incorporates THREE-STATE LOGIC.

tri-state logic see THREE-STATE LOGIC.

trivalent elements elements having three electrons in the outermost shell, acting as electron removers or hole donors in a semiconductor crystal.

troposcatter see TROPOSPHERIC SCATTER.

troposphere the region of the atmosphere between the Earth's surface and the *tropopause* at about 10km in altitude.

tropospheric scatter or **troposcatter** scattering of electromagnetic waves in the TROPOSPHERE because of the local variations in the refractive index. The scattering takes place in a forward direction, and can make possible communication distances of up to 2000 km for frequencies as high as 3GHz.

true RMS the measurement of the true ROOT MEAN SQUARE (sense 2) value of an ALTERNATING CURRENT quantity. Many AC meters operate by rectifying the AC and measuring the resulting unidirectional current. The meter resistors can be adjusted so that for a sine-wave input, the readings will correspond to the values of RMS current or voltage. This is not a true RMS reading, however, because using the meter on any other waveform with a different FORM FACTOR (sense 1) will give incorrect results. Only meters that operate on a square-law principle, such as MOVING IRON or HOT-WIRE INSTRUMENT will give true RMS values for any waveform.

trunk a main set of CABLES connecting from one main unit to another.

truth table a table that shows all of the possible inputs and outputs for a logic gate circuit. See also STATE TABLE.

Tschebycheff filter see TCHEBYCHEV RESPONSE.

T section a FILTER SECTION, one half-section of a LADDER FILTER, using two reactive elements in series and one in parallel, named after its shape. See also PI SECTION.

TT fuse a fuse that will rupture in 100 seconds for a twofold overload and in 150 milliseconds for a tenfold overload.

TTL see TRANSISTOR-TRANSISTOR LOGIC.

TTL levels the levels of +5V for logic 1 and 0V for logic 0, the normal operating levels assumed for TRANSISTOR-TRANSISTOR LOGIC digital devices.

T-type flip-flop a FLIP-FLOP circuit of the toggled (see TOGGLING) type. The T-type flip-flop has one input, the toggle input. Each pulse at this input will cause the output to reverse the output state between logic 0 and logic 1.

tube see CATHODE-RAY TUBE; VACUUM TUBE.

tube cathode poisoning failure of a cathode-ray tube due to surface contamination of the cathode. This can often be remedied by REACTIVATION, running the cathode at a temperature higher than normal for a short time, often with grid current flowing.

tubular capacitor a capacitor created by winding strips of metal and insulator into the form of the tube. See also PAPER CAPACITOR.

tubular plate battery a long life (15 years) version of lead-acid cell used for security systems.

tuned aerial (or **antenna)** or **resonant aerial (**or **antenna)** an aerial, such as a DIPOLE AERIAL, that is tuned in the sense of being cut to some multiple of the wavelength. This allows the formation of a STANDING WAVE on the aerial.

tuned amplifier an amplifier in which LOAD RESISTORS are replaced by RESONANT CIRCUITS so that amplification is a maximum at the frequency of resonance of the tuned circuit in each stage. See also STAGGER TUNING.

tuned circuit see RESONANT CIRCUIT.

tuned collector oscillator a form of OSCILLATOR with a RESONANT CIRCUIT connected to the COLLECTOR (DRAIN) with feedback to the BASE (GATE, sense 1) from an additional winding.

tuned filter a filter that is designed to accept or reject a very narrow frequency band. See also TRAP.

tuned-load oscillator a form of OSCILLATOR in which both INPUT (sense 1) and OUTPUT of an AMPLIFIER are tuned to the same FREQUENCY. The FEEDBACK through STRAY CAPACITANCE ensures that the circuit will oscillate at this frequency.

tuned radio frequency or **tuned RF amplifier** or **TRF** an early system for radio reception that used a set of circuits all tuned to the same radio frequency to receive transmission. This led to instability due to the FEEDBACK of signal from later stages to earlier stages, and was superseded by the SUPERHETERODYNE RECEIVER.

tuned transformer   a transformer for RF whose primary and/or secondary windings have a capacitor connected across each so that they will be resonant (see RESONANCE) at some frequency.

tuner   the portion of a RADIO RECEIVER that consists of the RF, IF, and DEMODULATOR stages. A separate tuner is often a part of a hi-fi system because, in general, the incorporation of a tuner and an amplifier in the same casing can lead to NOISE problems.

tuning capacitor   a VARIABLE CAPACITOR used for adjusting the frequency response of a RESONANT CIRCUIT.

tuning drift   variation of the tuned frequency of a RESONANT CIRCUIT, usually caused by changes in capacitance due to temperature change.

tuning indicator   a device used to indicate the accuracy of manual tuning. At one time, a form of vacuum device known as the *magic eye* was used for this purpose, but in the few examples where tuning indicators are still used they consist now of meters, solid-state displays, or modern forms of VACUUM-FLUORESCENT DISPLAY.

tuning memory   the NONVOLATILE memory used in a receiver to store tuning information.

tunnel diode   a heavily-doped (see DOPING) P-N JUNCTION diode that contains a NEGATIVE-RESISTANCE region in its current-voltage CHARACTERISTIC. Because of this negative-resistance region, the tunnel diode will oscillate when biased into the appropriate region, and by connecting a suitable RESONANT CIRCUIT, usually a resonant cavity, the oscillations can be tuned to any desired frequency. The tunnel diode is normally used as a very low power microwave LOCAL OSCILLATOR.

tunnelling   see QUANTUM TUNNELLING.

turn-off time   the time for current to stop flowing in a THYRISTOR or TRIAC once the turn-off conditions have been reached.

turn-on time   the time for current to reach its maximum level through a THYRISTOR or TRIAC following TRIGGERING.

turn-over frequency   the frequency at which PRE-EMPHASIS starts to be used on an audio signal.

turns ratio   the ratio of the number of secondary turns to primary turns in a TRANSFORMER.

turnstile aerial (or **antenna)**   a form of aerial that consists of two crossed half wave DIPOLEs with 90° phasing of signal, particularly effective as a RECEIVING AERIAL. See also SUPER TURNSTILE AERIAL.

turntable or **platter**   a revolving circular platform for supporting a (gramophone) VINYL DISC. Ideally, a turntable should be metallic and heavy so that it has a large rotational momentum, assisting in maintaining a steady speed.

turret tuner   a tuning system once used for TV receivers and FM tuners. This consisted of a cylinder that carried the tuning inductors inside with a set of connecting contacts outside. By rotating this cylinder inside a casing, the connections to each coil could be made, so tuning from one TV channel to another.

TV   see TELEVISION.

TV capture card or **TV card**   a card or board inserted into a computer in order to input and digitize television or video signals.

TV receiver   see TELEVISION RECEIVER.

tweak   to adjust for optimum performance.

tweeter   a LOUDSPEAKER intended to reproduce high-frequency notes. See also SUB-WOOFER; WOOFER.

twin cable or **twin line** or **twin feeder**   a CABLE made from two insulated close-spaced conductors. This cable has low radiation loss when used as a TRANSMISSION LINE. Compare COAXIAL CABLE.

twin core screened cable   cable used for low-level signals so that balanced signals can be used along with electrostatic screening.

twin feeder   see TWIN CABLE.

twin line   see TWIN CABLE.

twinned binary code a coding system that uses a LOW-PASS FILTER on a binary datastream to reduce the bandwidth and create a multi-level signal.

twin-T network or **parallel-T network** a form of FILTER network using resistors and capacitors that is frequency selective.

twin-T oscillator an OSCILLATOR circuit that uses the TWIN-T NETWORK in a FEEDBACK LOOP, and oscillates at the frequency of the twin-T filter resonance.

twisted-pair a cable consisting of a pair of insulated conductors twisted round each other and carrying a (usually) digital signal and its complement. This results in increased noise immunity, and such cables are used when serial DIGITAL DATA has to be transmitted by cable over distances greater than a few metres. For high-speed serial transmissions (see FIREWIRE; USB), twisted-pair cables are used even for short distances.

twisted-ring counter a form of digital COUNTER that uses FLIP-FLOPS connected in a circular arrangement, so that output of the last flip-flop is connected to the input of the first flip-flop with one Q-to-K and one Q̄-to-J connection.

two-channel stereo audio STEREO signals consisting only of left and right channel information.

two dimensional code a form of binary coding with an *inner code* to correct small BURST ERRORS and an *outer code* for correcting very LONG BURST ERRORS. See also REED-SOLOMON CODE.

two dimensional filter a type of filtering used for processing signals that are elements of an array or matrix. See also FINITE IMPULSE RESPONSE; INFINITE IMPULSE RESPONSE.

two-level code digital code that uses only two voltage levels to represent the binary digits 0 and 1.

two out of five code a BINARY CODED DECIMAL system in which each decimal character is represented by five bits, usually two 1s and three 0s.

two-phase (of an AC supply) using one live and one NEUTRAL (sense 3) line, as in the normal domestic AC supply.

two's complement a figure formed from a digital number by inverting each bit and adding 1 to the total value, so forming the negative equivalent of the number.

two way filtering removal of the PHASE change caused by a recursive digital filter by passing data through the same filter in the opposite direction.

two way key see PUBLIC KEY.

two-way microphone a form of microphone with separate diaphragms and transducers to cover the high and low frequencies respectively, combined by a CROSSOVER NETWORK. This produces a more consistent directivity pattern and better high frequency response than a single DIAPHRAGM type.

TWT see TRAVELLING-WAVE TUBE.

U and V signals the two COLOUR DIFFERENCE SIGNALS of the PAL colour TV system.

UART see UNIVERSAL ASYNCHRONOUS RECEIVER / TRANSMITTER.

UDMA or **ultra DMA** see ULTRA-DIRECT MEMORY ACCESS.

UHF see ULTRA HIGH FREQUENCY.

ULA see UNCOMMITTED LOGIC ARRAY.

ultra-direct memory access or **ultra DMA-3** or **ATA-4** a system developed by Quantum Corporation for very fast transfer of data between memory and the hard drive, now standard on all personal computers.

ultra DMA see ULTRA-DIRECT MEMORY ACCESS.

ultra-high definition a development of analogue television intended to enhance picture quality. In place of the existing line standards of 525 (USA and Japan) or 625 (Europe) lines per picture, ultra-high definition systems planned to use 1000 or more lines per picture, abandoning existing standards of bandwidth and frequency. The emergence of DIGITAL TELEVISION has squashed these proposals.

ultra-high frequency the frequency range of about 300MHz to 3GHz, 1m to 10cm wavelength. This range is widely used for television broadcasting.

ultra-linear connection a form of PUSH-PULL output stage using TETRODE THERMIONIC VALVES with the SCREEN GRIDS connected to tappings on the OUTPUT TRANSFORMER.

ultra-SCSI see SCSI.

ultrasonic (of an ACOUSTIC WAVE) having a frequency above the audible range. The ultrasonic range is usually taken as being 20kHz and above, but most ultrasonic devices use frequencies in the range 100kHz to 5MHz. The waves are generated by PIEZOELECTRIC CRYSTALS or, for the lower frequencies, magnetostrictive transducers (see MAGNETOSTRICTION).

ultrasonic cleaning bath a device for cleaning small components, consisting of a solvent or detergent in a container whose base is vibrated by an ULTRASONIC TRANSDUCER.

ultrasonic delay line a DELAY device for signals that makes use of ultrasonic waves. Because ultrasonic waves travel through solids or liquids at speeds that are much lower than the speed of radio waves in space or along conductors, a short length of ultrasonic wave path can cause a delay of several microseconds. The signals are converted to ultrasonic form by a TRANSDUCER, travel through a solid or liquid, and are then converted back into electromagnetic waves by a second transducer. The early ultrasonic delay lines used mercury as the wave medium, and were known as mumble-tubs. Later varieties have used glass and other solid materials. Such lines were at one time used as delay lines for PAL TV receivers, but have been superseded by digital delays. See also SURFACE ACOUSTIC WAVE DEVICE.

ultrasonic light valve a method of modulating a light beam, using ULTRASONIC waves to affect the polarizing (see POLARIZED, sense 1) properties of a CRYSTAL through which the light passes.

ultrasonic transducer a converter of electrical signals to vibration or vice versa, often using PIEZOELECTRIC CRYSTAL transducers. See also MAGNETOSTRICTION.

ultrasonic waves or **ultrasound** ACOUSTIC WAVES in a material at frequencies higher than 20 kHz.

ultrasound see ULTRASONIC WAVES.

ultra-violet the range of electromagnetic wave frequencies that lies between the violet end of the visible spectrum, and the start of the x-ray region. Ultra-violet radiation is of higher energy than light, and can have destructive effects on the eye and the skin. One important use is in erasing PROMS.

U-Matic™ a helical-scan video recorder devised and manufactured by Sony.

umbrella cell a CELLULAR PHONE system designed to minimize the number of changeovers from one cell to another along a traffic route.

U-MOS a variation of VV-MOS in which the GATE (sense 1) cross section has steeper sides, giving a lower value of forward resistance.

unbalanced circuit a circuit whose output and input consist of one signal connection and earth. Contrast BALANCED CIRCUIT.

unbalanced feeder or **unbalanced line** a TRANSMISSION LINE for which one wire carries signal voltage and the other is earthed, such as a coaxial line. See also BALANCED LINE; BALUN.

uncharged (of a material) having no electrical CHARGE. A neutral uncharged atom has the same number of orbiting ELECTRONS as it has PROTONS in the nucleus.

unclocked (of a gate circuit or flip-flop) not controlled by a CLOCK pulse. See also ASYNCHRONOUS.

uncommitted logic array (ULA) an INTEGRATED CIRCUIT that consists of a large number of gates whose interconnections are not made at the time of initial manufacture. The interconnection pattern can be specified by the customer, using a large chart, and then applied to the ICs by one final process. This permits the flexibility of custom-designed ICs at almost the price of mass-produced chips.

undercoupled see LOOSE COUPLED.

undercurrent release a contact breaker that operates when the current in a circuit is lower than a specified level. See also OVERCURRENT TRIP; TRIP.

underdamped (of a RESONANT circuit) oscillating for a few cycles after a sudden voltage change. See also DAMPED; OVERDAMPED; RINGING (sense 1).

underflow a number output from a digital process that is too small to represent in the binary code being used.

under-modulation modulation of a CARRIER (sense 1) that reduces the

amplitude of the carrier by a small percentage, resulting in feeble reception and inefficient use of the carrier.

under-run, buffer see BUFFER UNDER-RUN.

underscan a scan of a TV CAMERA TUBE or receiver tube with less than normal amplitude. This is usually avoided because of the danger of creating a visible boundary at the edge of the scan. Underscanning is not a problem for solid state camera devices.

undershoot a transient decrease of voltage at the trailing edge of a PULSE. Compare OVERSHOOT.

undervoltage release a CONTACT BREAKER that operates when the voltage in a circuit is below a set level. See also TRIP; UNDERCURRENT RELEASE.

undetected error rate see RESIDUAL ERROR RATE.

undistorted wave a WAVE whose WAVEFORM has not been changed in an electronic circuit.

UNI user network interface.

unidirectional (of a current, usually rectified alternating current) travelling in one direction.

unidirectional wave a wave with a DC component, so that all points on the wave are either at a varying positive voltage or all at a varying negative voltage.

uniform line a TRANSMISSION LINE whose constants of CAPACITANCE, INDUCTANCE and CHARACTERISTIC IMPEDANCE are the same throughout its length.

uniform spectrum (of electrical noise) having an amplitude/frequency response that is uniform over a large range of frequencies. See WHITE NOISE.

uniform waveguide a WAVEGUIDE whose characteristics are the same throughout all of its length.

unijunction or **unijunction transistor** or **double-base diode** a form of pulse generating semiconductor device. The unijunction consists of a bar of lightly-doped N-TYPE silicon with an OHMIC CONTACT at each end. Between these ohmic contacts, a junction is formed to a heavily-doped p-region, the emitter. The action is that the resistance between the two ohmic contacts is very high until carriers are injected from the junction. The unijunction is therefore nonconducting until the voltage at the emitter reaches a definite fraction of the voltage between the ohmic connections. This fraction is called the INTRINSIC STAND-OFF RATIO. When the emitter voltage reaches the value that causes conductivity, comparatively large current can flow both between emitter and the earthed base contact and between the two base contacts. The main application is in pulse generators and sawtooth oscillators.

unilateral network   a NETWORK (sense 1) that conducts in one direction only. This normally applies to signals, so that a transistor is a unilateral network in the sense that the direction of signal is from input to output, not the reverse. This is true only if the collector-base capacitance is low and collector-base resistance is high. At very high frequencies, a transistor may allow signal transfer through the collector-base capacitance, and the correction of this unwanted FEEDBACK is called *unilateralization*.

uninterruptible power supply (UPS) an auxiliary power supply, often fitted to a computer system, that consists of an INVERTER (sense 2), a set of storage cells, and a charger unit. When the mains power is interrupted, the UPS will take over and continue to run equipment for a limited time, in which time it can be shut down in an orderly way. The cells can be recharged when power is restored. See also OFF-LINE UPS, ON-LINE UPS.

unipolar   (of a SEMICONDUCTOR device) having the main current carried by MAJORITY CARRIERS in one polarity of material, without passing through a JUNCTION (sense 2). The FIELD-EFFECT TRANSISTOR is one example of a unipolar device.

unit   a physical quantity of strictly defined and reproducible size. The fundamental units are the kilogram, metre, second and ampere, and the lumen is added for purposes of light measurement.

unit-step   a sudden change of VOLTAGE between specified limits, such as logic 0 level to logic 1 level.

unity gain frequency   the (high) frequency for which an amplifier, usually an OPERATIONAL AMPLIFIER, has a gain of unity.

unity-gain preamplifier   a PREAMPLIFIER used for IMPEDANCE MATCHING rather than for GAIN.

universal aerial constant or **universal antenna**   a figure for a DIPOLE AERIAL, derived from effective area and wavelength, that can be used to calculate the gain of any other type of aerial.

universal asynchronous receiver transmitter or **UART**   a type of PORT (sense 1) chip for a computer that allows communication to and from the computer using SERIAL links. The serial signals do not have to be transmitted continuously, only when data is being sent. Many serial port chips are manufactured so that they can be used either in synchronous or asynchronous form. Compare USART; USRT.

universal bridge tester   a servicing instrument that can measure values of RESISTANCE, CAPACITANCE and INDUCTANCE, making use of a BRIDGE circuit.

universal LNB   a form of LOW NOISE BLOCK for satellite reception that uses a dual-frequency OSCILLATOR so that it can be operated on two bands, the low band (10.7 to 11.7 GHz) and the high band (11.7 to 12.75 GHz).

universal motor   an electric motor that operates on either AC or DC. A universal motor uses an electromagnet field coil rather than a permanent magnet, and a COMMUTATOR to feed the rotor coils. Compare AC MOTOR.

universal product code (UPC)   a form of BAR CODE applied to a wide range of applications.

universal serial bus (USB)   a fast type of SERIAL port connection for connecting external units to computers. Cables are inexpensive and can be up to 5 metres long. Up to a total of 127 devices can be connected one to another (*daisy-chained*) from one outlet. A later version, USB-2, is forty times faster and is now standardized in computers, replacing parallel and other types of serial connection systems.

universal shift register a SHIFT REGISTER with control logic that allows any of the four configurations of shift register to be used. See PARALLEL-IN PARALLEL-OUT; PARALLEL-IN SERIAL-OUT; SERIAL-IN PARALLEL-OUT; SERIAL-IN SERIAL-OUT.

universal shunt a meter SHUNT (sense 1) that is tapped so that the ratio of series to shunt resistance in the current path can be varied. This allows a MOVING-COIL METER connected to the shunt to be used for a whole set of current ranges.

universal synchronous/asynchronous receiver transmitter or **USART** a type of PORT (sense 1) chip for a computer that can send or receive signals along SERIAL links with either synchronous or asynchronous PROTOCOLS. Compare UART; USRT.

universal synthesizer interface (USI) a proposal for a standardized interconnection system for electronic musical instruments that led to the current MIDI system.

unloaded Q the value of Q FACTOR for a RESONANT CIRCUIT that is not supplying any form of load.

unmodulated carrier a pure sine wave CARRIER (sense 1).

unregulated output or **unstabilized output** an output from a power supply unit that is unregulated, and whose voltage will vary with changes in load and mains voltage.

unshielded twisted pair or **UTP** or **USP** the standard type of US telephone wire, sometimes used for small NETWORK (sense 2) connections on cost grounds. See also SHIELD.

unstabilized output see UNREGULATED OUTPUT.

untuned aerial an AERIAL whose dimensions are unrelated to the wavelength of the signal, as, for example, a long-wave transmitting or RECEIVING AERIAL.

untuned amplifier an amplifier that avoids frequency selective circuits or components so that it has a flat response over its intended bandwidth.

untuned circuit see APERIODIC CIRCUIT.

untuned oscillator see APERIODIC OSCILLATOR.

untuned transformer a transformer that is used for mains voltage conversion or for wideband use, as distinct to a TUNED TRANSFORMER.

U-numbers a coding system for cases for electronic equipment.

UPC see UNIVERSAL PRODUCT CODE.

up-convertor a SUPERHETERODYNE RECEIVER in which a conversion results in an INTERMEDIATE FREQUENCY that is the sum of the input signal frequency and the LOCAL OSCILLATOR frequency.

up-down counter a logic COUNTER based on FLIP-FLOPS that are interconnected by GATES (sense 2). The gates are controlled by a single line so that one voltage level on the line produces up-counting (incrementing), the opposite level produces down-counting (decrementing).

upgrading improvement of the speed or facilities of a computer or other device by adding new HARDWARE or SOFTWARE.

uploading the action of transmitting data from one computer to a website. Compare DOWNLOADING.

upper sideband the SIDEBAND of a modulated CARRIER (sense 1) whose frequencies are higher than the carrier frequency.

UPS see UNINTERRUPTIBLE POWER SUPPLY.

upstream (of a CIRCUIT) closer to the source of a signal. Contrast DOWNSTREAM.

upward spread the effect of frequency on MASKING, resulting in masking extending to higher frequencies as the interfering sound becomes louder.

USB see UNIVERSAL SERIAL BUS.

user specific integrated circuit (USIC) see APPLICATION SPECIFIC INTEGRATED CIRCUIT.

USI see UNIVERSAL SYNTHESIZER INTERFACE.

U signal the B–Y COLOUR DIFFERENCE SIGNAL in a PAL system, modulated on to the QUADRATURE phase of the SUBCARRIER.

UV see ULTRA-VIOLET.

U-wrap the half-drum circumference wrap of video tape around the DRUM (sense 1) of a VIDEO CASSETTE RECORDER, a shorter wrapping distance than OMEGA WRAP.

VA see VOLT-AMPERE.

vacuum capacitor a CAPACITOR that uses a vacuum as its insulating dielectric. Vacuum capacitors are widely used in transmitting circuits because they can be made variable (by varying their geometry), and because they do not suffer from any nonlinear effects.

vacuum diode a THERMIONIC VALVE consisting of CATHODE (sense 1) and ANODE (sense 1) only so that it can be used as a diode.

vacuum evaporation a method of depositing thin films, mainly of metals. The material that is to be deposited is attached to a tungsten filament that can be electrically heated. The surface to be coated is arranged at about 10–15cm distance, and the arrangement is enclosed and evacuated. When the filament is heated, the material on it evaporates and condenses as a thin film on the cool surface. See also METALLIZING; SPUTTERING.

vacuum fluorescent display any type of display for ALPHANUMERIC characters that uses a COLD CATHODE EMITTER whose electrons strike shaped ANODES coated with a phosphor material. Vacuum fluorescent displays have been widely used for pocket calculators and for metering indicators. They allow reasonably high brightness to be achieved at low power levels, and are often more satisfactory in this respect than LEDs. Their disadvantages are relative fragility and the need for a supply voltage that is higher than the normal +5V used in digital equipment.

vacuum switch a SWITCH whose contacts are in a VACUUM so as to avoid contact oxidation through sparking.

vacuum tube see THERMIONIC VALVE.

valence shell the outermost set of ELECTRONS of an ATOM, determining chemical reactivity and electrical characteristics.

valley point the minimum-current point in a TUNNEL DIODE characteristic.

valve see THERMIONIC VALVE.

valve microphone a CAPACITOR MICROPHONE with built in THERMIONIC VALVE amplifier, used because of its relative immunity to overload.

Van Allen belts two layers of charged particles emitted by the sun and trapped within the earth's magnetic field.

vapour axial deposition a method of producing OPTICAL FIBRE by pulling a thread away from a silica target heated by vaporized gases.

vapour cooling a method of cooling transmitter THERMIONIC VALVES. The ANODE is surrounded by a jacket through which vapour (usually water vapour) is circulated. The vapour can be circulated much faster than water, and acts as a much more efficient method of transferring heat. The method has more recently been applied to computer MICROPROCESSOR chips using 'heat-pipes' to a radiator with an external exhaust so that the heat from the chip does not have such a large effect on the temperature inside the case.

vapour phase epitaxy the deposition of SILICON atoms from a vapour onto a SUBSTRATE so as to extend a single crystal structure on the substrate.

vapour phase production a method of producing OPTICAL FIBRE using doping gases to control REFRACTIVE INDEX.

varactor a SEMICONDUCTOR diode with voltage-variable CAPACITANCE. The diode is operated with REVERSE BIAS, and the effect of the bias on the DEPLETION LAYER at the junction makes this layer act like a variable thickness of dielectric. The capacitance is therefore least with large reverse bias, and greatest with small reverse bias.

varactor tuning a form of tuning that makes use of an INDUCTOR and a VARACTOR. The varactor is normally connected in series with another capacitor to ensure DC isolation from the tuned circuit. Varactor tuning is widely used at VHF and UHF, where only small variations of capacitance are needed, and where AUTOMATIC FREQUENCY CONTROL circuits are essential.

variable capacitor a CAPACITOR whose value is mechanically variable. The usual variation method is to have a set of (fixed) *stator* plates and a set of (rotating) *rotor* plates whose meshing can be altered by rotating the shaft to which the rotor plates are connected. The rotor plates are normally earthed to avoid problems of BODY CAPACITANCE. TRIMMER CAPACITORS can use compression, in which a threaded bolt tightens or loosens plates that clamp a solid dielectric. The *beehive trimmer* uses concentric rings for rotor and stator and varies the interaction by screwing the rotor plates into or out of the stator plates. Variable capacitors may be ganged, see GANGED CIRCUITS.

variable density recording one of the two methods of recording a SOUND TRACK onto optical film by varying the density of shading according to the amplitude of signal. See also VARIABLE WIDTH RECORDING.

variable frequency oscillator or VFO an OSCILLATOR whose frequency can be easily varied, often using a VARIABLE CAPACITOR or VARIABLE INDUCTOR, or by using a VARICAP DIODE as part of oscillating circuit. Contrast CRYSTAL OSCILLATOR.

variable inductor an INDUCTOR whose value can be mechanically varied. The method of variation is normally to alter the position of a high-permeability core relative to the inductor windings.

variable-length coding a form of DIGITAL CODING that assigns the shortest codes to most common SYMBOL groups.

variable output regulator or variable voltage stabilizer a VOLTAGE REGULATOR circuit in which the regulated output voltage can be varied over a range of values.

variable reluctance the principle used for the MOVING IRON PICKUP. The movement of an armature that is part of a magnetic circuit alters the reluctance, the magnetic flux equivalent of resistance.

variable reluctance microphone a microphone with a DIAPHRAGM attached to an ARMATURE that is located in the gap of a permanent magnet. A coil wound on the magnet will generate a signal due to fluctuations of MAGNETIC FLUX when the armature is vibrated.

variable resistor a RESISTOR whose RESISTANCE value can be mechanically changed. The construction is as for a POTENTIOMETER (sense 1), but only one end and the moving tap of the potentiometer are used.

variable voltage stabilizer see VARIABLE OUTPUT REGULATOR.

variable width recording one of the two methods of recording a SOUND TRACK onto optical film by varying the width of the track according to the amplitude of signal. See also VARIABLE DENSITY RECORDING.

Variac™ a form of toroidally wound AUTOTRANSFORMER.

varicap diode a DIODE that is used with REVERSE BIAS and whose CAPACITANCE varies with the amount of bias.

varicap tuning a tuning system using a VARICAP DIODE in addition to a CAPACITOR so that tuning can be electrically controlled.

varigroove™ the system used for VINYL DISC recordings in which a wider spacing between grooves (groove pitch) is used just prior to a loud passage of music so as to avoid PRE-ECHO.

variometer an INDUCTOR whose value of SELF-INDUCTANCE is variable, seldom used now.

varistor a NON-OHMIC resistor. Varistors are made from semiconductor material, have an exponential current-voltage characteristic, and are used as over-voltage limiters, because the current through the varistor will greatly increase for a very small increase in the voltage across it. The METROSIL was an early form of varistor.

V band   the MICROWAVE band of wavelength range 53.6 to 63.2mm, frequency range 46 to 56GHz.

VCA   see VOLTAGE CONTROLLED AMPLIFIER.

VCD   see VIDEO COMPACT DISC.

VCF   see VOLTAGE CONTROLLED FILTER.

VCO   see VOLTAGE CONTROLLED OSCILLATOR.

VCR   see VIDEO CASSETTE RECORDER.

VCSEL   see VERTICAL CAVITY SURFACE EMITTING LASER.

VDU   see VISUAL DISPLAY UNIT.

vector   (of a physical quantity) having direction as well as size, such as MAGNETIC FIELD strength. Compare SCALAR.

vector diagram   a graphical display of a VECTOR quantity, using the length of a line to denote size and its angle to the x-axis to denote direction.

vector image display   an alternative to a RASTER display, drawing an image by a set of lines from point to point.

vector modulation analysis   a computer-controlled system of sampling modulated digital waveforms to provide displays of PHASE and AMPLITUDE.

velocity   speed in a specified direction.

velocity factor   the factor multiplied by the SPEED OF LIGHT in free space to express speed of ELECTROMAGNETIC WAVES in a DIELECTRIC. The factor is equal to: $1/_\varepsilon$ where ε is the RELATIVE PERMITTIVITY of the dielectric.

velocity modulation   the interaction between an ELECTRON BEAM and an electromagnetic wave. The velocity of electrons in the beam is modulated by the wave, causing the beam of electrons to become bunched. See BACKWARD-WAVE OSCILLATOR; CARCINOTRON; KLYSTRON; TRAVELLING-WAVE TUBE.

velocity modulation transistor or **VMT** a FIELD EFFECT TRANSISTOR with a double gallium arsenide/aluminium arsenide channel sandwiched between barrier layers of aluminium arsenide. The DRAIN current is modulated by changes in electron velocity and the device can achieve a switching rate of about one picosecond.

velocity of light   the figure of 3×10^8 metres per second taken as velocity of

light in free space. The velocity in denser media is lower, see REFRACTIVE INDEX.

velocity of sound   the velocity of sound in air is approximately 343 metres per second, but the velocity in denser media is considerably higher.

velocity operated microphone   a MICROPHONE that is operated by the velocity of air moving past it rather than by pressure. The essential feature of a velocity operated microphone is that the sound waves can strike all sides of the vibrating DIAPHRAGM. See also PRESSURE OPERATED MICROPHONE; RIBBON MICROPHONE.

velocity operation, microphone   see VELOCITY OPERATED MICROPHONE.

Veroboard™   a BREADBOARD system. The original Veroboard is a PRINTED CIRCUIT BOARD that consists of parallel strips of copper on an insulating sheet. The strips are drilled at regular intervals (originally 0.15″, later 0.1″) so that components can be inserted and soldered to the board. Strips can be cut across where necessary for isolation. Veroboard allows experimental circuits to be made and tested in a form that is closer to the final production shape than is usually possible with older breadboard systems.

vertical aerial (or **antenna)**   an UNBALANCED single vertical rod aerial usually fed by COAXIAL cable.

vertical aliasing   the flickering effect that makes the line structure of a conventional TV display (using a CATHODE-RAY TUBE) visible.

vertical blanking   the suppression of video signal in the time of the field or frame flyback. See RASTER; VERTICAL TIMEBASE.

vertical blanking interval   the time in the standard analogue television signal for which the field (vertical) SYNCHRONIZING PULSES are delivered and the video circuits are suppressed so that vertical FLYBACK can take place.

vertical cavity surface emitting laser or **VCSEL**   a SEMICONDUCTOR laser using ultra-thin layers of gallium arsenide, aluminium arsenide, aluminium gallium arsenide and indium aluminium gallium phosphide to provide emission perpendicular to the flat upper surface. Such lasers are commonly used in conjunction with optical fibres.

vertical FET see V-MOS.

vertical hold a TELEVISION RECEIVER control for the synchronization of the VERTICAL TIMEBASE.

vertical interval timecode or **VITC** the TIMECODE assigned to each FRAME (sense 1) in a CAMCORDER signal and in the VHS types carried on the unused lines of the FIELD BLANKING interval.

vertical resolution the ability to discern fine detail in the vertical direction of a TV screen, controlled by the number of VERTICAL SCAN lines or the number of vertical PIXELS.

vertical timebase the TIMEBASE circuit in a TELEVISION RECEIVER that generates the field (vertical scan) waveform. The WAVEFORM consists of a current sweep with a duration of about 20 milliseconds, followed by a rapid flyback.

vertical whip (aerial) an unbalanced form of aerial usually fed with coaxial feeder, and cut to one quarter of a wavelength long. This form of aerial is useful if a good ground can be arranged, and the metalwork of a vehicle is normally sufficiently good to give reasonable performance.

vertically polarized aerial (or **antenna)** an aerial whose main current-carrying structure is vertical so that the ELECTRIC FIELD component radiated from the aerial is vertically polarized.

very low frequency amplifier any amplifier designed to deal with DC or very low frequencies. The usual alternative to the DC coupled amplifier is the CHOPPER STABILIZED AMPLIFIER.

VESA Video Electronics Standards Association.

vestigial sideband (VSB) a method of TV signal transmission. The use of single sideband SUPPRESSED CARRIER TRANSMISSION methods, though advantageous from the point of view of efficiency, is impossible for TV signals because of the severe distortion that would be caused to the video signals. A compromise is to attenuate the modulated signal in such a way that the CARRIER (sense 1) amplitude is only half of its original amplitude, and the lower sideband contains only the lower frequencies of the video signal. This makes the lower sideband vestigial, and allows more efficient use of the transmitter power. See Fig. 117.

VFC see VOLTAGE TO FREQUENCY CONVERTER.

VFET see VERTICAL FET.

VFO see VARIABLE FREQUENCY OSCILLATOR.

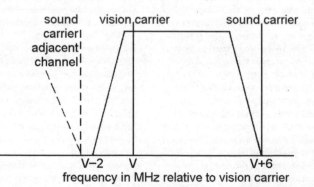

Fig. 117. **vestigial sideband**

VGA video graphics adapter: a standard of display adopted for computers that has now been considerably enhanced as an almost universal standard.

VHF very high frequency: the range of approximately 30MHz to 300MHz, 10m to 1m wavelength.

VHS video home system: a VIDEO CASSETTE RECORDER system devised by JVC.

VHS-C a miniature form of VHS cassette designed for use with a CAMCORDER but retaining compatibility with domestic VHS VIDEO CASSETTE RECORDERS.

VI see VIRTUAL INSTRUMENT.

via a SOLDER PAD on a PRINTED CIRCUIT BOARD that leads to the contacts on opposite sides, or a hole etched through a dielectric layer and filled with metal.

vibrator see CHOPPER.

video relating to or employed in the transmission of picture information, i.e. TV camera signals or any other signals (computer generated graphics, for example) that can produce an image. The video signal is of wide bandwidth, typically 5.5MHz or more, and may be a COMPOSITE SIGNAL with SYNCHRONIZING PULSES included.

video adapter see VIDEO CARD.

video amplifier a form of BROADBAND AMPLIFIER for video signals, typically in the range of DC to 5MHz. For TV purposes, the video amplifier need cater only for UNIDIRECTIONAL signals, so that TV video amplifiers can use AC coupling, with DC restoration at the output. For CATHODE-RAY OSCILLOSCOPES and other instruments, video amplifiers may have to be direct-coupled (see DIRECT COUPLING), capable of amplifying pulses of either polarity, and with an upper frequency limit of 30MHz or more.

video bandwidth the range of frequencies that is needed for video signals. The video bandwidth is measured in megahertz (MHz), and implies that any frequency from zero up to this limit will be present in a signal. For high resolution computer graphics and 80-column text, a video bandwidth of at least 18 MHz is desirable. This contrasts with the 5 MHz that is

normally available on a domestic television receiver. Most good quality monitors can achieve a bandwidth of 18 MHz, some more than 70 MHz.

video board see VIDEO CARD.

video camera a source of video signals using a lens to focus an image on a pickup device, formerly a vacuum tube device but now usually a CHARGE-COUPLED DEVICE. Circuitry in the camera provides scanning and amplification of video signals, along with adjustment of white balance and colour rendering. The lens is usually a zoom type with provision for electrically controlled focusing, zooming and aperture adjustment. See also CAMCORDER.

video capture the use of HARDWARE and SOFTWARE that will convert ANALOGUE signals from a camcorder, TV or VCR and convert them into digital format, typically MPEG.

video card or **video adapter** or **video board** a card added to a computer system to enhance the GRAPHICS display on a MONITOR.

video cassette recorder an analogue system that uses a cassette containing MAGNETIC TAPE for TV signal RECORDING. The system for domestic use in the UK is JVC's VHS, using half-inch wide tape at a speed in the region of 2.34cm/second. The recorder can take signals directly from an AERIAL, and has normal receiver circuits that will produce the LUMINANCE signal (black/white), CHROMINANCE SIGNAL (colour) and AUDIO signal (sound). The luminance signal is frequency modulated onto a CARRIER (sense 1) of around 6MHz. The colour signals are frequency-shifted to a lower frequency range, and then added to the FM luminance signals. The use of FM allows the luminance signals to be recorded at a constant amplitude, so avoiding the problems of the limited amplitude range of tape. The record/replay heads rotate, and the tape direction is skewed so that the recording tracks are across the tape at a shallow angle, allowing a high rate of tape scanning for a slow rate of tape movement.

The bandwidth of the system is limited, so that the resolution of the replayed picture is lower than that of a transmitted picture, typically about half of the resolution in terms of lines. The audio signal is separately recorded on one track that lies parallel to the length of the tape (see RECORDING OF VIDEO). A synchronizing control track is recorded in the same way on the other edge of the tape.

On replay, the two sets of video signals have to be reconstituted and modulated onto another UHF carrier, and the sound signal is also modulated so that the complete UHF video output can be used by any domestic receiver. Most recorders feature a SCART RGB output for direct connection to the video amplifier circuits of a TV receiver, permitting better quality than can be obtained by the process of modulation and demodulation. There is also usually a COMPOSITE VIDEO output so that a monitor can be used. At the time of writing, the video cassette recorder is being phased out in favour of DVD recorders and hard-drive recorders. See also CAMCORDER; DYNAMIC TRACKING.

video compact disc or **VCD** a form of COMPACT DISC that contains VIDEO signals in MPEG-1 format, used for storing files obtained from analogue camcorders and in the Far East for distributing short films. The quality of image is not so good as can be obtained using DVD, and the maximum length of video is about one hour. Software for writing CD-R or CD-RW discs often includes an option for creating VCDs.

video component any one of the separated parts of a video signal, typically LUMINANCE and CHROMINANCE or RGB, as distinct from COMPOSITE VIDEO signals.

video compression a form of compression (see COMPRESSED FILE) for DIGITAL VIDEO data that depends on the small differences between one FRAME (sense 2) and the next in a sequence. This allows a complete sequence to be coded using little more than is needed to describe the first frame. The best-known video compression standards make use of the MPEG standards.

videoconferencing a meeting of groups of people in different locations organized through a sound and vision link.

video coupling the methods by which a video signal may be passed from one unit to another. In order of ascending picture quality these are COMPOSITE VIDEO (using the CINCH SOCKET), S-VIDEO (using the Din or HOSIDEN socket), and RGB (using the SCART CONNECTOR).

videocrypt a SCRAMBLER system for ANALOGUE satellite transmissions.

video CVBS socket see CINCH SOCKET.

video demodulator the circuit within an analogue TELEVISION RECEIVER that recovers the video signal from the modulated carrier.

video disc any type of disc that is written on by means of a laser with a bit pattern that represents a video signal. The information is stored in digital form, as on a CD, and can be read using a low-power laser. By using compression techniques, a disc of audio CD size (see VIDEO COMPACT DISC) can carry a reasonable time of video signal that can be used in multimedia and interactive video displays. See also DVD.

video-8 a form of 8mm video cassette designed by Sony and intended for CAMCORDER use. See also DIGITAL-8; HI-8.

video frequency I. a frequency in the video range of about DC to 5MHz. **2.** (of a circuit) designed to cope with video signals.

video graphics card a set of circuits designed to provide an output to a MONITOR from a computer that provides the digital signals.

videography a general term for TELETEXT services.

video heads the magnetic writing and reading HEADs that are part of the rotating DRUM (sense 1) of a VIDEO CASSETTE RECORDER.

video mapping a computer technique applied to a RADAR display. A map or photographic image of the area is superimposed over a radar trace so that the geographical position of targets can be seen.

video memory or **video RAM** or **VRAM** memory, particularly for computer use, that can be read and written simultaneously so that graphics information fed to the memory can be used for display on a screen.

video monitor a unit using a high-quality CRT or LCD display with inputs that are either RGB, S-VHS or COMPOSITE VIDEO.

video on demand or **VOD** television pictures delivered to a viewer on demand as distinct from using scheduled times. See also NEAR VIDEO ON DEMAND; STAGGERCASTING.

video programming system (VPS) see PROGRAMME DELIVERY CONTROL (PDC).

video projector a display device using beams of high-intensity light (often from LASERs) that can be scanned (see SCAN) and modulated (see MODULATION) so as to project a large image on to a screen. See also BEAMER; DIGITAL SIGNAL PROCESSOR.

video ram see VIDEO MEMORY.

video recording see RECORDING OF VIDEO.

video signal a SIGNAL that can be used to provide a picture. The term usually denotes a COMPOSITE SIGNAL, that contains the video waveform along with colour signals and all of the synchronizing signals.

video spectrum the total BANDWIDTH of the transmitted PAL signal ranging from the suppressed lower SIDEBAND at about 1.25MHz below the vision CARRIER (sense 1) to the SOUND CARRIER at 6MHz above the vision carrier.

video tape a form of MAGNETIC TAPE for recording VIDEO SIGNALS. The tape is wider than audio tape, typically half-inch for video cassettes (see VIDEO CASSETTE RECORDER), and 50mm (just under 2 inch) for professional machines for broadcast use. The coating material is usually ferric oxide with cobalt oxide.

video timing reference signals or **VTRS** the signals used for SYNCHRONIZATION in a MULTIPLEXed datastream for a DIGITAL TELEVISION transmission. These contain information defining the FIELD BLANKING intervals.

video transition the change from one video shot to another, either live or later by editing.

VideoPlus™ an aid to programming a VIDEO CASSETTE RECORDER, using a code that is published by most newspapers to specify programme start time, channel and duration.

videotelephony a system of transmitting images along a telephone line using a lower image quality with a large amount of compression. See also QUARTER COMMON IMAGE FORMAT.

videowall a large area TV image formed from a group of display devices, usually a square matrix of monitors in very slim frames, with signals allocated so that each monitor shows only part of a picture.

vidicon a CAMERA TUBE for television, once almost universally used for colour cameras. A vidicon makes use of a photoconductive semiconductor, such as antimony trisulphide or lead oxide. The optical image from the camera lens is projected onto the flat faceplate of the vidicon, typically one inch in diameter, though $1/2$-inch vidicons have been used in smaller cameras. Inside the faceplate, a transparent conducting layer on the glass forms the output terminal, with a connection at the edge of the faceplate. The conducting layer is coated with the photoconducting material, the TARGET, which in turn can be scanned by a low-velocity ELECTRON BEAM. An optical image causes a corresponding pattern of low and high conductivity paths in the photoconductor, and these allow the inner surface to charge from the steady voltage at the target. The scanning electron beam discharges these parts of the inner surface, causing a signal voltage to appear by capacitive coupling on the conducting side. This signal voltage is the video signal out of the vidicon. The use of vidicons has now been almost totally superseded by solid-state methods, see CCD.

viewdata a graphics and text service similar to TELETEXT but transmitted over a telephone network.

vinyl disc · the form of SOUND RECORDING system developed from the older wax or shellac disks into a longer playing plastic surface in the 1940s. The signals from one or more microphones were used to modulate a spiral groove in a lacquer-covered metal disc, and this was used to make a master from which the final copies could be pressed.

virgin tape TAPE, particularly for BACKUP purposes that has never been recorded on.

virtual cathode an area of SPACE CHARGE that behaves as a supply of electrons.

virtual disk see SILICON DISK.

virtual earth or **virtual ground** or **Wagner earth** a point in a circuit at which there is no signal at any time, though the point is not directly connected to earth. An example is the INPUT (sense 1) to an operational amplifier in which large amounts of negative FEEDBACK are applied.

virtual earth amplifier an inverting amplifier circuit using an OPERATIONAL AMPLIFIER whose non-inverting input is at zero potential so that FEEDBACK ensures that the inverting input is also practically at zero potential, a VIRTUAL EARTH.

virtual instrument or **VI** a measuring instrument that is basically a COMPUTER provided with measuring software, allowing a vast range of measurement possibilities within one instrument.

virtual memory the use of a HARD DRIVE as a support to MEMORY, using the processor to move data from the hard drive into RAM for more rapid access.

virtual reality the use of a COMPUTER SYSTEM to simulate a realistic set of conditions, after the fashion of a flight simulator and using techniques from computer games. The most valuable applications are in the design of buildings (a prospective buyer can simulate walking through the building before it is constructed), working in dangerous spaces using a robot, and in medical teaching. The user of a virtual reality system needs to wear a helmet so that three-dimensional images can be presented to the eyes, and in some systems sensors are fitted to the hands so that images of arms in the picture can be realistically moved. See also DATA GLOVE.

virus a short program entered into a computer, usually illegally, so as to corrupt the operation of the computer and the data contained therein. The virus replicates itself and can usually be spread through a network.

visible spectrum the range of frequencies of electromagnetic waves that can be detected by the eye. The range is approximately from 400 THz (red) to 750 THz (violet) corresponding to wavelengths of 750 nm to 400 nm.

vision detector a synchronous detector (see SYNCHRONOUS DEMODULATION) used to provide the vision and sound outputs from the modulated colour television signal.

visual display unit (VDU) a CATHODE-RAY TUBE display or large screen LCD display for a computer.

VITC see VERTICAL INTERVAL TIME CODE.

Viterbi algorithm a type of MAXIMUM LIKELIHOOD DECODING algorithm devised in 1967 which has greatly increased the use of CONVOLUTION CODES. The algorithm uses a search method to calculate the DISTANCE between received and valid code words.

Viterbi coding see CONVOLUTIONAL CODING.

vitreous coated resistor a form of wire-wound resistor using a glass coating whose maximum surface temperature can be as high as 400°C.

VLF very low frequency: the range of approximately 3kHz to 30kHz, 100km to 10km wavelength. These frequencies are not particularly useful for surface radio use, but allow some degree of underwater communications.

VLSI very large scale integration: the SCALE OF INTEGRATION in which the number of ACTIVE COMPONENTS on one chip is a hundred-thousand ACTIVE COMPONENTS per chip. Though much larger scales of integration are in use, no suitable names have been coined.

V-MOS or **VFET** or **vertical FET** a FIELD EFFECT TRANSISTOR, particularly for power output stages, whose construction is arranged with layers at right angles to the surface so that the DRAIN is large and easily put into contact with a heat sink.

VMT see VELOCITY MODULATION TRANSISTOR.

vocoder (voice-coder) a processor for audio signals that extracts information which can be used to analyze and synthesize speech, or to use speech or other audio signals to modulate musical notes.

VOD see VIDEO ON DEMAND.

VOGAD see VOICE OPERATED GAIN ADJUSTING DEVICE.

voice-activated microphone a microphone whose output is muted by a level-sensitive GATE (sense 2) circuit until a pre-determined threshold sound level is exceeded. Such microphones are used for conference rooms, churches and security intruder detection.

voice coil the active part of a LOUDSPEAKER. The voice coil is wound on a tubular former, supported in the field of a magnet by a SPIDER and by the cone of the loudspeaker. An alternating current through the voice coil causes to and fro movement that displaces air, forming a sound wave. See also VOICE-COIL DRIVE.

voice-coil drive a method of moving the READ/WRITE HEAD of a HARD DRIVE that uses the coil and magnet construction similar to that of a LOUDSPEAKER. The advantage of such a drive is that it is quiet, fast and self-parking. The older STEPPER MOTOR drive is now obsolete.

voice grade channel a signal transmitting system that can use only a very limited BANDWIDTH, about 100 Hz to 2000 Hz, the range that is used by telephone systems for speech.

volatile (of a MEMORY using semiconductors) not retaining stored information when the power supply is switched off. Compare MAGNETIC MEMORY; NONVOLATILE; ROM.

volt the unit of ELECTRIC POTENTIAL and POTENTIAL DIFFERENCE. The volt is defined as the joule per coulomb, the amount of work done per unit charge in moving a charge from one place to another.

voltage see ELECTRIC POTENTIAL.

voltage adding converter or **weighted voltage addition converter** a form of ANALOGUE TO DIGITAL CONVERTER that uses FEEDBACK through a set of resistors arranged in weighted (1,2,4,8...) values. This scheme is adequate for a small number of bits but becomes impossible for eight bits or more due to the precision required in the resistors.

voltage amplifier an AMPLIFIER that has VOLTAGE GAIN. The output signal from a voltage amplifier will be a copy of the input signal, but with greater voltage amplitude.

voltage controlled amplifier (VCA) an AMPLIFIER whose gain can be changed by altering the level of a DC input.

voltage controlled filter (VCF) a form of ACTIVE FILTER in which the PASSBAND can be altered by applying a DC input.

voltage controlled oscillator (VCO) an OSCILLATOR whose frequency can be changed by altering the level of a DC input.

voltage depression phenomena see BATTERY MEMORY.

voltage-derived feedback feedback derived by taking a fraction of the output voltage from the output of a circuit to feed back to the input.

voltage divider a set of resistors in series connected across a supply so that a reduced voltage can be obtained at each junction of two resistors. See also ATTENUATOR.

voltage divider biasing a common system of biasing for a BIPOLAR JUNCTION TRANSISTOR in which the BASE is fed from a VOLTAGE DIVIDER that provides a constant voltage level, and the EMITTER (sense 1) is connected to earth through a resistor. The emitter current through the resistor will then ensure that the base to emitter voltage is maintained at a correct level.

voltage doubler a RECTIFIER circuit that provides double the peak voltage of the AC input. This is twice as much as would be obtained from a conventional half- or full-wave rectifier. See also VOLTAGE MULTIPLIER.

voltage drift a problem of a DC AMPLIFIER in which the output voltage varies slightly even while the input voltage is unchanged.

voltage drop the VOLTAGE between the ends of a CONDUCTOR or a COMPONENT. The voltage drop is due to the RESISTANCE or IMPEDANCE of the conductor or component when a current flows.

voltage feedback the FEEDBACK of a SIGNAL that is a selected fraction of the OUTPUT voltage signal, to the input of a circuit.

voltage follower a circuit in which the output is in the same PHASE as the input. See also EMITTER FOLLOWER.

voltage gain the ratio of OUTPUT signal voltage to INPUT (sense 1) signal voltage for an AMPLIFIER. The voltages must be measured in the same way, both peak-to-peak, or both RMS, and the ratio may be converted into decibels. Voltage GAIN takes no account of the phase between the output and the input.

voltage law see KIRCHOFF'S LAWS.

voltage level the signal VOLTAGE at some point in a CIRCUIT, compared to a standard level. For VIDEO SIGNALS, for example, the standard level is one volt peak-to-peak, ignoring synchronizing pulses.

voltage multiplier a RECTIFIER circuit whose DC output is several times the peak voltage of the AC input. The technique uses a chain of DIODES and CAPACITORS, with each rectifier having as its input the DC level of the previous rectifier, plus the original AC signal attenuated only slightly by the capacitor chain. See COCKROFT-WALTON VOLTAGE MULTIPLIER; DIODE PUMP MULTIPLIER; HICKMAN VOLTAGE MULTIPLIER.

voltage multiplier resistor a resistor used to extend the voltage measuring range of an analogue MOVING COIL METER.

voltage operated gain adjusting device or **VOGAD** a COMPRESSOR circuit that is controlled by an AUDIO input so that it provides an almost constant level of audio output signal from a range of input amplitudes.

voltage overload an excessive signal voltage that causes an ACTIVE stage to CUT OFF or SATURATION (sense 1).

voltage rating for an electronic component, the normal level of voltage that can be applied between the terminals.

voltage reference diode a diode using AVALANCHE BREAKDOWN. The diode is usually called a ZENER DIODE and catalogued as such. The voltage reference diode is operated with REVERSE BIAS, and the voltage across the diode is almost independent of the current. By using the diode with a current that is already partly regulated, a very precisely constant voltage value can be generated. The reference diode is used in VOLTAGE REGULATORS.

voltage regulator or **voltage stabilizer** a circuit whose output is a voltage, usually DC, that is steady. The output voltage should not, within limits, be affected by differing load currents or by changes in the AC supply voltage. Most voltage regulator circuits make use of NEGATIVE FEEDBACK amplifiers with direct coupling. A fraction of the output voltage is compared with the voltage of a VOLTAGE REFERENCE DIODE, and any difference is used to correct the output. The simplest designs make use of an EMITTER-FOLLOWER with the reference diode in the base circuit. Voltage regulators can be of series or shunt design, but are overwhelmingly of the series type. Circuits using such devices as SATURABLE REACTORS and THYRISTORS are used to regulate AC voltages.

voltage remanence see SOAKAGE.

voltage source a supply of approximately constant voltage or voltage signals. Contrast CURRENT SOURCE.

voltage stabilizer see VOLTAGE REGULATOR.

voltage standing wave ratio (VSWR) the STANDING WAVE RATIO measured from signal voltage amplitude levels.

voltage step a sudden change of voltage from one steady value to another.

voltage surge a pulse of voltage that can be particularly destructive to a semiconductor. A short-term voltage surge will not necessarily pass sufficient current to blow a FUSE, so that fast-acting surge protectors are required to avoid damage to circuits.

voltage surge protection circuitry designed to prevent damage to

SEMICONDUCTOR components when a current through an INDUCTOR is suddenly broken.

voltage to frequency converter   see SINGLE SLOPE A/D CONVERTER.

voltage to time A/D converter   see COUNTING A/D CONVERTER.

voltaic cell   see CELL.

volt-amp   see VOLT-AMPERE.

volt-ampere or **volt-amp** or **VA**   the product of VOLTS and AMPERES for a SIGNAL. Even if both quantities are measured as RMS quantities, the product is not necessarily equal to dissipated power because of PHASE DIFFERENCES. To obtain a figure for power, the volt-ampere figure must be multiplied by the POWER FACTOR, which is the cosine of the phase angle.

voltmeter   a METER for measuring potential difference (voltage). The older type is the (analogue) MOVING-COIL METER, with a set of DC ranges. A limited range of AC measurements are made possible by using a rectifier, but these readings are of lower precision and are affected by the frequency and waveform of the AC, see TRUE RMS. Digital voltmeters have now largely replaced the moving-coil type for DC measurements, and CATHODE-RAY OSCILLOSCOPEs are more suited for work with signals. Voltmeters with MOSFET inputs can be used for making measurements that require an exceptionally high input resistance. These meters have replaced the old valve voltmeters and the even older electrostatic voltmeters.

volume   1. the AMPLITUDE of sound as heard by the ear. For a sound of constant amplitude level, the effect on the ear is not constant but varies with frequency because of the NONLINEAR response of the ear. 2. the voltage or power amplitude of an AUDIO signal.

volume compressor   a CIRCUIT that reduces the range of amplitudes in an AUDIO signal. This is done typically by a NON-LINEAR AMPLIFIER, whose GAIN is inversely proportional to the signal amplitude. Volume compression is

extensively used in sound RECORDING, because no recording system or broadcasting system can cope with the full amplitude range (dynamic range) of orchestral music. See also COMPANDER; DBX; DOLBY SYSTEM; VOLUME EXPANDER; WHITE COMPRESSION.

volume control   the POTENTIOMETER (sense 1) control on sound reproduction equipment for adjusting the intensity of sound by altering the amplitude of AUDIO signals.

volume dependent amplitude modulation   see DYNAMIC AMPLITUDE MODULATION.

volume expander   a CIRCUIT that increases the AMPLITUDE range of SIGNALs. The volume expander is a NONLINEAR AMPLIFIER that has higher gain for larger amplitude signals. A volume expander is usually designed in conjunction with a VOLUME COMPRESSOR, to form a COMPANDER, so that a signal that has been compressed and then expanded will be restored to normal amplitude range. Companding is extensively used in tape RECORDING and optical film recording systems. See DBX; DOLBY SYSTEM.

volume limiter   a CIRCUIT that prevents the AMPLITUDE of a signal from exceeding a preset limit. This is commonly used for TELEPHONY, so that overmodulation of the CARRIER (sense 1) (which causes severe sideband distortion) is greatly reduced. Crude limiters simply clip the waveform, but modern types use a NONLINEAR AMPLIFIER that affects only the amplitude range near the limit.

volumetric detection   the use of a PASSIVE INFRA-RED intruder detection system covering a fan-shaped zone and covering a space with a detection angle of 90°. See also CORRIDOR; CURTAIN; PET ALLEY.

volumetric RADAR   a RADAR system that uses two stations simultaneously providing azimuth and elevation information to produce three-dimensional plots of targets.

volume-unit meter   a form of recording-level meter for a TAPE RECORDER. The meter measures the average signal level, and should give an indication that is proportional to the power level of the signal, so allowing for the differences between smooth and spiky waveforms.

von Neumann architecture the conventional scheme of COMPUTER design, in which each instruction is carried out in sequence. The alternative is some form of parallel architecture, and current research is devoted to the problems of parallel architecture (in which several instructions can be carried out simultaneously) and the computing languages that will be required to make efficient use of it. Named after John von Neumann (1903–1957), US mathematician.

voting type UPS see OFF-LINE UPS.

VRAM see VIDEO MEMORY.

VSAM video surveillance and monitoring.

V signal the weighted R – Y CHROMINANCE SIGNAL of the PAL system.

VSWR see VOLTAGE STANDING WAVE RATIO.

VU-meter see VOLUME-UNIT METER.

Wadley drift free loop an analogue FREQUENCY SYNTHESIZER technique that uses three MIXER stages and a VARIABLE FREQUENCY OSCILLATOR for tuning.

wafer a circular thin slice from a large crystal of SEMICONDUCTOR material. Wafers of, typically, 3" to 6" diameters are processed by PHOTOLITHOGRAPHY so that several hundred CHIPs (sense 1) can be formed in one set of operations. After the wafer processing, the individual chips are automatically tested by a machine that marks the rejects, and the chips are separated by ruling the wafer with a diamond cutter. The good chips are then selected and passed for mounting on to headers.

wafer scale integration or **WSI** a construction technique for ICs in which all the chips on one slice are integrated into a single circuit that incorporates a logic module that can bypass defective chips.

Wagner coding the use of a single PARITY bit for ERROR CORRECTION when it is known that one particular bit was received under abnormal conditions.

Wagner earth see VIRTUAL EARTH.

WAIS wide area information server.

walkie-talkie a miniature portable sound transmitter-receiver. The TV equivalent has been termed a *creepie-peepie*.

WAN see WIDE AREA NETWORK.

WAP see WIRELESS APPLICATION PROTOCOL.

warble a small variation in FREQUENCY, usually at an AUDIO rate. This can be due to speed variations in a motor of a film projector, gramophone disc player or TAPE RECORDER.

warm-up the time after switch-on during which characteristics of a CIRCUIT change. Warm-up time for a circuit that contains a CATHODE-RAY TUBE includes the time that is needed to heat the cathode until its electron emission is steady.

warping the distortion of an image in ways such as twisting and the lateral shifting of opposite ends of the image.

watchdog facility the use of devices such as a DIGITAL STORAGE OSCILLOSCOPE to detect TRANSIENT events such as a GLITCH.

watchdog timer a controller for a MICROPROCESSOR circuit that will reset the microprocessor automatically if it does not receive a logic signal. The reason for the watchdog is to avoid hanging up the system waiting for an input or becoming stuck in a software loop.

watt the unit of POWER. Electrically, the power value in watts is obtained by multiplying the DC voltage value in volts by the DC current value in amperes. For AC or signal quantities, ROOT-MEAN-SQUARE values must be used, and any differences in phase expressed by a POWER FACTOR correction.

wattage rating the rating of maximum POWER for a device.

watt-hour a unit of energy equal to 3600 JOULES.

wattless component the product of signal VOLTAGE and CURRENT when the PHASE DIFFERENCE is 90°. This quantity does not represent dissipated power because only the product of the IN-PHASE COMPONENT's (sense 1) voltage and current in phase gives the true figure of power dissipated. See also POWER FACTOR.

wattmeter any instrument that measures electrical power.

wave an alternating quantity whose effect can spread through a material, or through space. For electronics purposes, the most important waves are electromagnetic waves, which are the familiar radio waves used as CARRIERs (sense 1). See also ULTRASONIC.

wave analyzer an instrument, based on a CATHODE-RAY OSCILLOSCOPE display, that analyzes a wave into its components.

A typical output from a wave analyzer would be a set of vertical bars in which the height of each bar indicates the amplitude of a sine wave, and the bar position indicates frequency. In this way, the wave analyzer shows the amplitudes of the fundamental and each HARMONIC for a complex waveform. The CRO type of display is now being replaced by computer displays. See also FOURIER ANALYSIS.

waveband a range of frequencies used by a receiver.

waveband switching any method of altering the connections of RESONANT CIRCUITS so as to change the WAVEBAND that is tuned. Older radios and TV receivers used mechanical switches whose contacts frequently were a cause of poor reception.

wave filter see FILTER.

waveform or **waveshape** a graph-plot of wave AMPLITUDE against time for the time of one CYCLE. The common waveforms are sine, square, pulse and triangle.

waveform graph a graph of wave AMPLITUDE plotted against time, showing the shape of a WAVEFORM.

wavefront the line of advance of a WAVE through a material. The wavefront of a wave from a point source, for example, is in the shape of a sphere. The wavefront consists of all the points at which the wave has travelled through the material for the same time.

waveguide a hollow CONDUCTOR for MICROWAVES. Because of radiation and surface resistance, microwaves cannot be efficiently conducted along conventional open lines. A waveguide, consisting normally of a rectangular section metal tube, is much more efficient. The metal may be silver-plated to increase surface conductivity, and the wave is held inside the guide by reflections from the wall. The dimensions of the waveguide have to be chosen appropriately for the wavelengths that are to be propagated, and the ratio of width to depth for the cross section will determine the pattern (see MODE, sense 2) of electric and magnetic fields inside the waveguide.

waveguide feed see J-HOOK.

wave heating the heating of materials by means of MICROWAVE bombardment. This is used for fast-drying of damp materials, setting adhesives, and cooking food. See also MICROWAVE COOKER; RADIO GASTRONOMY.

wave interference the addition of amplitudes for waves of the same type that meet. If the waves are in phase, this will make the resultant of greater amplitude than either component; if the waves are in antiphase, the resultant will be small. If the phase varies, the resultant will change amplitude at a frequency equal to the difference between the frequencies of the constituent waves.

wavelength the distance between one wave peak and the next in a wave. The wavelength is a particularly easy feature of a wave to measure (see LECHER LINES), and its size determines many of the features of the wave, such as the ease of PROPAGATION. The value of wavelength multiplied by FREQUENCY gives speed of propagation in the medium in which wavelength is measured.

wavelength and time division multiplex or **WTDM** a method of increasing the use of BANDWIDTH on an OPTICAL FIBRE by transmitting a set of TIME DIVISION MULTIPLEX signals on to slightly different frequencies along the same fibre.

wavemeter a form of frequency METER. A RESONANT CIRCUIT is adjusted so as to resonate with an incoming wave, and the resonant current is displayed on a meter. The frequency can then be read from a dial. The wavemeter can be calibrated in terms of wavelength, assuming that the waves are in air.

wave propagation see PROPAGATION.

waveshape see WAVEFORM.

wave shaping the alteration of shapes of NON-SINUSOIDAL waves by passing them through NETWORKS (sense 1) that implement DIFFERENTIATION or INTEGRATION, FILTER action or CLIPPING.

wave soldering a soldering method in which SURFACE MOUNTED DEVICES are attached to soldering resist on a PRINTED CIRCUIT BOARD using an adhesive. The boards are then inverted and passed over a soldering bath in which waves have been induced by an ULTRASONIC TRANSDUCER while each joint is soldered.

wave tilt   the effects of DIFFRACTION and the conductivity of the Earth on an ELECTROMAGNETIC WAVE which causes it to tilt in a forward direction.

wavetime   see PERIOD.

wave train   a set of WAVES, usually implying a limited number.

wave trap   see NOTCH FILTER.

WAV file   an uncompressed DIGITAL AUDIO file, such as can be obtained from a CD and input to a computer.

ways, switch   the number of different connections the POLE (sense 3) of a switch can make.

W band   the range of 3mm to 5.36mm wavelength, 56 to 100GHz of MICROWAVE frequency.

WBFM   see WIDEBAND FM.

WDDX   Web distributed data exchange.

wear out region   the rise in failure rate at the far end of a BATHTUB DIAGRAM.

Weaver method   a method of obtaining SINGLE-SIDEBAND SUPPRESSED CARRIER modulation for telephone speech circuits using a set of balanced QUADRATURE modulators.

webcam   a simple form of CCD video camera controlled by a computer and used to provide images to Internet users.

weber   the unit of MAGNETIC FLUX, equal to the amount of flux that will induce an EMF of one volt when linked with a single turn of wire for one second.

weighted checksum   a form of CHECKSUM in which each data number is multiplied by a prime number so that the checksum carries information that will identify the position of an error.

weighted voltage addition converter   see VOLTAGE ADDING CONVERTER.

weighting   the process of adjusting values so as to conform to a desired norm. For example, the R–Y and B–Y signal amplitudes of PAL are multiplied by factors of 0.877 and 0.493 respectively so as to prevent OVERMODULATION of the transmitter on very light or very dark portions of a picture.

weighting curves   a method of adjusting measured SIGNAL-TO-NOISE RATIO to convert into a subjective value that provides a measure of nuisance value.

welding   the joining of metals by melting them together at a point or a seam, used as a more reliable alternative to SOLDERING for high-reliability assemblies.

Weston standard cell   see STANDARD CELL.

wet cell   a CELL that contains a liquid, such as a lead-acid cell.

Wheatstone bridge   the original and classical form of BRIDGE circuit used for resistance comparison.

whip aerial   a very thin vertical rod aerial that is free to flex easily. A typical application is to car radio.

whistle   an INTERFERENCE effect on a signal, caused by another CARRIER (sense 1). The beating of two carriers close to each other in frequency causes a whistle to be heard at the receiver. The *whistle frequency* is the difference between the carrier frequencies.

whistle filter   see SCRATCH FILTER.

whistler   a radio interference effect produced by radiation from a lightning strike, causing a whistle of descending frequency on an extra low frequency radio receiver.

white balance   a CAMCORDER and TELEVISION CAMERA facility that samples the ambient light and corrects the levels of signal accordingly.

white box testing or **clear box testing** or **glass box testing** or **logical testing** or **open box testing**   testing a system by using selected data, based on knowledge of the system. Contrast BLACK BOX TESTING.

white clip   a clipping action that removes a portion of a TV waveform corresponding to PEAK WHITE.

white compression   a form of volume compression (see VOLUME COMPRESSOR) on a VIDEO SIGNAL. This compresses the amplitudes that correspond to the white (brightest) areas of the picture.

white crushing   a lack of contrast between brighter areas of a TV picture, caused usually by NONLINEARITY in a VIDEO AMPLIFIER.

white light a mixture of all visible colours along with ultra-violet and infra-red radiation.

white noise an electrical or other form of NOISE (such as acoustical) that has a broad spectrum of frequencies and a uniform AMPLITUDE over the whole of the FREQUENCY range.

white peak an AMPLITUDE peak in a VIDEO SIGNAL that corresponds to a bright white part of the picture.

wide-angle tube a television CATHODE-RAY TUBE with a total DEFLECTION ANGLE of 110° or more, usually also with a flat screen.

wide area network or **WAN** any NETWORK (sense 2) that uses SERIAL links extending over large distances (typically more than 1 kilometre). See also LAN.

wideband see BROADBAND.

wideband amplifier an amplifier whose BANDWIDTH has been extended by careful design and choice of components. A TUNED AMPLIFIER will use such devices as STAGGER TUNING and RESISTIVE LOADING. An UNTUNED AMPLIFIER will use FEEDBACK and FREQUENCY COMPENSATION to achieve bandwidths that may extend from DC to several tens of MHz.

wideband FM or **WBFM** a FREQUENCY MODULATION system using DEVIATION (sense 2) of 75 kHz or more. See also NARROWBAND FM.

wide head the use of a wider head, typically 59μm, on a VIDEO CASSETTE RECORDER to facilitate TRACKING (sense 1) during a still frame.

wide-screen signalling decoder or **WSD** an 8-bit processor in a TV receiver that uses the WIDE-SCREEN SWITCHING FLAG to determine the ASPECT RATIO of the picture and switches scans accordingly.

wide-screen switching flag or **WSS flag** a BYTE carried within a TELETEXT signal that will cause a TV RECEIVER to set the amplitude of the FIELD (sense 2) and LINE (sense 2) timebases to suit a widescreen programme.

width control circuitry used for STEREO sound systems that will alter the apparent width of the sources.

Wien bridge a form of BRIDGE circuit used mainly as a FILTER or as a tuning circuit for a low-frequency OSCILLATOR. The circuit was originally used as a measuring bridge for frequency, hence its name. See Fig. 118.

wi-fi a very fast-changing computer technology that offers WIDEBAND Internet access with radio links. The service is up and running in several cities in the UK, but has a very limited range.

Winchester disk see HARD DRIVE.

winding a length of coiled CONDUCTOR that is used to produce a MAGNETIC FIELD or have a VOLTAGE induced in it by a magnetic field. See also PRIMARY WINDING; SECONDARY WINDING.

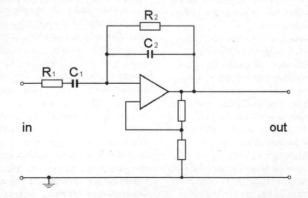

Fig. 118. **Wien bridge**

winding resistance   the resistance of a TRANSFORMER or other inductive winding.

window   1. a material that is transparent to radiation. 2. the range of frequencies that can pass through the IONOSPHERE from outer space, the 'radio window'. 3. the thin mica cover of a GEIGER-MÜLLER tube that allows ionizing particles and radiation to pass into the tube. 4. the faceplate of a TV camera tube. 5. a vacuum-sealed connection between a MICROWAVE generator and a WAVEGUIDE. 6. the frontal acceptance angle of a MICROPHONE.

window detector   a circuit that changes state when an input voltage is between two values.

window function   a form of weighting factor that corrects the output of a DIGITAL FILTER to reduce OVERSHOOT and OSCILLATIONS. See also BARTLETT; HAMMING; HANNING; RECTANGULAR; TRIANGULAR.

windowing   see WINDOW FUNCTION.

window operation   a FILTER action on a set of digital PIXEL values that computes new values based on the values of neighbouring pixels. See also CONVOLUTION.

wiping action   a SWITCH action in which the contacts are rubbed together as they are made or broken, maintaining a clean contact surface.

wire   1. a metal CONDUCTOR in wire form. 2. any connecting conductor that is not a strip in a PRINTED-CIRCUIT BOARD.

wire brittleness   a cause of broken wiring where stranded wire has become impregnated by solder.

wire broadcasting   the distribution of SIGNALS at radio frequencies by wire rather than through space.

wired   (of terminals) connected by wire.

wired logic   a method of providing more inputs to a GATE (sense 2) by wiring gates together in parallel and combining the outputs.

wired-OR   a method of connecting OUTPUTS from IC gates. Some types of gates with open-collector outputs (see OPEN-COLLECTOR DEVICE) can have their outputs connected to a common load. This allows the output voltage to be pulled down to logic 0 if any one of the

gates conducts, giving an OR logic action. Gates of conventional PUSH-PULL TTL stages may be destroyed if they are connected together and used in this way.

wire gauge   an old system of grading wire diameter by a reference number, see STANDARD WIRE GAUGE.

wireless   an old term for RADIO (sense 1), shortened from wireless (meaning without cables) telegraphy. The term is now revived in the sense of requiring no connecting wires, see WI-FI.

wireless application protocol (WAP)   a standard method of enabling INTERNET access by radio communication for such devices as mobile cellphones, pagers or PDA.

wireless in-building network or **WIN**   a low power radio communications link operating at around 18GHz to provide networking for computers in a single building.

wireless LAN   a form of LOCAL AREA NETWORK that uses a radio link, the *wireless local loop*, as part of its networking connections.

wireless microphone   a microphone connected to a miniature FM radio transmitter, allowing the use of a microphone anywhere within the range of the transmitter without connecting cables.

wireless security systems   intruder detectors and alarms that are linked by radio signals rather than by cable, using battery backup for any device that would fail in the absence of mains power.

wire-wound potentiometer   a POTENTIOMETER (sense 1) using a wire winding with a moveable metal tapping connected to the third terminal.

wire-wound resistor   a form of RESISTOR constructed by winding fine-gauge insulated wire around an insulating former. The POWER DISSIPATION of such a resistor can be large, but it is difficult to make the resistor NON-INDUCTIVE.

wire wrapping   connections made by wrapping a wire around a pin, an alternative to CRIMPING, WELDING or SOLDERING, particularly for automated assembly.

wiring diagram a diagram that shows the physical connection of wires in a circuit. Contrast CIRCUIT DIAGRAM.

WLAN see WIRELESS LAN.

WLL wireless local loop: see WIRELESS LAN.

wobble modulation see FREQUENCY MODULATION.

wobbulator an OSCILLATOR that uses FREQUENCY MODULATION to check the BANDWIDTH of a circuit. By using the wobbulator as an INPUT (sense 1) to a CIRCUIT, and displaying the AMPLITUDE of the OUTPUT on an oscilloscope whose TIMEBASE is provided by the wobbulator, a plot of amplitude against FREQUENCY can be obtained on which band limits can be marked. The wobbulator is particularly useful for checking the IF and video response of TV receivers.

woofer a LOUDSPEAKER that is particularly suitable for reproducing BASS notes. A woofer uses a large cone that is very freely suspended. At high frequencies, such a cone would resonate, with standing waves forming on it, so that the woofer is isolated from high frequencies by means of the CROSSOVER NETWORK. See also LOUDSPEAKER; TWEETER; SUB-WOOFER.

word a set of BITS, often 16 or 32, used as a unit of digital signal.

word display a form of LOGIC ANALYZER display that reads sampled signals at each CLOCK edge and displays the results as a binary WORD rather than as a waveform.

work function the amount of energy that is needed to liberate one ELECTRON from a material, usually quoted in terms of ELECTRONVOLTS.

working point the BIAS conditions on an ACTIVE COMPONENT that make it suitable for signal handling.

working voltage or **wv** the voltage at which a component such as a capacitor will achieve its rated life.

work station a servicing bench equipped for cleaning, soldering and testing and the handling of components that are sensitive to ELECTROSTATIC DISCHARGES.

WORM see WRITE ONCE READ MANY TIMES.

wound capacitor see ROLLED CAPACITOR.

wound core a TRANSFORMER core that consists of one ribbon of magnetic material wound into a core shape. See also E-CORE; I-CORE.

wow a slow frequency modulation of sound from a disc or tape source. Wow is caused by uneven disc or tape speed. Compare FLUTTER.

wrist strap a metal strap worn by an operator that is earthed through a high resistance, intended to avoid ELECTROSTATIC DAMAGE to sensitive components.

write to store data into a MEMORY or on a recordable CD or DVD. Compare READ.

write once read many times or **WORM** a form of OPTICAL drive that the user can write and read. The written data cannot, however, be erased. See also CD-R; DVD RECORDER.

writing current the signal current to the HEAD of a VIDEO CASSETTE RECORDER in the process of recording.

WSD see WIDE-SCREEN SIGNALLING DECODER.

WSI see WAFER SCALE INTEGRATION.

WSS flag see WIDE-SCREEN SWITCHING FLAG.

WTDM see WAVELENGTH AND TIME DIVISION MULTIPLEX.

Wyndom aerial (or antenna) a HALF WAVE DIPOLE suspended horizontally between two masts and fed offset from centre to match its impedance.

x-axis the horizontal axis of a graph or of a CATHODE-RAY TUBE display.

x band the MICROWAVE band range of 27.5mm to 57.7mm, 5.2GHz to 10.9GHz.

x coordinate a number indicating a distance along the X-AXIS of a graph.

X cut crystal a QUARTZ CRYSTAL cut with its large surface normal to the crystal x-axis.

x deflection the movement of an ELECTRON BEAM in a horizontal direction along the face of a CATHODE-RAY TUBE.

xenon headlamp a recent form of headlight for cars using a high-voltage GAS DISCHARGE through xenon gas to produce a light that looks blue when viewed from a distance. This achieves up to three times as much light output for the permitted electrical wattage as a conventional (halogen) bulb at the cost of an electronic voltage INVERTER (sense 2) and CONTROL GEAR.

xerography™ a method of paper-copying that relies on ELECTROSTATIC charging and PHOTOCONDUCTIVITY. The principle is also used in laser printers for computers.

XLR connectors connectors for professional AUDIO equipment available as three, four or five pin types with anchored pins and no loose springs or set screws.

XNOR gate a LOGIC GATE whose output is high when all inputs are high and whose output is high when all inputs are low. The output is low if any of the inputs differs from the others. The action is equivalent to an EXCLUSIVE OR GATE followed by an INVERTER (sense 1).

XOFF a signal sent to a remote computer along a communications link to indicate that no transfer should be made.

XON a signal sent to a remote computer along a communications link to indicate that a transfer can be made.

XOR a LOGIC action whose output is 1 if only one of its inputs is at logic 1. The output is zero for all other input combinations.

XOR gate see EXCLUSIVE OR.

x-plates the horizontal DEFLECTION PLATES of an INSTRUMENT TUBE. The timebase waveforms are normally applied to these plates.

x-ray the range of electromagnetic radiation with WAVELENGTHs much shorter than those of visible light. X-rays penetrate most materials, and cannot be focused, reflected or refracted by conventional methods.

x-ray tube a vacuum tube in which X-RAYS are generated. The tube generates a very high energy ELECTRON BEAM that is focused onto a metal ANODE, the TARGET. The bombardment of this target produces x-rays. The wavelength of the x-rays can be reduced by using higher voltages between cathode and target.

XS3 see EXCESS-3 CODE.

x-y coordinates see CARTESIAN COORDINATES.

xylene a volatile flammable liquid used as a solvent and cleaner.

x-y plotter an instrument that produces a two-dimensional plot on paper. The plot is similar to that produced by a CATHODE-RAY OSCILLOSCOPE, but the x–y plotter is more useful if the rate of production of the pattern is slow.

y adapter   a connector that allows a signal to be split into two paths.

yagi   a form of DIRECTIONAL AERIAL consisting of a DIPOLE AERIAL fitted with a REFLECTOR and several DIRECTORS. The direction of the yagi is the heading from reflector to director. The GAIN as compared to a simple dipole is large, and the directional properties of the aerial are very useful in overcoming interference problems.

y amplifier   the circuitry used to amplify the signal applied to the Y-PLATES of an instrument CATHODE-RAY TUBE. The input usually consists of a calibrated attenuator so that amplitudes can be measured from the screen scale (*graticule*).

y-axis   the vertical axis of graph paper or the TRACE on a CATHODE-RAY TUBE.

yellow   the complementary colour obtained from white – blue (or green + red).

Y-factor method   a method of measuring the NOISE TEMPERATURE of an AERIAL by comparing the noise output from a liquid-cooled noise source with that from the aerial.

YIG   see YTTRIUM-IRON-GARNET.

y-input   the input for signals to a CATHODE-RAY OSCILLOSCOPE.

yoke   a set of DEFLECTION COILS for a TV CATHODE-RAY TUBE.

y-parameters   a set of PARAMETERS formerly used for measuring TRANSISTOR characteristics.

y-plates   the vertical DEFLECTION PLATES for an instrument CATHODE-RAY TUBE.

yttrium-iron-garnet (YIG)   a magnetic crystal of the FERRITE type that is used in microwave circuits, and also for magnetic BUBBLE MEMORY applications.

YUV   the modulated signals on the SUBCARRIER of PAL and SECAM colour TV transmissions.

zap to remove or destroy.

z-axis a graph axis perpendicular to both x and y axes for a three-dimensional graph.

z coordinate a distance measured along the z-AXIS of a three-dimensional graph.

Z cut crystal a crystal cut along an axis perpendicular to both x and y axes.

Zener barrier the use of Zener diodes in PASSIVE INFRA-RED detectors to restrict the voltage and current to a low level so that such detectors can be used in a hazardous area.

Zener breakdown the reverse BREAKDOWN of a DIODE in which the p- and n-regions are heavily doped (see DOPING). Zener breakdown is more gradual than AVALANCHE BREAKDOWN, but the name of Zener is used for any diode in which reverse breakdown is used.

Zener diode any VOLTAGE REGULATOR DIODE that operates with REVERSE BIAS. The breakdown voltage of these diodes is almost independent of the amount of reverse current, so they can be used as voltage reference sources. See VOLTAGE REFERENCE DIODE. See Fig. 119.

Zeppelin aerial (or antenna) a form of half-wave DIPOLE AERIAL that is end fed with two open-wire feeders, the second terminated at a null point on the mast.

zero 1. the figure 0. 2. a minimum point on a POLE-ZERO DIAGRAM.

zero-crossing detector a form of COMPARATOR circuit, based on an operational amplifier and a diode, whose output will change state rapidly as the input passes through zero, used for generating SYNCHRONIZING pulses.

zero cross-over distortion a form of digital distortion that can occur due to nonlinearity when an analogue signal is in the zero region, because of the change of the MOST SIGNIFICANT BIT from zero in the positive half-cycle to 1 in the negative half-cycle.

zero disparity code a form of binary code in which each word consists of an even number of bits, and an equal number of 1s and 0s.

zero error a METER fault in which the needle of an ANALOGUE METER does not return to zero. Instruments that use

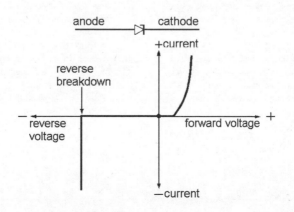

Fig. 119. **Zener diode**

DIGITAL displays may also exhibit zero errors so that the reading is not zero with the meter disconnected or short-circuited.

zero frequency (zf) a term often used to describe steady DC conditions, with no AC present.

zero IF receiver see DIRECT CONVERSION RECEIVER.

zeroing the action of restoring a setting to zero, particularly the reading of a meter when there is no input.

zero insertion force socket or **zif** a socket intended to allow easy insertion and removal of an IC. The zif socket allows the chip to be dropped into place and the connections made by clamping the pins after insertion. The clamp can be loosened to allow the chip to be pulled out.

zero level the level of comparison for SIGNALS. This need not necessarily be zero voltage, but the voltage of the signal BASELINE.

zero-level trigger a TRIGGER PULSE that is generated when an AC wave passes through the zero voltage level. Zero voltage triggers are used when a THYRISTOR is being switched in such a way as to generate little or no interference.

zero potential see EARTH POTENTIAL.

zero-slot network a primitive form of network using serial or parallel connections rather than a networking interface card.

zero suppression 1. the blanking of LEADING ZEROS in a number display. 2. the addition of extra 1s to a code to prevent a long string of 0s causing an increase in the BIT ERROR RATE.

zero temperature coefficient crystal or **ZTC crystal** a QUARTZ CRYSTAL cut in such a direction that it has a zero TEMPERATURE COEFFICIENT of frequency change.

zero-voltage switching see BURST CONTROL.

zf see ZERO FREQUENCY.

zif socket see ZERO INSERTION FORCE SOCKET.

zigzag symbol the shape of the older symbol for a resistor, still used in the USA.

zinc-carbon cell the conventional low-cost 1.5V cell using zinc as the CATHODE (sense 3) and carbon as the ANODE (sense 3) with an ammonium chloride ELECTROLYTE.

zipper noise the noise generated by signals passing through a DIGITAL FILTER, particularly a RECURSIVE FILTER.

z-modulation the MODULATION of the ELECTRON BEAM of a CATHODE-RAY TUBE, so changing screen brightness. The term particularly denotes the modulation of an INSTRUMENT TUBE, since TV cathode-ray tubes are normally modulated in this way.

Zobel network a series combination of a resistor and capacitor wired across a LOUDSPEAKER in order to correct PHASE characteristics of an OUTPUT STAGE.

Zolotarev filter see CAUER FILTER.

zone bit recording a method of recording VIDEO data on a HARD DRIVE so that speed of retrieval of video information can be faster.

zone plate see FRESNEL LENS.

zone plate aerial see FRESNEL ZONE PLATE AERIAL.

zoom microphone a development of the SHOTGUN MICROPHONE whose POLAR PATTERN can be varied from OMNIDIRECTIONAL to highly directional by changing the PHASE and level of the outputs from the microphone elements.

z-parameters a set of PARAMETERS formerly used for measurements of TRANSISTOR characteristics.

ZTC crystal see ZERO TEMPERATURE COEFFICIENT CRYSTAL.

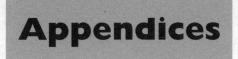

Appendices

APPENDIX A: Resistor Colour Code

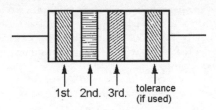

1st. 2nd. 3rd. tolerance (if used)

Band Coding

First band — first figure of resistance value (first *significant* figure)
Second band — second figure of resistance value (second *significant* figure)
Third band — number of zeros following second figure (*multiplier*)
Tolerance band — percentage tolerance of value (5% or 10%). No tolerance band is used if the resistor has 20% tolerance.

Note that these coding methods apply mainly to carbon composition resistors. Modern metal or carbon film resistors have the values printed onto the body of the component, as do many types of capacitors.

Code Colours (also used for capacitor values)

Figure	Colour
0	black
1	brown
2	red
3	orange
4	yellow
5	green
6	blue
7	violet
8	grey
9	white
0.01	silver
0.1	gold

} used as multipliers (3rd band) only

Tolerance

10%	silver
5%	gold

APPENDIX B: Resistance Value Coding

Resistance values on components and in component lists are often coded according to BS 1852. In this scheme no decimal points are used, and a value in ohms is indicated by R, kilohms by K (not k), and megohms by M. The letter R, K or M is used in place of the decimal point, with a zero in the leading position if the value is less than 1 ohm. For example:

1K5 = 1.5k or 1500 ohms; 2M2 = 2.2MΩ; 0R5 = 0.5 ohms.

APPENDIX C: Symbols

The use of symbols in electronics can be very confusing, and many manufacturers do not follow a coherent scheme. Most of the problems are caused by the use of letters such as R, C and L to denote components (resistors, capacitors, inductors) in circuit diagrams, and also to denote values of resistance, capacitance and inductance in equations. Another source of confusion is the use of a letter to denote both a quantity (such as voltage) and the unit used for measurement (volt). This is particularly noticeable on graphs, where, typically, a graph axis might be labelled as V/V, using the italic letter to mean the name of the quantity (voltage) and the roman letter to mean the unit (volts).

In this volume, the use of symbols is summarized in the following tables. The tables have been divided to show the use of symbols in circuit diagrams (roman letters), in equations (italics for scalars and bold for vectors or complex quantities), as abbreviations for units (roman letters), and graphical representation (see Appendix D). The symbols used in equations have been subdivided into separate tables for English and Greek symbols.

Circuit diagrams

The symbols used in this way employ roman letters, which may be followed by a number or letter identifier in a smaller type. This is indicated in each entry.

A,B,C	inputs to a digital circuit
C	carry output from an adder
C, C_1, C_b	capacitor
D, D_1, D_d	diode
E, E_1, E_c	EMF or voltage
I, I_1, I_b	current
L, L_1, L_e	self-inductor, coil
Q	main output from digital circuit
$\bar{Q}$	inverted output from digital circuit
Q, Q_1, Q_a	transistor
R, R_1, R_b	resistor
Sw_1, Sw_a	switch
T, T_1, T_b	transistor (alternative)
Tr, Tr_1	transformer or transistor
V, V_1, V_c	voltage level
ZD, ZD_1	zener diode

Symbols in equations

Roman letter use

Italic type denotes a scalar quantity, **bold type** a vector or complex number.
Principal meanings are given first. Note that these symbols are not always rigorously used outside textbooks.

Note the important distinction: dB= decibel (unit); **dB =** change of magnetic flux density.

In complex number notation, both i and j are used to mean the square root of -1.
In general, mathematicians use i, and engineers use j.

B	magnetic flux density
B	susceptance (inverse of reactance)
C	capacitance
c	velocity of light
D	electrostatic displacement
E	EMF; voltage
E	electrostatic field strength
F	mechanical force
f	frequency
F_m	magneto motive force (mmf)
G	conductance (inverse of resistance)
H	magnetic field strength
I	current
J	current density
k	coefficient of coupling
L	self-inductance
M	mutual inductance
P	dielectric polarization
Q	electric charge; quality factor of tuned circuit
R	resistance; magnetic circuit reluctance
T	period of an oscillation
V	potential difference (voltage)
X	reactance
Y	admittance (complex quantity)
Z	impedance (complex quantity)

Greek letters

ε	absolute permittivity
ε_0	permittivity of free space
ε_r	relative permittivity
θ	phase angle
κ	conductivity
λ	wavelength
μ	absolute permeability
μ_0	permeability of free space
μ_r	relative permeability
ν	frequency
ρ	resistivity; charge density
σ	conductivity; leakage coefficient
φ	magnetic flux; phase difference
χ	electrostatic susceptibility
ψ	electrostatic flux
ω	angular frequency

Symbols for units

Note the unit symbols that use upper-case (capital) letters are those which carry the name of the discoverer or researcher associated with the unit. The unit name itself uses a lower-case letter. All lettering for symbols is in roman.

Symbol	Unit name	Quantity
A	ampere	current
C	coulomb	electrostatic charge
cd	candela	luminous intensity
dB	decibel	comparative power
F	farad	electrostatic charge
H	henry	inductance (self or mutual)
Hz	hertz	frequency
J	joule	energy
K	kelvin	temperature (absolute)
kg	kilogram	mass
m	metre	length
mol	mole	amount of substance
N	newton	force
Pa	pascal	pressure
S	Siemens	conductivity (inverse ohm)
s	second	time
T	tesla	flux density
V	volt	potential; potential difference (voltage)
W	watt	power
Wb	weber	magnetic flux
Ω	ohm	resistance

Symbols

Appendix D: Graphical Symbols

AC	$\sim$	neon bulb	
AND gate		NOT gate (inverter)	
capacitor		operational amplifier	
cathode		OR gate	
connector terminals		positive pulse	
crystal		resistor	
DC	$=$	sawtooth wave	
diode		sine wave	
earth		square wave	
electrolytic capacitor		switch	
flip-flop		transformer	
heater		transistor (NPN)	
inductor		triangle wave	
lamp		tunnel diode	
meter		XOR gate	
meter *or* motor		Zener diode	
negative pulse			

Appendix E: Web Sites of Interest

The initial section of each address has been omitted, because it will be filled in by your browser.

Note that a few addresses occupy more than one line.

Aerials (antennae)
www.ee.surrey.ac.uk/Personal/D.Jefferies/antennas.html

Circuit theory
www.mitedu.freeserve.co.uk/adt.htm
www.circuit-magic.com/laws.htm
users.telenet.be/educypedia/electronics/electricitycircuits.htm

Electronics related software
hometown.aol.com/ledodd/eleclinks.htm#3.%20%20Software

Fast Fourier transforms
mathworld.wolfram.com/FastFourierTransform.html
aurora.phys.utk.edu/~forrest/papers/fourier/

Filters
ccrma.stanford.edu/~jos/filters/
www.newwaveinstruments.com/resources/rf_microwave_resources/sections/
    adaptive_filter_tutorial_theory_kalman_lms.htm
www-users.cs.york.ac.uk/~fisher/lcfilter/
www.maxim-ic.com/appnotes.cfm/appnote_number/1795

High voltage circuits
www.fortunecity.com/greenfield/bp/16/circuit.htm

Manufacturers' data sheets
www.ee.latrobe.edu.au/internal/workshop/datasheet.html
www.findchips.com/
www.datasheetarchive.com/
www.eeproductcenter.com/
www.datasheetlocator.com/

Pinouts and data, audio/TV
www.eio.com/repairfaq/REPAIR/F_chippins.html

Pole-zero theory
cnx.rice.edu/content/m10112/latest/

Practical circuits
www.repairfaq.org/REPAIR/F_samschem.html
hometown.aol.com/ledodd/eleclinks.htm#2
www.du.edu/~etuttle/electron/elecindx.htm

Repair work manuals
www.repairfaq.org/REPAIR/

Transistor equivalents
www.moyerelectronics.com/menu.html#

Transmission lines
www.newwaveinstruments.com/resources/rf_microwave_resources/sections/
  transmission_line_theory_equations_design.htm

Tutorials on electronics
www.iserv.net/~alexx/lib/tutorial.htm#top
www.educatorscorner.com/index.cgi?CONTENT_ID=3234
www.allaboutcircuits.com/

Waveguide theory
www.fnrf.science.cmu.ac.th/theory/waveguide/Waveguide%20theory%201.html

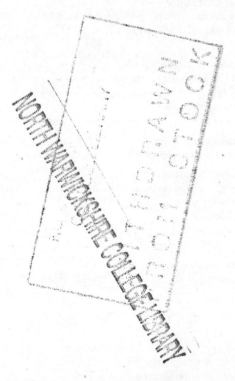